MATERNAL AND CHILD HEALTH

Programs, Problems, and Policy in Public Health

Edited by

Jonathan B. Kotch, MD, MPH

Department of Maternal and Child Health
The University of North Carolina at Chapel Hill
Chapel Hill, North Carolina

AN ASPEN PUBLICATION®
Aspen Publishers, Inc.
Gaithersburg, Maryland
1997

Library of Congress Cataloging-in-Publication Data

Maternal and child health : programs, problems, and policy in public
health / edited by Jonathan B. Kotch.
p.   cm.
Developed as core text for Master's program at the Dept. of
Maternal and Child Health, University of North Carolina at Chapel Hill.
Includes bibliographical references and index.
ISBN 0-8342-0771-0 (alk. paper)
1. Child health services—United States.   2. Maternal health
services—United States.   I. Kotch, Jonathan.   II. University of
North Carolina at Chapel Hill. Dept. of Maternal and Child Health.
[DNLM: 1. Child Health Services—United States.   2. Maternal
Health Services—United States.   3. Child Welfare—United States.
4. Maternal Welfare—United States.   WA 310 M4245   1997]
RJ102.M26   1997
362.1'9892'000973—dc21

DNLM/DLC
for Library of Congress   96-48785
CIP

Aspen Publishers, Inc., grants permission for photocopying for limited personal or internal use.
This consent does not extend to other kinds of copying, such as copying for general distribution,
for advertising or promotional purposes, for creating new collective works, or for resale.
For information, address Aspen Publishers, Inc., Permissions Department,
200 Orchard Ridge Drive, Suite 200, Gaithersburg, Maryland 20878.

Orders: (800) 638-8437
Customer Service: (800) 234-1660

About Aspen Publishers • For more than 35 years, Aspen has been a leading professional
publisher in a variety of disciplines. Aspen's vast information resources are available in both
print and electronic formats. We are committed to providing the highest quality information
available in the most appropriate format for our customers. Visit Aspen's Internet site for
more information resources, directories, articles, and a searchable version of Aspen's full
catalog, including the most recent publications: **http://www.aspenpub.com**
Aspen Publishers, Inc. • The hallmark of quality in publishing
Member of the worldwide Wolters Kluwer group

Editorial Resources: Lenda P. Hill
Library of Congress Catalog Card Number: 96-48785
ISBN: 0-8342-0771-0

Printed in the United States of America

1   2   3   4   5

Contents

Contributors

Greg R. Alexander, MPH, ScD
Professor
Department of Maternal and Child Health
School of Public Health
University of Alabama at Birmingham
Birmingham, Alabama

Trude Bennett, MSW, DrPH
Assistant Professor
Department of Maternal and Child Health
School of Public Health
University of North Carolina at Chapel Hill
Chapel Hill, North Carolina

Dorothy C. Browne, MSW, DrPH
Associate Professor
Department of Maternal and Child Health
School of Public Health
University of North Carolina at Chapel Hill
Chapel Hill, North Carolina

George P. Cole, MSW, DrPH
Department of Maternal and Child Health
School of Public Health
University of North Carolina at Chapel Hill
Chapel Hill, North Carolina

Deborah S. Cousins, BA
Graduate Research Assistant
Department of Epidemiology
School of Public Health
University of North Carolina at Chapel Hill
Chapel Hill, North Carolina

Larry Crum, PhD
Project Director
Minority Health Project
Department of Biostatistics
School of Public Health
University of North Carolina at Chapel Hill
Chapel Hill, North Carolina

Janice M. Dodds, EdD, RD
Associate Professor of Nutrition and
    Maternal and Child Health
Department of Nutrition
School of Public Health
University of North Carolina at Chapel Hill
Chapel Hill, North Carolina

Anita M. Farel, MSW, DrPH
Clinical Associate Professor
Department of Maternal and Child Health
School of Public Health
University of North Carolina at Chapel Hill
Chapel Hill, North Carolina

Charles Godue, MD
Regional Advisor
Pan American Health Organization
Human Resources Development Program
Washington, DC

Todd E. Gordon, MPH
Research Consultant
MACRO International Inc.
Atlanta, Georgia

David Knopf, LCSW, MPH
Department of Social Work
Division of Adolescent Medicine and
   National Adolescent Health Information
   Network
University of California, San Francisco
San Francisco, California

Jonathan B. Kotch, MD, MPH
Professor
Department of Maternal and Child Health
School of Public Health
University of North Carolina at Chapel Hill
Chapel Hill, North Carolina

Milton Kotelchuck, PhD, MPH
Professor
Department of Maternal and Child Health
School of Public Health
University of North Carolina at Chapel Hill
Chapel Hill, North Carolina

Barbara A. Laraia, RD, MPH
Registered Dietitian
Department of Nutrition
School of Public Health
University of North Carolina at Chapel Hill
Chapel Hill, North Carolina

Lewis H. Margolis, MD, MPH
Associate Professor
Department of Maternal and Child Health
School of Public Health
University of North Carolina at Chapel Hill
Chapel Hill, North Carolina

Sandra L. Martin, PhD
Assistant Professor
Department of Maternal and Child Health
School of Public Health
University of North Carolina at Chapel Hill
Chapel Hill, North Carolina

C. Arden Miller, MD
Professor Emeritus
Department of Maternal and Child Health
School of Public Health
University of North Carolina at Chapel Hill
Chapel Hill, North Carolina

Mary D. Peoples-Sheps, BSN, MS, DrPH
Associate Professor
Interdisciplinary Curriculum in Practice
   and Leadership and Department of
   Maternal and Child Health
School of Public Health
University of North Carolina at Chapel Hill
Chapel Hill, North Carolina

Donna J. Petersen, MHS, ScD
Visiting Associate Professor
Department of Maternal and Child Health
University of Alabama at Birmingham
Birmingham, Alabama

Jane Stein, DrPH
Lecturer
Department of Maternal and Child Health
School of Public Health
University of North Carolina at Chapel Hill
Chapel Hill, North Carolina

Joseph Telfair, MSW, MPH, DrPH
Assistant Professor
Department of Maternal and Child Health
School of Public Health
University of Alabama at Birmingham
Birmingham, Alabama

Amy Ong Tsui, MA, PhD
Associate Professor
Department of Maternal and Child Health
School of Public Health
University of North Carolina at Chapel Hill
Chapel Hill, North Carolina

Elizabeth L. Watkins, MSSA, MSc, DSc
Professor Emerita
Department of Maternal and Child Health
School of Public Health
University of North Carolina at Chapel Hill
Chapel Hill, North Carolina

B. Cecilia Zapata, MPH, DrPH
Assistant Professor
Department of Maternal and Child Health
School of Public Health
University of North Carolina at Chapel Hill
Chapel Hill, North Carolina

FOREWORD

The role of public health and its concepts, methods, and values have recently received increased recognition by policy makers and those responsible for the financing and delivery of health care. Books are being written and courses developed to prepare students and practitioners of public health to respond to this increased demand and to provide them with the necessary skills and knowledge to do so. The generalist public health professional of the future will need to have a broad understanding of public health issues and critical insights into diverse public health topics in order to intelligently relate to the various segments of the health care sector.

This volume, *Maternal and Child Health,* is special in that it is authored by University of North Carolina School of Public Health faculty and graduates who based their writings on the training offered at this university. It reflects both the philosophy and the structure of the maternal and child health curriculum at UNC, thus allowing the reader to experience this particular approach to the subject.

The field of maternal and child health is changing rapidly. The authors emphasize ethical and historical perspectives and supply analysis of policies and understanding of skills to help readers weather this rapid change. The emphasis on primary prevention to improve the health status of women, children, and families should equip the maternal and child health advocate with the necessary arguments to keep the field on the top of the list of national priorities.

The book is organized along the developmental life cycle but also addresses cross-cutting issues. The reader will find that the authors have done more than simply survey and superficially describe the various facets of maternal and child health. Careful in the selection of topics, these distinguished authors have provided in-depth information and critical analysis of events and their impact on public policy. They have authoritatively covered current issues and provided a glimpse of the future, giving students of maternal and child health and generalist public health students the proper perspective for anticipating the future.

Michel A. Ibrahim, MD, PhD
Professor of Epidemiology and Dean
University of North Carolina School of Public Health

PREFACE

Maternal and Child Health (MCH) is a profession rather than a discipline. It is a big tent, characterized by a multidisciplinary cast of characters who share a commitment to a vulnerable population. While a source of strength, the focus on a specific population rather than a theory or methodology can pose a threat. The lack of a unifying theoretical paradigm can be a weakness in an academic setting, placing MCH training programs on the defensive. Are MCH departments professional training programs, turning out generations of practitioners, or are they graduate departments, cloning future faculty and MCH researchers?

The answer, of course, is that they are both, for academic researchers and MCH practitioners each contribute, in their own ways, to the shared goal of improving the health status of women, children, and families. In doing so MCH borrows from many health and social science disciplines, but increasingly MCH is developing a set of knowledge and skills of its own. As recently as 1993, for example, the Association of Schools of Public Health (ASPH) and the Association of Teachers of Maternal and Child Health (ATMCH) developed the first set of competencies that MCH training programs across the country are striving to implement.

This book is an attempt to present, in a consolidated form, the way one such MCH training program, the Department of Maternal and Child Health of the School of Public Health of the University of North Carolina at Chapel Hill (UNC-CH), approaches the task of educating master's degree students in the core material necessary for entering the field of MCH. With only two exceptions, all of the contributors to this edited volume are either faculty, students, or alumni of UNC-CH. The chapters by and large correspond with courses that students at UNC must take to satisfy the requirements of the Master of Public Health degree in MCH. As such, the scope of this book is not intended to be comprehensive, nor is any individual topic pursued in depth. Rather, this book is an introduction to MCH for students, with some prior health training or experience, approaching formal training in MCH for the first time.

The structure of the book is straightforward. The first two chapters, which cover children's rights, justice, advocacy, and MCH history, provide the ethical and philosophical underpinnings without which MCH would be a mechanical exercise at best. The chapter on families provides background to the changing social context affecting the health and development of all children. The next five chapters follow the developmental cycle, beginning with family planning and proceeding through maternal and infant health, preschool, school-age, and adolescent health. In these chapters the authors have followed a similar, but not identical, outline, from demography to history to epidemiology, to programs, policy, and current or future issues.

The next chapters deal with issues which cross-cut the developmental stages of the previous five chapters and are more idiosyncratic in structure as befits the various topics—minority health, women's health, children with special needs, nutrition, and international health. Finally, the last two chapters present public health skills no MCH professional should leave home without, namely, research and program planning. While not complete expositions of MCH planning and research by themselves, these chapters should inspire readers to seek hands-on experience to complement the didactic presentations here.

As with any edited text, there are bound to be a variety of styles, but the faculty of the UNC Department of MCH and the other contributors have provided material of uniformly high quality, making my job as editor that much easier. It is a credit to the department, both to those currently in residence and to those who have since moved on, that such a book can be produced almost entirely from within.

Because the focus of the book is on how MCH is taught at UNC, there are many important areas which, in another format, would deserve chapters, indeed whole books, of their own. Injuries, HIV/AIDS, immunizations, dental public health, mental health, and other key public health issues overlap with core MCH areas and are discussed, to a greater or lesser extent, within one or more chapters. Yet none of these topics is unique to MCH. To do them justice, one would have to call upon the skills of disciplines such as health behavior, epidemiology, health policy and management, etc. In fact, this is exactly how courses in these areas are offered at UNC, sometimes with, and sometimes without, MCH faculty participation. There are only so many of us to go around.

We hope we have produced a readable introduction to MCH problems, programs, and policies for the beginning graduate student. If some of our readers go on to careers that promote and protect the health of women and children, then this effort will have been a success.

Jonathan B. Kotch

REFERENCE

Association of Teachers of Maternal and Child Health/Association of Schools of Public Health-MCH Council 1993. *Competencies for Education in Maternal and Child Health.* Arlington, VA: National Center for Education in Maternal and Child Health, November.

PART I

Foundations of Maternal and Child Health

CHAPTER 1

Children's Rights, Social Justice, and Advocacy in Maternal and Child Health

Lewis H. Margolis, George P. Cole, and Jonathan B. Kotch

Remember, that the human being is the most important of all products to turn out. I am eagerly anxious to do everything I can to wake up our people to the need of protecting the soil, protecting the forests, protecting the water; but first and foremost, protecting the people. If you do not have the right kind of citizens in the future, you cannot make any use of the natural resources. Protect the children—protect the boys; still more, protect the girls; because the greatest duty of this generation is to see to it that the next generation is of the proper kind to continue the work of this nation.

President Theodore Roosevelt, 1911

INTRODUCTION

In 1988, the Institute of Medicine (IOM) published *The Future of Public Health*, a study and critique of the state of the field of public health, accompanied by recommendations to enhance its effectiveness as the nation moves into the twenty-first century. The authors of the report articulated a definition of public health with three components—the mission, the substance, and the organizational framework. The mission was defined as "the fulfillment of society's interest in assuring the conditions in which people can be healthy" (IOM, 1988, p. 40). The substance was defined as "organized community efforts aimed at the prevention of disease and promotion of health" (IOM, 1988, p. 41). The organizational framework of public health encompasses "both activities undertaken within the formal structure of government and the associated efforts of private and voluntary organizations and individuals" (IOM, 1988, p. 42). Each component of this definition reflects the central dynamic or tension in the field of public health, that is, balancing the rights of individuals to pursue their private interests with the needs of communities to control the hazards that inevitably arise when groups of people pursue those interests.

3

It is only since the evolution of the recognition of children as individuals with interests and rights, potentially separate from those of their parents, that communities and nations have justified and conferred special protections and benefits on children through assorted public health, welfare, and education programs. In the United States, for example, the early twentieth century movement to ban child labor recognized that a child's right to an education and a right to protection from exploitation were both threatened by the collusion of those employers and politicians willing to take advantage of the desperate economic circumstances of poor families. Today's child advocates continue the tradition that argues that children never be treated as means to an end. Rather, optimal health, growth, and development in childhood are ends in themselves. This chapter will explore ethical principles underlying maternal and child health and relate those principles to advocacy for services on behalf of mothers and children.

RIGHTS

Rights are defined as valid claims (Feinberg, 1978) that imply a reciprocal duty. Such claims must be validated by rules obligating someone to respond. In the case of moral rights, such claims must be validated by moral rules. Similarly, legal rights are validated by legal rules. Although moral rights may make claims upon religion and social conscience, only legal rights are enforceable by the legal apparatus of the state.

Rights are classified as positive or negative, according to whether or not reciprocating a claimed right may require the transfer of resources. Therefore, positive rights are also referred to as subsistence rights or welfare rights, requiring some people to give up something of economic value in order to satisfy the legitimate claims of others. Negative rights, on the other hand, are option rights or rights of forbearance. A positive right is a right to something tangible, whereas a negative right is a right to be left alone.

Philosophers have argued about which came first, positive or negative rights. Historically, negative rights appeared in the Constitution of the United States and the Declaration of the Rights of Man before positive rights were codified in the United Nations (UN) charter and the constitution of the Soviet Union, but Bandman (1977) claims that logically some assurance of human subsistence must have preceded liberty, citing the Biblical tale of the gleaners, who had a moral right to pick up whatever produce was left behind after the fields had been harvested.

The distinction between positive and negative rights may not always be clearcut, especially in the case of children. For example, the Bill of Rights of the Constitution of the United States articulates negative rights in that Congress is prohibited from passing laws that restrict, for example, the freedoms of speech and assembly, and the free exercise of religion. These are rights to be left alone, not rights to economic resources. The ability of children, however, to exercise those negative rights is, more so than for adults, a direct function of education, housing, nourishment, and health care. Satisfying children's valid claims to these goods and services would involve their recognition by society as positive rights. The constitutions of socialist countries have attempted to ensure such positive rights as rights to housing, employment, and health care. Positive and negative rights are enumerated in the UN Convention on the Rights of the Child (Melton, 1991), ratified by the United Nations in 1989. Examples of positive rights are rights to:

- highest attainable standard of health and access to medical services
- where appropriate, social security
- an adequate standard of living
- education
- leisure, play, and participation in cultural and artistic activities

Examples of negative rights are rights to:

- legal protection against arbitrary or unlawful interference with privacy, family, home, or correspondence, or attacks on honor and reputation
- freedom of association
- express an opinion in matters affecting the child and to have that opinion heard

The issue of children's rights is further complicated by the fact that they cannot make claims on their own behalf. In other words, if children are to have rights at all, those rights must be claimed for them by someone else. In fact, a child's first claims are against its own parents, and the rights of parents in their own child derive from a prior duty to satisfy the legitimate needs of that child (Blackstone, 1968). Unlike the case with adults' rights, which require a reciprocal obligation on the part of another, a parent's right in a child requires an obligation on the part of that same parental rights-holder. "Parents' rights" therefore imply "parents' duties." Parents who do not satisfy their child's need for subsistence, indeed, for love and affection as well, risk losing their rights in that child, as in the case of a neglected child removed by the state child protective service from its home.

A parent, however, has not been required to act in the best interests of the child until recent history. Many ancient cultures codified aspects of the parent-child relationship by institutionalizing the absolute authority of the parent. Greek city-states condoned infanticide and even required it in the case of unwanted, illegitimate, and deformed children. In classical Sparta a defective child could be thrown from a cliff without penalty. In the Roman Empire a father had absolute legal authority over the life and death of his children (and, for that matter, his wife). In Egypt, the Middle East, China, and the Scandinavian countries, children were routinely sold into slavery, or, if without value on the open market, strangled, drowned or abandoned. European laws supported the right of parents to use lethal force in controlling adolescents, who were sometimes flogged or even executed for disobedience. Unwanted European newborns were discarded without penalty. There are accounts of infants left to die on trash heaps and dung heaps, or buried alive in the foundations of bridges and buildings for "good luck" (deMause, 1974; Leiby, 1976; Pfohl, 1976).

Children were not even depicted in archival art until after the eleventh century. The historian Barbara Tuchman has written that medieval illustrations show people in every contemporary human activity—making love and dying, sleeping and eating, in bed and in the bath, praying, hunting, dancing, plowing, in games and in combat, trading, traveling, reading, and writing—yet rarely with children. When children did appear they were portrayed as miniature adults in adult clothing. The concept of childhood as a developmental continuum simply did not exist, and children were pushed into adulthood as quickly as possible. Tuchman surmises that it just wasn't worth investing in individuals who were apt to die before they could actively participate in the adult struggle to survive. "Owing to the high infant mortality rate of the times, estimated at one or two in three, the investment of love in a young child may have been so unrewarding that by some ruse of nature . . . it was suppressed. Perhaps also the frequent childbearing put less value on the product. A child was born and died and another took its place" (Tuchman, 1978, p. 50).

Intermittently, children came under official protection. The Code of Hammurabi made it a crime for a mother to murder her newborn, and Tiberius ordered the death penalty for those caught sacrificing children to non-Roman gods. In thirteenth century England, so many infants were smothered by sleeping parents that it was made illegal to sleep with a swaddled child. By the sixteenth century there was a dawning recognition of the unique identity and developmental status of children. Christian reformers such as Martin Luther had for some time advocated for social concern and intervention, and there was a trend among contemporary secular philosophers and commentators to romanticize childhood. However, in the main, children were regarded as innately evil little adults, or the playthings of adults. There are accounts from the medical literature of injuries resulting from the popular pastime of "child tossing," and the violent control of children by parents continued largely unabated (deMause, 1974; Radbill, 1968).

Since the promulgation of Elizabethan Poor Laws, English tradition has vested ultimate guardianship over those incapable of acting on their own behalf in the sovereign (i.e., the king or queen). In the United States, it is the states, rather than the federal government, that have this power. Hence, it is the states that are ultimately responsible for public education, child welfare, and child protection. The early twentieth century saw the passage of a number of child welfare and child labor laws during what has since become known as the Progressive Era in U.S.

history. When enacted at the federal level, some of these, such as the National Child Labor Law, were ultimately declared unconstitutional. Although subsequently enacted during the Depression of the 1930s, in 1918 the Supreme Court ruled that the federal government had no jurisdiction to intervene in a decision (to make a child go to school instead of work) best left to parents (*Hammer v. Dagenhart,* 1918).

Nevertheless, the children's rights movement continued to gain momentum. The 1930 White House Conference on Children promulgated the Children's Charter, which declared, among other things, that every child should have "health protection from birth through adolescence, including: periodical health examinations and, where needed, care of specialists and hospital treatment; regular dental examinations and care of the teeth; protective and preventive measures among communicable diseases; the insuring of pure food, pure milk, and pure water" (Grotberg, 1977; p. 85). Recent U.S. Supreme Court decisions established certain constitutional rights of children, such as the right to due process in adult court (*Kent v. U.S.*, 1966) and the same rights as adults in criminal court (*In Re Gault,* 1967), rights that even parents may not overrule (*Planned Parenthood of Central Missouri v. Danforth,* 1976).

Legislation at the federal level has recognized some rights of children. Child abuse and neglect legislation, for example, establishes that children must be protected from abuse, and that parents may be prosecuted for failing to provide necessary food, clothing, shelter, medical care, and even love and affection, as determined by state governments. Protection from abuse corresponds with a negative right, whereas protection from neglect corresponds with the child's positive right to subsistence. Other rights established at the federal level include the right to a free, public education for all handicapped children; the right to the least restrictive placement, to rehabilitation, and to protection from cruel and unusual punishment for juveniles; and the right to some diagnostic and treatment services and to a barrier-free environment for children and adolescents with disabilities.

Satisfying positive rights to health care or education requires the expenditure of resources. Further, obligations to satisfy negative rights may clash with positive rights, as, for example, when crossing the thin line between family privacy (a negative right) and a child's right to at least minimal levels of care to avoid neglect (a positive right). In the face of limited resources, societies need rules for the fair allocation of resources and for resolving disputes involving conflicting rights. Such rules are called the *principles of social or distributive justice.*

THEORIES OF JUSTICE

As a matter of social policy, the question that must be answered is, "How can society justify taking resources legitimately earned by one person in order to purchase health care for another, or in this case, for the child of another?" For the purposes of analyzing and assessing distributive justice for children, it is useful to consider two basic theories of justice. (For an excellent discussion of ethical frameworks for professionals, see Applebaum and Lawton, 1990.) One theory is based on the principle of utility as developed by Jeremy Benthem and John Stuart Mill. This theory assumes that individuals act to maximize their own happiness or utility. A just allocation of resources within a community, therefore, derives from the calculation and balancing of positive and negative utilities for each of the individuals in the group. If the total of the positive utilities or benefits exceeds the total of the negative utilities or costs, then that allocation is deemed to be just or fair. Utilitarian theory is the basis for cost benefit analysis as a common and powerful tool in policy analysis. The benefits and costs to individuals may be judged in terms of a mixture of material principles such as equal shares, individual need, individual effort, social contribution, and merit (Beauchamp and Childress, 1983).

In the United States, the market is the mechanism for maximizing utility. To the extent that it rewards effort, merit, and social contribution, the market is the primary determinant of how health care resources are allocated. Other principles may, however, temper or exacerbate the results of market allocation. For example, the distributive principle of need argues that people who are ill or even at risk of becoming ill should have access to more medical care resources. Public support for health insurance for the poor through the Medicaid program, supplemental security income (SSI) for the disabled, or targeted services for children with special health care needs may be considered examples of redistribution of health care according to the principle of need. Under the principle of equal shares, every person in society would get the same amount of resources to spend on health care. A person who did not need his or her allocation could sell the remaining shares to a person who did. Such a system might result in people who were sick, whether or not through any fault of their own, winding up with insufficient health care should they not be able to purchase the necessary additional care.

A second basic theory, articulated by Immanuel Kant, is based on rules or duties. Unlike utilitarian theory that focuses on the consequences of resource allocation, Kant's focus is on fundamental duties. Kant asserted, "Act in such a way that you treat humanity, whether in your own person or in the person of any other, never simply as a means, but always at the same time as an end" (Applebaum and Lawton, 1990, p. 16). Kantian theory would emphasize individual need or perhaps merit as allocation principles.

Building upon the work of Kant, Rawls (1969), in *A Theory of Justice*, describes a "thought experiment" to explain how fair rules of distributive justice can be derived. In the "original position," rational adults come together behind a "veil of ignorance" for the sole purpose of making the rules that govern the distribution of goods and benefits. In such a position, with the decision makers ignorant of their statuses and roles in society, Rawls posits that all would agree with the following: that basic political liberties would be guaranteed, that desirable statuses and roles would be equally accessible to all, and that unequal distribution of resources would be tolerated to the extent that such inequalities benefit the least well off.

Rawls' formulation therefore provides a test of social policy, "Does such policy benefit the least well off?" In a real example, one would ask the question, "Would a proposed social policy that promotes an unequal distribution of benefits improve the lot of the have nots?" Take the case of infant mortality and its principal cause, low birth weight. Despite more than 30 years of concerted effort to reduce infant mortality, and despite the fact that infant mortality has declined significantly during the same period, the benefits have been relatively less for the African American community. Specifically, the gap in infant mortality rates between infants of African-American and European American extraction has increased. (See Chapter 5.) Further, there has been an absolute *increase* in the very low birth weight proportion. The combination of medical, social, and public health interventions has reduced infant mortality for both races, suggesting that these policies satisfy the Rawlsian criterion of benefiting the least well off, but the recent increase in very low birth weight argues otherwise.

Building upon the work of Rawls, Green (1976) has argued that society cannot withhold from children their fair share of health care resources because children, who are not rational, cannot participate in the original position. What would then be a child's "fair share"? Certainly a child's fair share of health care can be no less than that necessary for him or her to grow and develop to be able to fully exercise those political liberties and human rights guaranteed to all.

Unfortunately, it is not sufficient merely to assert rights on behalf of children. Inequities in the distribution of decision-making authority, economic resources, and information among different segments of a population behoove individuals and organizations to act as advocates for children in order to articulate their needs and interests, especially in the presence of opposition. Advocates attempt to influence the legislative, administrative and judicial processes of society to make children's rights a reality. We now turn to consideration of advocacy for mothers and children.

CHILD ADVOCACY

Defining Advocacy

Definitions of child advocacy, developed largely in the 1970s and 1980s, characterize the contemporary child advocate as operating at three levels:

1. On the individual or case level, an advocate is a person acting on behalf of a child . . . a defender, protector, mediator, supporter, investigator, negotia-

tor, monitor, promoter, enabler, and/or counselor (Fernandez, 1980). Individual or case advocacy is the process of challenging an organization on behalf of an individual, a process in which an individual or group attempts to obtain more responsive, adequate, and effective services for a child or a family.

2. On the organizational level, an advocate is a person or group attempting to alter and monitor legislative, budgetary, and administrative processes and, at times, to monitor professionals and professionalism (Kahn and McGowan, 1972).

3. Systems or class advocacy is the process of reforming an organization or a system to benefit a group of people, cases, or users of the organization or system. Class advocacy may begin with action on behalf of one individual and then move its focus to all members of a class of cases. Often, individuals with similar motivations for case advocacy organize in order to take advantage of the power of numbers and combined resources. Advocacy on behalf of a class is often precipitated by an event with broad public exposure and emotional impact. For example, a fundamental change in Medicaid policy occurred in the early 1980s when the mother of Katie Beckett was able to impress upon President Reagan the outrageous expenses resulting from the regulation that children with special health care needs be hospitalized for certain services when those same services could be provided less expensively and often more humanely at home (Roberts and Considine, 1997).

Since, as discussed above, children have special developmental and physical needs (that to a greater or lesser degree have been translated into positive rights by different communities and cultures), the fundamental value for child advocates would seem to be that goods and services ought to be distributed on the basis of need (Margolis and Salkind, 1996). Some organizations translate that value into *child saving*, emphasizing children's incompetence and vulnerability, and the role of assistance from the community or state. A second, albeit related, advocacy promotes *parents as savers*, arguing for policies that enable parents to address the vulnerabilities and thereby meet the needs of children. Others are *child liberators* who argue for policies that ensure the independence and autonomy of children, assuming that children have the right as well as the capability to determine and act upon their own needs. Yet others, however, advocate for *parental rights*, believing that the private domain of the family is the only appropriate arena in which to meet the needs of children.

The many organizations engaged in child advocacy are extremely diverse in the goals that they promote and the principles upon which they are based. Private, nonprofit organizations devoted almost exclusively to advocacy include groups such as the Children's Defense Fund and the National Association for Child Advocates. Organizations such as the March of Dimes, with broad missions involving community service, research, and education, also frequently play substantial advocacy roles. Professional organizations such as the American Academy of Pediatrics or the American Public Health Association, particularly through its Maternal and Child Health Section, allocate time and resources to advocacy for mothers and children. Religious or church-based organizations also support advocacy efforts. A cursory search on the World Wide Web generates dozens of organizations of multiple political and philosophical views engaged in advocacy on behalf of mothers and children.

The role of governments—whether federal, state, or local—in advocacy is problematic. Clearly, agency social workers or attorneys engaged in child protection are charged with the responsibility for individual children as case advocates. At the systems level, however, governmental advocacy is more controversial. The Centers for Disease Control and Prevention, for example, has supported advocacy institutes to teach individuals to influence policies regarding the use of tobacco by youth. These same institutes are roundly criticized by other government officials whose constituencies depend on the production and sale of tobacco products! The 1971 White House Conference on Children called for a formal system of child advocacy (White House Conference, 1971). The final report states: "This Forum believes independent representation for children, a *system of child advocacy* (emphasis added), is urgently needed and should be immediately created" (White House Conference, 1971, p. 390). Citing such basic child needs as parental care, a secure home, moral guidance, proper nutrition, health, discipline, and education, the Forum observed that "Government should be responsive to these needs" (White House Conference, 1971, p. 389). Among its recommendations were a Cabinet-level Department of Children and Youth, a National Advisory Council on Child Advocacy, an Office of Child Advocacy (specifically recommended for immediate establishment) within the new Department, federally funded State Advisory Councils on Child Advocacy, and local Advocacy Boards, funded by the State Councils, which would hire full-time, salaried Child Advocates to be responsible for children in a specific geographic region. Although these recommendations were never implemented, states and communities around the country have set up child advocacy agencies at the state and local levels.

Steps in the Child Advocacy Process

Child advocates may pursue a number of strategies that are neither mutually exclusive nor restricted to a particular order. Strategies include educating policy makers and citizens, lobbying for legislation and/or regulation, and adjudicating when rights or interests cannot be satisfied. Some advocates would add demonstrating on behalf of children as well.

Informed and strategic use of the media is today a necessary component of successful public education on behalf of children's causes. A successful public information campaign may be targeted to increased use of bicycle helmets, higher immunization rates, or reduction in adolescent cigarette smoking. An educational activity that may be the most important component of the advocate's armamentarium is the education of policy makers. Such an educational strategy, when exercised by the leadership of formal public health organizations, is part of public health's policy development function. Indeed, as envisioned by the Institute of Medicine, public health leadership includes "communication skills; knowledge of and skills in the public decision process, including its political dimensions; and the ability to marshal constituencies for effective action" (Institute of Medicine, 1988, p. 119).

As history and experience demonstrate, linking education with policy change at the legislative or regulatory levels can be more effective than public information campaigns alone. For example, seat belts and child auto safety restraints had been technologically feasible for decades before states began requiring their use. Prior to legislation, the percent of child passengers utilizing child auto safety restraints was in the teens. Today, in states like North Carolina with vigorous enforcement of legislative mandates and loaner programs for poor families, coupled with media campaigns, child auto safety restraint use may be as high as 80 percent.

Many large maternal and child health-related organizations have published handbooks and guides to effective advocacy (Children's Defense Fund, 1991; Michigan Council for Maternal and Child Health, n.d.). In 1981, the American Academy of Pediatrics produced an advocacy handbook for its state chapters (Government Affairs Committee, 1981). This manual outlines a strategic process for advocates to follow. Effective advocacy begins with identifying simple, specific, achievable objectives that "should benefit children directly and pediatricians indirectly, if at all" (Government Affairs Committee, 1981, p. 4). Next, advocates should develop data. Although data alone will not convince legislators, good data are necessary both to convince legislators and to gain the support of ancillary groups. Access to data enhances the credibility of advocates. Earning a reputation as a source of reliable information may lead to legislators and policy makers approaching the advocate for answers on the next child health issue.

Moving from a good idea and good data to a bill requires choosing an author to sponsor the legislation. One should select a legislator with authority and a place on the appropriate legislative committee. Working with or through a constituent from that legislator's home district, arrange a meeting, preceded by a letter outlining the proposal. Work with that legislator's staff to determine the feasibility of the proposal and the best ways to link the proposal with the legislator's personal interests. Once the meeting has taken place, assuming the legislator agrees, the staff then provide the technical support necessary for crafting the most appropriate language for the legislation.

When a proposal for legislation and a prospective sponsor have been secured, recruiting allies to the cause is a necessary next step. Natural allies for child advocacy are PTAs, Junior Leagues, March of Dimes chapters, state and local child advocacy councils, county boards of health, and educators. These allies can be key to marshaling additional constituent support at the local level for generating letters and phone calls and testifying at hearings. Coalitions of child advocacy groups can remain organized after the passage of the bill, both for monitoring implementation and for developing a legislative agenda for the future.

Success in the legislative arena does not guarantee the changes necessary for children to realize the benefits. Advocacy involves continuing struggle during the rule-making process. Advocates must now turn their attention to the administrative department charged with the responsibility of implementing the law. In order to influence and monitor the implementation of regulations that put the legislation into effect, meetings with administrative staff may be necessary. Proposed regulations must be publicized with an adequate period for public comment. Advocates need to keep the sponsoring legislator(s) informed of the implementation process, especially if it is not going well. Lapses in effective advocacy at this stage may be part of the reason for the failure of EPSDT (Early and Periodic Screening, Diagnosis, and Treatment) to reach more than 39 percent of eligible children (Hill, 1992), given the administrative decision to place primary responsibility for the program in the reimbursement-minded federal Medicaid agency rather than the public health-oriented Title V agency.

In contrast, active advocacy through the Consumer Product Safety Commission has resulted in numerous regulatory bans of dangerous products such as unsafe toys, infant cribs with entrapment and strangulation hazards, and three-wheel all-terrain vehicles. Contrary to the popular impression of regulations as illegitimate violations of personal liberties, much public health regulation has enjoyed widespread public support. The most conspicuous examples come from auto safety regulation, but even in an era of suspicion of government, clean air and water regulations and even regulation of handguns and of access to tobacco products by minors can be successful, if opposition by well-funded special interests can be matched by the organized activities of child and public health advocates.

Regulatory authority for public health, as is the case for many other governmental functions in the United States, is divided among the three levels: federal, state and local. Although most public health regulation resides at the state level, each level of government has a role to play. Advocates, therefore, need to be active at each level. While the federal government is legitimately involved in actions and services that are in the public interest of the entire nation, especially in the case of conditions that do not respect state boundaries, it is at the state level that responsibility for assessment, assurance, and policy development is vested, unless specifically delegated to the federal government. Child advocates with a national agenda may find the strategy of working up from the state level desirable. There are many examples of advocacy at the local level that not only succeeded in improving the health of children, but became precedents for action at the state level. The American Academy of Pediatrics has been a consistent supporter of legislative initiatives on behalf of children and families for over 65 years. Many of its successes can be traced to the advocacy activities of state pediatric societies. Among the triumphs at the state level that went on to become nationwide policy are health insurance coverage for newborns, child auto safety seat legislation, and vaccine liability legislation. In the case of preventing tap water burns, Dr. Murray Katcher, former Director of Maternal and Child Health for Wisconsin, started advocating for regulating the maximum setting of hot water heaters at 120 degrees in Wisconsin (Katcher et al., 1989). After a few other states joined ranks with Wisconsin, hot water heater manufacturers voluntarily agreed to a national standard that set the maximum temperature of new hot water heaters at the factory. Manufacturers realized it would be in their best interest to have a single standard rather than 50 different standards, and advocates achieved a success without resorting to federal regulation. Importantly, many policy and program decisions having to do with public schools are made at the local level.

In addition to educational and legislative/regulatory strategies, advocates can attempt to secure the rights or interests of mothers and children through the judicial process. Numerous advocacy victories have been won in court when legislatures were immovable. Some of these, in the areas of juvenile justice and reproductive health, have already been alluded to above. A good example from the area of children with special health care needs is the case of the Pennsylvania suit by parents that resulted in a ruling guaranteeing free public education for all handicapped children (Pennsylvania Association for Retarded Children, 1971). It was only *after* this landmark ruling that Congress passed PL 94-142, the Education for all Handicapped Act. (See Chapter 11.)

THE FUTURE

As argued by Preston (1984), the elderly, in contrast to children, have three willing cohorts of advocates for their interests—the elderly themselves, the adult children of the elderly who want assistance in the care of their parents, and the adult children of the elderly who see themselves as eventually becoming old and needing assistance. In order to realize the promise of children's rights for all, there will need to be a change in the prevailing model guiding the development of social policy in the United States. Richard Titmuss (1974), the architect of the British National Health Service (NHS), has described three such models of social policy. The first, the Residual Welfare Model, exemplified by the work of economists like Milton Friedman (1962) and Friedrich Hayek (1944) and policy analysts such as Charles Murray (1984), postulates that there are only two legitimate ways to meet people's needs, through the family and through the free market. When one or the other breaks down, social institutions provide the necessary resources to individuals on a temporary basis. Under this model, "the object of the welfare state is to teach people to do without it" (Titmuss, 1975, p. 31), and beneficiaries are expected to accept society's judgment that in some way or ways they have failed. This model has driven 1996 welfare reform legislation in the U.S. (P.L. 104-193, Personal Responsibility and Work Opportunity Reconciliation Act of 1996) which eliminated the entitlement to federal cash support that poor children had enjoyed, in one form or another, since 1935. Support for the elderly, in contrast, is based on the view that their social contributions entitle them to societal benefits, without consideration to the idea that they should learn to do without such benefits.

The second model is the Industrial Achievement-Performance model, which offers the social welfare system as an adjunct to the economy. Benefits are distributed on the basis of social contribution, such as work performance and productivity. In the United States, for example, the most prevalent source of health insurance is as a fringe benefit of employment. Insurance is prohibitively expensive when it must be purchased by an individual outside of a work-related group. Social Security Old Age benefits and Medicare, to the extent that they are derived from one's lifetime attachment to the labor force and are based to a limited degree on contributions made through payroll taxes while employed, also reflect the Industrial Achievement-Performance model.

Finally, Titmuss describes the Industrial-Redistributive model, which offers universalistic services outside of the market economy. Resources are distributed according to the principle of equity based on need (disproportionately more social benefits for the least well off). Under this model, social welfare is not stopgap, short term charity for individuals, but an instrument of a social policy which provides for the needs of society as a whole. For Titmuss this orientation is exemplified by the NHS itself, but in fact most western European countries, in one way or another, have created social policies which recognize access to basic health care as a right of all citizens, especially pregnant women and children (Miller, 1987). In the United States, since Social Security Old Age benefits and Medicare benefits greatly exceed their actuarial value, those programs represent the Industrial-Redistributive model in which resources are redistributed from the young to the old. In the case of these benefits, however, the redistribution is not based on need. The debate over converting those programs to need-based or means-tested programs has assumed great salience as the proportion of entitlements in the federal budget continues to grow (Bipartisan Commission on Entitlement and Tax Reform, 1994).

The future of the children is dependent on active and vibrant advocacy on their behalf. Children lack the developmental maturity to advocate for themselves. Partly as a result of that inadequacy, children are often excluded from the design and implementation of the very policies that affect them, making advocates essential. Promoting justice for children by distributing resources based on children's needs and by defining and securing rights for children is the central role that advocates play in policy debates. Not only should advocacy skills be taught to and practiced by public health officials, but they in turn should encourage the development of advocacy skills in the communities and among the parents with whom they work.

REFERENCES

American Academy of Pediatrics. Government Affairs Committee. 1981. *Pediatricians and the legislative process: A potent prescription for children.* Washington, DC: AAP.

Applebaum, D., and S.V. Lawton. 1990. *Ethics and the professions.* Englewood Cliffs, NJ: Prentice Hall.

Bandman, B. 1977. Some legal, moral, and intellectual rights of children. *Educational Theory 17,* 169–178.

Beauchamp, T., and J.F. Childress. 1983. *Principles of biomedical ethics.* New York: Oxford University Press.

Bipartison Commission on Entitlement Reform. August 1994. *Interim report to the President.* Washington, DC: Superintendent of Documents.

Blackstone, W. 1968. Blackstone on children and the rights and duties of parents. In *The child and the state.* Vol. I. Legal status in the family, apprenticeship and child labor, ed. G. Abbott, 9–13. New York, NY: Greenwood Press.

Children's Defense Fund. 1991. *An advocate's guide to lobbying and political activity for nonprofits: What you can and can't do.* Washington, DC: Author.

deMause, L. 1974. The evolution of childhood. In *The history of childhood,* ed. L. deMause. New York: Psychohistory Press.

Feinberg, J. 1978. Rights. In *Contemporary issues in bioethics,* eds. T. Beauchamp and L. Walters, 38–43. Encino, CA: Dickerson Publishing Co.

Fernandez, H.C. 1980. *The child advocacy handbook.* New York: The Pilgrim Press.

Friedman, M. 1962. *Capitalism and freedom.* Chicago: University of Chicago Press.

Green, R. 1976. In *Ethics and health policy,* eds. R.M. Veatch and R. Branson. Cambridge, MA: Ballinger.

Grotberg, E. 1977. *200 years of children.* Washington, DC: U.S. Department of Health, Education and Welfare.

Hammer v. Dagenhart, 247 US Reports 251, 268 (1918).

Hayek, F. A. 1944. *The road to serfdom.* Chicago: University of Chicago Press.

Hill, I.T. 1992. The role of Medicaid and other government programs in providing medical care for children and pregnant women. *The Future of Children, 2,* 134–153.

In Re Gault, 387 US 1 (1967).

Institute of Medicine. 1988. *The future of public health.* Washington, DC: National Academy Press.

Kahn, A., and S. McGowan. 1972. *Child advocacy: Report of a national baseline study.* Washington, DC: Columbia University School of Social Work and U.S. Department of Health, Education and Welfare, Office of Child Development, Children's Bureau. HEW Publication No. OCD 7318.

Katcher, M.L. et al. 1989. Liquid crystal thermometer use in pediatric office counseling about tap water burn prevention. *Pediatrics 83,* 766–771.

Kent v. US, US 383 541, 16 LE 2d 84, 86 S. Ct. 1045 (1966).

Leiby, J. 1976. History of social welfare. In *Encyclopedia of social work,* 18th ed., vol. 1. Silver Spring, MD: National Association of Social Workers.

Margolis, L.H., and N.J. Salkind. 1996. Parents as advocates for their children. *Journal for a Just and Caring Education 2,* 103–120.

Melton, G.B. 1991. Preserving the dignity of children around the world: The UN Convention on the Rights of the Child. *Child Abuse and Neglect 15,* 343–350.

Michigan Council for Maternal and Child Health. Undated. *From vision to action: A citizens' guidebook to grass roots advocacy.* Lansing, MI: Michigan Council for Maternal and Child Health.

Miller, C.A. 1987. *Maternal health and child survival.* Washington, DC: National Center for Clinical Infant Programs.

Murray, C. 1984. *Losing ground.* New York: Basic Books, Inc.

Pennsylvania Association for Retarded Children v. Pennsylvania, 334 F. Supp. 1257 E. D. Pa. (1971).

Pfohl, S.J. 1977. The "discovery" of child abuse. *Social Problems 24,* 310–323.

Planned Parenthood of Central Missouri v. Danforth, 428 US 52, 96 S. Ct. 2831 (1976).

Preston, S.H. 1984. Children and the elderly: divergent paths for America's dependents. *Demography 21,* 435–457.

Personal Responsibility and Work Opportunity Reconciliation Act, P.L. 104-193. 104th Congress, second session. August 22, 1996.

Radbill, S.X. 1968. A history of child abuse and infanticide. In *The battered child,* eds. R.E. Helfer and C.H. Kempe, Chicago, IL: The University of Chicago Press.

Rawls, J. 1969. *A theory of justice.* Cambridge, MA: Harvard University Press.

Roberts, B.S., and B.G. Considine. 1997. Public policy advocacy. In *Mosby's resource guide to children with disabilities and chronic illness,* eds. H.M. Wallace et al., 162–171. St. Louis, MO: Mosby.

Roosevelt, T. 1971. The conservation of childhood. In *Children and youth in America,* Vol. 2., ed. R. Bremner, 653–654. Cambridge, MA: Harvard University Press.

Titmuss, R. 1974. *Social policy: An introduction,* eds. B. Abel-Smith and K. Titmuss. New York: Pantheon Books.

Tuchman, B.W. 1978. *A distant mirror.* New York: Alfred A. Knopf.

U.S. Department of Health, Education and Welfare, Office of Child Development, Children's Bureau, National Center on Child Abuse and Neglect. 1976. Child abuse and neglect: An overview of the problem. In *The problem and its management,* vol. 1. Washington, DC: Author.

White House Conference on Children. 1971. *Report to the President.* Washington, DC: U.S. Government Printing Office.

Williams, G.J.R. 1983. Child protection: A journey into history. *Journal of Clinical Child Psychology 12.*

CHAPTER 2

Historical Foundations of Maternal and Child Health

Lewis H. Margolis, George P. Cole, and Jonathan B. Kotch

> *These questions of child health and protection are a complicated problem requiring much learning and action. And we need have great concern over this matter. Let no one believe that these are questions which should not stir a nation; that they are below the dignity of statesmen or governments. If we could have but one generation of properly born, trained, educated, and healthy children, a thousand other problems of government would vanish.*
>
> Herbert Hoover, 1931

INTRODUCTION

The development of policies to address the needs of mothers and children has played itself out in the unique political and social context of the United States. Three attributes in particular have influenced and continue to influence the development of maternal and child health policies. One attribute is federalism, that is, the fact that there are two major governmental entities—federal and state—that vie for influence within the structure outlined in the U.S. Constitution. This federal/state relationship is further complicated by the fact that there are thousands of county and city jurisdictions, each of which relates to both the federal government and its own state. The relative influence of these partners has waxed and waned, particularly during the twentieth century.

A second attribute is the independent judiciary that has served as the interpreter and upholder of the basic values infused in the Constitution. While the interpretation of certain constitutional limits has varied over the years, any given legislative action must pass judicial muster. The third attribute of the U.S. political and social scene is the high value placed on individualism, the free enterprise economic system, and the concomitant and dominant role of the private sector. Governmental influence in many spheres of life in the United States is generally justified in response to market failures rather than as a fundamental aspect of the social framework.

This chapter will characterize three phases in the development of U.S. health policy for mothers and children. First, the chapter reviews the origins of local, state, and federal participation in health care for mothers and children. Next, the discussion focuses on the emergence of the federal government as a major force in public maternal and child health (MCH) program development, with particular attention to the federal role in addressing equity. The chapter then concludes with consideration of the current political efforts to return power and responsibility for MCH policies, once again, to the states. Table 2–1 presents a chronology of the development of MCH services in the United States.

ORIGINS OF GOVERNMENTAL PARTICIPATION IN THE CARE OF MOTHERS AND CHILDREN

These attributes of social policy began to interact in prominent ways with regard to mothers and children following the Civil War. A series of developments prompted increased attention to the particular needs of children as distinct from adults. In the field of medicine, Dr. Abraham Jacobi and others began to articulate that the therapeutic needs of children differed from those of adults. Developments in the field of sanitation provided new understanding of determinants of infant mortality (Meckel, 1990). Fundamental discoveries in bacteriology and the prevention and control of infectious diseases provided a dramatic opportunity to demonstrate the possibilities of preventing infant deaths (Lesser, 1985). And while the discovery of the "germ theory" of disease gave public health a technological base, it became clear that prevention was not simply a medical research issue. Effective health promotion also demanded social mechanisms, the most important of which was public health education (Tratner, 1974).

In 1874, Henry Bergh, founder of the New York Society for the Prevention of Cruelty to Animals, personally intervened on behalf of a child who had been physically abused, bringing her situation to the attention of local authorities in New York City. Outrage over the absence of laws to protect children from such treatment prompted New York and other cities to enact laws prohibiting child cruelty and giving private agencies police authority to intervene in abusive situations (Williams, 1983). In New York, the new Society for the Prevention of Cruelty to Children (SPCC) assumed this responsibility.

Throughout history, children have been forced to provide menial or hazardous labor for their parents. The intense industrialization of the late nineteenth century drew many children into factories and mines, raising the concerns of child advocates and social reformers about the effects of working conditions on the health and education of children. Industrialization led to the creation of labor-intensive,

Table 2–1 A Chronology of Maternal and Child Health Services in the United States

1855	Founding of the Children's Hospital of Philadelphia
1869	State board of health established in Massachusetts
1879	Formation of a Section on Diseases of Children of the American Medical Association
1888	The American Pediatric Society founded to promote scientific inquiry into children's diseases
1893	First milk station established in New York City
1904	National Child Labor Committee organized to monitor effects of child labor on health and development
1907	First Bureau of Child Hygiene established in New York City
1909	First White House Conference on Children called by President Theodore Roosevelt
1912	Congress established the Children's Bureau
1921	First Maternity and Infancy Act (Sheppard-Towner)
1930	American Academy of Pediatrics founded
1935	Social Security Act, including Title V program, enacted
1943	Emergency Maternity and Infant Care program funded
1944	Association of Maternal and Child Health Programs founded as the Association of Directors of State and Territorial Maternal and Child Health and Crippled Children's Services
1951	American College of Obstetricians and Gynecologists founded
1954	Special appropriation to MCH programs for community services for children with mental retardation
1963	Special project grants for Maternity and Infant Care
1965	Title 18 (Medicare) and Title 19 (Medicaid) added to the Social Security Act. Amendments to Title V establish Children and Youth projects. First Neighborhood Health Center grant awarded.
1967	Office of Child Development created as a home for Head Start. Functions of the Children's Bureau distributed among four federal agencies.
1972	Special Supplemental Food Program for Women, Infants, and Children (WIC) established
1981	Maternal and Child Health Services Block Grant amendments to Title V enacted
1984	Beginning of a series of amendments to expand access to Medicaid
1989	Title V amended to increase accountability
1991	Healthy Start funded in 15 communities

low-paid jobs in mills, mines, and factories. Coupled with the high post–Civil War mortality experienced by working-age males, especially in the South, this situation resulted in the widespread employment of children in a number of out-of-home occupations (Schmidt and Wallace, 1988). By 1900, one in six 10- to 15-year-olds was employed, 40 percent in industry, 60 percent in agriculture, and children as young as 7 were employed in poor or hazardous work environments (Schmidt and Wallace, 1988).

In 1916 the Keating-Owen Act prohibited interstate commerce of goods produced by children. This legislation was controversial due to the necessity for children from poor families to work, and it was overturned by the U.S. Supreme Court in a 1918 case, *Hammer v. Dagenhart*, from textile-producing North Carolina (Berger and Johansson, 1980). It was not until the Depression forced unemployed adults to take jobs previously reserved for children that child labor was permanently constrained (Miller, 1988).

As immigrants poured into cities seeking new opportunities, the unmet health and educational needs of their children, as well as the potential threat to public health through the transmission of infectious diseases, became the subject of concern for reformers and politicians. The institutionalization of vital recordkeeping provided the first real evidence of the social impact of infant mortality. Infant death records revealed that in the United States in 1900, infant mortality averaged 150/1,000, was as high as 180/1,000 in some industrial cities, and claimed as many as 50 percent of the infants that had been abandoned or orphaned to the foundling hospitals that proliferated as a result of urbanization and immigration (Schmidt and Wallace, 1988). In this context, late nineteenth and early twentieth century social workers and public health officials joined forces. As social workers recognized that poverty and social dislocation engendered ill health, and that ill health caused poverty by creating economic burdens, they used their particular skills to combat poverty by promoting good health. They mobilized the lay leaders and residents of the community for the control of disease (Tratner, 1974). For example, recognizing the risk to infants of consuming spoiled milk and the heightened risk for poor infants because of the lack of adequate storage facilities, public health advocates urged municipalities and private individuals to fund milk stations where poor families could collect fresh milk (Grotberg, 1977).

The evolving concept of childhood as a special period of growth, socialization, and development provided a rational context for advocacy, while child labor, infant mortality, and child maltreatment provided highly visible targets for reform. A coalition of female reformers, the driving force behind the women's suffrage movement, lent energy, motivation, and critical mass to the ranks of settlement house workers, social workers, and public health nurses engaged in child advocacy. The first Bureau of Child Hygiene was established in 1907 in New York City, under the leadership of Dr. S. Josephine Baker. She had entered the New

York City Health Department after prejudice against female physicians had limited her ability to advance in academic medicine and private practice (Baker, 1994). One of the main strategies undertaken by Baker was to send public health nurses to visit the tenement homes of newborn babies in order to educate mothers about how to care for their new infants. The Bureau became involved in the care of school children, the supervision of midwives, and the regulation of children's institutions.

The convergence of social, economic, and political forces at the turn of the century resulted in the call for a federal role in promoting, if not ensuring, the well-being of children. In 1909, President Theodore Roosevelt convened the first White House Conference on Children. Emerging from the conference were calls for service programs and financial aid to protect the home environment and recommendations that the federal government take responsibility for gathering information on problems of infant and child health and welfare (Lesser, 1985; Schmidt and Wallace, 1988; Skocpol, 1992; Tratner, 1974). These recommendations gave rise to the Mother's Aid Movement and the American Association for the Study and Prevention of Infant Mortality. The former group drew attention to the benefits of keeping children in the family while pointing out the detrimental effects of dehumanizing institutions. The latter group drew attention to the unacceptably high rate of infant deaths (Lesser, 1985; Schmidt and Wallace, 1988; Tratner, 1974).

With advocacy from education, psychology, medicine, public health, labor, and social work, and over the opposition of groups opposing federal meddling in the private domain of parents, Congress followed another of the Conference's recommendations and enacted legislation establishing the Children's Bureau. Legislation for such an agency had been first introduced in 1906, but intense debate centering on the question of whether child welfare was a federal or state responsibility stalled its passage until 1912. Assigned to the Department of Commerce and Labor and reflecting the roots of the Bureau in concern over labor conditions for children, the Act charged the Children's Bureau to "investigate and report . . . upon all matters pertaining to the welfare of children and child life among all classes of our people, and . . . especially investigate the questions of infant mortality, the birth rate, orphanages, juvenile courts, desertion, dangerous occupations, accidents and diseases of children, employment, legislation affecting children in the several States and Territories" (U.S. Congress, 1912). The tension between public and private responsibility for children was reflected in the legislation that stated, "no official, or agent, or representative of said bureau shall, over the objection of the head of the family, enter any house used exclusively as a family residence."

Under the leadership of its first Chief, Julia Lathrop, the Children's Bureau embarked upon an active repertoire of investigations into the conditions of children. For example, the Bureau conducted a longitudinal study of the relationship between income and infant mortality (Lathrop, 1919). Other studies addressed child labor, working mothers, children's nutrition, services for crippled children, and juvenile delinquency. In 1915, as the result of Bureau studies that concluded that "to study infant mortality it is necessary to know how many babies have been born," the National Birth Registry was established (Bremner, 1970, p. 963).

While the mandate of the Bureau was to investigate and report, its leaders began to develop a legislative agenda to address identified problems. In 1918, Representative Jeanette Rankin of Montana introduced legislation to provide federal funds to the states to establish preventive health programs for mothers and infants (Wilson, 1989). This legislation was strongly supported by the suffragettes, but was opposed by the medical community because it would place responsibility for a health care program under the "non-medical" Children's Bureau (Lesser, 1985). In the midst of the debate over the legislation, the Second White House Conference on Children (1919) issued recommendations for minimum standards of maternal and child health care.

By 1920, sponsorship of the bill was assumed by Senator Morris Sheppard of Texas and Representative Horace Towner of Iowa. Subsequently, partially in recognition that the United States was not doing particularly well in responding to problems of maternal and infant (M&I) health, and partially out of fear of a feminine voting bloc backlash, Congress passed the Maternity and Infancy Act (also known as the Sheppard-Towner Act) in November 1921 (Schmidt and Wallace, 1988).

The Sheppard-Towner Act authorized grants paid "to the several States for the purpose of cooperating with them in promoting the welfare and hygiene of maternity and infancy as hereinafter provided" (Bremner, 1971). Under the Act, each state that elected to receive these funds was required to establish a child welfare or child hygiene agency, representing the first federal effort to develop an MCH infrastructure within the states. The monies were allocated as a grant in two parts. Under the first part, each state received an equal share of a $480,000 appropriation. Under the second part, totaling $1,000,000, each state received $5,000, plus an amount proportionate to that state's population in the census of 1920. States were required to match the funds provided under the second part of the Act. Funds were distributed in response "to detailed plans for carrying out the provisions of this Act within such State." Although the Sheppard-Towner Act did not regulate the content of these plans beyond "promoting the welfare and hygiene of maternity and infancy," the legislation was quite explicit in what states were not permitted to do. Continuing the attention to individual liberty instilled in the Children's Bureau authorization, the Act asserted that, "No official, agent, or representative of the Children's Bureau shall by virtue of this Act have any right to enter any home over the objection of the owner thereof, or to take charge of any children over the objection of the parents, or either of them, or of the person standing in loco parentis or having custody of such child. Nothing in this Act shall be construed as limiting the power of a parent or guardian or person standing in loco parentis to determine what treatment or correction shall be provided for a child or the agency or agencies to be employed for such purpose." Second, states were not permitted to spend monies on buildings or "payment of any maternity or infancy pension, stipend, or gratuity."

The Congressional debate over the Sheppard-Towner Act replicated the heated encounters that occurred over the establishment of the Children's Bureau. On one side were those who argued for a federal role in promoting the welfare of mothers and children. This argument was presented in economic terms, that is, that the federal government plays a role in agricultural and commercial activities in order to promote economic development, and children represent no less valuable a resource. The opposition to Sheppard-Towner was argued on several grounds. Some were opposed to any governmental role, i.e., interference, in the relationship between children and their parents. In this view, the family was a private domain, and responsibility for children resided with their parents or local family members or charities. Another source of opposition was organized medicine through the American Medical Association (AMA). Exploiting the uncertainty and fear stemming from the Communist revolution in Russia in 1917, the AMA decried the law as an "imported socialistic scheme unsuited to our form of government" (JAMA, 1922, p. 1709). Further, the AMA sought to protect practitioners from what was perceived as the potential for governmental interference or control over the practice of medicine, despite the fact that Sheppard-Towner support for primary care (as opposed to preventive care) was expressly forbidden. Furthermore, the bill was also assailed because it required services to be available to all citizens. When it was re-considered in 1929, the Maternity and Infancy Act was defeated (Schmidt and Wallace, 1988).

The debate within the AMA over Sheppard-Towner spawned the birth of the American Academy of Pediatrics (Hughes, 1980). During the 1922 meeting of the AMA, the Pediatric Section debated and endorsed Sheppard-Towner, concluding that it was in the best interests of mothers and children. The AMA House of Delegates, however, not only condemned the Act, but also repudiated the Pediatric Section for its endorsement without the approval of the governing House. Recognizing that the AMA was not prepared to speak for the welfare of children, pediatricians met over the next eight years and finally convened the first meeting of the American Academy of Pediatrics in Detroit in 1930, which became a powerful and consistent supporter of MCH policies and programs (Lesser, 1985; Schmidt and Wallace, 1988).

The Sheppard-Towner Act passed handily in 1921, in part due to uncertainty over how newly enfranchised women would vote. Passage of this legislation was the first national political issue to follow the passage of the nineteenth amendment the previous year, granting women the right to vote. Another factor that facilitated its passage was the effort to assuage organized medicine by emphasizing the preventive nature of this legislation in an attempt to avoid a conflict with the private practice of medicine. Whereas physicians were viewed as the appropriate source of care for sick infants and parturient women, the educational and screening activities envisioned in the bill were presented as complements and enhancements of traditional medical care. Nevertheless, opposition intensified throughout the 1920s. Physicians began to recognize the competitive potential that the provision of preventive services had for the development of their practices. Opposition also grew within the Catholic Church, fearful of a governmental role in the provision of historically church-based charitable services. A third source of protest came from within the Public Health Service, annoyed at the dissemination of health services through this program of the Department of Commerce and Labor. As a result, the Act was not renewed after 1929. The defeat of the Maternity and Infancy Act established the hegemony of both the medical community and the medical model in MCH policy development, and established the publicly funded use of private providers as the preferred method of health care delivery.

The accomplishments of the Sheppard-Towner Act were reviewed in the Eighteenth Annual Report of the Children's Bureau. Birth registration increased from 30 states, covering 72 percent of the births in 1922, to 46 states, representing 95 percent of the population. By 1920, child hygiene bureaus had been established in 28 states, 16 of them in 1919 alone, a result of Children's Bureau leadership. After the implementation of the Act, another 19 states established such bureaus. Hundreds of maternal and/or child health consultation centers were established, often in conjunction with local health agencies. Even after expiration of the appropriation, 19 states continued to fund the efforts implemented under the Act.

THE EMERGENCE OF THE FEDERAL GOVERNMENT IN COMMUNITY ASSESSMENT, POLICY DEVELOPMENT, AND ASSURANCE FOR MOTHERS AND CHILDREN

With the descent into the Great Depression in 1929, many states and local communities were confronted by the challenge of rising health needs in the face of catastrophic levels of unemployment and devastated budgets as state and local governments witnessed the decimation of their tax bases. State programs for indigent parents and children existed, but without Maternity and Infancy Act funds, health services for mothers and infants were drastically reduced. By 1934, "23 states appropriated virtually no MCH funds" for such services (Lesser, 1985, p. 592). The Depression impoverished 40 percent of the population.

After his election in 1932, President Franklin D. Roosevelt recommended legislation designed to provide temporary assistance to the "deserving" poor and ongoing economic insurance to those who were making it but might need help in the future. He charged the Economic Security Committee to address "security for men, women and children . . . against several of the great disturbing factors of life—especially those which relate to unemployment and old age" (Grotberg, 1977, p. 87). Consultation with Grace Abbott and other representatives of the Children's Bureau resulted in the incorporation of Bureau plans into the Social Security Act of 1935. The Bureau proposed three major sets of activities: (1) aid to dependent children; (2) welfare services for children needing special care; and (3) maternal and child health services including services for crippled children. These were incorporated into the Social Security Act, enacted on August 14, 1935 (Hutchins, 1994). Title IV provided cash payments to mothers who had lost fathers' support for their children. Responsibility for this Title was given to the newly created Social Security Board, rather than the Children's Bureau. Title V consisted of four parts. Part 1, Maternal and Child Health Services, represented an expansion of the programs established under the Sheppard-Towner Act. Part 2, Services for Crippled Children,[1] enabled states to improve services for locating crippled children and "for providing medical, surgical, corrective, and other services and care, and facilities for diagnosis, hospitalization, and aftercare, for children who are crippled or who are suffering from conditions which lead to crippling" (United States Congress, 1935, p. 631). Part 3, Child-Welfare Services, enabled states to provide services for "the protection and care of homeless, dependent, and neglected children, and children in danger of becoming delinquent" (United States Congress, 1935, p. 633). Part 4, Vocational Rehabilitation, enabled states to strengthen programs of vocational rehabilitation of the physically disabled, although the administration of this part was not under the Children's Bureau.

A broad base of public support existed for the child health, welfare, and economic security components of the Social Security Act. Support for Titles IV and V was especially strong. All the leading women's organizations were represented at the Congressional hearings to express their support. Opposition to Titles IV and V, which might have been expected given the history of the Maternity and Infancy Act, did not materialize. The AMA was preoccupied with the broader issue of blocking any possibility of national health insurance (Witte, 1963).

The funding formula for Title V had several components. One set of funds sent an equal share to each state. A second set was distributed on the basis of live

---

[1]During the 1980s, the name of the Crippled Children's Program was changed to Children with Special Health Care Needs to reflect the multifaceted aspects of care for these children.

births and required a dollar-for-dollar match. A third set of funds was allocated based on financial need and the number of live births, without a required match. Finally, Crippled Children's funds provided an equal share as well as an allotment based on the number of children served, building an incentive to locate and treat children. The Secretary of Labor retained up to 15 percent of the appropriation for training, research, and demonstrations, including Special Projects of Regional and National Significance (SPRANS).

The onset of World War II created a new challenge in addressing the health needs of mothers and children. With the mobilization of millions of soldiers, many military wives, dislocated from their homes, were in need of maternity care. Although the Bureau attempted to provide support for medical care and hospitalization of these women through Title V funds, the amounts were inadequate. In 1943, Congress appropriated additional funds for the Emergency Maternity and Infant Care (EMIC) Program. These funds, allocated from general revenues and distributed through the states with no required match, paid for medical care for the wives of servicemen in the lowest four pay grades. By the time the program was phased out in 1949, it had provided care in 1.5 million maternity cases, approximately one of every seven births in the United States at its peak.

Federal initiatives following World War II were rather limited. While Title V secured and encouraged the development of MCH agencies within state health departments, the federal government directed its efforts mainly at the support of research and services for particular diseases. For example, the Crippled Children's Program adopted many conditions beyond the orthopedic problems that were the first targets of its programs. Epilepsy, congenital and rheumatic heart disease, hearing impairments, premature newborn care, and other conditions were incorporated into state programs (Lesser, 1985).

Also following the Second World War, the Children's Bureau began a slow but steady decline from its position of prominence in the national health and welfare arena. At its founding in 1912, the Director of the Bureau reported directly to the Secretary of Commerce and Labor and then, after the Department split in 1913, to the Secretary of Labor. Although arguments were raised about the appropriateness of the Children's Bureau within Labor as opposed to the Public Health Service, the early leaders of the Bureau maintained its leadership role in a wide range of maternal and child interests. During the 1930s, consideration was given to dividing the health, education, and welfare activities of the Bureau among various agencies, but the political pressure both without and within the federal bureaucracy was not sufficient to effect this change until the late 1940s. The Bureau was moved to the newly created Federal Security Administration in 1945. Although it did retain control, temporarily, of the various grant-in-aid programs that it had developed and administered, this marked the beginning of the decline of the influence of the Children's Bureau.

SOCIAL ACTIVISM, EQUITY, AND THE DEVELOPMENT OF MATERNAL AND CHILD HEALTH POLICY IN THE 1960s

Special Projects under Title V of the Social Security Act

President Kennedy's interest in mental retardation, stirred in part by the efforts of his parents to provide for their mentally retarded daughter, provided the Bureau with the opportunity to launch new initiatives. Arguing that mental retardation could be prevented, in part, by adequate prenatal care, the administration developed a program of special grants through Title V. Different from the traditional Bureau focus on preventive services, these M&I care projects, authorized by PL 88-156 in 1963, were designed to provide comprehensive services including prenatal, intrapartum, and postpartum medical care and hospitalization. By 1969, 53 projects had served 100,000 impoverished women and their infants nationwide (Lesser, 1985). Not only did the scope of supported activities change with the introduction of these projects, but also the administration of Bureau activities changed. Rather than allocating funds through state health agencies, the Bureau distributed M&I funds directly to the service agencies. Further, funds for these demonstration projects could be allocated to private, nonprofit institutions. Comparable projects for children and youth (C&Y) were inaugurated in 1965. By 1969, 58 C&Y projects had provided preventive and primary medical care to 335,000 children (Lesser, 1985). Funded as "demonstration" projects, the M&I projects in particular reported notable improvements in infant health (Sokol et al., 1980). Special projects for neonatal intensive care, family planning, and dental care followed. The M&I and C&Y projects expanded in number during the 1960s and early 1970s, but were never extended beyond their demonstration status to become the general policy.

Public Health and Child Protection

The period from 1960 to 1974 was much like the earlier Social Reform Era in its public expression of social malcontent and institutional mistrust. Civil rights advocates established that otherwise disenfranchised adults and children had rights that could be enforced by legal and administrative means. Further, by gaining legal access to bureaucratic decision making, those same advocates challenged the complacency of professionals who purportedly served disenfranchised adults and children.

At the same time, medical and public health professionals were challenged to reconsider the relationship of child health and social phenomena. In 1946, John Caffey, a pediatric radiologist, published a paper describing traumatic long bone fractures in infants. In 1953, a paper by Silverman, also a radiologist, discussed the possibility that such fractures might be parent-induced. In 1955, Wooley and

Evans concluded that infants suffering from repeated fractures often come from homes with aggressive, immature, or emotionally ill adults. In 1957, Caffey recapitulated his earlier findings, urging physicians to consider parental abuse when diagnosing injured infants (Pfohl, 1976; Williams, 1983).

However, it was not until 1962, with the publication of Henry Kempe's paper, "The Battered Child Syndrome," that the incidence of physically abused children seen in the nation's hospitals caught the attention of child health professionals and the public everywhere (Kempe et al., 1962). "The Battered Child Syndrome" challenged the belief that parental abuse ". . . was a deplorable fact of the past" (Rosenheim, 1977, p. 453). It also documented the medical community's unwillingness to implicate parents in diagnosing abuse (Pfohl, 1976; Williams, 1983).

The public health community's response to Kempe's "discovery" of child abuse was immediate and dramatic, and within a decade child protection had become a national priority. In 1962, the Children's Bureau prepared and disseminated a model child abuse reporting law, and the Social Security Amendments of 1962 required each state to make child welfare services available to all children, including the abused child. In 1963, 18 bills to protect abused children were introduced in Congress, 11 of which passed, and subsequently states developed or expanded their capacities to respond to reports of child abuse. By 1967, all states had child abuse reporting laws (Williams, 1983).

In 1973, widely publicized hearings were chaired by Sen. Walter Mondale (D.-Minnesota) on proposed legislation to establish federal leadership in child protection. In 1974, with the support of virtually every children's advocacy group and the AMA, the Child Abuse Prevention and Treatment Act was passed, creating a structure for responding to the problem of child maltreatment much like the original Children's Bureau had been a structure for responding to MCH needs (Williams, 1983).

Title XVIII (Medicare) and Title XIX (Medicaid)

Culminating three decades of debate over the nature of the federal role in providing health insurance, Congress enacted Medicare, Title XVIII of the Social Security Act, in 1965. Unique among Western nations with compulsory health insurance, the United States limits its coverage to the elderly. Medicare provides coverage for short-term hospitalization and medical services. Hospitalization is financed through employment taxes, and physician services are financed jointly through premiums (approximately 25 percent of the actuarial cost) and general federal revenues (the remaining cost). Unlike Title V, states play no role in the financing, administering, or standard-setting for this program.

Since the political struggle over the federal role in health care was waged in the arena of Medicare, the accompanying legislation to establish Medicaid, a program of health insurance assistance for the poor, was shielded from controversy. Enacted as Title XIX of the Social Security Act, the structure of the Medicaid program built upon earlier federal support to the states for low income elderly. In contrast to Medicare, the Medicaid program involves joint federal-state financing and state development of standards within guidelines established by the federal government. A third characteristic of Medicaid (a characteristic that has gradually changed through a series of alterations during the 1980s) was the linkage of eligibility for Medicaid to eligibility for Aid for Families with Dependent Children (AFDC). Consistent with the state-federal partnership, criteria for welfare eligibility are established by the states so that state welfare regulations have a direct effect on eligibility for the federal Medicaid program. The welfare eligibility requirement severely limited eligibility for Medicaid. As Davis and Schoen (1978) note in *Health and the War on Poverty*, a majority of states limited AFDC to families without a father in the home. The income and assets requirements further limited access to the program. For example, in 1985, the cutoff for eligibility for Medicaid ranged among states from a low of only 16 percent of the federal poverty income guidelines to 97 percent (Rosenbaum and Johnson, 1986).

Soon after the implementation of Medicaid, it became apparent that its focus on acute medical care rather than preventive services impeded its effectiveness for children. Social Security amendments submitted by President Lyndon Johnson in 1967 modified Medicaid and Title V Crippled Children's programs to include a new benefit, the Early and Periodic Screening, Diagnosis, and Treatment (EPSDT) program. Building upon language in the original Crippled Children's legislation of 1935, the EPSDT program has been described as "potentially the most comprehensive child health care program the government had ever undertaken" (Foltz, 1975, p. 35). The program called for specific services such as physical and developmental exams, vision and hearing screening, appropriate laboratory tests, dental referral for children under three, immunizations, and payment for other services covered by each state's Medicaid program. Further, the services had to be provided according to a periodicity schedule consistent with reasonable standards of care. Finally, states were expected actively to enroll Medicaid-eligible children into their programs.

Unfortunately, the implementation of EPSDT was slowed by several issues. First, the program was cobbled together through changes in programs (Medicaid and Title V) with different missions and different bureaucracies. In particular, the Medicaid program was anchored in the welfare system with its restrictive eligibility criteria, impairing the ability of this bold screening, referral, and treatment program to reach broad groups of children in need. Second, the costs of such an ambitious screening and treatment program were daunting to the states that were required to pay for these new services under the shared financing structure of Medicaid. As Rosenbaum and Johnson (1986) have emphasized, however, the main obstacle to the successful implementation of EPSDT as a program to address the preventive health needs of poor children was the fact that the proportion of poor children who were Medicaid-eligible remained low.

In spite of the limitations of the Medicaid program, it did increase access to medical care for poor children. According to a review conducted by the Office of Technology Assessment (U.S. Congress, 1988) and published in *Healthy Children: Investing in the Future*, children with Medicaid were similar to middle-income insured children with regard to general check-ups and immunizations. Further, Medicaid recipients with health problems were more likely to have seen a physician than were uninsured children. Although use of services increased for Medicaid recipients, the sites of care tended to be public health clinics, emergency rooms, and hospital outpatient departments rather than private physician offices (Orr and Miller, 1981), resulting in the further evolution of a dual system of health care. Studies of the effectiveness of EPSDT in particular suggest that participation in the program decreased the likelihood of referral for specialized care over time (Keller, 1983; Irwin and Conroy-Hughes, 1982). Others studies confirm that this screening and prevention program has not achieved the goals originally envisioned. For example, a review of California's screening program indicated that 30 percent of the children under age one enrolled in Medicaid reported a preventive service and only 65 percent of children age one to four were up-to-date on their immunizations (Yudkowsky and Fleming, 1990).

Neighborhood/Community Health Centers

Although Medicaid quickly became the financial underpinning of medical services for poor mothers and children, several additional health programs arose out of the political and social activism of the early 1960s. The Economic Opportunity Act of 1964 established the Office of Economic Opportunity (OEO). Recognizing medical care as only one of many determinants of health, OEO funded a series of Neighborhood Health Centers. While these centers provided comprehensive medical services including prevention and treatment of physical and mental conditions, their mission was much broader. The Neighborhood Health Centers provided employment opportunities in their low income catchment areas and served as the focus for other community and economic development activities. In addition to the broad service mandate, several other characteristics made these centers a unique approach to health services for the poor. For example, independent of state and local governments, the centers were supposed to be governed by boards of community members. Further, services were supposed to be without cost to the users.

A key administrative and political aspect of these centers was that their federal support came directly to the local community organizations that had solicited the funds. Unlike the Title V program and Medicaid that allocated funds to states and required a state match, the establishment of Neighborhood Health Centers enabled federal policy makers to leap over potential state level bureaucratic impediments to addressing local conditions, as well as social and political attitudes and prejudices that had disenfranchised the poor people who needed the services provided by these health centers (Sardell, 1988).

As political support for the War on Poverty declined with the election of Richard Nixon in 1968, the legislative base for Neighborhood Health Centers changed. As Sardell (1988) notes, the centers achieved their own authorization under PL 94-63 and were renamed Community Health Centers. Unfortunately, attempts to rationalize the administration and oversight of the centers through the delineation of two types of financial support for (1) required and (2) supplemental services resulted in disproportionate emphasis on required, traditional medical services in contrast to the supplemental services such as health education, social services, and outreach. The appeal of the infrastructure established by the centers was strong, however, and Congress has occasionally appropriated funds for special infant mortality initiatives by them.

Special Supplemental Food Program for Women, Infants, and Children (WIC)

Created in 1972, the Special Supplemental Food Program for Women, Infants, and Children (WIC) has become a fundamental component of government support for mothers and children. The program provides supplemental food, nutrition education, and access to medical care. Under eligibility guidelines established by the federal government and through federally appropriated funds, states distribute food (or coupons for selected, nutritious foods) to low income pregnant women, nursing mothers, infants, and children considered at nutritional risk. The key economic risk factor is family income under 185 percent of the federal poverty level. WIC has been associated with health improvements reflected in decreased rates of low birth weight (Rush, 1988) and anemia (Yip et al., 1987). From a services perspective there has been difficulty in incorporating WIC into other MCH programs. As indicated below in the discussion of major policy changes in the 1980s, administrative efforts are underway to make the supplemental food program a more cohesive part of services for mothers and children. For example, studies of the linkage of the provision of WIC services with immunization have, not surprisingly, shown marked improvement in immunization rates (Kotch and Whiteman, 1982).

Head Start

Analogous to the attention to Community Health Centers as sites around which to organize efforts to address the more far-reaching determinants of health was the focus on early childhood as a time during which key social and economic influences might be altered to promote the later well-being of children. Project Head Start was launched as a summer program in 1965, to provide an intellectually stimulating and healthful environment for preschool children in centers established for that purpose. Proposed for 100,000 children, the popularity was such that over 560,000 children enrolled during that first summer. In spite of controversy over the intellectual benefits of Head Start, this federal effort has grown steadily since its inception. An often overlooked impact of Head Start has been its effect on health. In a review of Head Start studies, Ron Haskins (1989), a staff analyst with the Committee on Ways and Means of the House of Representatives, noted that children attending Head Start were "more likely to get medical and dental exams, speech and developmental assessments, nutrition evaluations, and vision and hearing screenings." Further, Head Start programs are well targeted toward poor children and provide many jobs as teachers and staff for low income community members.

With the implementation of Head Start, the Children's Bureau met its functional, if not legislative, demise. Bureau responsibilities had focused increasingly on the area of welfare, even though the actual administration of AFDC fell within the purview of another agency. As reviewed by Steiner (1976), there was reluctance to assign a prominent and potentially substantial initiative such as Head Start to the Children's Bureau. Secretary of Health, Education and Welfare Robert Finch, lacking strong political support for the Children's Bureau, delegated Head Start to the newly created Office of Child Development, also assigning the Children's Bureau, a shell of its former self, to this newly created office. The Title V Maternal and Child Health and Crippled Children's programs were assigned to the Health Services and Mental Health Administration of the Public Health Service. Child Welfare Services and the Juvenile Delinquency Service were assigned to the Social and Rehabilitation Service (Hutchins, 1994). What remained of the Children's Bureau was left with its responsibilities limited to that of a clearinghouse for agency information about children's health and welfare.

REDEFINING THE ROLES OF STATES

The election of Ronald Reagan as President in 1980 was followed by changes in Title V and Medicaid. As part of the Reagan effort to decrease the size of the federal government, reduce federal spending for social programs, and return power to the states, many categorical grants were combined into a series of block grants. The initial proposal by the President was to create two health block grants, converting 11 health services grants and 15 preventive health programs, respectively. Negotiations with Congress resulted in the consolidation of 21 programs into four health block grants: (1) alcohol, drug abuse, and mental health; (2) primary care; (3) preventive health; and (4) maternal and child health.

The MCH Services Block Grant consolidated seven programs: Maternal and Child Health Services and Crippled Children's Services under Title V, Supplemental Security Income Disabled Children's Services, Hemophilia, Sudden Infant Death Syndrome, Prevention of Lead-Based Paint Poisoning, Genetic Disease, and Adolescent Health Services. Federal regulations covering the content of the programs in this block grant were minimal, permitting states to establish their own priorities. Funding for the block grant was reduced from $454.9 million in FY 1981 to $373.7 million in FY 1982, under the rationale that reduced federal regulation would enable states to undertake these activities more efficiently (Peterson et al., 1986). States were permitted, however, to transfer other block grant funds into the MCH block grant, although transfers of funds from MCH were prohibited. As the decade progressed, Congress increased MCH block grant funding to a high of $687 million in 1994. Political forces in the 104th Congress threatened to cut the 1997 appropriation for Title V by 50 percent, but MCH advocates succeeded in reducing the proposed reduction to 1 percent.

The allocation formula for Title V funds with the MCH Services Block Grant as the current incarnation has undergone several revisions. The initial formula described above was altered in 1963 when Congress authorized that project grants could be distributed directly to local health agencies and various public and non-profit organizations, providing the funding base for the M&I Care Projects and the C&Y Projects mentioned previously. As described by Klerman (1981) in her lucid review of the development of Title V, Congress decided in 1967 to re-allocate these special project funds back into the basic formula grant. States were required to have a "Program of Projects" in M&I care, neonatal intensive care, family planning, health of children and youth, and dental health of children, although by no means was the intent or expectation that these were to extend statewide, beyond the "demonstration" mode. Funds were provided to ensure that each state undertook these required programs, but states with large urban populations were at risk of receiving smaller allocations than they had received under the previous scheme. The Section 516 allotment was added to ensure that no state received less through the formula grants than it had received through its previous formula and project grants.

With the creation of the MCH Services Block Grant in 1981, the allocation formula was again based on previous allocations under the categorical programs. States were held "harmless" in that they would receive the same proportion of funds as under the prior legislation. As excess funds became available, they were to be distributed on the basis of the low income population, but as the General Accounting Office (GAO) noted, in 1990 90 percent of the MCH block grants were allocated on the basis of their previous allocations, rather than adjustments for the low income population. In a provocative study of allocation, the GAO (1992) examined what allocations would look like if done on the basis of three simple "at-risk" indicators—proportion of low birth weight children, proportion of children living in poverty, and proportion of the state's population under the age of 21 (compared to the U.S. population). The GAO determined that 14 percent of the block grant funds would shift from lower risk to higher risk states, with decreases in 37 states and increases in 14.

The Medicaid program also was the object of major change in 1981. Mothers and children were directly affected by adverse changes in the eligibility requirements for AFDC. Since eligibility for AFDC was the major criterion for participation in Medicaid, loss of AFDC meant a loss of Medicaid coverage, resulting in a decline in the proportion of poor people covered by Medicaid early in the 1980s.

Changes in Title V and Medicaid during the 1980s reflected the ongoing tension between the White House, controlled by Republicans, and the Congress, controlled by Democrats. The back-to-back economic recessions of 1979 through 1982 were accompanied by deterioration in several fundamental maternal and child health indicators. For example, although the national infant mortality rate continued to decline, several states experienced increases or plateauing rates. The proportion of children covered by health insurance declined. Pressured by governors and advocates for mothers and children, Congress turned to the Medicaid program as the structure on which to address some of the glaring gaps in health services for mothers and children. The budget reconciliation process produced the changes shown in Table 2–2. In 1986, Congress severed the link between AFDC and Medicaid by permitting states to enroll pregnant women in Medicaid whose incomes were up to 100 percent of the federal poverty level even if their incomes were greater than the state income limit. The 1989 Omnibus Budget Reconciliation Act (OBRA) was noteworthy in that it set a national floor for Medicaid eligibility. By April 1990, states were required to extend Medicaid coverage to all pregnant women and children up to age six with family incomes below 133 percent of the federal poverty level.

The Medicaid expansions of the 1980s were effective in increasing access to care for poor pregnant women and children. As Cartland and coworkers (1993) have reported, Medicaid added five million recipients, half of whom were children. In 1990, 7 percent of the children enrolled in Medicaid were recipients as a result of the expansions of the 1980s. The proportion of recipients as a result of AFDC eligibility decreased from 90 percent in 1979 to 72 percent in 1990, although this population accounted for 29.8 percent of the increased costs, in contrast to 26.8 percent by the expansion children. The remaining increased costs were accounted for by children not receiving cash assistance (19.4 percent) and medically needy (24.0 percent). In 1994, children constituted 50 percent of the 25 million beneficiaries. Reflecting the persistent emphasis in Medicaid on treatment and rehabilitation as well as the lesser health care needs of the young, children accounted for only 15 percent of the expenditures (Families USA, 1995).

Table 2–2 Changes in Medicaid Eligibility during the 1980s

1984	Required states to provide Medicaid coverage to single pregnant women, women in two-parent unemployed families, and all children born after 9/30/83, if their incomes would have made them eligible for AFDC, according to each state's income guidelines.
1985	Required states to provide Medicaid coverage to all remaining pregnant women with family income below each state's AFDC eligibility levels and immediate coverage of all children under age five with AFDC-level income or below.
1986	Allowed states to cover pregnant women, infants up to age one, and on an incremental basis, children up to age five living in families with incomes above the state's AFDC income levels, but below 100 percent of the FPL, effectively severing the link between AFDC eligibility and Medicaid eligibility. Also permitted states to make pregnant women presumptively eligible for prenatal care upon application and permitted states to eliminate the assets tests for poverty-related eligible pregnant women and children, allowing shortened application forms.
1987	Permitted states to increase the upper limit on income for pregnant women and infants up to age one from 100 percent to 185 percent of the FPL.
1989	Required states to provide Medicaid coverage to all pregnant women and children up to age six with family incomes below 133 percent of the FPL by April 1990.
1990	Increased eligibility level for pregnant women and infants to 185 percent of the FPL, for children ages one to six to 133 percent of the FPL.

Source: The Alpha Center. The Medical Expansions for Pregnant Women and Children, Washington, D.C.: Alpha Center, Undated.

OBRA 1989 also mandated changes in the design and implementation of the MCH Services Block Grant. States were required to allocate 30 percent of their funds to children's preventive/primary care services and 30 percent to children with special health care needs. For appropriations greater than $600 million, 12.75 percent was set aside for four targeted initiatives. One set of initiatives expanded maternal and infant home visiting programs as well as enhanced the abilities of states to provide a range of health and social services using the "one-stop shopping" model. A second set of initiatives was aimed at increasing the participation of obstetricians and pediatricians in Medicaid. Third, monies were directed at the enhancement of rural projects for the care of pregnant women and infants and the development of maternal and child health centers at nonprofit hospitals. The fourth targeted area was to expand outpatient and community-based services (including day care) for children with special health needs. Further, the Act required states to undertake a statewide needs assessment and to formulate a plan for the use of Title V funds that was based on the identified needs. In addition to these specific MCH mandates to improve access to care, OBRA 1989 directed the Secretary of Health and Human Services (HHS) to develop a uniform, simple application for use by Medicaid, MCH, WIC, Head Start, Migrant and Community Health Centers, and Health Care Programs for the Homeless. A final initiative to promote accessibility required state Title V agencies to coordinate their activities with Medicaid. For example, state Title V agencies were expected to work with Medicaid agencies to achieve specified enrollment goals for the EPSDT program.

OBRA 1989 mandated changes to hold states and the Maternal and Child Health Bureau (MCHB) more accountable for the block grant expenditures. Annual reports were required to address progress toward their state goals, particularly as linked to the goals articulated in *Healthy People 2000* (USDHHS, 1991). Required reporting elements included a variety of MCH status indicators by class of individuals (pregnant women, infants up to age one, children with special health care needs, and other children under 22 years of age), provider information, and the numbers served as well as health insurance status, including enrollment to Medicaid. The Secretary is also required to provide the House Energy and Commerce and Senate Finance Committees with detailed summaries of states' annual reports, a compilation of national MCH data by health status indicators (including an assessment of progress toward *Healthy People 2000* goals), and detailed results of each SPRANS project.

Concern over infant mortality, particularly the persistence of areas of strikingly high rates, prompted President George Bush to launch a targeted infant mortality initiative of substantial size. The Healthy Start program, administered by the MCHB, selected 15 communities (13 urban and 2 rural) and provided over $200 million dollars annually to facilitate community-driven approaches to infant mortality reduction. Building upon the lessons of Sheppard-Towner and M&I projects, Healthy Start has provided social and educational interventions as well as medical services. Employment of community members as outreach workers reflects economic development as yet another component of this substantial initiative. The effects of Healthy Start on infant mortality and low birth weight should become known in 1997.

Since the inception of Title V in 1935, there have been three major motivations behind federal involvement in health services for children. Arising out of the Great Depression, Title V was the first in a series of federal initiatives that attempted to address inequities in health outcomes and services. With the globalization of the economy in the 1970s and 1980s, the motivation shifted to a recognition that a healthy work force was needed in order to remain competitive. While Medicaid expansions certainly addressed inequities, the broadening of eligibility represented a strategy to invest in the health of the potential work force. As health care costs continued to grow at an alarming rate, with Medicaid and Medicare in particular escalating at annual rates of 21 percent and 10 percent, respectively, the motivating force behind health care reform became cost control. Bill Clinton's election to the presidency in 1992 was motivated, in part, by a growing concern over access to health care, particularly as escalating costs impeded the abilities of employers to offer health care as a benefit, state governments to finance Medicaid and other state health care programs, and individuals to purchase needed care.

Soon after his election, President Clinton proposed the Health Security Act, a sweeping reorganization of the health care system. The primary goal was to ensure that every citizen would have access to health insurance. Stemming from the work of Enthoven and Kronick (1989), the proposal promoted the concept of managed competition, with a substantial federal role. Large "accountable health partnerships," consisting of providers of health services (physicians, hospitals, etc.) and managers of payment systems (insurance companies, large health maintenance organizations [HMOS]), would compete with one another to offer packages of services to those who pay for services (employers, governments, and individuals). The "managed" part reflects the imposition of standardized packages of services and in some models the requirement that all populations be served. The "competition" takes place among the partnerships, since they would adjust their prices (and to some degree their packages of services within the established guidelines) in order to attract those who pay for services. As Iglehart explains, "Managed competition is price competition, but the price it focuses on is the annual premium for comprehensive health care services, not the price for each service" (Iglehart, 1993, p. 1220). Each partnership was required to provide several "packages" from which consumers might choose on the basis of price. The packages were required to include one choice that was without cost to the consumer, for example, an HMO where costs could be strictly controlled. Other packages could include the equivalent of fee-for-service options in which consumers could choose among physicians, but they would bear the additional cost through premiums.

Since the Health Security Act fell victim to the political struggle leading up to the 1994 midterm elections, many of the details of its potential effects on mothers and children in general and the low income population in particular remained unanswered. For example, it is crucial to consider the effects of the managed competition proposal on Medicaid as the major source of health care funds for low income members of the MCH population. Under the proposal, insurance coverage would be secured through the place of employment. Medicaid funds were to be blended with premiums from employers so that each employee of a given employer would choose among the same packages. Families eligible for Medicaid would have their premiums covered through this mechanism. Unemployed individuals, e.g., single mothers, would have retained their categorical eligibility by virtue of their enrollment in AFDC. Ironically, this proposal represented a return to the circumstances prior to 1986, before the link between Medicaid eligibility and AFDC was severed. As another example, support for core public health functions such as community assessment, policy development, and health assurance were not well articulated in legislation.

The 1994 Congressional elections represented a watershed in national and local politics. The Republicans gained the majority in the House of Representatives for the first time in 50 years and regained the majority in the Senate, which they had maintained from 1981 to 1986. No Republican incumbent governors lost re-election bids, and Republicans ended up controlling 31 states. Responding to the public belief that the role of the federal government must be reduced and that responsibility for health and welfare should return to states and even local communities, the Republicans proposed an end to the entitlement status for AFDC and Medicaid, creating instead block grants to the states to address these issues as they deemed appropriate. In addition to the termination of these entitlements, federal guidelines would be minimal to nonexistent, and state contributions would not be required. As of this writing, legislation ending 60 years of guaranteed federal support for dependent children has been signed into law. The attempt to replace Medicaid with a block grant did not succeed.

CONCLUSION

The end of the twentieth century finds the population of U.S. mothers and children at the center of the same debate that raged over the establishment of the Children's Bureau at the beginning of this century. On one side are those that argue that children represent a community resource, a type of public good, the support of which is a responsibility of all citizens. On the other side are those who assert that the care and nurturance of children, while a community resource, are most effectively undertaken by families and their local communities. With the implementation of block grants for AFDC, and in particular the elimination of the categorical entitlements to income support for poor, dependent children, efforts to ensure minimum health and welfare services for children now move to the state capitals. While state and local governments are indeed "closer" to the people that they serve, it is the federal government through the Congress and the Supreme Court that has traditionally articulated and enforced children's rights to the special services and protections that are the prerequisites of their healthy growth and development. With the devolution of responsibility to the states, it remains to be seen who will ensure, and to what degree, that all children, the most vulnerable and innocent among us, receive the social and health benefits they need to become productive members of society (Nathan, 1996).

REFERENCES

Baker, J.P. 1994. Women and the invention of well child care. *Pediatrics 94*, 527–31.

Berger, L., and S.R. Johansson. 1980. *Journal of Health Politics, Policy and Law 5*, 81–97.

Bremner, R.H., ed. 1971. *Children and youth in America*. Cambridge, MA: Harvard University Press.

Cartland, J.D.C. et al. 1993. A decade of Medicaid in perspective: What have been the effects on children? *Pediatrics 91*, 287–295.

Davis, K., and C. Schoen. 1978. *Health and the war on poverty*. Washington, DC: Brookings Institution.

Enthoven, A. and R. Kronick. 1989. A consumer-choice health plan for the 1990s. *New England Journal of Medicine 320*, 29–37.

Families USA. 1995. *Hurting real people*. Washington, DC: Families USA Foundation.

Foltz, A. 1975. The development of ambiguous federal policy: Early and Periodic Screening, Diagnosis and Treatment (EPSDT). *Milbank Memorial Fund Quarterly 53*, 35–64.

Grotberg, E. 1977. *200 years of children*. Washington, DC: U.S. Department of Health, Education and Welfare.

Haskins, R. 1989. Beyond metaphor. *American Psychologist 44*, 274–282.

Hoover, H. 1931. In *White House Conference on Child Health and Protection*. New York: Century Company.

Hughes, J.G. 1980. *American Academy of Pediatrics: The first 50 years*. Elk Grove Village, IL: American Academy of Pediatrics.

Hutchins, V. 1994. Maternal and Child Health Bureau: Roots. *Pediatrics 94*, 695–699.

Iglehart, J.K. 1993. Managed competition. *New England Journal of Medicine 328*, 1208–1212.

Irwin, P., and R. Conroy-Hughes. 1982. EPSDT impact on health status: Estimates based on secondary analysis of administratively generated data. *Medical Care 20*, 216–234.

Journal of American Medical Association. 1922. *78*, 1709, editorial.

Keller, W. 1983. Study of selected outcomes of the EPSDT program in Michigan. *Public Health Reports 28*, 110–118.

Kempe, C.H. et al. 1962. The battered child syndrome. *Journal of the American Medical Association 181*, 17–24.

Klerman, L. 1981. Title V. The Maternal and Child Health and Crippled Children's Services Section of the Social Security Act: Problems and Opportunities. In Select Panel for the Promotion of Child Health. *Better health for our children: A national strategy*. DHHS (PHS) Publication No. 79-55071. Washington, DC: U.S. Department of Health and Human Services.

Kotch, J.B., and D. Whiteman. 1982. Effect of the WIC program on children's clinic activity in a local health department. *Medical Care 20*, 691–698.

Lathrop, J. 1919. Income and infant mortality. *American Journal of Public Health 19*, 270–274.

Lesser, A.J. 1985. The origin and development of maternal and child health programs in the United States. *American Journal of Public Health 75*, 590–598.

Meckel, R. 1990. *"Saving babies": American public health and the prevention of infant mortality*. Baltimore, MD: The Johns Hopkins University Press.

Miller, C.A. 1988. Development of MCH services and policy in the United States. In *Maternal and child health practices*, 3rd ed., eds. H.M. Wallace, G.M. Ryan, and A. Olgesby. Oakland, CA: Third Party Publishing Co.

Nathan, R. 1996. The "devolution revolution". *Rockefeller Institute Bulletin*. Albany, NY: The Nelson A. Rockefeller Institute of Government.

Orr, S.T., and C.A. Miller. 1981. Utilization of health services by poor children since advent of Medicaid. *Medical Care 19*, 583–590.

Peterson, G.E. et al. 1986. *The Reagan block grants: What have we learned?* Washington, DC: Urban Institute Press.

Pfohl, S.J. 1976. The "discovery" of child abuse. *Social Problems 24*, 310–323.

Rosenbaum, S., and K. Johnson. 1986. Providing health care for low-income children: Reconciling child health goals with child health financing realities. *Milbank Quarterly 64*, 442–478.

Rosenheim, M.K. 1977. The child and the law. In *200 years of children*, ed. E.H. Grotberg. Washington, DC: Office of Child Development, U.S. Department Health, Education and Welfare.

Rush, D. et al. 1988. The national WIC evaluation: Evaluation of the Special Supplemental Food Program for Women, Infants, and Children. *American Journal of Clinical Nutrition 48*, 389–519.

Sardell, A. 1988. *The U.S. experiment in social medicine*. Pittsburgh, PA: University of Pittsburgh Press.

Schmidt, W.M., and H.M. Wallace. 1988. The development of health services for mothers and children in the U.S. In *Maternal and child health practices*, 3rd ed., eds. H.M. Wallace, G.M. Ryan, and A. Oglesby. Oakland, CA: Third Party Publishing Co.

Skocpol, T. 1992. *Protecting soldiers and mothers: The political origins of social policy in the U.S.* Cambridge, MA: Harvard University Press.

Sokol, R.J. et al. 1980. Risk, antepartum care, and outcome: Impact of a maternity and infant care project. *Obstetrics and Gynecology 56*, 150–156.

Steiner, G. 1976. *The children's cause*. Washington, DC: Brookings Institution.

Tratner, W.I. 1974. The public health movement. From poor laws to welfare state. In *A history of social welfare in America*. New York: The Free Press.

U.S. Congress. 1912. *An act to establish in the Department of Commerce and Labor a bureau to be known as the Children's Bureau*. 37 US Statutes 79.

U.S. Congress. 1935. Grants to states for maternal and child welfare. *Social Security Act*. 49 US Statutes 633, Title V.

U.S. Congress, Office of Technology Assessment. 1988. *Healthy children: Investing in the future*. OTA-H-345. Washington, DC: Government Printing Office.

U.S. Department of Health and Human Services. 1991. *Healthy people 2000: National health promotion and disease prevention objectives*. DHHS Publication No. (PHS) 91-50212. Washington, DC: Author.

U.S. Department of Health, Education and Welfare, Office of Child Development, Children's Bureau, National Center on Child Abuse and Neglect. 1976. Child abuse and neglect: An overview of the problem. In *The problem and its management*. vol. 1. Washington, DC: Author.

U.S. General Accounting Office. 1992. *Maternal and child health: Block grant funds should be distributed more equitably*. GAO/HRD-92-5. Washington, DC: Author, April.

Williams, G.J.R. 1983. Child protection: A journey into history. *Journal of Clinical Child Psychology 12*, 236–243.

Wilson, A.L. 1989. Development of the U.S. federal role in chldren's health care: A critical appraisal. In *Children and health care*. eds. L. Kopelman and J. Moskop. Boston, MA: Kluwer Academic Publishers.

Witte, E.E. 1963. *The development of the Social Security Act.* Madison, WI: University of Wisconsin Press.

Yip, R. et al. 1987. Declining prevalence of anemia among low income children in the US. *Journal of American Medical Association 258,* 1619–1623.

Yudkowsky B., and G. Fleming. 1990. Preventive health care for Medicaid children. *Health Care Financing Review,* Annual Supplement, 89–96.

CHAPTER 3

Families and Health

Joseph Telfair and Elizabeth L. Watkins

A family is not an association of independent people. It is a human commitment designed to make possible the rearing of moral healthy children. . . . Governments care—or ought to care—about families for this reason, and scarcely any other.

James Q. Wilson [in Roberts, 1993]

INTRODUCTION

Historical and ethical concern with the needs of children is inextricably linked with the family, the social institution most basic to the study and practice of maternal and child health (MCH). A family has been defined as a small, usually kinship-structured group, whose key function is nuturant socialization (Reiss and Lee, 1988). Contrary to the theory that the extended family was the prevalent structure in pre-industrial society, in the United States the predominant family system has always been the nuclear family (i.e., social positions of husband-father, wife-mother, and offspring). Relationships with extended kin had importance, but as mobility of families has increased, accessibility to these relationships has decreased.

The nuclear family, or more appropriately the "nuclear household" (Hareven, 1984), has been the definitive unit of analysis in the social scientific study of kinship relationships of the past several centuries. Much of what we know about the social health and overall well-being of children has come from these household studies, which have portrayed the family as the foundation for understanding human social development in modern American society.

The family is an institution beneficial to both individuals and society; however, it is an institution that is under great stress from the significant changes that have taken place in recent times. The increase in single parent units, the intensification

45

of economic hardships, the exacerbation of racial divisions, and the rise in rates of divorce and separation are all changes that are shaking the foundation of families as we have come to know them.

With the current political emphasis on "family values" connoting the more idealized "traditional" family unit, it has become necessary for practitioners in the field of MCH to develop an empirical understanding of the reality of the composition of the family in the United States today. It is of value in MCH practice to recognize that as a system-level foundation for social development, a healthy, nurturing family is essential to a child's as well as a parent's normal physical, emotional, and social development. Consistent, supportive relationships, as well as adequate nutrition, safe environments, and healthy lifestyles, are as important to children's and parents' well-being as timely access to appropriate medical care (Center for the Future of Children, 1992).

This chapter will describe the characteristics of current American families. As part of these descriptions, there will be a discussion of health and health service issues (including emerging trends) as they affect families and whether these services meet their needs. Emerging trends in family services also will be examined.

FAMILY TRENDS IN THE HISTORICAL CONTEXT

World Wars I and II

Until World War I, the United States was primarily a society of farms and small towns with a few big urban centers. In these early communities the typical form of household structure was the nuclear family. These were family units consisting of parents and their children, or of a childless couple, or one parent and children. Interestingly, the most important distinguishing feature of the nuclear family was the absence of extended kin. The nuclear *family* (discussed above) should not, however, be seen as identical to the nuclear *household*, since the latter may have included nonrelatives (Laslett and Wall, 1972; Hareven, 1984).

By the time of the 1920 U.S. census, the majority of the U.S. population had shifted from rural to urban areas (*World Almanac*, 1990). Prior to World War II, the nuclear household served the economic purpose of members working together on the farm (in rural areas) or in family businesses or for others (in urban areas). Adult children tended to live near their parents, creating communities with multigenerational kinship ties. There was a continuity of shared values and prescribed family roles. For example, men were seen as the major wage earners and women remained at home, if possible, with the responsibility of rearing the children. Further, because of the values of close family bonds, mutual support, and the overall well-being of the community, the care of poor children and families was not always seen as a responsibilty to be shared by the community and the government. However, the impact of World War II on the economic and social structure of America brought significant change to kinship and community relations on the one hand and government responsibilities on the other.

The continuing urbanization of America during and after World War II led to many changes that significantly affected the family unit and its functional roles and responsibilities. The increased mobility of families over the last three decades, spurred by the need to seek employment wherever it could be found, led to less spacial and temporal continuity and communal security (McNally, 1980). Further, the lure of opportunity and the need to survive within a rapidly changing society have led to a redefinition of the role of family members and to a new understanding of family structure and life.

American Family Composition

The make-up of American families has changed significantly since the end of World War II. In 1990, 71 percent (66.1 million) of households contained families (households having at least two members, including at least one relative of the head of household). This was down from 74 percent in 1980 and 81 percent in 1970. One-parent family households rose from 4 to 8 percent of all households during the three decades of 1960 to 1990 (Lugaila, 1992). Further, families maintained by women with no husband present doubled from 1970 to 1990 (5.5 million to 10.9 million) and rose from 13 percent of family households in 1970 to 15 percent in 1980 to 30 percent in 1993 (Rawlings, 1993). Women alone maintained 25 percent of white families, 63 percent of black families, and 35 percent of Hispanic families in 1993 (Rawlings, 1993).

The proportion of children living with two parents has decreased in each decade since 1960. Even the proportion living with only their father grew from 1.1 percent in 1960 and 1970 to 3.1 percent in 1990. Because there are fewer children per family, more one-parent families, and a growing number of persons living alone, the average sizes of households and families have declined.

The trend toward smaller families and households began in the mid-1960s with the end of the post-war baby boom and has continued to the present, reaching a level of 2.63 persons per household, on average, in 1990 and 3.17 persons per family. The proportion of families in 1990 with one or two children was 80 percent. In 1960, the proportion was not quite two-thirds (64 percent). The proportion of families with three or more children was only 20 percent in 1990, compared to 36 percent in 1960. During the last 30 years the percent of families with children under 18 present declined. In 1990, only 49 percent of all families had one to two children under 18 years of age present. The decline since 1960 in the proportion of total families and married-couple families with children under 18 present occurred for all parental age groups.

There were 34.7 million family groups with children under age 8 in 1990; 9.7 million, or 28 percent, of these were maintained by one parent, with 8.4 million of these maintained by the mother (U.S. Bureau of the Census, 1990). Interestingly, these family groups comprised 2.4 million 'subfamilies' in which the children were not the children of the householder (U.S. Bureau of the Census, 1990). In 1970, there were 3.8 million one-parent family groups, only 13 percent of the 29.6 million total. In 1990, the proportions of family groups maintained by one parent were 23 percent for whites, 61 percent for blacks, and 33 percent for Hispanics (U.S. Bureau of the Census, 1990).

Between 1970 and 1990, the proportion of two-parent family groups declined for whites, blacks, and persons of Hispanic origin (who may be of any race), while father-child and mother-child family groups have increased. Mother-child family groups have increased most dramatically due to the rise in divorce and births outside of marriage. There is a high proportion of births to women who never married. In 1990, 32 percent of children were living in homes where the mother never married. This varied by race of the child, with 53 percent of black children, 37 percent of Hispanic children, and 22 percent of white children living in family households with never-married mothers between the ages of 14 and 44 (Lugaila, 1992). Possible reasons for the increase for all races have been noted as: (1) increased sexual activity at earlier ages; (2) less social stigma toward out-of-wedlock birth than in previous decades; and (3) the emotional gratification of relationships with the male partner and the baby may be the only positive relationships in the woman's life (Donovan, 1995).

Marriage, Divorce, and Remarriage

In the decades since World War II, changes in the social and technological fabric of American society have led to dramatic challenges and changes for families. Opportunities for women to delay (choosing to marry at a later age) or not pursue marriage as the path to having a family have increased dramatically. These opportunities were the result of the changing social perceptions of the role of women. The chance for many more women to pursue higher education and careers rose significantly between 1960 and 1990.

Married-couple families dropped from 87 percent in 1970 to 82 percent in 1980 and 79 percent in the first quarter of 1990 (U.S. Bureau of the Census, 1990). In the past two decades the overall marriage rate has had a two-fold decrease, from a rate of 76 percent of all women 15 years of age and older in 1970 to 52.3 percent of women 15 years of age and older in 1992 (Rawlings, 1993). For both men and women, the median ages at first marriage were lowest in the mid-

1950s and have been rising since (Lugaila, 1992). The median age at first marriage has increased three full years for both men and women in the past two decades, from 24.6 years for men and 21 years for men and women (respectively) in 1970 to 26.1 for men and 23.9 for women (respectively) in 1990 (Lugaila, 1992). Rates of first marriage and remarriage declined after the mid-1960s (from 118 per thousand in 1960 to 78 per thousand women 14 to 44 years old in 1990 for first marriages and from 158 per thousand in 1966 to 110 per thousand widowed and divorced women 14 to 44 years old in 1990 for remarriages) but have remained fairly constant from 1980 to 1990 (at about 80 per thousand for first marriages and 110 per thousand for remarriages) (Lugaila, 1992). The high rate of remarriage has resulted in an increase of "blended family" units with the new spouses bringing into the household children from previous marriages.

Just as age at first marriage has been rising, so are the proportions of men and women who have never married. Increases have occurred for each five-year age group between ages 20 and 34 in the proportions who have never married. For women, only 23 percent had never married in 1960 compared to 63 percent in 1990. For men, 53 percent had never married in 1960 compared to 79 percent in 1990.

Change in social mores and the dissipation of some of the earlier taboos against single parenthood and divorce have allowed for both to become more socially acceptable. The discarding of traditional social constraints and the availability of medical methods of contraception led to more acceptance of cohabitation without marriage. There was less bias against out-of-wedlock pregnancy and a trend for single mothers to keep their babies rather than placing such children for adoption or in long-term child care homes (Schorr and Schorr, 1988). Divorce rates have increased since 1921, with the sharpest increases occurring from the mid-1960s to the late 1970s (Lugaila, 1992; Schorr and Schorr, 1988). The rate of divorce has risen dramatically over the last three decades from approximately 15 percent of all marriages in 1960 to a rate of approximately 50 percent of all marriages in 1990 (that is, currently 4.6 out of every 10 marriages ends in divorce), and the children of these divorces will typically live in one-parent families (Lugaila, 1992). Relatedly, a high percentage of remarriages fail. In 1991, 37 percent of remarriages versus 30 percent of first marriages failed. Studies suggest that children growing up in divorced families and in stepfamilies have greater difficulties in social relations, achievement, and behavioral adjustment (Hetherington and Jodl, 1994). Researchers caution, however, that the results of these studies have small effect on sizes and diversity in outcome. There is considerable variation in the balance of risk and protective factors within family structures, and individual and policy decisions should not be based on these findings alone (Amato, 1994).

Of children living with two parents in 1990, 16 percent lived with a stepparent. The vast majority of these stepfamily situations consists of a biological mother and a stepfather combination, because children usually remain with their mother after divorce. In the case of unmarried parents, the children also usually remain with the mother. In 1990 the majority of children living with one parent were living with a parent who was divorced or whose spouse was absent (either separated or living elsewhere). The proportion living with a widowed parent declined during the past 20 years, from 20 percent to 7 percent. The proportion of children in one-parent families who lived with a never-married mother increased from 7 percent in 1970 to 32 percent in 1990 (Lugaila, 1992).

Finally, the increased availability of artificial insemination technology and the number of states allowing adoption by same sex couples provided many single women the chance to have a family without a commitment to marriage. On the other hand, the development of an effective oral contraceptive and the initiation of public policy allowing the use of tax funds to support family planning clinics gave couples the opportunity to avoid pregnancy. Both of these trends have contributed to the increasing proportion of children living with single, never-married mothers.

Family Income and Employment

Median family income increased by 104 percent during the 26 years between 1947 and 1973. The median income of married-couple families increased by 115 percent. Despite these fluctuations and the increase in wives' labor force participation, by 1990 the median income for all families was only 6 percent more than in 1973, and the median income for married-couple families was only 11 percent greater than in 1973. Among families with female householders and no spouse present, median family income grew by 37 percent between 1947 and 1973, but increased only by 5 percent between 1973 and 1990. Despite an increase in the annual rate of inflation (9 percent), the median family income (in dollars adjusted for inflation) for all races over the last five years has been going down. In 1989, the median family income was $33,585; in 1992 the median family income was $31,553; and in 1993, the median family income was $31,241. The 1993 median family income differs by race: Asians at $38,347, whites at $32,960, Hispanics at $22,886, and blacks at $19,532 (U.S. Bureau of the Census, 1994).

The proportion of households with a low relative income (less than half the median income for a family relative to family size) increased from 15 percent in 1969 to 24 percent in 1989, while the proportion of households with a high relative income increased from 8 to 10 percent during the same time period. The rates of low relative income varied significantly by race. For whites, the proportion of relatively low income families increased from 13 percent in 1969 to 15 percent in 1989; for Hispanics the increase was from 33 percent in 1979 to 38 percent in 1989 (1969 numbers were not available); and for blacks the increase was from 42 percent in 1974 to 44 percent in 1989 (1969 numbers were not available) (U.S. Bureau of the Census, 1991b). The proportion of families with a relative income in the middle range declined from 77 percent in 1969 to 66 percent in 1989 for all families.

An increasing number of women have entered the work force since 1950. The percentage of married mothers with children under 18 in the work force in 1960 was less than 30 percent; in 1970 the number was 40 percent; and in 1990 it was 59 percent. The percentage of married mothers with children age 6 to 17 years who were employed rose from less than 30 percent in 1960 to 49 percent in 1970 and to 74 percent in 1990 (Lugaila, 1992). These data indicate that labor force participation by married women is increasing, especially for those women with children less than six years old. Between 1970 and 1990, among married women with preschool children in the home, the proportion of those in the labor force doubled, from 30 percent in 1970 to 59 percent in 1990. Further, by 1990, 74 percent of all married women with school-age children were in the labor force (Lugaila, 1992).

Among married-couple families with children in 1990, the proportion in which both the husband and wife worked was 70 percent. In 1990, 28 percent of married-couple families with children had both husbands and wives who worked year-round full-time (Lugaila, 1992). A substantially smaller proportion of married-couple families with related children (21 percent) had husbands who worked year-round full-time and wives who did not work (Lugaila, 1992). A majority of female householder families with children had householders who worked. However, substantial proportions of female householder families with children had no one in the home who had worked during the previous year. Further, poor family householders were much less likely to work than nonpoor householders, regardless of family composition. Among poor family householders, 50.4 percent worked in 1991, and 15.8 percent worked year-round, full-time. In contrast, 80.5 percent of nonpoor family householders worked, and 61.1 percent worked year-round, full-time. At least one person worked in 69.2 percent of poor married-couple families in 1991; both spouses worked in 24 percent of these families. In poor families maintained by women with no spouse present, 42.4 percent of the householders worked with only 9.5 percent working year-round, full-time. For the nonpoor householders in this category, 76.1 percent worked in 1991, and 54.5 percent worked year-round, full-time (U.S. Bureau of the Census, 1994).

Only 21 percent of current families fit the traditional model of the husband working full-time year round and the wife not working. Further, the women's liberation and civil rights movements led to legislation forbidding discrimination against women and minorities in employment, opening many more career opportunities for them. Increase in the cost of living and decreasing purchasing power of stagnant wages prompted the need for all adult members of the household to seek work.

In 1990, among poor married-couple families with children, 27 percent received means-tested cash assistance[1], but 78 percent had one or more members who worked to earn wages or salaries (Baugher, 1993.) Poor female-headed households with children, on the other hand, were more likely to have received means-tested cash assistance than to have one or more members with income earned through work (67 percent versus 49 percent). Of the total income of poor families, about 80 percent was received from these two sources. The remaining 20 percent of total income for poor families with children came from other sources, such as Social Security.

Poverty

Families with children under 18 years of age experienced a decline in poverty from 20.3 percent in 1959 to 10.8 percent in 1966. Between 1966 and 1979, the poverty rate remained within 2.5 percentage points of this previous low, varying from 10.8 to 13.3 percent. Poverty estimates based on the current definition date back to the early 1960s. The poverty rate fell dramatically during the 1960s, from 22.2 percent in 1960 to 12.1 percent in 1969. From 1970 to 1978, changes in poverty were relatively small, with the poverty rates ranging between 12.6 percent in 1970 and 11.7 percent in 1979. This was followed by a rapid increase in the poverty rate as the number of persons in poverty increased to a total of 35.3 million in 1983. The poverty rate in 1983, 15.2 percent, was the highest since 1965. Although the poverty rate in 1991 (14.2 percent) was lower than this recent peak, it remained well above the 1978 level of 11.4 percent, a recent low point (U.S. Bureau of the Census, 1994).

During the period of 1965 to 1990, white families had the lowest poverty rates (14 percent in 1965 to 12 percent in 1990), and black families had the highest poverty rates (40 percent in 1965 to 38 percent in 1990[2]). In 1980 the poverty rate for all families with children rose to 14.7 percent, and between 1981 and 1990 the poverty rate for families with children varied from 15.5 percent to 17.9 percent, respectively (Baugher, 1993; Lugaila, 1992).

Despite a decrease in overall poverty rates since 1966, poverty rates for white, black, and Hispanic married-couple families with children have been much lower than corresponding poverty rates for female-headed families with children, from 17 percent in 1959 to 8 percent in 1990 for all married-couple families with children and from 60 percent in 1959 to 45 percent in 1990 for female-headed families with children (Lugaila, 1992; U.S. Bureau of the Census, 1991b; U.S. Bureau of the Census, 1990). But within these two family types, the poverty rates for

---

[1]Means-tested cash assistance includes public assistance or welfare payments and Supplemental Security Income.

[2]Estimates are for all white and all black families during this time period.

blacks and Hispanics have been substantially higher than for whites. For example, from 1975 to 1990 the poverty rate for married-couple families has remained stable at 8 percent, while the poverty rate for black married couples has remained stable at 15 percent (U.S. Bureau of the Census, 1991a).[3] In addition, in 1991, 40.9 percent of all poor families were maintained by a married couple, whereas 54.0 percent were headed by a female householder, no spouse present. In contrast, only 12.7 percent of nonpoor families were maintained by women. After leveling off in the early 1980s, the proportion of female-householder families among all poor families has grown from 48.1 percent in 1985 to 54.1 percent in 1991. Further, in 1991 female-headed households constituted 78.3 percent of all poor black families, compared with 45.7 percent of poor Hispanic-origin families and 28.4 percent of poor white families (Baugher, 1993).

In 1990, white, black, and Hispanic-origin family householders age 25 years and over with higher educational attainments were each less likely to live in poverty, but within educational levels the poverty rates for blacks and Hispanics were much greater than for whites. For example, for high school graduates the rate of poverty for Hispanic families was 15 percent, the rate for white families was 7 percent, and the rate for black families was 26 percent. However, the overall poverty rate for white, black, and Hispanic families with at least a high school education fell in 1990 to 9 percent. Families with children had very different poverty rates in 1990 depending on the work status of their adult family members, and their race or ethnicity. In married-couple families with children where both parents worked, poverty rates were particularly low, although they varied notably for whites, blacks, and Hispanics (3 percent for white families, 5 percent for black families, and 10 percent for Hispanic families). Poverty rates were much larger among married-couple families with children where only the husband worked (12.6 percent for white families, 25.7 percent for black families, and 30.5 percent for Hispanic families). Poverty rates were also higher among two family types with children that depended mainly on female workers: two-parent families where only the wife worked (24.3 percent for white families, 42.2 percent for black families, and 36 percent for Hispanic families), and female-headed household families where the head of household worked (24.7 percent for white families, 38.4 percent for black families, and 35.7 percent for Hispanic families) (U.S. Bureau of the Census, 1991a). Since all of these families had one or more workers, the poor ones were all working poor families (Lugaila, 1992). Because the vast majority (93 percent) of family households with children included one or more workers in 1990, a large majority of poor families with children (63 percent) were working poor families. Families maintained by nonworkers had even higher poverty rates (Lugaila, 1992).

---

[3]The exception in both cases is the increase in the rate of poverty for all families by five percentage points from 1975 to 1985.

Lastly, in 1988, approximately 34 million persons participated in major assistance programs.[4] Participation was highest for Food Stamps and Medicaid, followed by Aid to Families with Dependent Children (AFDC) (U.S. Bureau of the Census, 1994). During this same time period, the relationship between poverty status and program participation is correlated with family type. Most single-parent families are maintained by a female householder with no husband present (79.3 percent), and participation in major assistance programs is higher for persons in female-householder families than for persons in married-couple families and unrelated individuals. Although close to 42 percent of persons in female-householder families received assistance during 1988, only 9 percent of persons in married-couple families received assistance.

The median combined family benefits for persons in female-householder families amounted to $466 in 1988, which is substantially higher than the $284 received by persons in married-couple families. Of importance is the fact that, despite significantly higher participation rates for blacks and persons of Hispanic origin, 62.4 percent of all participants were white. Also, children under 18 constituted 26 percent of the population but 42 percent of all program participants in 1988.

Child Care

The increase of parents in the work force led to schools and other institutions (e.g., child day care) having an increased share of the responsibility for caring for children. The increase in labor force participation among mothers with preschool children was not limited to mothers with older preschoolers. In 1976 (only 14 years earlier), the proportion of women with children under age 1 who were in the labor force was only 31 percent. However, the rapid increase in the proportion of women with infants and children under 1 year of age, jumping to 53 percent in 1990, has produced a corresponding increase in the demand for child care for children under age 1. Data collected in the fall of 1987 show that there were an estimated 52 million children under age 15 living in families with their mothers present.[5] About 29 million of these children (59 percent) had mothers who were employed; 9 million of the children were under 5 years of age and not in school full time (U.S. Bureau of the Census, 1991a).

---

[4]Persons are counted as participants in a major assistance program if they live in public housing or are beneficiaries of one of the following programs: Aid to Families with Dependent Children, General Assistance, Supplemental Security Income (SSI), Medicaid, Food Stamps, and federal or state rent assistance.

[5]Data from the Survey of Income and Program Participation were collected only for the three youngest children under age 15 in each household and represent 94 percent of all children under age 15 in households.

Between 1987–1990 among all preschoolers, 30 percent were cared for in their own homes (about one-half of this care was provided by their fathers), and 36 percent were cared for in another home, usually by someone not related to the child (U.S. Bureau of the Census, 1991a). Another 9 percent of preschoolers were cared for by their mothers while working, either at home or away from home (U.S. Bureau of the Census, 1991a). Sixteen percent (1,465,000) of preschoolers were in group child care centers, and another 8 percent (755,000) were enrolled in nursery/preschool programs. Sixty percent of preschoolers in organized child care facilities were 3 and 4 year olds, 31 percent were 1 and 2 year olds, and 9 percent were under 1 year of age.

Of the 20 million school-age children of employed mothers, 14 million were in school most of the time their mothers were at work. Nevertheless, 6 million of these children (43 percent) needed a secondary arrangement either before or after school. Most often, the secondary arrangement was care in the child's home by an adult (38 percent). In addition, another 22 percent cared for themselves before or after school while their mothers were at work. Of the remaining 5.7 million children who were not in school during their mothers' work hours, 2.7 million had their primary care arrangement in their own home; half of this care was provided by their fathers. About 800,000 children were left unsupervised most of the time their mothers were at work (U.S. Bureau of the Census, 1991a).

The cost of child care was significant. Of the 18.5 million employed women with children under 15 years old in the fall of 1987, 6.2 million (33 percent) made a cash payment for child care for at least one of their children. The average cost per week for families paying for child care services was $49, an increase of $8 per week since the last Survey of Income and Program Participation was conducted in 1984–1985. The monthly family income of women who paid for child care averaged about $3,200, so child care represented about 7 percent of their family income (U.S. Bureau of the Census, 1991a). Women with preschool-age children paid more per week (ranging from $51 with youngest child 3 or 4 years old to $58 with youngest child under 1 year) and spent a higher proportion of their monthly income (7 to 8 percent) on child care than did women whose youngest child was 5 years old or over ($35 per week and 4.5 percent of family income) (U.S. Bureau of the Census, 1991a; Lugaila, 1992).

Low income families are less likely to arrange paid child care. One-fourth of employed mothers living in families with income below the poverty level paid for child care. Among employed women living in families with income at 125 percent of poverty level and over, one-third paid for child care.[6] Average weekly child care payments for these women were $35 and $50, respectively. Poor women

---

[6]In this report, persons living in near poverty are defined as those living in households from 100 up to 125 percent of poverty level.

spent 25 percent of their monthly family income on child care, compared with 6 percent among women who were not poor. About 15 percent of poor families used organized child care facilities for their children under 5, compared with 26 percent for families who were not poor. Children living in poverty in the fall of 1987 depended more on care in their own home provided by their grandparents and other relatives (19 percent) than did children who were not poor (7 percent).

Health Insurance Coverage

At the end of 1990, 87 percent of Americans were covered at a given point in time by health insurance of all types. About 6 in 8 of all insured persons were covered by private insurance. Stable full-time employment improved the chances of having continuous coverage (Short, 1993). From mid-1987 to the end of 1990, only 14 percent of those who worked full time—35 hours or more per week—for all 28 months experienced lapses in coverage. In contrast, 43 percent of those who spent a month or more without a job experienced a lapse in health insurance coverage (Short, 1993). Further, taking into account the changing system of employer-provided dependent coverage, Newson and Harvey (1994) point out the following:

> Currently, 60 percent of all Americans obtain insurance through their own or a family member's employment. This arrangement, however, is seriously threatened. Employers concerned with rising health care costs are either dropping dependent health insurance, reducing the benefit packages, or increasing the employee's share of the premium for dependent coverage. In 1980, 72 percent of medium- and large-sized firms paid the full cost of health insurance for their workers, and 51 percent paid the full cost of dependent coverage. By 1991, fully paid individual insurance dropped to 45 percent of firms, and family coverage to 23 percent. While employer-provided health insurance is declining, even plans that do cover dependents often fail to meet the health care needs of children, which are not the same as those of adults. Most child health services are provided in an ambulatory setting, and services rendered in such a setting are often not covered by health insurance. Because health insurance plans tend to be designed for adults, children's needs are often addressed inadequately (pp. 11–12).

Therefore, there is concern that as a result of the current health care reform climate, poor and nonpoor families with children are at risk of having no source of health insurance for their dependents.

In 1990, poor families with children were twice as likely as nonpoor families with children not to be covered by private or public health insurance at any given time during the year (22 percent versus 11 percent) (Lugaila, 1992; Short, 1993;

U.S. Bureau of the Census, 1991b). Among nonpoor families with children, those in female-headed household families were about twice as likely as those in married-couple families not to be covered by health insurance at any given time during the year (17 percent versus 9 percent). The reverse held true for poor families with children. It should be noted that some families with children covered by health insurance during 1990 had coverage for only part of the year. Hence, the proportions of families with children not covered at any given time (or at all) during the year, and discussed here, are certainly smaller than the proportions who did not have coverage for the full year. In addition, families with children who did not have health insurance coverage may also differ in the extent to which specific health care costs were fully, partially, or not paid by their health insurance (Short, 1993). Between 1987 and 1991, approximately 22.2 million children had no health insurance during some part of each year (Flint, 1992; Short, 1993). Contrary to what many believe, access to health care is not primarily a problem of the poor. The majority of uninsured children live in two-parent families, in which at least one parent is employed full time and earns an income above the poverty line (Foley, 1991). Seventy percent of the uninsured have family incomes above the poverty level (Darman, 1992).

Poor children in married-couple families were more than twice as likely as poor children in female-householder families not to be covered by health insurance during the year (33 percent versus 13 percent) (Short, 1993). However, Cunningham and Hahn (1994) point out that, "Research has shown that children in single-parent families use fewer health care services than children in two-parent families, but it is unknown whether this is a result of medical need, the dramatically lower economic resources of single-parent families, or other noneconomic characteristics" (p. 25). Whatever the reason for this low use of services, of those who participated at some point in a major assistance program in 1990—AFDC, General Assistance, SSI, Food Stamps, or housing assistance—49 percent lacked continuous coverage compared with 22 percent who did not participate at all. Those who participated in all 28 months, however, were nearly as likely to be continuously covered as those who never participated. Six in ten of these persons were covered by Medicaid for the entire period. AFDC beneficiaries represented 49 percent of the recipients of Medicaid yet account for only 16 percent of the expenditures. Average expenditure per year per recipient in 1990 was $971.

COMMUNITY SERVICES

Historical Background

The most basic social agency available in every community is the tax-supported public welfare agency. However, voluntary, nonprofit agencies have played an important role in the history and current provision of social services in the United States. Because of the greater need, they have flourished mainly in urban areas. Nonetheless, the public welfare agency remains the one resource available nationwide.

The public welfare system of the United States is based on the English poor laws of the seventeenth century, which placed the responsibility for care of the needy on the local community and stated that the income of persons receiving assistance should not be greater than the lowest income of a self-sufficient person (Reisch, 1995). In the United States, public welfare was administered entirely by local and state agencies until the Social Security Act was passed in 1935. The reason for this change was that there was great inequity in criteria for eligibility and benefits. Interestingly, the belief that the state or local community is better situated to assess the needs of and benefits for dependent persons, and the use of a means test to determine need, form the basis for much of current welfare reform policies. Thus, the U.S.'s welfare system is founded on the Residual Welfare Model, described in Chapter 1 of this text, and there is still adherence to some of these principles, whereas England and other western European countries have adopted the principles of the Industrial Redistributive Model (Kahn, 1973).

In the eighteenth and early nineteenth centuries, the American welfare system also used institutional care for the elderly, chronically ill, and dependent children, e.g., almshouses and orphanages. With the industrial revolution and the wave of immigration, private agencies were developed to help people in their own homes. The Community Organization Societies, which developed into today's Family Service Agencies, and Children's Aid Societies (antecedents of United Way), were major resources offering financial assistance as well as other services in kind. The development of private child protection agencies such as the Society for the Prevention of Cruelty to Children is described in Chapter 2.

With the onset of the Great Depression in the 1930s, private organizations found they were unable to meet the financial needs of the masses of unemployed persons. After the passage of the Social Security Act, private agencies made the policy decision not to provide income maintenance but to provide only counseling and supplementary services. In turn the original Social Security Act provided only financial assistance, not services (Meyer, 1995).

The Social Security Act established the responsibility of the federal government to provide funds to all states for the support of certain groups and the policy of entitlement, i.e., that all persons who met eligibility criteria were entitled to benefits (Reisch, 1995). Originally the Social Security Act provided funds for three groups in the population—the aged (Old Age Assistance), the blind (Aid to the Blind), and dependent children (Aid to Dependent Children). In 1950 a third group, disabled persons (Aid to the Permanently and Totally Disabled) was added. These programs were administered by the states. That is, under general federal guidelines states established eligibility criteria and benefits. In answer to complaints about the wide variation in benefits according to the economic status of a state, Old Age Assistance, Aid to the Blind, and Aid to the Permanently and Totally Disabled were "federalized" in 1974 under the SSI program (Meyer, 1995). It is administered directly by the Social Security Administration, whose primary responsibilities are to: (1) set eligibility criteria, (2) establish a basic measure of income maintenance, and (3) mail checks directly to recipients. States can supplement the amount of SSI benefit; however, states which gave higher benefits before 1974 were required to supplement the new federal level in order to remain at that level (Meyer, 1995).

The Aid to Dependent Children (ADC) program originally provided benefits only for the children, but in 1950 funds for the caretaker in the family were also included and the name was changed to Aid to Families with Dependent Children. It has not been "federalized" as were the other programs because of the moral and political feelings expressed by communities toward the population group served by this program. "To qualify for assistance, a child in a single parent household must be deprived of support because the parent is deceased, continually absent from the home, or suffering a mental or physical incapacity that is expected to last more than 30 days. Under limited conditions, a two-parent family can receive aid if principal wage earner is unemployed." (Abramovitz, 1995, p. 184). In 1935, one of the goals of the Social Security Act was to remove from the labor pool economically dependent persons, thus freeing employment opportunities for the able-bodied. In the beginning, mothers of dependent children continued to work because they were not included as recipients of the ADC benefits. They were included in 1950 because of the culture of that era. That is, it was believed to be better for the development of children if the mother remained at home to care for them. Also, the role of women as homemakers was encouraged as a means of removing women from the labor pool after World War II in order to increase opportunities for returning veterans.

The demographics of AFDC also changed between 1935 and 1990. The AFDC program subsumed the population previously served by Mothers Pensions programs, which states had initiated as a result of the 1909 White House Conference on Children. These programs were focused primarily on widows who otherwise would have had to place their children in orphanages. The proportion of widows with children was high under the original ADC program but diminished as this group became eligible for survivors' benefits under the Social Security insurance program. Currently the children in the AFDC caseload are primarily those of divorced, separated, or never-married women. The average monthly AFDC family caseload for calendar year 1992 was 4,829,000, up 8.1 percent from the preceding year (U.S. Department of Health and Human Services, Social Security Administration, 1994). The AFDC recipient count averaged 13,773,000 in 1992.

In 1992 payments to AFDC recipients totaled $21,655.9 million, an increase of $725.3 million or 3.5 percent above 1991 (U.S. Department of Health and Human Services, Social Security Administration, 1994). However, the average monthly payment per family was down $16.73 (−4.3 percent) to $373.71 for 1992 from the 1991 level of $390.44 (Abramovitz, 1995; U.S. Department of Health and Human Services, Social Security Administration, 1994).

The role of public welfare agencies in providing social services not only to its own beneficiaries but also the population in general has varied in recent years. Beginning in 1956 the federal government offered to match a certain percentage of state funds spent on counseling, rehabilitation, and other direct services to persons receiving public welfare benefits. These services were always perceived as services to individual cases for purposes of rehabilitation and control. In the 1960s, in the era of the War on Poverty and the Great Society, there was more of an interest among academicians and policy makers in dealing with the problem of social dependency on a systems basis (Reisch, 1995). A leader in the systems approach was Dr. Alfred J. Kahn, professor at the Columbia University School of Social Work, who was influenced by the work of Titmuss cited in Chapter 1. He believed that a function of public welfare was the socialization and development of society, regardless of an individual's economic status. His ultimate goal was the Industrial Redistributive Model, but as an intermediary phase he recommended that governmental units be responsible for providing "social utilities," that is, services that are needed to meet emerging needs and are generally accepted as representing social infrastructure (Kahn, 1973). Public social utilities may be divided into those available at user options (e.g., museums, community centers) and others by user status (day care, centers for the aged). He stresses that the user is a citizen, not a client or patient (Kahn, 1973).

This concept of public welfare offering services to all citizens was incorporated into Title XX of the Social Security Act passed in 1975. The services of information and referral, family planning, and protective services for children and the aged were provided to all families regardless of income. Other developmental services were available to people with incomes up to 115 percent of a median state's income; persons with 80–115 percent of the state's median income paid a sliding fee for services. Title XX legislation led to many innovative programs with a preventive approach. However, it was an open-ended appropriation. In the 1980s it was placed in a block grant with all other provision for social services under the Social Security Act and a cap was placed on appropriations (Reisch, 1995). Current programs are more limited.

The history of child welfare services for the protection and enhancement of the lives of children has a history similar to income maintenance. Services, such as they were, were provided by the local judicial and welfare system with use of institutional care. Private nonprofit, including religious, agencies developed protective and custodial care. Until the 1930s these varied according to the state and locality. The child welfare provisions under Title V of the Social Security Act required each state to have a statewide agency responsible for public child welfare services. Originally administered by the Children's Bureau, this program offered mainly guidance and staff training in foster care, adoption, maternity homes, day care centers, homemaker services, etc. Its relatively small budget was used to try to upgrade the quality of staffs of public child welfare agencies, providing funds for the employment of social workers with master's degrees. It did not provide funds for the payment of foster care or to assist adoptive parents. Studies in the 1970s that tracked children throughout their experiences in foster care documented the inadequacy of foster homes, the agencies' tendencies to "lose children" and not provide continuous service to the child. It also found that if children were not returned to their parents within their first two years in foster care, they were likely never to be returned. These findings resulted in the Child Welfare and Adoption Assistance Act in the 1980s. Federal funds were appropriated for payment of foster care. Agencies were required to establish registers and tracking systems. Plans had to be made to review cases by the time the child was in foster care for 18 months to see whether there was potential for the child to be returned to his or her parents or plans made for placement in an adoptive home. Funds were provided to assist adoptive parents with the cost of care of children with special needs.

The original placement of Child Welfare Services and MCH Services in the Children's Bureau was a felicitous one in that the two programs had so many areas of mutual concern, such as services to unwed mothers, standards for foster homes, adoption, day care centers, and homemaker services. During the 1960s they both received funds to expand services for mentally retarded children. The Social Work Section of the MCH Division was able to work closely with the social workers in the Child Welfare Division on these issues (Kadushin, 1980). Since 1973, when Child Welfare Services was transferred to the Administration for Children and Families and MCH was transferred to the Public Health Service, these two programs have had to collaborate through interagency committees.

When initiated in 1935, the Social Work Section of the Children's Bureau was concerned mainly with the program for children with special health care needs (then called the Crippled Children's Program), because many of the states had incorporated social work positions into their clinical services. The impetus for the development of social work positions in state MCH agencies came with the initiation of the Program of Special Projects in the 1960s. Because of the nature of the programs, the federal administrators of MCH services always insisted on the multidisciplinary approach. Social work positions were created in state health departments to give guidance and supervision to the social workers employed in the special projects. After the end of the Program of Projects with the initiation of block grants to the states in the 1980s, state-level positions for public health social workers remained important in assessing the impact of health and social policy on the health status and social needs of low income families. For example, data gathered by public health social workers in the southeastern states regarding rates of premature birth and infant death occurring to women not eligible for Medicaid were used in the development of legislation for the expansion of Medicaid to include married women and women with incomes up to 185 percent of poverty. The provision of payment for case-management services to Medicaid patients led to an increase in the number of social work positions in local public health departments providing MCH services (Watkins, 1993; Schmidt and Wallace, 1994). These public health social workers provided information about and referral to other community resources as well as counseling and follow-up. They work closely with other community agencies in developing new resources for families as well as working to changing policies that may serve as barriers. The current trend for states to assign the Medicaid population to managed care programs is leading to a reduction of the availability of public health social work and other "wrap-around" services that facilitate the accessibility and effectiveness of medical care for low income populations.

Current Issues

The current attack on "the welfare system" and the proposal to fund Medicaid through block grants to the states threaten the health and social resources available to young low-income families. Politicians expressing the need to "reform the welfare system" are referring to the AFDC program, since other dependent populations are now covered by the SSI program. Two major factors account for the negative atmosphere surrounding the AFDC program. One is that the more socially acceptable group of women, i.e., widows, is now cared for by Survivors Insurance, which leaves the politically unacceptable group of divorced, separated, and unmarried women as the primary recipients of AFDC. This group of women is targeted for "reform" despite the fact that their numbers reflect a social phenomenon that is occurring in all economic groups. Second, the recipients are perceived negatively because of their high rate of unemployment. Today, greater numbers of women work outside the home, so AFDC recipients are seen as not meeting society's expectations, even though the early intention of the AFDC program was to enable mothers to stay home and raise their children. Since the passage of Family Support legislation in 1988, recipients whose children are over three years of age have been required to participate in the Job Opportunity and Basic Skills program. However, these efforts have not led to any greater numbers obtaining employment. Current proposals have a more punitive approach, i.e., cutting off benefits if the woman does not return to work within a certain time limit (e.g., two years), or if she has additional children while receiving benefits.

Legislation passed in 1996 (Public Law 104-193, "Personal Responsibility and Work Opportunity Reconciliation Act, 1996) gave administration of AFDC to the states, with minimal federal guidelines, reduced funds, employment requirements, and time limits on assistance, ending entitlements for those most in need. There now is a question as to whether state legislatures will be willing to raise taxes to replace lost federal revenue with state funds and to meet the new demands of the law (training, employment, child care, etc.). The resources of private organizations are inadequate and too unevenly distributed to meet nationwide needs. Efforts to help recipients enter employment or return to school require training programs and provision of child day care services that are not guaranteed by the new legislation.

The proposal to fund Medicaid through block grants to the states would lead to similar problems of inequity in criteria for eligibility and benefits. Mothers and children excluded from AFDC assistance may find they are also excluded from a state's Medicaid program. Although converting Medicaid to a block grant was originally considered as part of the welfare reform legislation, it was omitted from the final version of PL 104-193.

The increase in acquired immune deficiency syndrome (AIDS), drug abuse, and family violence has placed a great strain on child welfare agencies (Reiss and Lee, 1988). Children in these families often have to be removed from these threatening environments temporarily or permanently. There are insufficient qualified foster homes to meet this demand. A high proportion of caseworkers in child welfare agencies have not had formal social work training and are given responsibility for solving problems in family relationships far beyond their abilities. There is frequent turnover in staff, and children in care often become lost in the system. Also, the policy that a decision must be made to either return the child to his or her biological parents or place him or her in a permanent adoptive home after 18 months in foster care often leads to the child's being returned to the original hazardous environment. Current approaches to remedying this situation include closer case management and monitoring, crisis and long-term family counseling, parental life-skill training, and permanency planning that involves the family's biological and "other kinship/support network."

CONCLUSION

American family life has changed dramatically during the past three decades. Age at first marriage for women has increased, as well as age at first pregnancy for married women. Since 1970, small families with one or two children increased sharply as a proportion of all families with children. In contrast, there are high rates of divorce and births to unmarried mothers, which are largely responsible for the growing proportion of families headed by single, mostly female, parents. As noted, these families are a heterogeneous group in terms of income, education, employment, and race. However, black and Hispanic-origin families are disproportionately represented (Cunningham and Hahn, 1994). Thus, given the continuing high levels of divorce and premarital childbearing, the proportion of children living with a lone parent doubled between 1970 and 1990, reaching about 25 percent (Lugaila, 1992).

There has been an increase in the proportion of women in general, and mothers in particular, participating in the labor force since 1970. This increase in mothers in the labor force corresponded with the increased need for child care, especially for children under five. Further, in 1990, nearly 30 percent of married-couple families had both spouses working year-round. Also, the number of parents with at least some college education increased during the 1970s and 1980s. Despite the increases in mothers and married-couples in the labor force, and higher educational attainment of parents, the overall median family income was only 6 percent above what it was in 1970. That this increase was so small was predominantly due to the rise in single-parent households.

The disparity in poverty rates between married and unmarried women has increased, with unmarried women far more likely to have incomes below the poverty level or to be receiving public assistance than married women. Similarly, the disparity in poverty rates between employed and unemployed women with children has also increased. As with many other demographic trends over the last 30 years, blacks and Hispanic-origin women and children were disproportionately represented among the ranks of the poor. The latter is particularly poignant since blacks have much lower median family incomes and higher rates of poverty than whites with similar educational attainment and patterns of work (Lugaila, 1992). Lack of health insurance coverage is often noted as a problem for poor children living in mother-only families, but even among children living in married-couple families, the proportion not covered by health insurance anytime during 1990 was 9 percent for the nonpoor and 3 percent for poor.

Stable family relationships and adequate financial support are essential for the healthy development of children. In the United States, changes in family structure and in the economic system are weakening supports for families. Current social systems, such as public assistance, tax-supported medical care, and child welfare services, are being questioned and restructured, possibly placing some families at risk. Public health professionals in the field of MCH are challenged with the tasks of assessing the impact of these proposed changes on the health status of families and initiating policies and programs that will promote and protect their well-being.

REFERENCES

Abramovitz, M. 1995. Aid to Families with Dependent Children. In *Encyclopedia of social work*, 19th ed., vol. 1. Washington, DC: National Association of Social Workers.

Amato, P.R. 1994. The implications of research findings on children in stepfamilies. In *Stepfamilies: Who benefits? Who does not?*, eds. A. Booth and J. Dunn, 81–88. Hillsdale, NJ: Lawrence Erlbaum Associates, Publishers.

Baugher, E. 1993. Population profile of the US 1993: Poverty. In *Current population reports: Population characteristics*, Special Studies Series P-23, No. 185. Washington, DC: U.S. Department of Commerce, Economics and Statistics Administration, Bureau of the Census.

Center for the Future of Children. Winter 1992. *U.S. health care for children*, Vol. 2, No. 2. Los Altos, CA: The David and Lucille Packard Foundation.

Cunningham, P.J., and B.A. Hahn. 1994. The changing American family: Implication for children's health insurance coverage and the use of ambulatory care services. *The Future of Children 4*, 24–42.

Darman, R. 1992. *Comprehensive health reform: Observations about the problem and alternative approaches to solution.* Testimony before the U.S. House of Representatives, Committee on Ways and Means, Washington, DC, January 17, p. 6.

Donovan, P. 1995. *The politics of blame: Family planning, abortion, and the poor.* New York: Alan Guttmacher Institute.

Flint, S. 1992. Decline in uninsured children registered in 1990. *Child health financing report*, Vol. IX, No. 1. Elk Grove Village, IL: American Academy of Pediatrics, p. 5.

Foley, J.D. 1991. *Uninsured in the United States: The nonelderly population without health insurance. Analysis of the March 1990 current population survey.* Special Report SR-10. Washington, DC: Employee Benefit Research Institute.

Hareven, T.K. 1984. Themes in the historical development of the family. In *The review of child development*, Vol. 7, *The family,* ed. R.D. Parke, 137–178. Chicago: The University of Chicago Press.

Hetherington, E.M., and K.M. Jodl. 1994. Stepfamilies as settings for child development. In *Stepfamilies: Who benefits? Who does not?*, eds. A. Booth and J. Dunn, 55–80. Hillsdale, NJ: Lawrence Erlbaum Associates, Publishers.

Kadushin, A. 1980. *Child welfare services.* 3rd ed. New York: Macmillan Publishing Co., Inc.

Kahn, A.J. 1973. *Social policy and social services.* New York: Random House.

Laslett, P., and R. Wall. 1972. *Households and families in past times.* Cambridge, UK: Cambridge University Press.

Lugaila, T. 1992. Households, families, and children: A 30-year perspective. *In Current population reports: Population characteristics,* Special Studies Series P-23, No. 181. Washington, DC: U.S. Department of Commerce, Bureau of the Census.

McNally, S.J. (1980). Historical perspectives on the family. In *Family focused care*, eds. J.R. Miller and E.H. Janosik. New York: McGraw-Hill Book Co.

Meyer, D. 1995. Supplemental Security Income. In *Encyclopedia of social work,* 19th ed., Vol. 3. Washington, DC: National Association of Social Workers.

Newson, G., and B. Harvey. 1994. Assuring access to health care. In *Maternal and child health practices,* 4th ed., eds. H.M. Wallace et al. Oakland, CA: Third Party Publishers.

Rawlings, S. 1993. Population profile of the U.S. 1993: Households and families. In *Current population reports: Population characteristics,* Special Studies Series P-23, No. 185. Washington, DC: U.S. Department of Commerce, Bureau of the Census.

Reisch, M. 1995. Public social services. In *Encyclopedia of social work,* 19th ed., Vol. 3. Washington, DC: National Association of Social Workers.

Reiss, I., and G. Lee. 1988. *Family systems in America.* New York: Holt, Rinehart and Winston, Inc.

Roberts, S. 1993. *Who we are.* New York: Times Books.

Schmidt, W.M., and H.M. Wallace. 1994. The development of health services for mothers and children in the U.S. In *Maternal and child health practices,* 4th ed., eds. H.M. Wallace et al. Oakland, CA: Third Party Publishers.

Schorr, L.B., and D. Schorr. 1988. *Within our reach: Breaking the cycle of disadvantage.* New York: Anchor Press, Doubleday.

Short, E. 1993. Population profile of the U.S. 1993: Health insurance. In *Current population reports: Population characteristics,* Special Studies Series P-23, No. 185. Washington, DC: U.S. Department of Commerce, Bureau of the Census.

U.S. Bureau of the Census. 1990. How we are changing: Demographic state of the nation: 1990. *Current population reports,* Special Studies Series P-23, No. 170. Washington, DC: U.S. Department of Commerce.

U.S. Bureau of the Census. 1991a. Poverty in the U.S.: 1990. *Current population reports,* Consumer Income Series P-60, No. 175. Washington, DC: U.S. Department of Commerce.

U.S. Bureau of the Census. 1991b. Trends in relative income: 1964–1989. *Current population reports,* Consumer Income Series P-60, No. 177. Washington, DC: Government Printing Office.

U.S. Bureau of the Census. 1994. Demographic state of the nation: 1995. *Current population reports,* Special Studies Series P-23, No. 188. Washington, DC: Government Printing Office.

U.S. Congress. 1996. *Personal Responsibility and Work Opportunity Reconciliation Act,* 104-193.

U.S. Department of Health and Human Services, Social Security Administration. August 1994. Annual statistical supplement. *Social Security Bulletin.* SSA Pub. No. 13-71700.

U.S. Department of Health and Human Services. 1994. *Health United States 1993 Chartbook.* DHHS Pub. No. PHS 94-1232-1. Hyattsville, MD: U.S. Public Health Service, National Center for Health Statistics.

Watkins, E. 1993. The history of maternal and child health: The role of public health social workers. In *Social problems with health consequences: Program design, implementation, and evaluation,* ed. J.J. Fickling. Proceedings of the 1990 Bi-Regional Conference for Public Health Social Workers in Regions IV and VI. Columbia, SC: College of Social Work, University of South Carolina.

World almanac and book of facts 1990. 1990. New York: Pharos Books, 551.

PART II

Determinants of Health and Health Services: The Developmental Cycle

CHAPTER 4

Family Planning

C. Arden Miller and Amy Ong Tsui

The predominant influences which led to the improvement in health in the past three centuries were nutritional, environmental (particularly control of water and food) and behavioral; the last through the change in reproductive practices which limited population growth.

T. McKeown, 1976

INTRODUCTION

The next section of this textbook groups chapters according to the maternal and child health (MCH) developmental cycle and appropriately begins with a discussion of family planning, organized programs to enable limitation of fertility. Family planning represents a key component of reproductive health services in the United States and elsewhere. Emphasis here will feature needs and programs in the United States, although some reference will be made to international situations.

Although contraceptive use has increased in the United States, so too has the percentage of births that are unwanted. At the same time public spending on contraceptive services declined by 27 percent during the 1980s and continues to be in jeopardy of further cuts. This chapter will present some of the history of the family planning movement not covered in Chapter 2 and will review the status of family planning services in the United States in terms of their availability and barriers to their access. It will also describe current and past levels and trends of contraceptive practice, the characteristics of users, the methods adopted, and sources of services. The likely future of family planning in the United States will be discussed in terms of the critical policy issues that prevent the U.S. population from achieving the status of an appropriately contracepting society. The chapter ends with a call to advocacy.

69

Clarification of terms is appropriate in this chapter. *Unintended* or *unplanned pregnancies* include those that are unwanted and those that are mistimed. *Unwanted pregnancies* and *unwanted childbearing* occur among women who report that they never intended to give birth or to continue childbearing. *Mistimed pregnancies* occur among women who report that they at some time in the future intended to bear one or more children but not at the time this pregnancy occurred. Data on these issues are based on surveys that in part require recall of intent, a procedure with a degree of uncertainty among some women and their partners.

About 60 percent of pregnancies in the U.S. are unintended. About half of these are terminated by abortion, but even so the proportion of births from unintended pregnancies appears to be increasing (Institute of Medicine, 1995). About 40 percent of all births are the result of unintended pregnancies. The proportion is higher among women in poverty, those never married, and among teenagers. About 28 percent of births are the result of mistimed pregnancies and another 12 percent are births from unwanted pregnancies. The consequences of these circumstances are dire for many women and children, and underscore a pressing need for more effective programs of family planning (Kost and Forrest, 1995).

BACKGROUND

Efforts to control fertility date from earliest recorded history. Egyptian papyri recommend the insertion of a vaginal suppository containing crocodile's dung and honey mixed with sodium carbonate, or the insertion of acacia tips. Soranos, a Greek physician writing in the second century, advised that for the prevention of conception, coitus should be avoided during critical times in the menstrual cycle. Other suggested methods included anointing the cervix with astringent materials or closing the os uteri with cotton (Major, 1954). The contraceptive effect of coitus interruptus has been known since antiquity. By an account in Genesis, Onan, required by tribal custom to sleep with his deceased brother's widow but not wishing to establish a collateral family line, chose to spill his seed upon the ground. Throughout history various penile sheaths, often from strips of linen or animal membranes, have been tried as contraceptives.

The prevailing motivations for promoting access to contraception have changed from time to time. Concern for the well-being of unwanted children is one of them. Boswell estimates that from antiquity through the Renaissance about one quarter of liveborn children were abandoned. Some of these children survived, but many did not. Medieval chronicles report a harvest of infant corpses yielded by rivers such as the Nile and the Arno. Child abandonment was not a socially reprehensible method for coping with unwanted fertility. Rousseau, the noted eighteenth century French philosopher, wrote without apparent shame or regret that he abandoned all five of his children. It was a practice not much condemned by theologians, except for risk of committing the grave sin of incest by inadvertently having sexual relations with a previously abandoned daughter or son (Boswell, 1988).

Circumstances in the United States through the early decades of this century can be interpreted as evidence of socially sanctioned infanticide. Nearly every large city accommodated a foundling hospital, often with convenient provision for depositing unwanted infants. The mortality rates in those hospitals approached 90 percent (English, 1984). During the same period upper class French women boarded their unplanned infants with peasant families, a practice with a comparably high mortality rate (Klaus, 1993).

SUPPORTIVE RATIONALE

Some less stark considerations relate to unplanned childbearing. Infants and children have better survival rates and survivors are healthier if they are born to mothers who are not at the extremes of the childbearing age span, if there is spacing of two years between births, and if family size is limited. Unwanted childbearing poses health burdens beyond those that can be attributed to social and economic characteristics of the mother. For an unwanted pregnancy the mother is less likely to seek prenatal care and is more likely to expose the fetus to harmful substances such as tobacco and alcohol. The child of an unwanted conception is more likely to be of low birth weight, to die in the first year of life, and to be abused. The risks and outcomes for mistimed conception are of a similar nature but of lesser magnitude (Institute of Medicine, 1995).

Concern about the effects of unwanted, mistimed, or excessive childbearing on the health of women has been conspicuous in the policy dynamics of family planning programs in this century. Childbearing and parenthood are low risk and rewarding experiences for people who want them. The risks and rewards become adverse for women at the extremes of the childbearing years, women experiencing short interpregnancy intervals, for women with health problems such as diabetes or hypertension, for women with multiple pregnancies, and for those women whose pregnancies are unwanted or mistimed. The adversities are biological, psychological (depression), economic, and social. Educational and career prospects for women are curtailed by unplanned childbearing. Women whose pregnancies are unwanted or mistimed are four times as likely as women with a planned pregnancy to be physically abused by their husband or partner (Gazmararian et al., 1995).

Maternal deaths from major complications of pregnancy (uncontrolled bleeding, blood clots to the lungs, and toxemia with high blood pressure and convulsions) are concentrated among fourth and higher order births and among very young women and those in the upper ranges of the childbearing years. These hazards are minimized among women given access to family planning.

When women have access to contraceptive services, they have reduced likelihood of resorting to dangerous illegal abortions for control of fertility. Under safe conditions, induced abortion is a low risk procedure—with even fewer complications than childbearing. When access to abortion is limited, many women resort to unsafe procedures in order to avert pregnancy. Accurate data on illegal procedures are not readily available, but some estimates place the total number of illegal abortions the world over to be in the range of 20 million each year. Associated deaths are estimated to number over 70,000, nearly one fifth of the half a million maternal deaths that occur annually worldwide (World Health Organization, 1993).

When Margaret Sanger worked as a public health nurse in the poorest sectors of New York City during the early years of this century, she confronted appalling evidence of the plight of women caught in lives of excessive and unwanted fertility. She began promoting family planning, a cause which attracted many followers. Her work led to the formation of The Family Planning Federation, an organization which sponsored family planning clinics in nearly every U.S. community and in many other countries. It continues under the name of Planned Parenthood Federation of America as one of this country's largest organized providers of family planning services.

The eugenics theme has played a part in the promotion of family planning. In the early decades of this century, the view developed that society would be improved if only the "right" people were encouraged to propagate. This view today is greatly diminished but is not entirely absent. Voices from developing countries and from U.S. minority populations sometimes charge that the promotion of family planning is a covert expression of genocidal intent.

Concern about overpopulation is a strong motivating force for family planning, especially in densely populated countries such as China, India, Indonesia, and Bangladesh. Malthus was one of the earliest (1798) analysts to point out that the growth of a population could outstrip resources to support it. This consideration figured prominently in the United States during the 1970s when public programs to enable access to family planning both domestically and internationally were greatly expanded. As rational as the population theme may be in support of family planning, it is not now a strong influence in this country. The size of the U.S. population would be stable if it were not for immigration. Historically, some countries have been more concerned about too little population than too much. Nationalistic rivalries in Europe during the late nineteenth and early twentieth centuries caused many countries to adopt pronatalist policies, which offered strong inducements for childbearing, even among unmarried women (Klaus, 1993). These inducements and supportive services formed the basis for protections that contribute to favorable pregnancy outcomes and that persist to this day.

Feminists currently provide the strongest advocacy for abortion rights. Their concern is fortified by data on the health and well-being of women, but the cause is largely argued on the basis of human rights, an argument that the political process has tended to uphold in a climate of increasing contention. Proponents maintain that women are entitled to sexual fulfillment that is free from the risks of unintended pregnancy. Denial of pregnancy prevention services is interpreted by some voices as a form of social control over women by a male-dominated society. Advocacy for abortion services, for family planning, and for family planning services for poor women remains an urgent policy priority for workers in MCH.

SOCIAL AND POLITICAL CONTEXT

Public health workers are apt to find the supportive rationale for family planning so compelling that countervailing forces are underestimated. These forces are considerable. In 1873 Anthony Comstock, secretary of the New York Society for the Suppression of Vice, induced Congress to pass an act prohibiting the use of the mails for obscene matter. Any content dealing with sex education or family planning was declared pornographic and was prohibited under provisions of the act. Comstockery (George Bernard Shaw's term) found even more stringent expression in various state laws. Margaret Sanger was arrested a number of times for lecturing and distributing pamphlets on family planning. As recently as the 1940s, an obstetrician in Connecticut was jailed for prescribing contraceptives for a married woman.

The tenets of nearly every organized religion are construed by some as supportive of family planning. Conversely nearly every organized religion produces other voices that raise opposition. For many decades the Catholic Church has been the strongest force in opposition. The official position of the church is supportive of family planning except by "unnatural" means. These include all currently available methods of contraception that are most effective. The "natural" methods approved by the church include periodic abstinence and breastfeeding, which tends to delay ovulation in some women. These methods have some effectiveness on a population-wide basis, but they are all high risk for individual couples who seek protection from unwanted childbearing. It is not surprising, as a consequence, that Catholic women in the United States have a rate of abortion 29 percent higher than Protestant women (Henshaw and Kost, 1996). Women of all ages, socioeconomic circumstances, religions, and races may find it necessary to have an abortion when faced with an unwanted pregnancy.

Withdrawal from intercourse before ejaculation is another "natural" method of attempted contraception. The annual failure rate for withdrawal is 24 percent, which means that 24 out of 100 women will experience a pregnancy while using this method. Practicing this method over three years produces a cumulative failure rate of 56 percent. More than one half of such contraceptors will have an unwanted pregnancy.

The social reforms of the 1960s (e.g., Medicare, Medicaid, Head Start, the War on Poverty) included a prevailing attitude that family planning and population policy were appropriate matters for government action (Rosoff, 1988). Presidents Kennedy (the nation's only Catholic president) and Johnson spoke frequently in support of government-sponsored family planning programs. Support was bipartisan. President Nixon declared, "No American woman should be denied access to family planning assistance because of her economic condition. I believe, therefore, that we should establish as a national goal the provision of family planning services . . . to all who want but cannot afford them" (Rosoff, 1988, p. 313). Former presidents Truman and Eisenhower served as honorary co-chairmen of Planned Parenthood Federation of America. As part of the War on Poverty, the Maternal and Child Health provisions of the Social Security Act were required to allocate to family planning a minimum of six percent of available funds and to offer services to "all appropriate cases." Congressman George Bush lent his support to a national program of government support for family planning clinics. Prior to 1980 he also supported the Supreme Court's decision of 1973, which protected a woman's constitutional right to abortion. Abortion remains a procedure not generally regarded as an appropriate method of family planning in the United States (unlike some countries in Eastern Europe) except as an alternative to be considered when contraception fails.

In 1970 Congress enacted Title X of the Public Health Service Act, which provided funds and implementation authority for a nationwide program of family planning clinics for poor women. Under this act teenage women were generally eligible for services regardless of their parents' resources. The program expanded rapidly throughout the 1970s.

The political climate began to change toward the end of the decade. In 1976 Congress prohibited the use of Medicaid funds to pay for abortions. Aspirants to elective office began to reassess their positions supportive of family planning. Controversy over abortion grew as a conspicuous political issue. These changes were driven by the growing influence of a conservative political coalition given finance and voice by a Christian fundamentalist movement. The movement garnered support from a growing radio and television audience for charismatic media evangelists.

The election of Ronald Reagan to the presidency in 1980 marked a watershed in government policy. He omitted family planning funds from all of his budgets and spoke energetically in opposition to abortion. The "right to life," formulated around the abortion issue, became confusedly linked with negative attitudes toward family planning. As vice-president, George Bush changed his position on both abortion and family planning.

During each year in the next decade and a half, a Democratic-majority Congress succeeded in restoring funds to Title X, holding them only to the 1981 funding level. After considering inflation, however, real financial support for the program dwindled by 72 percent. This decrease was only partially offset by increases in Medicaid funding for family planning services (Daley and Gold, 1993). The election of a Republican Congress in 1994, strongly beholden to ultraconservative influences, brought new and real threats to the existence of publicly supported programs for family planning.

The issue is not easily resolved. A strongly articulated view holds that easy access to contraception, especially for teenagers, has promoted irresponsible behavior, increasing early and extramarital sexual activity and, paradoxically, an increase in extramarital teenage childbearing. It is true that during the 1970s and 1980s more teenagers were engaging in sexual intercourse at earlier ages than in previous years (Alan Guttmacher Institute, 1994). It is also true that many difficult-to-measure influences other than access to contraception were brought to bear during those years. Ubiquitous media programming and advertising, often with provocative sexual content, and sexual maturation at younger ages are among the possible factors contributing to intercourse at earlier ages.

An opposing view holds that access to contraception is not the problem, but is in fact the solution. It is certainly true that during the 1980s programs to promote "just say no," generously financed during the Reagan administration, did not reverse trends in sexual behavior. It is also true that teenage fertility in this country has been at a stable level for many decades, increasing only slightly during the late 1980s, and decreasing again in the mid-1990s. The problem appears larger than it really may be because older women have reduced their fertility so much more than young women, resulting in an increased proportion of newborns with teenage mothers.

Few good studies are available to resolve this controversy to everyone's satisfaction. Many public health workers are attracted by the findings of a controlled study by Zabin and colleagues on the influence of a school-linked program of counseling and clinical services that included contraception. Onset of the age of first intercourse by participants in the study population was delayed by 13 months (Zabin et al., 1986). More such studies are needed. This one suggests that when young people have information and related clinical services, their behavior becomes more responsible than without them. Experience from other industrialized nations is relevant. Many of them provide school-based sex education beginning at young ages and access to contraception when teenagers choose to become sexually active. Under these circumstances the average age of first intercourse is no younger than in the United States, but teenage pregnancy and abortion rates are much lower (Jones et al., 1988). The U.S. experience with teenage pregnancy prevention programs includes very few that were effective. They are reviewed by Frost and Forrest (1995).

METHODS OF FAMILY PLANNING

Readers who are not thoroughly familiar with the physiology of sexual maturation, menstruation, and childbearing are urged to take time to study these processes with a standard text of physiology. Understanding the successes, failures, indications, and possible complications of various contraceptives is not possible without knowledge, for example, of the hormonal orchestration of reproduction. Some of the most widely used contraceptives manipulate female hormonal balances.

Successful family planning programs make available a variety of methods. No one of them is entirely satisfactory for all women or for all circumstances. Most women make use of different methods at different stages of their reproductive history. Condoms or diaphragms may be useful for relationships that are intermittent; a daily contraceptive pill may be convenient for stable, continuing partnerships; and surgical sterilization may be chosen when plans for family formation are completed. Surgical sterilization, more often female than male, is the most commonly used method of contraception in the United States. Latex condoms and diaphragms are also useful for protection against sexually transmitted disease (STD).

Some methods rely on preventing union of the ovum and sperm in normally ovulating women. Such methods include periodic abstinence (often identified as the rhythm method because it attempts to confine coitus to phases of the menstrual cycle when the woman is presumed not to be ovulating) and withdrawal, or onanism, when the male discontinues vaginal penetration before ejaculation. More effective methods of preventing union between ovum and sperm provide barriers such as the male and female condom, diaphragm, or cervical cap (the last infrequently used).

One of the most widely used contraceptive methods prevents ovulation by replacing the woman's normal hormonal cycle with an imposed one by means of a daily sequence of oral hormonal pills. The method is highly effective, but it requires diligence to remember to take the pills according to the prescribed schedule. Lapses reduce effectiveness; guidance on how to correct for lapses has no firm scientific basis. This problem is averted by adaptations of the hormonal method, such as the provision of the replacement hormones in a long-acting injection, effective for several months, or in subcutaneous implants, which can be effective for up to five years. If during this period a couple desires to conceive, the implants can be removed and fertility restored.

Various chemical agents can deactivate the sperm and hence prevent conception. These agents are prepared as vaginal foams or jellies, to be inserted into the vagina before intercourse, or more commonly to be used in conjunction with other methods, such as the diaphragm or the condom.

The mode of action of some methods is not precisely known. For example, some models of the intrauterine device (IUD) may not actually prevent fertilization but act by disrupting implantation of the conceptum in the uterine wall. This matter has relevance to some people who take a microscopic view of a "right to life," charging that the device is not a contraceptive but an abortifacient. This view is contradicted when chemical agents, such as copper, are incorporated into the intrauterine device. This is a highly effective method which acts by chemical, as well as by mechanical, means. IUDs currently available in the United States are contraceptives, not abortifacients (Sivin, 1989).

A postcoital "morning after" regimen for taking certain oral contraceptive pills can also avert pregnancy. The method is widely used in Europe and is available in this country, but its use is not much promoted and its availability is not known to many sexually active couples. Only twenty percent of U.S. family planning clinics offer the postcoital pill (Henshaw and Torres, 1994). More recently the contraceptive pill has been publicized as a means of "emergency contraception" for women having unprotected intercourse in the past 72 hours (Ellertson, 1996).

Surgical sterilization by ligating the fallopian tubes or by severing the vas deferens is a choice elected by many individuals who have no further desire for family formation. The method is rarely ineffective, but it has the disadvantage of being almost irreversible if circumstances change and a couple decides they desire a pregnancy.

About 90 percent of women at risk of unintended pregnancy use a contraceptive at least some of the time. The methods they choose are shown in Table 4–1, ranked according to frequency of use in 1990. Note that the most frequently used methods (surgical sterilization and the pill) require a medical visit. (In many countries the pill is available without a medical prescription.) Note should be taken also that use patterns change rapidly, particularly in response to concerns about sexually transmitted disease. For people who are not in a stable monogamous relationship, use of latex condoms is strongly recommended as the best protection next to abstinence to prevent venereal infection, including human immunodeficiency virus (HIV). Hormonal and other nonbarrier methods are not protective against venereal disease.

Use patterns also change rapidly in response to fear of complications. All of the methods described have greater health benefits than health risks that are rare, but in past years, with a regime of higher dose hormonal pills than those now in use, some women experienced uncomfortable side effects. An IUD, the Dalkon shield, no longer manufactured, caused serious pelvic complications in some women. That experience has contributed to the unpopularity in the United States of all IUDs, both among users and providers.

Use patterns also respond to changes in contraceptive technology. Some of the most effective means of contraception have been available for only a few decades. Among currently married users between surveys of 1973 and 1988, reliance on sterilization increased from 23.5 percent to 42.4 percent; use of the hormonal pill

Table 4-1 Contraceptive Use in the United States, 1990

Method	# of Users (in Thousands)	% of Users
Sterilization	14,596	42.0
Tubal	(10,217)	(29.4)
Vasectomy	(4,379)	(12.6)
Pill	9,866	28.4
Condom	6,130	17.6
Diaphragm	992	2.9
Periodic abstinence	934	2.7
Spermicides	759	2.1
IUD	467	1.3
Sponge	467	1.3
Withdrawal	350	1.0
Other methods	117	0.5
TOTAL USERS	34,678	100.0

Note: Distribution of users of spermicides, sponge, and other methods estimated using 1988 figures.

Source: Reprinted from L.S. Peterson, Contraceptive Use in the U.S.: 1982–1990, Advance Data, No. 260, National Center for Health Statistics, February 14, 1995.

declined from 36.1 percent to 20.4 percent; IUD use decreased from 9.6 percent to 2.0 percent; and diaphragm use increased from 3.4 percent to 6.2 percent. Reliance on periodic abstinence dropped during the same period from 4.0 percent to 2.8 percent. Comparable data for the same period are not available for nonmarried users. Among all users between 1982 and 1988, use of the pill remained high (28.0 percent to 30.7 percent), and use of the condom increased from 12.0 percent to 14.6 percent (Mosher, 1990). Further rapid change in use patterns is anticipated as a result of recent approved access to long-acting injectable hormonal contraceptives. Use of the condom since 1988 has increased as a result of educational campaigns urging protection against acquired immune deficiency syndrome (AIDS).

Malcolm Potts (1988) emphasizes that U.S. women, compared with those in other developed countries, are inefficient contraceptors. Contributing factors include limitations in the United States on contraceptive information and services as well as restrictions on the methods available. The choices available to European women are greater and include easy access to postcoital contraceptives, a wider range of IUDs, and injectable or implanted contraceptives, only recently approved for use in the United States.

Table 4–2 Contraceptive Failure Rates* (1988)

Method	Perfect Use	Average Use
No method (chance)	85.0	85.0
Spermicides	3.0	30.0
Sponge	8.0	24.0
Withdrawal	4.0	24.0
Periodic abstinence	9.0	19.0
Cervical cap	6.0	18.0
Diaphragm	6.0	18.0
Condom	2.0	16.0
Pill	1.0	6.0
IUD	0.8	4.0
Injectables	0.3	0.4
Tubal sterilization	0.2	0.5
Vasectomy	0.1	0.2
Implants	0.04	0.05

* Estimated percentage of women experiencing an unintended pregnancy in the first year of use.

Source: Reprinted from *Facts in Brief, 1993,* Alan Guttmacher Institute.

The effectiveness of different family planning methods varies greatly. Failure rates of the most widely used methods are indicated in Table 4–2. Note that even for the most protective methods the failure rates are substantial unless usage conforms perfectly to guidance. Note also that failure rates are calculated only for the first year of use. As noted earlier, when failures are accumulated over multiple years of the reproductive life span, they are greatly increased. This circumstance is alarmingly confirmed by the finding that 47 percent of unintended pregnancies occur among women who are attempting some form of reversible contraception (Institute of Medicine, 1995). This dismal record helps explain this country's high abortion rate. One in four pregnancies is terminated by induced abortion; one in two among pregnant teenagers. Improving this record suggests the need for more effective contraception.

FAMILY PLANNING PROVIDERS

Most users of reversible contraceptives obtain them from private physicians or managed care organizations. Little is known about the scope or quality of those services. About one user in three obtains services from a family planning clinic; the proportion is much higher for poor people, for teenagers, and for minority populations. A great deal is known about those clinics and their users. Accurate data are available on U.S. family planning agencies and their funding sources through 1991 (Henshaw and Torres, 1994). Those studies show that:

- 2,614 agencies provide family planning services in 5,460 clinics.
- Health departments operate 52 percent of the clinic sites; Planned Parenthood affiliates, 15 percent; hospitals, 6 percent; and other agencies, largely community and migrant health centers, 27 percent.
- Most sites offer family planning services in clinic sessions devoted specifically to that purpose.
- Planned Parenthood clinics serve on average three times the number of clients as the next largest provider.
- Clinics offer on average seven to nine different family planning methods.

Most family planning clinics offer a great deal more than contraceptives. A usual cluster of services would include pregnancy testing; screening for breast and cervical cancer; screening and treatment for STDs; screening for hypertension, anemia, and kidney disease; infertility and genetic counseling; abortion; and sometimes prenatal and postpartum care. This extensive array of services has led some analysts to suggest that family planning clinics should become comprehensive primary care centers for women. In truth family planning clinics are now the only or major source of care for many women of reproductive age. The prospect of expanding the role for family planning clinics has some appeal, but it presents many problems. Among them is funding. Family planning is a low-cost service. As other more expensive services draw on the same resources, the family planning mission is diluted. A case can be made that the cause of family planning can best be served, as in many countries, by narrowly focused programs that strive for the widest possible participation of the population in need, leaving provision of other appropriate services to other providers.

The funding issue is central to consideration of the family planning mission. The most important single funding source for clinics is the federal Title X program, which contributes support to three-fourths of the agencies. More than half of all family planning provider agencies receive more than 20 percent of their support from Title X. The next largest source of funding comes from state and local governments; 40 percent of provider agencies receive more than 20 percent of their funds from those sources. Nearly all agencies receive some fee income from Medicaid, but only 15 percent derive more than 20 percent of their total budget from that source. (When considering all providers, not just the public clinics, the funding role of Medicaid increases appreciably.) Other fee income and private

contributions are minor sources of support, as are the MCH and Social Services Block grants (Henshaw and Torres, 1994).

The number of women who received their most recent family planning services at a publicly subsidized clinic rose from 6.1 million in 1982 to 7.1 million in 1988 (Alan Guttmacher Institute, 1995). Title X clinics are especially important sources of care for low income women and teenagers. While 18 percent of all women who made a family planning visit in 1987 went to a Title X clinic, 35 percent of women under the poverty level, 34 percent of black women, and 39 percent of teenage visitors utilized Title X clinics.

Since the 1980s family planning clinics have been caught in a squeeze between increased demand for more costly services and reduced funding (Donovan, 1991). As a result, some clinics have had to resort to increased fee income with resultant threats to nonpaying clients for services. Gold and Daley estimate that, after adjusting for inflation, public support for contraceptive services and supplies diminished by one-third during the 1980s (Gold and Daley, 1991).

NEEDS AND PROSPECTS

The fact that a high proportion of sexually active people practice contraception at least part of the time suggests that the need for it is widely known. The fact that such a high proportion of pregnancies is unintended and that the abortion rate is so high suggests that the effective practice of contraception is poorly understood and that utilization of family planning services is insufficient. Utilization is especially low among women in households with incomes below 200 percent of poverty. For some women access to family planning can be an expensive procedure, not always covered by health insurance, especially for young women and those of low income. Waiting times for an appointment at family planning clinics have lengthened as clinic resources have shrunk. The need for a renewed national effort to enable planned childbearing is well established (Institute of Medicine, 1995).

Ever since the second Nixon administration in the early 1970s, a policy theme has gained strength to diminish the role of government, especially at the federal level, and to privatize as many public programs as possible. This theme had found expression, along with the political power to implement it, in the mid-1990s, with Congressional intent to make draconian cuts in the federal budget. Title X has been slated for elimination, or failing that, being folded into the MCH Block Grant. At the very best this alternative would place public family planning at the uncertain discretion of different state governments. In many states Planned Parenthood Federation affiliates, major providers of clinic services, would be shunted out of the funding stream. In other states services in the public clinics would face serious political constraints. A consistent national policy and funding source for family planning would be lost. No strong private initiative shows promise of replacing it. What traditionally has been regarded as a public good now becomes an individual responsibility.

Threats and uncertainties come from another direction. The Clinton administration's health care reform proposal provided for everyone to be enrolled in a managed care plan that would provide all indicated personal health services. The reform was initially proposed for legislative action, which failed, but the managed care movement gains strength without it. Favorable experience with managed care rests largely on the record of early models of Health Maintenance Organizations, which ordinarily enrolled working families and which provided services financed at a fixed per capita rate.

Enrollees who had the resources and inclination could opt out of the program to purchase selected services from other providers. The new managed care plans are of a different sort. For the most part they are not providers of services, but financial intermediaries for services that are rendered under contract with a variety of providers. Enrollees increasingly are low-income people, often Medicaid recipients, who are locked into the system without resources to purchase services independent of the plan. The inclination and expertise of these plans to render family planning services is largely unknown. There was even controversy over whether some providers (such as Catholic hospitals) may refuse to include family planning services under circumstances when beneficiaries' choices of alternative providers were limited. Prospects for availability of family planning services through managed care plans should not be underestimated, however. Service priorities under managed care will be driven by considerations of cost, if not profit. Nearly all methods for averting unwanted childbearing, including abortion, are less costly than maternity care (Trussell et al., 1995). For this reason insurance companies that do not explicitly cover the costs of abortion will sometimes do so if asked. Still, financing abortions is a less appealing prospect than preventing unplanned pregnancies.

The need for family planning clinics to continue functioning outside managed care plans, or under contract with them, is an ongoing concern. No matter how the issue is resolved, there is room here for expert influence from public health. Insofar as managed care plans are currently influenced by standards that define benefits, they are framed around considerations of cost to enable employers to purchase economical plans on behalf of employees and their families. Standards for Medicaid managed care are still in development. A strong influence protective of user interests has not yet coalesced.

Standards for family planning, well established in Planned Parenthood clinics, need to be developed for managed care plans. A pressing commitment for public health workers would be to define those standards, see to their incorporation into managed care benefits and contracts, arrange to participate in quality reviews, develop data systems that enable accountability and outcome evaluations, train personnel capable of performing these tasks, and monitor the quality and outcome of services. All this awaits doing at the same time the mission of existing family planning clinics and their funding sources are reviewed. Nothing in the history of this country suggests that the family planning needs of the population are likely to be met without the strongest possible advocacy.

REFERENCES

Alan Guttmacher Institute. 1994. *Sex and America's teenagers.* New York and Washington, DC: Author.

Alan Guttmacher Institute. 1995. The U.S. family planning program faces challenges and change. *Issues in brief.* Washington, DC: Author.

Boswell, J. 1988. *The kindness of strangers.* New York: Pantheon.

Daley, D., and R.B. Gold. 1993. Public funding for contraceptive, sterilization, and abortion services, fiscal year 1992. *Family Planning Perspectives 25,* 244–251.

Donovan P. 1991. Family planning clinics: Facing higher costs and sicker patients. *Family Planning Perspectives 23,* 198–203.

Ellertson, C. 1996. History and efficacy of emergency contraception: Beyond Coca-Cola. *Family Planning Perspectives 28,* 44–48.

English, P.C. 1984. Pediatrics and the unwanted child in history: Foundling homes, disease, and the origins of foster care in New York City, 1860 to 1920. *Pediatrics 73,* 699–711.

Frost, J.J., and J.P. Forrest. 1995. Understanding the impact of effective teenage pregnancy prevention programs. *Family Planning Perspectives 27,* 188–195.

Gazmararian, J.A. et al. 1995. The relationship between pregnancy intendedness and physical violence in mothers of newborns. *Obstetrics and Gynecology 85,* 1031–1038.

Gold, R.B., and D. Daley. 1991. Public funding of contraceptive, sterilization, and abortion services, fiscal year 1990–1991. *Family Planning Perspectives 23,* 204–211.

Henshaw, S.K., and A. Torres. 1994. Family planning agencies: Services, policies, and funding. *Family Planning Perspectives 26,* 52–82.

Henshaw, S.K., and K. Kost. 1996. Abortion patients in 1994–1995: Characteristics and contraceptive use. *Family Planning Perspectives 20,* 158–168.

Institute of Medicine. 1995. *The best intentions. Unintended pregnancy and the well-being of children and families.* Washington, DC: National Academy Press.

Jones, E.F. et al. 1988. Unintended pregnancy, contraceptive practice, and family planning services in developed countries. *Family Planning Perspectives 20,* 53–67.

Klaus, A. 1993. *Every child a lion: The origins of maternal and infant health policy in the United States and France, 1890–1920.* Ithaca, NY: Cornell University Press.

Kost, K., and J.D. Forrest. 1995. Intention status of U.S. births in 1988: Differences by mothers' socioeconomic and demographic characteristics. *Family Planning Perspectives 27,* 11–17.

Major, R.H. 1954. *A history of medicine,* Vol 1. Springfield, IL: Charles C Thomas.

McKeown, T. 1976. *The role of medicine: Dream, mirage, or nemesis.* London, UK: The Nuffield Provincial Hospitals Trust.

Mosher, W.D. 1990. Contraceptive practice in the U.S., 1982–1988. *Family Planning Perspectives 22,* 198–205.

Potts, M. 1988. Birth control methods in the U.S. *Family Planning Perspectives 20,* 288–296.

Rosoff, J. 1988. The politics of birth control. *Family Planning Perspectives 20,* 312–320.

Sivin, I. 1989. IUDs are contraceptives, not abortifacients: A comment on research and belief. *Studies in Family Planning 20,* 355–359.

Trussell, J. et al. 1995. The economic value of contraception: A comparison of 15 methods. *American Journal of Public Health 85,* 494–503.

World Health Organization. 1993. *Abortion. A tabulation of available data on the frequency and mortality of unsafe abortion.* WHO/FHE/MSM/92.13. Geneva: Author, 1–14.

Zabin, L.S. et al. 1986. Evaluation of a pregnancy prevention program for urban teenagers. *Family Planning Perspectives 18,* 119–126.

CHAPTER 5

Mothers and Infants

Trude Bennett and Milton Kotelchuck

At the present time medical schools do not prepare students for the work of preventing infant mortality. . . . In short, preventive pediatrics must be taught. This becomes possible only when it is a required course based upon the present-day needs of the community. To be successful the preventive work in pediatrics must have a foundation in the knowledge that the faulty social structure is at the basis of many of the ills that are thrust upon infant flesh.

Wile, 1910 [in Bremner, 1971]

I am 37 years old and I am so worried and filled with perfect horror at the prospects ahead. So many of my neighbors die at giving birth to their children. I have a baby 11 months old in my keeping now, whose mother died. When I reached their cabin last Nov. it was 22 below zero, and I had to ride 7 miles horse back. She was nearly dead when I got there, and died after giving birth to a 14 lb. boy.

Mrs. A-C-P, 1916 [in Bremner, 1971]

INTRODUCTION

At the beginning of this century, childbirth was still a life-threatening event for women in the United States. The risk of death to mothers and infants was substantial, and the available information and treatments were not adequate to assuage women's fears. Although the uneven distribution of risks has always placed disadvantaged groups in greatest jeopardy, the tragedy of a maternal or infant death elicits universal sympathy. Dr. Sara Josephine Baker, who became director of the New York City Bureau of Child Hygiene in 1908, coined the slogan "No Mother's Baby Is Safe Until Every Mother's Baby Is Safe" (Wertz and Wertz, 1982, p. 228). A pamphlet published by the United States Children's Bureau in 1913 proclaimed, "The infant death rate is the truest index of the welfare of any community" (Bremner, 1971, p. 966).

Infant deaths remain a widely used indicator of the general health and well-being of society. Infant mortality continues to plague developing countries at alarming rates, exacting significant social and economic costs and curtailing overall life expectancy. Although both maternal and infant mortality have been markedly reduced in this country, major racial and socioeconomic disparities persist as a gauge of social inequality. The slipping international ranking of the United States in infant mortality rates has been a source of national embarrassment. The last two decades have seen a great deal of effort targeted toward lowering the U.S. infant mortality rate, and especially toward reducing the extremely high death rates of African American infants. The maternal and child health (MCH) community has focused on equalizing the life circumstances of mothers and the life chances of infants as a starting point toward greater social equity in the United States.

This chapter provides an overview of reproductive outcomes that are used as health indicators for mothers and infants. Definitions are provided, and epidemiological trends and salient policy issues are briefly discussed. The notion of reproductive risk is explored and its usefulness examined in relation to the defined outcomes. The chapter concludes with a review of current interventions in the field and some of the controversies we face in setting program and policy priorities in the search for equity.

OUTCOMES

Definitions

Formal efforts to study the health of populations began in Europe and the United States in the 1840s with the development of vital statistics systems in which the state, as opposed to the church, began to record births and deaths. The well-being of children has always been recognized as critical to a society's vitality and continuity, and the measurement of early death has been an important topic from the beginning of birth registration systems. In an era with no vaccinations or cures for infectious childhood diseases, the first efforts to examine the health of a state's youngest citizens focused on deaths of children under five. *Childhood mortality,* still calculated as a rate of such deaths per 1,000 children from birth to five years, is an important measure of a society's health. The World Health Organization (WHO) uses childhood mortality as part of a child survival index to make cross-national comparisons.

One can view the efforts of public health professionals over the past century as an effort to refine this broad child health measure to better assess infant health status. As we have increasingly been able to affect the health of mothers and newborns, our ability to define and measure relevant components of infant health and morbidity has also improved. Measurement of MCH events is intended not only to enhance scientific understanding, but also to facilitate effective interventions. By the 1870s the present concept of *infant mortality*, the number of infant deaths per 1,000 live births, came into use. The turn of the twentieth century brought into focus the role of infectious diseases and poor nutrition, which took a heavy toll on infants throughout their first year. The MCH community began to divide infant mortality into *neonatal mortality* (deaths in the first 27 days of life per 1,000 live births) and *postneonatal mortality* (deaths from 28 to 364 days per 1,000 live births minus neonatal deaths). Neonatal deaths were generally attributed to biological birth complications and postneonatal deaths to environmental conditions and infectious diseases.

International comparisons are troubled by different historical and cultural perspectives on the meaning of infants' lives and deaths. In China, newborns are counted as being one year old at the time of birth. In some societies an infant is not considered to be alive (and age is not calculated) until the time of christening, circumcision, or naming. A baby that dies before achieving the required status would not be enumerated as an infant death, and classification of neonatal and postneonatal deaths would be skewed by varying definitions.

Birth weight has been universally recognized as an important predictor of infant mortality and morbidity. Historically, all societies have known that tiny babies were more likely to die and that small infants who survived were developmentally vulnerable. In industrialized countries, the growth of specialized services for newborns and neonatal intensive care units in the 1950s and 1960s increased the focus on *low birth weight* and *prematurity.* Specific measures of newborn morbidity status arose in tandem with these developments. Differential categorizations of small size that became popularized included definitions based on birth weight, gestational age or prematurity, and growth (birth weight levels corresponding to gestational age).

In 1948, the WHO established 2,500 grams as the threshold for normal births. At first low birth weight was the only criterion used to define infant size. But with improved registration and use of computerized databases, more detailed and sophisticated birth weight measures developed. Birth weight categories are generally defined as *normal birth weight* or NBW (2,500 grams or more; 5 lb., 8.5 oz.); *low birth weight* or LBW (less than 2,500 grams); *moderately low birth weight* or MLBW (1,500–2,499 grams), *very low birth weight* or VLBW (less than 1,500 grams; 3 lb., 4.5 oz.), and occasionally *extra low birth weight* or ELBW (less than 750 grams). Births at less than 500 grams are sometimes considered marginally viable and excluded from live births, and infants weighing 4,000 grams or greater are sometimes considered separately as a high-weight group with potential health risks. Birth weight rates (more properly called *proportions*) are defined as the percentages of births in a weight category (i.e., number of births in a given weight range per 100 live births).

LBW can be thought of as being due to two possible causes, infants born too soon (prematurity) or born too small (*intrauterine growth retardation* or IUGR). Interest in the measurement of prematurity is increasing with the recognition that most infant deaths are due to low gestational age and immaturity of the fetus, not size per se. Prematurity has been defined somewhat arbitrarily based on 40 weeks as the average length of pregnancy. Normal gestation is defined as 37–41 weeks. The criterion for *premature* gestation is 36 weeks or less and for *extremely premature,* 32 weeks or less. Births at 42+ weeks of gestation are classified as *postmature.* Rates of prematurity are usually calculated as the number of premature births per total live births x 100.

Prematurity is more difficult to measure accurately than birth weight. Gestational age is usually defined as the difference between the last menstrual period (LMP) less two weeks and the birthdate. The completeness and accuracy of birth certificate and medical record data on LMP vary according to mothers' ability to recall this information. Ultrasonography and newborn observational criteria, such as the Dubowitz scoring system, can also be used to estimate gestational age.

Growth measures, which define IUGR or *small for gestational age* (SGA), use percentages to rank infant birth weights for a given gestational age based on national norms. For example, among all infants born at 39 weeks gestation, 50 percent weighed more than 3,600 grams. Babies are usually defined as SGA if they rank in the lowest tenth percentile for a given gestational age. The distinction between prematurity and growth retardation has important implications for prevention efforts and for subsequent morbidity and treatment of the infant. Premature infants are more vulnerable to mortality, but if they survive their life course may be quite normal. SGA infants have better survival rates but more subsequent developmental and health problems. Growth retardation often makes a greater contribution to low birth weight rates in developing countries compared with the United States. However, the utility of these growth measures is limited by the lack of international comparative norms as well as the need for fairly sophisticated data collection systems.

Public health analysts have attempted to capture the relationship between infant birth size and infant mortality by defining *birth weight-specific mortality* or BWSM, the number of infant deaths per 1,000 live births in a given weight category. For example, in the United States today approximately 100 infants die per every 1,000 born at LBW, compared to only 5 deaths per 1,000 infants born at LBW. BWSM is a very effective measure of a society's capacity to keep small infants alive.

Technically, infant mortality can thus be defined as IM = Σ(BWSM $\times$ BW). That is, the total infant mortality in society is the sum of all the infant mortality rates within each birthweight group. The overall impact of death rates for different groups is thus influenced by the frequency of births in each weight category.

This formula is important because it suggests two approaches to improve infant mortality, reducing the number of small babies through prenatal interventions and improving neonatal health services to keep small babies alive. Both elements are critical to improving infant mortality rates in any society.

The timing of the loss of a product of pregnancy is also important. One should think along an embryogenic timeline. (Issues of conception are discussed in Chapter 4.) About 15 percent of fertilized eggs do not successfully implant. Of the 85 percent that do implant, it is estimated that 27 percent end in spontaneous abortions, often called *miscarriages*, although the reasons are not well understood (Hertz-Picciotto, 1988). Spontaneous abortions frequently present a serious psychological loss for the mother and family. In spite of the high frequency of early loss, general inattention to this important topic in women's health has hindered the development of any standardized measurement of rates in this area. The MCH field has a very limited understanding of the causes, risk factors, and distribution of early fetal loss.

Deaths after 20 weeks, but prior to birth, are defined as *fetal deaths* and are also rather poorly understood. Fetal death rates are approximately equal to neonatal death rates, but are much less frequently studied. An arbitrary division is made between *early* (20–27 weeks) and *late* (28+ weeks) fetal deaths. Late fetal deaths are often called *stillbirths*. Historically based on fetal viability, these distinctions have become less clear with the increased potential for early surgical interventions on the fetus. In many European countries, the term *perinatal mortality* is used to refer to all deaths from 28 weeks gestation through 7 days of life (number of perinatal deaths per 1,000 births plus late fetal deaths). U.S. studies sometimes use this term but with varying definitions.

As with indicators of infant health status, the definition of maternal outcomes has been evolving over time. *Maternal mortality* has traditionally been used as the sole indicator, with measures estimating rates of maternal deaths per 100,000 live births or women's average lifetime risks of dying from maternal causes. However, definitions used for maternal mortality have not been consistent. In 1974, a statistical working group in Geneva declared a maternal death to be "the death of a woman while pregnant or within 42 days of termination of pregnancy . . ." (Royston and Armstrong, 1989, p. 12). By including "all known deaths of women known to be pregnant," this group recommended a definition based purely on the timing of death, parallel to infant mortality. A limit of 42 days postpartum, however, is a narrow window to capture deaths related to the sequelae of pregnancy and childbearing. Studies that have extended the postpartum period to a full year have identified 6–11 percent additional deaths after 42 days (Atrash et al., 1990; Rochat et al., 1988). The International Classification of Diseases, 10th ed., Clinical Modification (ICD-10-CM), which will appear in 1997, has revised the time frame upward to one year postdelivery.

Like the ICD-9 (World Health Organization, 1977) and earlier versions, this widely used classification system divides maternal deaths into two groups. The first category is made up of *direct obstetric deaths* resulting from obstetric complications of the pregnant state (pregnancy, labor, and puerperium), from interventions, omissions, incorrect treatment, or from a chain of events resulting from any of the above. The second classification is *indirect obstetric deaths* resulting from previous existing disease or disease that developed during pregnancy, which was not due to direct obstetric causes, but which was aggravated by the physiologic effects of pregnancy. Deaths from accidental or incidental causes presumed to be independent of childbearing are excluded, an omission that provides conservative estimates. Studies have shown that maternal mortality increases considerably with inclusion of deaths to pregnant and postpartum women caused by drugs, violence, and injury (Chavkin and Allen, 1993).

As maternal deaths have become more rare in developed countries, a new measure has been developed—the *reproductive mortality rate*. The concept of reproductive mortality includes risks sustained by women trying to avoid pregnancy, or deaths related to contraceptive use. The rate consists of the number of reproductive deaths per 100,000 women in a given age group. In the United States, mortality risks sustained by women trying to avoid or delay pregnancy have become as important as pregnancy-associated risks. "Whereas in 1955, 99 percent of the reproductive deaths in the U.S. were pregnancy-related, only slightly more than one-half (53 percent) were so in 1975. Virtually all of the remainder (45 percent) were related to oral contraceptive use" (Royston and Armstrong, 1989, p. 16).

The decline of maternal mortality calls for more sensitive measures of maternal morbidity, an area which has been relatively understudied. *Severe pregnancy complications* are measured by the ratio of pregnancy-related hospitalizations per 100 deliveries, but reductions in hospital admissions may reflect changes in hospital policy and standards of medical practice rather than a true decline in morbidity. Cost containment policies and shifts to outpatient management of many conditions could mask health problems while lowering hospitalization rates.

Epidemiologic Trends

Infant Mortality

The provisional estimate of 31,400 infant deaths in 1994 was the lowest annual number ever recorded in the United States; the corresponding rate of 7.9 per 1,000 live births represented a 5 percent decrease from the 1993 rate of 8.3 (Guyer et al., 1995). The decline was found solely among neonatal deaths. Causes of death with lowered rates were respiratory distress syndrome, for which new treatments have been developed, and sudden infant death syndrome (SIDS), which may have been affected by recent recommendations on infants' sleeping position (Guyer et al., 1995).

Major racial disparities in infant morality show no sign of lessening. In 1992, African-American infants were 2.4 times as likely to die in the first year as white infants (16.8 versus 6.9 deaths per 1,000 live births). Racial comparisons in infant mortality usually focus on black/white differences because of the extreme gap in outcomes. Numbers of births in other racial and ethnic minority groups tend to be too small for statistical analysis, and the accuracy and completeness of reporting for many other groups are often questionable. Overall mortality rates for Asian American, Native American, and Latino infants are similar to the white rate, though regional and subgroup variations underlie the appearance of homogeneity. (See Chapter 9.) For example, in 1989–1991 the Native American infant mortality rate for the Aberdeen Area of the Indian Health Service (IHS) (North Dakota, South Dakota, Nebraska, and Iowa) was 17.5 per 1000 live births, compared with a rate of 10.2 for all IHS areas (Indian Health Service, 1994). In an analysis of California vital statistics, Samoan infants were found to have much higher infant mortality rates than other Asian or Pacific Islander groups (Asian American Health Forum, n.d.).

Infant mortality rates in the United States also vary by geography. The highest rates tend to cluster among states in the south and midwest. In 1994, the lowest rates occurred in Massachusetts (5.4 per 1,000 births) and Washington state (5.7) (Guyer et al., 1995). Both remote rural areas and metropolitan centers with large pockets of poverty and unemployment tend to have extremely high rates. African-American infant mortality rates in rural areas of Georgia are as high as 22 per 1,000 (Boettcher, 1993); in 1994, the infant mortality rate reached 20.1 in Washington, D.C. (Guyer et al., 1995). Variations by state also exist for race-specific rates. African Americans consistently fare worse, but the racial gap is more severe in some states than in others.

Infant mortality rates have not improved steadily in the twentieth century in the United States. In the 1950s the United States ranked seventh worldwide; by 1989, the United States had slipped to twenty-fourth place (March of Dimes, 1993). Infant mortality has had three periods of limited or no decline: during the Great Depression in the 1930s, the period from the 1950s to the mid-1960s, and the 1980s. Nonetheless, the reduction of infant mortality rates from 150/1,000 in 1900 to less than 10/1,000 is one of the great public health success stories in the United States. Infant mortality has gone from being a common to a relatively rare event over this century.

With greater control over environmental conditions and infectious diseases, the timing of infant mortality has shifted historically toward early deaths that have stronger biological determinants. Currently most infant deaths occur in the neonatal (5.4 deaths/1,000 births in 1992) rather than the postneonatal period (3.1

deaths/1,000 births in 1992); more than half of neonatal deaths occur on the first day of life. In recent years, improvements in infant mortality have been concentrated in the neonatal period, perhaps due to rapid improvements in neonatology and enhanced regionalization of tertiary care.

In 1990, congenital anomalies or birth defects were the leading cause of infant mortality (21.5 percent). SIDS was the second most frequent cause (14.1 percent), followed by prematurity and low birth weight (10.5 percent) and respiratory distress syndrome (7.4 percent) (March of Dimes, 1993). The principal causes of neonatal deaths are congenital anomalies, respiratory distress syndrome, disorders relating to short gestation, and effects of maternal complications. Post-neonatal causes include SIDS, congenital anomalies, injuries, and infection (*Healthy People 2000*, 1991). Between 1993 and 1994, the overall infant death rate from injury rose by 35 percent (Guyer et al., 1995).

Low Birth Weight

In 1993, 7.2 percent of all U.S. infants were born at LBW (less than 2,500 grams); 1.3 percent of those were VLBW (under 1,500 grams) and 5.9 percent were MLBW (1,500–2,499 grams). About three-quarters of all neonatal deaths stem from low-weight births (Guyer et al., 1995). African Americans have substantially higher rates of LBW than whites (13.3 percent versus 6.0 percent in 1993). The rate of VLBW births for African Americans is threefold the rate for whites (3 percent v. 1 percent). Regardless of race, about 350 of every 1,000 infants in the vulnerable VLBW group do not survive (March of Dimes, 1993). Rates of LBW have not changed appreciably over the past 20 years. The gap between African-Americans and whites increased during the 1990s, especially with respect to VLBW. However, since 1991, there has been a slight improvement in the black/white LBW ratio (NCHS, 1996). This persistent problem has presented a frustrating challenge to the MCH community in its efforts to improve birth outcomes and eliminate inequities.

Gestational Age

In 1991, 10.7 percent of all U.S. births were under 37 weeks gestation—9.1 percent of births to white women and 18.9 percent of births to African-American women. Almost two percent (1.9 percent) of all births occurred before 32 weeks of gestational age. In 1990, 62 percent of all LBW births were premature (<37 weeks) (March of Dimes, 1993).

Birth Weight-Specific Mortality

Birth outcomes differ dramatically by birth weight. The majority of infants who die are both premature and LBW—born too early *and* too small. Among infants weighing 3,000–4,000 grams (7–9 lbs.), one death occurs per 1,000 live births, while mortality for infants weighing 1,000–1,500 grams is 150 per 1,000. Over two-thirds of all infant deaths are to LBW babies. Only 1 percent of infants are VLBW, but they account for 53 percent of all neonatal deaths and 59 percent of all infant deaths.

Though progress in reducing LBW has been forestalled, dramatic declines in birthweight-specific mortality occurred between 1960 and 1987 (the last year the United States compiled national data on BWSM). The reduction of infant mortality rates during that period averaged above 60 percent in every weight category. Due to sophisticated neonatal intensive care technologies, the likelihood of survival is now 35 percent for infants 500–749 grams (under 2 lbs.), 65 percent at 750–999 grams, 85 percent at 1,000–1,249 grams, and 90 percent at 1,250–1,499 grams. These dramatic improvements explain the overall decline in infant mortality over the last several decades.

In comparison with whites, African Americans appear to have slightly better survival rates in lower weight categories but higher death rates in the normal weight range. While there is much debate over the explanation for these differences, the reality is that survival rates of African-Americans and whites of similar birth weight are not markedly different. The major source of the racial gap in infant mortality is clearly due to birthweight differentials, specifically the extent of LBW and prematurity among African Americans.

An excess of LBW in the entire U.S. population explains our low international ranking in infant mortality. The U.S. rate of LBW ranks thirtieth in the world. Developed European and Asian countries have substantially lower rates. Ethnic diversity does not explain the differences, as many European countries are as diverse as the United States. The United States would rank only seventeenth if the national rate were the same as the rate for white births. Birth weight-specific mortality rates in the United States compare well with rates in Germany, Norway, and Denmark—all countries with lower infant mortality. The dissemination of high-technology neonatal and infant health services in the United States rivals any other country, but our population-based prevention efforts lag behind many regions.

Maternal Mortality

An estimated 500,000 women worldwide die of maternal causes each year; 99 percent of these deaths occur in developing countries. Regional and national variations are extreme, ranging from average estimates of 55 deaths per 100,000 live births in East Asia to 700/100,000 in West Africa. Leading causes of death in developing countries are hemorrhage; sepsis or infection; toxemia and hypertensive disease; illegal and unsafe abortion; and obstructed labor/ruptured uterus. The vast majority of these deaths would be preventable with better health and transportation systems, as well as additional societal resources to improve nutrition, education, and the overall health status of women (Royston and Armstrong, 1989).

In the developed world as a whole, the average maternal death rate is 30 deaths per 100,000 births (Royston and Armstrong, 1989). The official U.S. rate for 1987 was 6.6, an incredible decline from 619 deaths per 100,000 births in 1933 (*Healthy People 2000*, 1991; Enkin, 1994). However, a large racial differential exists in the United States. In 1987 the African-American rate was 14.2, compared with 5.1 for whites (*Healthy People 2000*, 1991).

Maternal mortality is known to be underestimated in all countries' registration systems, including U.S. statistics. According to studies of mortality surveillance, the actual U.S. rate may be 25 percent higher than reported (Royston and Armstrong, 1989). In a study of U.S. maternal deaths from 1979–1986, Atrash et al. (1990) confirmed that the leading causes of maternal death were pulmonary embolism, pregnancy-induced hypertension, hemorrhage, and ectopic pregnancy complications. Sachs et al. (1987) examined maternal mortality in Massachusetts between 1954 and 1985 and noted a recent shift to trauma (suicide, homicide, motor vehicle injuries) and pulmonary embolus as leading causes of death. Inadequate prenatal care also assumed greater prominence as a risk factor in Massachusetts, and one-third to one-half of the deaths were judged to be preventable.

REPRODUCTIVE RISK

Extensive research has established many associations between maternal characteristics and infant health outcomes. The listing of principal risk factors for LBW from the 1985 Institute of Medicine report, *Preventing Low Birthweight*, is reproduced in Table 5–1. This list is organized by type of risk—demographic factors, medical conditions preceding and arising during pregnancy, behavioral and environmental exposures, health care characteristics, and newly evolving concepts of risk, such as stress, that are not yet well understood. Table 5–2 classifies risk factors for preterm birth according to the certainty of association demonstrated by current research (Berkowitz and Papiernik, 1993).

According to Kramer (1987), less than a third of premature deliveries in developed countries can be predicted by these risk factors. In the section below on prenatal interventions, we discuss the strengths and limitations of risk assessments for clinical predictions based on known factors. First we wish to examine the notion of risk in the context of MCH. A close look at the items listed in Tables 5–1 and 5–2 reveals a heterogeneous mixture of elements with unclear causal links to LBW and prematurity.

Krieger (1994) has traced the historical evolution of explanatory models in medical research from the mechanistic "doctrine of specific etiology" to a more complex understanding of "multiple causation" in epidemiology. Risk factors

Table 5–1 Principal Risk Factors for Low Birth Weight

I. Demographic Risks
   A. Age (less than 17; over 34)
   B. Race (black)
   C. Low socioeconomic status
   D. Unmarried
   E. Low level of education

II. Medical Risks Predating Pregnancy
   A. Parity (0 or more than 4)
   B. Low weight for height
   C. Genitourinary anomalies/surgery
   D. Selected diseases such as diabetes, chronic hypertension
   E. Nonimmune status for selected infections such as rubella
   F. Poor obstetric history, including previous low birth weight infant, multiple spontaneous abortions
   G. Maternal genetic factors (such as low maternal weight at own birth)

III. Medical Risks in Current Pregnancy
   A. Multiple pregnancy
   B. Poor weight gain
   C. Short interpregnancy interval
   D. Hypotension
   E. Hypertension/preeclampsia/toxemia
   F. Selected infections such as symptomatic bacteriuria, rubella, and cytomegalovirus
   G. First or second trimester bleeding
   H. Placental problems such as placenta previa, abruptio placentae
   I. Hyperemesis
   J. Oligohydramnios/polyhydramnios
   K. Anemia/abnormal hemoglobin
   L. Isoimmunization
   M. Fetal anomalies
   N. Incompetent cervix
   O. Spontaneous premature rupture of membranes

IV. Behavioral and Environmental Risks
   A. Smoking
   B. Poor nutritional status
   C. Alcohol and other substance abuse
   D. DES exposure and other toxic exposures, including occupational hazards
   E. High altitude

continues

Table 5–1 continued

V. Health Care Risks
    A. Absent or inadequate prenatal care
    B. Iatrogenic prematurity

VI. Evolving Concepts of Risk
    A. Stress, physical and psychosocial
    B. Uterine irritability
    C. Events triggering uterine contractions
    D. Cervical changes detected before onset of labor
    E. Selected infections such as mycoplasma and Chlamydia trachomatis
    F. Inadequate plasma volume expansion
    G. Progesterone deficiency

Source: Committee to Study the Prevention of Low Birthweight, Division of Health Promotion and Disease Prevention, Institute of Medicine (1985). *Preventing Low Birthweight.* Washington, DC: National Academy Press, p. 7.

---

tend to be viewed as independent entities, though in reality they often cluster together and interact with one another. For many of the listed risks, we know little about the causal mechanisms that contribute to outcomes. Some of these are "risk markers" that indicate certain problems may be present. For example, unmarried status is often accompanied by mother's low income. Reliability of risk markers is changeable, and the amenability of risk factors to interventions is variable. We often use available information as a proxy for missing data (e.g., marital status to represent income, or race/ethnicity to substitute for socioeconomic status), but fail to measure relevant factors. Emanuel et al. (1989) note that we seldom take into account significant aspects of mothers' childhood and adult environments preceding pregnancy; similarly, we are generally unaware of many potential difficulties during pregnancy, such as domestic violence.

A potential problem with risk factor analysis is the narrow focus on single outcomes rather than a more holistic context. The search to explain LBW and prematurity is extremely important, but not to the exclusion of other concerns. For example, alcohol consumption may not be associated with preterm delivery, but fetal alcohol syndrome and fetal alcohol effect are serious problems for infant development. Conclusive evidence may not exist to implicate anemia in prematurity, but—like alcohol abuse—anemia is not only a risk for LBW, it is also a danger to women's subsequent health.

Wise (1993) has pointed out that the relevance of individual risks must be evaluated in terms of their prevalence in the larger population, not just the magnitude

Table 5–2 Risk Factors for Preterm Birth

Established risk factors
  Black race
  Single marital status
  Low socioeconomic status
  Previous low birth weight or preterm delivery
  Multiple second trimester spontaneous abortions
  In vitro fertilization pregnancy
  Placental abnormalities
  Gestational bleeding
  Cervical and uterine anomalies
  In utero diethylstilbestrol exposure
  Multiple gestations
  Cigarette smoking
Probable risk factors
  Urogenital infections
  Cocaine use
  No prenatal care or inadequate prenatal care
  Seasonality
Factors weakly associated or not associated with preterm birth
  Maternal age
  Infant sex
  Maternal weight gain
  Dietary intake
  Parity
  Short interpregnancy interval
  Prior first trimester induced abortion
  Alcohol consumption
  Caffeine intake
  Sexual activity during late pregnancy
Inconclusive risk factors
  Psychosocial stress
  Short stature
  Low prepregnancy weight/low body mass index
  Anemia
  Employment-related physical activity
Factors for which there are insufficient data
  Familial and intergenerational factors
  History of infertility
  Use of marijuana and other illicit drugs
  Leisure-time physical activity
  Occupational and environmental toxicants

Source: Reprinted with permission from G.S. Berkowitz and E. Papiernik, Epidemiology of Preterm Birth, *Epidemiologic Reviews,* Vol. 15, p. 434, © 1993.

of risk in extreme cases. For example, women who use illicit drugs or receive no prenatal care are frequently cited as being central to the infant mortality problem; yet overall, a very small proportion of infant deaths is attributable to women in those situations. Though these serious problems need to be addressed, a distortion of their extent in the population often serves a moralistic or judgmental rather than a preventive purpose. It is also notable that the root causes of many health risks—social inequalities and discrimination—are missing from the usual lists of risk factors.

In an ethnographic study at a public teaching hospital, Handwerker (1994) concluded that the labeling of low income pregnant women as "high risk" has a stigmatizing function, to the extent of blaming and even prosecuting women who suffer fetal or infant deaths after failure to follow medical advice. "While addiction or other 'high risk' behavior occurring in white middle class women is often considered a health problem, poor women of color are increasingly viewed as criminals" (Handwerker, 1994, p. 672). Health professionals' values and training may influence risk classification at least as much as scientific criteria. For pregnant women, identification as high risk determines the nature of their prenatal care and delivery experience, exposure to technological interventions, relationship with health care providers, and even their ability to maintain custody of their infants. The recent focus on unintended pregnancy as a risk factor, while meant to be supportive of women's right to reproductive choice, can imply that women in "high risk" populations should be discouraged from childbearing.

Enkin (1994) has also critiqued the framework of risk in pregnancy because it suggests the need for control by professionals rather than women and families, and it interferes with birth as a natural process. "Objecting to the risk management approach to childbirth is difficult, because the idea of risk management is a product of the culture in which we live. . . . Perhaps it is time to look for alternatives. It is essentially a question of strengthening the woman to give birth and to take care of her own baby" (Enkin, 1994, pp. 133–134).

INTERVENTIONS

The manifestation of a poor pregnancy outcome is a function both of the maternal risks and any intervention that ameliorates those risks. Interventions to improve pregnancy outcomes have probably existed since the earliest days of humanity, and folk traditions still abound. The histories of both public health and modern medicine are intimately tied to efforts to enhance the safety of mothers and newborns. The dramatic reduction of infant mortality in the twentieth century testifies to the cumulative effects of multiple interventions.

Today a very wide range of interventions takes place to ensure a successful pregnancy for mothers and infants. Some of these interventions are tied directly to specific risk amelioration, while others are more closely associated with general health promotion. We can divide interventions into four broad groups, reflecting the developmental course of pregnancy and birth: preconception, antepartum or prenatal, intrapartum, and postpartum.

Optimal reproductive outcomes result from a continuous process of health promotion and disease prevention throughout the entire course of women's lives. (See Chapter 10.) Infant health is intimately related to mothers' well-being from the time of their own conceptions, and the lifetime effects of childbearing are influenced by all of the self-care and health care that mothers receive. Continuity of primary preventive care and adequate access to family planning services are essential for women's well-being before pregnancy occurs.

Preconceptional Health Care

We now recognize the critical nature of early fetal development completed before many women enter prenatal care, or even know with certainty that they are pregnant. "The period of greatest environmental sensitivity for the developing fetus is between 17 and 56 days after fertilization. Cell organization, cell differentiation, and organogenesis take place during this period, and any insult, whether nutritional, drug-related, or viral, can jeopardize fetal development. . . . By the end of the eighth week after conception and certainly by the end of the first trimester, any major structural anomalies in the fetus have already developed" (Cefalo and Moos, 1994, pp. 2–3).

Like LBW, congenital anomalies represent a major infant morbidity that has not improved in response to recent technological developments. Little change has occurred in the overall incidence of birth defects, and some increases have been observed in rates of specific anomalies. A new model of preconceptional health care has been introduced in hopes of shifting medical care and counseling to an earlier period with greater potential for primary prevention of early fetal loss, birth defects, and other adverse pregnancy outcomes (Cefalo and Moos, 1994).

Cefalo and Moos (1994), authors of a guide to "Preconceptional Counseling for Informed Decision Making," stress the importance of adequate information in assuring full reproductive choice. The goal of preconceptional counseling is to give women a clear sense of the extent to which they can increase the chances of a healthy pregnancy and birth outcome. Women must also be helped to understand that some occurrences are beyond their control and that medical professionals also have significant limitations in their capacity to predict and prevent problems. Skill and training are required to implement preconceptional health promotion successfully, but this new approach offers an opportunity to empower parents and improve birth outcomes.

One example is the potential for nutritional counseling, specifically the recent recommendation that women contemplating pregnancy take folic acid supplements. Folate is a B vitamin needed to make DNA, the building block of cells. A deficiency of folate causes macrocytic anemia. In the fetus, folate has also been found to play a key role in the development of the neural tube. Folate must be present during the development of the neural tube and before it closes at eight weeks gestation, a time when many women are not yet aware that they are pregnant. A deficiency of folate during this period may cause neural tube defects, e.g., spina bifida, which can result in serious disability. A recommended daily supplement of 0.4 to 0.8 mg of folate for all women has been shown to reduce the risk of a first occurrence, and a 4 mg dose has been recommended for women who have had a neural defect occur in a previous pregnancy. In order to ensure adequate supplementation, women must be educated about and encouraged to take folate before pregnancy and throughout the first trimester. Hopefully, this extension of prenatal health care can provide a bridge to more continuous services for women's general health needs—nutritional counseling during preconception could have lifelong benefits for women.

Prenatal Care

The American College of Obstetricians and Gynecologists (ACOG) describes four functions of prenatal care: *risk assessment, serial surveillance, health education*, and *psychosocial support* (Brann and Cefalo, 1992). The goals of risk assessment are to screen women in order to detect specific pregnancy risks for poor birth outcomes and to determine the most appropriate level of prenatal care, e.g., to determine which women are medically at high risk needing specialized tertiary prenatal or obstetric care and which women have psychosocial needs requiring specialized social services. The task of comprehensive prenatal care programs is to provide treatment for women appropriate to the level of need. Formal risk assessment is usually conducted at the first prenatal care visit. Currently there are several popular screening tools, such as the Problem-Oriented Prenatal Risk Assessment System (POPRAS), which identify and weigh a variety of demographic, medical, psychosocial, and behavioral risks using a standardized protocol.

Currently risk-screening tools have relatively low predictive value. At best, 54 percent of women experiencing perinatal deaths can be identified by existing instruments. Screening systems have inherent problems and limitations (Selwyn, 1990). Risk assessments are limited by our relatively weak understanding of the mechanisms explaining poor pregnancy outcomes. Currently, the strongest predictors of adverse pregnancy outcomes are prior poor obstetric history, use of substances, including cigarettes, and multiple gestations (i.e., twins, etc.). Thus, predictions are much stronger for multiparous women than for primiparous women (i.e., those having their first child).

Selwyn (1990) has outlined several dilemmas associated with risk assessment instruments based on the trade-off between sensitivity and specificity. The greater the chance of identifying women who are actually at risk (i.e., those who have a preterm birth), the lower the likelihood of accurately classifying low-risk women (i.e., those with full-term deliveries). In other words, in selecting the cutoff points for measuring risks, providers must choose between overdiagnosis with unnecessary treatment of *false positives* as opposed to underdiagnosis and missed opportunities for preventive treatment of *false negatives*. Both of these possibilities carry the risk of medical complications and psychological distress. Repeated screening may be one way to improve the accuracy of risk assessment.

Serial surveillance is successive monitoring of the pregnant women and fetus to ensure that they are progressing properly through the normal developmental stages. The purpose of this screening is to detect deviations and then to make appropriate referrals or provide treatments for any identified problems of the pregnancy. For most women this routine surveillance involves urine analysis, fundal height measurement, weighing, and sometimes other tests such as alpha-fetoprotein (AFP) screening and ultrasound. Both ACOG and the U.S. Public Health Service (PHS) Expert Panel on the Content of Prenatal Care have developed detailed protocols for the timing and content of prenatal surveillance (Public Health Service, 1989).

Health education is the provision of health information about the impact of pregnancy on women's health and physical changes, advice on behaviors to promote a healthy pregnancy and healthy infant (including nutrition, weight gain, exercise, substance use, etc.), preparation for the delivery, and knowledge of newborn care. Pregnancy provides a significant opportunity for instruction and advice to improve the health of the mother, her future offspring, and the entire family. Studies repeatedly show that pregnancy is a receptive period for health behavior change.

Currently in the United States, ACOG recommends 13 prenatal visits during pregnancy: the initial visit in the first six weeks, one visit per month until the twenty-eighth week, one visit every two weeks until the thirty-sixth week, and one visit per week thereafter. This standardized universal visit schedule was developed in the early part of the century in order to prevent maternal mortality, especially from eclampsia, a hypertensive disorder generally manifesting toward the end of pregnancy. It is important to note that this prenatal care schedule was developed primarily to improve maternal, not infant, health.

Recently there have been some suggestions to change the visitation pattern. The U.S. PHS report, *Caring for Our Future: The Content of Prenatal Care*, suggested fewer but more intensive prenatal care visits (Public Health Service, 1989). According to the report, the timing of care should be shifted to increase visits toward the beginning of the pregnancy, including a preconceptional visit, in order to focus more on maternal health promotion activities. The PHS also recommended the establishment of different visitation schedules for primiparous and multiparous women. This proposal to modify the standard schedule met with strong opposition from the organized obstetric community, even though the United States recommends more prenatal care visits than many European countries.

Prenatal care can be conceptualized very broadly or very narrowly. Narrowly defined, prenatal care represents only the ACOG recommended visits to a medical provider, i.e., the provision of medical care during pregnancy. Broadly conceptualized, prenatal care comprises any intervention during pregnancy that enhances the health and well-being of mothers and their offspring. A comprehensive definition of prenatal care would include nutrition counseling and food supplementation, childbirth preparation classes, mentoring and advice from a "resource mother," home visitation, and an array of other services.

In general, the MCH field has taken a very broad view of prenatal care and encourages the inclusion of psychosocial, nutrition, health education, case management, and other services. Defining the scope of prenatal care reflects fundamental beliefs about what is truly necessary to ensure a successful pregnancy. A strictly biomedical orientation has until recently been reinforced by third-party payment policies, with reimbursement available only for medical visits. Now Medicaid and certain private insurers, including some Health Maintenance Organizations (HMOs), provide coverage for more comprehensive prenatal care services. We appear to be at the beginning of a major period of exploring the content of prenatal care, including both psychosocial inputs and advances in medical technology.

There is widespread agreement that prenatal care is positive and effective, but there is surprisingly little research documenting the efficacy of prenatal care utilization or the effectiveness of specific interventions. This is actually quite a difficult area to study. Randomized clinical trials assigning some women to nonintervention groups are not possible or desirable for ethical reasons. The Institute of Medicine's Committee to Study the Prevention of Low Birthweight (1985) concluded their analysis by simply noting that any prenatal care was better than none; that earlier prenatal care was better than later prenatal care; and that more prenatal care was better than less. Kotelchuck (1994) showed that the impact of prenatal care on birth outcomes is a U-shaped function; women with inadequate and intensive care have the poorest birth outcomes. Inadequate care is often a marker for psychosocial and socioeconomic difficulties that may result in medical conditions. Lack of preventive care and early treatment may exacerbate those problems. Women with intensive care are likely to have severe medical needs and complications. Their outcomes, though not optimal, would undoubtedly be worse without the intensive treatment they receive.

Researchers have begun to address the content of prenatal care, another understudied area, in order to understand what is measured by the quantity of care. The MCH field, especially in this era of health care reorganization, is being challenged to demonstrate the effectiveness of specific components of prenatal care.

In general, there is strong research evidence that comprehensive prenatal care approaches are effective in improving birth outcomes (Korenbrot, 1984; Peoples and Siegel, 1983; Sokol et al., 1980). Most of the evaluation studies reflect comprehensive care settings with multiple interventions; it is difficult to know what specific aspects of prenatal care content are most effective, or whether they would remain effective in isolation.

The Special Supplemental Food Program for Women, Infants, and Children (WIC) program has been consistently associated with reduced rates of LBW and infant mortality, as well as more adequate prenatal care utilization (Kotelchuck et al., 1984; Rush, 1988). Women's utilization of comprehensive or enhanced services is often facilitated through care coordination or case management. Baby Love, a collaborative MCH-Medicaid maternity care coordination program in North Carolina, has shown better birth weight outcomes for program participants compared with other Medicaid patients (Buescher et al., 1991).

Comprehensive prenatal care most often takes place in health departments or community health centers. Birth outcomes for low income women appear better if care is provided in such community-based clinics rather than private practice settings (Buescher et al., 1987). In the private provider community, practitioners need extensive referral and support networks in order to implement this model of care.

Recent findings from national survey data (Kogan et al., 1994) indicate that receipt of health advice from prenatal care providers is an important contributor to LBW prevention. Unfortunately, research suggests that the ACOG prenatal care recommendations, especially for risk assessments and health education, are not routinely followed (Peoples-Sheps et al., 1996). Kogan et al. (1994) found that African-American women were more likely than white women to have the recommended prenatal medical procedures performed, but less likely to receive advice about health behaviors.

Efforts to enhance the effectiveness of prenatal care have also included recent developments in prenatal treatment and technology focused on the prevention of preterm labor. A growing number of clinical trials are testing the use of antibiotics to treat sexually transmitted diseases (STDs) and other vaginal infections that can precipitate early labor. Toco-belts are a new device used by women to monitor preterm contractions at home. The use of tocolytic drugs (e.g., ritodrine) to reduce the onset of early labor is now widespread, though major improvements in preterm delivery and LBW are not expected to result from tocolysis (Klein and Goldenberg, 1990). Recent national trials of a prematurity prevention intervention involving weekly vaginal examinations for women assessed as high risk have had mixed success.

Most of the prenatal care literature is restricted to outpatient or ambulatory care and focuses on "normal" pregnancies; yet many women experience complications, and the likelihood of hospitalization during pregnancy is relatively high.

Over a fifth (22 percent) of women receive more than ACOG's recommended number of visits, and account for 43 percent of all LBW infants (Kotelchuck, 1994). Fourteen percent of women are hospitalized during the course of their pregnancies, 5 percent more than one time. Among women with LBW infants in 1991–1992, a third were hospitalized at least once while pregnant (Bennett et al., unpublished data). For women receiving inpatient and more intensive outpatient care, many opportunities exist to improve birth outcomes, to monitor long-term health issues, and to address psychosocial needs.

Intrapartum Interventions

The delivery or intrapartum period is also an important period of interventions to improve birth outcomes for mothers and infants. Many of these are pharmacological protocols and surgical procedures to augment the speed and safety of the birth process. There is much controversy about interventions in this period, reflecting conflicting ideologies and values about childbirth. Proponents of natural childbirth can cite evidence of the psychological and medical benefits of nonintervention, though most would recommend that women receive the highest quality of medical services at the first indication of need. In contrast, some providers advocate for routine use of the latest medical technologies as an attempt to prevent any possible risk to the infant during delivery. Liability concerns, changing hospital practices, and trends in consumer demand influence the balance between these two orientations.

This chapter will not review the literature about obstetric delivery practices other than to note that there is much debate over the use of specific technologies during delivery. Electronic fetal monitoring is very widely used to assess fetal heart rate during delivery, though it has not been recommended for universal usage. Some argue for routine monitoring in order to alert providers to fetal distress; others are concerned about unnecessary C-sections resulting from misreadings. Induction and augmentation of labor are widespread, but the use of drugs—no matter how benign—is controversial because of the potential impact on mothers and subsequent health and development of newborns. Yet pain control and length of delivery are important issues for most women. Forceps deliveries have declined in recent years as C-section rates have increased, but the use of forceps is still relatively common.

Cesarean sections are very widely performed in the United States. One of the National Health Promotion and Disease Prevention Objectives for the Year 2000 is to reduce the cesarean delivery rate to no more than 15 per 100 deliveries from the baseline rate of 24.4 per 100 deliveries in 1987 (*Healthy People 2000*, 1991). There is very strong evidence that C-sections reduce maternal and infant mortality in specific delivery situations, such as obstructed labor and eclamptic conditions. However, the optimal level of C-sections is subject to much debate since the surgery introduces new risks to both mothers and infants (e.g., anesthesia complications, infection, iatrogenic prematurity).

Most European countries have much lower rates of C-sections than the United States (10 percent in the Netherlands, 15 percent in Great Britain), though their rates are rising rapidly. High cesarean rates have alarmed many obstetricians, prompting the initiation of a series of second opinion programs that have succeeded in reducing C-section rates. There has also been a growing willingness to allow trials for vaginal birth after caesarean (VBACS) in the United States. Rates of caesarean delivery appear to have stabilized in the United States after increasing rapidly for many years, though many financial and legal incentives still make it a popular procedure.

Controversy over the desirability of obstetric interventions and hospital competition has led both to more home births and to marketing of more home-like and humane birthing practices within hospitals. Debate continues, however, about optimal settings and attendants for deliveries. For low-risk women, tertiary centers have been shown to have better birth outcomes but also more surgical interventions (Albers and Savitz, 1991). The National Birth Center Study examined outcomes of care in 84 U.S. nonhospital birth centers that deliver "family-centered" maternity care to medically low-risk women. Nearly 80 percent of deliveries of the 12,000 women in the study were attended by nurse-midwives. The rest of the women were cared for by obstetricians or other physicians, other midwives, or registered nurses. The total rate of C-sections was only 4.4 per 100 deliveries, and rates of low birth weight and infant mortality were extremely low. When surveyed, 99 percent of the women said they would recommend the birth center to a friend (Rooks et al., 1989).

For women at high risk—those whose conditions are recognized during crises in labor as well as those identified through early assessment—regionalization of obstetric and postpartum care has been very successful in improving birth outcomes. Regionalized care is a system of coordination among hospitals for the transfer of high risk mothers or newborns to more appropriate levels of care, including air transport for women in isolated rural areas. Hospitals are designated as Level I, II, or III. Level III hospitals are tertiary care centers with fully staffed neonatal intensive care units. Ideally, all women deliver at the appropriate level hospital after having been screened throughout pregnancy for their risks and needs. Regionalization of obstetric services became widespread in the 1960s–1970s and dramatically reduced infant mortality by making tertiary neonatal services available for all births. In North Carolina, for example, 70 percent of VLBW infants are now born in Level III hospitals. Favorable rates of

BWSM in the United States reflect both our high level of technology and our regionalization programs, which give the entire population access to that technology. Wise (1990) has cautioned that improvements in infant mortality may level off, and even that mortality could increase, if we achieve the maximum benefits of neonatal technology without rectifying social risks to health and deficiencies in preventive health care.

Two major advances in fetal medicine have had significant effects on fetal survivability. The use of steroids to mature the lungs of the fetus has become widespread in anticipation of a premature delivery. This treatment, coupled with the use of tocolytic agents to delay labor for a limited time period, has lowered the incidence of respiratory distress syndrome (RDS). Similarly, surfactant, an agent which enhances the elasticity of fetal lung surface, has had a major impact on infants with RDS. It is estimated that 50 percent of the decrease in U.S. infant mortality rates in the 1990s was due to the introduction of surfactants. The broad efficacy of important new treatments such as steroids and surfactants depends on the regular involvement of all women in high quality prenatal and obstetric care. Any inequities in access to new advances in maternal and fetal medicine will reinforce social injustices and impair the overall improvement of MCH outcomes.

Postpartum Care

In addition to the regionalized access to neonatal intensive care units for high risk infants discussed above, a wide range of postpartum treatments can influence birth outcomes. Also critical for the care of high-risk infants are linkages to early intervention programs (which are discussed in the next chapter). For routine uncomplicated deliveries, the postpartum period is also extremely important as the initiation into parenthood for new mothers, their partners, and their families.

The postpartum hospitalization represents a time for physical recovery and stabilization of the mother and newborn, psychological adaptation, maternal education, and observation of the mother's and infant's health status. Current insurance and hospital policies allow little time for any of these functions, and duration of delivery hospitalizations has become a major public health issue. The average length of stay for a hospital delivery is now about 2 days for a vaginal birth and 4 days for a C-section, much shorter than the manifestation of many problems that require medical care and advice. Many women are discharged more quickly. In the Western states, 12 to 24 hours is a typical stay for vaginal delivery without complications (Braveman et al., 1995).

Initially, early discharge programs were offered only to low-risk women in order to free hospital beds and to meet consumer demand for a less medicalized birth experience. In such programs in the 1970s, women were carefully screened for participation and received extensive in-home follow-up services. As cost containment pressures have become more dominant, early discharge has become routine and involuntary for almost all women without serious medical complications.

Margolis and Kotelchuck (1994) have shown that women discharged early are actually more likely to have risk characteristics, such as teen childbearing and lack of private health insurance. The consequences of this fiscally driven policy for maternal and child health are unknown. In an extensive review of literature on early discharge, Braveman et al. (1995) concluded, "No adequately designed studies have examined discharge before 48 hours after delivery without additional postdischarge services. . . . Some studies suggested adverse outcomes associated with early discharge even with early follow-up." (p. 716) Several states (and recently each house of the U.S. Congress) have passed legislation mandating minimum stays of 48 hours for vaginal deliveries and 96 hours for C-sections. Since those mandates still constitute early discharge compared with previous policies and international standards, MCH advocates need to ensure the development, rigorous evaluation, and assurance of reimbursement for postpartum home visitation and other follow-up programs.

Issues in Intervention Policy

Location of Preconceptional Health Care

Preconceptional care addresses general health promotion for women, family planning needs, and preparation for pregnancy. In an integrated health system with comprehensive coverage, preconceptional care could easily fit into a continuum of services. In our current categorical and underfunded public health care system, we face a major policy decision about the inclusion of preconceptional health care as part of Title X family planning services or Title V prenatal care services. Family planning reaches a broader population, but still places women's health in the context of reproduction. In the current health system, no sector acts as guarantor of women's health outside of the maternal role. Tension arises over whether preconceptional (i.e., women's) health must always be linked to a maternity focus, as well as over the question of who will pay for these new services.

Timing and Number of Visits

Should the current ACOG recommendations on timing and number of prenatal care visits be modified? These recommendations were based on protection of the mother's health (especially mortality due to pre-eclampsia) with an emphasis on frequency of visits in late pregnancy. Maternal mortality has been significantly reduced with largely effective management of hypertensive conditions. Should the recommendation be changed to encourage more visits early in pregnancy (as suggested by the PHS) in order to promote infant health through maternal behavioral changes and social support? Is there a chance that women's health could be impaired by decreased surveillance near term?

Balancing Visions and Risks of Childbirth

How should the MCH community balance the competing visions of birth as a natural process or as a risky event requiring the most advanced medical techniques available? Both views of the birth process capture a truth and express concern for the health of mothers and newborns. Women who have been historically excluded from high quality health services may rightfully perceive an equal entitlement to technology. To some, natural childbirth is seen as the most psychologically and physically healthy manner to have a child; to others it represents an unnecessary endangerment of both mother and child. This debate is shaped by strong ideological views and personal experiences as well as strong professional identities and economic interests. How can we continue to reduce mortality and morbidity without disempowering women in the experience of pregnancy and birth?

Setting Priorities for Prenatal Services

The MCH field has advocated for broadening the range of prenatal care services. Now we are being asked to justify and prioritize well-established services, even though it is difficult to evaluate the individual effectiveness of each. In an era of fiscal restraint, which of these services should be maintained? Enhanced services such as home visitation, case management, psychosocial counseling, nutrition education, and smoking cessation are personnel-intensive and require adequate funding for quality programs. Can we establish and compare their cost-effectiveness, and should that be our only criterion for decision making? Do programs such as these fit within the rubric of managed care? Will health care reform turn out to be a means to reverse hard-won services for poor women?

Who Shall Live?

Neonatal technology has allowed society to keep smaller and smaller babies alive. These tiny premature infants have the highest risks of dying, and those who survive often have significant health burdens. Many attempts to save 500–750 gram infants are still very experimental and invasive. Should we be striving to keep all premature infants alive? Is it wrong to question whether heroic and costly efforts to save infants are always worthwhile? What sacrifices are we making against other urgent needs that cannot be met with limited resources? Should research funding be allocated to extend fetal viability at younger ages? Who should decide when it is time to let a child die—the parents, the physicians, the federal government via the Baby Doe Law, hospital committees? These ethical issues are part of the responsibility undertaken by MCH professionals.

OUTSTANDING CONCERNS

Racial Disparities in Birth Outcomes

What are the causes of racial disparities in birth outcomes between African Americans and whites in the United States, and how can these disparities be eliminated? The racial gap has confounded the MCH field for many decades. Historically, biological and genetic explanations were offered but later shown to be scientifically invalid. Economic explanations became predominant in the 1960s, with the focus on high poverty rates in black communities. Race is often viewed as a proxy for socioeconomic status, since African Americans are less likely on average than whites to have private health insurance coverage or access to services and are more likely to be exposed to environmental hazards.

Recent analyses have suggested that race is not simply a marker of social class; for example, the racial gap in LBW rates is highest among college-educated women (Schoendorf et al., 1992). The "Hispanic paradox" of good birth outcomes in relatively poor and underinsured Latino communities also challenges the assumption of a simple relationship between social class and birth outcomes. Recent attention has turned to the role of psychosocial stressors, including the experience of racist treatment, in determining African-American health outcomes such as prematurity (McLean, 1993). New research paradigms are being developed to determine the interactive effects of racism, sexism, and class discrimination on women's reproductive health (e.g., differential treatment by prenatal care providers, vulnerability to infections), as well as the protective influence of cultural beliefs and responses (e.g., low rates of tobacco use, intergenerational supports) (Krieger et al., 1993). The continued existence of severe disparities remains an unacceptable burden in the African American community, a stark reminder of societal inequities and a compelling challenge to MCH.

Intransigence of Low Birth Weight and Prematurity Rates

Can any public health initiative reduce our unacceptable LBW and prematurity rates? For the past 30 years, since the War on Poverty, wide-ranging public health programs have aimed to improve these birth outcomes. In spite of interventions to improve: (1) nutrition (e.g., WIC); (2) access to medical care (via expanded eligibility for Medicaid maternity coverage); and, (3) content of prenatal care (e.g., home visitation, comprehensive services), birthweight distributions have barely changed. Are birth outcomes impervious to public health interventions? The success of European experiences with comprehensive health and social benefits for mothers and families suggests otherwise. Yet identifying key factors that influence birth weight and are amenable to change still eludes us in the United States. Perhaps the impact of our interventions has been obscured by countervailing pressures such as overutilization of C-section, increasing substance use, or environmental assaults. LBW and prematurity, with their lifetime consequences for children and families, will hinder national progress until we can solve this puzzle and mobilize the will to support necessary solutions.

Prevention versus Treatment

What is the wisest allocation of resources for improving birth outcomes? Both prevention to reduce LBW and treatment to lower BWSM rates are crucial in the fight against infant mortality. These aspects of prevention should not be seen as mutually exclusive, but the two domains are quite distinct and often competitive in the professional and political process of funding decisions. Almost all of our recent improvements in infant mortality have been due to developments in neonatal treatment and access to care. Pressures to abandon regionalized care networks that have made newborn tertiary care almost universally available could have devastating consequences, especially in poor and rural communities.

Should we continue to invest new funds in enhanced neonatal treatment, or have we maximized the effectiveness of this strategy? To what extent are we producing serious new morbidity by saving increasingly smaller infants? Should we assume that further technological expenses are justified, or should we spend money on uncertain experiments in hopes of preventing LBW and prematurity? Epidemiological findings can not provide a final answer to this dilemma, which rests on values as well as science.

Measurement Issues

Some researchers do not believe that our nation's infant mortality ranking is an accurate indicator. Equivalent definitions of infant mortality become critical when making national comparisons. Japan, for example, defines infant deaths only as those occurring to babies born weighing at least 1,000 grams. Since death rates are highest at low weights, Japan's low infant mortality rate could be in part an artifact of this convention.

With extensive use of C-sections and other prenatal and intrapartum technology, a fetus in distress may be surgically removed from the mother as a live birth, only to die shortly thereafter. Previously that fetus might have been considered a fetal death; now it is counted as an infant death. Cities and states in the United States vary widely in the extent to which they report infants born under 500 grams as live births. These are problems of measurement, not biology. Should we adopt the European measure of perinatal mortality to avoid the distinction between live births and fetal deaths? Could we obscure our infant mortality problem—or define it away—by changing our measurement system?

Many measurement issues cloud our debates over MCH strategies. At what gestational age should pregnancy losses be considered fetal deaths? Should the definition of fetal deaths be tied to the age of viability? Should we collect MCH data by race, ethnicity, and/or social class? Do these categories highlight real population differences or only reinforce social stereotypes? As the number of infant deaths declines, classification decisions become more critical to the perception and estimation of infant mortality.

Women's Health

Why do we study maternal health as a component of infant health rather than women's health? This analysis of the epidemiology of infant mortality indicates the relative paucity of information on maternal health and morbidity, and particularly on the long-term impact of pregnancy on women's health. Maternal mortality is no longer sufficient to describe maternal health. Yet what other universal measures of maternal health are available? Hospitalization rates? Specific morbidity rates for high blood pressure or diabetes? The MCH field hasn't developed broad measures of women's health during pregnancy. Connecting maternal morbidity to subsequent issues in women's health, not simply infant death, remains a challenge for the field. (See Chapter 10.)

Early Pregnancy Loss

What is the epidemiology of miscarriages? For all of our sophistication about infant morbidity and mortality, we still lack a full assessment of the outcomes of all conceptions. The MCH field is simply inadequate in its measurements of early pregnancy loss. We don't really know how many early pregnancy losses occur; what the nature of their geographic and temporal trends is; or their true impact on the subsequent physical, mental, and reproductive health of women. Does this deficiency simply reflect technical measurement issues, or does it indicate a lack of attention to a major issue for women and the health of the entire population? The environmental disaster at Love Canal was detected, after all, by elevated miscarriage rates in the community. Measuring early fetal loss is another challenge for MCH research and an important health topic for mothers and families.

Multisectoral Collaboration for MCH Goals

How do we foster more far-reaching community-based strategies for infant morality reduction instead of our predominantly medical focus? In developing countries, the current approach to infant mortality is to involve multiple sectors of society in collective efforts. Women's organizations, community development groups, educators, religious leaders, and others join with the health sector to tackle the social roots of the problem. The challenge for MCH in the United States is to mobilize entire communities, including medical professionals, in initiatives that attack the full range of health risks and barriers to health care. One of the tasks of community coalitions will be to work toward social policies that achieve their goals. In Europe, social welfare policies are integrated with health planning to reduce social inequities that manifest in health differentials. Women in most European countries have universal entitlements such as child allowances and paid maternity leave; single mothers and others with greater need receive special benefits. As welfare reforms are enacted in the United States, federal benefit dollars will shrink and state program variations will increase. Public health advocates will need to monitor carefully the potential health effects on women and children of changing program requirements and benefits, including eligibility restrictions for income supports and associated health coverage.

REFERENCES

Albers, L.L., and D.A. Savitz. 1991. Hospital setting for birth and use of medical procedures in low-risk women. *Journal of Nurse-Midwifery 36*, 327–333.

Asian American Health Forum, Inc. Undated. Final report: Cooperative agreement between National Center for Health Statistics and Asian American Health Forum, Inc. to advance the understanding of the Asian and Pacific Islander American population. San Francisco.

Atrash, H.K. et al. 1990. Maternal mortality in the United States, 1979–1986. *American Journal of Obstetrics and Gynecology 76,* 1055–1060.

Berkowitz, G.S., and E. Papiernik. 1993. Epidemiology of preterm birth. *Epidemiologic Reviews 15,* 414–443.

Boettcher, J.H. 1993. Promoting maternal infant health in rural communities: The Rural Health Outreach Program. *Nursing Clinics of North America 28,* 199–209.

Brann, A.W., and R.C. Cefalo, eds. 1992. *Guidelines for perinatal care,* 3rd ed. Evanston, IL, and Washington, DC: American Academy of Pediatrics and American College of Obstetricians and Gynecologists.

Braveman, P. et al. 1995. Early discharge of newborns and mothers: A critical review of the literature. *Pediatrics 96,* 716–729.

Bremner, R.H., ed. 1971. *Children and youth in America: A documentary history,* Vol. II, Part 8. Cambridge, MA: Harvard University Press.

Buescher, P.A. et al. 1987. Source of prenatal care and infant birth weight: The case of a North Carolina county. *American Journal of Obstetrics and Gynecology 156,* 204–210.

Buescher, P.A. et al. 1991. An evaluation of the impact of maternity care coordination on Medicaid birth outcomes in North Carolina. *American Journal of Public Health 81,* 1625–1629.

Cefalo, R.C., and M.K. Moos. 1994. *Preconceptional health care: A practical guide.* St. Louis, MO: Mosby.

Chavkin, W., and M. Allen. 1993. Questionable category of nonmaternal death. (Letter). *American Journal of Obstetrics and Gynecology 168,* 1640–1641.

Committee to Study the Prevention of Low Birthweight, Division of Health Promotion and Disease Prevention, Institute of Medicine (1985). *Preventing low birthweight.* Washington, DC: National Academy Press.

Emanuel, I. et al. 1989. Poor birth outcomes of American black women: An alternative explanation. *Journal of Public Health Policy 10*, 299–308.

Enkin, M.W. 1994. Risk in pregnancy: The reality, the perception, and the concept. *Birth 21*, 131–134.

Guyer, B. et al. 1995. Annual summary of vital statistics—1994. *Pediatrics 96*, 1029–1039.

Handwerker, L. 1994. Medical risk: Implicating poor pregnant women. *Social Science and Medicine 38*, 665–675.

Healthy people 2000: National health promotion and disease prevention objectives. 1991. Washington, DC: U.S. Department of Health and Human Services, Public Health Service.

Hertz-Picciotto, I. 1988. Incidence of early pregnancy loss (letter). *New England Journal of Medicine 319*, 1483–1484.

Indian Health Service. 1994. *Regional differences in Indian health: 1994.* Rockville, MD: Indian Health Service.

Klein, L., and R.L. Goldenberg. 1990. Prenatal care and its effect on preterm birth and low birth weight. In *New perspectives on prenatal care,* eds. I.R. Merkatz and J.E. Thompson. New York: Elsevier.

Kogan, M.D. et al. 1994. Comparing mothers' reports on the content of prenatal care received with recommended national guidelines for care. *Public Health Reports 109*, 637–646.

Korenbrot, C.C. 1984. Risk reduction in pregnancies of low-income women: Comprehensive prenatal care through the OB Access Project. *Mobius 4*, 34–43.

Kotelchuck, M. 1994. The adequacy of prenatal care utilization index: Its US distribution and association with low birthweight. *American Journal of Public Health 84*, 1486–1489.

Kotelchuck, M. et al. 1984. WIC participation and pregnancy outcomes: Massachusetts statewide evaluation study. *American Journal of Public Health 74*, 1086–1092.

Kramer, M.S. 1987. Determinants of low birth weight: Methodological assessment and meta-analysis. *Bulletin of the World Health Organization 65*, 663–737.

Krieger, N. 1994. Epidemiology and the web of causation. *Social Science and Medicine 39*, 887–903.

Krieger, N. et al. 1993. Racism, sexism, and social class: Implications for studies of health, disease, and well-being. In *Racial differences in preterm delivery: Developing a new research paradigm,* eds. D. Rowley and H. Tosteson, 82–122. New York: Oxford University Press.

March of Dimes Birth Defects Foundation. 1993. *March of Dimes statBook: Statistics for healthier mothers and babies.* White Plains, NY: March of Dimes Birth Defects Foundation.

Margolis, L.H., and M. Kotelchuck. 1994. *Which mothers experience early postpartum discharge?* Paper presented at the 122nd annual Meeting of the American Public Health Association, Washington, DC, November.

McLean, D.E. 1993. Psychosocial measurement: Implications for the study of preterm delivery in black women. In *Racial differences in preterm delivery: Developing a new research paradigm,* eds. D. Rowley and H. Tosteson, 39–81. New York: Oxford University Press.

Mrs. A-C-P to Julia Lathrop, Chief of the U.S. Children's Bureau. June 24, 1971. October 19, 1916, folder 634, Ethel S. Dummer Papers. Schlesinger Library, Radcliffe College. In *Children and youth in America: A documentary history,* ed. R.H. Bremner, 1071. Cambridge, MA: Harvard University Press.

National Center for Health Statistics. 1996. *Monthly Vital Statistics Report 44* (11s), 75.

Peoples, M.D., and E. Siegel. 1983. Measuring the impact of programs for mothers and infants on prenatal care and low birthweight: The value of refined analyses. *Medical Care 21*, 586–605.

Peoples-Sheps, M.D., V.K. Hogan, and N. Ng'andu. 1996. Content of prenatal care during the initial work-up. *American Journal of Obstetrics and Gynecology 174*, 220–226.

Public Health Service Expert Panel on the Content of Prenatal Care. 1989. *Caring for our future: The content of prenatal care.* Washington, DC: U.S. Public Health Service.

Rochat, R. et al. 1988. Maternal mortality in the United States: Report from the Maternal Mortality Collaborative. *Obstetrics and Gynecology 72*, 91–97.

Rooks, J.P. et al. 1989. Outcomes of care in birth centers: The National Birth Center Study. *The New England Journal of Medicine 321*, 1804–1811.

Royston, E., and S. Armstrong, eds. 1989. *Preventing maternal deaths.* Geneva: World Health Organization.

Rush, D. et al. 1988. The national WIC evaluation: Evaluation of the Special Supplemental Food Program for Women, Infants and Children. *American Journal of Clinical Nutrition 48*, 389–519.

Sachs, B.P. et al. 1987. Maternal mortality in Massachusetts: Trends and prevention. *The New England Journal of Medicine 316*, 667–672.

Schoendorf, K. et al. 1992. Infant mortality in college educated families: Narrowing the racial gap. *The New England Journal of Medicine 326*, 1522–1526.

Selwyn, B.J. 1990. The accuracy of obstetric risk assessment instruments for predicting mortality, low birth weight, and preterm birth. In *New perspectives on prenatal care*, eds. I.R. Merkatz and J.E. Thompson. New York: Elsevier.

Sokol, R.J. et al. 1980. Risk, antepartum care, and outcome: Impact of a maternity and infant care project. *Obstetrics and Gynecology 56*, 150–156.

Wertz, R.W., and D.C. Wertz. 1982. *Lying-In: A history of childbirth in America.* New York: Schocken Books.

Wile, I.S. 1971. Do medical schools adequately train students for the prevention of infant mortality? Transactions of the American Association for Study and Prevention of Infant Mortality, 1910, 1, 222–223. In *Children and youth in America: A documentary history*, Vol. II, Part 8, ed. R.H. Bremner, 965–966. Cambridge, MA: Harvard University Press.

Wise, P.H. 1990. Poverty, technology and recent trends in the United States infant mortality rate. *Paediatric and Perinatal Epidemiology 4*, 390–401.

Wise, P.H. 1993. Confronting racial disparities in infant mortality: Reconciling science and politics. In *Racial differences in preterm delivery: Developing a new research paradigm*, eds. R. Rowley and H. Tosteson, 7–16. New York: Oxford University Press.

World Health Organization. 1977. *International Classification of Diseases: Manual of the International Statistical Classification of Diseases, Injuries, and Causes of Death.* Ninth revision: Geneva. World Health Organization.

CHAPTER 6

The Child from One to Four: The Toddler and Preschool Years

Anita M. Farel and Jonathan B. Kotch

American society did not then generally recognize (as much of it still does not) that children might not be fully responsible for their own actions and decisions: childhood has never been viewed by most Americans as a separate and special stage of growth, fundamentally different from adulthood and subject to its own rules and laws. By and large, children are seen as miniature adults.

C. Carr, 1994

INTRODUCTION

The child's greatest growth and development between birth and adolescence takes place during that child's first five years. By the time the child is five years old, for example, the brain will have reached 90 percent of its adult weight. Although the child's rate of growth will have already begun to slow before birth, the preschool years will witness growth rates not experienced again until the adolescent growth spurt. The importance of this period for any person's future health cannot be overstated. During early childhood the child, born totally helpless and dependent, develops language, locomotion, social relations, and the knowledge and skills that make successful school entry possible. It is also a period of great risk, not only because inadequate nutrition or health care can dispose the preschool child to potential health problems that compromise future growth and development, but also because inadequate or incompetent parenting or inadequate social and cognitive stimulation can jeopardize the successful transition to school and lead to subsequent academic and social problems.

According to Erikson (1950), the preschool child's developmental tasks are to achieve a sense of autonomy and to experience individual initiative. The successful completion of these tasks is a necessary prerequisite to the individuality and purposeful activity that will be called upon when the child enters school. The interpersonal relationships that the child develops during this period will be long lasting, as in the case of family relationships, or will be models for future relationships. Health habits initiated during this period, most importantly nutrition and attitudes toward physical activity and aggression, are associated with adult obesity, cardiovascular disease, and even interpersonal violence respectively (Margolis et al., 1989). Whereas the role of preventive health services, exemplified by immunizations, is most prominent in this age period, it is also true that, as children approach school age, the greatest threat to their lives becomes intentional and unintentional injury, which at best can only modestly be affected by personal health care. Similarly, many of the leading causes of morbidity in this period either seem resistant to medical intervention or are increasing in prevalence as a result of advances in medical technology and treatment. All these circumstances suggest the need to consider community-based prevention strategies and social policy as interventions of choice in this age group. In this chapter, we describe the demographics, history, and health status of one- to four-year-olds in the United States, their access to health services, and programs and policies relevant to this age group.

DEMOGRAPHICS

Although children under five decreased in number between 1970 and 1980, between 1980 and 1990 their numbers increased again as a result of the rising number of births experienced in this country since the late 1970s. In 1975, before the number of births started increasing again, there were 3,154,198 infants born alive in the United States. In 1991, that number was 4,110,907 (National Center for Health Statistics, 1995b). As a result of this trend, the estimated 14,268,000 one- to four-year-olds in 1985 were 1.5 million more than in 1980 (Fingerhut, 1989). There are slightly more boys born than girls, 51.2 percent of all births, but since boys have a higher mortality rate, females become the majority by the age of 30. According to the U.S. Bureau of the Census (1994), the racial distribution of children under five in the United States is as follows:

White	15,454,000
Black	3,099,000
Asian/Pacific Islander	740,000
Native American/Eskimo/Aleut	219,000

Among these were 2,809,000 children of Hispanic origin, who could have been of any race (U.S. Bureau of the Census, 1994).

Demographic trends indicate that the ethnic composition of the preschool population, and consequently of all children in the United States, is shifting toward non-white. "By the year 2000, the proportion of whites among America's children will shrink to less than two-thirds (it is already one-half or less in three states: Texas, California, and New Mexico). By the middle of the next century, no ethnic or racial group will constitute a majority" (Roberts, 1994, p. 246).

The fact that young children in poverty tend to be disproportionately minority (U.S. General Accounting Office, 1994) has dire consequences for the health status of the emerging majority of nonwhite children. The single most powerful predictor of the health status for young children is poverty, and poverty is increasing among preschool children in the United States, from 18 percent of all children under six in 1979 to 23 percent in 1990 (National Center for Children in Poverty, 1993). The percent of all persons in poverty in the U.S. increased from 13.5 percent in 1990 to 15.1 percent in 1993, according to the way the U.S. government determines poverty (State of North Carolina Office of State Planning, 1995). The World Bank, in order to perform cross-national comparisons, calculates poverty as less than half of the national median income. Using this measure, the United States has the highest percent of its population in poverty among a representative group of industrialized democracies (Wolff et al., 1992).

Poverty is the underlying cause of preventable illness in children in the United States. Beginning with the landmark study of infant deaths in 1913 by the Children's Bureau (U.S. Department of Health, Education and Welfare, 1976), many studies, summarized in Gortmaker and Wise (1994), have repeatedly documented this association, not only for natural causes of mortality and morbidity (Starfield, 1982), but also for external causes (Nelson, 1992; Nersesian et al., 1985). Yet, there is debate over the precise dynamics of the relationship between poverty and child illness. One controversy is over whether, within limits, it is absolute or relative deprivation that is key. In Denmark, for example, child health statistics remained favorable even during economic hardship. Gortmaker and Wise (1994) attribute this to redistribution of resources in this very egalitarian society. Consistent with this observation is the recent documentation that, rather than mean income, the gap between the highest and lowest income groups in a society is more closely correlated with health status data such as infant mortality (Waldmann, 1992). Over the past 20 years, there has been a sharp rise in income inequality in the United States. By the mid-1990s, the share of the nation's wealth held by the top one percent of the population was double what it had been in the mid-1970s (Thurow, 1995), whereas the bottom 20 percent were earning a lower share of total family income than had been the case in the 1960s (Wolff et al., 1992). Finally, Brenner (1973) has shown that unemployment rates are associated with increasing infant mortality, when an appropriate lag time is built into the analysis. But no matter which indicator of poverty one chooses, the association with poor child health status can be demonstrated.

The relationship between poverty and health status has ominous implications for the future of children's health and well-being, given the increasing number of people in the United States who are poor. Between 1990 and 1993, the number of persons in poverty in the United States increased from 13.5 percent of the population to 15.1 percent. Within this increasing population of the poor, children are the single largest age group. Major adjustments in the economy, such as the replacement of skilled, unionized manufacturing jobs with lower-paid, lesser-skilled, nonunionized service sector jobs, coupled with increasing proportions of children living with one parent, usually the mother, and failure of social welfare programs to keep pace with inflation, conspire to keep approximately one in five children (and one in four minority children) in poverty.

Poverty is associated with many risks for poor health among young children. For example, poor children are more likely to have inadequate or inappropriate nutrition. Malnutrition is associated with iron deficiency anemia, weakness, fatigue, growth retardation, impaired social development, slow learning, and increased susceptibility to infection (Oberg, 1987). Children from poor families are 73 percent more likely to experience severe chronic conditions. Children with chronic health conditions are more likely to be without a usual source of routine or sick care and more likely to experience discontinuity between routine and sick care sources (Newacheck, 1994). Poverty is also associated with increased exposure to health risks such as higher levels of morbidity and mortality from illness, injury, and environmental toxins. Injuries associated with hazardous housing conditions, such as malfunctioning heating and electrical systems, use of alternative sources of heat such as space heaters, makeshift wood stoves and kitchen ovens—all of which can lead to housefires—are more prevalent among children in low-income families (Wise and Meyers, 1988). Young children from very poor families are nine times as likely to have significantly elevated blood lead levels than children from higher income families (Miller et al., 1985). Children living in poverty experience double jeopardy. They are exposed more frequently to such risks as illnesses, family stress, and inadequate social support, and they experience more serious consequences from these risks than do children from higher socioeconomic status. The synergistic double jeopardy of increased exposure to and greater sequelae of environmental risks predisposes children living in poverty to adverse developmental outcomes (Parker et al., 1988).

HEALTH STATUS

Historical Changes

The improvement in the health status of preschool age children in the United States in this century is the greatest of any infant or child age bracket. Using fatality as a proxy measure of health status, it may be said that preschool children in the United States are healthier now than ever before. Fatalities among one- to four-year-olds fell 97 percent from 1900 to 1985 (Fingerhut, 1989). Indisputably, the story behind this modern public health miracle is the control of infectious diseases. Ninety three of the 97 percent decline occurred prior to 1950, approximately the time of the introduction of antibiotics to the general public. Therefore, the lives saved and morbidities prevented are attributable almost entirely to improved public health services such as sanitation, immunization, and the promotion of personal hygiene by public health workers on the one hand, and improved living standards resulting in reductions in family size, improved nutrition, and improved housing conditions on the other. There is no credible basis for the claim that personal medical care made anything more than a marginal contribution to this remarkable improvement in health and life expectancy enjoyed by U.S. children.

In her autobiography, Dr. Sara Josephine Baker (1873–1945), the first woman to receive a doctorate in public health and founder of New York City's Division of Child Hygiene, the first government-sponsored agency in the world dedicated to child health, described the activities contributing to the improvement of the health of children in her jurisdiction (Baker, 1995). These included training 30 public health nurses to teach recent immigrants preventive health practices such as proper ventilation, bathing, breastfeeding, and clothing for infants and young children. Her Division of Child Hygiene offered health education and advice, screening and referral, and pure milk in the "baby hygiene stations" she set up. She trained midwives, introduced hygiene into New York City classrooms, isolated schoolchildren with infectious diseases by keeping them out of school, and placed orphaned children from hospitals with loving foster mothers. By the time of her retirement in 1923, New York's child death rate was the lowest of any city in the United States or Europe (Grolier, 1994).

In her comprehensive review of trends in childhood mortality in the United States, Fingerhut (1989) documents the precipitous drop in death rates for the one-to-four-year age group, from 1980 per 100,000 (based on death registration states, which included 26 percent of the U.S. population) in 1900 to 50 per 100,000 in 1985. Yet, preschool children in the United States experience higher mortality rates than their peers in other Western countries, primarily due to excess injury deaths. The success in reducing the death rate in this age group represents primarily the success in reducing natural causes of death. Improved living standards and sanitation, immunizations, and antibiotics account for the remarkable success in nearly eradicating the killer diseases of childhood. In 1900 natural causes accounted for 93 percent of all one- to four-year-old deaths in the United States. Diphtheria, diarrhea, enteritis, and pneumonia together caused 10 percent of all one-to-four-year-old deaths. By 1985, however, all natural causes (including but not limited to infectious diseases) accounted for 55 percent of all one-to-four-year-old deaths. The leading causes of death in this age group, in order, have become motor vehicle crash injuries, congenital anomalies, burns, drowning, malignant neoplasms, and homicide, reflecting the relatively greater success in preventing natural causes of death compared with external causes (Fingerhut, 1989). The relative status of these six conditions remained the same in 1991, and the rate of every one of them decreased with the single exception of homicide. The one-to-four-year-old homicide rate increased from 2.4 per 100,000 in 1985 to 2.8 in 1991 (U.S. Department of Health and Human Services, 1994).

Epidemiology of Major Health Problems

Infectious Diseases

Excluding routine visits, the five leading reasons for visiting pediatricians are infectious diseases. In 1988 the Child Health Supplement of the National Health Interview Survey asked questions about nine of the more common childhood infectious diseases (Hardy, 1991). Among preschool children, about half of all doctor visits are for infectious illness. The annual incidence of repeated ear infections for the birth-to-four-year-old age group, 16 per 100 per year, is the highest in all of childhood. Nearly 30 percent of all U.S. preschoolers have had repeated ear infections, and they visited the doctor on average more than five times per year. Among infectious conditions, preschool children in the United States (including infants) visited the doctor next most often for repeated tonsillitis, followed by mononucleosis, frequent diarrhea or colic, pneumonia, and bladder or urinary tract infection (in descending order) (Hardy, 1991).

Infectious illness takes its toll in other ways. Preschool children who are ill due to infectious disease may miss preschool or day care, or experience activity limitation and days in bed, requiring working parents to lose days at work. A high proportion of preschoolers with infectious disease take prescribed medications (over 90 percent of those with ear infections, tonsillitis, and pneumonia), and some (less than 5 percent) require surgery (Hardy, 1991). Hospitalization, although infrequent, does occur, most commonly for pneumonia, which is the leading cause of hospitalization in this age group (Maternal and Child Health Bureau, 1994). And infectious disease is still a killer, the underlying cause of 10 percent of deaths among one-to-four-year-old children.

Congenital Conditions

Birth defects account for one-fifth of all infant deaths and are the leading cause of infant mortality (CDC, 1992). Although most children with birth defects do not die in infancy, many of the more serious congenital malformations contribute substantially to childhood morbidity and long-term disability and thus have health care, social, and economic implications. Children with birth defects account for 25–30 percent of pediatric hospital admissions (Flynt et al., 1987). Costs for care for individuals with birth defects include expenses associated with a range of services including diagnosis and treatment, possible hospitalization, special education, rehabilitation, and residential placement.

Three percent of infants are diagnosed with birth defects during the first year of life. By the age of two, five to seven percent are diagnosed and by the age of five, seven to ten percent of all children have recognizable birth defects. The prevalence of birth defects is affected by diverse demographic and environmental factors, genetics, and type of defects. Birth defects include structural malformations, metabolic disorders, and other conditions that originate during the prenatal period. The etiology of only a small proportion of birth defects is understood (Nelson and Holmes, 1989). In addition to certain teratogens, risk factors such as gender, birth rank, and mother's age have been identified. Most defects are identified within codes 740.0–759.9 of the International Classification of Diseases, Ninth revision, Clinical Modification (U.S. Public Health Service, 1991).

Increasing awareness of the relationship between the incidence of birth defects and teratogenic factors, such as use of thalidomide in the 1960s, and infectious diseases, such as rubella in the 1950s, stimulated the development of surveillance programs. Organized in 1974, the International Clearinghouse for Birth Defects Monitoring Systems now includes 24 programs from around the world. Over half of all state health departments also have developed their own birth defects surveillance systems. Surveillance programs are important for documenting the incidence of birth defects, examining potential etiologic agents, and assessing the effectiveness of interventions. When risk factors are identified, preventive interventions can be implemented. Program managers can use data from surveillance programs to evaluate the success of programs in reaching populations targeted for services. Information collected by different monitoring programs is useful for tracking changes in the incidence of anomalies that are detected at birth and demographic variations among conditions. Although initially developed as a means for determining the etiology of certain birth defects, surveillance systems have evolved into a means for monitoring the effectiveness of interventions (Lynberg and Edmonds, 1992). Progress in understanding the etiology of some birth defects has led to campaigns such as that directed at the consumption of folic acid to prevent spina bifida (CDC, 1992b).

Significant measurement issues surround the reporting of birth defects. Birth defects that involve structural malformations are more easily identified than, for example, subtle metabolic disorders. Surveillance systems that use multiple ascertainment methods, such as the Metropolitan Atlanta Congenital Defects Program (MACDP), will be more accurate than programs that use only newborn hospital discharge information. The MACDP is a population-based surveillance system for birth defects and other perinatal conditions that occur in infants born to women who live in the five-county metropolitan Atlanta area. The program has statutory authority to conduct program activities such as reviewing records from maternity units, newborn nurseries, and genetic counseling (Edmonds et al., 1981).

The Centers for Disease Control and Prevention (CDC) conducts the Birth Defects Monitoring Program (BDMP). This program monitors the incidence of congenital anomalies and other conditions of prenatal origin across the United States. On a regular basis, computerized newborn hospital discharge abstracts collected by the Commission of Professional and Hospital Activities are sent to the CDC. These data are only collected for birth defects diagnosed during the newborn period and are neither population-based nor collected from a random sample of hospitals.

Chronic Illness

Estimates of the number of children with chronic illness or disabilities vary widely since most conditions are rare and reported prevalence rates have been generated from diverse sources (Newacheck and Taylor, 1992). Further, except for conditions that are readily diagnosed, children between one and four years may be identified as being *at risk* for health or developmental problems or developmental delay to qualify for special services. A firm diagnosis of a particular condition is often not made until children are in school. Although not all eligible children between one and four are served by early intervention programs, annual reports to Congress by state education programs are useful sources of data about the number of children with chronic health or developmental conditions. Approximately one to three percent of all infants and toddlers are served by the Part H Infant/Toddler Program; and three to eight percent are served by the Part B Preschool Program, under the Individuals with Disabilities Education Act (IDEA). The larger number of children served by Part B is likely a result of the availability of more accurate screening and assessment instruments, parental concern about the course of a child's development and behavior as children get older, and variable eligibility policies between the two programs (Harbin and Danaher, 1994).

Mental Health

Attention to the prevalence and distribution of mental health disorders among preschool-age children is relatively new. Studies conducted in London, Hong Kong, and both rural and urban areas of the United States estimate the prevalence rates for mental health disorders at 22–24 percent of three-year-olds, with 5 percent to 7 percent having a moderate to severe disorder and 15 percent to 18 percent a mild disorder (Anderson and Werry, 1994). Commonly identified problems include overactivity, restlessness, attention-seeking and difficult-to-control behavior, bedwetting, daytime wetting, food fads, difficulty settling down at bedtime, and night waking. These problems are most frequently associated with maternal depression, poor family relationships, and marital disharmony.

Future work on the prevalence and concomitants of mental health problems will be aided by *Diagnostic Classification 0-3* (1994), a new, systematic, developmentally-based approach to classifying mental health and developmental difficulties in the first four years of life. Designed by a multidisciplinary task force, this diagnostic framework complements existing medical and developmental frameworks for understanding mental health and developmental problems in early childhood.

Developmental Disabilities

Mental retardation is one among a group of diverse conditions termed developmental disabilities that are attributable to mental and/or physical impairments, manifest between birth and 21 years of age, and likely to continue indefinitely (Decoufle et al., 1994). Mental retardation is a broad classification including conditions for which the etiologies are numerous and diverse. Legislative and social initiatives can reduce the incidence of some conditions associated with mental retardation such as preterm births and alcohol consumption during pregnancy, but most cases of mental retardation have no known cause. In addition to mental retardation, neuromuscular disorders such as muscular dystrophy, sensory impairments such as blindness and deafness, learning disabilities, and conditions such as epilepsy and autism all fall under the developmental disabilities classification.

In the 1960s, intelligence tests were used to identify children with mental retardation, and services were offered primarily in special schools or residential institutions. The current practice of mainstreaming children with mental retardation grew out of concern that the segregated environment of special classes or institutions deprived children with mental retardation of experiences necessary for effective socialization. Widespread use of IQ testing as the criterion for decisions about services was also criticized for having stigmatizing consequences that were difficult to overcome. While there is not a consistent viewpoint about classifying children with mild mental retardation, severe mental retardation (SMR), defined as IQ <50, is usually recognizable before children reach school age. The prevalence of preschool-age children with SMR ranges from three to five per 1,000 children. However, the definition of SMR as IQ <50 is problematic because IQ alone does not describe individual differences in adaptive skills or the presence of other conditions that may impede effective coping by a child whose IQ is above this cutoff.

Precise prevalence rates for developmental disabilities are not available. Children with developmental disabilities have functional limitations in at least three of the following seven areas: self-care, receptive or expressive language, learning, mobility, self-direction, capacity for independent living, and economic self-sufficiency (Crocker, 1989). Based on records from local special education programs, an estimated 8–16 percent of school-age children with developmental disabilities receive special education services. Since legislative mandates to provide educational services to all school-age children with specific physical, emotional, or cognitive impairments, Decoufle et al. (1994) argue that school records provide the most comprehensive means to identify school-age children with developmental disabilities. Consequently, recent mandates to provide preschool special education services may also generate useful data about children under four with developmental disabilities.

Surveillance of developmental disabilities is difficult because case definitions for developmental disabilities often rely on clinical judgment, and there are no standard national or state-specific definitions for developmental disabilities. Further, developmental disabilities may not be manifest at age one and only become apparent as the child matures. In the United States, the Centers for Disease Control and Prevention has conducted the Metropolitan Atlanta Developmental Disabilities Surveillance Program (MADDSP), a population-based surveillance system for mental retardation, cerebral palsy, vision impairment, and hearing impairment among children aged three to ten years whose parents are residents of the Atlanta metropolitan area. Educational, medical, and social services records are used to ascertain cases.

External Causes

Injuries are the single leading cause of death among all children over the age of six months. In the one-to-four-year-old age group, intentional and unintentional injuries combined account for nearly half of all deaths. Motor vehicle injury, burns, drowning, and homicide are the most common injury causes of death among preschoolers. Deaths due to the first two causes have been declining, whereas drowning deaths have been stable since the 1980s and homicides have increased (Fingerhut, 1989).

Among these increasing homicides perhaps the most tragic is child abuse, defined here as physical harm deliberately inflicted by a caretaker. Although many parents whose use of corporal punishment may have led to the death of a child might not have "intended" to kill the child, the result is the same. The difference between the intention to teach the child a lesson by hurting him and deliberately intending to harm him is merely semantic. Unfortunately, many cases of child abuse fail to achieve the medical examiner's threshold for diagnosing child maltreatment as the cause of death, resulting in underreporting of the incidence of fatal child abuse (Kotch et al., 1993; Herman-Giddens, 1991). The proliferation of child fatality teams in the United States is evidence of the recognition that fatal child abuse is preventable if, by more accurate identification, we can learn who is at risk and when to intervene.

There is no doubt that both the awareness of abuse and the real incidence of abuse are increasing. Far more injuries are nonfatal than fatal, but the causes and incidence of nonfatal injury are less well documented than those of fatal injury.

Leading causes of emergency room visits and hospitalizations for injury in this age group include falls, burns, motor vehicle injury, and poisoning. Although less serious medically, nonfatal injuries, the leading cause of disability after congenital and perinatal causes, actually cost the United States more in indirect costs than fatal injuries, given that the present value of total lost productivity due to nonfatal injuries is greater than that due to fatal injuries. In fact, of the over $4 billion lifetime cost of injury in the birth-to-four-year-old age group in 1985, 33 percent is the indirect cost of injury morbidity, compared to 23 percent for injury mortality (Rice et al., 1989).

HEALTH CARE ACCESS

Among the uninsured in the United States, children are the largest group. In 1993, nearly 15 percent of all children living in the United States lacked health insurance for the entire year; many more were covered for only a portion of the year (National Governors' Association, 1995). The consequences of uninsuredness are serious. Children without health insurance are less likely to receive necessary preventive and primary health care. The potential need for chronic and acute care services as these children grow older, and the need for time off from work among their parents, both rise exponentially.

Many children are *underinsured* in that their current health insurance covers only major medical and catastrophic coverage. Preventive health care, including immunizations, may not be covered under such plans, or the deductible may be so high that parents postpone well child visits because the cost-sharing requirements are prohibitive (Oberg, 1990).

From 1989 to 1993, the percentage of children covered by employer-based health insurance decreased from 63.2 percent to 57.6 percent (U.S. General Accounting Office, 1995). In 1993, nearly 90 percent of uninsured children lived in a family where at least one parent worked. Through a combination of state-level expansions and increased federal mandates, Medicaid has covered health care for more children in working poor families. From 1989 to 1993, the number of children enrolled in Medicaid increased by 54 percent (National Governors' Association, 1995). However, Medicaid was never intended to provide health care coverage for all uninsured individuals. Modifications in Medicaid eligibility and state ingenuity in brokering Medicaid funds have increased the size of the population enrolled in Medicaid, but a concurrent reduction in employer health care coverage has reduced total health care coverage for children.

A survey by the National Governors' Association (1995) of state health insurance programs for children described a range of strategies that states are implementing to address uninsuredness. Almost all programs cover routine primary and preventive care. Outpatient surgery, hearing care, emergency care, and prescription drugs are frequently included; dental care, hospitalization, and transportation are less frequently provided. In 1995, a unique, private program sponsored and administered by Blue Cross and Blue Shield, *Caring Programs for Children,* was operating in 23 states (Hill and Breyel, 1991). Children are issued a standard Blue Cross Blue Shield plan identification card to mitigate stigma associated with being poor. Enrolled children typically live at home with their families. They are not eligible for Medicaid, and their families cannot afford private health insurance.

Although they consume less than one-quarter of total Medicaid spending, children represent half of all Medicaid beneficiaries. Some states are creating new programs through Section 1115 (a) waivers, which expand Medicaid coverage to specific populations, or Section 1902 (r) (2) of the Social Security Act, which permits more generous Medicaid eligibility criteria for pregnant women and children without a waiver. States are also using Section 1115 (a) waivers to create Medicaid managed care systems.

Particular concern about Medicaid managed care revolves around the extent to which comprehensive benefits through the Early and Periodic Screening, Diagnosis, and Treatment (EPSDT) program are assured. Since 1989, states are required to cover all services needed to treat conditions identified during an EPSDT screen regardless of whether the services are covered by the state Medicaid plan. The extent to which state Medicaid agencies incorporated all the requirements for the EPSDT program into contracts with managed care plans was examined by Rivera et al. (1995). Since these contracts document the service obligations of the managed care plan, clarity about the responsibilities assigned to the state agency and the out-of-plan providers on the one hand, and those assigned to the managed care plan on the other, is critical. Children may lose crucial benefits and services if contracts are ambiguous or incomplete. Thirty-three contracts from 23 states and the District of Columbia were examined for coverage of services, quality of care, and patient support services. Analyses of the findings revealed that 25 of the 29 plans that identified case management as a required activity defined case management as a gatekeeping function (that is, requiring prior authorization for services). The majority of contracts specified that medical case managers must have a medical credential. However, none of the contracts included language instructing the plans that pediatricians must be available as primary care providers; none of the contracts required coordination with other health and social programs such as WIC or Part H and Part B of IDEA; among the contracts referring to EPSDT, only a little over half (59 percent) required plans to furnish periodic screens, a basic EPSDT service, and only a small proportion identified all of the screening components. Noting the failure of many state contracts to delineate responsibility for providing EPSDT services, the authors urge that state Medicaid agencies improve their contracting procedures so families and providers are not misled about the care enrolled children can receive, and that the Health Care Financing Administration (HCFA) provide the oversight necessary to develop strong managed care contracts for children. Without managed care contracts that are consistent with Medicaid law and the purposes of the EPSDT program, children's access to continuous care will be jeopardized.

A recent study by Kogan et al. (1995) used the 1991 Longitudinal Follow-up of the National Maternal and Infant Health Survey (NMIHS) to examine the relationship between having gaps in health insurance and continuity of a regular source of care for children. Nearly one-fifth of the preschool children sampled had three or more sites of care, suggesting a lack of continuous care, increased geographic mobility, or need and use of specialty care. Gaps in insurance undermine a child's access to preventive and primary care services such as vision, hearing, and developmental screening, early intervention, and immunizations. The magnitude of the childhood population experiencing gaps in continuity of care, lack of insurance, and underinsurance all reinforce the urgency of addressing and correcting the current restrictive, categorical health care delivery system.

PROGRAMS AND SERVICES

Several federal programs are of particular importance for this age group.

Immunizations

Immunizations are the *sine qua non* of a personal preventive health intervention. Immunizations exemplify disease prevention, the delivery of a direct service to individuals for the purpose of preventing a specific disease. Immunizations have been proven to be cost beneficial and are the basis for the routine schedule of health maintenance services recommended for preschool children by the American Academy of Pediatrics and others. Despite the existence of the CDC's Childhood Immunization Initiative, achievement of the Healthy People 2000 immunization goals (90 percent by age two) remains elusive. For every child in the United States to receive on time all the recommended doses of available vaccines for the prevention of polio, diphtheria/pertussis/tetanus (DPT), measles/mumps/rubella (MMR), Haemophilis influenza type (Hib), chicken pox and hepatitis B, a more organized child health services delivery system is necessary. Although the up-to-date immunization rate of three-year olds in the United States went up from 37 percent in 1991 to 55.3 percent in 1992 (U.S. Bureau of the Census, 1994) and 67 percent in 1993, these levels are 20 percent lower for poor children (National Center for Health Statistics, 1995a). Public health officials and policy makers cannot agree on a strategy to bring this up to the level at which "herd immunity" would protect those who remain unimmunized. As a result, from January to October 1995, there were 6 cases of congenital rubella syndrome, 280 cases of measles, 685 cases of mumps, 3,398 cases of pertussis, 135 cases of rubella, and 26 cases of tetanus among U.S. children under 5. The numbers for congenital rubella and pertussis represent increases over the same period in 1994 (CDC, 1995a).

Individuals with Disabilities Education Act (IDEA) (See Chapter 11.)

Many health programs address the needs of particular populations and target services to eligible groups. In contrast, all children are entitled to public education. For children with disabilities, significant amendments to the Education of the Handicapped Act (EHA) in 1986 (P.L. 99-457) extended these entitlements to three-to-five-year-olds (Preschool Grants Program, Section 619 of Part B), offered states funding to plan systems of services for infants and toddlers from birth to two years of age (Part H, Infant and Toddler Program), and provided funds for special demonstration projects, training, and research in the Early Education Program for Children with Disabilities (EEPCD, Part C).

Part B. Preschool Grants Program

Compelling evidence over the past 50 years has affirmed that special interventions for young children with disabilities and their families during the preschool years increase the child's developmental and educational gains. In 1986, the federal government reinforced the importance of preschool services for children with developmental delays or disabilities by establishing the Preschool Grants Program (Section 619 of Part B) under amendments to the EHA, referred to as IDEA since 1990. This legislation expanded earlier incentives to encourage states to entitle all three- through five-year-old children with disabilities to a free, appropriate public education (FAPE). By 1995, every state and jurisdiction assured FAPE for all preschoolers with disabilities. The Preschool Grants Program is the only federal program exclusively serving preschool-age children with disabilities. State education agencies are awarded formula grants from the U.S. Department of Education to implement the program through local education agencies and other community service agencies. The Preschool Grants Program is the second largest Federal program focusing on three- through five-year-old children.

Services provided under Part B may include, but are not limited to, assistive technology devices and services, audiology, counseling services, early identification and assessment, medical services for diagnosis or evaluation, occupational therapy, parent counseling and training, physical therapy, psychological services, recreation, rehabilitation counseling services, school health services, social work services in schools, special education, speech pathology, and transportation. All children who are eligible for services under Part B must have an Individualized Education Plan (IEP) developed by parents and providers to develop goals for a child's program of services and to determine which special education and related services are necessary to reach these goals, and the setting(s) in which these services will be provided. Related services are provided when they are necessary to assist a child to benefit from special education. As a result of successful outreach and child find campaigns, the number of children being served under the Preschool Grants Program grew from 261,000 in 1986 to 525,000 in 1994. Innovations and increased interagency collaboration have ensured that services are comprehensive and cost effective. However, some difficult issues persist. Translating the vision of inclusion is difficult in many communities where, historically, children with disabilities may have been placed in more segregated, distinct settings. Although local school systems may be integrating older children into the public school classrooms, child care settings have traditionally been more autonomous. This situation is compounded by the dearth of preschool or child care resources, particularly in rural areas. Further, providing services for children with more rare conditions requires establishing channels of communication among diverse providers, resources in the public and private sector, and families. Communities where day care rather than preschool services is the norm require special collaborative initiatives between health care and educational providers.

Capitalizing on possibilities for flexibility in use of Part B funds to translate the spirit of the legislation into action requires skills in collaboration and a comprehensive, less categorical vision of a child's and family's needs. In response to concerns that eligibility for services under Part B required identifying a specific disability in order for a preschool-age child to be eligible for services, thus possibly stigmatizing a child, creating a self-fulfilling prophecy, or prematurely assigning a diagnosis, amendments to the law retracted the requirement that states report the numbers of three- through five-year-old children served by disability category and subsequently allowed states to incorporate an additional *preschool-specific category* for children experiencing developmental delays. Such amendments have made it possible for programs to use more flexible, noncategorical eligibility criteria. In 1995, only seven states used Part B disability categories exclusively to determine eligibility for preschool services (Danaher, 1995).

Part H. Infant and Toddler Program

Part H, the infant/toddler section of IDEA, is a mechanism for developing systems of family-centered services for infants and toddlers, with or at risk for disabilities, and their families. The 1986 legislation required states that chose to participate in the Part H program to develop state and local infrastructures to respond to the requirement for service delivery systems. Over the course of the five-year planning period, states were required to apply for continued funding from the U.S. Department of Education and to document their progress in developing the different elements of the system required by the legislation. At the end of the five-year program implementation process, all eligible infants, toddlers, and their families were expected to be entitled to a gamut of comprehensive, coordinated services. By 1992, the complicated process of developing appropriate policies, including interagency agreements, at the state and local levels slowed progress toward full implementation of the law. Further, budget constraints experienced by many federal and state programs forced states to narrow their conceptualization of appropriate populations to serve. In fact, only 11 states opted ultimately to serve infants and toddlers "at risk" for developmental problems (Shackelford, 1995).

All states are required to address 14 minimum requirements in their state plans. States are required to identify a "lead agency" for the Part H program. In more than half the states, the health department is the lead agency. An Individualized Family Service Plan (IFSP) for each eligible child must be developed with families in order to assure its responsiveness to families' unique concerns, priorities, and needs. Extensive regulations direct state early intervention programs to improve community awareness and identification of children with or at risk for developmental disabilities. For example, under IDEA, the child-find system requires each state to ensure that all children with disabilities or suspected of having disabilities are located, identified, and evaluated. Explicit regulations for community outreach, participation of diverse early childhood personnel, and development and monitoring of IFSPs have shaped the implementation and evaluation of early intervention programs. The IFSP has several components related to health care. For example, the IFSP must describe the child's physical development. Health care services that would enable the child to benefit from other early intervention services must be provided. Medical services, in so far as they are necessary for diagnostic and assessment purposes, are also included in early intervention services. Other services that the child needs, such as well-child care or surgery, must also be documented in the IFSP. Such information helps provide a more complete picture of the child and family's need for services, and for tracking a child's health status, particularly when the child does not have a primary care physician.

Part C. Early Education Program for Children with Disabilities

This part of special education legislation funds model-demonstration projects, research institutes, outreach activities, statewide data systems, and technical assistance. Currently, there are 114 EEPCD projects nationwide. Approximately 85 percent of the EEPCD projects have continued to provide services after the federal grant period terminated (Trohanis, 1995).

Early Intervention

Early intervention refers to the provision of educational, health care, supportive, social, and therapeutic services to young children between birth and three years with or at risk for developmental disabilities and their families. The health care system has historically been the first point of professional contact for families with young children with developmental problems. Initially, services for young children with disabilities were primarily rehabilitative, segregated, and emphasized functional and cognitive development (Hutt and Gibby, 1976). In the 1960s, the importance of the interaction between the child and caregiver was recognized as the single most important factor in developmental achievement. Consequently, children with mental retardation were no longer segregated in separate preschool programs, nor were children considered to be at risk for poor development because of social disadvantage. Assessing a child's needs and resources in the context of the family shifted the orientation of the relationship between caregivers and interventionists and fostered the development of identification and assessment procedures for infants and preschool children.

Whereas federal law includes infants: (1) with established conditions that are likely to lead to delay, (2) with developmental delay, and (3) at risk for developmental delay, states are given considerable discretion in establishing eligibility criteria among these groups. However, identifying accurate, culturally sensitive risk factors has been difficult. Although there is agreement that early intervention programs should be provided for infants with disabilities and those at some level of identifiable risk for developmental problems (Guralnick and Bennett, 1987), identifying less easily defined potential risk factors in order to determine who should be served by an early intervention program has proved elusive (Upshur, 1990).

The use of perinatal factors, such as low birth weight or preterm birth, to estimate number of children at risk has proved to be relatively insensitive (Scott and Masi, 1979). Some of the best-studied registries were those instituted by Great Britain in the early 1960s to identify children who would need medical care and other attention. The limited predictive value of indices such as low birth weight, traumatic delivery, and environmental risk factors led to recommendations that registries be abandoned or redesigned for other purposes related to children with disabilities (Knox and Mahon, 1970). Similarly, Werner et al. (1971) reported that only 15 percent of all school problems in a group of children followed from birth through age 18 could be attributed to children with high perinatal risk indicators.

Projections based on socioeconomic indicators alone have been no more successful (Finkelstein and Ramey, 1980; Ramey et al., 1978). Most recent early intervention initiatives have addressed the child's needs *in the context of the family* (Ramey et al., 1992; Shonkoff and Hauser-Cram, 1987). Bronfenbrenner et al.

(1984) reinforced the complex interaction among risk factors for developmental problems by emphasizing that the family is embedded in neighborhoods and communities that have broad social and cultural influences. Precursors of developmental delay have been identified more accurately by including the impact of multiple, family risk factors, such as stressful life events, mother's educational level, mother's mental health status, and father's presence in the home. A family's role in identifying and monitoring interventions is reinforced by the implementation of IFSPs. Research has documented the long-term effects and broad consensus that early intervention is a "cost-effective method" for mitigating the effects of poverty early in life (Zigler and Muenchow, 1992). Early intervention programs have increasingly stronger empirical bases, are the focus of interprogram initiatives at the state and community levels, and continue to enjoy renewed funding (Trohanis, 1995).

Community-Based Services

Increased federal involvement has generated a myriad of programs that address the health and development of children under five. However, categorical, as opposed to comprehensive, blueprints for services have meant that a child's malnutrition may be addressed but not her need for age-appropriate peer interaction. For families, disparate eligibility requirements and forms create frustration. While the detrimental consequences of fragmentation have been documented (Gliedman and Roth, 1980; Schorr and Schorr, 1988), funding may be jeopardized if a program that initiates cooperative agreements to improve continuity of care, for example, cannot verify that it is meeting the requirements of a particular federal program. Block grant funding has been promoted as a way for states to regain some autonomy in making decisions about allocation of funds. But the lack of accountability inherent in this funding mechanism has reduced the documentation of progress made in reducing duplication, closing gaps, or describing outcomes of interagency agreements.

Attempts to reduce the splintering that characterizes the federal, categorical legislative process are occurring through the development of community-based services. Legislation, such as Part H of IDEA, requires states to develop an Interagency Coordinating Council at the state level, mirrored in interagency councils at the local level. The maternal and child health block grant application has required states to describe how they work with communities to promote collaboration and the development of service delivery systems at the local level.

Initiatives for improving community outreach and responsiveness at the local level are increasing. Although current financing mechanisms offer few incentives for child health professionals to spend time in community-focused interventions or activities outside the traditional clinical setting, there are some signs of progress. The American Academy of Pediatrics is working to justify "cognitive procedures" as legitimately billable procedures so child health professionals can rearrange schedules to attend, for example, an IEP meeting—typically an expensive endeavor for a physician. Some health maintenance organization (HMO) practices are initiating community outreach to promote healthy behavior. The Harvard Community Health Plan in Massachusetts has produced a set of health education materials and collaborated with the Boston Children's Museum to promote better understanding of diversity and disability (Palfrey, 1994).

WIC

The Special Supplemental Food Program for Women, Infants, and Children (WIC) began as a demonstration in 1972. The goal was to improve the health of pregnant and lactating women, as well as infants and children, by combining nutrition supplements, nutrition education, and access to health services. From its inception, WIC was conceived of as a food and nutrition program with a necessary connection to health services. Congress deliberately chose to avoid any stigma associated with welfare programs by administratively placing WIC in the Food and Nutrition Service (FNS) of the Department of Agriculture. As Senator Hubert H. Humphrey, one of the architects of the new program, said at the time, such placement would ensure that the program would "not be mismanaged in terms of some other programs" (*Congressional Record*, 1972).

Since 1972, thanks in part to a series of lawsuits to overcome the Nixon administration's deliberate impounding of WIC funds, the program has expanded rapidly. Today it serves almost 6 million clients at an annual cost of over $2 billion. A beneficiary of the combined forces of agricultural interests, retail stores, child health and nutrition advocates, and drug companies that produce infant formula, WIC has survived major policy challenges, including threats of budget cuts in 1995. The success of WIC is undoubtedly attributable also to the fact that it is the most evaluated program of all federal social programs, and most of those evaluations have demonstrated the health benefits and the cost-effectiveness of WIC.

The overwhelming majority of these evaluations have focused on pregnancy outcome. During pregnancy, WIC services include vouchers for milk, cheese, eggs, fruit juice, dried peas, beans or peanut butter, and iron-fortified grain products. In addition, WIC services are offered as an adjunct to health care, so women attracted by free food also receive prenatal care, as well as group and individual nutrition education. The evaluations of WIC have not attempted to disaggregate the separate contributions of health care, nutrition supplements, and nutrition education, but as a package WIC has been shown to increase the mean birth weight and mean gestational age of newborns (Kennedy and Kotelchuck, 1984; Rush et al., 1988). WIC also has been shown to reduce Medicaid expenses for newborns in the first year of life (Schramm, 1986), hence the assertion that, in addition to providing a net health benefit, WIC also saves money.

There is less evidence about the benefits of WIC for the preschool child. As with the pregnant woman, an eligible child, who has a nutritional risk and is income eligible (<185 percent of the Federal Poverty Income Guidelines in most states), is entitled to food vouchers for milk and milk products, eggs, peanut butter, iron-fortified cereals and vitamin C-rich juices. In addition, the parent or guardian (and in some cases the child) participates in nutrition education, and the child must have access to medical care. One study demonstrated that the requirement for access to medical care increased immunization rates for children in a local health department (Kotch and Whiteman, 1982). Rush's National WIC Evaluation included the tantalizing suggestion that children's head circumferences were 1/2 cm larger if they were on WIC in utero, and he attempted to link that finding with the observation that older children on WIC performed better on some cognitive tests such as digit memory (Rush et al., 1988). However, due to issues of confidentiality and cost, these findings were never followed up, and in 1989 the Congress refused to fund studies of the WIC impact on children that had been solicited by the FNS.

Head Start

An important initiative of the War on Poverty in the 1960s addressed the need for comprehensive group preschool programs for children at socioeconomic disadvantage. The goals of Project Head Start include promoting social and behavioral competence among children to ensure that they enter school with a similar foundation as their more economically advantaged peers. To that end, objectives were formulated in four areas: education, parent involvement, social services, and health. Almost unique among child care programs, health services were a fundamental theme in Head Start programming. They include: (1) a comprehensive health services program that encompasses a broad range of medical, dental, nutrition, and mental health services, including children with disabilities; (2) preventive health services and early intervention; and (3) linking the child's family to an ongoing health care system to ensure that the child continues to receive comprehensive health care even after leaving Head Start (Zigler et al., 1994). Ten percent of Head Start enrollment is reserved for children with disabilities, most of whom have hearing or speech/language impairments. Evidence from studies of some Head Start programs indicated that the need for special education placements and grade retentions when disabled Head Start children reached public school were reduced. Head Start programs also have been credited with helping children complete school and reducing juvenile delinquency. In 1990, under the Head Start Expansion and Quality Improvement Act, Congress gave Head Start its largest budget increase to date. While the budget for Head Start doubled between 1986 and 1990, Edward Zigler, an architect of Head Start, raised concern about the sacrifice of program quality to program expansion (Zigler and Muenchow, 1992). Salaries and benefits that would attract and retain lead teachers with professional training must be offered. Full-day, full-year services and stronger relationships with a broad range of job training programs would promote economic self-sufficiency among parents as well as social competence among enrolled children. Directing program expansion toward infants and toddlers would address the needs of families that are particularly disadvantaged—a growing population among enrollees. Almost half (49 percent) of the parents of Head Start children are enrolled in Aid to Families with Dependent Children (AFDC). The parent involvement component, which has usually been developed in terms of engaging parents as classroom volunteers or as recipients of home visits, is not effective when parents are expected to be employed full-time or enrolled in job training. Younger children's parents are more likely to benefit from home visits and more likely to have the time to volunteer.

The Head Start program includes a model nutrition program that addresses the nutritional needs of enrolled children through the food served, classroom activities that teach about good nutrition, and demonstrations of model meals. In response to reports of a Head Start program that served foods with high sugar, salt, fat, and refined grain content, and where staff members drank soda with meals and failed to include nutritional content in the curriculum, a nutrition policy based on the standards set by the Head Start program was established. Information about the new program, including appropriate food for holiday celebrations, was sent to parents. Weekly healthy food activities, trips to grocery stores, and an appropriately stocked refrigerator at the program reinforced these program changes (Wardle and Winegarner, 1992).

Home Visiting

Home visiting is a strategy for offering support to families with young children in order to promote healthy early child development. Funded by both public and private sources, home visiting is integral to many programs serving families. At the turn of the century, the special needs of new immigrant populations brought about by poverty, contagious disease, and infant mortality were addressed by home visiting programs. The impetus for such services was the belief that ameliorating environmental conditions could significantly improve the family's ability to cope with personal problems (Wasik et al., 1990). The model of parents and children as passive recipients of services delivered by an expert was modified during the 1950s. Parents' critical roles in social and intellectual development were reinforced by service delivery models that emphasized the family as a resource as well as a target for intervention. The rationale for incorporating home visiting into a comprehensive program includes identifying and reaching out to families who might not otherwise seek a service provider, fitting services to individual needs, and bridging the gap between individualized services and other community-based providers (Olds and Kitzman, 1993).

Programs with a home visiting component continue to proliferate. Olds and Kitzman (1990) found that home visiting programs for children with medical risks led to enhanced cognitive and motor development as measured by scores on standardized tests of infant development. However, programs targeting children with social risks produced more mixed results. Benefits in child development in these studies were accompanied by positive changes in the interaction of parents with their children and/or in the conduciveness of the home environments to child rearing. However, only about 20 percent of the studies demonstrated increased use of preventive health services such as immunizations and well-baby care. Home visiting programs appear to be more effective if they are comprehensive. For example, programs that focus on a child's cognitive development but fail to address the child's physical health needs will produce, by and large, short-term or only modest effects. Effective home visiting programs approach comprehensively a child's and family's needs across many dimensions.

OUTSTANDING ISSUES

Child Abuse and Neglect

Public involvement in child protection in the United States can be traced to the case of Mary Ellen, a beaten, emaciated New York City child who was found chained to a bed in her tenement apartment. The New York Society for the Prevention of Cruelty to Animals, in the absence of any analogous agency—public or private—dedicated to the prevention of cruelty to children, took the case to court and won. Subsequently, the N.Y. Society for the Prevention of Cruelty to Children emerged, later becoming the American Humane Association. Child protection remained primarily a responsibility of voluntary agencies until the outcry prompted by the publication of Kempe's seminal article, "The Battered Child Syndrome," resulted in local and state social service involvement (Kempe et al., 1962).

The federal government has been directly involved in child abuse and neglect services since 1973, when model Child Abuse and Neglect legislation was first passed (U.S. Congress, 1973). Because social services are under state jurisdiction, the federal government is limited to providing child maltreatment services through grants-in-aid. In the model legislation, the Congress provided funds for state child protective services (CPS), which defined child maltreatment more or less the same way that the model legislation does, and included mandatory reporting in state legislation. As a result every state now has a mandatory reporting law, and federal support for child maltreatment services is channeled to states through the social services block grant (Title XX of the Social Security Act).

Overworked and under-staffed CPS agencies are constrained to investigate every legitimate report and to provide services to the substantiated cases (about 40 percent of all reports), leaving little time, money, or energy for prevention. Public health has been in the forefront of prevention services for families at risk of abuse and neglect (Barber-Madden et al., 1988), but identifying such families remains a crude science at best. Although there is some evidence that home visiting services can reduce reporting rates among at-risk families, there is no evidence that, short of removing the child from the home, CPS interventions actually reduce the risk of subsequent abuse. Approximately one-third of CPS cases are re-reported, and since there is little interest and no funding for rigorous evaluation of CPS, there is no way of knowing if this recidivism rate is higher or lower than would be the case without CPS.

AIDS/HIV

Human immunodeficiency virus (HIV) infection will assume increasing prominence among the health and social problems affecting children under five. HIV is a leading cause of death for young children. In 1991, approximately 1 percent of all AIDS cases reported to the CDC were among children under 13, 83 percent of whom were under five. In the same year, HIV infection was the second leading cause of death among black children one through four years of age in New Jersey, Massachusetts, New York, and Florida, and among Hispanic children in this age group in New York (CDC, 1995b). In 1992, HIV was the seventh leading cause of death among all children one through four years of age (National Center for Health Statistics, 1994). HIV infection among children can be attributed almost completely to perinatal transmission. From 1989 to 1992, over 20,000 HIV-infected women gave birth in the United States. Assuming a perinatal transmission rate of 15–30 percent, 1,000 to 2,000 HIV-infected infants were born annually during these years (CDC, 1995b). The median incubation period development of AIDS is 12 months. Most (90 percent) perinatally infected children will be symptomatic by four years of age, half of whom will come to medical attention in the first year of life (Sicklick and Rubenstein, 1992). Although it is theoretically possible to reduce in-utero HIV transmission to children to one-third with drug therapy during pregnancy, whether a real decrease in incidence is possible in this hard-to-reach population remains to be seen.

Young children with HIV infection and their families require the resources of diverse human services, child care, and health care delivery programs. Barriers to coordinated, comprehensive prenatal and pediatric health care services for minority, disadvantaged, and drug-using populations are compounded for young children with HIV infection and their parents. Issues surrounding care for this population include attention to confidentiality and the development of trust and confidence in the health care system. Further, since AIDS disproportionately affects minority populations, understanding and respecting the family's cultural belief system, values, traditions, and coping styles is of crucial importance. Social support for family members afflicted with guilt, isolation, poor health, and ostracism is also necessary. Arrangements for respite and child care services are essential for families, particularly where the only adult is a single mother, likely undergoing treatment for acquired immune deficiency syndrome (AIDS) herself. Anxiety for families is heightened by the fact that it is not always possible to distinguish HIV-infected children from the much larger group of HIV-positive children during the perinatal period (Cohen, 1994).

While the Academy of Pediatrics and the CDC support the enrollment of children with HIV infection in day care and preschool, planning for these children requires the consistent and informed involvement of teachers, families, primary caregivers, and administrators. Depending on the extent to which the infection interferes with a child's ability to participate in a preschool experience, special education resources may also be needed.

HIV disease has features of both chronic and terminal illnesses. Similar to many chronic illnesses, medical advances have lengthened the life span of children with HIV infection. Affected children are alternately free of problems or experience periods of acute exacerbation, functional limitations, and physical impairments that rarely dissipate entirely. Most children with HIV disease experience neurologic effects, cognitive deficits, loss of previously achieved developmental milestones, and/or developmental delays.

Generally, service delivery around a specific presenting problem without coordinating efforts with other involved providers has resulted in fragmented services that often overlap or fail to address family needs. Such a model has proven especially problematic and unsuccessful with families affected by drug use and AIDS. For example, most drug treatment programs were designed for men and did not take into account women's multiple roles and responsibilities. Newer models have emphasized the importance of family support. Programs that include support around parenting and relational issues, life skills, and vocational training report encouraging results (Woodruff and Sterzin, 1993).

Day Care

Increasing numbers of preschool children are being cared for outside the home. This is a consequence of increasing numbers of women with young children entering the labor force, itself a consequence of stagnation of wages since the 1970s. Over half of U.S. mothers of infants are in the labor force (U.S. Bureau of the Census, 1986). By 1993, 59.6 percent of married women with children under six, and 47.4 percent of single women with children under six, were in the labor force (U.S. Bureau of the Census, 1994). Approximately 60 percent of the children of these women received care outside of their own homes (Dawson and Cain, 1990). For infants and toddlers, most such care in 1991 was in another home, but by the time children reach the age of three to four years, 32.9 percent are being cared for in organized child care centers, compared with 24.5 percent in homes other than their own (U.S. Bureau of the Census, 1994).

Use of child day care is not without risk. There is strong evidence that group child care increases the frequency of infectious diseases among young children. For example, a typical toddler raised at home in the United States may have two episodes of diarrhea a year, whereas a day care-reared child may have four or more (Haskins and Kotch, 1986). Similarly, the risk of upper respiratory infection is increased among children attending day care. Most of these illnesses that children are exposed to in day care are annoying but benign. However, the same mode of transmission that increases the risk of diarrhea also increases the risk of hepatitis A. The same mode of transmission that increases the risk of upper respiratory infection also increases the risk of otitis media and meningitis.

The means to prevent the most common form of meningitis in preschoolers, Hib meningitis, is straightforward—immunization. There is no immunization for diarrhea, however, which may be caused by any of a number of parasites, viruses, and bacteria. Most prevention strategies rely on scrupulous handwashing, which was shown in one study (Black et al., 1981) to reduce diarrhea in day care 50 percent. However, when Bartlett et al. (1988) replicated their own similar study, they discovered that training child day care workers to monitor diarrhea episodes in their classrooms resulted in the same reduction in diarrhea that the classrooms whose workers had been trained to wash their hands enjoyed. In the only randomized, controlled trial of handwashing, Kotch et al. (1994) demonstrated a small but significant decrease in severe diarrhea, but no effect on mild diarrhea. The mechanism responsible for these improvements remains to be isolated.

The picture with respect to injuries among children in out-of-home care is even less clear, given the absence of any U.S. studies based on community-wide samples of children. The studies of injury risk in child care centers that do exist (Rivara et al., 1989; Sachs et al., 1989) identify the playground and particularly playground equipment as potentially hazardous, but injury rates controlled for exposure are actually less than the injury rates reported for similarly aged children in other communities (Gallagher et al., 1984). The injury rates of children in family day care homes are unknown, but are likely to be closer to the rates of children reared in their own homes than to the rates of center-reared children. Adult supervision, safer playground equipment and impact absorbing playground surfaces, scheduled activities, barriers to exposure to household hazards such as poisonous cleaning substances and medications, and less time spent in the car all contribute to reduced injury risk for children in organized child day care centers.

Homelessness

In the 1990s, families with young children comprise the most rapidly growing segment of the homeless population (Fantasia and Isserman, 1994). The rising number of homeless families can be attributed in large part to the growth of American families headed by women and the economic hardship incurred by single-parent households. Homeless mothers are typically single, in their late twenties, and have two to three children, most of whom are under five. The percentage of women in the homeless population grew from 3 percent in the 1950s to 20 percent in the 1990s. In the 30 cities surveyed by the U.S. Conference of Mayors in 1994, families with children accounted for, on average, about 39 percent of the homeless population (Children's Defense Fund, 1995).

Estimates of the number of young children whose families are homeless vary. According to the U.S. Department of Housing and Urban Development, for the past two decades homelessness has increased faster among families with children than among any other group. Separation from their families is one of the devastating consequences of homelessness for children. Many women who live in shelters for single adults have children in foster care and other living arrangements. In more than half of the cities surveyed by the U.S. Conference of Mayors in 1994, homeless families sometimes had to separate to stay in emergency shelters. The survey reported that 15–30 percent of children in foster care were removed from their families or remained in foster care primarily because of housing problems. Among the myriad problems they face, homeless children have more severe health problems and less chance of being immunized than other poor children. A study comparing the dietary intake, height and weight of homeless, three- to five-year-old children in two emergency shelters and transitional shelters showed that the overall nutritional adequacy of children's diets met or exceeded the recommended dietary allowances (RDAs) for children; however, this level of nutritional adequacy reflected their consumption of nutrient-fortified ready-to-eat cereals (Taylor and Koblinsky, 1993). In fact, many of the homeless mothers reported giving their children sweets as treats in lieu of the toys they could not afford. Although the height-for-age and weight-for-age measurements of homeless children in this study were comparable to those of a national sample of low-income children, 9 percent of children living in emergency shelters were below the fifth percentile for height and weight. Children in homeless shelters in Philadelphia were reported to have high rates of injuries, lead toxicity, burns, and developmental delay (Palfrey, 1994).

CONCLUSION

A social problem becomes a part of a nation's policy agenda when a particular issue catches public attention, or a group with a special interest advocates for its own particular cause. We do not have a national agenda with a child health focus. The United States alone among developed countries has not ensured access to a minimum level of health services, nor committed itself to achievable health status standards, for its youngest citizens. Rather, it has chosen a categorical approach to child health, ignoring opportunities for addressing the underlying causes of suboptimal child health. The current legislative process, through U.S. House and Senate committee structures, perpetuates the practice of addressing pervasive social problems from the fragmented perspectives of the many different health and developmental outcomes occurring at the furthest ends of the chain of causality. In fact, the broad array of public programs supported by the federal government is symptomatic of the fact that health status for growing subpopulations of preschool children in the United States has been deteriorating. Perhaps the most serious criticism leveled against the U.S. child health system is that it is neither equitable nor efficient. That is, children who need comprehensive health services the most do not have access to them because of varied program eligibility requirements and inconsistent benefits, and those who do have access pay more than any other children in the developed world. In his address to the American Academy of Pediatrics, President-elect Harvey (1991) argued that the health promotion and disease prevention objectives developed for the Year 2000 should be used as a foundation for developing cohesive child health goals that ensure universal eligibility and adequate benefits. But even before committing itself to achieving child health goals, the United States must make a national commitment to children themselves. As of this writing, the country is moving away from such a commitment.

REFERENCES

Anderson, J., and J.S. Werry. 1994. Emotional and behavioral disorders. In *The epidemiology of childhood disorders*, ed. I.B. Pless, 304–338. New York: Oxford University Press.

Baker, S.J. 1995. *Fighting for life.* Temecula, CA: Reprint Services Corporation. (First Published in 1939).

Barber-Madden, R. et al. 1988. Prevention of child abuse: A public health agenda. *Journal of Public Health Policy 9* 167–176.

Bartlett, A.V. et al. 1988. Diarrheal illness among infants and toddlers in day care centers: Effects of active surveillance and staff training without subsequent monitoring. *American Journal of Epidemiology 127*, 808–817.

Black, R.E. et al. 1981. Hand washing to prevent diarrhea in day care centers. *American Journal of Epidemiology 113*, 445–451.

Brenner, M.H. 1973. Fetal, infant and maternal mortality during periods of economic stress. *International Journal of Health Services 3,* 145–159.

Bronfenbrenner, U. et al. 1984. Child, family, and community. In *Review of child development research,* Vol. 7. *Handbook of early childhood intervention,* ed. R.D. Parke, 283–328. Chicago: University of Chicago Press.

Carr, C. 1994. *The alienist.* New York: Random House.

Centers for Disease Control and Prevention. 1992a. Annual summary of births, marriages, divorces, and deaths: United States, 1991. *Monthly Vital Statistics Report, 40.* Hyattsville, MD: U.S. Department of Health and Human Services, U.S. Public Health Service, CDC.

Centers for Disease Control and Prevention. 1992b. Recommendations for the use of folic acid to reduce the number of cases of spina bifida and other neural tube defects. *Morbidity and Mortality Weekly Report 41,* RR-14, 1–7, September 11.

Centers for Disease Control and Prevention. 1995a. Monthly immunization table. *Morbidity and Mortality Weekly Report 44,* 903, December 8.

Centers for Disease Control and Prevention. 1995b. U.S. Public Health Service recommendations for human immunodeficiency virus counseling and voluntary testing for pregnant women. *Morbidity and Mortality Weekly Reports 44,* RR-7, 1–13, July 7.

Children's Defense Fund. 1995. Wasting America's future: The Children's Defense Fund report on the costs of child poverty. In *The state of America's children yearbook.* Washington, DC: Author.

Cohen, F.L. 1994. Research on families and pediatric human immunodeficiency virus disease: A review and needed directions. *Developmental and Behavioral Pediatrics 15,* S34–S42.

Congressional Record. 92d Cong., 2d sess., 16 August 1972, S28588. Vol. 118, part 22.

Crocker, A. 1989. The spectrum of medical care for developmental disabilities. In *Developmental disabilities: Delivery of medical care for children and adults.* eds. I.L. Rubin and A.C. Crocker, London: Lea & Febiger.

Danaher, J. 1995. *Preschool special education eligibility classifications and criteria.* Chapel Hill, NC: National Early Childhood Technical Assistance System (NEC*TAS), University of North Carolina at Chapel Hill, No. 6 revised, September.

Dawson, D.A., and V.S. Cain. 1990. *Child care arrangements: Health of our nation's children—United States, 1988.* Hyattsville, MD: Centers for Disease Control and Prevention.

Decoufle, P. et al. 1994. Developmental disabilities. In *From data to action,* eds. L.S. Wilcox and J.S. Marks. Atlanta, GA: Centers for Disease Control and Prevention.

Edmonds, L.D. et al. 1981. Congenital malformations surveillance: Two American systems. *International Journal of Epidemiology 10,* 247–252.

Erikson, E.H. 1950. *Childhood and society,* 2d ed. New York: W.W. Norton and Co., Inc.

Fantasia, R., and M. Isserman. 1994. *Homelessness: A sourcebook.* New York: Facts on File, Inc.

Fingerhut, L.A., National Center for Health Statistics, 1989. *Trends and current status in childhood mortality, United States, 1900–1985.* Vital and health statistics. Series 3, No. 26. DHHS Pub. No. (PHS).

Finkelstein, N.W., and C.T. Ramey. 1980. Learning to control the environment in infancy. *Child Development 48,* 806–819.

Flynt, J.W. et al. 1987. *State surveillance of birth defects and other adverse reproductive outcomes: April 1987.* Washington, D.C: U.S. Department of Health and Human Services, Office of the Assistant Secretary for Planning and Evaluation.

Gallagher, S.S. et al. 1984. The incidence of injuries among 87,000 Massachusetts children and adolescents: Results of the 1980–81 statewide childhood injury prevention program surveillance system. *American Journal of Public Health 74*, 1340–1347.

Gliedman, J. et al. 1980. *The unexpected minority: Handicapped children in America.* New York: Harcourt Brace Jovanovich.

Gortmaker, S., and P. Wise. 1994. *The first economic injustice: Socioeconomic disparities in infant mortality in the United States: Theoretical and policy perspectives.* Society and Health Working Paper Series No. 94–4. Boston, MA: Society and Health Working Group, The Health Institute, New England Medical Center and Harvard School of Public Health.

Grolier Library of North American Biographies. 1994. Baker, Sara Josephine, In *Activists,* vol. 1. Danbury, CT: Grolier Educational Corporation.

Guralnick, M.J., and F.C. Bennett. 1987. A framework for early intervention. In *The effectiveness of early intervention for at-risk and handicapped children.* eds. M.J. Guralnick and F.C. Bennett, 3–32. Orlando, FL: Academic Press.

Harbin, G., and J. Danaher. 1994. Comparison of eligibility policies for infant/toddler programs and preschool special education programs. *Topics in Early Childhood Special Education 14* 455–471.

Hardy, A.M. 1991. *Incidence and impact of selected infectious diseases in childhood.* Vital and health statistics, Series 10, No. 180. DHHS Pub. No. (PHS) 91-1508.

Harvey, B. 1991. Why we need a national child health policy. *Pediatrics 87,* 1–6.

Haskins, R., and J.B. Kotch. 1986. Day care and illness: Evidence, costs, and public policy. *Pediatrics 77* (6, suppl), 951–982.

Head Start Expansion and Quality Improvement Act of 1990. 101-501. U.S. Department of Health and Human Services.

Heekin, S., and J. Ward-Newton. 1995. *Section 619 profile sixth edition.* Chapel Hill, NC: National Early Childhood Technical Assistance System (NEC*TAS), University of North Carolina at Chapel Hill.

Herman-Giddens, M.E. 1991. Underreporting of child abuse and neglect fatalities in North Carolina. *North Carolina Medical Journal 52,* 634–639.

Hill, I.T., and J.M. Breyel. 1991. *Caring for kids.* Washington, DC: National Governors' Association.

Hutt, M.L., and R.G. Gibby. 1976. *The mentally retarded child: Development, education and treatment,* 3rd ed. Boston, MA: Allyn and Bacon.

Kempe, C.H. et al. 1962. The battered child syndrome. *Journal of American Medical Association 181,* 17–24.

Kennedy, E.T., and M. Kotelchuck. 1984. The effect of WIC supplemental feeding on birth weight: A case-control analysis. *American Journal of Clinical Nutrition 40,* 579–585.

Knox, E.G., and D.F. Mahon. 1970. Evaluation of "infant at risk" registers. *Archives of disease in childhood 45,* 634–639.

Kogan, M.D. et al. 1995. The effect of gaps in health insurance on continuity of a regular source of care among preschool-aged children in the United States. *Journal of American Medical Association 18,* 1429–1435.

Kotch, J.B. et al. 1993. Morbidity and death due to child abuse in New Zealand. *Child Abuse and Neglect 17,* 233–247.

Kotch, J.B. et al. 1994. Evaluation of an hygienic intervention in child day-care centers. *Pediatrics 94* (6, suppl), 991–994.

Kotch, J.B., and D. Whiteman. 1982. Effect of the WIC program on children's clinic activity in a local health department. *Medical Care 20,* 691–698.

Lynberg, M.C., and L.D. Edmonds. 1992. Surveillance of birth defects. In *Public health surveillance*, eds. W. Halperin and E. Baker. New York: Van Nostrand Reinhold.

Margolis, L.H. et al. 1989. *Growing into healthy adults: Pediatric antecedents of adult disease*. Lansing, MI: Michigan Department of Public Health.

Miller, C.A. et al. 1985. *Monitoring children's health: Key indicators*, 2nd ed. Washington, DC: American Public Health Association.

National Center for Children in Poverty. 1993. Young children still live in poverty despite parental employment. *News and Issues*, winter/spring.

National Center for Health Statistics. 1994. *Advance report of final mortality statistics, 1992*. Monthly vital statistics report, vol. 43, no. 6S. Hyattsville, MD: U.S. Department of Health and Human Services Public Health Service, CDC.

National Center for Health Statistics. 1995a. *Health, United States, 1994*. Hyattsville, MD: US Public Health Service.

National Center for Health Statistics. 1995b. *Vital statistics of the United States, 1991*, Vol. 1, natality. Washington, DC: US Public Health Service.

National Center for Health Statistics. 1988. National Health Interview Survey, Child Health Supplement. Washington, DC: US Public Health Service.

National Early Childhood Technical Assistance System (NEC*TAS). April 1995. *Helping our nation's infants and toddlers with disabilities and their families*. Federal Interagency Coordinating Council: A briefing paper on Part H of the Individuals with Disabilities Education Act (IDEA) 1986–1995. Chapel Hill, NC: University of North Carolina at Chapel Hill.

National Early Childhood Technical Assistance System (NEC*TAS). August 1995. *Assisting our nation's preschool children with disabilities and their families*. Ad Hoc 619 Work Group for Federal Interagency Coordinating Council: A briefing paper on section 619 of Part B of the Individuals with Disabilities Act (IDEA), 1986–1995. Chapel Hill, NC: University of North Carolina at Chapel Hill.

National Early Childhood Technical Assistance System (NEC*TAS). November 1995. *Part H updates*. Chapel Hill, NC: University of North Carolina at Chapel Hill.

National Governors' Association. May 1995. *Issue brief. Providing health insurance coverage to uninsured children*. Washington, DC: Author.

Nelson, M.D. 1992. Socioeconomic status and childhood mortality in North Carolina. *American Journal of Public Health 82*, 1131–1133.

Nelson, K., and L.B. Holmes. 1989. Malformation due to presumed spontaneous mutations in newborn infants. *New England Journal of Medicine 320*, 19–23.

Nersesian, W.S. et al. 1985. Childhood death and poverty: A study of childhood deaths in Maine, 1976–1980. *Pediatrics 75*, 41–50.

Newacheck, P. 1994. Poverty and childhood chronic illness. *Archives of Pediatric and Adolescent Medicine 148*, 1143–1150.

Newacheck, P., and W.R. Taylor. 1992. Childhood chronic illness: Prevalence, severity, and access to health services. *Pediatrics 84*, 872–881.

Oberg, C.N. 1987. Pediatrics and poverty. *Pediatrics 79*, 567–569.

Oberg, C.N. 1990. Medically uninsured children in the United States: A challenge to the public policy. *Pediatrics 85*, 824–833.

Olds, D.I., and H. Kitzman. 1990. Can home visitation improve the health of women and children at environmental risk? *Pediatrics 86*, 108–116.

Olds, D.I., and H. Kitzman. 1993. Review of research on home visiting for pregnant women and parents of young children. *The Future of Children 3*, 53–90.

Palfrey, J.S. 1994. *Community child health: An action plan for today*. Westport, CT: Praeger.

Parker, S. et al. 1988. Double jeopardy: The impact of poverty on early child development. *Pediatric Clinics of North America 35,* 1227–1240.

Ramey, C.T. et al. 1978. Predicting school failure from information available at birth. *American Journal of Mental Deficiency 82,* 524–534.

Ramey, C.T. et al. 1992. Infant health and development program for low-birthweight, premature infants: Program elements, family participation, and child intelligence. *Pediatrics 89,* 454–465.

Richardson, S.A. et al. 1984. Career paths through mental retardation services: An epidemiological perspective. *Applied Research Mental Retardation 5,* 53–67.

Rice, D.P. et al. 1989. *Cost of injury in the United States: A report to Congress.* San Francisco, CA: Institute for Health and Aging, University of California and Injury Prevention Center, The Johns Hopkins University.

Rivara, F.P. et al. 1989. Risk of injury to children less than five years of age in day care versus home care settings. *Pediatrics 84,* 1011–1016.

Rivera, L. et al. 1995. *Managed care and children's health: An analysis of early and periodic screening, diagnosis, and treatment services under state Medicaid managed care contracts.* Los Angeles, CA: National Health Law Program.

Roberts, S. 1994. *Who we are.* New York: The New York Times.

Roth, L. 1990. Children of homeless families: Health status and access to health care. *Journal of Community Health 15,* 275–284.

Rush, D. et al. 1988. The national WIC evaluation: Evaluation of the Special Supplemental Food Program for Women, Infants and Children. *American Journal of Clinical Nutrition 48,* 389–519.

Sachs, J.J. et al. 1989. The epidemiology of injuries in Atlanta day care centers. *Journal of American Medical Association 262,* 1641–1645.

Schorr, L.B., and D. Schorr. 1988. *Within our reach: Breaking the cycle of disadvantage.* New York: Anchor Press, Doubleday.

Schramm, W.F. 1986. Prenatal participation in WIC related to Medicaid costs for Missouri newborns: 1982 update. *Public Health Reports 101,* 607–615.

Scott, K.G., and W. Masi. 1979. The outcome from and utility of registers of risk. In *Infants born at risk,* eds. T.M. Field et al. New York: Spectrum Publications.

Shackelford, J. November 5, 1995. *State Jurisdiction Eligibility Definitions for Part H,* revised. Chapel Hill, NC: National Early Childhood Technical Assistance System (NEC*TAS), University of North Carolina at Chapel Hill.

Shonkoff, J., and P. Hauser-Cram. 1987. Early intervention for disabled infants and their families: A quantitative analysis. *Pediatrics 80,* 650–658.

Sicklick, M.J., and A. Rubenstein. 1992. Types of HIV infection and the course of the disease. In *HIV infection and developmental disabilities,* eds. A.C. Crocker et al. Baltimore, MD: Brookes Publishing Company.

Starfield, B. 1982. Family income, ill health, and medical care of U.S. children. *Journal of Public Health Policy 3,* 244–259.

State of North Carolina Office of State Planning. Fall 1995. Trends and implications. *State Planning Newsletter 2,* 2–3, Raleigh, NC: Author.

Taylor, M.L., and S.A. Koblinsky. 1993. Dietary intake and growth status of young homeless children. *Journal of American Dietetic Association 93,* 464–466.

Thurow, L. "Why their world might crumble." *New York Times Magazine,* 1 November 1995, 78–79.

Trohanis, P.L. May 1995. *Progress in providing services to young children with special needs and their families,* No. 7. Chapel Hill, NC: National Early Childhood Technical Assistance System (NEC*TAS).

Upshur, C.C. 1990. Early intervention as preventive intervention. In *Handbook of early childhood intervention,* eds. S.J. Meisels and J.P. Shonkoff. New York: Cambridge University Press.

U.S. Bureau of the Census. 1986. *Current population reports,* Series P-25, No. 985, Washington, DC: Author.

U.S. Bureau of the Census. 1994. *Statistical abstract of the United States: 1994,* 114th ed. Washington, DC: Government Printing Office.

U.S. Congress. 1973. *Child Abuse Prevention and Treatment Act,* 93-247.

U.S. Department of Education. 1995. *17th annual report to Congress on the implementation of the Individuals with Disabilities Education Act.* Washington, DC: Government Printing Office.

U.S. Department of Health and Human Services Health Care Financing Administration, Medicaid Bureau, Office of Managed Care. 1994. *Medicaid Managed Care Enrollment Report Summary Statistics as of June 30, 1994.* Washington, DC.

U.S. Department of Health and Human Services, Maternal and Child Health Bureau, Health Resources and Services Administration, Public Health Service, *Child health USA '93.* DHHS Pub. No. HRSA-MCH-94-1. Washington, DC: Government Printing Office, 1994.

U.S. Department of Health, Education and Welfare, Public Health Service, Health Services Administration, Bureau of Community Health Services. 1976. *Child health in America.* Rockville, MD: DHEW Publication No. (HSA) 76-5015.

U.S. General Accounting Office. April 1994. *Infants and toddlers: Dramatic increases in numbers living in poverty.* Pub. No. GAO/HEHS-94-74. Washington, DC: U.S. General Accounting Office.

U.S. General Accounting Office, Health, Education, and Human Services Division. February 14, 1995. *Uninsured children on Medicaid,* HEHS-95-83R. Washington, DC: General Accounting Office.

U.S. Public Health Service. 1991. *International classsification of disease, ninth revision, clinical modification.* U.S. Department of Health and Human Services, Health Care Financing Administration. DHHS Publication No. (PHS) 91–1260.

Waldmann, R.J. 1992. Income distribution and infant mortality. *Quarterly Journal of Economics 107,* 1283–1302.

Wardle, F., and N. Winegarner. 1992. Nutrition and Head Start. *Children Today 21,* 5–7.

Wasik, B.H. et al. 1990. *Home visiting: Procedures for helping families.* Newbury Park, CA: Sage Publishing Company.

Werner, E.E. et a!. 1971. *The children of Kauai: A longitudinal study from the prenatal period to age ten.* Honolulu, HI: University of Hawaii Press.

Wise, P.H., and A. Meyers. 1988. Poverty and child health. *Pediatric Clinics of North America 35,* 1169–1186.

Wolff, M. et al., and the World Bank Research Team. 1992. *Where we stand.* New York: Bantam Books.

Woodruff, G., and E.D. Sterzin. 1993. Family support services for drug- and AIDS-affected families. In *Families living with drugs and HIV,* eds. R.P. Barth et al. New York: Guilford Press.

Zero to Three/National Center for Clinical Infant Programs. 1994. *Diagnostic classification: 0–3. Diagnostic classification of mental health and developmental disorders of infancy and early childhood.* Arlington, VA: Author.

Zigler, E., and S. Muenchow. 1992. *Head Start: The inside story of America's most successful educational experiment.* New York: Basic Books.

Zigler, E. et al. 1994. Health services in Head Start. *Annual Review of Public Health 15,* 511–534.

CHAPTER 7

The School-Age Child from Five to Nine

Joseph Telfair and Jonathan B. Kotch

> *. . . When I was born in 1920, if you wanted to visit your family on Sundays you . . . went to the graveyard . . . My brother and sister died when I was 7. Half of my family was gone! Tell me, dear children, how many of your friends died while you were growing up?"*
> "None," said Rodney at last.
> "None! You hear that? . . . Six of my best friends died by the time I was ten!"
>
> R. Bradbury, 1994

INTRODUCTION

The transition to school for any child, whether reared primarily at home or with significant experience in out-of-home care, is the most profound transition for most children until the transition to work or residential college. Upon school entry the child becomes a worker, responsible for "producing things" (Erikson 1950). Although success in making this transition does not guarantee future health and happiness, in the developed world it is a rare individual these days who can become a healthy and productive adult following a failed career in school. Indeed, years of completed education is a powerful predictor of health status. Applying regression techniques to data from the National Vital Statistics System, the National Longitudinal Mortality Study, and the Area Resource File, Singh and Yu (1996) concluded, "The lower the level of educational attainment and the greater the poverty, the higher the childhood mortality rates."

The child entering the realm of formal education moves from a learning style based mostly on personal contacts to one based on symbols. The child's world expands from the familiar, circumscribed environment of direct experience to one whose history extends back over centuries and forward infinitely in time and space (Dewey 1956). As his or her physical and intellectual worlds expand, so do physical risks. It is in the school years that injury becomes the cause of over half of childhood deaths (U.S. DHHS 1991). In this chapter we review the demography, health status, health services, and health programs affecting U.S. children five to nine years of age.

DEMOGRAPHICS

Children five- to nine-years-old constitute 7.2 percent of the American population (U.S. DHHS 1995). The U.S. population of children five to nine declined from 1970 to 1980, and then went up again in 1990. By 1992, U.S. children five to nine numbered approximately 18,350,000. There were 9,396,000 boys and 8,954,000 girls (U.S. Bureau of the Census 1994). The racial composition of this population is as follows: there were 14,688,000 White children, 2,782,000 Black children, 215,000 American Indian/Eskimo/Aleut children, and 665,000 Asian/Pacific Islander children. Among these were 2,325,000 children of Hispanic origin, who could have been of any race (U.S. Bureau of the Census 1994).

Family Structure

During the last 30 years the percent of families with children under 18 percent declined. In 1990, 49 percent of all families had children under 18 years of age present. The decline since 1960 in the proportion of total families and married-couple families with children under 18 present occurred for all parental age groups (U.S. Department of Commerce 1992). There were 34.7 million family groups with children under age 8 in 1990; 9.7 million, or 28 percent, of these were maintained by one parent, with 8.4 million of these maintained by the mother. (In 1970, there were 3.8 million one-parent family groups, only 13 percent of the 29.6 million total.) In 1990, the proportions of family groups maintained by one-parent varied greatly by race with 23 percent for Whites, 61 percent for Blacks, and 33 percent for Hispanics (U.S. Bureau of the Census 1990).

Children and Poverty

In 1991, the overall poverty rate for children under 18 was 21.8 percent (U.S. Department of Commerce 1992). This rate indicates that more than one in five U.S. children live below the federal poverty line. This rate varies greatly by race and family type. Children in White families had the lowest poverty rates (15.9 percent), and children in Black families had the highest poverty rates (44.8 percent), with children in Hispanic families having rates closer to those of Whites (38.4 percent). The overall poverty rate in 1990 for children under 18 was much smaller for children in married-couple families (10.2 percent) than for children in female householder families (53.4 percent). Further, as indicated in the table below, poverty rates were much lower for children living in married-couple families than those living in single-parent households, over 85 percent of which were female-headed (U.S. Bureau of the Census, 1990). However, in all categories of household type, poverty rates were much higher for Black and Hispanic children (who may be of any race) than for White children (see Table 7–1).

HEALTH STATUS

The years from five to nine are the healthiest of any age bracket in the United States, if judged by the mortality rate, 0.2 per 1,000 in 1985 (National Center for Health Statistics 1989). Major concerns in child health have shifted from natural causes (infectious diseases primarily) to the so-called new morbidities (injury-related mortality and morbidity; psychological, emotional, and learning disorders; and chronic physical and developmental conditions) (U.S. DHHS 1991). Improved living standards, community-based prevention, and effective immunization against infectious diseases all have made major contributions to reducing childhood mortality in this century. Yet the United States is still behind other industrialized nations in childhood mortality, primarily due to excess deaths attributable to injury (Williams and Kotch 1990). A quarter of these deaths result from motor vehicle injuries alone. Though seat belt use and other safety measures (such as childproof safety caps, smoke detectors, bicycle helmets, flame-retardant clothing, etc.) have reduced mortality rates due to unintentional injury, rates of death due to violence have been rising among children (U.S. DHHS 1989).

Table 7–1 Percent of Poverty by Household Type and Race for U.S. Children 1990

Household Type	All (%)	White (%)	Hispanic (%)	Black (%)
All	19.9 (%)	15.1 (%)	37.7 (%)	44.2 (%)
Married	10.2 (%)	9.2 (%)	26.5 (%)	18.1 (%)
Female-headed household	53.4 (%)	46.0 (%)	68.5 (%)	64.8 (%)

Source: Reprinted from U.S. Bureau of the Census 1990, Demographic State of the Nation: 1990, *Current Population Reports,* Special Studies Series, P-23, No. 170, U.S. Department of Commerce.

Epidemiology of Major Health Problems

Natural Causes

Death rates in this age group declined 66 percent from 1900 to 1933, 62.5 percent between 1933 and 1950, 33.3 percent from 1950 to 1970, and 50 percent from 1970 to 1985 (National Center for Health Statistics 1989). That 50 percent decline was the highest of any age bracket among all people in the United States. Because natural causes were declining faster than external causes (69 percent between 1933 and 1950 for natural causes, compared with 35 percent for external causes), the proportion of all deaths attributable to external causes has been increasing. In 1900 an estimated 89.9 percent of child deaths were due to natural causes. Sometime between 1970 and 1971, natural causes resulted in fewer than 50 percent of deaths among U.S. five- to nine-year-olds for the first time in history (National Center for Health Statistics 1989).

Infectious Diseases

In 1900 diphtheria alone caused 10 percent of all deaths in U.S. school-age children (National Center for Health Statistics 1989). By 1992 there was no infectious disease among the top five killers of such children (U.S. DHHS 1995). On the other hand, infectious disease is the leading cause of visits to the doctor for sick care (Hardy 1991) and a major cause of hospitalization in this age group (U.S. DHHS 1995).

The 1988 Child Health Supplement to the National Health Interview Survey (NHIS-CHS) (National Center for Health Statistics 1989) asked respondents about nine of the most common childhood infectious diseases. Using a seven-year age bracket (5–11), the survey discovered that repeated ear infections were the most common complaint in the past year (8.8 percent), followed by repeated tonsillitis (5.5 percent). Half of school-age children who had either condition had to limit their activity. Pneumonia was the leading infectious disease cause of hospitalization, but children with mononucleosis were hospitalized longer. Children in the 5–11-year-old bracket were the age group most likely to have surgery for repeated tonsillitis or repeated ear infections, to lose the most school days and spend more time in bed due to mononucleosis, and to see the doctor for repeated tonsillitis and bladder or urinary infections (Hardy 1991).

Chronic Illness

Preliminary data from the new National Health Interview Survey on Disability (NHIS-D 1994) suggest that 16 to 18 percent of U.S. children under age 18 have chronic physical, developmental, behavioral, or emotional conditions having some degree of functional impact or requiring services. Eschewing one definition of disability developed by Stein et al. (1993), the questionnaire identifies children with disabilities or special needs through questions in the following areas: limitation of activity (from the NHIS core), impairments (for example, vision, hearing, mobility), activities of daily living (children > 5 years of age), a condition list, special health care needs, special education services, and early child development (Simpson 1993). For children under the age of 18, the most prevalent conditions included respiratory allergies (9.7 percent), asthma (4.2 percent), eczema and skin allergies (3.3 percent), frequent or severe headaches (2.5 percent), and speech defects (2.6 percent). Diabetes (0.1 percent), sickle cell disease (0.1 percent), and cerebral palsy (0.2 percent) were among the less prevalent conditions (Newacheck and Taylor 1992; Silverman and Koretz 1989). However, the prevalence of these conditions is higher in certain populations (e.g., the prevalence of sickle cell disease for Blacks is 1 in 400). Further, the severity of chronic conditions for children under 18 years of age varies. For example, 20 percent were mildly affected, 9 percent of children experienced more than occasional bother or limitation of activity, but not both, and 2 percent were severely affected (Newacheck and Taylor 1992).

The absolute numbers of children with chronic illness is not expected to change dramatically in the coming decades (Newacheck and Taylor 1992). Although more children with chronic conditions will survive due to improvements in medical technology and practice, these increases will be offset by demographic trends leading to fewer births (National Center for Health Statistics 1995). Nonetheless, the *prevalence* of children with chronic conditions, or the percentage of this population affected at a particular time, continues to increase. Growing populations of children with special health care needs include those with human immunodeficiency virus (HIV) infection and the population of children who are dependent upon advanced medical technology such as ventilators, gastrostomies, and tracheostomies (Palfrey et al. 1991). However, improvements in diagnosis (e.g., asthma hearing impairments) and longer survival due to medical advances (e.g., cystic fibrosis) are credited in the increasing prevalence of certain diseases (Richardson 1989; Schidlow and Fiel 1990).

Mental Health

In previous decades, emotional and behavioral problems among children were treated because they were seen as precursors of adult disorders. More recently, these problems have come to be seen as important in their own right (Drotar and Bush 1985). The Institute of Medicine, the Office of Technology Assessment, and other groups have estimated that 12 to 15 percent of U.S. children suffer from mental disorders (Zill and Schoenborn 1990). The comparable proportion in the 1988 NHIS-CHS was 10 percent, indicating that the use of psychological assistance for children had increased by more than 50 percent between the two surveys (Zill and Schoenborn 1990).

Data from the 1988 NHIS-CHS indicate that the cumulative proportion of children who have ever had emotional or behavioral problems should increase fairly steadily with age. The proportion of children who had ever had an emotional or behavioral problem rose from 5.3 percent at ages 3–5 years, to 12.7 percent at ages 6–11 years, to 18.5 percent at ages 12–17 years. One-quarter emerged during the preschool years (3–5) and another quarter during the early elementary years (6–8). Twenty-two percent became evident during the adolescent years (12–17). Increases in childhood psychological disorders have been attributed to the growing proportions of children who experience parental divorce, were born outside of marriage, or are raised in conflict-filled families or low-income, low-education, single-parent households (Zill and Schoenborn 1990).

NHIS-CHS data also indicate that the prevalence of childhood emotional and behavioral problems showed significant variation across family income groups, with children from less advantaged backgrounds standing a somewhat greater chance of exhibiting such problems. The prevalence declined from 15.8 percent among children from families with incomes less than $10,000 per year or 12.8 percent among those with family incomes of $40,000 or more (Zill and Schoenborn 1990). Income-related differences were more pronounced among elementary school children and adolescents than among preschoolers.

Further, the 1988 NHIS-CHS indicates that prevalence of childhood emotional and behavioral problems varied by differences in family structure. The prevalence of emotional and behavioral problems was 8.3 percent in mother-father families, 19.1 percent in mother-only families, 23.6 percent in mother-stepfather families, and 22.2 percent in other family situations (Zill and Schoenborn 1990). However, the frequency of problems among children in mother-only families may have been understated because of the large proportions of Black and Hispanic persons in this group.

Although mental health problems are relatively common among children, especially among those with health problems (Drotar and Bush 1985), most cases are mild and resolve without treatment. Nonetheless, there is a core of persistent, disabling disorders—notably conduct disorder, multiple disorders, autism, and childhood schizophrenia—that require focused and sustained treatment. Data from the 1988 NHIS-CHS indicate that although the overall prevalence with regard to emotional or behavioral problems was 13.4 percent of all children 3 to 17 years of age, just 10 percent had ever received counseling or treatment (Zill and Schoenborn 1990). This fact should be of great concern to maternal and child health (MCH) practitioners, in that: (1) the etiology of most childhood emotional and behavioral problems is not well understood; (2) many providers have not been adequately trained to recognize and deal with these types of problems; and (3) procedures for referring children for psychological diagnosis and treatment are not standardized. Thus, there is believed to be a substantial group of young people with developmental or behavioral disorders whose problems go untreated and perhaps even unrecognized (Silverman and Koretz 1989). Because of the significant life stresses faced by children with emotional and behavioral difficulties, untreated mental health problems can often lead to further difficulties in adolescence and adulthood. Prevention at all levels can play a major role in reducing the prevalence of, or the exacerbation of, these problems.

Developmental Disabilities

In 1984, the Developmental Disabilities Act (PL 98-527) referred to a developmental disability as a "severe, chronic condition attributable to a mental or physical impairment, manifest before the age of 22 and likely to continue indefinitely." In recent amendments to this legislation (PL 101-496, 1990), infants at risk for developmental disabilities, including preterm children, and infants born to mothers who used substances are also included for state planning purpose. Prevalence-estimate data from the 1988 NHIS-CHS indicate that 4.0 percent of U.S. children ages 17 years and under have had a delay in their growth or development, that is, there is an estimated 2.5 million children who have developmental delays. The 1988 NHIS-CHS indicates that the proportion of children with developmental delays was 4.1 percent at ages 6–11 years, and 3.6 percent in the adolescent years, ages 12–17 (Zill and Schoenborn 1990).

The 1988 NHIS-CHS also indicated that prevalence of developmental delay varied by differences in family income and education, but these differences were relatively small. Among family income groups, only the comparison between the lowest category—less than $10,000 per year—and the highest—$40,000 or more per year—showed (statistically) significant differences (Zill and Schoenborn 1990). That is, of the children in the less than $10,000 per year families, 5.4 percent had developmental delays, but of those in the $40,000 or more per year families, 3.9 percent had developmental delays. Further, in regard to family structure, 1988 NHIS-CHS data indicated that the prevalence of developmental delays showed little significant variation across family types. The prevalence of developmental delays was 3.8 percent among children from mother-father families, 4.5 percent among children in mother-only families, 3.7 percent in mother-stepfather families, and 4.8 percent in all other family situations (children living with fathers only, or fathers and stepmothers, with grandparents or other relatives, or in adoptive or foster families).

In the 1988 NHIS-CHS, Black parents were less likely than White parents to report that their children had developmental delays. Hispanic parents also reported slightly fewer developmental problems in their children than did non-Hispanic parents. Thus, the overall prevalence of developmental delays was 2.1 percent among Black and 4.4 percent among White children; 3.4 percent among Hispanic and 4.2 percent among non-Hispanic children (Zill and Schoenborn 1990). The proportion was 6.2 percent among Black and 6.7 percent among White children; 5.8 percent among Hispanic and 6.6 percent among non-Hispanic children. The proportion of children ages 3–17 years reported to have had emotional and behavioral problems was 10.3 percent among Black and 14.2 percent among White children; 12.0 percent among Hispanic and 13.6 percent among non-Hispanic children. When all three types of childhood conditions were examined, the prevalence was 14.9 percent among Black, 20.7 percent among White, and 17.2 percent among non-Hispanic children.

Lastly, in the 1988 NHIS-CHS, two percent of all children ages 17 years and under had ever received treatment or counseling for a delay in growth or development. That is, less than half (49 percent) of those reported to have had such a delay received some form of treatment, with half of this group receiving treatment in the previous 12 months. As with mental health problems, this low rate of treatment for these problems should be of concern to MCH practitioners.

Learning Disabilities

The proportion of children who were reported in 1988 NHIS-CHS to have learning disabilities was higher than the proportion known to be receiving special educational services according to school record data. Of total public school children, 4.8 percent were recorded as receiving special educational services for learning disabilities in 1987, more than double the 1.8 percent recorded in 1977. However, 6.5 percent of all children ages 3–17 years (or 3.4 million) were reported in the 1988 NHIS-CHS to have learning disabilities, and 5.5 percent of those ages 6–17 years were reported to have attended special classes or a special school because of such disabilities (Zill and Schoenborn 1990). Further, in contrast to developmental delays, most learning disabilities are not fully apparent until the child gets to school and starts trying to read, write, and calculate. Therefore, a substantial rise in the prevalence of learning disabilities as children reached school age was expected. This is what was found. The proportion of children with learning disabilities jumped from 1.6 percent at ages 3–5 years to 6.8 percent in the elementary school ages, 6–11 years. There was a further increase to 8.8 percent in the junior high and high school ages, 12–17 years. One-quarter of the learning disabilities became apparent during the nursery school or kindergarten years (ages 3–5 years), and another 45 percent were first noticed in early elementary school (ages 6–8 years).

The prevalence of learning disabilities also varied by family structure. In the 1988 NHIS-CHS the prevalence of learning disabilities was 5.5 percent among children in mother-father families, 7.5 percent in mother-only families, 9.1 percent in mother-stepfather families, and 8.3 percent in other family situations (Zill and Schoenborn 1990). Further, learning disabilities varied significantly by parental education and family income. Overall, the prevalence of learning problems decreased with increasing years of education or increasing income. That is, the proportion of children reported to have learning disabilities was 8.7 percent of children with mothers with less than 12 years of schooling, 6.8 percent for those whose mothers had more than 12 years of schooling. The prevalence of learning disabilities was 8.4 percent among children from families with incomes less than $10,000 per year and decreased as income rose, with 5.8 percent among children in families with incomes of $40,000 or more (Zill and Schoenborn 1990).

Moreover, Zill and Schoenborn point out that despite the apparent excess of learning disabilities in the 1988 NHIS-CHS data, there is evidence that learning disabilities were underidentified in populations of color. The reason for this is that with regard to the risk factors for learning disabilities—low parental education and income levels, low birth weight, single-parenthood, etc.—Blacks and Hispanics have higher rates than Whites. However, Black parents were about equally as likely as White parents to report learning disabilities, and Hispanic parents reported slightly fewer developmental problems in their children than did non-Hispanic parents. Thus, the overall prevalence of children ages 3–17 with learning disabilities was 6.2 percent among Black and 6.7 percent among White children, with 5.8 percent among Hispanic children and 6.6 percent among non-Hispanic children. Explanations of the reporting differences have included lack of familiarity with the terms used to describe learning disabilities and differential recall of past events between Whites and peoples of color (Zill and Schoenborn 1990). However, it is important to keep in mind the different cultural perceptions and mores of Whites and persons of color regarding what constitutes a learning deficiency (how it is both perceived and defined) and how much and what type of information should be shared with strangers (Jackson 1981; Jones and Roberts 1994; Nettles 1994; Telfair and Nash 1996). Finally, given more limited access to medical care (see below), children of color may be less likely to have had a learning disability diagnosed than White children.

Lastly, in the 1988 NHIS-CHS about 5 percent of all children ages 3–17 years, or more than three-quarters of those with learning disabilities, had received treatment or counseling for their disabilities and most of these children (three-fifths) had received treatment or counseling in the previous 12 months (Zill and Schoenborn 1990).

External Causes

External causes (including both intentional and unintentional injury) are the leading causes of death in the 5–9 age group. Unintentional injury causes the most deaths (within which motor vehicle injury is the single leading cause of death, followed by fires, burns, and drowning). The fourth leading injury cause of death in this age group is homicide (U.S. DHHS 1995).

Community-based strategies to prevent injury death have been largely successful in reducing death rates. Examples of such successes include seat belt use and other safety measures that have lowered traffic fatalities, smoke detectors to reduce deaths due to house fires, childproof caps on medications, and bicycle helmets. On the other hand, rates of death due to homicide have risen among children 5–14 by a factor of two to three (Singh and Yu 1996).

Injuries more often are not fatal. In this age group (5–9), injury is the second leading cause of hospitalization, resulting in 60,000 hospital discharges a year (U.S. DHHS 1995). Unfortunately, not all of these children are discharged healthy. Injury is the leading cause of acquired disability among school-age children. In addition to hospitalization, injury may result in an emergency room or doctor visit, activity limitation, days lost from school, bed-disability days, etc.

HEALTH CARE ACCESS AND UTILIZATION

Use of health services by children is qualitatively different from that of adults. Children use proportionately more ambulatory and preventive care and less hospital care than adults (U.S. DHHS 1981). As a direct result, annual health care costs for children (excluding infants) are less than those of adults, even of adults under 65. For children ages 6–17, total annual health care expenditures in 1987, $730, was less than that of any other age group. Yet, more than half of that expense was paid out-of-pocket (Lefkowitz and Monheit 1991).

The need for immunizations, and indeed for routine well-child visits in general, declines in the school years. This explains why older school-age children (8–11) were the least likely age group among all children under 18 to have had a routine doctor visit in 1988 (Bloom 1990). Another reason for lack of a doctor visit for routine medical care, or for not having a regular source of routine health care in the first place, is uninsuredness. Not surprisingly, privately insured children were more likely to use health care than either the uninsured or the publicly insured (predominantly those on Medicaid), despite the fact that privately insured children are reported to experience more favorable health status (Lefkowitz and Monheit 1991). This inequity seems to characterize the nation's approach to children's health care needs in general. Children are disproportionately uninsured. There is a big drop in Medicaid coverage between those under 5 (25 percent coverage) and 5–14 year olds (15.6 percent), which is not made up for by a proportionate increase in private insurance coverage (National Center for Health Statistics 1994). In fact, private insurance coverage of all children under 18, particularly employer-based health insurance coverage, is decreasing steadily. Private health insurance coverage of all children under 18 declined from 73.5 percent in 1988 to 69.3 percent in 1992 (Newacheck et al. 1995). Although Medicaid and other public insurance has been able to compensate so far, policy initiatives at the national level to cut Medicaid funding and eliminate federal entitlements to Medicaid are ominous.

Medicaid has unquestionably been a boon to poor children. Poor children have reached near parity with nonpoor children in average number of doctor visits, thanks in large part to Medicaid. Medicaid served a total of 14,481,000 children, 21.6 percent of all children under 18, in 1992 (Newacheck et al. 1995). However, this parity does not take need for care into account. Poor children, who have poorer health status, should be seeing physicians and other health care providers more than their nonpoor counterparts if need for care were the driving principle. In fact, poor children experience fewer doctor visits for well-child care, report using clinics and other institutional settings for routine care more often, and utilize more days in a hospital than nonpoor children (U.S. DHHS 1981).

Similar concerns attend upon privately insured children, since even they may not be covered for preventive care, or may have to pay a substantial copayment. Parents are more likely to put off so-called "patient-initiated" doctor visits for well-child care that they themselves have to pay for. The Rand Health Insurance Experiment attempted to measure the effect of insurance copayments on utilization and health status of participants. Children whose parents were in an indemnity-type insurance plan with higher copayments had fewer doctor visits, but in general their health status was no worse. However, there was a footnote to these findings. Although the numbers of poor children were too small to permit a significant statistical test, there were indications in the findings that, for poor children whose utilization of care suffered from the imposition of copayments, health status did suffer (Valdez et al. 1985).

Community-Based Services for Children and Families

Community-based services are those provided to children and families outside of traditional institutional settings and in proximity to where clients live. These services include those provided by local health departments, community clinics, social service satellite programs, specialized umbrella programs, etc. Community-based services for children and their families are best exemplified by the model of the Family Resource Center (FRC). FRCs (depending on size and range of services), like most community-based programs, attempt to encompass a holistic or ecological approach to serving children and families that includes both health and human services. Precursors of FRCs were the community family service agencies that had as their primary mission assistance to families after they have experienced a crisis. The primary goal was to provide whatever services the family needed that would enable them to stay together after the crisis experience (Weiss and Halpern 1990; Weissbourd and Patrick 1988).

In the mid-1960s, as the war on poverty heated up and the concept of empowerment entered the human services repertoire (Kadushin 1980), there was a recognition of the need for a broad range of programs that should be available to families on a continuum from prevention through early intervention to crisis management and long-term supportive measures. This recognition led to the current emphasis of prevention and building on the strengths of families. Preventive programs, the first of the programs on the continuum, are designed to help families before they are in crisis by attempting to reach all families (program access) and to reflect the strengths, needs, and culture of the families whom they serve (cultural access). An overall goal of these programs is to assess families' competencies and strengths and to empower them (through the provision of support services) to function adeptly within their existing environments. They focus on the building, preserving, reinforcing, and maintaining of family strengths, sense of worth, and competence. Current family resource programs, like other community-based services programs, may take a variety of forms or service emphases. These include: (1) comprehensive drop-in centers; (2) parent education; (3) crisis intervention services; (4) support groups services; (5) home visitors services; (6) information and referral services; (7) parent advocacy services; (8) other family-centered service delivery models; and (9) any combination of these emphases. Given the range of program or service emphasis, family resource and other community-based service programs having a family-centered and public health focus and rely on a number of basic principles. These principles are:

- *Focus on prevention.* Family resource programs clearly emphasize prevention over treatment. Such programs seek to assist families to meet their needs and head off problems before they develop. Yet, they also go one step further and embrace the concept of *optimalism.* Optimalism means "providing an environment conducive to the optimal development of children through the support of the family and maintenance of a viable community" (Weiss and Halpern 1990; Weissbourd and Patrick 1988). This definition does not specify a target population as it implies that all children have the right to an optimal environment in which they can grow into healthy adults. Thus, family resource programs serve all families regardless of economic status, race ethnicity, composition, or capabilities.
- *Recognition of the importance of the early years.* Research has demonstrated that strong, healthy attachments and positive experiences in the early years provide a solid foundation for further positive social, cognitive, and emotional development. As a result, family resource programs often provide support programs and services for extended periods of time, primarily during pregnancy and through the preschool years, so as to help establish an optimal reciprocal relationship between parents and their young children.
- *Ecological approach.* Children do not exist in a vacuum, but are embedded in families and communities. If a child is to develop in a truly healthy manner, then attention must be paid to the family and community in which that child lives. Such attention takes two forms in the context of family resource programs. First, family resource programs respect the cultural and social tra-

ditions of the many diverse groups that currently reside in the United States. Secondly, family resource programs seek to build up communities by strengthening the bonds between people and the services in the community in which they live, thereby strengthening the informal support system of communities.

- *Holistic view of parents.* Family resource programs take a holistic view of parents. Parents have their own needs, desires, and interests aside from those of their children, and they are more than vessels into which to pour information. They learn from experience as well as from facts and tend to assimilate information as it relates to their lives. Adults who have positive self-esteem and express confidence in their child-rearing skills in turn enhance their children's social and cognitive development.
- *Value of support.* Family support services help reduce social isolation, provide information, and enhance coping abilities. They seek to build upon family strengths rather than emphasize deficits. The ability of a family to develop friendships, to make linkages with other groups, and to seek advice and information is considered a strength. Parents may become empowered to take control of their lives on a neighborhood or national level through their experiences with a family resource program.

Lastly, because of the advantages of access (physical and cultural) and emphases of prevention, empowerment, and support, community-based programs play an important role in the provision of needed services to school-age children and their families.

School Health

School health activities were one of the earliest public health interventions targeted specifically at children. Leading the way were Dr. Sara Josephine Baker (see Chapter 1) and Lillian Wald, who, based in New York's Henry Street Settlement, organized in 1893 the first visiting nurse service and subsequently the first school health nursing program in the country. These early efforts (1) used the school setting to short-cut infectious disease surveillance strategies in an effort to identify and quarantine children whose diseases were a threat to others; and (2) directed health education, screening, and disease prevention activities for the benefit of the children served and their families.

Public school entry is the first time since birth that virtually all children in the United States are within the purview of an institutional setting. This creates an opportunity for proactive health intervention that has only partly been taken advantage of in this country. Traditional school health activities, such as screening tests and routine medical history and examination, are of "low effectiveness" and "limited value" respectively (American Academy of Pediatrics 1981). On the other hand, a comprehensive school health program cannot only promote a child's achievement of health literacy, "the capacity to obtain, interpret, and understand basic health information and services and the competence to use such information and services in ways which enhance health" (Joint Committee 1995, p. 5). It can also make a direct contribution to the general education of the child. According to J. Michael McGinnis, former Director of Disease Prevention and Health Promotion of the U.S. Public Health Service, a child who is not healthy will not "profit optimally from the educational process" (American School Health Association 1994, p. 224).

The goals of a comprehensive school health program are to promote health, prevent injury and disease, prevent high risk behavior, intervene to help children in need or at risk, help those with special needs, and promote positive health and safety behaviors. The program has eight separate components: school environment; health education; health services; physical education; counseling, guidance, and mental health; food service and nutrition; worksite health promotion; and integration of school and community activities. The school environment addresses not only the safety of the physical environment but a supportive psychosocial environment as well. Health education is to be integrated into the academic curriculum and to result in changes in students' knowledge, attitudes, behaviors, and skills (American School Health Association 1994).

Physical education should devote at least 60 percent of its time to instruction that can translate into a program of lifelong, health-related physical activity. Counseling, guidance, and mental health addresses direct services to students with psychosocial needs, in conjunction with other community-based resources. School food service and nutrition includes both nutritionally appropriate meals at a reasonable price, and education in making responsible, healthy food choices. Worksite health promotion is directed at school district employees. Integration of school and community health activities seeks to maximize health and health-related services for school-age children through coordination, integration, and communication with existing health resources, including parents (American School Health Association 1994).

School health services are a special case. These may vary from the minimum required by law (such as dental, hearing, vision, and spinal screening, and sports physicals) to the delivery of hands-on personal health services on school grounds. School-based and school-linked health centers, totaling about 30 in the early 1980s, now number in the hundreds (U.S. General Accounting Office 1994). Although more common in middle and high schools, school-based clinics are not unknown at the elementary level. About 9 percent of all school-based and school-linked health centers serve primary school children, and another 12 percent serve both primary and secondary school students (U.S. General Accounting Office 1994).

There are many different school-based and school-linked health center models. They may be staffed by school district employees or local health department employees, may be available to a specific subpopulation of the student body or to all (with parental consent), and may be limited to screening and referral for initial complaints or provide comprehensive primary and preventive care. In most cases mid-level providers, primarily nurse practitioners and physician assistants, provide the bulk of the services. The most controversial issue, which has to be confronted in establishing a school-based health center (SBHC) at the high school level—the provision of reproductive health services—is less of a problem at the elementary school level. Financing, staffing, third-party reimbursement, and responding to dental and mental health needs are continuing problems. Nevertheless, the SBHCs are low cost, convenient, and "can improve children's access to health care . . . especially those who are poor or uninsured" (U.S. General Accounting Office 1994, p. 5).

OUTSTANDING ISSUES

Child Abuse and Neglect

Child abuse and neglect are continuing to increase in the United States, and the data do not reflect only an increased awareness and willingness to report (National Center for Health Statistics 1995). In her re-analysis of the 1986 national incidence study, Sedlak (1991) concluded that the countable incidence of child maltreatment, 22.6 per 1,000, increased 51 percent over the 1980 incidence rate. Although the increase could have been caused by increased recognition by professionals of maltreatment leading to moderate injury, "the possibility remained that the findings reflected increases in the incidence of occurrence of moderate injury cases" (Sedlak 1991, pp. 3–15). Subsequent to Sedlak's analysis, a Gallup poll reported that a survey of parents revealed a rate of abuse 16 times that estimated by official statistics (Lewin 1995).

There are different patterns of abuse among school-age children compared with infants and preschoolers. Older children are significantly more likely to experience physical abuse than those in younger age groups; yet the youngest children are more likely to be fatally abused, and the older more likely to experience moderate injury (Sedlak 1991). Overall, there were no age differences for neglect, but two subcategories, emotional and educational neglect, were higher for older children. Finally, sexual abuse rates also increased with age (Sedlak 1991).

In order to qualify for federal child protective services funding, states must implement child abuse and neglect legislation that mandates reporting, conforms with federal definitions of abuse and neglect, and provides prevention and treatment services within the guidelines of the law (U.S. Congress 1973). Unfortunately, CPS agencies as currently constituted are inadequate to the task. Problems include underfunding; inadequate and inadequately trained staff; lack of coordination among the legal, criminal justice, health, social service, and education communities; inadequate or conflicting laws and policies; and lack of responsibility among the general public (U.S. Advisory Board 1995). Many cases reported to CPS are not substantiated, and, according to McCurdy and Daro (1992), hundreds of thousands of substantiated cases do not even receive basic services.

The answer to child maltreatment is prevention, but prevention requires knowing the underlying causes. Yet few resources have been expended to understand the etiology of abuse and neglect. Not only are the funds available for child abuse and neglect research inadequate, but the very agency designated by Congress to lead the national effort to investigate the phenomenon of child maltreatment, the National Center on Child Abuse and Neglect (NCCAN), was abolished by the welfare reform legislation that emerged from the 1996 Congress. Nevertheless, it is clear that child abuse and neglect cannot be overcome without attention to social and economic conditions (poverty, substandard housing, inadequate education, broken families, unemployment, substance abuse) that put children and families at risk of a myriad of health problems. In addition, stressful life events and lack of social support have been shown to contribute to the risk of abuse and neglect (Kotch et al. 1995).

AIDS/HIV

Pediatric AIDS (acquired immune deficiency syndrome) is defined as clinical AIDS in children under 13 years of age. AIDS was not recognized in children until well after its initial description in adults (Work Group on HIV/AIDS 1988). Initially it was difficult to distinguish AIDS from other rare congenital immunodeficiency diseases in children, but several researchers convincingly demonstrated that HIV affects the pediatric as well as the adult population (Work Group on HIV/AIDS, 1988). Nationally, the number of infants and children with AIDS from birth through age 13 represents about 1.4 percent of AIDS cases in the United States (U.S. DHHS 1995). In some metropolitan areas, however, the percentage of pediatric AIDS cases may be as high as 4 percent of total AIDS cases, a variation that reflects a correlation between perinatal transmission of HIV and the number of adult drug users who are infected with HIV. Recent studies demonstrate that HIV seropositivity has reached alarming levels among childbearing women in some major cities.

Of the more than 74,000 cases of AIDS reported to the Centers for Disease Control and Prevention (CDC) as of late September 1988, 1,185 were in infants and children under 13 years of age at the time of diagnosis. More than half of those in the 0–12 year age group (672) were known to have died. As of June 30, 1994, the CDC reported that there were 5,734 cases of AIDS in children younger than 13 years of age. This number indicated an almost fivefold increase in the number of children diagnosed with AIDS. Further, this count reflects only those children with AIDS who have been reported to CDC. It does not include other infected children who are either asymptomatic or symptomatic at any of the earlier stages of disease. It is likely that for every child who meets the definition of AIDS, another 2 to 10 are infected with HIV (Work Group on HIV/AIDS, 1988).

The face of pediatric AIDS is changing. When first recognized in children, HIV infections were seen primarily among hemophiliacs and neonatal intensive care unit graduates, as these were children who had multiple exposures to blood products. Effective screening and processing of the blood supply has largely eliminated this vector of transmission (Stuber 1989). It is now well understood that HIV in children is transmitted by three routes: (1) from mothers to infants during the perinatal period; (2) through parenteral exposure to infected body fluids, primarily blood; and (3) through sexual contact (Rogers 1987). Rogers points out that perinatal transmission accounts nationwide for about three-quarters of cases of HIV infection in prepubertal children.

Recent reports indicate that prenatal transmission remains the primary form of transmission of HIV in children. Evidence suggests that HIV is transmitted from infected mothers to their infants in utero by transplacental passage of the virus; during labor and delivery through exposure to infected maternal blood and/or vaginal secretions; and, although infrequently reported, postnatally through breastfeeding. The remainder of infants and children have been infected primarily through blood transfusions or use of blood products. Rogers adds that the epidemiologic characteristics of these children closely parallel those of heterosexual adults with AIDS, particularly women. As of June 30, 1986, over half (65 percent) of reported cases of AIDS in women, 69 percent of heterosexual men with AIDS, and 73 percent of perinatally acquired AIDS cases in children were related to IV (intravenous) drug abuse and sexual contact with IV drug abusers (by the parent).

Pediatric HIV disease including AIDS differs from the disease in adults in a variety of ways. Children with AIDS often develop severe bacterial infections, and a large proportion have mental or motor retardation. The natural history of the disease is not only different in children; it is less well understood than in adults. Moreover, AIDS progresses very differently in different children. Most of the children reported with perinatally acquired AIDS (87 percent) had met the CDC case definition for AIDS before their third birthday, while three percent were diagnosed after their sixth birthday.

However, promising therapy that may dramatically affect this high rate of transmission is emerging. Peckham and Gibb (1995) report that randomized, placebo-controlled trials of the antiretroviral drug Azidothymidine (AZT) given to pregnant women in the United States and France resulted in the reduction of the risk of transmission from 25.5 percent to 8.3 percent. This promise of more than a threefold decrease in the number of infants born with HIV is significant, but will have an effect only if those mothers in the most at-risk groups receive this and other promising therapies.

The pediatric AIDS crisis is one small part of the overall crisis of AIDS, and it is also distinct from it. Today, most children with AIDS were born with HIV infection—born into families often living in poverty in which one or both parents may be HIV infected and drug dependent (Oleske 1989). Minority children, many of whom face urban poverty, poor health, lack of access to adequate health care, and educational disadvantages, comprise the majority of pediatric AIDS cases (Work Group on HIV/AIDS 1988). While Black children constitute 15 percent of the total U.S. child population, they represent 53 percent of all childhood AIDS cases; Hispanic children are 10 percent of the U.S. child population and represent 23 percent of all childhood AIDS cases.

Children with AIDS become sicker and die faster than do adults. However, infected infants and children who receive comprehensive health care have markedly fewer hospitalizations and experience an improved quality of life. However, this care comes at a price. Oleske (1989), Osterholm and MacDonald (1987), and Boland et al. (1992), point out that on average, the lengths of hospital stay for children with AIDS are longer and their bills are higher than comparable children with acute or other chronic conditions. Anecdotal data cited by Oleske (1989) suggest that inpatient hospital care for children with AIDS can run between $775 and $1,200 per day; or $16,000 to $18,000 per discharge. Further, using 1992 dollars, Boland et al. (1992) studied 136 children diagnosed with HIV, 44 of whom had full-blown AIDS, treated at New Jersey's Children's Hospital from 1988 to 1990. Although much of the care for these children was paid for by Medicaid, annualized hospital cost for children with AIDS was on average $44,403, compared to only $2,831 for asymptomatic children and $10,768 for symptomatic children. Given the natural history and complexity of the condition, the cost of providing a full range of services for the pediatric population with AIDS is expected to be high. However, the Work Group on HIV/AIDS (1988) points out that comprehensive ambulatory care and community-based services could considerably reduce in-hospital occupancy and its attendant costs.

Further, in regard to research-related treatment, Oleske (1989) observed that, because the route of infection with children is different from adults, because its impact on the child is complicated by the child's immature development, and because of the more limited access of children to drug treatment trials, the research needs of children are unique and often more expensive. However, 6 percent of all federal National Institutes of Health AIDS research dollars are devoted specifically to the problems of pediatric AIDS. That is, federal policy has only begun to address the challenges to health care financing for children with AIDS, the research challenges of children with AIDS, and the welfare as well as the health of whole families with AIDS (parents, children, and siblings).

The Pediatric Section of the Work Group on HIV/AIDS (1988) and others (Boland et al. 1992; Osterholm and MacDonald 1987; Stuber 1989) point out that coordination of care for these children and mothers is complicated by the precautions necessary to protect confidentiality and by the sheer enormity and complexity of the problems encountered. In addition, Stuber (1989) states that there is an enormous emotional cost of dealing with the problems involved in the treatment of HIV-infected patients as a group, especially children in families. These authors all believe that the expertise of many disciplines is needed to provide optimal care, including (but not limited to) nursing, social work, nutrition, psychiatry, psychology, child development, law, ethics, immunology, infectious disease, and obstetrics. Stuber (1989) argues that a multidisciplinary team can provide the mutual education, support, and understanding needed to overcome the fear and exhaustion reported by many health care professionals when they work with HIV infection or AIDS in this under-13 age group. Lastly, in her discussion of the development of a Maternal-Child HIV Task Force, Stuber (1989) states that the most efficient collaboration of such a diverse group requires some sort of forum in which they can meet and work.

MCH practitioners must keep in mind that children with AIDS have a particular dependency—in many cases, virtually total dependency—on the community and on government. This unique dependency arises from the complexity of their health care needs and the high costs of treatment, the stigma that they often face, the fragility of their families, and the poverty into which they are so often born. Further, as paraphrased from Osterholm and MacDonald (1987), MCH practitioners must first realize in a straightforward but compassionate manner that the great weight of pediatric AIDS will continue to fall on our communities of color, particularly in the innercity. It will be important for both those working with these communities and the communities themselves to take ownership in developing creative solutions to addressing the complex problems associated with pediatric HIV/AIDS and public health support, and to begin addressing its many complexities. In other words, individuals, communities, MCH practitioners, and government all need to respond.

Homelessness

Because of adverse phenomena faced by many Americans, including an increase in rates of poverty, increasing unemployment, rapidly rising housing prices, substance abuse, domestic violence, and diminished federal housing subsidies, a rapidly increasing number of Americans (estimated at about 3 million, in

1985) are homeless (Committee on Health Care for Homeless People, 1988; Redlender 1994; U.S. Bureau of the Census 1990). Recent attention to this problem has revealed a changing composition of the homeless population. What once consisted largely of older males now consists of increasing numbers of young men, women, and children. The fastest growing segment of the homeless are families, most commonly single mothers with two or three children. In 1986, nationwide, members of families with children represented an estimated 28 percent of the homeless population (Alperstein and Arnstein 1988) with children representing about one-third to one-half of homeless families (Reyes and Waxman 1987). It is generally acknowledged that the latter statisitic may be a gross undercount because it does not account for children and families living in rural areas, abandoned shacks, bus terminals, and street shanties or for runaway or "throwaway" adolescent youth (Children's Defense Fund 1988).

The largest number of homeless families reside in the major urban areas that include New York City, Denver, Philadephia, San Francisco, St. Paul, Salt Lake City, San Antonio, Seattle, and Washington, D.C. (Alperstein and Arnstein 1988). For example, according to Alperstein and Arnstein (1988), it is estimated that in New York State there are 50,000 homeless, of whom 85 percent are in New York City. Of these, the fastest-growing segment of the homeless is families, most commonly single mothers with two or three children, who now comprise 40 to 45 percent of that city's homeless population. In addition, the Committee on Health Care for Homeless People (1988) reports that in Washington, D.C., the number of families seeking shelter jumped 500 percent during 1986. Current figures are not available, but it is suspected that, given the increase in factors that put families at risk for homelessness, the number of families with no home in the United States is well over 1 million.

In these urban areas there is a significant lack of appropriate shelters for families with children. It has only been within the last decade that "welfare hotels" (those willing to take government subsidies to house homeless persons) and homeless shelters have had to make accommodation for women and children. These facilities are generally dilapidated, overcrowded, lack privacy or cooking facilities, and are breeding grounds for unsafe behaviors like substance abuse, violence, and prostitution. Many of these facilities provide day-to-day temporary sheltering, that is, families must stay outside of the shelters during daytime hours (for a number of reasons, including encouraging children to attend school and parent to search for jobs) (Alperstein and Arnstein 1988; Committee on Health Care for Homeless People, 1988). On average most of these facilities have an upper time limit for how long a family can stay (e.g., 14 months). However, in cities such as New York, families have stayed for as long as five years (Alperstein and Arnstein 1988). The experience of unstable housing, however long, has a significant impact on the health, education, and emotional development of children.

Homeless children, compared to domiciled children of poor families, are generally less healthy and experience greater psychosocial stress as a result of living under more adverse conditions (Acker et al. 1987; Alperstein and Arnstein 1988; Committee on Health Care for Homeless People, 1988; Redlender 1994). Very little is known, and even less has been published on the health status of children who are also homeless. Alperstein and Arnstein (1988) and Redlender (1994) report that, from what little is known, a disturbing pattern describing the health conditions of these young homeless children has emerged. These children have limited access to primary care. As a result, chronic health problems that include delayed immunizations, poor hygiene, anemia, poor diet and nutrition, and undetected and untreated emotional difficulties are much more likely in this population than in their domiciled, poor, same-age peers (Committee on Health Care for Homeless People, 1988). In addition, due to overcrowding, inadequate toilet facilities, and lack of knowledge of good hygiene, homeless children are also at high risk for various contagious diseases, such as enteric illness, childhood exanthems, and possibly tuberculosis (Alperstein and Arnstein 1988).

Alperstein and Arnstein (1988) point out that, if care is obtained, these children are more likely to use emergency health care providers than are domiciled poor families. Further, the difficulties of access to health care for the poor are exacerbated by their homelessness. Homeless families also have to deal with the difficulties of finding their way around unfamiliar neighborhoods to reach health providers. Thus, already overburdened by frequent changes in abode, the daily searches for affordable food, and the periodic attempts to find housing, parents are unlikely to be able to manage the health care system except for emergency care. Lastly, emotional difficulties experienced by all family members can threaten not only the well-being of the child but also can lead to temporary or permanent family dissolution. Like most problems experienced by children in general, homelessness affects the "whole health" of the child, his/her physical, psychological, spiritual, and social health.

Housing instability often interferes with a child's opportunity for education. Frequent moving does not allow a child to establish a base of relationships with teachers or peers, nor does it allow the school to put in place the necessary supports needed to allow the child to "catch up" academically with his/her peers. Unfortunately, as the Committee on Health Care for Homeless People (1988) states, many school systems may be indifferent to homeless children and, with some exceptions, are not equipped to help these children continue their education. Even for homeless children who are able to continue their education, their poor living conditions and poor health, hygiene, and nutrition make it difficult for them to keep up with the required work. In addition, emotional difficulties (e.g., depression) resulting from living under adverse conditions and exacerbated by stigmatization and teasing from peers only make a focus on learning much more difficult.

Children who are homeless have significant health and human service needs related to a number of factors including profound poverty, the stress of unstable housing, lack of a peer system, interrupted schooling, and living in a generally unsafe environment. MCH practitioners should take a holistic approach to addressing the needs of these children and families. This approach must include efforts to ensure that health, welfare, and education systems are sensitive to the egregious circumstances of familial homelessness. Interventions that attempt to create a welcoming environment also should provide advocacy for the empowerment of families and the amelioration of their problems.

CONCLUSION

Although on average, school-age children in the United States may be the healthiest population group in the country, they are also among the most vulnerable. While benefiting to an unprecedented extent from public health advances in the areas of infectious disease and other natural causes of morbidity and mortality, injuries—both intentional and unintentional—remain important threats to these children. Chronic illness and handicapping conditions, behavioral morbidities including social and emotional problems, learning disabilities, and social problems such as hunger and homelessness, and abuse and exploitation demand attention.

Yet it is during the school-age years that enormous potential exists for reaching vast numbers of children with services and health-promoting strategies, for it is in this age group, for the first time since birth, that children in the United States are nearly universally accessible through a helping institution. The success of utilizing the schools to enforce immunization requirements demonstrates the opportunity to reach children and their families at this stage of their development. Recognizing this, Freedman et al. (1988) proposed that public schools be used to define insurable groups for the purpose of obtaining health care coverage for uninsured and underinsured children and their families. Initiatives like this could be expanded to include setting the stage for healthier adolescence and adulthood by emphasizing injury prevention, physical activity, dental health, good nutrition, and healthful, prosocial interpersonal relationships. Teachers and others in schools see children every day and would be appropriate sources for early referral for health, developmental, social, and emotional problems, were there resources available to respond. Inadequate funding and preoccupation with so-called family rights has prevented the United States from maximizing the potential of generations of children.

REFERENCES

Acker, R.J. et al. 1987. An assessment of parameters of health care and nutrition in homeless children. *American Journal of Diseases in Children* 141:388.

Alperstein, G., and E. Arnstein. 1988. Homeless children—a challenge for pediatricians. *Pediatric Clinics of North America* 35:1413–1425.

American Academy of Pediatrics. 1981. *School health: A guide for health professionals.* Evanston, IL: Author.

American School Health Association. 1994. *Guidelines for comprehensive school health programs.* 2d ed. Kent, OH.

Bloom, B. 1990. *Health insurance and medical care: Health of our nation's children, United States, 1988.* Advance data from vital and health statistics, No. 188. Hyattsville, MD: National Center for Health Statistics.

Boland, M. et al. 1992. Care needs of HIV-infected children at New Jersey Children's Hospital. *Aids and Public Policy Journal* 7:7–17.

Bradbury, R. 1994. No news, or what killed the dog? *American Way* 27:133, 135.

Children's Defense Fund. 1988. *The children's defense budget: An analysis of our nation's investment in children.* Washington, DC: Author.

Committee on Health Care for Homeless People. 1988. Homelessness, Health, and Human Needs. Institute of Medicine. Washington, DC: National Academy Press.

Dewey, J. 1956. *The child and the curriculum.* Chicago: University of Chicago Press.

Drotar, D., and M. Bush. 1985. Mental health issues and services. In *Issues in the care of children with chronic illness*, eds. N. Hobbs and J.M. Perrin. San Francisco: Jossey-Bass Publishers.

Erikson, E.H. 1950. *Childhood and society.* 2d ed. New York: W.W. Norton and Co., Inc.

Freedman, S.A. et al. 1988. Coverage of the uninsured and underinsured. A proposal for school enroll-ment-based family health insurance. *New England Journal of Medicine* 318:843–847.

Hardy, A.M., National Center for Health Statistics. 1991. *Incidence and impact of selected infectious diseases in childhood. Vital and health statistics*, Series 10, No. 173.

Jackson, J.J. 1981. Urban black Americans. In *Ethnicity and medical care*, ed. A. Harwood. Cam-bridge, MA: Harvard University Press.

Joint Committee on National Health Education Standards. 1995. *National health education stan-dards: Achieving health literacy.* American Cancer Society.

Jones, D.J., and V.A. Roberts. 1994. Black children: Growth, development, and health. In *Handbook of black American health: The mosaic of conditions, issues, policies, and prospects*, ed. L. Liv-ingston. Westport, CT: Greenwood Press.

Kadushin, A. 1980. *Child welfare services.* 3rd ed. New York: McMillan Publishing Co., Inc.

Kotch, J.B. et al. 1995. Risk of child abuse or neglect among a cohort of low income infants. *Child Abuse and Neglect* 19:1115–1130.

Lefkowitz, D., and A. Monheit. 1991. *Health insurance, use of health services, and health care expen-ditures.* (AHCPR Pub. No. 92-0017). National Medical Expenditure Survey Research Findings 12. Rockville, MD: Agency for Health Care Policy and Research, U.S. Public Health Service.

Lewin, T. 1995, 7 Dec. "Parents poll shows high incidence of child abuse," *New York Times.* National Edition, Section B, 16.

McCurdy, K., and D. Daro. 1992. *Current trends in child abuse reporting and fatalities: The results of the 1991 Annual Fifty State Survey.* Chicago: National Center on Child Abuse Prevention Research.

National Center for Health Statistics. L Fingerhut. 1989. *Trends and current status in childhood mor-tality, United States, 1900–1985.* Vital and health statistics, Series 3, No. 26. DHHS Pub. No. (PHS) 89-1410. Washington, DC: Government Printing Office.

National Center for Health Statistics. 1989. *Current estimates from the National Health Interview Survey: United States, 1988.* Vital and health statistics, Series 10, No. 173.

National Center for Health Statistics. 1995. *Health, United States, 1994.* Hyattsville, MD: U.S. Public Health Service.

National Health Interview Survey-Disability Supplement. 1994. Rockville, MD: National Center for Health Statistics.

Nettles, A. 1994. Scholastic performance of children with sickle cell disease. *Journal of Health and Social Policy* 5:123–140.

Newacheck, P.W. et al. 1995. Children and health insurance: An overview of recent trends. *Health policy and child health.* Washington, DC: Center for Health Policy Research, The George Washington University, spring.

Newacheck, P.W., and W.R. Taylor. 1992. Childhood chronic illness: Prevalence, Severity, and impact. *American Journal of Public Health* 82:364–370.

Oleske, J.M. 1989. Children with HIV infection: Dilemmas in management. *Caring* VIII:32–35.

Osterholm, M.T., and K.L. MacDonald. 1987. Facing the complex issues of pediatric AIDS: A public health perspective. *Journal of American Medical Association* 258:2736–2737.

Palfrey, J.S. et al. 1991. Technology's children: Report of a statewide census of childen dependent on medical supports. *Pediatrics* 87:611–618.

Peckham, C., and D. Gibb. 1995. Mother-to-child transmission of the Human Immunodeficiency Virus. *New England Journal of Medicine* 333:298–302.

Redlender, I. 1994. Health care of homeless women and children. In *Maternal and child health practices.* 4th ed. Eds. H.M. Wallace et al. Oakland, CA: Third Party Publishing Company.

Reyes, L.M., and L.D. Waxman. 1987. *The continuing growth of hunger, homelessness, and poverty in American Cities: 1986.* Washington, DC: U.S. Conference of Mayors.

Richardson, S.A. 1989. Transition to adulthood. In *Caring for children with chronic illness: Issues and strategies*, ed. R.E.K. Stein. New York: Springer Publishing Company.

Rogers, M.F. 1987. Transmission of Human Immunodeficiency Virus infection in the U.S. In *Report of the Surgeon General's Workshop on Children with HIV infection and their families.* Rockville, MD: U.S. Department of Health and Human Services, Public Health Service, Health Resources and Services Administration, Bureau of Health Care Delivery and Assistance, Division of Maternal and Child Health.

Schidlow, D., and S. Fiel. 1990. Life beyond pediatrics: Transition of chronically ill adolescents from pediatric to adult care systems. *Medical Clinics of North America* 74:1113.

Sedlak, A. 1991. *National incidence and prevalence of child abuse and neglect: 1988.* Revised report. Rockville, MD: Westat, Inc., Sept. 5.

Silverman, M.M., and D.S. Koretz. 1989. Preventing mental health problems. In *Caring for children with chronic illness: Issues and strategies*, ed. R.E.K. Stein. New York: Springer Publishing Company.

Simpson, G. 1993. *Determining childhood disability and special needs children in the 1994–95 NHIS on disability.* Paper presented at the ASA annual meeting, winter.

Singh, G.K., and S.M. Yu. 1996. U.S. childhood mortality, 1950–1993: Trends and socioeconomic differentials. *American Journal of Public Health* 86:505–512.

Stein, R.E.K. et al. 1993. Framework for identifying children who have chronic conditions: The case for a new definition. *Journal of Pediatrics* 122:342–347.

Stuber, M.L. 1989. Coordination of care for pediatric AIDS: The development of a maternal-child HIV task force. *Developmental and Behavioral Pediatrics* 10:201–204.

Telfair, J., and K.B. Nash. 1996. Delivery of genetic services to African Americans. In *Ethnic and cultural diversity and its impact on the delivery of genetic services*, ed. N.L. Fisher. Baltimore: The Johns Hopkins University Press.

U.S. Advisory Board on Child Abuse and Neglect. 1995. *A nation's shame: Fatal child abuse and neglect in the U.S.* Executive Summary. Washington, DC.

U.S. Bureau of the Census. 1990. Demographic state of the nation: 1990. *Current population reports.* Special Studies Series, P-23, No. 170. Washington, DC: Government Printing Office.

U.S. Bureau of the Census. 1993. Demographic state of the nation: 1993. *Current population reports.* Special Studies Series, P-23, No. 185. Washington, DC: Government Printing Office.

U.S. Bureau of the Census. 1994. *Statistical Abstract of the United States: 1994.* 114th ed. Washington, DC: Government Printing Office.

U.S. Congress. 1973. *Child Abuse Prevention and Treatment Act*, PL 93–247. 93rd Cong., 31 January 1974.

U.S. Department of Commerce. 1992. Households, families, and children: A 30-year perspective, by T. Lugaila. *Current population reports: Population characteristics.* Washington, DC.

U.S. Department of Health and Human Services. 1981. Use of health services, by M.G. Kovar. In *Better health for our children: A national strategy.* The Report of the Select Panel for the Promotion of Child Health, Vol. 4. Washington, DC: Government Printing Office.

U.S. Department of Health and Human Services, U.S. Public Health Service. 1989. *Healthy People 2000.* National Health Promotion and Disease Prevention Objectives. Washington, DC.

U.S. Department of Health and Human Services, Health Resources and Services Administration. 1991. Public Health Service, Maternal and Child Health Bureau. *Healthy Children 2000.* DHHS Pub. No. HRSA-M-CH-91-2. Washington, DC: Government Printing Office.

U.S. Department of Health and Human Services, Public Health Service, Health Resources and Services Administration, Maternal and Child Health Bureau. 1995. *Child Health U.S.A '94.* DHHS Pub. No. HRSA-MCH-95-1. Washington DC: Government Printing Office.

U.S. General Accounting Office. 1994. *Health care reform: School-based health centers can promote-access to care.* GAO/HEHS-94-166. Washington, DC: Author.

Valdez, R., et al. 1985. Consequences of cost-sharing for children's health. *Pediatrics* 75:952–961.

Weiss and Halpern. 1990 Community-based family support and education programs: Something old or something new? *National Center for Children in Poverty.* New York, NY: Columbia University School of Public Health.

Weissbourd, B., and M. Patrick. 1988. In the best interest of the family: The emergence of the family resource programs. *Infants and Young Children* 1:46–54.

Work Group on HIV/AIDS (1988). Pediatric AIDS. *Public Health Reports* 103 (suppl 1):94–98.

Williams, B., and J.B. Kotch. 1990. Excess injury mortality among children in the U.S.: Comparison of recent international statistics. *Pediatrics* 86 suppl:1067–1073.

Zill, N., and C.A. Schoenborn. 1990. Developmental, learning, and emotional problems. *Health of our nation's children, U.S., 1988.* Advance data from vital and health statistics, No. 190. Hyattsville, MD: National Center for Health Statistics.

CHAPTER 8

Adolescent Health

David Knopf and Todd E. Gordon

I would there were no age between ten and three-and-twenty, or that youth would sleep out the rest; for there is nothing in between but getting wenches with child, wronging the ancientry, stealing, fighting.

Shakespeare, *Winter's Tale,* act 3, scene 3

Adolescence is a new birth, for the higher and completely human traits are now born. . . . These years are the best decade of life. No age is so responsive to all the best and wisest adult endeavor.

Hall, 1904, pages xiii and xviii

INTRODUCTION

No age group is more maligned or idealized than adolescence. This cultural ambivalence has profound implications for the health of adolescents, resulting in sometimes dismissing adolescent problems as inevitable and sometimes minimizing adolescent concerns and issues as trivial. Despite this, adolescent health is often injected into the core political/cultural debates regarding justice and the range and role of government in such areas as abortion, sexuality, family values, poverty, and social opportunity. Clearly, adolescents have significant problems as a population, and these problems have significant repercussions for young people and society now and in the future. Despite the romanticization of America as youth-obsessed, relatively few resources have been devoted to the problems of adolescents. Public health professionals and advocates have long sought to improve the health of adolescents and increase concern for their needs.

Compared to other age groups, adolescents are generally healthy, but they should be of high public health concern for several reasons. Certain populations of adolescents have poor health status, and many of these are in the direct care of public agencies, such as the incarcerated, those in foster care, and Native Americans. Many of the major health problems of adolescents are psychosocially based and thus should be amenable to prevention efforts. Since many of the behaviors that cause significant adult morbidity and mortality begin in adolescence and may be less well embedded in younger people, changes within adolescence may pay long dividends for the public's health.

Another important reason to attend closely to adolescent health is that adolescents are the immediate next pool of parents, workers, and citizens, so their health will very soon affect the health of succeeding generations, the economy, and the body politic. Adolescent problems such as juvenile crime, motor vehicle injuries, pregnancy, and sexually transmitted diseases often affect the other generations directly. Finally, just as parents feel some urgency—as the opportunity to influence the development of their offspring draws to a close in adolescence—to complete the unfinished business of socialization (Smetana 1989), so too should society.

In this chapter, we shall consider the importance, nature, and context of adolescent development. The epidemiology of adolescent health problems will illustrate the pervasiveness of psychosocial factors in mortality, morbidity, risk behavior, and factors that influence the severity of problems. A consideration of the state of current health care for adolescents will show the lack of access and underutilization of relevant health care and illustrate the need for broadly conceived, comprehensive, youth-oriented approaches that address health promotion, prevention, primary care, and treatment services. Recent efforts to develop such approaches have been advocated by several national commissions and have been attempted at federal, state, and local levels. Major problem areas of injury and violence, adolescent pregnancy, risk behaviors, and services for stigmatized populations will be considered in light of key public health concepts and tools.

But first, who are adolescents? Some use biological markers such as the beginning and completion of puberty. Others would use social definitions such as leaving the family of origin, becoming economically independent, or becoming a legally responsible adult (usually at age 21). Some would even combine in the adolescent group both teenagers and youth and thus include those up to their mid-twenties, reflecting the continued lack of true independence of many in their early twenties. For public health purposes, age-based definitions, though crude, are easiest to apply, but even age definitions vary. Some sources such as the Centers for Disease Control and Prevention (CDC) typically report health data in varying age blocks such as <18, 5–14, 15–24, or even 15–64, thus confusing and obscuring many data with issues of other ages. For the purposes here, adolescence will usually refer to those in the second decade of life.

HISTORICAL PERSPECTIVES ON ADOLESCENCE

Some have argued that adolescence is a recent invention (Kett 1993), but historical reviews illustrate a long awareness of unique issues in the second decade of life and some important differences over time. The term *adolescent* was not in common use until G. Stanley Hall's publication in 1904 of a two-volume text, *Adolescence: Its Psychology, and Its Relations to Anthropology, Sex, Crime, Religion, and Education* (Hall 1904). Prior to this time, the age group was more often referred to as *Youth*, which had a connotation of semi-independent participation in economic activities and typically ranged from age 12 to the early to mid-20s (Modell and Goodman 1990). The transition by youth to full adulthood prior to industrialization often included fostering out of the family to apprenticeships for working class youth and to boarding school for the elite, both of which were seen as semi-autonomous phases still monitored by adults. With industrialization, urbanization, and the expansion of the middle class in the late nineteen century, such transitions faded, and youth became increasingly dependent on their families and marginalized economically. Age-segregated training became the norm for the second decade of life, and the class-heterogeneous American public high school emerged as the uniquely American means to foster upward social mobility for the working and middle classes. Hall's publication became an important part of the movement, which focused on the character development of an age group that was seen as vulnerable and malleable (until working-class youth did not respond to these bourgeois reformers' attempts, at which point they were again seen as troublesome, and the label of *juvenile delinquent* developed). Hall believed adolescents should be protected from precocity—too early adult experiences and responsibilities. This view fit well with the changing needs of the economy for fewer unskilled laborers and the changing view of the family as less an economic unit and more an emotional refuge to protect children. Contrary to the popular imagination, protected child development, family stability, and multigenerational relationships have only become a possible norm within the last century. This is due to life spans increasing, birth rates falling, desertion becoming more formalized into legally prescribed divorce, and parents surviving predictably throughout the course of childhood. (In 1900, 25 percent of parents died before the eighteenth birthday of their children [Harevan 1982].) This changing view of adolescence as a protected transition time may not be universally accepted and may be particularly difficult for non-European immigrants, who come from different historical, economic, and cultural traditions.

DEMOGRAPHICS OF ADOLESCENCE

For the first time in two decades, adolescents are increasing as a percentage of the overall population, and projections are for this increase to continue for the next decade. In 1994 there were 37 million persons between the ages of 10 and 19, 14 percent of the entire U.S. population. The adolescent population will become increasingly heterogeneous, with the percentage of those who do not consider their heritage primarily European going from 18.5 percent in 1980 to 47 per-

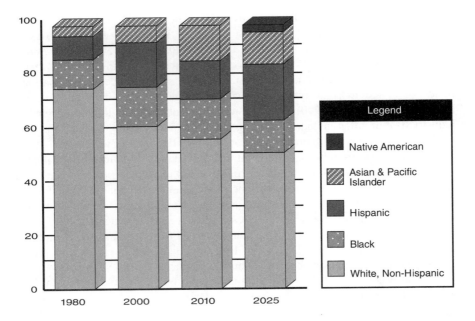

Figure 8–1 Adolescent Ethnicity, 1980–2025. *Note:* 1980 based on total population age 10–19; 2000–2050 based on projected population age 14–17. *Source:* Reprinted from U.S. Census Bureau, *Statistical Abstracts, 1995,* Tables 23 and 25.

cent by 2025 according to Census Bureau projections (U.S. Census Bureau 1995). (See Figure 8–1.) This change may result in adolescents' being seen as even more alien and becoming more marginalized.

Although most young people under 18 lived with two parents in 1994 (69 percent), this percentage is down considerably since 1970, when 87.1 percent lived with two parents. Like other minors, adolescents increasingly experience poverty—in 1993, 22 percent of those under 18 were poor compared to 17.9 percent in 1980. There are also large differences by race and ethnicity in both family composition and poverty levels. Only 33 percent of African Americans live with two parents, and 63 percent of Hispanics live with two parents, while 76 percent of non-Hispanic Whites live with two parents. African Americans and Hispanics under 18 are three times as likely to live in poor families as Whites (31 percent and 27 percent respectively v. 9.4 percent) (U.S. Census Bureau 1995). Since studies rarely include data regarding economic status but do include ethnic identity data, it should always be questioned whether ethnic data reflect the interacting and confounding problems of poverty and family structure.

THE CONTEXT OF ADOLESCENT DEVELOPMENT

Part of the difficulty in approaching adolescence has been in understanding the nature of adolescence. Anna Freud once wrote that normality in adolescence is abnormal (Freud 1958), basing her interpretation of normality on clinical samples. Many still think of adolescents not as people but as monstrosities to be avoided at best, endured and controlled at worst. Population-based studies do not confirm this negative view of normal adolescence. Most adolescents do not describe extreme moodiness but rather describe positive relationships with their parents; most parents describe their own adolescents in mostly positive terms. Numerous studies find that 80 percent of adolescents are growing up and becoming responsible adults without major difficulty (Offer and Schonert-Reichl 1992). The consequence of the view that adolescence is inevitably a time of "storm and stress" for most youth is that problems are dismissed as inherent to adolescence rather than seen as signs of significant difficulties that may continue. A more rounded view has developed recently in the social psychological literature of adolescence as a time of transitions with occasional perturbations (Steinberg 1990), needing a "prolonged supportive environment with graded steps toward autonomy" (Irwin 1987, p. 2).

Biological Development

Biological changes, particularly the development of the reproductive and endocrine systems, are often considered the engine for the train of many issues related to adolescent development. For females, the normal process may begin as early as age 8 with the first stages of breast development. Height spurts commonly occur between ages 9.5 to 14.5, and menarche between 10.5 and 15.5 years of age. Males are usually a little later, with testicular enlargement between 10.5 and 13.5 years of age and rapid growth in height and other dimensions about a year after that (U.S. Congress, 1991b). Although the process takes a predictable course, there is much variation in timing between individuals such that normal puberty may be considered anywhere from years 8 to 18.

There are also significant historical and environmental variations in the timing of puberty. At the beginning of the twentieth century, menarche averaged 14.5 years in the United States, and thus puberty was often not completed until near the end of high school. Currently the average age of menarche is 12.5 years, so that the process is now often completed *prior* to high school. The exact causes of this change are unknown but are usually attributed to reductions in infectious disease and improvement in overall nutrition. It is generally believed that this declining age of menarche has reached a plateau (U.S. Congress 1991b). Although this phenomenon has been noted primarily in industrialized countries, now it may be also happening in developing countries (Tanner and Falkner 1986).

Psychological and Social Health and Development

Since so much of public health work regarding adolescence is focused on the behavioral changes of adolescents, it is necessary for public health workers to have an understanding of adolescent psychological and social development. Although the growth and development of the reproductive system is widely recognized, few appreciate the increasing complexity of mental operations made possible by neurological and cognitive maturation in adolescence, a process that facilitates the transformations during adolescence in identity, personal relationships, and social roles. Until the last decade most thinking about young people's cognitive ability has followed Piaget's developmental stage theories of a necessary and inevitable sequence from concrete thinking through simple abstractions, cognitive comparisons, perspective taking, and empathy, to formal operations and synthesis using self-awareness, experience, judgment about the thinking process, and multiple strategies for making logical inferences. More recent work now suggests that the processes are much more environmentally supported or hindered than previously thought, and much more specific to content areas of interest (Keating 1990). Rampant relativism, questioning everything, intolerance of inconsistency, literalism, and difficulty with understanding inferences and consequences, all common to earlier adolescents, may be seen as expected signs of incomplete cognitive maturity. Since these same adolescents are increasingly independent and exposed to risky situations, those attempting to influence health behavior who do not take cognitive differences into account will have difficulty being effective.

Much psychological research and theorizing has described various aspects of normal developmental tasks of adolescents that accompany cognitive and biological changes. In early adolescence the central tasks are described as coming to terms with physical changes, the accompanying need for a changing body image, and increased cognitive abilities. Ego development is described as frequently impulsive and self-focused (Sayer et al. 1995). In middle adolescence the central task are developing independent relationships with peers and establishing a sexual identity while balancing continuing relationships with family. Ego development is described as conformist because it is usually group- and peer-centered and thus externally imposed. Late adolescence is often described as having the central task of completing the establishment of autonomy by determining vocational orientations and planning to exit the family of origin. The ego in late adolescence is described as postconformist in that there is increased internal control, greater reliance on internalized principles, appreciation of more subtle differences in motivation, and awareness of multiple causation. Developmental maturation usually results in an adequate resolution and integration of the various tasks, but as Hauser notes, severe trauma, stress, emotional deprivation, and severely restricted environments can result in *arrested* ego development marked by impulsiveness and self-protection, *foreclosed* ego development with excessive peer orientation and steady conformity, or *regressive* ego development marked by decreasing internal strengths (Hauser et al. 1991).

Development theorists seem to imply that the goal of maturity is an independent identity, which has several implications challenged by feminist theorists. Gilligan has suggested that maturity is more related to the development of *inter*dependence, the ability to care and be connected, so the excessive attention to independence as a goal of development reflects an excessively individualistic approach based on building theories that look only at middle class male development (Gilligan 1987).

During adolescence, there is a significant increase in human sexual interest, arousal, and behavior (Miller et al. 1993). Adolescents are exposed to considerable sexually oriented advertisements and entertainment, yet adolescents receive inconsistent messages from adults about the acceptability of sexual expression. This American cultural contradiction between a sexualized environment and the unacceptability of sexual behavior places youth in a double bind, tends to drive sexual decision making away from adult influence, and makes accessing contraceptives psychologically difficult for many. Developmental challenges related to the sexual unfolding of adolescents have been defined as (1) developing positive feelings about one's body, (2) learning to manage feelings of sexual arousal and desire, (3) developing new forms of autonomy and intimacy, and (4) developing skills to control the consequences of sexual behavior (Brooks-Gunn and Paikoff 1993).

National studies on the sexual behaviors of adolescents have assumed all adolescent respondents are heterosexual. Although seldom considered, unless as pariahs, a significant number of youth are struggling with issues of sexual orientation, identity, and behavior (Savin-Williams and Rodriguez 1993). A large survey of high school students in Minnesota found that 4.5 percent considered themselves "predominantly homosexual," and 10.7 percent "weren't sure" of their sexual orientation (Remefedi 1992). The concept of normal, healthy homosexual behavior is rarely discussed, but a few attempts have noted parallel issues to heterosexuals in coming to terms with one's self-identity, being able to achieve intimacy, and planning for the consequences of sexual activity. The massive stigmatization, alienation from supportive adults, and violence toward those with different sexual orientations result in greater difficulty achieving a healthy sexual identity, and lead to distinctive subcultures offering different forms of community supports (Remefedi 1989).

Social relationships also go through changes in adolescence. Families continue to be important and, as noted above, relationships are generally positive, but still there are significant changes. Boundaries become more permeable such that adolescents and their families often have to find ways to accommodate new relationships. Conflict increases somewhat during early adolescence, particularly between mothers and daughters, usually about household chores. The conflict is defined by the adolescent as about issues of personal choice, and by parents the conflict is usually defined as about issues of social propriety. Parent-adolescent conflict usually subsides by middle adolescence and is seldom threatening to family cohesion (Smetana 1989). A substantial amount of research has attempted to define parenting correlates of adolescent competency, usually defined in terms of school achievement, psychological health, and healthy behavior (Baumrind 1987; Darling and Steinberg 1993; Lamborn et al. 1991). Using both longitudinal convenience samples and large-scale school population-based samples, these studies analyzed parenting on two dimensions—amount of control or demandingness, and amount of nurturance or warmth. This approach identified four basic types of parenting—*authoritative* (sometimes called democratic) parents who are demanding but warm and nurturant, *authoritarian* families who may be demanding but are not seen by the adolescent as warm or nurturant, *permissive* parents who are nurturant but not demanding, and *neglectful* parents who are neither demanding nor warm toward the adolescents. Adolescents with authoritarian or authoritative parents generally achieve better than the other two groups, but young people with authoritative parents score higher on measures of psychological health and healthy behavior. The youth who fared the worst were those with neglectful parents. The degree of effect in most studies is rather low, and the distinctions between types somewhat imprecise, since most parents fall toward the middle on the two dimensions. This has been replicated among other cultural groups with similar results, but the positive impact of authoritative parenting is even more modest among African American families (Steinberg et al. 1991).

Environmental Context of Adolescent Health and Development

The context of adolescent lives is also affected by the larger society. Legal structures, schools, neighborhoods, the economy, and the media all have influence on the young people and are at various times described as the cause of adolescent problems.

Legal Structure

The legal structure affects adolescent development by establishing a series of regulatory steps designed to reduce risky behavior until the young person is deemed by age to be capable. Statutes related to tobacco, alcohol, driving, sexual consent, medical consent, and financial responsibility are all based on judgments about adolescent developmental abilities and needs for protection. Although states differ, generally beginning about age 12, adolescents begin to have more legal rights (such as the ability to get confidential treatment for sexually transmitted diseases), and they progress in the direction of increasing legal autonomy in the areas of driving privileges (usually from 16 to 18), consent for medical treatment (from 14 to 18), sexual consent (from 13 to 18), confidentiality (from 14 to 18), contracts (18), purchase of controlled substances such as tobacco (18), and the last legal right in most states, buying alcohol (21) (English and Matthews 1995). On the surface, such variation seems inconsistent, which can be quite irritating to some youth, but such inconsistency reflects attempts at accommodation between the reality of increasing adolescent autonomy and the need for continued parental involvement and responsibility. All states require those under 18 to have parental consent for medical treatment, but there are significant exceptions which vary widely by state. Most important, most states do recognize the need for minors to have confidentiality regarding sexual health issues, but mechanisms to allow independent and confidential access to public or private health insurance vary greatly. Some states have specific provisions for *mature minors* who are living independently to obtain adult legal standing, or emancipation. The trend in the law has been to increase legal rights for young people. Nevertheless, the legal right for young people to seek medical treatment, especially regarding sexuality and abortion, continues to be highly controversial. The important issue of legal obligation to pay for services and the ability of minors to qualify for state-funded health care also vary widely, but without provisions for independent qualification, confidentiality provisions are rather hollow because the bill may be sent home.

Schools

Schools have a major influence on adolescent health and development and are often a major site for public health interventions. Poor school adaptation as shown through dropping out, grade retention, and lack of participation in school activities has been associated with pregnancy, delinquency, substance use, unemployment, and reduced earnings (U.S. Congress, 1991b).

Public schools in American are often described as "in crisis," "besieged," and "failing." Such viewpoints ignore the long controversial history of public schools and their sizable achievements documented by population-based studies. A recent review of the results of the National Educational Longitudinal Survey 1970–1990 found significant improvements in academic achievement for all groups, particularly for minority groups (Grissmer et al. 1995). Nevertheless, there still are significant problems and inequalities in American schools. Differences are widespread in resources devoted to poor and minority youth, to poorer school districts in poorer communities in urban and some rural areas, and to noncollege youth.

Especially difficult are times of transitions for those going into middle school/junior high school and for those exiting high school.

Although the problems of poor school adaptation may be most related to social class issues, some factors of the school structure and environment have been associated with poorer adaptation, as reviewed by the Office of Technology Assessment (U.S. Congress, 1991b). Efforts to increase academic standards by using standardized testing, requiring more courses, and tracking by ability have increased academic performance for a few, but have also increased grade retention, school dropout, and alienation among more marginal students. Larger schools are problematic. Somewhat smaller schools, 500 to 1000 students, generally have more social cohesion and participation in school activities than larger schools and have fewer behavioral problems, delinquency, dropping out, or health problems. Policies that facilitate participation by teachers, students, and parents in decision making have shown similar benefits. Schools that have more transitions—between classes, teachers, subjects, and/or grade level—tend to have worse behavior and less achievement, particularly among early adolescent girls and among poorer students. Studies of the effects of class size in adolescence have shown mixed results, but the negative impact is worse again on the more marginal students.

Seldom recognized has been the significant improvement in educational performance of minorities. Already mentioned was the greater improvement on standardized test scores by African American youth, although Blacks still average two to three grade levels behind Whites (Entwisle 1990). This improvement may more reflect the tremendous discrepancy between Whites and Blacks under mostly segregated conditions in 1970, but it may also reflect the results of some investment in education for all over the last 20 years. Minority graduation rates have improved dramatically. After controlling for income, Blacks and Hispanics have better high school graduation rates than Whites, and African American graduation rates now nearly equal White graduation rates (National Research Council 1993a).

Neighborhood and Community

Neighborhood and community effects on adolescent development are most studied in terms of the consequences of concentrations of poverty in urban environments. Seldom studied are rural/urban differences. Nevertheless, the data on poor neighborhoods are distressing. Neighborhoods with a high concentration of people in poverty (>40 percent) have increased markedly since 1970. Such neighborhoods have more single mothers, greater number of unemployed men, more substance abuse, and fewer positive role models (National Research Council, 1993a). The consequences on adolescents of living in high-poverty-concentration environments are more exposure to risky behavior, which in turn affects educational achievement, pregnancy rates, employment, delinquency, and violent crime. The negative effects may be more related to other factors in social organization than just income. A study of small cities in the Midwest found important differences between communities, with some having more support for families, some facilitating positive interactions with and between youth, and some endorsing prosocial values (Blyth 1993). Communities that had more strengths tended also to have lower frequency of risk behaviors, substance abuse, pregnancy, antisocial behavior, depression, and vandalism.

Economic Influences

Economic influences on adolescent health and development are poorly understood because researchers seldom obtain income data directly and instead use proxy measures such as parental education or race. Nevertheless, the influence on health and development is considerable. The poorer the adolescent, the more likely the youth will be disabled, have a chronic condition, have school problems, get pregnant, or be arrested (U.S. Congress 1991c). Economic changes affect family behavior. Due to declining wage structure, increasing single parenthood, and skyrocketing housing prices in many areas, more family caretakers need to be employed outside of the home. By the mid-1980s, 70 percent of mothers with children between 6 and 17 were in the labor force, leaving three-fourths of 13- to 14-year-olds at home by themselves or with a younger sibling (Millstein et al. 1991). Adolescents at home without adult supervision are more likely to engage in risk behavior, regardless of economic status (Richardson et al. 1993). Economic problems also affect family behavior. Studies of middle-class Iowa families who had major decreases in income found increased parental depression and hostility, particularly among the men, which resulted in greater negativity by the father toward the adolescent children in the family, which in turn was associated with more antisocial behavior and depression among the adolescents (Elder et al. 1992). Other studies have associated poverty with fewer positive role models for adolescents, restricted geographic mobility resulting in exposure to riskier neighborhoods, greater disengagement from society (particularly among African American males), and greater difficulty with becoming employed (Sum and Fogg 1991). Although poverty increases the risks of poor transitions, it should be recognized that two-thirds of poor adolescents are not poor as adults (Edelman and Ladner 1991).

The Media

The media, particularly television, are also often seen as a major influence on adolescent development, usually in terms of stimulating desire, fostering violence, socializing adolescents into the market economy, and fostering passivity. American teenagers watch about 22 hours of television per week. Although this is less than other age groups, it is still more time than is spent in classrooms (Strasburger 1993). For many parents, particularly those of early adolescents in middle school, the television has become the after-school plan to "keep kids out of trouble." A variety of studies using a variety of methodologies have established a relationship between television watching and violence, particularly the amount of violent programming watched in third grade and aggressive behavior at ages 19 and 30 (Huesman and Eron 1986). Some researchers have identified negative effects of television on academic performance and weight, and many have raised concern through content analysis about the possibility of television increasing gender and racial stereotyping, inappropriate sexual behavior, substance use (particularly alcohol), and consumerism (Strasburger 1993).

EPIDEMIOLOGY OF ADOLESCENT HEALTH ISSUES

Unlike every other age group, adolescent overall mortality has not improved dramatically in the last 40 years (Singh and Yu 1996). What has changed are the causes of death—from infectious disease-related causes in 1950 to injury, both intentional and nonintentional, today. Epidemiologic analysis of adolescent health problems indicates the pervasiveness of behavioral factors in the morbidity and mortality of adolescents, and many of these same behaviors initiated during adolescence contribute to the morbidities and mortalities experienced in adulthood. These behaviors include actions that lead to injuries; tobacco use; alcohol and other drug use; sexual behaviors that contribute to unintended pregnancy and sexually transmitted infections (STI), which include human immunodeficiency virus (HIV) and acquired immune deficiency syndrome (AIDS); unhealthy dietary behaviors; and physical inactivity (Kann et al. 1995). Although most adolescents are healthy, certain individuals and groups contribute a disproportionate share to morbidity and mortality data. The large variation associated with ethnicity is undoubtedly confounded by the pervasiveness of economic and social inequality in the United States, but economic status data are seldom reported, so it is often difficult to determine the direction of influence of these factors.

Important national data sources include vital statistics data reported by the National Center for Health Statistics (NCHS) and CDC surveillance data reported in the *Morbidity and Mortality Weekly Report (MMWR)*. To date, the most comprehensive assessment of adolescent health behaviors has been the CDC's Youth Risk Behavior Surveillance System (YRBSS). The YRBSS measures the incidence and prevalence of the specific behaviors among adolescents that lead to their most important health problems, using national, state, and local samples of youth throughout the United States. The YRBSS is also used by schools, communities, and states to assess health risk status and to target interventions. An important limitation of the YRBSS has been that it does not include higher risk, out-of-school youth who may be incarcerated, homeless, or working. Another important national data source is the National Health Interview Survey (NHIS), carried out at regular intervals by the NCHS. This survey obtains baseline health data and information on varying topics, such as a youth risk inventory in 1992, and includes out-of-school youth. Other important annual surveys include the National Survey of Family Growth, the National Household Drug Use Survey, and the University of Michigan's Monitoring the Future project, which evaluates substance use trends yearly.

Research on adolescent health has been increasing over the last several years. However, there are several limitations, including the continued use of differing age categories, limited data on non-African American minority populations, and poor data on socioeconomic status of adolescents' families (Gans et al. 1990). Cultural controversy has emerged, with some arguing that surveys of youth are a violation of parental confidentiality and should require active parental consent. Some surveys, particularly those regarding sexual behavior, have been withdrawn from the field.

Injuries

In 1987–1988 injuries were the cause of 77 percent of all deaths among adolescents ages 10 to 24 including deaths from motor vehicle crashes (37 percent), homicide (14 percent), suicide (12 percent), and other injuries (12 percent) (CDC 1995b). Information on nonfatal injuries is much less complete than information on deaths due to injury. It is estimated that for every fatal injury there are 41 adolescents hospitalized for an injury (Runyan and Gerken 1991). It is important to distinguish between those behaviors related to unintentional injuries (motor vehicle crashes, other transportation, occupational) and intentional injuries (homicide, suicide, and other forms of assault).

Unintentional Injuries

Unintentional injuries are the leading cause of death among adolescents in the United States. The most common is motor vehicle crashes (73 percent), drowning (8 percent), unintentional firearm injuries (4 percent), and fires/burns (4 percent) (U.S. Congress 1991b). With a 38 percent decrease in motor vehicle fatalities from 1979 to 1991, a result attributed to a one-third reduction in alcohol fatalities among other factors, unintentional fatalities are one of the few areas of mortality data showing improvement (Sells and Blum 1996) (See Figure 8–2.) Factors associated with unintentional injury include demographic and behavioral characteristics. Males and older adolescents are more likely to die from both intentional and unintentional injuries. Females and those in early adolescence are more likely to attempt suicide (U.S. Congress, 1991b). Whites have a higher rate of vehicle-related injuries.

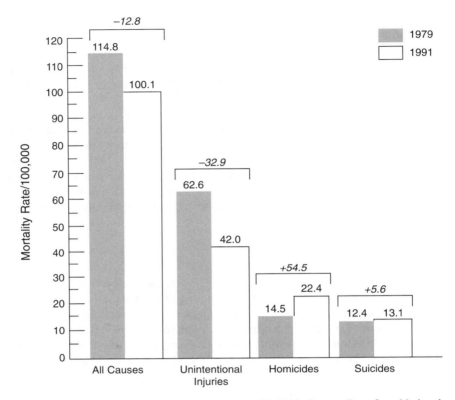

Figure 8–2 Changing Mortality of Adolescents, 1979–1991. *Source:* Data from National Center for Health Statistics, Advance Report of Final Mortality Statistics, 1991, *Monthly Vital Stat Rep.* 1993; 42(2, suppl).

Behavioral characteristics that contribute to unintentional injuries include lack of seat belt use, lack of motorcycle helmet or bicycle helmet use, and riding with a driver who has been drinking alcohol. Table 8–1 describes selected YRBSS data relating to risky behaviors.

Intentional Injuries and Violence

Intentional injuries are defined as injuries resulting from interpersonal violence, including homicide and the self-directed violence of suicide. In 1991 there were 8,159 homicides in the 15–24 age group, or 22 young people per day (O'Carroll et al. 1993). The rate for adolescent males 15–19 is 32.8 per 100,000.

Table 8–1 Risk Behaviors—U.S. 9th to 12th Graders, Youth Risk Behavior Surveillance Surveys, 1993

Behavior	All	Gender		Grade		White	Ethnicity	
		Male	Female	9th	12th		Hispanic	Black
Injury related behaviors								
Rarely use safety belt	19%	24%	14%	20%	19%	17%	20%	30%
Ever ridden with driver who had been drinking	35	36	34	32	39	34	42	39
Carried a weapon last month	22	34	9.2	26	20	20	24	28
Ever made suicide attempt	8.9	5	12	10	6.7	7.7	14	8.4
Substance use related behaviors								
Smoked cigarette last month	30	30	31	28	34	34	29	15
Drank alcohol last month	48	50	46	40	56	50	51	42
5 or more drinks at a time within the last month	30	34	26	22	39	33	33	19
Smoked marijuana last month	18	21	15	13	22	17	19	19
Used cocaine last month	1.9	2.3	1.4	1.6	2.1	1.6	4.6	1.0
Sexual behaviors								
Intercourse in last 3 months	38	38	38	25	53	34	39	59
Condom use last intercourse	53	59	46	62	46	52	46	56
Nutrition and exercise-related behaviors								
Attempted weight loss	40	23	59	41	40	41	47	32
Lower fat diet	66	58	76	65	68	66	73	59
Regular vigorous physical activity	66	75	56	74	58	68	59	60

Note: n = 16,296
Percentages >10 rounded.
Source: Reprinted from Centers for Disease Control and Prevention, Youth Risk Behavior Surveillance Survey, *Morbidity and Mortality Weekly Report*, Vol. 44, No. SS-1, 1993.

The United States has by far the highest rate of any industrialized country—more than one hundred times the lowest rate, which was Austria, and five times the second highest, which was Scotland. Males are three to four times more likely to be victims, and Blacks are seven to eight times as likely as Whites to be killed (National Adolescent Health Information Center 1995b). Guns are involved in approximately three out of four homicides, and three out of four firearm deaths are with small handguns. Most victims know their assailant; 60 percent of the shooting deaths follow an argument. Interestingly, the rate of assaults in Denmark is similar to that of Ohio, but the homicide rate is about one-fifth as high, suggesting that the availability of guns rather than violent behavior *per se* is the predominant factor for increased homicide (Cohall and Cohall 1995).

Suicide has been identified as the third leading cause of death among adolescents, and rates have been increasing in the last 30 years (CDC, 1995c). Suicide rates are higher for males than females, more frequent in Western states, much higher among Native Americans, and somewhat higher among Hispanics and Whites than among African American adolescent. Attempted suicide is even more common, with 8.6 percent of all adolescent students surveyed as part of the 1993 YRBSS reporting a suicide attempt, and twice as many females as males making an attempt (Kann et al. 1995). Prior history of suicide attempt, substance abuse, presence of firearms in the home, family history of suicide, antisocial behavior, and psychiatric disorders have all been associated with increased risk for suicide (Kachur et al. 1995). A handgun is the weapon used in 70 percent of all suicides among 15- to- 24-year-olds (Wintemute et al. 1988).

Chronic Illness and Disabilities

Chronic conditions include a wide spectrum of physical and mental health problems, including hay fever, asthma, cancer, cardiovascular disease, learning disabilities, epilepsy, juvenile onset diabetes, hearing and visual impairments, sickle cell disease, leukemia, chronic kidney disease, and cystic fibrosis. Many of these disabilities result in a substantially reduced quality of life for the adolescent. Additionally, chronically ill adolescents may be more dependent upon the health care and social service systems.

The Survey of Income and Program Participation for 1991–1992 collected information about chronic conditions, including the functional limitations related to those conditions for children and adolescents 17 years of age (CDC, 1995b). Of 10,067 15–17-year-old adolescents surveyed, 933 (93 percent) were identified as having a disability that included limitation in the ability to do regular school work, problems in personal care, personal management (activities of daily living), and the use of assistance aids (e.g., wheelchairs).

The condition most frequently identified as a cause of functional limitation among all children age 17 years was learning disability (29.5 percent), followed by speech problems (13.1 percent), mental retardation (6.8 percent), asthma (6.4 percent), and mental or emotional problems (6.3 percent). Of the 6.2 percent of all adolescents age 10–17 identified in the 1988 Child Health Survey as limited in activities due to a chronic condition, the disabled were more likely poor (8.6 percent vs. 5.9 percent). One in seven disabled adolescents had no private or public health insurance in 1984 (Newacheck 1989).

Mental Health

Many youth also experience serious emotional disturbance during adolescence. Research over the past 20 years has been unable to demonstrate that emotional disturbance is inevitably a part of adolescence, but a substantial proportion of the adolescent population has been identified as suffering from psychological problems serious enough to warrant mental health treatment (U.S. Congress 1991b).

No national prevalence studies have been conducted to assess specific diagnosable mental disorders in adolescents. The NHIS attempts to assess lifetime prevalence of mental health problems based on parental responses to questions regarding emotional and mental health. The 1988 NHIS found a lifetime prevalence rate for 12- to 17-year-olds of 18.5 percent, a figure considered comparable to adult prevalence rates (Zill and Schoenborn 1990). Among these learning disorders, affecting 8.8 percent of 12- to 17-year-olds, are the most common, followed by major depression, anxiety disorders, and eating disorders. Prolonged depressed mood within the last 6 months has been estimated to affect between 10 to 20 percent of adolescents, and between 3 to 8 percent of adolescents could be depressed enough to meet psychiatric criteria for major depressive disorder (Petersen et al. 1993). Eating restriction is common in adolescence, with 63 percent of high school girls saying they have dieted, 20 percent having fasted, and 17 percent having used diet pills. About 0.3 to 1 percent of high school girls meet psychiatric criteria for the diagnosis of anorexia nervosa, and about 4 to 10 percent struggle with bulimia (Whitaker 1992).

Sexual Behavior and Its Health Consequences

There has been a significant rise in adolescent sexual activity, but more than half are still sexually abstinent until age 17. Among 15- to 19-year-olds in 1990, one half of the unmarried women and 75 percent of the unmarried men reported having had sexual intercourse, compared to about 25 percent of females who reported in 1970 ever having had intercourse (U.S. Congress, 1991b). The 1993 YRBSS reports that among ninth graders, 32 percent of the females and 43 percent of the males have had sexual intercourse, and 18.8 percent of all youth in grades 9–12 have had four or more sexual partners (Kann et al. 1995). (See Table 8–1.) These rates are substantially similar to European rates, although as we shall see, the consequences are very different. The initiation of sexual behaviors among youth is related to several variables including age, sex, physical development, race/ethnicity, and socioeconomic level (Brooks-Gunn and Furstenberg 1989; Forrest and Singh 1990).

Two-thirds of the more than 12 million cases annually of sexually transmitted infections occur in people under 25 years of age, and about one in four sexually active teens will get a STI by the age 20 (CDC, Division of STD/HIV, 1994). All states require reporting of gonorrhea, syphilis, and AIDS to county public health departments, and most states require reporting of chlamydia infection, but there is no consensus among the states on reporting other sexually transmitted diseases such as herpes, human papillomavirus, chancroid, or HIV. In spite of major increases in sexual activity, changes in the rates of these diseases present a mixed picture, with increases in some diseases and among some groups, and decreases or leveling off in others (U.S. Congress 1991b). Gonorrhea, for instance, has decreased slightly overall, but it increased dramatically among 10- to 14-year-olds. Syphilis rates appear to have decreased among males but increased among females. HIV rates are unknown because of the low rate of testing among adolescents, but it is known that the HIV and AIDS diagnoses have increased among the 20–25-year-old group, many of whom were exposed to the diseases in their teens. There are also significant regional and racial differences in sexually transmitted infections, with the South Americans and African Americans generally having higher rates.

Nearly 1 million adolescents become pregnant each year, with half of these pregnancies resulting in live births (National Research Council 1987). The rates of pregnancy, birth, abortion, and miscarriage among 15- to 19-year-olds are about twice those of most European countries. Although adolescents in the past decade have been initiating intercourse earlier and in higher percentages, the ratio of births to sexually active adolescent women 15–19 has decreased from 189 per 1,000 in 1980 to 175 per 1,000 in 1990. Because the number of sexually active women in this age group increased, the overall pregnancy rate of adolescent females increased, from 89 per 1,000 in 1980 to 96 per thousand in 1990 (Spitz et al. 1996) but leveled off in 1991–1993 (CDC 1995a). In 1990, 77 percent of female students reported using contraception during last intercourse (National Adolescent Health Information Center 1995a). The total number of pregnancies to non-Hispanic whites exceeds African American and Hispanic pregnancies, but the rate of these two groups is twice the White rate. Being poor increases the birth rate among teens, with 83 percent of births to teens in families with income less than $25,000 and half of all births to teens in families with income less than $12,000.

Tobacco, Alcohol, and Other Drug Use

High prevalences of tobacco, alcohol, and other substance use by adolescents have been identified as serious threats to the health of youth (Blum 1987). Alcohol and other drugs frequently contribute to the causes of unintentional and intentional injuries, including motor vehicle-related injuries, homicide, and suicide; may be a factor in unintended pregnancy; and lead to a variety of medical, psychological, and social morbidities. The trend in substance use has been generally down during the 1980s, but there have been some increases reported in the 1990s, particularly in marijuana and tobacco use and among early adolescents (Johnson et al. 1996).

Existing data on the incidence and prevalence of tobacco, alcohol, and other drugs used by adolescents are based on self-reports. Self-reported data may not be entirely accurate due to adolescents' attempts to provide socially desirable responses. Adolescents may also report engaging in behaviors to counteract what is socially desirable. When reviewing self-reported data, it is necessary to consider the potential biases that may exist.

The most frequently used drugs by adolescents are those that eventually will be legal for them to use. Although two-thirds of students have tried cigarettes and four-fifths have drunk alcohol at least once, regular and current use is less (Kann et al. 1995). Out-of-school adolescents were significantly more likely than in-school adolescents to have reported ever having smoked cigarettes (57.7 percent vs. 50.9 percent) or used alcohol (62.9 percent vs. 55.2 percent) in their lifetimes (CDC 1994). Nearly one-third of students are current smokers, and nearly half have drunk alcohol within the last month. White and Hispanic students, older students, and out-of-school adolescents were significantly more likely than African American students to be current users of cigarettes. (See Table 8–1.)

Illicit substance use is not as prevalent as use of alcohol and tobacco, but a significant number of adolescents reported use of marijuana and/or cocaine. Nearly one-third (32.8 percent) of students surveyed had used marijuana during their lifetimes, and 17.7 percent were current users of marijuana. Older, male, and out-of school youth are more likely than others to report ever having used marijuana (31.4 percent vs. 15.9 percent). Overall, 4.9 percent of students surveyed had used cocaine during their lifetime, and 1.9 percent were current cocaine users. Hispanic male and female students were significantly more likely than White or African American students to have tried cocaine. Despite the stereotype of cocaine as a problem of only urban Blacks, White youth were significantly more likely than African American young people to report ever having used cocaine. Out-of-school adolescents were over three times more likely than in-school adolescents to have reported ever having used cocaine (7.1 percent vs. 2.1 percent) (CDC 1994).

Nutrition and Physical Activity

The nutritional and activity statuses of adolescents are important for several reasons. First, adolescent growth and development require an increase in energy and an increase in nutrients, particularly iron, calcium, and certain other minerals (Pipes, 1989). Second, as adolescents make more independent food choices, patterns are developing that could play important roles in several chronic diseases in adulthood. Third, eating habits may have even more direct effects on health during adolescence, such as obesity or deficits during pregnancy. The fourth area of concern about nutrition and physical activity is changing patterns that may be detrimental to long-term health.

Chronic diseases begin to develop during childhood and adolescence. Autopsies of young men in their early twenties, taken during the of wars of Korea and Vietnam, showed fatty streaks indicative of atherosclerosis, thus confirming that this chronic disease starts early. Certain types of cancer, stroke, diabetes mellitus, and osteoporosis have been associated with long-term dietary behaviors. Certain chronic diseases, particularly diabetes, need careful attention to nutritional issues. Good bone development related to physical activity and calcium-rich diets in adolescence results in less osteoporosis in adult life (National Research Council 1989).

Eating patterns that relate to the development of obesity are often established in adolescence. Fifteen to 25 percent of American adolescents are obese, an increase over the past 20 years. Obese youth older than 12 years of age have four times the risk of adult obesity compared to obese children younger than 12 years (U.S. Congress 1991b). Television watching, maternal inactivity, and irregular eating patterns have been associated with obesity. Among irregular eating patterns are three behaviors that are common during adolescence—skipping meals, snacking, and eating high fat food, particularly "fast food." The National Adolescent School Health Survey (NASHS) reported that 5 percent of adolescents chronically skip meals. Ninety percent of the adolescents reported eating between meals. Most of the snacks consisted of calorie dense "junk foods," containing high fat, sugar, and sodium content, and one-third of the daily intake of adolescents comes from such snacks, according to a U.S. Department of Agriculture survey. Fast foods, like many snack foods, are high in fat, sugar, and sodium. During pregnancy, nutritional needs for women increase, particularly for folic acid, but the general adolescent diet is low in this and other important nutrients. This is particularly important during the first several months when many do not know (or do not wish to know) they are pregnant.

Although adolescents generally have more physical activity than other age groups, the percentage of those with vigorous physical activity has been decreasing, a trend attributed to television and to the decrease in required physical education activities in school for older adolescents. Seldom noticed are other forms of activity—particularly intense athletics, physical exercise, or dance—which have physiologic effects similar to those of eating disorders by interrupting menses and depleting nutritional status, thus creating potential for bone damage and other nutrition-related problems.

Interrelatedness of Health Risk Behaviors and Risk-Taking Theory

Adolescent health risk behaviors are substantially interrelated. While young people may be labeled or identified in terms of a particular set of behaviors, research data confirm what youth service providers, parents, and teenagers have long known, that the adolescent with the drug problem is often the one with the school problem, with the STI, enmeshed in the juvenile justice system, and with a tumultuous relationship with parents. Some risk behaviors such as alcohol use and sexual activity are only associated with other risk behaviors if present in early adolescence. While the etiology of these behaviors and events is complex and multifaceted, the ubiquitousness of the cluster of riskiness is not (Jessor and Jessor 1977; Irwin 1990). Although the correlations between risk behaviors are high, the ability of various measures of riskiness to correctly identify behaviors that lead to health problems without over-identifying risky behaviors that do not result in health problems is still problematic. To establish both sensitivity and specificity will require greater use of longitudinal studies with larger populations. Antecedents of high risk behavior include early school failure and behavioral problems in elementary school, smoking tobacco in late childhood and early adolescence, and early puberty in girls, all of which suggest potential for early intervention focused on these factors and evaluation of programs for younger children that monitor behavioral outcomes well into adolescence.

Attempts to explain adolescent risk taking have usually been psychologically based. Some cognitive psychologists such as Elkind believe the adolescent's "personal fable" about exemption from natural laws may put him or her at higher risk (Elkind 1967), but others have noted that adolescent perception of risk is very similar to adult perception of risk (Quadrel et al. 1993). Other models of risk-taking behavior have been proposed, including the dispositional, ecological, and biological models, which may be integrated into a "biopsycho-social model" in which "biological changes trigger psychological and social changes, which themselves have both direct and indirect effects on risk" (Millstein and Igra 1996). Risk taking may be particularly important for adolescent development in that it may assist with expectations regarding familial emancipation and help develop autonomy, mastery, and intimacy. Along these lines, Donovan and Jessor have argued that "problem behavior" should be seen as a functional aspect of development in that these behaviors may be means of achieving otherwise blocked goal obtainment, may be ways of expressing opposition to adult authority, may be ways of gaining access to peers and youth culture, and may be means of confirming self-identity (Donovan and Jessor 1985). From this perspective, interventions aimed at reducing risk behaviors will need to more dramatically address the developmental needs of adolescents for mastery, peer relationships, and identity.

Resilience

An important concept related to risk behavior emerging from longitudinal research is that of resilience. It has been noted that even among high-risk youth in high-risk environments, some young people succeed. One such study of high-risk children in Hawaii identified one-third of the youth as high risk due to having four or more situations thought to be unfavorable to development—family situations such as poverty, conflict, alcoholism, or mental illness. These children showed signs of emotional distress in childhood, but at age 18 one-third were doing well and at age 32 nearly one-half "loved well, worked well, played well, and expected well" (Werner 1992). Five clusters of protective factors were identified, including (1) temperamental factors that seemed to elicit positive responses from caring adults; (2) skills and values that led to use of their abilities; (3) parents who fostered self-esteem and structure; (4) contact with supportive adults through school, extended family, church, or youth service programs; and (5) a "second chance" through adult education in community colleges and/or military service. These clusters enabled the protective processes, identified in other longitudinal studies, that reduce the impact of risk situations. These processes are those that reduce the likelihood of negative chain reactions, promote self-efficacy, and open up opportunities—factors that are at the base of most intervention programs with youth (Rutter 1987).

ADOLESCENT HEALTH CARE SERVICES

The change in health problems from infectious diseases to psychosocially based morbidities requires a broader array of health promotion, prevention, and treatment services. Although there may be problems with the appropriate "fit" between current health care needs and health care services, it remains to be seen if emerging changes in health care delivery will create a better or worse fit.

Use of Health Care Services

Adolescents use health care services for the treatment of acute (sore throat, injury, etc.) and chronic (hypertension, asthma, diabetes, etc.) conditions as well as for preventive services, including dental services, mental health services, substance abuse services, and reproductive health services. However, adolescents tend to average fewer visits for health services than any other age group, three visits each year (U.S. Congress 1991a). Despite having worse health status, poor and minorities youth have more time elapsed between visits to health care and fewer hospitalizations than White and nonpoor youth. Rural and Southern youth are also less likely to receive such health care services.

Adolescents seek out health services in a variety of places including physicians' offices, emergency rooms, neighborhood and community health centers, public health departments, and school-based clinics, but care is generally episodic rather than preventive. The most common health concerns and conditions prompting adolescent visits to a physician's office include colds and sore throats (8 percent), skin problems (7 percent), general medical examinations (7 percent), pregnancy-related services (6 percent), allergies (4 percent), ear infections (3 percent), vision disorders (2 percent), STIs (2 percent), and other diagnoses (61 percent). Other diagnoses include a wide array of concerns and conditions (none accounting for more than 2 percent of visits) including injuries, back problems, anxiety, nervousness, etc. (Nelson 1991). Very few services in office-based practices could be considered preventive health care, with only 2 percent of visits including discussions about smoking cessation, weight control, nutrition, or HIV transmission (Igra and Millstein 1993). Of all office-based visits by adolescents age 11–20, 35 percent were with family physicians, 18 percent with pediatricians, 8 percent with OB/GYN physicians, 4 percent with internal medicine physicians, and 34 percent with other specialists (Gans et al. 1991). Early adolescents are more likely to see pediatricians and late adolescents more likely to see family physicians and OB/GYN doctors. Adolescents' reasons for visits to school-based clinics include acute illness or injury (25 percent), mental health (20 percent), reproductive health (13 percent), physical exams (12 percent), chronic conditions (5 percent), skin conditions (4 percent), nutrition (3 percent), and other preventive care, including hearing and vision testing (18 percent) (Lear 1989).

Barriers to Health Care

Barriers to access to health care have been categorized as financial and nonfinancial (Gans et al. 1991). Financial barriers include:

- *Lack of insurance coverage and inadequate coverage.* Fifteen percent of adolescents (4.7 million) are uninsured and these numbers continue to rise. These adolescents tend to be living at or below the poverty level, are minorities, and are in poorer health overall. The lack of health insurance is attributed to ineligibility for public insurance and ineligibility for or inability to afford private insurance. Copayments, deductibles, and specific exclusions of many private insurance plans and some public insurance plans effectively exclude many from primary and preventive care.

- *Quality of insurance coverage.* Although public and private insurance may generally both provide good coverage for traditional medical services, coverage for preventive services, mental health and substance abuse treatment services, and other services not usually provided by a physician tend to not be as well covered.
- *Limited provider reimbursement.* Many physicians are discouraged from screening and treating adolescents who require services that are more time-intensive, based on inadequate reimbursement rates in fee-for-service systems or time pressures in managed care environments.

Nonfinancial barriers include:

- *Confidentiality.* Adolescents who do not feel that their health concerns will remain confidential may be hesitant to seek medical care. In one survey in central Massachusetts, more than one-half of the students reported they had health concerns they did not want their parents to know about, and more than one-fourth of these students said they would not seek health care for fear their parents might find out (Cheng et al. 1993). Earlier studies have found even greater health care avoidance rates because of concerns about confidentiality (Council of Scientific Affairs 1993). Only a third of the students in the Massachusetts study knew they could get confidential care for STIs. Interestingly, an even higher percentage of youth said they did not want their friends to know their health concerns, a finding which needs to be considered in the development of school-based and school-linked health services and peer education programs.
- *Lack of coordination.* Many adolescents require a multitude of services that include health, mental health, social services, substance abuse treatment, and juvenile justice. A lack of coordination between providers may leave gaps in services and create unnecessary duplication of services.
- *Professional training in adolescent health.* Many providers lack significant training in adolescent health and preventive services, and many reflect the stereotypes and fears of the society at large regarding adolescents (Hein 1994). Few physicians or other health care providers receive training in adolescent medicine, and many feel that their specialty training did not prepare them with the necessary skills to manage effectively the complex social and emotional problems of adolescents.
- *Provider sensitivity.* Providers' sensitivity to the developmental issues and cultural backgrounds of adolescent clients may directly affect their ability to communicate with adolescents and the adolescent's willingness to comply with prevention and treatment protocols.
- *Fear and inexperience.* Fear of health problems and providers along with the adolescent's lack of experience and ability to recognize health problems may delay or prevent the adolescent from seeking necessary care.

Improving Accessibility to Health Care

The Society for Adolescent Medicine (SAM) has identified the following components as key criteria for improving access to care for adolescents (Klein et al. 1992):

- *Availability*. Age-appropriate services and trained health care providers.
- *Visibility*. Health services for adolescents must be recognizable, convenient, and should not require complex planning by adolescents or their parents.
- *Quality*. A basic level of service must be provided to all youth, and adolescents should be satisfied with the care they receive.
- *Confidentiality*. Adolescents should be encouraged to involve their families in health decisions, but confidentiality must be ensured.
- *Affordability*. Public and private insurance programs must provide adolescents with both preventive and other services designed to promote health behaviors and decrease morbidity and mortality.
- *Flexibility*. Services, providers, and delivery sites must consider the developmental, cultural, ethnic, and social diversity among adolescents.
- *Coordination*. Service providers must ensure that comprehensive services are available to adolescents.

As noted by SAM, the complexity of many adolescent health problems and the nature of these problems that often involve several institutions—schools, courts, clinics, social services, recreation programs—mean coordinated services that are comprehensive must be available for adolescents. Comprehensive services should include treatment and both primary and secondary prevention of the major health concerns of adolescents.

Some have expressed concern that various health care system changes, such as a half-hearted attempt at national health insurance or the *de facto* reform of managed care, could increase barriers for adolescence (Fox and Wicks 1994; Irwin et al. 1994). Complicated, inflexible systems of care, with copayments that are proportionately much higher for poorer adolescents, with a limited list of generalists who may or may not have an interest in adolescents and who are under significant time and system pressures to minimize services, may discourage adolescents from seeking care. On the other hand, large, organized health care systems have the potential to specialize in teen programs, may be able to market confidential services more efficiently than fee-for-service systems, and may be able to better integrate a wide range of psychosocial services. Since health care systems have more of a total cost perspective than traditional fee-for-service, there is potential for more efficient risk screening, preventive service delivery, and collaborative community-based programs as ways to avoid secondary and tertiary level care for high-cost problems such as unintended pregnancy, injuries, and psychiatric hospitalizations due to suicide. The actual implementation of any health care system will undoubtedly be more mixed. A survey of state adolescent health coordinators regarding implementation of Medicaid-managed care found that the systems rated poorly on most of the SAM criteria, but the ratings were similar to estimates of the state's services for adolescents prior to managed care implementation (Knopf 1996).

PUBLIC HEALTH PROGRAMS FOR ADOLESCENTS

Federal Programs

A sometimes bewildering number of federal agencies, ranging from the Department of Agriculture to the Department of Transportation, have programs related to adolescent health care—roughly 2 percent of the federal human resources budget was spent on adolescent health initiatives according to a review by the Office of Technology Assessment (U.S. Congress, 1991c). The primary funder of direct health care is the U.S. Department of Health and Human Services' (DHHS) Health Care Financing Administration (HCFA). In the Public Health Service of DHHS are numerous programs directed toward assessment, assurance, and policy development, including programs within the Alcohol, Drug Abuse, and Mental Health Administration, within the CDC (particularly its Division of Adolescent and School Health), and within the Health Resources and Services Administration (HRSA), the most important of which for adolescents is the Maternal and Child Health Bureau (MCHB).

Maternal and Child Health Bureau (MCHB) and Adolescents

MCHB administers Title V of the Social Security Act, which underwrites most public health work for adolescents in the United States. Using both block grants to the states and Special Projects of Regional and National Significance (SPRANS) grants for infrastructure development and demonstration projects, MCHB has been the key federal agency for developing adolescent health as an area of concern. Some of the projects within the Office of Adolescent Health include establishing Adolescent Health Coordinators in each state to develop plans for meeting adolescent health care needs, establishing national centers to promote continuing education regarding adolescent health (Center for Continuing Education in Adolescent Health in Cincinnati), administering to special needs populations (National Center for Youth with Disabilities in Minnesota), and supporting adolescent health policy (National Adolescent Health Information Center in San Francisco). Several other MCHB projects, such as the National Center for Education in Maternal and Child Health and the National Center for Child Health Policy, both in the Washington, D.C., area, have also been active with adolescent health issues. Demonstration grants from the SPRANS program have modeled a wide variety of maternal and child health (MCH) programs, including projects for adolescents regarding violence, male African Americans, homeless youth, physically disabled coordination services, pregnancy prevention, and public health data and infrastructure development projects regarding adolescents. MCHB sponsors publications, conferences, and grants regarding minority adolescent health programs and has also developed programs, National Centers, and grants for work with special needs adolescents, pediatric/adolescent AIDS, and injury and violence prevention.

One important part of the federal role has been to support health care training. The epidemiology of adolescent health presented in this chapter underscores the importance of addressing the complex psychosocial mortalities and morbidities with more broadly based training than traditional medically based models, so the federal government sponsors several programs to increase interdisciplinary training. These include the Center for Continuing Education in Adolescent Health Care in Cincinnati, the REACH (Resources for Enhancement of Adolescent Community Health) Center (currently called LEAP—Leadership Education for Adolescent Programs) in the Colorado Department of Health, and the Adolescent Health Training Programs (AHTPs) in seven university-based sites (Boston, Baltimore, Cincinnati, Indianapolis, Minneapolis, Seattle, and San Francisco). Begun in 1978, AHTPs train graduate and postgraduate nurses, nutritionists, physicians, psychologists, and social workers to provide leadership in interdisciplinary work in adolescent health care.

The MCHB also funds programs at 11 schools of public health, and these programs are more likely to include course material on adolescence, as shown in a survey of the Association of Schools of Public Health (Gordon 1996). In schools of public health receiving MCHB funding, 54 percent offer a course focused on adolescent health, and all have MCH courses that discuss various issues of adolescent health. Only one of the schools with no additional MCHB funding has an adolescent health course, and one additional school discusses adolescent health as part of its MCH courses. Additional differences between programs include time devoted to adolescent health and various adolescent health topics. Courses ranged from full semester or quarter courses (Adolescent Health and Health Behavior, Adolescent Health and Social Issues, Public Health Issues in Adolescent Health, Seminar in Adolescent Health), to one- and two-day minicourses (Adolescent Substance Abuse, Teen Pregnancy) and individual lectures as part of other courses (Foundations of MCH, Pediatrics, Issues in MCH, Public Health Aspects of Reproductive Health).

Professional associations have paralleled the increasing attention to adolescents within the federal government. Beginning in 1995 pediatric residents have a minimum requirement for training experiences in adolescent health care settings. Many physicians interested in adolescence have evolved practices specializing in youth, but to date, there are no comprehensive data that describe the number of adolescent health specialists or the nature of their training. In 1995 the American Academy of Pediatrics and the Society of Internal Medicine established a subspecialty board of Adolescent Medicine, which qualified 232 physicians in its first yearly examination. The move toward specialty boards goes against the effort to minimize specialty boards in medicine and emphasize the generalist primary care provider, so it is expected that the role of the specialist will be focused increasingly on consultation, program development, training, and research. It is unclear if other primary care training programs provide specific instruction in adolescent health care to heed the call of health care reformers to provide "interdisciplinary training in adolescent health as a designated component of all primary care disciplines to improve the quality of care received by adolescents" (Irwin et al. 1994, p. 14).

Office of Technology Assessment Report

Responding to a bipartisan petition in 1989, Congress authorized a major study by the Office of Technology Assessment (OTA) to review the status of adolescent health and recommend options for the federal government (U.S. Congress 1991a, b, c). The resulting three volumes describe in detail the background and options to fulfill this mandate. Three major options that OTA believes Congress may want to consider are (1) improving adolescents' access to health services, (2) restructuring and invigorating federal efforts to improve adolescent health, and (3) improving adolescents' environments. Such an approach generally assumes a leadership role of the federal government, but many of the findings and recommendations could be implemented by state governments in various mixes of federal/state cooperation.

Other Federal Programs and Services

Several other programs sponsored by the federal government have relevance to adolescents including Early Periodic Screening, Diagnosis, and Treatment (EPSDT), the Medicaid expansions of the Omnibus Budget Reconciliation Act of 1989 (OBRA 89), school-based/linked health care, nutrition initiatives, and efforts with nonfederal participants to specify and expand preventive and primary care.

EPSDT had a long-delayed expansion in OBRA 89, which mandated states to provide outreach, screening, treatment, and case management services with simplified and expanded needs-based eligibility (state option to 200 percent of poverty). Screening is supposed to include several areas of particular relevance to adolescents, including reproductive health and mental health (English 1993). Unfortunately, even with improved funding the program has reached only a small percentage of eligible adolescents, and few states have established mental health screening protocols. Requirements for newer Medicaid managed care organizations to comply with EPSDT guidelines could result in significant improvements for adolescents (Perkins and Rivera 1995). Enforcement of such guidelines will depend on the nature of the federal role in any block grant reforms under consideration by Congress in 1996, on the nature of Medicaid administrative waivers granted to states seeking to establish their own Medicaid policies, and on the work of advocates trying to enforce compliance with existing law.

Another categorical program that has significant implications for adolescent financial access to care was the plan in OBRA 89 to expand Medicaid eligibility to up to 200 percent of poverty (with state buy-in), initially for mothers and infants but then adding 1 year of age each year. Adolescents are the last to be added, but proposals such as the 1996 plan of the National Governors' Association to suspend the program to reduce the deficit and require some form of coverage only until age 13 may mean adolescents lose any Medicaid coverage (unless they become pregnant!).

Another area of federal initiative has been to support school-based/linked health care services. After initial reports suggesting such services may reduce sexual activity and pregnancy, the federal government joined private foundations, state governments, and local school districts in funding sites so that by 1994 there were 607 schools with school-based health centers, two-thirds of which served secondary schools (Schlitt et al. 1994). These clinics vary in the amount of services provided and have often proven quite controversial because of concern from some that they would provide reproductive health care services and thus increase sexual activity. Subsequent evaluations have found that school health clinics do achieve accessible, acceptable, comprehensive health care for adolescents, do not increase sexual activity among the students, and may decrease pregnancy rates (U.S. Congress, 1991c).

Other federal efforts to reduce teen pregnancy include several programs and funding sources in addition to those above. Title X of the Public Health Service Act began in 1970 to fund family planning clinics, which in 1989 served 1.4 million adolescents. Title XX of the Public Health Services Act of 1981 created the Adolescent Family Life Program, which funds both prevention programs and services for adolescents who are pregnant or parenting. Funding for this program has been cut drastically to $4.5 million in 1995 compared to $14.7 million in 1985. Block grants to the states for MCH services and for social services are often used for adolescent pregnancy prevention efforts as are SPRANS grants. The federal government also has created special initiatives that include teen pregnancy reduction efforts, often as part of other projects such as Healthy Start, Healthy Schools, Healthy Communities, and in 1995 the Community Coalition Partnership Program with $6.5 million for 13 communities to plan adolescent pregnancy community-wide interventions. The funding levels for these programs indicate a rather timid approach, particularly when compared to the 1995 requirement by Congress for states to use $75 million of the MCH Title V Block Grants for unproven abstinence-only education, part of the Clinton-vetoed welfare bill, H.R. 4.

Other National Efforts To Improve Adolescent Health

There have been several efforts on a national basis to improve adolescent health through attempting to heighten awareness and focus concern on policy, research, program development, and clinical activities for adolescents. One set of activities has been attempts to achieve consensus on key policy issues. The other has been to establish professional guidelines for primary and preventive care.

National Commission Attempts To Build Consensus

From 1985 to 1995 there were approximately 100 different national consensus reports, commissions, or studies regarding adolescent health. Some of these groups, such as the Carnegie Corporation of New York, have made significant commitments over time to adolescent issues (Carnegie Council on Adolescent Development 1989; Carnegie Council on Adolescent Development 1995). Others are event-reports of time-limited formal collaboration, such as the study by the National Commission on the Role of the School and Community in Improving Adolescent Health (1990). Other examples include parts of the National Commission on Children's report (1991), several National Research Council (NRC) studies (National Research Council 1987; National Research Council 1993a; 1993b), and the W.T. Grant Foundation's report on "the other half" who are not college-oriented (W.T. Grant Commission on Work, Family and Citizenship 1988).

Although each sponsoring agency or configuration of participants has resulted in slightly different approaches, an analysis of these reports indicates that these groups have collectively achieved a consensus on the key issues and policy needs for adolescents. A synthesis of these documents has identified over 1,000 different, often overlapping recommendations that can be distilled to six major areas.

1. *Improve access to health care* by ensuring high quality services, by providing access to comprehensive services, and by providing improved financial access. These services need to ensure confidentiality, be acceptable to adolescents, and be adolescent-specific.
2. *Improve adolescent environments* by supporting families, improving economic conditions, enhancing communities where adolescents live, reducing violence, and encouraging understanding and less discrimination toward adolescents.
3. *Increase the role of schools in adolescent health* through educational policies that encourage success for all through links with parents and the community, through comprehensive health education, and through the establishment of more school-based/linked health centers.
4. *Promote positive adolescent health* by including adolescent health in lifetime health promotion efforts, by increasing adolescent-positive norms, by

educating and facilitating adolescent decision making, and by targeting adolescents in health promotion and disease prevention efforts.

5. *Improve adolescent transitions* through improved service opportunities, better employment opportunities, more transitional independent living programs for out-of-home adolescents, and more attention to life options and career choice development.

6. *Improve collaborative relationships* within communities, between the public and private sectors, between and within various levels of government, and within and between the professions (Brindis et al. 1996).

These efforts have generally been made from the viewpoint that government and society are capable of addressing social problems, a viewpoint that is not necessarily accepted by a majority of the voting public. Although such recommendations may summarize a possible consensus of the academic, direct service, and policy communities' viewpoints on adolescents' needs after considerable deliberation and research, these do not necessarily represent a consensus regarding the value conflicts within the larger society regarding sexuality, parenting, or the role of government. They could, however, define the knowledge basis for national, state, and local efforts to reach accommodation on these issues.

GAPS and Bright Futures and the Development of Primary Care

Another related set of initiatives has been to define and support the expansion of prevention within primary health care. The American Academy of Pediatrics, in cooperation with funding agencies of the federal government such as MCHB and others, has created a set of guidelines and materials regarding primary care for all of pediatrics, including adolescents, called *Bright Futures*. A cooperative effort with the American Medical Association as the lead agency has worked toward defining, educating, and implementing preventive services within primary care, called Guidelines for Adolescent Preventive Services (GAPS) (Elster and Kuznets 1994). This program includes training, resources materials, and guidebooks for a primary care provider. (See Table 8–2.)

Together these two sets of guidelines establish a professional standard that recognizes the special needs of adolescents for regular prevention-oriented health care that includes periodic evaluation, risk screening, health education, and anticipatory guidance. It is recognized that implementation will require significant training for providers of health care. These guidelines assume thorough links with health education and social services that may be stigmatizing or poorly coordinated with health care delivery. Proving the cost-benefit of this type of clinic-based preventive care should be possible in part because the high cost of many preventable adolescent problems (premature birth, motor vehicle injuries, cancer from smoking for 30 years) and the long exposure to costs mean that a small effect

Table 8–2 Essential Components of a GAPS Visit

Visit Orientation
Adolescents and their parents should be informed of the nature and purpose of each annual GAPS visit. This can be done with a reminder letter or postcard, by telephone, and/or upon arrival at the office.

Medical History
At the initial visit, information about current health status, past medical history, and family history should be obtained. This information should be updated at each subsequent GAPS visit through use of a self-administered questionnaire, clinical interview, or a combination of both.

Adolescent Interview
Adolescents should be asked annually about current health concerns as well as behaviors that may compromise health. These discussions should take place without the parent present and should be confidential to ensure that adolescents discuss sensitive issues candidly.

Parent Interview
Parents should be interviewed alone at least twice during their child's adolescence to clarify past medical or family history, provide health guidance, and elicit parental concerns about the adolescent's health, behavior, and development.

Measurements
All adolescents should have annual blood pressure, height, and weight measurements. The Body Mass Index (BMI), weight/height^2, should be used to determine the weight status of adolescents.

Physical Examination
Adolescents should receive three complete physical examinations between the ages of 11 and 21 to identify deviations in growth and development and early onset of biomedical and emotional disorders.

Management Plan
Information obtained from the history, clinical interviews, and physical examination should be used to develop a management plan. This plan might include the need for immunizations, laboratory tests, TB skin test, follow-up visits for further assessment, targeted counseling, treatment, or referral.

Health Guidance
GAPS recommends that all adolescents and parents receive health guidance on growth and development, lifestyles, and injuries. In addition, targeted counseling should be given to those adolescents and parents with specific needs as identified during clinical visits.

Source: Reprinted with permission from A.B. Elster and N.J. Kuznets, *AMA Guidelines for Adolescent Preventive Services: Recommendations and Rationale,* chart p. XXV, © 1994, Williams and Wilkins.

of 5–7 percent in changing a high-risk behavior may in fact be very cost effective for society as a whole over the long run (Downs and Klein 1995). The difficulty may be that most cost benefit analyses of interest to those who finance health care usually look to shorter term benefits. Showing shorter term benefits will require greater immediate effectiveness, which will be more difficult to demonstrate.

CURRENT ISSUES IN ADOLESCENT HEALTH: APPLICATION OF KEY PUBLIC HEALTH CONCEPTS

Injuries and the Haddon Matrix

As noted above, injuries account for over 75 percent of all adolescent deaths. Injuries include both *unintentional* events, such as motor vehicle and bicycle crashes, drowning, and occupational safety failures, as well as *intentional* injuries, such as homicide, suicide, and abuse. Since the frequency and severity of injury in the population are predictable, public health workers focused on primary prevention and avoiding use of the word "accident," preferring the term, "injury event." By intersecting the three time phases of the injury event—pre-event, event, and post-event—with the agent, host, and environment factors from the epidemiologic model, the Haddon matrix has been a successful public health tool for identifying strategies for injury prevention. Several applications of the Haddon matrix to intentional and unintentional injury problems of adolescence follow.

Motor Vehicle Injuries

As a result of interventions suggested by a public health approach such as the Haddon matrix (see Table 8–3), unintentional motor vehicle fatalities in the 15- to 19-year-old age group have declined 30 percent from 1979 to 1991 (Lescohier and Gallagher 1996). Population-based strategies of benefit to all ages, such as improvements in highway design (interstate highways have one-third the fatality rate of rural highways), automobile crash safety design, seat belt use and passive restraint systems (40–50 percent less fatality), and emergency medical service can be derived from this type of analysis. Efforts to reduce drunk driving by raising the drinking age, lowering the permissible blood alcohol levels, making the identification of a "designated driver" the social norm, sponsoring alcohol-free events, and even restricting automobile travel time are ways to improve the human pre-event factors related to injury. Efforts to increase the human factor of seat belt use during the event are only minimally successful unless they are also accompanied by a pre-event social environment with legal sanctions for noncompliance. Interestingly, driver education classes have not been shown to improve safety and in fact may decrease safety by enabling adolescents to drive at an earlier age (U.S. Congress, 1991a). The federal requirement of passive restraints and air bags is based

Table 8–3 Modified Haddon Matrix of Factors Related to Likelihood of Motor Vehicle Injuries and Their Outcomes

	Host Factors	Agent or Vehicle Factors	Physical Environment Factors	Socio-Cultural Environment Factors
Pre-Event	driver vision alcohol intoxication experience and judgment amount of travel	brakes, tires center of gravity jack-knife tendency speed capability ease of control	visibility of hazards road curve and grade surface divided hwy signals intersection access control	attitudes about alcohol enforcement of speeding laws laws re graduated driver licensing
Event	safety-belt use age sex	speed on impact vehicle size automatic restraints air bag type of contact rollover	recovery areas guard rails median barriers roadside embankments speed limits	attitudes about safety-belt use laws about safety-belt use enforcement of safety-belt use
Post-Event	age physical condition severity of injury body region injured	fuel system integrity	emergency transport system quality of EMS distance to trauma center rehabilitation programs	support for trauma care systems skill of EMS personnel laws and attitudes re disability school integration

Source: National Committee for Injury Prevention and Control, *Injury Prevention: Meeting the Challenge,* p. 8, © 1989, by permission of Oxford University Press.

on the consideration of rapid energy exchange as the "agent" of injury at the time of the crash, and may be one of the most significant factors for harm reduction.

Other efforts such as restricting the hours of motor vehicle operation for adolescents ("graduated driver licensing") have been suggested, but these are likely to be quite provocative to many adolescents. The importance of transportation in conflict with parents has a long history, as illustrated by the story told of Socrates, who asked a youth named Lysis whether his parents gratified all his wishes. In response, Lysis complained that, even though his parents seemed to want him to be happy, his father would not let him ride the family's horses (quoted in Hall 1904).

Occupational Injuries of Adolescents

A seldom considered aspect of injuries for adolescents is occupational injury. Five million children and adolescents under 18 are legally employed, and an estimated 1 million other youth are employed illegally, often in agriculture, sweatshops, and more recently, chain restaurants and grocery stores with sweatshop conditions (Landrigan et al. 1995). In 1992, 64,000 teenagers ages 14–17 were treated in emergency departments of hospitals for occupational related injuries, including 26 percent of all 17-year-olds treated for emergencies (Layne et al. 1994). Of these injuries, two-thirds were of males; 54 percent were cuts, lacerations, and burns in the retail trades, mostly restaurant businesses; and 20 percent were in service industries. Illegally employed youth are particularly vulnerable with a 10 times greater risk of injury than the legally employed. Agricultural workers, often exempt from child labor laws, are another risk group with significant injury, including 300 deaths, mostly from tractors and other farm equipment. Hearing loss among high school farm workers from exposure to noisy machinery is another common but seldom recognized problem. An overlooked aspect of occupational health is the impact in adolescence of work on other risk behaviors. Although evaluations of the effect of work on academic progress are mixed, one extensive study found increased substance abuse, sexual behavior, and increased hostility toward the world of work among adolescents who worked more than 15–20 hours per week (Fine et al. 1990). Since adolescents are often new to jobs, inexperienced, ignorant of their legal rights, and often trusting and/or easily intimidated by employers, they may be particularly vulnerable to occupational injuries and reluctant to identify and report unsafe practices and injuries. Work permits, often required by the state until age 18, which must be signed by a school office and sometimes by a physician, are often overlooked opportunities for anticipatory guidance and other preventive efforts.

Homicide

As described in the epidemiology section, homicides have increased dramatically from 1985 to 1995, and victims are overwhelmingly male, African American, older adolescent, known to the assailant, and killed with a handgun following an argument when the victim and/or the assailant has been drinking alcohol (Cohall and Cohall 1995). Nonfatal assaults, knife homicides, and other violent crimes in general have not in fact increased dramatically during this time period, but the increased availability of small, powerful handguns leads to the conclusion that the marketing of these weapons is the most likely cause of the increased homicide rate (Fingerhut et al. 1992). Although usually seen as a criminal justice problem, increasingly homicide is also being seen as a public health problem requiring multidimensional responses from a variety of sectors in the community. Table 8–4 presents a Haddon matrix of public health interventions regarding gun violence. Some of these ideas may not be feasible, but use of the matrix as a brainstorming tool can help broaden the range of ideas to be considered.

A wide range of efforts have been made to reduce gun-related homicide. These are usually founded on ideas to improve the community, change the youth, and restrict gun access. In many ways the least controversial and the easiest to implement politically are efforts to modify youth behavior, although evaluation efforts have been limited (Stiffman et al. 1996). Some examples are teaching conflict resolution skills, engaging youth in more positive activities inconsistent with violence or gang activity such as recreation programs or service programs, and developing life-option enhancement programs. Despite good evidence that limiting gun access reduces violence (Sloan et al. 1988; Christoffel 1991), efforts such as requiring registration, realistic background checks, and seller liability, as well as efforts to improve product safety by mandating devices such as automatic locking mechanisms (which could eliminate the value of stolen guns and thus make registration programs effective) have run into such controversy that it is clear guns have a significant symbolic value that is poorly understood.

Suicide

Efforts to reduce suicide usually involve improving identification and treatment related to mental health problems. Although suicide prevention efforts have had difficulty proving effectiveness scientifically, some promising results have been shown in reducing risk factors, reducing nonfatal risk behaviors, and in identifying and treating substance abuse disorders and affective disorders related to suicide (Kachur et al. 1995). Attempting to reduce youth suicide, the CDC has identified several basic strategies (Berman and Jobes 1991).

1. *Training school and community gatekeepers* such as teachers, coaches, and youth workers in suicide and mental health problem recognition. Too often problems of distressed youth are dismissed as "just adolescence," but it is hoped that those who work regularly with youth would more readily be able to recognize the differences.

Table 8–4 Modified Haddon Matrix of Factors Related to Firearm-Related Homicide

	Host Factors	Agent or Energy Factors	Physical Environment Factors	Socio-Cultural Environment Factors
Pre-Event	Train people to recognize potential assault situations and respond in a self-protective manner Teach conflict resolution skills Provide positive activities (clubs, recreation, service, education) Teach secure gun storage Identify and treat at-risk youth Provide mentoring programs Employment programs for youth, particularly minority urban youth	Modify guns so they cannot be easily concealed Require default locking to reduce stolen gun value Require gun loaded indicator Prohibit assault ammunition (large "footprint" bullets)	Provide bullet-proof shields Regular police patrols Surveillance systems Make metal detectors more common	National gun owner ID laws Limit gun sale, ownership, and access to teens Reduce TV violence Pass and enforce civil liability laws for illegal sale End consumer safety law exemptions Adequately fund background check systems Register ammunition sales Establish curfew laws to reduce high risk exposure times Establish "safe area" activity programs and neighborhood watch programs

continues

Table 8–4 continued

Factors	Host Factors	Agent or Energy Factors	Physical Environment Factors	Socio-Cultural Environment Factors
Event	Provide people with bullet-proof vests Train people in self defense Train community conflict mediators Promulgate conflict de-escalation rituals	Modify guns or bullets so they do not injure	Police patrols to catch events in-progress Surveillance cameras for quick response	Change societal norms regarding resistance to assault
Post-Event	Increase first-aid training Promulgate conflict de-escalation systems Provide post-traumatic stress treatment	Modify guns so they require reloading more often	Nearby emergency care Rapid EMS deployment	Ensure emergency medical care access to all Sue dealer, assaulter, manufacturer for damages Increase penalties for unsafe or illegal gun use

Source: Reprinted with permission from C.W. Runyan and E.A. Gerken, Injuries, in *The Health of Adolescents: Understanding and Facilitating Biological, Behavioral, and Social Development,* W.R. Hendee and Associates, p. 326, © 1991, American Medical Association, published by Jossey-Bass Inc., Publishers.

2. *General, untargeted education* regarding suicide. These have included education about the relationship of depression, substance abuse, and conduct disorders to suicide; publicizing ways to access help; and more general health promotion focusing on stress management, social skills, assertiveness training, and problem-solving skills. Evaluations of the effectiveness of such programs have been mixed, and some have expressed concern about possible iatrogenic effects in that some suicide attempters have developed more positive attitudes about suicide after exposure to such programs (U.S. Congress, 1991b).

3. *Screening* with standardized tools. Although such tools usually have a very high false positive rate (U.S. Task Force on Preventive Services 1996), they may still be useful in identifying those who still have significant mental health needs.

4. *Peer support* to help with a variety of risk behaviors. Peer support has shown some effectiveness in reducing some forms of risk behavior and is usually well received, but again the link to suicidal behavior has not been established.

5. *Crisis centers and hotlines.* Again, evaluation studies are rare and show mixed results in follow-up studies of callers, but one study showed that communities that began such centers had a statistically significant, albeit small, reduction in suicides (U.S. Congress, 1991b).

6. *Restriction of access to lethal means.* This has been effective in several locations, including Great Britain where the method of choice—cooking gas with carbon monoxide—was made less lethal, Australia where sedatives were more strictly regulated, and certain U.S. communities after firearms were more strictly controlled (Kachur et al. 1995).

7. *Postvention* after suicide to identify others at risk and to prevent clustering of attempts. Although the phenomenon of clustering is commonly reported, much doubt has been expressed by researchers regarding the phenomenon (Berman and Jobes 1991).

Other strategies would be to improve coordination of services for those who have attempted suicide and to enhance the availability and acceptability of mental health services to at-risk populations, such as Native American youth, gay and lesbian youth, incarcerated youth.

Adolescent Pregnancy and the Continuum of Services

Adolescent pregnancy is another public health problem that has become politicized, with much misinformation and distortion related to political expressions of concern. Since American sexual activity rates are similar to European rates yet

U.S. pregnancy rates are substantially higher, American adolescent pregnancy rates can hardly be attributed to the nature of adolescence, to the supposed generosity of the American welfare system compared to European welfare systems, or to greater promiscuity and related immoralities. Instead the higher rates should be attributed to factors more unique to the American experience, particularly widespread poverty and inequality, American attitudes about sexual behavior of adolescents, and the lack of universally available and accessible health care services, including family planning education and methods. Despite the controversy, the NRC notes that most adolescent pregnancy prevention programs enjoy wide support from the majority of Americans, and that even those who did not initially support these programs can often find common ground with the idea that every child should be born to a welcoming family ready and able to care for it (Brown and Eisenberg 1995).

Some have challenged the assumptions behind much of the public's concern. Since pregnancy rates are generally down and sexual activity up, pregnancy prevention efforts could claim a little success. Increases in unmarried pregnancy reflect changing societal patterns and the lack of employment opportunities more than they reflect adolescent ineptitude. Geronimus has argued that the negative consequences of teen parenting have been greatly exaggerated because researchers have not accounted for selection bias in that they have failed to recognize that those who become pregnant by and large are the poorest, least achieving young people even before they became pregnant (Geronimus 1987). Geronimus also has suggested that teen parenting may in fact be an adaptive response for adolescent African Americans with little hope for the future because they get more respect as mothers and are more likely to receive extended family support for parenting in adolescence than they would receive in their twenties. The frequently made claim by politicians that welfare causes teen pregnancy has been challenged by those who note large increases in the unmarried child-bearing rate among nonwelfare mothers, and lower pregnancy rates in countries and states with more generous welfare benefits. There does seem to be a weak effect of the availability of welfare benefits on decreasing the marriage rate of teen parents (Duncan et al. 1988).

Nevertheless, there is a general consensus among researchers that adolescent pregnancy has consequences that may have been exaggerated but that are still significant (Furstenburg 1991). Adolescents mothers themselves say their lives would have been better had they waited. Although controlling for income does reduce much of the difference in birth outcomes between adolescent and adult mothers, early adolescents still are at significantly greater risk for complications of pregnancy and for delivering small infants (U.S. Congress, 1991b; Fraser et al. 1995). Long-term follow-up studies of adolescents who give birth tend to show that they finish fewer total years of schooling, have lower income, and are more welfare dependent than those who don't give birth, but much variability and an impressive resilience in the face of adversity has been noted among many adolescent mothers. The discrepancy for poor outcomes has been noted to be less between African American adolescent and adult mothers than between White adolescent and adult mothers. The children of teen mothers have been shown to have less academic achievement, but again, controlling for the selection bias of socioeconomic status has been difficult. Achievement for males who father has also been shown to be affected but less so than for females (National Research Council 1987).

Numerous major reviews have reached general agreement on best ways to prevent adolescent pregnancies (National Research Council 1987; Brown and Eisenberg 1995). Each has affirmed that there is not one strategy, but multiple, communitywide approaches needed, which include the classic public health service continuum of health promotion, prevention, treatment, and secondary prevention.

First, echoing Marion Wright Edelman's often repeated comment that the best contraception is hope, adolescent pregnancy prevention strategies need to promote life options for at-risk adolescents by increasing employment and educational opportunities, training in specific skills, and providing support for youth in transition. One such program in 30 states, the Teen Outreach Program, emphasized small discussion groups and community service while reducing pregnancy rates, school failure, and school dropout by 30–50 percent compared to comparison groups (Allen et al. 1990).

Second, prevention programs based on comprehensive education are needed. Most current sex education programs are too short, too late, and too cognitively based. Effective programs include values discussion urging abstinence and delaying sexual activity as well as training in social skills, assertiveness, and peer pressure resistance and specific information on contraceptive use and access. Typically such programs include didactic information, role playing, and small group discussions. "Reducing the Risk," aimed at grades 9–12, and "Postponing Sexual Involvement," targeted to early adolescents, are examples of such programs (Howard and McCabe 1991; Kirby et al. 1991).

The third strategy is to increase access to contraceptives for the sizable number of adolescents who are already sexually active. Education about their use, confidentiality in obtaining health care services, readily available services such as those of school clinics, and payment mechanisms are critical to achieve this. In a model program that integrated school educational programs and contraceptive services at a nearby clinic, three-year pregnancy rates declined by 30 percent among enrolled students compared to a 58 percent increase among nonenrolled students (Zabin and Hayward 1993).

The fourth strategy, secondary prevention, is to provide comprehensive medical, educational, and social services to teen parents. Most such programs use the intermediate goal of completing education as the way to reduce the likelihood of a second pregnancy and to reduce the negative consequences to the infant of having a teen mother. They try to achieve these by a range of services including mentoring, tutoring, case management, counseling, support groups, financial incentives (and disincentives), child care, and employment assistance for young fathers. Follow-up studies as long as 20 years later indicate improved outcomes compared to controls (Seitz and Apfel 1993). Linking education to incentives may be a particularly useful approach to welfare reform, reducing second pregnancies and reducing the negative consequences of early childbearing (Aber et al. 1995).

Health Promotion and Problem Behaviors—Substance Abuse, Mental Health, Maltreatment

Although problems such as substance abuse and mental health problems are diverse, their consequences often follow similar pathways to expensive secondary level medical and social treatments. The pervasiveness of these psycho-social problems means interventions based solely on individual treatment approaches will require extensive and thus expensive use of professional time in systems that are frequently plagued by dyscoordination, difficulties in equality of access, and frequent lack of sensitivity to adolescent concerns. Treatment-based approaches, which currently reach only a small percentage of those needing such services, may be necessary and in need of expansion and improvement, but such services should not be expected to significantly reduce the prevalence of these problems. Focusing too much on psychopathologies such as depression, eating disorders, conduct disorders, and addictions misses the dearth of opportunities, skills, and internal strengths needed by adolescents to resist much of their toxic social environments. Even primary prevention programs based on individual anticipatory guidance and health education, screening, and referral to treatment, though necessary, will be insufficient to reduce these problems in a major way. Activities broadly based on skills for promoting health offer a paradigm for programs that have led to significant improvements in a variety of areas, particularly when such programs are integrated and reinforced in school, community, home, and medical settings (Elster et al. 1993).

Views of what constitutes health promotion depend on views of health. Usually the term is used to contrast with illness. Instead, emphasis should be placed on the experience of well-being, the capacity to perform expected roles and tasks, and the ability to fulfill one's potential (Millstein 1993). For adolescents the definition varies by development, by culture, and by domain of personal experience. What constitutes health regarding sexual expression or alcohol is different for 12-year-olds than it is for 19-year-olds, is different in cultures where customs differ, and is different in domains such as body image and athletics. Positive mental health for adolescents has been defined as having the skills of emotional regulation, flexible problem solving, and use of social resources to protect oneself from stress as well as having the skills to involve oneself in personally meaningful activities (Compras 1993).

Most programs aimed at increasing skills for coping with stress emphasize interactive learning, role playing, peer leadership, modeling, practice, and small group discussions in addition to some didactic education. The Life Skills Training program and the Yale-New Haven Social Problem-Solving Project are two examples of programs using these concepts to teach and practice specific social competency skills to deal with stress. Life Skills Training has demonstrated significantly less substance use among participants than among control groups and has been replicated. Participants in the Yale-New Haven Social Problem-Solving Project had increased problem-solving skills, better academic achievement, and less misbehavior in school than controls. Sustaining changes over time has been difficult unless the interventions continue or have "booster sessions" and involve opportunities within the environment to use the skills learned under supportive conditions. Reviews of substance abuse prevention programs found that programs that teach interactively and that target social influences such as media and peer pressure are able to reduce use of gateway substances (tobacco, alcohol, and marijuana) between 20 to 67 percent (Compras 1993).

Designing programs so that school, community, home, and medical interventions reinforce each other and create "webs of influence" has been an important part of health promotion strategies (Price et al. 1993). The Midwestern Prevention Project in Kansas City, an experimental program using random assignment of schools to intervention strategies, added a social institution intervention each year including mass media campaigns, school programs, parent programs, community organization interventions, and areawide policy changes. The program showed the most changes in cigarette smoking, alcohol, and marijuana use in the groups that were exposed to the most interventions (Pentz 1993).

Support for families and enhancing parenting skills is another important area for health promotion, given the importance of families for healthy development and the tremendous consequences of parental maltreatment. Adolescents of parents who abuse them, neglect them, or fail to supervise them show increased risk behavior and too often individual and social destructiveness (National Research Council 1993b). Although physical abuse of adolescents is less common than abuse of younger children, child abuse reporting systems indicate adolescents are neglected more often than younger children are abused, either by parents expelling them, ignoring behavioral problems, failing to provide food and shelter, or just leaving them (Finkelhor et al. 1995). A review of family support programs indicates most teach communication skills of parents, a few teach monitoring skills, but very few address the skills needed to fulfill the responsibilities of parents to provide for basic needs, protection, or advocacy (Small and Eastin 1991). A broader approach to healthy parenting is recommended in the last report of the

Carnegie Council of Adolescent Development, which recommends major efforts to re-engage adults and families in the lives of young people by more specific parenting support classes, groups, networks, and resource centers, particularly at the middle school; by increasing work schedule flexibility; by specifically including parents in school and agency governance; by emphasizing the need for community responsibility for after-school programs; and by extending the child care credit past the current age of 12 (Carnegie Council on Adolescent Development 1995).

Special Populations and the Core Responsibilities of Public Health

Although public health uses population-based approaches, the population is heterogeneous and certain groups of the population have worse health status, often based on being excluded from social resources, stigmatized, and blamed for their conditions. These special populations include groups such as ethnic and racial minorities, immigrants and migrants, the poor, the learning disabled, the incarcerated, pregnant and parenting youth, the mentally ill, foster youth, maltreated youth, and youth with different sexual orientations. For youth, the multiplicity of special population identities is probably the most significant factor in risk. For example, the Native American, learning disabled youth in the foster care system who is pregnant would be considered at "multiple jeopardy." Owing to the alienated and/or outcast nature of many of these groups, public health work is particularly concerned with assessing the needs of these populations, ensuring that appropriate, quality services are provided, and creating policies that attempt to create a link with the larger society. Sometimes the assurance function leads public health agencies to provide direct services to some of these groups to demonstrate the feasibility of services, and thereby establish a beginning point for wider collaboration. In this way groups that are considered "too difficult" for traditional health care providers are served.

Furthermore, because of the degree of social alienation experienced by many of these groups, special efforts need to be made to establish collaborative relationships for health. The population of homeless youth, for instance, is difficult to assess because many avoid contact with adults for fear of being turned over to the police and returned to their homes. Efforts to understand their health problems will need significant street outreach and work with peers. Likewise, ensuring quality may be more difficult with certain ethnic groups with traditions of alternative views of health and with traditions of not appearing to disagree with authority. Policy development regarding some particularly stigmatized groups such as the incarcerated creates many controversies beyond their immediate health care needs. Working with key people trusted by those within the group, recognizing existing community networks and supports, and engaging in collaborative processes around jointly identified problems have been ways that public health workers have tried to develop epidemiological analysis, a continuum of care, and health promotion activities for special populations.

FUTURE DIRECTIONS

Despite the widespread call for increased access to health care and improved environments for adolescents, the continuing cultural conflict about the role of government, the degree of individual versus social causation for problems, and adolescent sexual behavior will likely continue and make access for adolescents to health care difficult. Public health initiatives have had the most success when they deliberately and systematically build a wide base at the local, state, or national level. This may be time-consuming and unpredictable, but it may also lead to stronger, continuing support.

Another future direction of public health work with adolescents will be an effort to include adolescent needs in any future system of health care reform— managed care, national health insurance, or whatever combination emerges. Particularly important is establishing systems of confidentiality for adolescents; enabling and training providers to have a working knowledge of adolescents' needs, abilities, and limitations; and establishing primary care with risk screening, health guidance, and coordination with appropriate ameliorative programs. Identifying adolescent health indicators and adolescent-specific evaluations will be important avenues to pursue in efforts to keep health care systems accountable to serving adolescents. Since these problems and solutions often cross institutional boundaries, creating partnerships and a broader view of social cost will be important areas for future program implementation and evaluations.

Ultimately adolescent health status may be affected more by broader social issues than by direct contact with the health care system. Factors that seem to increase health among adolescents have been described as not just the absence of maltreatment, infection, stress, or social oppression, but the presence of adults who maintain caring and connectedness with them within the community. Those wanting to improve the health of adolescents will need to find ways to institutionalize these traits and find ways to enhance resilience, reduce the harm, secure the environment, and establish a sense of engagement in the lives of adolescents.

ACKNOWLEDGMENTS

From the Division of Adolescent Medicine, Department of Social Work, and the National Adolescent Health Information Center, University of California, San Francisco. (Knopf)

Supported in part by the United States Maternal and Child Health Bureau grants MCJ 063 A80 and MC 000 978A, and by the Murdoch Endowment, Department of Social Work, University of California, San Francisco.

REFERENCES

Aber, J.L. et al. 1995. Effects of welfare reform on teenage parents and their children. *Future of Children* 5:53–71.

Allen, J.P. et al. 1990. School based prevention of teenage pregnancy and school drop out: Process evaluation of the National Replication of the Teen Outreach Program. *Community Psychology* 18:4.

Baumrind, D. 1987. Rearing competent children. In Adolescent social behavior and health. *New directions for child development,* Vol. 37, ed. C.E. Irwin, Jr. San Francisco, CA: Jossey-Bass.

Berman, A.L., and D.A. Jobes. 1991. *Adolescent suicide assessment and intervention.* Washington, DC: American Psychological Association.

Blum, R. 1987. Contemporary threats to adolescent health in the United States. *Journal of American Medical Association* 257:3390–3395.

Blyth, D.A. 1993. *Healthy communities, healthy youth: How communities contribute to positive youth development.* Minneapolis: Search Institute.

Brindis, C.B. et al. 1996. *Improving adolescent lives: A synthesis of health policy recommendations.* (Working Document). San Francisco: National Adolescent Health Information Center.

Brooks-Gunn, J., and F.F. Furstenberg, Jr. 1989. Adolescent sexual behavior. *American Psychologist* 44:249–257.

Brooks-Gunn, J., and R.L. Paikoff. 1993. "Sex is a gamble, kissing is a game": Adolescent sexuality and health promotion. In *Promoting the health of adolescents: New directions for the twenty-first century,* eds. S.G. Millstein et al. New York: Oxford University Press.

Brown, S.S., and L. Eisenberg. 1995. *The best intentions: Unintended pregnancy and the well-being of children and families.* Washington, DC: National Academy Press.

Carnegie Council on Adolescent Development. 1989. *Turning points. Preparing American youth for the twenty-first century: The report of the Task Force on Education of Young Adolescents.* Washington, DC: Carnegie Council on Adolescent Development.

Carnegie Council on Adolescent Development. 1995. *Great transitions: Preparing adolescents for a new century/concluding report of the Carnegie Council on Adolescent Development.* New York: Carnegie Corporation of New York.

Centers for Disease Control and Prevention. 1994. Health risk behaviors among adolescents who do and do not attend school—U.S., 1992. *Morbidity and Mortality Weekly Report* 43:129–132.

Centers for Disease Control and Prevention, Division of STD/HIV Prevention. 1994. *Annual Report, 1993.* Atlanta, GA.

Centers for Disease Control and Prevention. 1995a. State specific pregnancy and birth rates among teenagers—United States 1991–1992. *Morbidity and Mortality Weekly Report* 44:676–684.

Centers for Disease Control and Prevention. 1995b. Disabilities among children aged 17 years—U.S., 1991–1992. *Morbidity and Mortality Weekly Report* 44:609–613.

Centers for Disease Control and Prevention. 1995c. Mortality trends, causes of death, and related risk behaviors among U.S. adolescents, 1993. *Adolescent Health: State of the Nation Monograph Series,* No. 1. Centers for Disease Control and Prevention Publication No. 099-4112. Atlanta, GA: Author.

Cheng, T.L. et al. 1993. Confidentiality in health care: A survey of knowledge, perceptions, and attitudes among high school students. *Journal of American Medical Association* 269:1404–1407.

Christoffel, K.K. 1991. Toward reducing pediatric firearm injuries: Charting a legislative and regulatory course. *Pediatrics* 88:294.

Cohall, A.T., and R.M Cohall. 1995. Number one with a bullet. Adolescent injury: Epidemiology and prevention, eds. K.K. Christoffel and C.W. Runyan. *Adolescent Medicine: State of the Art Reviews* 6:183–198.

Compras, B.E. 1993. Promoting positive mental health during adolescence. In *Promoting the health of adolescents: New directions for the 21st century*, eds. S.G. Millstein et al. New York: Oxford University Press.

Council of Scientific Affairs. 1993. Confidential health care services for adolescents. *Journal of American Medical Association* 269:1420–1424.

Darling, N., and L. Steinberg. 1993. Parenting style as context: An integrative model. *Psychological Bulletin* 113:487–496.

Donovan, J.E., and R. Jessor. 1985. Structure of problem behavior in adolescence and young adulthood. *Journal of Consulting and Clinical Psychology* 53:890–904.

Downs, S.M., and J.D. Klein. 1995. Clinical preventive services efficacy and adolescent risk behaviors. *Archives of Pediatric and Adolescent Medicine* 149:374–379.

Duncan, G.J. et al. 1988. Welfare dependence within and across generations. *Science* 1:467–471.

Edelman, P., and J. Ladner, eds. 1991. *Adolescence and Poverty.* Washington, DC: Center for National Policy Press.

Elder, G.H. et al. 1992. Families under economic pressure. *Journal of Family Issues* 13:5–37.

Elkind, D. 1967. Egocentrism in adolescence. *Child Development* 38:1025–1034.

Elster, A.B., and N.J. Kuznets, eds. 1994. *AMA guidelines for adolescent preventive services (GAPS): Recommendations and rationale.* Baltimore: Williams and Wilkins.

Elster, A. et al., eds. 1993. *American Medical Association state-of-the-art conference on adolescent health promotion: Proceedings.* Arlington, VA: National Center for Education in Maternal and Child Health.

English, A. 1993. Early and Periodic Screening, Diagnosis and Treatment: A model for improving adolescents' access to health care. *Journal of Adolescent Health* 14:524–527.

English, A., and M. Matthews. 1995. *State minor consent statutes: A summary.* Cincinnati, OH: Center for Continuing Education in Adolescent Health.

Entwisle, D.R. 1990. Schools and the adolescent. In *At the threshold: The developing adolescent*, eds. S.S. Feldman and G.R. Elliot. Cambridge, MA: Harvard University Press.

Fine, G.A. et al. 1990. Leisure, work, and the mass media. In *At the threshold: The developing adolescent*, eds. S.S. Feldman and G.R. Elliot. Cambridge, MA: Harvard University Press.

Fingerhut, L.A. et al. 1992. Firearm and non-firearm homicide among persons 15–19 years of age. *Journal of American Medical Association* 267:48–53.

Finkelhor, D. et al. 1995. *Missing, abducted, runaway, throwaway children in America.* Washington, DC: Office of Juvenile Justice and Delinquency Prevention Programs.

Forrest, J.D., and S. Singh. 1990. The sexual and reproductive behaviors of American women, 1982–1988. *Family Planning Perspectives* 22:206–214.

Fox, H.B., and L.B. Wicks. 1994. *Serving Medicaid eligible adolescents through managed care.* Portland, ME: National Academy for State Health Policy.

Fraser, A.M. et al. 1995. Association of young maternal age with adverse reproductive outcomes. *New England Journal of Medicine* 332:1113–1117.

Freud, A. 1958. Adolescence. In *Psychoanalytic study of the child,* Vol. 13. New York, NY: International Universities.

Furstenberg, F.F. 1991. As the pendulum swings: Teenage childbearing and social concern. *Human Relations* 40:127–138.

Gans, J.E. et al. 1990. *America's adolescents: How healthy are they?* Chicago: American Medical Association.

Gans, J.E. et al. 1991. *Adolescent health care: Use, costs, and problems of access.* Chicago, IL: American Medical Association.

Geronimus, A.T. 1987. On teenage childbearing in the United States. *Population and Development Review* 13:54–61.

Gilligan, C. 1987. Adolescent development reconsidered. In Adolescent social behavior and health. *New directions in child development,* Vol. 37., ed. C.E. Irwin, Jr. San Francisco: Jossey-Bass.

Gordon, T.E. 1996. The need for adolescent health education and training among health professionals. *American Journal of Public Health* (In Press).

Grissmer, D.W. et al. 1995. *Student achievement and the changing American family.* Santa Monica, CA: Rand Corporation.

Hall, G.S. 1904. *Adolescence: Its psychology, and its relations to anthropology, sex, crime, religion, and education.* New York: Appleton and Company.

Harevan, T.K. 1982. American families in transition: Historical perspectives on change. In *Normal family processes,* ed. F. Walsh. New York: Guilford Press.

Hauser, S.T. et al. 1991. *Adolescents and their families: Paths of ego development.* New York: Free Press.

Hein, K. 1994. Training in the era of health care reform. In *Health care reform: Opportunities for improving adolescent health,* eds. C.E. Irwin, Jr. et al. Arlington, VA: National Center for Education in Maternal and Child Health.

Howard, M., and J. McCabe. 1990. Helping teenagers postpone sexual involvement. *Family Planning Perspectives* 22:21–26.

Huesman, L.R., and L.D. Eron, eds. 1986. *Television and the aggressive child: A cross national comparison.* Hillsdale, NJ: Lawrence Erlbaum.

Igra, V., and S.G. Millstein. 1993. Current status and approaches to improving preventive services for adolescents. *Journal of American Medical Association* 9:1408–1412.

Irwin, C.E., Jr. 1987. Editor's notes: Adolescent health and behavior. In *New directions for child development.* Vol. 37., ed. C.E. Irwin, Jr. San Francisco: Jossey-Bass.

Irwin, C.E., Jr. 1990. The theoretical concept of at-risk adolescents. *Adolescent medicine: State of the art reviews* 1:1–14.

Irwin, C.E., Jr. et al., eds. 1994. *Health care reform: Opportunities for improving adolescent health.* Arlington, VA: National Center for Education in Maternal and Child Health.

Jessor, R., and S. Jessor. 1977. *Problem behavior and psycho-social development: A longitudinal study of youth.* New York: Academic Press.

Johnson, L.D. et al. 1996. *National survey results from monitoring the future study: 1975–1995. II. College and Young Adults.* Washington, DC: National Institute of Drug Abuse.

Kachur, S.P. et al. 1995. Suicide: Epidemiology, prevention and treatment. *Adolescent Medicine: State of the Art Reviews* 6:171–182.

Kann, E. et al. 1995. Youth risk behavior surveillance—United States, 1993. Centers for Disease Control and Prevention Surveillance Summaries. *Morbidity and Mortality Weekly Report* 44 (SS-a): 1–49.

Keating, D.P. 1990. Adolescent thinking. In *At the threshold: The developing adolescent,* eds. S.S. Feldman and C.R. Elliot. Cambridge, MA: Harvard University Press.

Kett, J.F. 1993. Discovery and invention in the history of adolescence. *Journal of Adolescent Health* 14:605–612.

Kirby, D. et al. 1991. Reducing the risk: A new curriculum to prevent sexual risk-taking. *Family Planning Perspectives* 23:253–263.

Klein, J.D. et al. 1992. Access to health care for adolescents. A position paper of the Society for Adolescent Medicine. *Journal of Adolescent Health* 13:162–170.

Knopf, D. 1996. *State adolescent health coordinators annual survey, 1996: Medicaid managed care; Special Populations. Preliminary report.* San Francisco: National Adolescent Health Information Center.

Lamborn, S.D. et al. 1991. Patterns of competence and adjustment among adolescents from authoritative, authoritarian, indulgent, and neglectful families. *Child Development* 62:1049–1065.

Landrigan, P.J. et al. 1995. Occupational injuries: Epidemiology, preventions, treatment. In Adolescent injuries: Epidemiology and prevention, eds. K.K. Christoffel and C.W. Runyan. *Adolescent Medicine State of the Art Reviews* 6:207–214.

Layne, L.A. et al. 1994. Adolescent occupational injuries requiring emergency department treatment: A nationally representative sample. *American Journal of Public Health* 84:657–660.

Lear, J.G. ed. 1989. *The school-based adolescent health care program.* Proceedings from the 1989 Adolescent Health Coordinators Conference. Washington, DC: National Center for Education in Maternal and Child Health.

Lescohier, D., and S.S. Gallagher. 1996. Unintentional injury. In *Handbook of adolescent risk behavior*, eds. R.J. Diclemente et al. New York: Plenum Press.

Miller, B.C. et al. 1993. Sexual behavior in adolescence. In *Adolescent sexuality*, ed. T.P. Gullota. Newbury Park, CA: Sage Publishing.

Millstein, S.G. et al. 1993. *Promoting the health of adolescents: New directions for the 21st century.* New York: Oxford University Press.

Millstein, S.G. et al. 1991. Sociodemographic trends and projections in the adolescent population. In *The health of adolescents*, ed. W.R. Hendee. San Francisco: Jossey-Bass.

Millstein, S.G., and V. Igra. 1996. Theoretical models of adolescent risk-behavior. In *Adolescent health problems: Behavioral perspectives*, eds. J.L. Wallander and L.J. Siegal. New York: Guilford Press.

Modell, J., and M. Goodman. 1990. Historical perspective. In *At the threshold: The developing adolescent*, eds. S.S. Feldman and G.R. Elliot. Cambridge, MA: Harvard University Press.

National Adolescent Health Information Center. 1995a. *Fact sheet on adolescent pregnancy prevention: Effective strategies.* San Francisco: University of California.

National Adolescent Health Information Center. 1995b. *Fact sheet on adolescent homicide.* San Francisco: University of California.

National Commission on Children. 1991. *Beyond rhetoric: A new American agenda for children and families. Final report.* Washington, DC: Government Printing Office.

National Commission on the Role of the School and Community in Improving Adolescent Health, National Association of School Boards of Education and the American Medical Society. 1990. *Code blue: Uniting for healthier youth.* Washington, DC: National Association of School Boards of Education.

National Research Council. Panel on Adolescent Pregnancy and Childbearing, Committee on Child Development and Research, Commission on Behavioral and Social Sciences. 1987. *Risking the future: Adolescent sexuality, pregnancy, and childbearing.* Washington, DC: National Academy Press.

National Research Council. 1989. *Diet and health: Implications for reducing chronic disease risk.* Washington, DC: National Academy Press.

National Research Council, Commission on Behavioral and Social Sciences and Education. 1993a. *Losing generations.* Washington, DC: National Academy Press.

National Research Council, Panel on Research on Child Abuse and Neglect. 1993b. *Understanding child abuse and neglect.* Washington, DC: National Academy Press.

Nelson, C. 1991. Office visits by adolescents. *Advance Data* 11:1–11, April.

Newacheck, P.W. 1989. Adolescents with special health care needs: Prevalence, severity, and access to health services. *Pediatrics* 84:872–881.

Offer, D., and K.A. Schonert-Reichl. 1992. Debunking the myths of adolescence: Findings from recent research. *Journal of American Academy of Child and Adolescent Psychiatry* 31:1003–1014.

O'Carroll, P.W. et al. 1993. Measuring adolescent health behavior related to intentional injuries. *Public Health Reports* 108 (suppl. 1):15–19.

Pentz, MA. 1993. Benefits of integrating strategies in different settings. In *American Medical Association state-of-the-art conference on adolescent health promotion, Proceedings,* eds. A. Elster et al. Arlington, VA: National Center for Education in Maternal and Child Health.

Perkins, J., and E. Rivera. 1995. EPSDT and managed care: Do plans know what they are getting into? *Clearinghouse Review* 21:1248–1260, March.

Petersen, A.C. et al. 1993. Depression in adolescence. *American Psychologist* 48:155–168.

Pipes, P.L. 1989. *Nutrition in infancy and childhood.* St. Louis, MO: Times Mirror/Mosby College Publishing.

Price, R.H. et al. 1993. Webs of influence: School and community programs that enhance adolescent health and education. *Teacher's College Record* 94:487–520.

Quadrel, M.J. et al. 1993. Adolescent (in)vulnerability. *American Psychologist* 43:102–116.

Remefedi, G. 1989. The healthy sexual development of gay and lesbian adolescents. *SIECUS Report* 17:7–8.

Remefedi, G. 1992. Demography of sexual orientation in adolescence. *Pediatrics* 89:714.

Richardson, J.L. et al. 1993. Relationship between after-school care of adolescents and substance use, risk taking, depressed mood and academic achievement. *Pediatrics* 92:32–38.

Runyan, C.W., and E.A. Gerken. 1991. Injuries. In *The health of adolescents,* ed. W.R. Hendee, San Francisco: Jossey-Bass.

Rutter, M. 1987. Psycho-social resilience and protective mechanism. *American Journal of Orthopsychiatry* 57:316–331.

Savin-Williams R.C., and R.G. Rodriguez. 1993. A developmental, clinical perspective on lesbian, gay male, and bisexual youths. In *Adolescent sexuality,* eds. T.P. Gullota et al. Newbury Park, CA: Sage Publications.

Sayer, A.G. et al. 1995. Developmental influences on adolescent health. In *Adolescent health problems: Behavioral perspectives,* eds. S.T. Hauser et al. New York, NY: Guilford Press.

Schlitt, J.J. et al. 1994. *State initiatives to support school-based health centers: A national survey.* Washington, DC: Making the Grade National Program Office.

Seitz, V., and N.H. Apfel. 1993. Adolescent mothers and repeated childbearing: Effects of a school-based intervention program. *American Journal of Orthopsychiatry* 63:572–581.

Sells, C.W., and R.W. Blum. 1996. Morbidity and mortality among U.S. adolescents: An overview of data and trends. *American Journal of Public Health,* 86:513–519.

Singh, G.K., and S.M. Yu. 1996. Trends and differentials in adolescent and young adult mortality in the United States, 1950–1993. *American Journal of Public Health* 86:560–564.

Sloan, J.H. et al. 1988. Handgun regulations, crime, assaults, and homicide: A tale of two cities. *New England Journal of Medicine.* 319:1256.

Small, S.A., and G. Eastin. 1991. Rearing adolescents in contemporary society: A conceptual frame-work for understanding the responsibilities and needs of parents. *Human Relations* 40:455–462.

Smetana, J.G. 1989. Adolescents' and parents' reasoning about actual family conflict. *Child Development* 60:1052–1067.

Spitz, A.M. et al. 1996. Pregnancy, abortion, and birth rates among U.S. adolescents—1980, 1985, and 1990. *Journal of American Medical Association* 275:989–1117.

Steinberg, L. 1990. Autonomy, conflict, and harmony. In *At the threshold: The developing adolescent*, eds. S.S. Feldman and G.R. Elliot. Cambridge, MA: Harvard University Press.

Steinberg, L. et al. 1991. Authoritative parenting and adolescent adjustment across varied ecological niches. *Journal of Research on Adolescence* 1:19–36.

Stiffman, A.R. et al. 1996. Adolescent violence. In *Handbook of adolescent health risk behavior*, eds. R.J. Diclemente et al. New York: Plenum Press.

Strasburger, V.C. 1993. Children, adolescents, and the media: Five crucial issues. *Adolescent Medicine State of the Art Reviews* 4:479–494.

Sum, A.M., and W.N. Fogg. 1991. The adolescent poor and the transition to early adulthood. In *Adolescence and poverty: Challenge for the 1990s*, eds. P. Edelman and J. Ladner, Washington, DC: Center for National Policy Press, 37–109.

Tanner, J.M., and F. Falkner. 1986. *Human growth: A comprehensive treatise.* New York: Plenum.

U.S. Census Bureau. 1995. *Statistical Abstracts, 1995.* Washington, DC: Government Printing Office.

U.S. Congress, Office of Technology Assessment. 1991a. *Adolescent Health - Volume I: Summary and Policy Options.* OTA-H-468. Washington, DC: Government Printing Office.

U.S. Congress, Office of Technology Assessment. 1991b. *Adolescent Health - Volume II: Background and the Effectiveness of Selected Prevention and Treatment Services.* OTA-H-468. Washington, DC: Government Printing Office.

U.S. Congress, Office of Technology Assessment. 1991c. *Adolescent Health - Volume III: Crosscutting Issues in the Delivery of Health and Related Services.* OTA-H-468. Washington, DC: Government Printing Office.

U.S. Task Force on Preventive Services. 1996. *Guide to clinical preventive services,* 2d ed. Fairfax, VA: International Medical Publishers.

Weissberg, R.P. et al. 1991. Promoting competent young people in competence-enhancing environments: A system-based perspective on primary prevention. *Journal of Consulting and Clinical Psychology* 59:830–841.

Werner, E.E. 1992. The children of Kauai: Resiliency and recovery in adolescence and adulthood. *Journal of Adolescent Health* 22:262–268.

Whitaker, A.H. 1992. An epidemiological study of anorectic and bulimia symptoms in adolescent girls: Implications for pediatricians. *Pediatric Annals* 21:752–759.

Wintemute, G.J. et al. 1988. Choice of weapons in firearm suicides. *American Journal of Public Health* 78:824–825.

W.T. Grant Foundation, Commission on Work, Family, and Citizenship (1988). *The forgotten half: Pathways to success for America's youth and young families.* Washington, DC.

Zabin, L.S., and S.C. Hayward. 1993. *Adolescent sexual behavior and childbearing.* Newbury Park, CA: Sage Publications.

Zill, N., and C.A. Schoenborn. 1990. Developmental, learning, and emotional problems. Health of our nation's children. United States 1988. *Advance Data* 16:1–18.

PART III

Cross-Cutting Issues

CHAPTER 9

Minority Health

Dorothy C. Browne, Larry Crum, and Deborah S. Cousins

The health of the Indians as compared with that of the general population is bad. Although accurate mortality and morbidity statistics are commonly lacking, the existing evidence warrants the statement that both the general death rate and infant mortality rate are high.

L. Meriam, 1928

INTRODUCTION

The observation made in 1928 by Lewis Meriam, then technical director of the Survey Staff of the Institute for Government Research, Brookings Institution, was met with a great deal of concern and commitment to redress the health status of Native Americans (Bremner 1971). Unfortunately Meriam's observation regarding the health status of Native Americans is just as accurate today as it was 69 years ago. In fact, today the health status of Native Americans and other ethnic and racial groups is a prominent item on the national public health agenda. Although substantial progress has been made in improving the health of various ethnic and racial groups, there is still room for improvement. For example, Blacks, when compared with Whites, continue to bear a higher burden of death, disease, and disability. *The Report of the Secretary's Task Force on Black and Minority Health* documented persistent (and, in some cases, growing) disadvantages in indicators of morbidity, mortality, and access to health services for the Black population (U.S. Department of Health and Human Services [U.S. DHHS] 1985). This document noted that racial and ethnic populations other than Blacks also experience poor health status compared with the White population.

The report used the concept of excess deaths to denote differences between the actual number of deaths in a minority population and the number of deaths that would have occurred if the mortality experience of that group were the same as that for the White population. Excess deaths for those younger than 70 years were 42.3 percent among Blacks, 14 percent for the Spanish-surnamed, 2 percent among Cuban-born persons, 7.2 percent for those Mexican-born, and 25 percent for Native Americans. The rate of excess deaths was particularly high (i.e., 43 percent) for Native Americans younger than 45 years. There were no excess deaths for the Asian/Pacific Islander populations, suggesting that this group possesses a healthier mortality profile than all other racial or ethnic subgroups. However, the statistics might be an artifact of the aggregation of data from various groups comprising the category of Asians/Pacific Islanders. That is, when the data are examined for each of the separate groups comprising the category of Asians/Pacific Islanders, one or more of the groups might present a profile that is similar to that for other ethnic and racial groups. For example, data from the U.S. Public Health Service (1991) reveal that the homicide rate for the category of Asians/Pacific Islanders, ages 15 to 24, is substantially lower than that for African Americans. As indicated in Table 9–1, the mortality rate for all Asians/Pacific Islanders combined was 17 per 100,000 vs. 86 per 100,000 for African Americans. However, an examination of each of the subgroups represented in the overall category indicates that the homicide rates for Samoans and other Pacific Islanders differ dramatically from the overall group of Asians/Pacific Islanders. That is, the homicide rates for the Samoans and other Pacific Islanders are 54 and 73, respectively. Their rates are high and worthy of concern while somewhat lower than those for African Americans. Just looking at the summary statistics for the total category masks the diversity within the category of Asians and Pacific Islanders.

The fact that racial and ethnic groups have inequalities of health status and lack adequate access to health care was recognized by the public health community in its initiative known as Healthy People 2000. In the publication, *Healthy People 2000: National Health Promotion and Disease Prevention Objectives* (U.S. DHHS, 1991), the Public Health Service set a number of objectives designed to

Table 9–1 Mortality Rates from Homicide for 15–24-Year-Olds in California

Race/Ethnicity	Deaths Per 100,000
Asian or Pacific Islander	17
Chinese American	6
Japanese American	13
Samoan	54
Other Pacific Islander	73
African American	86

Source: Reprinted from U.S. Public Health Service, National Center for Health Statistics, 1991.

reduce the disparities in risk factors, morbidity, mortality, and disability for ethnic and racial populations. As noted in this document and subsequent publications (Office of Minority Health [OMH], Centers for Disease Control and Prevention [CDC] 1993a, 1993b; U.S. DHHS 1992; U.S. Public Health Service), a number of diseases still disproportionately strike racial and ethnic minorities, including acquired immune deficiency syndrome (AIDS), tuberculosis, high blood pressure, and cardiovascular disease. Furthermore, the mortality rates for diseases and conditions such as cancer, cardiovascular diseases, substance use, homicide, diabetes, suicide and unintentional injuries, and the low birth weight rate are higher for many of the ethnic and racial groups. *Healthy People 2000* noted that one of the goals of the nation is the reduction of the disparities in health for subgroups of the U.S. population, including ethnic and racial minorities.

The purpose of this chapter is to discuss the general health status of various racial and ethnic groups. The changing demographics will be discussed, given their implications for the health of minorities. In addition, the nature and the extent of salient disparities in health status and health outcomes for various ethnic and racial groups are presented. Some of the methodological and conceptual challenges affecting the understanding of the health disparities among minorities are enumerated. The chapter concludes with recommendations for training and educating maternal and child health professionals in an effort to increase knowledge of and improve the health of various ethnic and racial groups.

CHANGING DEMOGRAPHICS

Population Projections

As we move toward the year 2000, the inability to effectively address and reduce the disparities in health and improve the health outcomes for the four major racial and ethnic populations—Asians/Pacific Islanders, African Americans, Hispanics, and Native Americans—looms as a challenge and a concern due to the changing demographics of the U.S. population. According to the U.S. Census Bureau, in 1990 African Americans were 12 percent of the U.S. population or 28.6 million; Hispanics represented almost 9 percent of the mainland U.S. population or 21.4 million (U.S. Department of Commerce, 1990). The Hispanic category comprises five main groups. They are Mexican Americans (64 percent), Central and Southern Americans (14 percent), mainland Puerto Ricans (11 percent), Cuban Americans (5 percent), and other groups of Hispanic origin (7 percent). Asians and Pacific Islanders make up 3 percent of the population and consist of 25 groups. Some of the groups included in this category are Chinese, Filipino, Japanese, Asian, Indian, Korean, and Vietnamese. The three largest groups of the Pacific Islander portion of this category are Hawaiians, Samoans, and Guamanians. The Native American population is 1 percent of the U.S. population. Represented in this 1 percent are individuals from over 400 federally recognized tribes; 35 percent of the tribes live near or on reservations (U.S. Department of Commerce 1992a).

Population projections based on assumed rates of natural increase and continued immigration show further increases in the size of the ethnic and racial population. In the next 50 years, the non-Hispanic White population is projected to decrease from the 1990 figure of 75 percent to 59 percent of the U.S. population (Edmonston et al. 1996). The relative size of the minority population is projected to change significantly as Asian and Hispanic groups grow rapidly, and the Black population remains at its current relative size. Projections for 2040 for racial and ethnic populations are as follows: Hispanics, 18 percent; African Americans, 12 percent; Asian and Pacific Islanders, 10 percent; American Indians and Alaska Natives, 1 percent (Edmonston and Passel 1994). This change in demographics is compounded by the fact that the U.S. White population is becoming older while the racial and ethnic minority populations have larger proportions of younger children and adolescents. Minority children accounted for approximately 30 percent of the population under 19 years of age in 1990 (U.S. Public Health Service 1991). It is estimated that by year 2020, minority children will constitute 40 percent of the child population in the United States (U.S. Department of Commerce 1992b).

The elementary and middle school population of children, ages 5 to 13, is expected to rise from about 32 million to over 36 million by the year 2000. It is also estimated that this number will decline slightly starting in 2003 because of the smaller cohorts born in the late 1990s, but will rise again in 2015, reaching over 38 million in 2020, and over 45 million in 2050. The high school age population, i.e., children 14 to 17 years of age, is likely to increase from now until 2050. In fact, data indicate that this population will grow from about 14 million to about 17 million in 2005, then decline for a short time. However, numbers in this age group are estimated to reach almost 21 million by year 2050. Again, it has been noted that the child population between the ages of 5 and 17 will be increasingly composed of racial and ethnic groups other than non-Hispanic Whites. Demographically, the racial and ethnic groups will have much in common, such as being younger than the White population and having a high proportion of individuals who are less than 15 years of age. In addition, these groups are projected to grow faster than the White population during the next five decades (U.S. Department of Commerce 1992b). The rate of increase is such that in a matter of years, the population groups characterized as minorities will no longer be minorities, but as a group will constitute a majority of the population. In fact, it is projected that half of the U.S. population will be made up of minority groups by the year 2050 (Nickens 1995).

Socioeconomic status (SES) is another characteristic in which there are commonalities as well as differences within and across ethnic and racial groups. With the exception of Asian Americans and Pacific Islanders, a lower percentage of ethnic and racial minorities have 12 or more years of formal education than do White Americans, and higher percentages live below the poverty level (U.S. DHHS, 1992a). Specifically, Blacks are disproportionately more disadvantaged than Whites (O'Hare et al. 1991; U.S. Department of Commerce 1993). In addition, African Americans earn less than Whites regardless of educational levels attained. Thus, African American individuals and their families are more likely to be classified as poor. Data from the U.S. Census indicate that 32 percent of African American individuals and 29 percent of their families are classified as poor, as compared to 11 percent of White individuals and 8 percent of White families. Similarly, 32 percent of Native Americans were below the poverty line in 1990, as compared to 13 percent for all races. Nearly 1 in 3 American Indians and Alaska Natives lived below the poverty level in 1990, whereas 1 in 10 White Americans lived below the poverty level. Furthermore, the percentage of American Indians and Alaska Natives who have a high school education or higher is smaller than the 65 percent of people in the general population who do (U.S. Department of Commerce 1992a; 1993).

Socioeconomic diversity exists across and within the Hispanic population subgroups, although educational attainment is lower for Hispanics than non-Hispanic Whites, and among the three main subgroups comprising the Hispanic category, Puerto Ricans have the lowest socioeconomic status and Cubans have a high socioeconomic status, as determined by years of formal education, income, and home ownership. Unemployment rates, poverty rates, and the number of households headed by women are the highest among the Puerto Rican individuals.

Current socioeconomic indicators among Asians and Pacific Islanders in the United States range from relative affluence to dire poverty. Although Asians and Pacific Islanders are often depicted as the model minority, i.e., hard working, self-reliant and overachieving, data show a wide range of values for socioeconomic indicators across and within subgroups. For example, data from the 1990 census show that 14 percent of Asian Americans and 17 percent of Pacific Islanders lived in poverty. The highest poverty rates were among the Hmong (63.6 percent), Cambodian (42.6 percent), and Laotian (34 percent) ethnic groups. On the other hand, the poverty rates of the Japanese and the Filipino populations were 7 percent and 6.4 percent, respectively. Both Asian Americans (77.6 percent) and Pacific Islanders (76.1 percent) age 25 years and older have slightly higher rates of completing high school than do persons in the general population (75 percent). However, the level of education varies widely among persons within the subgroups. While diversity in socioeconomic status exists among ethnic and minority groups, most minorities currently experience and will continue to experience economic hardship. In addition, many of these ethnic and racial groups are at risk of remaining in poverty since they tend to be employed in low income jobs, are immigrants or refugees, have limited English language skills, and are not familiar with Western norms and practices (Galai and Yehiele 1995).

Implications of Changing Demographics

The rapidly changing demographics in the United States have important implications, not only for the health of the individuals who compose these ethnic and racial groups, but for the overall population. With an increase in the number of ethnic and racial minorities in the United States, barriers that currently exist are likely to persist for some time. The existence of these barriers, such as access to health care and prevention services, will compromise the health status of various racial and ethnic groups and place surrounding populations and communities at risk for infectious diseases and other conditions. These barriers to gaining access range from language to culturally based factors (Galai and Yehiele 1995). With increased numbers of individuals representing diverse groups, there will be large numbers of individuals speaking languages other than English. For example, 60 percent of Hispanics in the United States speak Spanish at home. The inability to converse in English can be a significant obstacle to Hispanic and other non-English speaking individuals. Failure to provide translation services will mean that minority and racial groups might have difficulty accessing appropriate care and conversing with professionals about their health needs and health concerns. Barriers such as these can cause individuals to delay seeking services, thus leading to increased costs of these services and negative health outcomes.

Similarly, profound socioeconomic and sociocultural barriers exist for selected ethnic and racial groups. Every cultural subgroup has health beliefs and practices that shape their responses to health and illness. Many of these practices and beliefs are inconsistent with those based on Western values. Adherence to these beliefs and practices could represent major impediments to intervening effectively to improve health outcomes for the various ethnic and racial groups. The fact that poverty is disproportionately found among minority populations could affect their capacity to seek health services. As most members of the racial and ethnic minorities are low-paid, less well-educated, and working class, they will be at risk of experiencing greater morbidity and mortality rates from chronic diseases. Additionally, the facts that the ethnic and racial populations are decidedly younger than the White population and that the fertility rates for women of certain segments of the ethnic and racial communities are higher mean that rates of pediatric, reproductive, and other health problems commonly observed in mothers and children will be much higher. Therefore, publicly funded programs (e.g., Medicaid, Special Supplemental Food Program for Women, Infants and Children [WIC]) undoubtedly will continue to be important in the improvement of the health and well-being of minority mothers and children.

HEALTH STATUS OF MINORITY GROUPS

The following section presents selected mortality data for various ethnic and racial groups. When available or appropriate, mortality and morbidity statistics are for the maternal and child health (MCH) populations within these racial and ethnic groups. Mortality data are used to identify the leading causes of death among the various racial and ethnic groups. By examining sex, age, and cause-specific mortality rates by racial/ethnic groups for important diseases and conditions, public health practitioners can determine how best to achieve the national objectives detailed in *Healthy People 2000* and improve the health of special populations.

Infant Mortality

Infant mortality, the rate at which children die before their first birthday, serves both as a national and an international indicator of the overall status of health of a community or nation. The significance of infant mortality as a key indicator of a nation's health status and well-being is well accepted in social and biomedical sciences (CDC 1991; Klein and Hawk 1992; Nersessian 1988; Singh et al. 1994). Although the infant mortality rate for all Americans has been declining, the rate of decline has leveled off in recent years. The mortality rate for Black infants is twice the rate for White infants, and there is evidence that the difference is increasing (U.S. Public Health Service 1993). In addition, the proportion of live births that are low or very low birth weight is disturbingly high for Blacks when compared to all races combined.

Until recently, the focus on infant mortality was on the differentials between Whites and Blacks. The failure to show differentials for other racial and ethnic groups is partly due to the small numbers of deaths and the unavailability of reliable population counts for the various subgroups. For example, race- and ethnic-specific mortality data contained on death and birth certificates have also been questioned, with claims that the death rates for American Indians and Asians and Pacific Islanders are grossly underestimated (Bennett 1993; Sorlie et al. 1992). Addressing the issue of small numbers for selected subgroup groups, Singh and Yu (1996) aggregated three years of mortality data to provide stable estimates of infant mortality for various ethnic and racial groups.

As shown in Table 9–2, compared to White infants, Chinese, Japanese, and Filipino infants had lower mortality rates. However, Hawaiian, American Indian, and Black infants fared much more poorly in their mortality, with their rates being significantly higher than those for White infants. Similar ethnic and racial differences were found in neonatal mortality, with Chinese, Japanese, and Filipinos showing significantly lower risks of neonatal death than Whites, Blacks, American Indians, and Hawaiians. Relative differences in postneonatal mortality among

Table 9-2 Infant Mortality Rate by Age at Death and Cause of Death by Maternal Race and Ethnicity: U.S., 1985–1987

	White	Black	American Indian	Chinese	Japanese	Filipino	Other Asian	Hawaiian
Infant Mortality Rate[1]	8.4	19.1	13.9	6.0	6.6	7.2	8.1	11.4
Neonatal Mortality Rate	5.5	12.0	6.1	3.4	3.9	4.7	5.0	7.1
Postneonatal Mortality Rate	2.8	7.1	7.8	2.6	2.7	2.5	3.1	4.3
Cause of Infant Death								
Perinatal Conditions[2]	3.9	11.0	4.1	2.2	2.6	2.9	3.3	5.0
Congenital anomalies[3]	1.9	1.9	2.8	1.6	1.7	2.1	2.2	2.2
SIDS[4]	1.0	2.5	3.5	0.9	1.3	0.9	0.9	1.9
Other causes	1.5	3.7	3.6	1.2	1.0	1.3	1.6	2.2

Source: Reprinted from G. Singh and S. Yu, *Trends and Projections of Infant Childhood, Adolescent and Young Adulthood, and Maternal Mortality by Sex, Race, and Ethnicity, Education, Family Income and Cause of Death*, U.S. Paper commissioned by the Maternal and Child Health Bureau, Health Resources and Services Administration, USDHHS, for the Fourth National Title V Maternal and Child Health Research Priorities Conference, June 21–29, 1994.

[1] Rate per 1,000 live births
[2] Perinatal conditions (ICD-9 codes 760–779)
[3] Congenital anomalies (ICD-9 codes 740–759)
[4] SIDS: Sudden Infant Death Syndrome (ICD-9 code 798.0)

Chinese, Japanese, Filipino, other Asians, and Whites were somewhat smaller, with only Filipinos showing significantly lower postneonatal mortality than Whites. Relative differences in postneonatal mortality between Whites on the one hand and Hawaiians, American Indians, and Blacks on the other hand were wider than the corresponding differences in infant mortality and neonatal mortality rates. As with infant and neonatal mortality, American Indians, African Americans, and Hawaiians infants had the highest postneonatal mortality rates.

An examination of the cause-specific infant mortality rates is also shown in Table 9–2. The data reveal that, compared to White infants, Chinese, Japanese, and Filipino infants were significantly less likely to die from perinatal conditions. Black and Hawaiian infants, on the other hand, were almost 3 and 1.3 times respectively more likely to die from perinatal conditions. Ethnic and racial differentials in congenital anomalies were rather small, with only American Indian babies dying from this cause and at a significantly higher rate compared to other racial and ethnic groups. Of all groups, American Indian infants were at the highest risk of dying from Sudden Infant Death Syndrome (SIDS), with a mortality risk that is three times as great as that for White infants. The risk of dying from SIDS was 2.5 times greater for Blacks than for Whites. Among Asians/Pacific Islanders, Hawaiians and Japanese infants reported higher mortality rates from SIDS than other Asian and White populations.

Childhood

Early and late childhood mortality rates indicate an improvement in the health status of the child population, yet despite overall reductions in childhood mortality, there are substantial differentials across racial and ethnic groups. As noted by Singh and Yu (1996) in a recent examination of data from the National Vital Statistics System, the National Longitudinal Mortality Study and the Area Resource File, Asians and Pacific Islanders, 1–4 years, have the lowest child mortality rate of all racial and ethnic groups for the periods of 1979–1981 and 1989–1991. However, mortality varied greatly within the category of Asians and Pacific Islanders. Chinese, Japanese, and Filipino children, 1–4 years, have lower death rates than Hawaiians and other Asians. This was the case for both boys and girls. Black, American Indian, and Hawaiian male and female children had the highest death rates for the two time periods. Among Hispanics, Cuban children had lower death rates than their White counterparts, and Puerto Rican and Central and South American children had higher rates in both time periods examined.

As in the case of younger children, Asian and Pacific Islander children, 1–4 years, have the lowest mortality rates. Specifically, Chinese, Japanese, and Filipino children had significantly lower death rates than Whites, Blacks, Hawaiians, and American Indians (Singh and Yu 1996). This was true among female and male children. Black, American Indian, and Hawaiian male and female children had the highest death rate for the periods of 1979 through 1981 and 1989 through 1991, while Cuban children had significantly lower rates than other Hispanics (Singh and Yu 1996).

An examination of the leading causes of death among children 1–4 years and 5–14 years indicates that for children 1–4, the leading causes of death during 1989 and 1991 were motor vehicle fatalities, other unintentional injuries, congenital anomalies, homicide, cancer, pneumonia and influenza, and human immunodeficiency virus (HIV). For children 5–14 years, the list contained some of the same causes except that added to this list was suicide, cerebrovascular disease, and pulmonary disease (Singh and Yu 1996). It is of note that the leading health problems affecting the preadolescent and adolescent youth have less to do with the medical etiologies and more with environmental, behavioral, and lifestyle practices. For racial and ethnic youth, injuries, intentional and nonintentional, are of major concern.

Injuries are a major cause of death for children in the early and later childhood periods, and there are major disparities in the mortality rates for Blacks and Whites. Homicide is the leading cause of death and disability among Black male adolescents. The Black homicide rate decreased by 22 percent between 1970 and 1985, from its peak of 102.5 to 66.11; however, since then this rate has been rising, reaching 112.4 for Black males 15–24 in 1989 (Greenberg and Schneider 1994). White homicide rates increased by 30 percent from 7.9 to 11.2 in the same period (CDC 1986). Statistics on homicide collected at the national level have consistently shown significantly higher victimization rates for African Americans than for Whites or other ethnic groups, regardless of age or gender (U.S. Public Health Service 1995). For both male and female African Americans between the ages of 15 and 34 years of age, homicide has been the leading cause of death since 1978. In 1992, the homicide rate for African American males, ages 15–34 years, was 134.2. The rate for African American females was 22.7 per 100,000 (U.S. Public Health Service 1995). For African Americans as well as the general population, it is much more difficult to estimate the extent of assaultive violence that does not result in death. However, it is estimated that for every homicide, there are 100 nonfatal assaultive injuries.

As with comprehensive demographics on Hispanics and other racial and ethnic groups, national data on violence victimization by race and ethnicity are not yet systematically collected. Health, juvenile justice, and crime data typically provide aggregate national statistics and in some circumstances will provide a breakdown by race, primarily Black and White comparisons. Only rarely are data provided for ethnic groups or subgroups such as Hispanics (Soriano 1994). While systematic national data are unavailable, regional data indicate that the homicide rates for Hispanics are relatively high. Block (1988) showed that when, compared with

African American or white non-Hispanic youth of the same age, Hispanics age 15–19 years had the highest homicide rates (104 per 100,000 for Hispanics, 62 for African Americans, and 12 per white non-Hispanic youth). Unfortunately, until better data are obtained, the above statistics for Hispanics are estimates. Similarly, data are lacking that would present a picture of violence among Native Americans. Estimates on the risk of homicide for Native Americans are derived from data gathered in regional or tribal studies. Many studies have suggested that the relative risk for homicide for Native Americans is 1.5 to 3 times that for all Americans (Indian Health Service 1990; U.S. DHHS 1991; Wallace et al. 1993). Although homicide rates for Native Americans have been found to be lower than those for African Americans and about equal to those for Latinos, one study indicated that Native Americans had higher rates of homicide than whites or other racial and ethnic groups. Becker et al. (1990) studied homicide over a 30-year period and found substantially higher rates for both male and female Native Americans than for U.S. Latino and non-Latino women. National statistics on Asians/Pacific Islanders are difficult to interpret in that the rates of suicide and homicide are combined. Among 15- to 24-year-old Asians/Pacific Islanders, the combined suicide and homicide rates per 100,000 were 15.5 in 1987, 13.2 in 1988, and 17.5 in 1989 (U.S. Department of Education 1992b).

The above review demonstrates that data on the prevalence of violence among ethnic minority group members are not comprehensive, in large part because of the method of data collection (e.g., official records tend to have race/ethnic categories of "Black," "White," and "Other"). Moreover, the data often do not specify the age of the victims, and thus data that are often presented are not specific to youth.

HIV Infection and AIDS

For minority populations that are already plagued by violence and other indicators of poor health status, HIV infection and AIDS are additional handicaps. In the United States, the majority of AIDS cases still occur in the White population, yet individual minority groups are grossly over-represented in AIDS statistics. Blacks compose approximately 12 percent of the population and make up almost 26 percent of the reported AIDS cases (Ross-Lee et al. 1994). Of minority AIDS cases, 66 percent are African Americans, 32 percent are Hispanics, 1 percent are Asian/Pacific Islanders, and 1 percent are American Indian/Alaska Native (CDC, 1993a). The risk of AIDS in Hispanic and African American men is approximately three times that of white men (Ross-Lee et al. 1994).

HIV/AIDS in minority women has made a significant impact on their communities since infection and disease occur most often in women of childbearing age. Death rates due to AIDS for U.S. women between the ages of 15 and 44 have steadily risen (Chu et al. 1990). AIDS is the sixth leading cause of death among women of reproductive age in the United States, surpassed only by cancer, injury, heart disease, suicide, and homicide (Rogers et al. 1994). In Black women between the ages of 15 and 44, the death rate due to HIV/AIDS is 10 times that of White women (Pizzi, 1992). Hispanic women are four times more likely to be diagnosed with AIDS than White women (Pizzi, 1992). More specifically, 20 to 21 percent of women with AIDS are Latino, and 52 to 53 percent are Black (Ross-Lee et al. 1994; Pizzi 1992).

In addition to having a short survival time, women with HIV infection often face problems that HIV-infected men do not. For example, women are less likely to be diagnosed because gynecological infections and conditions are not always recognized by health professionals as signs of HIV infection. Also, since in many homes they are the sole providers for their families, women will have to deal with decisions regarding custody of their children in addition to maintaining their physical health (Pizzi 1992). Because of this, HIV/AIDS has a devastating impact on minority families and communities. In lower income families, there is a higher risk of HIV infection and a more adverse economic impact due to HIV infection (Mann et al. 1992). Dependent children are the most frequently and most significantly affected by HIV infection in the family. In addition to economic hardships due to medical bills and lost wages of the sick parent, children are often required to assume the responsibilities of the adult, including that of nurturer (Mann et al. 1992). This has ramifications for children's educational and social futures. It also has psychological ramifications, as children are often forced to experience the early and painful death of one or both parents in a society that has both stigmatized HIV/AIDS and discriminated against its victims.

Children with HIV infection are a growing problem. Currently AIDS ranks seventh for cause of mortality in children age 1–4 years. In some areas of the United States, AIDS ranks among the top five causes of death (Rogers et al. 1994). In minority populations, the outlook for pediatric HIV/AIDS is even more grim. For example, the pediatric segment of the Black community has been especially hard hit, as 52 percent of children with AIDS in this country are African American (Ross-Lee et al. 1994).

In most cases, HIV/AIDS in children is directly associated with HIV infection in their parents (Rogers et al. 1994). There are a number of cases of pediatric HIV infection from blood and blood products, other partner exposure to infected blood, or from sexual abuse (Rogers et al. 1994), but the majority of cases have been transmitted to children by their mothers by perinatal or vertical transmission (Rogers et al. 1994). Children with HIV infection do not live as long as adults. Fifty percent die before the age of 2, and 30 percent die before the age of 5 (Mann et al. 1992). AIDS is the sixth leading cause of death in young adults between the ages of 15 and 24 (U.S. Public Health Service 1993). Of all AIDS cases, 20 percent are in individuals age 20–29, most having acquired the disease during adolescence (Kolbe 1992).

African American and Hispanic youth are disproportionately represented in the number of AIDS cases among young people age 13–24. African Americans account for one-third of the cases reported among males and more than half (i.e., 55 percent) of all cases are among females. Similarly, of all reported cases by sex, Hispanic males represent 20 percent and Hispanic females represent 21 percent (Kolbe 1992).

Chronic Diseases

Table 9–3 shows disparities of age-adjusted mortality rates for major chronic diseases among Whites and minority groups for 1990. As indicated, the mortality rates for the chronic diseases are not uniformly higher for minority groups than for Whites. Asians/Pacific Islanders and American Indians/Alaska Natives had mortality rates below those for White Americans, while African Americans had rates well above the rates for Whites. Hispanic Americans, on the other hand, had rates on these selected chronic diseases similar to those of Whites. These profiles show that minority groups are quite heterogeneous when it comes to health status, and for the conditions specified in the above, not all ethnic and racial groups are at a disadvantage.

Of course, as noted earlier, mortality rates such as those shown in Table 9–3 can be artifacts of the classification system used to categorize individuals into racial/ethnic groups. For example, it is known that refugees from Southeast Asia have very different health profiles than Japanese Americans, and differences also exist among the major groups making up the Hispanic population. Thus, caution should be exercised when making generalizations about the relative health status of the generally accepted categories. More issues related to classification are discussed later in this chapter.

Reasons for Health Status Differentials

Given the deplorable discrepancies that exist in the health status of some minority groups when compared to Whites, one is first compelled to explain these discrepancies in terms of the prevalence of risk factors within these various groups. The prevalence rates for White and minority groups of several risk factors known to be associated with chronic disease are shown in Table 9–4. Note that the nonuniform profiles for minority groups compared to Whites shown for chronic diseases is also reflected for behavioral risk factors. Minority group members are more likely than Whites to report a sedentary lifestyle and being overweight, while (except for American Indians and Alaska Natives) minority groups are less likely than Whites to report current cigarette smoking or chronic drinking. In addition, African Americans and Asians and Pacific Islanders are less likely than Whites to report binge drinking.

Table 9–3 Age-Adjusted Mortality Rates* for Major Chronic Diseases for White and Minority Groups, by Underlying Cause of Death, U.S., 1990

Indicator	White American	African American	American Indian/Alaska Native	Asian/Pacific Islander	Hispanic American†
Ischemic heart disease	177.4	180.7	104.0	93.7	181.2
Stroke	48.5	76.0	33.3	45.8	47.4
Chronic obstructive pulmonary disease	32.6	24.8	21.5	15.8	22.6
Diabetes	15.9	35.7	30.3	12.4	28.3
Cirrhosis	9.4	14.5	21.2	4.7	19.0
Lung cancer	54.0	67.5	27.9	26.8	35.6
Colorectal cancer	20.6	26.6	10.1	12.6	18.2
Breast cancer	16.3	19.5	6.6	6.5	13.9
Cervical cancer	1.1	1.8	0.7	0.5	0.9
Prostate cancer	10.7	23.5	5.8	6.0	10.2
Total	386.5	470.6	261.4	224.8	377.3

*Age-adjusted to the 1980 U.S. standard populations; rate per 100,000 persons.
†Persons of Hispanic origin may be of any race.
Source: CDC, NCHS, National Vital Statistics Systems, 1990.

Table 9–4 Weighted Prevalence of Behavioral Risk Factors for White and Minority Groups, U.S., 1991–1992

Indicator	White American	African American	American Indian/Alaska Native	Asian/Pacific Islander	Hispanic American*
Cigarette smoking†	23.0	23.0	34.3	14.8	18.1
Sedentary lifestyle‡	56.3	65.5	57.4	60.5	61.7
Alcohol use:					
Chronic drinking◆	3.8	2.3	4.4	1.4	3.2
Binge drinking¶	15.0	9.4	17.2	8.4	16.6
Overweight**	23.2	33.6	32.0	10.4	25.2
High cholesterol††	26.5	23.9	27.5	26.6	24.4

*Persons of Hispanic origin may be of any race.

†Cigarette smoking—ever smoked 100 cigarettes and currently smoke regularly.

‡Sedentary lifestyle—fewer than three 20-minute sessions of leisure-time physical activity per week.

◆Chronic drinking—60 or more drinks of alcohol during the past month.

¶Binge drinking—consumption of five or more alcoholic beverages on at least one occasion during the past month.

**Overweight—body mass index ≥27.8 for men and ≥27.3 for women (body mass index = weight in kilograms divided by height in meters squared).

††High cholesterol awareness—respondents ever told by a health professional that their cholesterol is elevated.

Source: Reprinted from CDC, Behavioral Risk Factor Surveillance System, State-Aggregate Data for 1991–1992.

There are several theories as to why the health status of some minority groups is poor relative to Whites and other minority groups. All reflect the typical problems of groups that battle poverty, lack social resources and adequate education, and experience discrimination by mainstream society. Reasons may include differences in medical care-seeking behavior, difference in sexual behavior (Moran et al. 1989), differences in knowledge about disease transmission (Ford and Norris 1993), lack of grassroots organization, and lack of medical resources (Perrow and Guillen 1990). These reasons can be exacerbated by various cultural attitudes that exist in some minority communities. For example, in some Black and Hispanic communities, male dominance may lead to couples not using condoms during sexual acts (Perrow and Guillen 1990). Inability of the female partner to insist on the use of condoms may be difficult or next to impossible, as doing so may imply mistrust of the male partner (Weeks et al. 1995). This may be especially true for women whose sexual partners provide financial support (Kline et al. 1992). It may also reflect the need for improvement of negotiating skills in sexually active women who do not use condoms. Other cultural barriers to safer sex practices and reduced HIV infection are language differences and the fact that, in some minority communities, the mention of sexual practices is taboo outside of the bedroom (Pizzi 1992). Removing these barriers and changing attitudes will be crucial steps in preventing future HIV infection in minority women.

Lack of education and living in poverty also have predictable detrimental effects on the health status of minority groups. Illiteracy often prevents mothers from obtaining information about behaviors that can put them or their infants at risk, and poverty too often prevents mothers from seeking treatments for their families until health problems are severe (and more costly to treat).

To a large extent the racial gap in mortality is a function of economic inequalities such as poverty, lack of educational and employment opportunities, substandard housing, and inability to access health care. However, in addition to the economic inequalities, there are certain noneconomic factors such as differences in lifestyle, diet, and microlevel or behavioral variables such as substance use that explain the differentials in health status between racial and ethnic subgroups on the one hand and the White population on the other.

RACIAL AND ETHNIC DIFFERENCES IN ACCESS TO CARE

Reasons that have been proposed in an attempt to explain the observed racial and ethnic differences in physician and hospital care access include the lack of health insurance and other economic factors, small number of Black physicians, restrictions in hospital admissions, changes in hospital locations, individual perceptions of symptoms and disease status, long waiting periods, inconvenient hours, racial discrimination, lack of continuity of care, inadequate privacy, dissatisfaction with physician treatment, and physician bias (Mirvis et al. 1994).

Lack of trust may be an issue as a result of the U.S. Public Health Service's 40-year study of untreated syphilis in African Americans at the Tuskegee Veterans Administration hospital (LaViest et al. 1993). Significant differences in physician-patient relationships have been observed between Whites and nonwhites; however, it is unclear whether or not discordance in race or ethnicity between physician and patient ultimately causes differences in care (Weddington and Gabel 1991).

Compared to White children, African American and Hispanic children are less likely to receive prescribed medication and receive fewer medications (Hahn 1995). These differences were found to exist after such factors as SES, health status, and number of physicians were controlled for suggesting that persons of color are less likely than Whites to receive medical services (Hahn 1995). Also, African American mothers have been observed to experience inadequate and delayed prenatal care as compared to White mothers (LaViest et al. 1993). Research has not been sufficient to explain these differences in access to prenatal care; however, it is thought that lower education, lack of private medical insurance, and unavailability of MCH clinics may be the main problems. It was thought that Medicare and Medicaid would narrow racial differences, although race is still observed to be a factor in quality of health care. Blacks are more likely to seek care in hospital outpatient clinics and emergency rooms than Whites (LaViest et al. 1993).

DEBATE SURROUNDING THE COLLECTION OF RACIAL AND ETHNIC DATA

Despite the increase in our knowledge of various health disparities across and within various racial and ethnic subgroups, gaps still exist in our understanding of the factors that contribute to the observed differences. That is, while we are aware of some of the determinants of poor health status and outcomes for minorities, there is still a need to understand the "why" of the disparities in health status among racial and ethnic groups. To what extent is it poverty, the lack of access to medical and health services and facilities, the provision of poor quality of care, or the lack of prevention and intervention strategies? What is the contribution of cultural factors (e.g., language, religion, beliefs, and norms) or structural inequalities (i.e., racism and discrimination)? Recent studies indicate that culture, perceptions, and beliefs affect the health status of individuals. Yet, there is still a lack of data to aid in understanding the extent to which these and other less frequently examined factors affect the health status of the minority population in general, and specific subgroups of racial and ethnic populations in particular.

Unfortunately, our knowledge regarding the reasons for the racial and ethnic differences in health outcomes is compromised by some of the challenges associated with collecting data on race and ethnicity. These challenges include debates surrounding the appropriateness of collecting and analyzing data by race and ethnicity and the use of questionable strategies and approaches for collecting data on ethnic and racial subpopulations. Aggregating data for ethnic and racial subpopulations such that one cannot examine the health status of a particular subgroup or the prevalence of a particular health condition and failure to supplement racial and ethnicity data with the use of culturally sensitive and appropriate instruments are other areas of concern.

The collection of health information by racial and ethnic categories is an important component of public health surveillance. Sources for this surveillance information regarding the health status of the overall population and racial and ethnic subgroups are state agencies and a myriad of federal agencies, including the CDC, the Bureau of the Census, the Indian Health Service, and the National Center for Health Statistics. Census data systems and those from other federal and nonfederal statistical systems are closely related and interdependent. In fact, this interdependence is demonstrated by the use of census data as the denominators for virtually all birth, mortality, and morbidity rates. In turn, these rates are used to develop the Census Bureau's population estimates and projections (Edmonston et al. 1996.) Additionally, federal agencies use census data as the baseline for designing sampling frames for their data collection efforts. For example, birth, death, and immigration data are combined to get estimates of postcensal population counts. Census data are also used to assess the completeness of natality registration and survival rates (Hahn and Stroup 1994).

The collection of data by race and ethnicity is advocated by many since such information can assist in public health efforts to recognize disparities and address their causes by targeting resources to affected communities and populations. While few public health practitioners and data users would refute the value in collecting data by ethnic and racial identifiers, some scholars argue that race should not be a variable in health research and that race as a concept should be deleted from all classification schemes. In his classic article, Terris (1973) advocates for an abandonment of the practices of collecting and analyzing data by racial categories. According to Terris, the concept of race is unscientific, accepts unsubstantiated beliefs of biological distinctness, promotes racial discrimination, and obscures the real causes of racial differences in health outcomes. Although Terris took this position approximately 24 years ago, he remains unchanged in his commitment to abandoning the use of race.

Terris' position is supported by Osborne and Feit (1992). According to them, when race is used as a variable in research, there is a tendency to assume that the results obtained are manifestations of differences in biology, whereas the confounding effects of other factors are often not made explicit when the data are interpreted. That is, using race as a variable implies that there is a genetic reason for the observed differences in incidence, prevalence, or severity of health conditions. Although widely shared in our society, the belief that races in human populations differ from each other primarily in terms of genetics is without scientific basis (Gould 1977; Latter 1980; Lewontin 1982; Littlefield et al. 1982). In fact there is more genetic variation within than between races. Lewontin and others (1982) contend that the fact that we know what race an individual belongs to tells us more about our society than about his or her genetic makeup. Nonetheless, without saying so, researchers and readers of various material discussing racial differences often conclude that certain racial groups have predispositions, risks, or susceptibilities to illnesses, conditions, and diseases being studied. According to Terris (1973) and Osborne and Feit (1992), this presupposition is seldom warranted, and comparisons of racial groups, without providing explanations, may represent a subtle form of discrimination, reinforce stereotypes, and could lead to political consequences for these groups, such as quarantining and "blaming the victims."

Osborne and Feit (1992) continue by saying that constant attention to racial and ethnic groups being disproportionately affected by certain diseases often leads to the belief that one of the best efforts to reduce or eliminate the observed differentials is to focus primarily on creating and/or revamping health programs for these groups. By doing this, there is less attention given to addressing the virulent societal problems such as economic and social inequalities that predispose to those diseases. For example, factors contributing to the high rate of violence among ethnic and racial groups of youth include poverty, joblessness, and interpersonal problems in ethnic and racial families. Race, in and of itself, should not be considered a causal or risk factor for violence. Thus, as noted by Osborne and Feit (1992), to avoid erroneous conclusions it is essential that researchers and users of racial identifiers in their analyses clarify terms, state clearly the reasons for examining racial disparities, and make clear that race and ethnicity are not risk factors, but are instead *risk markers*. Race as a risk marker means that race represents many underlying problems of greater relevance to health, including SES and cultural and behavioral characteristics that are social and not biological in nature.

STRATEGIES AND APPROACHES FOR CLASSIFYING RACE

Depending on the data source, collecting racial and ethnic identifiers presents methodological problems. Issues of misclassification come into play in the calculations of rates of any kind because rates require compatible data for the numerator and denominator. Often, however, the numerator and denominator come from different sources. For example, data for demographic estimates at the national level come from vital statistics collected by individual states, which may use different race and ethnicity categories. Often, census data are used as the principal source of numbers for the denominator, which can lead to systematically poor estimation if the collection procedures used for the numerator do not gather data in the same manner as the census. The case of infant mortality is often cited as an example of inaccuracies that result from inconsistent racial and ethnic reporting. Beginning in 1989, births have been categorized by the race of the mother as recorded on the birth certificate. If the mother does not state her race on the certificate, then the baby's race is listed as the race of the father. If neither parent's race is reported on the birth certificate, the baby's race is listed as that of the mother on the preceding record that indicates race. However, racial classification of death, unlike births, is designated by an outside party, usually attending physicians or funeral home directors, on the basis of information provided by relatives or their own observation. The reliance on visual identification or the possibility of inadequate information from relatives has resulted in an overassignment of deaths to Black and White categories and an underassignment of deaths to American Indian and Asian/Pacific Islander categories. Hahn (1994) notes that before the 1989 change in classifying parents of the same race, almost 10 percent of American Indian infant deaths were incorrectly classified when both parents were American Indians, and the inconsistent assignment of Asian infant deaths varied from almost 20 percent for Japanese to almost 40 percent for Chinese. Changes introduced in 1989, whereby infants were assigned the same race as their mothers, have failed to reduce the level of incorrect assignment. As a result the infant mortality rates—even when both parents are Asian or American Indian—are substantially lower than the actual levels. Hahn also noted that the level of inconsistent classification of infant death by race is even greater for children of mixed heritage. The result of this inconsistency is only a slight overestimation of Black and White infants' mortality rates, since the numbers of births are so large. For the smaller racial and ethnic groups, however, the under-reporting of infant mortality rates will produce inaccurate results and have major ramifications for calculations made by Social Security and private insurance industry actuaries. One suggestion for improving or reducing inconsistencies is to collect more data on ancestral background or to institute the same kinds of requirements for data collection across data systems to allow for consistent racial and ethnic identification.

One of the most troublesome issues in the area of minority health is the imprecise nature of many existing classification systems as well as the varying of the categories, such that it is difficult to collect reliable data or to conduct highly targeted and focused analyses of minority populations. In many classification systems, small populations of diverse minority groups are often clustered together under one category with only Whites and Blacks being separated. Given the increasing ethnic diversity, data collection utilizing broad and crude racial categories is inadequate. Using broad categories makes it impossible to recognize important differences within racial groups. Because of limitations in detail, within-group heterogeneity cannot be recognized, and differences within racial groups are masked.

Research and data collection activities related to ethnic and racial classification currently do a poor job differentiating race/ethnicity from SES variables in addressing minority populations. The co-mingling of race/ethnicity and SES has important ramifications for understanding and improving the health of minority groups. Race may be a confounding factor that can operate in concert with other factors that are rarely used to measure SES. Since low SES and poverty have been associated with poor health, and minorities are disproportionately represented in low SES groups, then low SES and race have often been used synonymously in the research literature. The inability to sort out the differential impact of these two variables obscures the ability to understand how to intervene and to develop appropriate mechanisms to measure and monitor the effectiveness of interventions, especially in minority populations. Some people have called for a decreased emphasis on race with a corresponding increase in attention to SES. However, such an action is inappropriate for several reasons. First, the widely used SES indicators are not equivalent across races (Williams 1992; LaViest 1992). The standard measures of socioeconomic status are income, education, and occupational status or some combination of the three. These concepts may be misused or misleading when applied to minority populations, and there is a need to identify and use more accurate indicators of SES for racial/ethnic groups. David Williams (1992), a sociologist who devotes a great deal of time and attention to the issue of SES and ethnic/racial groups, suggests that African Americans, even though they might have a certain income, might have higher costs in terms of being charged more for food, housing, and other services such as insurance. In addition, middle class African Americans are often involved in the provision of material support for poorer family members, and a similar pattern exists for other minority groups. Thus, when income status is determined, attention must be given to the extent to which nonhousehold residents are supported by a given household income. Furthermore, the fact that middle class African Americans are more likely to be the first generation in that status suggests that a disproportionate share of the African American middle class experienced poorer living conditions in childhood.

SES is not stable or constant during the life course, and a measure of current SES does not capture lifetime exposure to deprived living conditions. Nancy Krieger et al. (1991), in the article "Racism, Sexism, and Social Class: Implications for Studies of Health and Disease and Well-being," points out that we know that Black women are twice as likely as White women to experience the loss of their infants before the infants reach the age of one year. To explain this finding researchers have invoked two well-known facts. One, infant mortality is higher among poor and less well-educated women, and two, Black women in the United States have persistently higher levels of poverty than White women. However, on closer inspection of the data we observe that Black women have problematic birth outcomes regardless of their socioeconomic status. They fare worse than White women at every economic level, and the disadvantage persists even among the most highly educated Black women. Thus, a major issue is how socioeconomic status is defined and operationalized. Some people like Williams (1992) have recommended using a variety of measures, including assets, and measuring SES over time.

Another major challenge to increasing our knowledge and understanding of differentials in health status is the use of culturally sensitive approaches and the development of culturally appropriate instruments for obtaining data from various ethnic and racial groups. A large number of research projects and data collection efforts are being conducted without attention to cultural factors of the minorities and/or racial groups being studied. That is, there is no information collected on ancestral backgrounds, their group-specific attitudes, perceptions, expectations, norms, and values or linguistic preferences. One of the critical issues in national surveys is whether the answers or responses to questions are clearly understood by respondents. Often the survey questions and measurement instruments are not "formed" on minority/racial populations, and there are issues of whether the language of the questions and scales used to measure health events is measuring the same phenomena across all populations. For example, researchers have found a marked difference between the way African Americans respond to the words *hypertension* and *high blood pressure* (U.S. Public Health Service 1993). These two terms have significantly different connotations. It is also clear that there may be significant translation problems in questions intended for the English-speaking/White population. It is important that questions that are relevant to health on national surveys be designed specifically to fit the unique lifestyles, histories, and cultures of specific racial and ethnic groups, including mixed heritage or peculiar life experiences. Comparable if not identical questions that are theoretically and racially relevant need to be formulated for different racial and ethnic groups to ensure that equivalent phenomena are really being measured. Culturally sensitive instruments would also recognize the use of alternative health systems and the extent of identification with one's ethnic and racial heritage, norms, values, and beliefs.

IMPLICATIONS FOR THE TRAINING OF MCH PROFESSIONALS

With their concern for the health and well-being of mothers and children, MCH training programs are well-positioned to prepare individuals to play a unique role in research, service, and teaching. Given this unique role, the following recommendations are offered for strengthening the information pertaining to the health of minorities and improving the health status and health outcomes of these groups.

1. Curricula in MCH programs should be expanded to include courses in culturally sensitive communication and assessment that acknowledge cultural beliefs and values. Courses in acculturation and assimilation should be part of the curriculum.
2. Opportunities should be made available to MCH students, practitioners, and faculty to better understand the rapidly changing communities in which they work, culturally determined perceptions of disease, and the cultural barriers to adherence to prevention and treatment programs.
3. MCH programs are in a unique position to train individuals in innovative techniques relevant to minority research and health services. MCH professionals must be trained to create and validate more culturally sensitive instruments and tools for data collection. In addition, MCH professionals must create and validate culturally sensitive approaches for interviewing individuals from ethnic and racially diverse populations. Additionally, new studies are required to investigate racial and multicultural determinants of illness and disease in terms of causation and treatment in ethnic populations.
4. MCH programs must expand the pool of minority researchers. Currently the number of minority researchers involved in the collection and analyzing of data is far too few. Minority students must be encouraged to pursue their doctorates and become engaged in innovative, important research related to the health of women and children, including racial and ethnic minorities.

In conclusion, MCH training programs can and should play a pivotal role in influencing the health of the nation, through conducting specialized and important research and preparing students to assume roles and positions that will affect positively the nation's rapidly diversifying population.

REFERENCES

Becker, T. et al. 1990. Violent death in the west: Suicide and homicide in New Mexico, 1958–1987. *Suicide and Life Threatening Behavior* 20:324–334.

Bennett, T. 1993. *American Indians in California: Health status and access to health.* San Francisco, CA: Monograph Series, Institute for Health Policy Studies, University of California, September.

Block, C.R. 1988. Lethal violence in a Chicago community, 1965 to 1981. In *Research conference proceedings. Violence and homicide in Hispanic communities.* Los Angeles, CA: University of California Press.

Bremner, R.H. 1971. *Children and youth in America.* Vol. II (1866–1932). Boston: Harvard University Press.

Centers for Disease Control and Prevention. 1986. *Homicide surveillance: High risk racial and ethnic groups–Blacks and Hispanics, 1970 to 1983.* Atlanta, GA: Author.

Centers for Disease Control and Prevention. 1991. Consensus set of health status indicators for the general assessment of community health status—U.S. *Morbidity and Mortality Weekly Report* 40: 449–451.

Centers for Disease Control and Prevention. 1993a. AIDS among racial/ethnic minorities—U.S. *Morbidity and Mortality Weekly Report* 43:644–647, 653–655.

Centers for Disease Control and Prevention. 1993b. Tuberculosis morbidity—U.S., 1992. *Morbidity and Mortality Weekly Report* 42:696–704.

Chu, S.Y. et al. 1990. The impact of the human immunodeficiency virus epidemic on mortality of women of reproductive age. U.S. *Journal of American Medical Association* 264:225–229.

Edmonston, B. et al. 1996. *Spotlight on heterogeneity: The federal standards for racial and ethnic classification.* Washington, DC: National Academy Press.

Edmonston, B., and J. Passel, eds. 1994. *Immigration and ethnicity: The integration of America's newest arrivals.* Washington, DC: The Urban Institute Press.

Ford, K., and A.E. Norris. 1993. Knowledge of AIDS transmission, risk behavior and perceptions of risk among urban, low-income, African American and Hispanic youth. *American Journal of Preventive Medicine* 915:297–306.

Galai, G., and M. Yehiele. 1995. The role of public health schools in meeting the needs of rapidly developing communities. In *Race and ethnicity in America: Meeting the challenge in the 21st century,* ed. G.E. Thomas, Washington, DC: Taylor and Francis.

Gould, S.J. 1977. Why we should not name human races—a biological view. In *Ever since Darwin,* ed. S.J. Gould, 231–236. New York: Norton.

Greenberg, M., and D. Schneider. 1994. Violence in American cities: Young black males is the answer, but what is the question? *Social Science Medicine,* 39:179–187.

Hahn, R. 1995. Children's health: Racial and ethnic differences in the use of prescription medication. *Pediatrics* 95:727–732.

Hahn, R., and D. Stroup. 1994. Race and ethnicity in public health. Surveillance criteria for the scientific use of social categories. *CDC-Agency for Toxic Substances Disease Registry (ATSDR) Workshop* 109:11–15.

Indian Health Service. 1990. *Injuries among American Indians and Alaska Natives 1990.* Rockville, MD: U.S. Public Health Service.

Klein, J., and S. Hawk. 1992. *Statistical notes, health status indicators, definitions and national data.* Vol. 1, No. 3. Hyattsville, MD: U.S. Public Health Service, National Center for Health Statistics.

Kline, A. et al. 1992. Minority women and sexual choice in the age of AIDS. *Social Science Medicine* 34:447–457.

Krieger, N. et al. 1993. Racism, sexism, and social class: Implications for studies of health, disease, and well-being. *American Journal of Preventive Medicine* 9 (suppl):82–122.

Kolbe, L.J. 1992. The role of the federal government in promoting health through the schools: Report from the Division of Adolescent and School Health, Centers for Disease Control. *Journal of School Health* 62:135–137.

Latter, D.H. 1980. Genetic differences within and between populations of the major human subgroups. *American Naturalist* 116:220–237.

LaViest, T. 1992. Segregation, poverty, and empowerment: Health consequences for African Americans. Mapping a new territory. *American Journal of Sociology* 94:1080–1095.

LaViest, T. et al. 1993. Black/white differences in prenatal care utilization: An assessment of predisposing and enabling factors. *Health Services Research* 30:43–58.

Lewontin, R. 1982. Human diversity. In *Introduction to physical anthropology,* eds. H. Nelson and R. Jarman. St. Paul, MN: West Publishing.

Littlefield et al. 1982. Redefining race: The potential demise of a concept in physical anthropology. *Current Anthropology* 23:641–655.

Mann, J.M. et al., eds. 1992. *AIDS in the world.* Cambridge, MA: Harvard University Press.

Meriam, L. 1928. *The problem of Indian administration.* Washington, DC: Brookings Institution, Institute for Government Research, 3–4.

Mirvis, D. et al. 1994. Variation in utilization of cardiac procedures in the Department of Veterans Affairs health care system: Effect of race. *Journal of American College of Cardiology* 24:1297–1304.

Moran, J.S. et al. 1989. The impact of sexually transmitted diseases on minority populations. *Public Health Reports* 104:560–565.

National Center for Health Statistics. 1992. *Setting a research agenda: Challenges for the minority health statistics grants program.* Proceedings from a workshop held December 4–6, manuscript.

Nersessian, W. 1988. Infant mortality in socially vulnerable populations. *Annual Review of Public Health* 9:361–377.

Nickens, H.W. 1995. The role of race/ethnicity and social class in minority health status. *Health Services Research* 30:151–162.

O'Hare, W. et al. 1991. African Americans in the 1900s. *Population Bulletin* 46:3–5.

Osborne, N.G., and M.D. Feit. 1992. The use of race in medical research. *Journal of American Medical Association* 672:275–279.

Perrow, C., and M.F. Guillen. 1990. *The AIDS disaster.* New Haven, CT: Yale University Press.

Pizzi, M. 1992. HIV infection and AIDS: Tapestries of life, death, and empowerment. *American Journal of Occupational Therapy* 46:1021–1027.

Rogers, M.F. et al. 1994. Epidemiology of pediatric human immunodeficiency virus infection in the U.S. *Acta Paediatrica Suppl,* 40:5–7.

Ross-Lee, B. et al. 1994. Should health care reform be "color-blind"? Addressing the barriers to improving minority health. *Journal of American Osteopathic Association* 94: 664–671.

Singh, G. et al. 1994. Comparative analysis of infant mortality in major Ohio cities: Significance of nonbiological factors. *Applied Behavioral Science Review* 2:63–80.

Singh, G., and S. Yu. 1994. *Trends and projections of infant, childhood, adolescent and young adulthood, and maternal mortality by sex, race and ethnicity, education, family income and cause of death, U.S.* Paper commissioned by the Maternal and Child Health Bureau, Health Resources and Services Administration, USDHHS, for the Fourth National Title V Maternal and Child Health Research Priorities Conference, June 27–29.

Singh, G., and S. Yu. 1996. Childhood mortality 1950 through 1993: Trends and socioeconomic differentials. *American Journal of Public Health* 86:505–512.

Soriano, F. 1994. U.S. Latinos. In *Reason to hope: A psychological perspective on violence and youth,* eds. L.D. Eron et al. Washington, DC: American Psychological Association.

Sorlie, P. et al. 1992. Validity of demographic characteristics on the death certificate. *Epidemiology* 3: 181–184.

Terris, M. 1994. Personal communication in conversation with Trude Bennett, June.

Terris, M. 1973. Desegregating health statistics. *American Journal of Public Health* 63:477–480.

U.S. Department of Commerce, Bureau of the Census. 1990. *Decennial census of population and housing. Public use microdata sample.* Washington, DC: Author.

U.S. Department of Commerce, Bureau of the Census, Population Division. 1992a. *American Indian population, by tribe for United States regions, divisions, and states, 1990.* CHP L-99. Washington, DC: Author.

U.S. Department of Commerce, Bureau of the Census. 1992b. Population projections of the U.S. by age, sex, and race, 1992–2050. *Current population reports*. Series P25, No. 1092b. Washington, DC: Government Printing Office.

U.S. Department of Commerce, Bureau of Census. 1993. *We, the First Americans*. Washington, DC: Government Printing Office.

U.S. Department of Education, National Center of Educational Statistics. 1992. *The condition of education*. Washington, DC: Government Printing Office.

U.S. Department of Health and Human Services. 1985. *Report of the secretary's task force on black and minority health*. Washington, DC: Government Printing Office.

U.S. Department of Health and Human Services. National Center for Health Statistics. 1990. Prevention profile. *Health United States 1989*. Washington, DC: Government Printing Office.

U.S. Department of Health and Human Services. 1991. *Healthy People 2000: National Health Promotion and Disease Prevention Objectives*. Washington, DC: U.S. Public Health Service.

U.S. Department of Health and Human Services. 1992a. *Improving minority health statistics. Report of the public health statistics task force on minority health data*. Washington, DC: Government Printing Office.

U.S. Department of Health and Human Services. 1992b. *Report from the National Center for Injury Prevention and Control*. Atlanta, GA: Centers for Disease Control and Prevention.

U.S. Public Health Service. National Center for Health Statistics. 1991. *Healthy People 2000 Review, 1991*. Hyattsville, MD: Government Printing Office.

U.S. Public Health Service. National Center for Health Statistics. 1993. *Healthy People 2000 Review, 1992*. Hyattsville, MD: Government Printing Office.

U.S. Public Health Service. National Center for Health Statistics 1995. *Healthy People 2000 Review, 1994*. Hyattsville, MD: Government Printing Office.

Wallace, D. et al. 1993. *Injury Mortality Atlas. Indian Health Services Areas 1979–87*. Atlanta, GA: National Center for Injury Prevention and Control, Centers for Disease Control and Prevention.

Weddington, W.H., and L.L. Gabel. 1991. Racial differences in physicians and patients in relationship to quality of care. *Journal of National Medical Association* 83:569–572.

Weeks, M.R. et al. 1995. AIDS prevention for African American and Latino women: Building culturally and gender-appropriate intervention. *AIDS Education and Prevention* 7:251–263.

Williams, D. 1992. *The Concept of Race in Health Services Research: 1966–1990*. Presented at the Annual Meeting of the Association for Health Services Research, Chicago, IL.

CHAPTER 10

Women's Health: A Life Cycle

B. Cecilia Zapata and Trude Bennett

We must recognize that, in some large measure, problems with infant ill health are a legacy of women's ill health generally. Cross-disciplinary investigations that can examine the interactions between the general health of women and childbearing are needed urgently.

P. Wise, 1993, p. 14

INTRODUCTION

Why a chapter on women's health in a textbook on maternal and child health (MCH)? For a number of reasons, some MCH practitioners in recent years have been pressing for the inclusion of general women's health issues. MCH advocates who approach the field from the maternal perspective seek assurance that broad women's health concerns will be promoted in public health. They note that gender discrimination may cause women's health to fall through the cracks of other disciplines and research arenas, whether they be specific to populations, diseases, or methodologies. A logical extension of the MCH mission may be health promotion and disease prevention for women throughout the life cycle.

Proponents of a more traditional definition are concerned that the special needs of pregnant women may receive too little emphasis if MCH is defined too broadly. However, the need for a comprehensive reproductive health framework is recognized by international and domestic MCH fields. Maternal outcomes are clearly influenced by a complex web of socioeconomic and environmental influences that precede a woman's pregnancy, perhaps by generations. Chronic illness and underlying health status, including psychological health, are important elements in the creation or exacerbation of pregnancy-related risks. Exclusion of pre-pregnancy and nonobstetric factors restricts our understanding of maternal health unnecessarily.

In most women's lives, the period of *childbearing* is much shorter than the duration of *childrearing*. Yet maternal outcomes are usually measured only by immediate pregnancy consequences. The mental and physical stresses and benefits of the childrearing years are seldom considered as part of maternal health. Furthermore, a growing proportion of U.S. women are delaying childbearing or choosing not to have children. In an analysis of national survey data, Forrest (1993) found that half of all U.S. women were childless at age 26. By the age of 30, half stated they had completed their intended childbearing. Before they reached the age of 36, half of all women reported that they were sterile.

Thus today many more "woman-years" than previously are spent outside the reproductive domain, and many women never enter the realm of maternity care. Since the United States lacks a universal system of health care, maternity services provide entry for many women into primary care they might otherwise lack. Women's health concerns in MCH include continuity of care and access to services before, after, and independent of childbearing. It seems unreasonable to expect women to invest their trust in a health system that expresses concern about them only during pregnancy.

An important insight from the international health field has been the critical role of the status of women in determining MCH outcomes. If women are not socially valued, they are likely to face limitations in reproductive decision making and hazards to their general and reproductive health status. Unless women command respect and equity in their roles as daughters, students, wives, and workers, they are not likely to experience the physical and mental health advantages predictive of optimal child health. Some observers view the inclusion of women's health in MCH as yet another attempt to confine women to the maternal definition and role, yet no one can deny that any improvements in the overall determinants of women's health will benefit their offspring. The opposite, however, is not necessarily the case:

> In discussions of MCH it is commonly assumed that whatever is good for the child is good for the mother. However, not only are the causes of maternal death quite different from those of child death but so are the potential remedies.
>
> A. Rosenfield and D. Maine, 1985, p. 83

Examples exist of developing countries that have experienced impressive improvements in infant mortality while maternal mortality remains tragically high. This situation has caused commentators to ask, "Where is the M in MCH?" (Rosenfield and Maine, 1985) and to demand a sharper focus on questions of maternal mortality and morbidity. In the United States, the lack of emphasis on the "M in MCH" is reflected in our poor understanding of the marked differentials in maternal and infant health outcomes according to mothers' socioeconomic status, race, and ethnicity. Both women and children would be better served by identifying all of the women's health factors that potentially contribute to pregnancy outcomes.

A more holistic approach to maternal health requires much closer investigation of nonobstetric conditions. In a study of all the deaths to women ages 15–44 in Boston between 1980 and 1989, Katz et al. (1995) found that only 7 of the 1,234 total deaths were attributable to causes related to childbearing. These researchers concluded that neglect of the comprehensive health needs of women of reproductive age results in many preventable deaths.

> . . . this study challenges the current view that the health needs of young women should be defined principally in relation to childbearing and instead highlights the concept that these needs transcend reproductive care.
>
> Katz et al. 1995, p. 1138

A final argument for including women's health in MCH is the importance of considering pregnancy and childbearing as potential risk factors for women's health in later life. This reversal of the usual paradigm creates opportunities for exploring poorly understood aspects of women's health, life expectancy, and quality of life. Beral (1985) and Green et al. (1988) have found that parity appears to present elevated risks for certain chronic and acute diseases in women and protection against other conditions. "These data suggest that there may be residual and cumulative effects of childbearing which influence patterns of disease in the long-term" (Green et al. 1988, p. 391).

THE WOMEN'S HEALTH MOVEMENT

Historically, interest in women's health has revolved around fertility and maternity (i.e., pregnancy, childbirth, and the postpartum period). According to feminist historians, the reproductive life of western women prior to the twentieth century was embedded in a female culture, which provided women with sympathetic support and guidance throughout their reproductive cycle (Ruzek 1978). Although social class and culture influenced women's experiences, a common value was shared—women assisted other women through the maternity process (Alexander and LaRosa 1994). Thus, maternity was part of women's domestic and social responsibilities. Women were bound together in mutual support in order to endure frequent pregnancies and childbirth, breastfeeding, and menopause. Women healers and midwives took care of women's reproductive health from menarche through menopause.

By the mid-eighteenth century, the western world started to question women's unique role in maternity care. European woman began to deliver babies in hospitals with the assistance of midwives under the watchful eyes of physicians who themselves had little experience in childbirth. French physicians took advantage of delivery hospitalizations to study childbirth as a natural process, while the English engaged in the development of surgical procedures and technological tools such as the forceps (Alexander and LaRosa 1994). By the end of the eighteenth century, physicians attended deliveries along with midwives. This was the beginning of physician control over birthing—and the medicalization of women's lives.

The female culture lost strength by the twentieth century, in part due to the new role of male physicians in women's reproductive lives. In the United States doctors were able to begin a monopoly in medicine through their new power and prestige. Physicians (men and women) were instrumental in the passing of laws requiring a medical degree for the practice of obstetrics. The new laws replaced midwives with physicians, who were eager to use medications and surgical procedures not fully mastered and understood. More deaths were caused by these procedures at the hands of physicians than by infections in the care of midwives (Alexander and LaRosa 1994; Ruzek 1978).

In the United States, medicine became almost exclusively a white male profession by 1920. The Flexner report (an evaluation of medical schools by the Carnegie Foundation) was responsible for the closure of six of the eight Black medical schools and the majority of church-affiliated medical schools, which were more willing to train women. As childbirth moved away from the home to the hospital, women's sense of helplessness and lack of control over their bodies increased. The medical presence brought into maternity care a number of interventions, including drugs, anesthesia, and birthing instruments. This was a major intensification of the medicalization of women's lives. The trend continued uninterrupted until the 1960s, when women began to question and openly express their dissatisfaction with the medical profession's approach to women's reproductive health.

Since the 1960s, a multifaceted women's health movement has framed women's health issues in a variety of ways. The second wave women's liberation movement of the 1960s and 1970s, inspired by the civil rights movement, offered a critique of gender inequalities and oppression in all aspects of women's lives. Through the lens of a gendered analysis, grassroots groups all over the country began to question women's treatment by medical professionals. Springing from women's desire to define their own sexuality and to reclaim the birthing experience, many of the earliest challenges focused on reproductive health issues. Groups like the Boston Women's Health Collective, which authored *Our Bodies, Ourselves* (Boston Women's Health Collective, 1984), began to develop their own knowledge base and to encourage women's self-confidence related to health matters.

To combat the unnecessary medicalization of women's lives stemming from the hegemony of the medical profession, the women's health movement spawned numerous self-help activities related to gynecological health. A national network of Feminist Women's Health Clinics developed new models of self-examination and treatment. A revival of midwifery and home-birth was accompanied by pressure on hospitals to allow natural childbirth, partners' presence and participation at births, and other conditions giving more control to women and their families. Central to the changes enacted by the women's health movement was a salutogenic or health-promoting orientation in contrast with the prevailing disease-oriented medical model. Inherent in the framework of self-education and self-help are notions of prevention that include diet, herbal remedies, exercise, and stress reduction techniques to ease the discomforts of conditions ranging from menstrual cramps to menopause.

As in all social movements, the beliefs and methods promoted by the different segments of the women's health movement are widely variable. For example, feminist health advocates disagree about the safety and desirability of many new reproductive technologies. Some groups are working to ban the development and implementation of such technologies while others are working to achieve broader diffusion of expensive infertility treatments. Differences exist in the emphasis on developing alternatives to traditional medicine versus demanding changes in the health care system. Some groups have worked to create new models through their own counter-institutions, while others have concentrated their efforts at the legislative level or targeted their demands toward professional associations, hospitals, or drug companies.

The politically charged issue of abortion illustrates the effectiveness of a dual strategy involving both approaches. Before the legalization of abortion in 1973, many women's networks made referrals to providers who were willing to perform abortions and who were known to be competent and trustworthy. At least one group, the Jane Collective in Chicago, became trained as lay abortion providers and helped thousands of women terminate their pregnancies without medical complications or economic exploitation. At the same time, broad coalitions were organizing and demonstrating to change the country's laws in order to achieve legal and safe abortions that would become available to a much broader spectrum of women after 1973.

After abortion was legalized, some women in the abortion rights movement expanded their agenda to encompass more comprehensive reproductive rights required for women to decide freely whether or not to have children. True reproductive freedom was understood to imply the guarantee of adequate income, housing, child care, health services, schools, and other necessities for bringing up children. The reproductive rights movement recognized the need to join with other groups struggling to ensure such conditions, and attempted to address social disparities in access to health and other services. In recent years, groups such as the National Black Women's Health Project, National Latina Health Organization, Native American Women's Health Education Resource Center, and Asian-Pacific Women for Reproductive Health have provided new leadership to invigorate the reproductive rights movement and expand the agenda of the women's health movement to be more responsive to women in different communities (Fried 1990; Worcester and Whatley 1994).

Attention to inequities in health outcomes and access to health care has expanded the purview of the women's health movement beyond reproductive issues and into the areas of health care financing, health care delivery systems, and medical research. The National Women's Health Network and other groups have investigated, developed policy positions, and testified at Congressional hearings on diverse women's health issues. Recent issues of concern have included estrogen replacement therapy and the design of experimental research testing the effectiveness of the drug tamoxifen in preventing breast cancer. Campaigns to improve maternity care services have recently branched out into consumer movements to force insurance companies to cover longer postpartum hospitalizations.

The legislative attempts to enact universal health insurance coverage mobilized activists to advocate for women's needs in health care reform. Since the failure of health care reform, potential changes in the Medicaid system have raised alarm about the insurance status and access to care for low-income women. Medicaid currently finances prenatal care and deliveries for a large proportion of U.S. women, and it also funds family planning and other services for many others. Lack of health care coverage is a threat for many women; lack of scientific knowledge as the basis for appropriate health care services also places women in jeopardy. The advantages of a women's health specialty within organized medicine have been hotly debated in professional circles. Some think such a new field would legitimize women's health needs and fill important gaps, while others fear it would "marginalize the care of women and leave the mainstream to men" (Angell 1993, p. 272). This fear is based on the idea that

> . . . clinical research has over the years improperly excluded women. According to this view, women have been discriminated against in three ways: diseases that affect them disproportionately are less likely to be studied; women are less likely to be included as participants in clinical trials; and they are less likely to be senior investigators conducting the trials (Angell 1993, p. 271).

Several recent developments have aimed to address these problems. The National Institutes of Health (NIH) established the Office of Research on Women's Health in 1990. The following year NIH Director Bernadine Healy launched the Women's Health Initiative, "a massive 15-year study of 160,000 women that will cost more than $600 million and include the largest clinical trial ever conducted" (Angell 1993, p. 271). The Women's Health Initiative represents a national commitment to begin to address the impact on women of all major morbidities, not just reproductive risks. In 1994, NIH published "Guidelines on the Inclusion of

Women and Minorities as Subjects in Clinical Research." These guidelines establish a policy that women as well as minority populations and subpopulations must be included in all human research funded by NIH unless a compelling reason is given that such inclusion is "inappropriate with respect to the health of the subjects or the purpose of the research." The policy specifically prevents routine exclusion of "women of childbearing potential" from clinical research.

The development and refinement of these NIH guidelines in the early 1990s has been both a response and a spur to increasing surveillance of women's health needs. In 1994 a national conference was convened under the leadership of the American Psychological Association "aimed at developing a specific agenda to address the psychosocial aspects of women's health care" (Voelker 1994, p. 7). The Centers for Disease Control and Prevention (CDC) also announced the opening of an Office on Women's Health. According to Reuben Warren, the CDC's associate director for Minority Health, "Without an effective women's health movement, the health of the nation cannot improve" (Voelker 1994, p. 7).

Finally, the U.S. women's health movement has expanded its scope by forging stronger links with international women's health advocacy groups. Consciousness about the interrelationship of women here and abroad has been heightened by issues such as the testing of contraceptives on women in developing countries prior to Food and Drug Administration (FDA) approval for U.S. distribution, and the international targeting of women as potential consumers of exported cigarettes while outreach increases to warn U.S. women about the hazards of smoking. At the same time that U.S. policies endanger the health of women in the developing world, grassroots empowerment of women in many parts of the globe provide inspiration for organizing efforts in the international gatherings, such as the recent meetings on international population issues in Cairo and on women's rights in Beijing. Combined with electronic communication and computer technology, these efforts have increasingly united women to improve their health and social status throughout the world.

Women's health cannot be adequately understood without discussing the role of gender on the maintenance of health and the prevention and treatment of disease (Strickland 1988; Verbrugge 1989; Verbrugge and Wingard 1987). Since the 1980s, sex and gender have been among the most applied but poorly understood concepts within health research. Sex differentials in morbidity and mortality have been widely researched. Some examples are: *health and well-being* (Grimmell and Stern 1992; Lane and Meleis 1991; Nakano 1990; Rathgeber and Vlassoff 1993; Williams et al. 1992); *mental health and stress* (Allgood et al. 1990; Anson et al. 1990; Avison and McAlpine 1992; Barnett and Marshall 1992; Costello 1991; Gillespie and Eisler 1992; Groer et al. 1992; Janes 1990; Kane 1991; Napholz 1992; Nuess and Zubenko 1992; Radke-Yarrow et al. 1993; Woods et al. 1993; Zimmerman-Tansella and Lattanzi 1991); and *cardiovascular disease*

(Elliott 1994; Helmers et al. 1993; Knox and Follmann 1993; Suarez et al. 1993; Theorell 1991). *Sex* and *gender* have been used as synonymous terms in most of these studies. However, sex and gender have very different meanings and measure very distinct components of the continuum of health and disease.

Sex is biologically determined. It can usually be measured easily by using the biological categories of male and female. The construct of sex is determined by the laws of genetics, through the arrangement of chromosomes that result in phenotypes (groups of people with similar genetically and environmentally produced physical appearances) and genotypes (groups of people with similar genetic structures) (de los Rios 1994; de los Rios and Gomez 1992; Gomez 1990; Kane 1991). Thus, sex (female or male) has a biologic base and is clearly defined by specific anatomic and physiologic traits.

In contrast, gender is socially determined. It is rooted in the biological differences between the sexes, but it relates to the roles assigned by society to the female and male sexes. As yet, universal measurements of gender are not well defined. Gender is expressed through relations of power and subordination, which translate into assigned roles, norms, activities, and behaviors expected to be performed by women and men in each society (Alexander and LaRosa 1994; Amit et al. 1989; Arango 1992; Canadian Council for International Co-operation 1991; de los Rios 1994; de los Rios and Gomez 1992; Gomez 1990; 1994; J.E. Austin Associates and The Collaborative for Development Action, Inc. 1989; Kane 1991; Moser 1989; Rathgeber and Vlassoff 1993). The conditions of women's and men's daily lives and their positions within society are expressed in beliefs, attitudes, and behaviors (de los Rios and Gomez 1992; Gomez 1990; Moser, 1989). To be a man or a woman is to be associated with different behaviors and attitudes in public and private life. The construct of gender has been shaped by historical circumstance and is susceptible to changes in policies associated with social, economic, judicial, and political events. According to de los Rios and Gomez (1992), the core of the gender construct is the sex-based division of labor, which is expressed in the segregation of social functions on the basis of belonging to either the female or male sex. The sexual division of labor is a historical product—not a natural aspect of society (Castellanos 1987). It is the basis by which societies ensure their social reproduction. It guarantees both the biologic reproduction (childbearing and rearing responsibilities) and the social reproduction of society, which shapes its production mode, social and political institutions, and patterns of social relationships (Castellanos 1987; de los Rios and Gomez 1992).

As a means of ensuring the social reproduction of society, women's lives are structured to revolve around multiple social roles, needs, and expectations (J.E. Austin Associates and The Collaborative for Development Action, Inc. 1989). These roles form a dynamic web bringing together sex and gender attributes, including age and physical environments (de los Rios and Gomez 1992). Age is directly related to the cycles in women's lives that trigger not only biological but also political and social changes at the individual and societal levels (Arango 1992; Directorate General for International Cooperation 1989). Throughout the world the social roles assigned to most women dictate their use of physical space (Arango 1992; de los Rios and Gomez 1992; Directorate General for International Cooperation 1989). The spaces where women spend most of their time are directly influenced by social class, race, ethnicity, and family dynamics. Private and public spaces (e.g., school, home, church, work places) are the cradles of socialization for girls and women. In addition, physical environments influence women's social support and networks, which can be affective, social, or occupational in nature.

The options that shape women's lives, including marital status, religion, and political ideology, are directly linked to gender constructs. Gender relations and identities are not universal, but vary from culture to culture, and sometimes from community to community. They are dynamic and change over time (de los Rios and Gomez 1992; Gomez 1994). The analysis of gender in research needs to take into account all these aspects as well as women's heterogeneity. The construct of gender assumes specific meaning depending on political milieu, culture, race, ethnicity, and social class (de los Rios 1994; de los Rios and Gomez 1992; Gomez 1994). Despite their heterogeneity, in most societies women are generally disadvantaged compared to men in relation to social and sex roles and, subsequently, with regard to services and opportunities. Thus women are exposed more than men to interpersonal violence, sexual discrimination, social displacement, and poverty (de los Rios and Gomez 1992; Directorate General for International Cooperation 1989).

WOMEN'S HEALTH: A LIFE CYCLE

To do justice in one chapter to women's health throughout the life cycle is an impossible task. Thus, the aim of this section is to highlight aspects of women's health from the life cycle perspective.

The influence of biology, cultural roles and behaviors, and social status on health differs greatly between women and men. Women live longer than men worldwide. In addition, as life expectancy increases for both women and men, the gap tends to widen. However, the biological responsibility for human reproduction has been historically a primary cause of women's morbidity and mortality. This was documented in 1662 by John Graunt, when he stated, "Yes I have heard *Physicians* say, that they have two women patients to one man, which Assertion seems very likely; for that women have either the *Greensickness*, or other Distempers, are sick of *Breedings, Abortions, Child-bearing, Sorebreasts, Whites, Obstructions, Fits of the Mother and the like*" (quoted by Kane, 1991, p. 1).

Graunt concluded that men die because of their vices and women because of the disease of their sex (Kane 1991). Although reproductive mortality and morbidity are still realities for women in many countries, the differences between women's and men's health exist from the time of conception to death, and human reproduction is only part of the life cycle. The conceptualization of women's health throughout life reflects the interconnection of the different life stages and their relation to the health of women and future generations.

In Utero, Infancy, and Childhood

In Utero

Biologists tell us that the sex ratio estimate at conception (primary sex ratio) is 120 male embryos per every 100 female embryos (Overfield 1995; Strickland 1988). Although miscarriages in the first month of pregnancy are thought to be frequent, little is known about their sex distribution. Males are more likely to be stillborn due to difficult labor, birth injuries, and diseases or injuries of the mother, while deaths of females *in utero* are more likely to be caused by congenital malformations (Kane 1991). In some countries, female fetuses are targets of abortions for the purpose of sex selection. For example, "a report from Bombay in 1984 on abortion after prenatal sex determination stated that 7,999 out of 8,000 of the aborted fetuses were females. Sex determination has become a lucrative business" (World Health Organization, 1992). Most of the clients for this expensive procedure are women from the middle and lower classes. Thus, fetal survival is related to biological and genetic factors and influenced by maternal health, personal decisions, social values, obstetrical care, and other environmental factors.

Infancy

More males than females are born. The sex ratio of live births (secondary sex ratio) is approximately 104–106 males to 100 females (Dolnick 1994). However, this ratio is not universal. In some Asian countries, including China and India, the ratio is higher than average; in some African countries, it is lower (Kane 1991). The sex ratio difference could be due to ineffective birth registration systems. People may not register births that are followed by the death of the infant. Parents may be less likely to register an infant girl in countries where girl children are less valued than males, since a girl has a lower chance of survival in such countries. Presently, there are 100 million females unaccounted for worldwide and sex preference may be the reason. The preference for a son is associated with the perception of women's meager economic potential. Both women and men have expressed a strong preference for boys in many countries. However, the son preference is especially prevalent in Hindu, Moslem, and Chinese societies (Kane 1991). (See Table 10–1.)

Table 10–1 Preference for the Sex of Children

Country	Index of Son Preference*	Country	Index of Son Preference*
Strong Son Preference		Malaysia	1.2
Pakistan	4.9	Mexico	1.2
Nepal	4.0	Morocco	1.2
Bangladesh	3.3		
Korea	3.3	*Equal Preference*	
Syria	2.3	Guyana	1.1
Jordan	1.9	Indonesia	1.1
		Kenya	1.1
Moderate Son Preference		Peru	1.1
Egypt	1.5	Trinidad and Tobago	1.1
Lesotho	1.5	Colombia	1.0
Senegal	1.5	Costa Rica	1.0
Sri Lanka	1.5	Ghana	1.0
Sudan	1.5	Panama	1.0
Thailand	1.4	Paraguay	1.0
Turkey	1.4	Portugal	1.0
Fiji	1.3	Haiti	0.9
Nigeria	1.3	Philippines	0.9
Tunisia	1.3		
Yemen A.R.	1.3	*Daughter Preference*	
Cameroon	1.2	Venezuela	0.8
Dominican Republic	1.2	Jamaica	0.7
Ivory Coast	1.2		

*Index of son preference=Ratio of the number of mothers who prefer the next child to be male to the number of mothers who prefer the next child to be female.

Source: Reprinted with permission from E. Royston and S. Armstrong, *Preventing Maternal Deaths,* p. 51, © 1989, World Health Organization.

Infants of both sexes are at risk of dying during the early weeks after birth. The causes of death are related to complications of pregnancy, childbirth, congenital abnormalities, prematurity, low weight for gestational age, and inadequate postnatal care. Male infants are more likely to die of causes related to low birth weight and congenital abnormalities, indicating that female fetuses with congenital malformations may be more likely to be miscarried. Infant mortality in general is also associated with poverty, social inequities, and lack of access to adequate sources of health care (Kane 1991).

Childhood

Death rates begin to fall after the first year of life. The risk of dying is two times higher for children age 1–4 than children age 5–14 (Kane 1991). However, there are sex differentials in child survival favoring boys. According to the World Health Organization (1992, p. 20), "Gender discrimination is found throughout the world, from birth onwards. Research on disease prevalence, health care utilization and family resource allocation indicates that girls are treated differently from boys, with negative results that last for a lifetime." In societies with son-preference, baby girls may be breastfed for a shorter time, and thus may be exposed at an early age to contaminated or poor quality foods. In addition, a daughter may get less food and less medical and preventive health care (Frongillo and Bégin 1993; Kane 1991; Shrestha 1990; Singh 1990). It has been argued by some that better feeding and caring for boys is not so much discrimination against girls as it is a way to compensate for boys' biological disadvantages. However, it is difficult to accept these practices as an impartial way to deal with boys' vulnerabilities. (See Table 10–2.)

Health information about school-age children (5–14) is limited; studies and reports rarely address sex differentials among them. Selwyn (1990) found in

Table 10–2 Annual Death Rate per 1000 among 2- to 5-Year-Olds, by Sex

Country	Girls	Boys
Bangladesh	68.6	57.7
Colombia	24.8	20.5
Costa Rica	8.1	4.8
Dominican Republic	20.2	17.2
Haiti	61.2	47.8
Mexico	16.7	14.7
Nepal	60.7	57.7
Pakistan	54.4	36.9
Panama	8.7	7.6
Peru	30.8	28.8
Philippines	21.9	19.1
Republic of Korea	12.7	11.8
Sri Lanka	18.7	16.3
Syrian Arab Republic	14.6	9.3
Thailand	26.8	17.3
Turkey	19.5	18.4
Venezuela	8.4	7.6

Source: Reprinted with permission from United Nations (1991), *The World's Women 1970–1990, Trends and Statistics,* Social Statistics and Indicators, Series K, No. 8, New York, NY: Author, p. 60, based on the United Nations Children's Fund analyses of World Fertility Survey results.

reviewing community surveys that the incidence rates of acute and upper respiratory infections were only slightly higher for boys than girls, but boys were very often the main users of inpatient or outpatient hospital services for those conditions. In England, boys age 0–14 have higher total rates of hospitalization than girls (Kane 1991). The main causes of illness and hospitalization among school-age children are infections and parasitic diseases, upper and lower respiratory infections, congenital anomalies, symptoms and ill-defined conditions, and injury and poisoning. There is evidence that many countries underreport illness episodes for school-age girls, suggesting that illness among boys tends to be taken more seriously than sickness among girls (Williams et al. 1994).

Children are frequent targets of violence, abuse, and neglect. With respect to sexual abuse in particular, the situation is much worse for girls (Wong 1990). Presently, 1.6 million children in the United States annually experience some form of abuse or neglect. According to Alexander and LaRosa (1994, p. 169) "Childhood sexual abuse is estimated to occur in about 40 percent of girls before the age of 17." Research indicates that as abused children become adolescents, they have elevated risks of substance use, suicide attempts, aggressive behavior, anorexia and bulimia, pregnancy, and running away. Child abuse and neglect cuts across gender, race/ethnicity, and socioeconomic lines internationally.

In some countries, girls and young women experience cultural practices that place them at risk of morbidity and mortality (Toubia 1994). The practice of female circumcision is one example. Worldwide, approximately 100 million women and girls have undergone genital mutilation through this practice in around 40 African countries, Malaysia, Indonesia, Yemen, parts of Mexico, Brazil, and Peru (Crossete 1995). Immigrants from these countries continue this practice in Europe and North America (Crossete 1995). England and France have responded by outlawing genital mutilation.

There is not a set age for this cultural practice, which ranges from infancy to the sixth month of a woman's first pregnancy. The surgical procedures are usually performed by women known to the girl, in her home and without anesthesia. A few wealthy families have their daughters' operations done under anesthesia by medical personnel. There are three types of female circumcision: clitoridectomy—removal of the skin over the clitoris or the tip of the clitoris; excision—removal of the entire clitoris and the labia minora without closing the vulva; and infibulation—encompassing the two previous mutilations plus removing part of the labia majora and stitching it together, leaving just a small opening to allow the secretion of urine and menstrual fluid (Smyke 1993; Toubia 1994).

Women undergoing these procedures experience short- and long-term effects. Soon after the surgery, women may experience pain, shock, hemorrhage, retention of urine, infection, fever, or tetanus. Death may be an outcome if the girl or woman does not have appropriate medical care to deal with complications.

Throughout the life cycle women subsequently experience pelvic infections, sometimes so severe that the fallopian tubes get blocked. Urinary tract infections are common, and women develop cysts and scar tissue. Most women experience problems with the flow of menstrual blood. The first intercourse is extremely painful for women who have undergone infibulation. If the vaginal opening is too small, the husband or midwife has to cut the scar to enlarge the opening. These women also tend to have labor complications. The most common is obstructed labor, which may bring additional complications (hemorrhage, tearing of the perineal tissue, urinary or rectal fistulae, and possible prolapsed uterus [Toubia 1994]). Giving birth does not free infibulated women; they are stitched back into their prebirth status. Though most circumcised women do not feel free to talk about sexual matters, a few understandably have reported unresponsiveness and anxiety connected with intercourse (Toubia 1994).

Tradition is the main reason for the perpetuation of a practice that inflicts pain, suffering, a sequelae of health problems, and sometimes even death on girls and women. For some women and men it is a symbol of belonging and shared heritage. For example, in the western part of Sierra Leone, 90 percent of women are circumcised (Smyke 1993). In this region female circumcision is the ritual of passage into women's secret societies, and the desire to be accepted into the society outweighs any doubt. Another reason often given is religion. However, according to Muslim and Christian scholars, nowhere in the Qu'ran or the Bible is there a female circumcision requirement (Smyke 1993). Parents often state that they have the girl's best interest in mind—a girl who does not undergo the procedure will be socially unacceptable without a chance for marriage. The cultural issue has been challenged by Dr. Nafis Sadikon, who stated at the Fourth World Women's Conference that "The function of culture and tradition is to provide a framework for human well-being. If they are used against us, we will reject them" (Crossete 1995, p. 18). Many African and Asian women reject the claim that female mutilation must be understood in a cultural context. Furthermore, women health professionals from Africa have been outspoken against the practice of female circumcision. The Inter-African Committee on Traditional Practices Affecting the Health of Women and Children (IAC) has been established to unite and to empower Africans working to abolish female circumcision and other dangerous cultural practices.

Teen Years

Adolescence has been recognized as the most turbulent stage in the life cycle due to the extent of physiological changes and social role development (Muuss 1988). Young women and men go through drastic biological changes during their adolescence. The sex hormones responsible for these major changes—estrogens and androgens—are present in both sexes (Whatley 1994). Women tend to have higher levels of estrogens than androgens and men the reverse; however, there is not a defined ratio of these hormones, and there is a great deal of individual variation. Unfortunately, much of the emphasis has been placed on the differences and very little on the similarities between adolescent boys and girls. Consequently, sexuality becomes defined in terms of hormones and culturally circumscribed sex roles, instead of common areas such as affection, love, and sexual rights and responsibilities.

Worldwide, teenagers contribute 13.7 percent of all live births (Mahowald 1993). According to Mahowald (1993), it is important to take into consideration gynecological and social age as well as chronological age when evaluating the impact of pregnancy on adolescent women. Gynecological age determines the biological maturity of the young woman and the number of years between the onset of menarche and pregnancy. Though pregnancy is a natural and healthy process among biologically mature women, inadequate gynecological age contributes to morbidity and mortality among pregnant adolescent women. Social age relates to the developmental milestones achieved by the teenager. Social age can be detrimental to the well-being of pregnant adolescents due to embarrassment, social ostracism, education interruptions, and economic pressures.

Although the teen years have been associated with the best physical health status within the life cycle continuum, adolescents are notorious for their risk-taking behavior. Injury and poisoning are major causes of death in the teen years. Morbidity associated with risk-taking behavior is exemplified by the high rates of sexually transmitted diseases (STDs) and the spread of human immunodeficiency virus/acquired immune deficiency syndrome (HIV/AIDS) among young people. According to the CDC, more than 12 million instances of STDs occur among the U.S. population each year, and more than 3 million of those are among teenagers (Alexander and LaRosa 1994). In 1990, the annual estimates of sexually transmitted infections worldwide were as follows: 120 million cases of trichomoniasis; 50 million cases of genital chlamydia; 30 million cases of genital papillomavirus; 25 million cases of Gonorrhea, 20 million cases of Genital Herpes; 3.5 million cases of syphilis; and 2 million cases of chancroid (World Health Organization 1992). Worldwide, women age 15–24 have the highest rates of gonorrhea (World Health Organization 1992), and bear a disproportionate share of the increase in reported cases of syphilis (Smyke 1993). STDs present greater risk and complications to women than men. Women experience pain, infertility, increased risk of etopic pregnancy, pelvic inflammatory disease, and psychological distress. Because most societies have a sexual double standard for women and men, STDs can be a source of shame and embarrassment for women. When a woman finds out that she has STD, she may experience denial, hurt, feelings of victimization, anger, fear, shame, or loss of control over her sexuality. Infection and the ensuing distress are compounded by the fact that women are more likely than men to live in poverty and they have less access to comprehensive health care, including diagnostic screening, treatment, and follow-up services for STDs (Williams et al. 1994; World Health Organization 1992). (See Tables 10–3a and 3b.)

Teenagers face difficult gender role expectations. Appearance can be a source of unhealthy practices among teenagers. For example, in the U.S. and European cultures, tall and well-muscled physiques are socially desirable for males; women are exhorted to be thin (Mahowald 1993; Alexander and LaRosa, 1994). Unfortunately, some adolescents pay a high price for such characteristics and consequently develop serious health problems. Young men may seek growth hormone therapy to increase their height and/or steroidal treatment to increase their muscle mass. Young women may develop anorexia nervosa or bulimia attempting to keep their weight down. Both eating disorders are identified with extreme preoccupation with food and body figure and image (Alexander and LaRosa 1994). Anorexics may purge after eating even a small portion of food, while bulimics tend to starve themselves before a binge. Anorexia is very difficult to cure. It is a physically and psychologically debilitating disease. According to research in the United States the feeling of being "fat" increases with age among young women, from 50 percent at age 14 to 70 percent at age 18 (Mahowald 1993).

Teenagers today are faced with a range of choices that were not even dreamt of two generations ago. At the same time adolescents experience high levels of alienation, depression, injuries, and death. Furthermore, teenagers are being targeted as consumers for cigarettes, illicit drugs, alcohol, cars, and daring sports

---

Table 10–3a Percentage of Pregnant Women with Bacteriological Evidence of C. Trachomatis in Specific Studies

Country	Percentage Positive
Fiji	45.1
Gabon	9.9
Gambia	6.9
Ghana	7.7
Kenya	29.0
Nigeria	6.5
Somalia	18.8
Thailand	12.8

Source: Reprinted with permission from A. De Schryver and A. Meheus, Epidemiology of Sexually Transmitted Diseases: The Global Picture, *Bulletin of the World Health Organization,* 68, pp. 639–654, © 1990 World Health Organization.

Table 10–3b Prevalence of Gonorrhea in Studies of Pregnant Women

Country	Prevalence (%)
Cameroon	15.0
Central African Republic	9.5
Fiji	2.3
Gambia	6.7
Gabon	5.5
Ghana	4.4
Jamaica	11.0
Kenya	6.6
Malaysia	0.5
Nigeria	5.2
Senegal	2.1
Singapore	0.8
South Africa	11.7
Swaziland	3.9
Thailand	11.9
Uganda	40.0
United Republic of Tanzania	6.0
Zambia	11.3
Zimbabwe	7.0

Source: Reprinted with permission from A. DeSchryver and A. Meheus. Epidemiology of Sexually Transmitted Diseases: The Global Picture. *Bulletin of the World Health Organization* 68, pp. 639–654, © 1990, World Health Organization.

and physical activities. There is an increase in illicit drugs and the use of alcohol, sedatives, and cigarettes among teenagers, including young women (Worcester and Whatley 1994).

Middle Years

In their middle years women and men assume a number of new social roles and responsibilities and are the main contributors to the economic well-being of their societies. This stage of the life cycle has traditionally been associated with issues of human reproduction, marriage, and career. In the last hundred years, women's time spent in childbearing has been reduced from half to one-sixth of their lives. It was not so long ago that women could not expect to live long enough to enjoy their grandchildren. Presently, in many cultures, women survive pregnancy and childbirth and have increased lifespans, partly because of the implementation of public health interventions and partly due to access to advances in medicine and medical technology.

Reproductive tract infections (RTIs) are hidden in the "culture of silence" (World Health Organization 1992). RTIs do not discriminate among women based on their social class, race and/or ethnicity, education, or country of origin. The prevalence of RTIs is high. For example, chlamydia (4–23 percent in Africa, 2–14 percent in Asia), gonorrhea (40 percent in Africa, 0.3–12 percent in Asia, 2–18 percent in Latin America), trichomoniasis (2–50 percent in Africa, 5–30 percent in Asia, 3–24 percent in Latin America). Untreated RTIs are a source of infection and have serious short-and long-term consequences for women's general health. Infertility has been associated with RTIs and STDs. Worldwide, there are approximately 70 million married couples with infertility problems. Women are usually the targets for infertility screening and treatments; however, a World Health Organization (WHO) study of 10,000 infertile couples found that 33 percent of the causes were attributable to the male partner and 25 percent to the female (Smyke 1993). (See Table 10–4.)

Women assume multiple roles in most societies today. In order to fulfill their many roles, women perform 67 percent of the world's labor. However, they earn only 10 percent of the world's income, and own 1 percent of the world's property (Canadian Council for International Co-operation 1991; Williams et al. 1994). Female heads of households earn much less than men. International data show a direct relationship between female family headship and poverty (Williams et al. 1994).

Table 10–4 Prevalence of Reproductive Tract Infections (RTIs) among Selected Female Populations* in Developing Countries

Infection	Africa	Asia	Latin America
Gonorrhea			
Prevalence	40%	0.3–12%	2–18%
Number of studies	39	9	5
Chlamydia			
Prevalence	4–23%	2–14%	
Number of studies	5	2	
Trichomoniasis			
Prevalence	2–50%	5–30%	3–24%
Number of studies	15	4	5

*Populations include family planning clients, gynecology clients, prenatal clinic patients, women giving birth in clinical settings, and community-based populations. Studies on female populations presenting specifically with pelvic inflammatory disease or puerperal sepsis have been excluded from this summary as have clients of sexually transmitted disease clinics.

Source: Data from Wasserheit, J. (1989). Significance and scope of reproductive tract infections among third world women. *International Journal of Gynaecology and Obstetrics* 3 (suppl): 154.

Dixon-Mueller, R., and Wasserheit, J. (1991). *The Culture of Silence. Reproductive Tract Infections among Women in the Third World.* New York: International Women's Health Coalition.

In general, having a paid job and being married both have health benefits for women and men. Men, however, tend to benefit more from being married (Haber 1991; Klonoff and Landrine 1991; Martikainen 1995; Rosenfeld 1992). According to Kane (1991), paid work and marriage generally have a synergistic and positive effect on the health status of women and men, but unemployed married men have worse health outcomes than unemployed unmarried men. By contrast, women who are either single and employed or married and unemployed have more acute and chronic disabilities than married and employed women. These findings suggest that multiple roles may be related to women's status in the household. In African and Latin American countries where women are responsible for childbearing, at least 70 percent of food production and approximately 50 percent of animal husbandry, the interaction between overwork, pregnancy, and malnutrition has serious health consequences.

Women everywhere work long hours. The workday of women in most countries is 16 hours. Despite modern appliances, western housewives spend 56 hours per week working, while their counterparts in Pakistan work just 6 hours more (62 hours) per week (Williams et al. 1994). Furthermore, it is important to note that the distribution of health and illness is influenced by social class, race and ethnicity, geographical location, and social indicators such as education, access to health services, occupational hazards, environmental factors, and a range of personal circumstances.

Women are responsible for the biological reproduction of humankind. The United Nations Decade for Women provided an international focus on women's reproductive health issues and the right to reproductive health. The following United Nations (UN) Conferences have had major impact on women's reproductive lives: Mexico City (1975), Copenhagen (1980), Nairobi (1985), Rio de Janeiro (1992), Vienna (1993), Cairo (1994), and Beijing (1995). For discussions of reproductive health, please refer to the chapters on Mothers and Infants and International Health (Chapters 5 and 13).

Transitional Years

Significant changes in women's life patterns have occurred in the last 100 years. As mentioned earlier, women's life expectancy surpasses that of men in most countries, and women currently have about 30 years more to live compared with women a century ago. For example, in the United States today there are 43 million women in the age of perimenopause (Alexander and LaRosa 1994)—"changes in menstrual flow or frequency during the last 12 months" (Morse et al.

1994, p. 164), and each day, 3,500 women enter menopause (Braus 1993)—"no menses for twelve consecutive months or longer" (Morse et al. 1994, p. 164). It is women at the perimenopausal age who are challenging how society deals with the natural process of aging. It is a major phobia in the United States, while in some societies women's status increases with age.

Menopause (natural or surgically induced) has been until recently a social taboo—women talked about it only in whispers. Not long ago, physicians viewed menopause as the "death of the woman in the woman" (Braus 1993, p. 46). Avis and McKinlay (1995) conducted the largest and most comprehensive prospective cohort study on menopause. They found that natural menopause did not have a major impact on the health or health behavior of women. The majority of women undergoing menopause did not seek medical help, and their attitudes were over-whelmingly positive or neutral. Some women experienced transitional depression; rate of depression decreased as women moved away from the peri-menopausal to the post-menopause stage.

Endocrine changes of menopause are the main causes of physical and psycho-logical symptoms (e.g., hot flashes, vaginal atrophy, weight gain, insomnia, mood changes, depression), but not all women experience these symptoms. However, all women do have a drastic decline in estrogen levels. Low levels of estrogen are associated with an increased risk of osteoporosis and cardiovascular diseases. Hormone replacement therapy (HRT) has become the "magic bullet" to combat these risks. It has been argued that HRT maintains the high density lipoprotein (HDL) and low density lipoprotein (LDL) levels at the premenopausal stage. Results from a prospective study following 50,000 women found that women using estrogen had half the risk of major coronary artery disease or fatal cardio-vascular disease and no increased risk of stroke compared with nonestrogen users (Alexander and LaRosa 1994). Parke-Davis is marketing a low-dose birth control pill designated for women in transition between pre-and post-menopause. This pill offers both estrogen supplements and contraceptive protection.

There is no consensus in the women's health movement or within the medical community about the use of HRT. It is important to note that very little research has been conducted on menopause-related issues. Two major research efforts have been sponsored by NIH to answer some questions related to menopause. The HRT study is the first large-scale clinical trial, and it will provide much-needed infor-mation to make decisions on the benefits and counterindications of hormonal therapy. Another study—PEPI (Postmenopausal Estrogen/Progestin Interven-tion)—measures the effects of estrogen and progestin on cholesterol, blood pres-sure, bone density, and breast and uterine cancers. It will be several years before the results of these studies will be available to health providers and women. The results are critical for decision making regarding issues on the quality of life and health for a growing number of women worldwide.

Elderly Women

Elderly women live longer and are poorer than elderly men. For example, widows make up 25 percent of the adult female population in Africa (Smyke 1993). Worldwide, millions of elderly women experience poverty, social isolation, and ill health. In the United States, three of every five women age 65 years and over are without spouses, while three of every four men in the same age group are married or living with a partner (Jecker 1991). Over half of elderly women in the United States live below the poverty level (Arendell and Estes 1991; Sidel 1994). Furthermore, a higher percent of Latin and African American women age 65 and over live in poverty (Hunter and Sundel 1994). According to Arendell and Estes (1991, p. 62), "being old, female, and a member of a minority group represents a triple jeopardy." The two poorest groups in the United States are women over 65 years of age and children under 5. In the United States, elderly women represent 11 percent of the population, but they are prescribed 25 percent of legal drugs. Prescriptions are given to elderly women at a rate 2.5 times that for elderly men. Some of the unintended outcomes of prescription drug use among elderly women are drug reactions, impairment of cognitive and motor functions, insomnia, affective disturbance, and suicide.

The lives of elderly women are affected by cultural attitudes toward women and the elderly, economic development, and social organizations. For example, in Fiji, Korea, and the Philippines, only 2 percent of persons age 60 and over live away from their families, while in the United States over one-third live alone. In the United Kingdom, 80 percent of all elderly persons living alone are women (Smyke 1993).

The views of a society regarding elderly women are not necessarily shared by the women themselves. Most elderly women do not consider themselves old if they are in good health (Moen et al. 1992; UN 1985). For this population, health is the key to remaining active and to participating meaningfully in society. Older women are organizing themselves and joining forces with women of all ages to improve their lives and to create a world where women can hold their rightful place in society (UN 1985).

EMERGING ISSUES

Because women's health is heavily influenced by socioeconomic and environmental trends as well as gender dynamics and other social relations, new issues are constantly rising to the fore. In the last two decades, technological and political changes have had a tremendous impact, making available new means of reproduction, such as in vitro fertilization and surrogacy, and restricting access to abortion and family planning services as legislative mandates and funding have fluctuated. New legal and ethical dilemmas have arisen with the development and approval of long-acting hormonal contraceptives such as Norplant® and Depo-Provera®, which offer new forms of coitus-independent protection but also new potential for coercion in reproductive decision making.

Women compose an increasing proportion of the population affected by HIV infection. The tragedies of women's vulnerability to HIV/AIDS and their role in perinatal transmission have accentuated stark disparities in health—disproportionate numbers of poor women of color and their children are affected by HIV. The plague of substance abuse in these women's communities and soaring rates of other STDs enhance their risk of HIV infection. Models of appropriate drug treatment services for women now exist, but moral judgments compound class and racial discrimination in restricting resource allocation for such badly needed services.

Social prejudices against women have also been identified as barriers to adequate health services for lesbians and to the medical community's responsibility for dealing with violence against women as a public health concern. Little is known about the health effects of the combination of work and family responsibilities that most women now assume, and the concentration of women in low-wage, low-status occupations creates additional physical and psychological stresses. Advocacy by and for women continues to seek redress for health inequities and to pursue the long-term goal of universal health care for all women and their families.

REFERENCES

Alexander, L.L., and J.H. LaRosa. 1994. *New dimensions in women's health*. Boston and London: Jones and Bartlett Publishers.

Allgood, M.B. et al. 1990. Sex differences and adolescent depression. *Journal of Abnormal Psychology* 99:56–63.

Amit, H.R. et al. 1989. *A handbook for social/gender analysis*. Ottawa: Social and Human Resources Development Division, Canadian International Development Agency.

Angell, M. 1993. Caring for women's health—what is the problem? *The New England Journal of Medicine* 329:271–272.

Anson, O. et al. 1990. Gender and health on the kibbutz. *Sex-Roles*, 22, no. 3–4:213–235.

Arango, Y. 1992. Autocuidado: Una toma de decisión de la mujer frente a su salud. In *Mujer, Salud y Autocuidado: Memorias,* ed. Y. Arango, 81–101. Washington, DC: Pan American Health Organization.

Arendell, T., and C.L. Estes. 1991. Older women in the post-Reagan era. *International Journal of Health Services* 21:59–73.

Avis, N.E., and S.M. McKinlay. 1995. The Massachusetts women's health study: An epidemiologic investigation of the menopause. *Journal of American Medical Women's Association* 50:45–49.

Avison, W.R., and D.D. McAlpine. 1992. Gender differences in symptoms of depression among adolescents. *Journal of Health Social Behavior* 33:77–96.

Barnett, R., and N.L. Marshall. 1992. Worker and mother roles, spill over effects, and psychological distress. *Women and Health* 18, no. 2:9–40.

Beral, V. 1985. Long-term effects of childbearing on health. *Journal of Epidemiology Community Health* 39:343–346.

Boston Women's Health Collective. 1984. *Our bodies, ourselves: A book by and for women.* New York: Simon and Schuster.

Braus, P. 1993. Facing M. *American Demographics* 15:44–48, March.

Canadian Council for International Co-operation. 1991. *Two halves make whole: Balancing gender relations in development.* Ottawa: MATCH International, and Association Québécoise des Organismes de Coopération Internationale.

Castellanos, P. 1987. Sobre el concepto de salud-enfermedad: Un punto de vista epidemiologico. *Fifth World Congress of Social Medicine.* Medellin, Colombia, mimeo.

Costello, E.J. 1991. Married with children: Predictors of mental and physical health in middle-aged women. *Psychiatry* 54:292–305.

Crossete, B. Female genital mutilation by immigrants is becoming cause for concern in the U.S. *New York Times,* 10 December 1995, p. 18.

de los Rios, R. 1994. Gender, health, and development: An approach in the making. In *Gender, Women, and Health in the Americas,* ed. E. Gomez, 3–17. Washington, DC: Pan American Health Organization.

de los Rios, R., and E. Gomez. 1992. Mujer en la salud y el desarrollo. In *Mujer, Salud y Autocuidado: Memorias,* ed. Y. Arango, 107–123. Washington, DC: Pan American Health Organization.

Directorate General for International Cooperation. 1989. Women and health. In *Sector Paper, Women and Development,* No. 3, Ministry of Foreign Affairs, The Netherlands.

Dolnick, E. 1994. Super women. In *Women's health—Readings on social, economic, and political issues,* 2nd ed., eds. N. Worcester and M. Whatley. Dubuque, IO: Kendall/Hunt Publishing Company.

Elliott, S.J. 1994. Psychosocial stress, women and heart health: A critical review. *Social Science Medicine* 40:115.

Forrest, J.D. 1993. Timing of reproductive life stages. *Obstetrics and Gynecology* 82:105–110.

Fried, M.G., ed. 1990. *From abortion to reproductive freedom: Transforming a movement.* Boston: South End Press.

Frongillo, E.A., Jr., and F. Bégin. 1993. Gender bias in food intake favors male preschool Guatemalan children. *Journal of Nutrition* 123:189–196.

Gillespie, B.L., and R.M. Eisler. 1992. Development of the feminine gender role stress scale: A cognitive-behavioral measure of stress, appraisal, and coping for women. *Behavioral Analysis and Modification* 16:426–438.

Gomez, E. 1990. *Perfil epidemiologico de la salud de la mujer en la region de las Americas.* Washington, DC: Pan American Health Organization, 1–3, 221–237.

Gomez, E. 1994. Introduction in *Gender, Women, and Health in the Americas,* ed. E. Gomez, ix–xviii. Washington, DC: Pan American Health Organization.

Green, A. et al. 1988. Mortality in women in relation to their childbearing history. *British Medical Journal* 297:391–395.

Grimmell, D., and G.S. Stern. 1992. The relationship between gender role ideals and psychological well-being. *Sex Roles* 27:487–497.

Groer, M.W. et al. 1992. Adolescent stress and coping: A longitudinal study. *Research in Nursing and Health* 15:209–217.

Haber, L.C. 1991. The effect of employment on the relationship between gender-role preference and self-esteem in married women. *J Advanced Nursing* 16:606–613.

Helmers, K.F. et al. 1993. Hostility and myocardial ischemia in coronary artery disease patients: evaluation by gender and ischemic index. *Psychosomatic Medicine* 55:29–36.

Hunter, S., and M. Sundel. 1994. Midlife for women: A new perspective. *Affilia* 9:113–128.

Janes, C.R. 1990. Migration, changing gender roles and stress: The Samoan case. *Medical Anthropology* 12:217–248.

J.E. Austin Associates and The Collaborative for Development Action, Inc. 1989. *Gender analysis for project design: UNFPA training manual.* Prepared for UNFPA. Cambridge, MA: Author.

Jecker, N.S. 1991. Age-based rationing and women. *Journal of American Medical Association* 266: 3012–3015.

Kane, P. 1991. *Women's health: From womb to tomb.* New York: St. Martin's Press.

Katz, M.E. et al. 1995. Mortality rates among 15- to 44-year-old women in Boston: Looking beyond reproductive status. *American Journal of Public Health* 85:1135–1138.

Klonoff, E.A., and H. Landrine. 1991. Sex roles, occupational roles, and symptom-reporting: A test of competing hypothesis on sex difference. *Journal of Behavioral Medicine* 15:355–364.

Knox, S.S., and D. Follmann. 1993. Gender difference in the psychosocial variance of framingham and bortner type A measures. *Journal of Psychosomatic Research* 37:709–716.

Lane, S.D., and A. Meleis. 1991. Roles, work, health perceptions and health resources of women: A Study in an Egyptian delta hamlet. *Social Science Medicine* 33:1197–1208.

Mahowald, M.B. 1993. *Women and children in health care: An unequal majority.* New York: Oxford University Press, 242–254.

Martikainen, P. 1995. Women's employment, marriage, motherhood and mortality: A test of multiple role and role accumulation hypotheses. *Social Science Medicine* 40:199–212.

Moen, P. et al. 1992. Successful aging: A life-course perspective on women's multiple roles and health. *American Journal of Sociology* 97:1612–1638.

Morse, C.A. et al. 1994. The treatment-seeking women at menopause. *Maturitas* 18:161–173.

Moser, C.O. 1989. Gender planning in the third world: Meeting practical and strategic gender needs. *World Development* 17:1799–1825.

Muuss, R.E. 1988. Carol Gilligan's theory of sex differences in the development of moral reasoning during adolescence. *Adolescence* XXIII:229–243.

Nakano, K. 1990. Type A behavior, hardiness, and psychological well-being in Japanese women. *Psychological Reports* 67:367–370.

Napholz, L. 1992. Locus of control and depression as a function of sex role orientation in tubert S. *Acta-Psiquiatrica y Psicologica de America Latina* 38:205–212, abstract.

NIH/ADAMHA. 1994. Guidelines on the inclusion of women and minorities as subjects in clinical research. *NIH Guide for Grants and Contracts.* Bethesda, MD: Author.

Nuess, W.S., and G.S. Zubenko. 1992. Correlates of persistent depression symptoms in widows. *American Journal of Psychiatry* 149:346–351.

Overfield, T. 1995. *Biologic variation in health and illness: Race, age, and sex differences,* 2nd ed. Boca Raton, LA: CRS Press.

Radke-Yarrow, M. et al. 1993. Affective interactions of depressed and nondepressed mothers and their children. *Journal of Abnormal Child Psychology* 21:683–695.

Rathgeber, E.M., and C. Vlassoff. 1993. Gender and tropical diseases: A new research focus. *Social Science Medicine* 37:513–520.

Rosenfeld, J.A. 1992. Maternal work outside the home and its effect on women and their families. *Journal of American Medical Women's Association* 47:47–53.

Rosenfield, A., and D. Maine. 1985. Maternal mortality—a neglected tragedy: Where is the M in MCH? *The Lancet* 2, no. 8446:83–85.

Ruzek, S.B. 1978. *The women's health movement.* New York: Praeger Publishers.

Selwyn, B.J. 1990. The epidemiology of acute respiratory tract infection in young children: Comparison of findings from several developing countries. *Review of Infectious Diseases* 12 (suppl. 8): S877.

Shrestha, N.M. 1990. The girl child. *Asian-Pacific Journal of Public Health* 4:205–208.

Sidel, R. 1994. The special plight of older women. In *Women's health—readings on social, economic, and political issues,* 2nd ed., eds. N. Worcester and M. Whatley, 97–103. Dubuque, IO: Kendall/Hunt Publishing Company.

Singh, I. 1990. Sociocultural factors affecting girl children in Nepal. *Asian-Pacific Journal of Public Health* 4:251–254.

Smyke, P. 1993. *Women and health, 2nd impression.* Atlantic Highlands, NJ: Zed Books Ltd.

Strickland, B.R. 1988. Sex-related differences in health and illness. *Psychology of Women Quarterly* 12:381–399.

Suarez, E.C. et al. 1993. Cardiovascular and emotional responses in women: The role of hostility and harassment. *Health Psychology* 12:459–468.

Theorell, T. 1991. Cardiovascular health in women: Results from epidemiological and psychosocial studies in Sweden. In *Women, work and health: Stress and opportunities,* eds. M. Frankenhaeuser, U. Lundberg, and M.A. Chesney. New York, NY: Plenum Press, abstract.

Toubia, N. 1994. Female circumcision as a public health issue. *The New England Journal of Medicine* 331:712–716.

United Nations. 1985. *UN Decade for Women Bulletin, 11.* New York.

Verbrugge, L.M. 1989. The twain meet: Empirical explanations of sex differences in health and mortality. *Journal of Health and Social Behavior* 30:282–304.

Verbrugge, L.M., and D.L. Wingard. 1987. Sex differentials in health and mortality. *Women and Health* 12:103–144.

Voelker, R. 1994. A new agenda for women's health. *Journal of American Medical Association* 272:7.

Whatley, M.H. 1994. Male and female hormones: Misinterpretation of biology in school health and sex education. In *Women's health—Readings on social, economic, and political issues,* 2nd ed., eds. N. Worcester and M. Whatley, 97–103. Dubuque, IO: Kendall/Hunt Publishing Company.

Williams, C.D. et al. 1994. *Mother and child health: Delivering the services,* 3rd ed. New York: Oxford University Press.

Williams, P.G. et al. 1992. Coping processes as mediators of the relationship between hardiness and health. *Journal of Behavioral Medicine* 15:237–255.

Wise, P. 1993. Confronting racial disparities in infant mortality: Reconciling science and politics. In Racial differences in preterm delivery: Developing a new research paradigm, eds. D. Rowley and H. Tosteson. *American Journal of Preventive Medicine*, Supplement, 9:7–16, November/December.

Wong, Y.L. 1990. Girl abuse: The Malaysian situation. *Asian-Pacific Journal of Public Health* 4: 258–264.

Woods, N.F. et al. 1993. The new woman: Health-promotion and health-damaging. *Health Care for Women International* 14:389–405.

Worcester, N., and M.H. Whatley, eds. 1994. *Women's health: Readings on social, economic, and political issues,* 2nd ed. Dubuque, IO: Kendall/Hunt Publishing Company.

World Health Organization. 1992. *Women's health: Across age and frontier.* Geneva, Switzerland.

Zimmerman-Tansella, C., and M. Lattanzi. 1991. The Ryle Marital Patterns Test as a predictor of symptoms of anxiety and depression in couples in the community. *Social Psychiatry and Psychiatric Epidemiology* 26:221–229.

CHAPTER 11

Children with Special Health Care Needs

Anita M. Farel

The details of this struggle are personal, but the story itself is not unique. Every family with a handicapped or chronically ill child shares the same problems: lack of money, isolation from the community of the healthy, prejudice, misunderstanding in the schools, loneliness, boredom, depression.

R. Massie and S. Massie, 1975

INTRODUCTION

Issues relating to children with special health care needs and their families are salient in current deliberations about health care policy, long-term care, and program development. Public policy and the orientation of public programs continue to be shaped by increased understanding of the impact of a broad array of chronic conditions among children and of ways to identify and address the needs of these children and their families. This chapter will provide an overview of the evolution of public policy guiding the development of programs to meet the needs of this population, the epidemiology of childhood conditions, and the persistent and emerging issues in service delivery.

EVOLUTION OF PUBLIC POLICY

Legislative History

Maternal and child health (MCH) and Crippled Children's Services (CCS) programs were initiated as part of Title V of the Social Security Act in 1935. Since that time, the federal government has played an active role in financing, organizing, and delivering services for children with special health care needs and their families. Although the legislation fostering the development of state CCS programs incorporated a broad vision of how the needs of children with, or at risk for, chronic health conditions could be addressed, funds for the CCS program were originally designated primarily for children who would benefit most from treatment. The program was oriented toward direct services and depended primarily on the private sector to provide specialty care. Decisions about which chronic health conditions could best be treated were left to state discretion. Because the effects of polio were of paramount concern, most of the CCS programs emphasized treatment for orthopedic conditions such as those that affected child survivors of polio.

Medical advances in the 1940s and 1950s continued to broaden the focus of CCS programs to include newly treatable pediatric conditions, such as rheumatic heart conditions and congenital cardiac anomalies. Through the 1940s, 80 percent of all children served were treated for orthopedic conditions, but this percentage was reduced to less than 50 percent in 1959 by the development of the polio vaccine (Ireys 1980). Other medical and surgical advances continued to modify the context within which the state CCS programs operated and broadened perceptions about the population that should be served and the range of services that should be offered.

During the first three decades of its existence, Title V was the sole source of federal funding for children with special health care needs. The enactment in 1965 of Medicaid (Title XIX of the Social Security Act) provided states with a source of funding for medical care for needy individuals, which absorbed many of the reimbursement and direct service provision functions of CCS programs. State CCS programs were thus relieved of some of the financing concerns that had dominated program planning and were able to redouble their efforts consistent with the original Title V mandate to "extend and improve services" through program planning for children with chronic health conditions. An amendment to Medicaid in 1967, the Early and Periodic Screening, Diagnosis, and Treatment (EPSDT) program, was designed to strengthen Medicaid's preventive care component for children.

Since 1974, the Supplemental Security Income (SSI) childhood disability program (Title XVI of the Social Security Act), administered by the Social Security Administration at the federal level, has provided monthly cash payments to low-income children with disabilities and special health care needs (Jameson and King 1989). In almost all states, SSI eligibility qualifies a child for Medicaid benefits. A child (birth to 21 years of age) is considered disabled if the physical, mental, or chronic medical condition has lasted or is expected to last at least 12 months or to result in death. Whereas the Medicaid program reimburses providers, the SSI monthly cash benefit can be used to help defray family costs incurred in caring for a child with special health needs, such as transportation for specialty care, special equipment, or respite care.

In 1976, funds were provided through the Supplemental Security Income/Disabled Children's Program (SSI/DCP) to ensure that low-income children under the age of seven receiving SSI cash benefits would be referred to the state's Title V agency for service coordination. Each child's need for services was assessed and an individual service plan (ISP) was prepared to guide the coordination of services. Thus, children enrolled in the SSI program were ensured both a linkage to Medicaid and to services offered under the state's CCS program. Funding for the SSI/DCP program included only children up to the age of seven; however, when the SSI/DCP was folded into the MCH Services Block Grant in 1981, rehabilitative services were extended to all children under age 16.

Although Title V programs continued to develop community-based services for children with chronic conditions, services for children with mental retardation emphasized institutional care. In the 1950s, under the leadership of the Children's Bureau, states started child development clinics to provide health and related care by multidisciplinary teams for children with mental retardation. Subsequent appropriations to build University Affiliated Facilities (UAFs)—within which exemplary services, research, and professional training in the treatment and prevention of mental retardation would occur—were based on evidence that a multidisciplinary team approach was the most effective way to serve this population of children and their families. To reduce the incidence of mental retardation, a new five-year program of Maternal and Infant Care (M&I) special projects grants was implemented in the 1960s by the Children's Bureau to provide prenatal care for low income, pregnant women. In the 1970s, developmental disabilities (DD) legislation (PL 91-517, 1970; PL 94-103, 1975) generated a multifaceted mandate to organize services for individuals with developmental disabilities attributable to mental retardation, cerebral palsy, and epilepsy and established state DD Councils. By 1978, developmental disabilities were defined functionally and included all conditions attributable to a mental or physical impairment manifested before age 22 that resulted in substantial functional limitations in three or more areas of major life activity (PL 95-602, 1978). Under DD legislation, state DD Councils, which include individuals with disabilities, parents of children with disabilities, and representatives from diverse state agencies including Title V, education, and social services, develop a comprehensive state plan identifying services needed by the population with disabilities.

In 1975, a Congressional finding that "more than half of the children with disabilities in the United States do not receive appropriate educational services" (20 U.S.C. § 1400(b)(3)) quickened the enactment of the Education for All Handicapped Children Act (PL 94-142, 1975). Renamed the Individuals with Disabilities Education Act (IDEA) in 1990, the law guarantees a free, appropriate education for all school-age children with disabilities. Multidisciplinary assessments must be conducted for all children who may need special services. An individualized education plan (IEP) that identifies services needed to address issues raised in the assessment must be developed by a multidisciplinary group, including teachers, counselors, and allied health professionals. Parents or guardians are invited to be a part of this process. As a result of this legislation, new collaborative relationships among teachers and health care professionals were forged, and schools began to assume certain responsibilities previously relegated to the health services sector, such as administering medications and treatment regimens. While this legislation is far-reaching in scope, several unresolved areas in its application have been identified (U.S. General Accounting Office 1981a; U.S. General Accounting Office 1981b).

The *related services* provisions of PL 94-142 refer to services that are necessary for a child to benefit from special education. Related services may include, for example, transportation, counseling services, and assistive technology, and must be included in a student's IEP. All decisions about related services must be made on an individualized basis depending upon a particular child's needs. Although schools are not required to provide health services that are usually conducted during nonschool hours or treatment that must be conducted by a physician or in a hospital setting, the cost of providing these services may strain the ability of local school systems (Mesibov 1994). One of the criteria for determining if a child with a chronic health condition would gain from special services is whether the condition is considered, under the law, to be an "other health impairment" such as asthma, sickle cell anemia, epilepsy, diabetes, and lead poisoning that adversely affects a child's educational performance. However, limited guidance to schools and inconsistent criteria for determining the child's functional status undermine consistent implementation of special education services. Children with chronic illnesses who are enrolled in school systems with inadequate health and pupil personnel services may be at the greatest risk for not having their conditions monitored effectively (Walker and Jacobs 1984).

Since the passage of special education legislation in 1975, states had been encouraged to plan for extending services to birth. In 1986, reauthorization of the special education legislation under PL 99-457 required states to serve children between 3 and 5 years of age and encouraged states to apply for funds to plan early intervention programs. Evidence that potential developmental problems could be prevented or ameliorated by early intervention stimulated interest in extending the special education entitlement to birth. Early intervention services focus on reducing the impact of or eliminating developmental delay and helping identified children and their families make the transition to preschool and kindergarten programs. By 1995, all states provided an entitlement to early intervention services for children, birth through 2 years of age (Trohanis 1995).

In recognition of the increasingly broader childhood population with special needs, the program title, Crippled Children's Services, was changed to Children with Special Health Care Needs (CSHCN) programs in 1985. However, continued medical advances, escalating professional specialization, program expansion, and services that were increasingly fragmented threatened to undermine the ability of state programs to offer comprehensive and continuous services. In response, Surgeon General Koop (U.S. DHHS 1987) convened a national conference in 1987 to develop a *national agenda* for children with special health care needs that by 1989 had redirected the mission of the CSHCN program.

The Omnibus Budget Reconciliation Act of 1989 (OBRA89) reinforced the leadership role of state CSHCN programs in (1) the development of community-based systems of services for all children with special health care needs, regardless of socioeconomic status, and (2) the implementation of the program's mission to promote and provide family-centered, community-based, coordinated, comprehensive, and culturally competent services. Explicitly acknowledging the diverse conditions composing the population of children with special health care needs, 30 percent of the MCH Services Block Grant was to be directed toward children with disabilities, chronic illnesses and conditions, and health-related educational and behavioral problems.

Additional features of OBRA89, with implications for children with special health care needs, included the requirement that any medically necessary service required to treat a condition identified through an EPSDT screen, even if the service were an optional one that the state had not otherwise chosen to cover in its Medicaid program, must be provided (42 U.S.C. § 1396d (r) (5)).

Although the SSI program experienced periods of heightened attention and languished at other times, it was greatly expanded in the wake of OBRA89 and the 1990 Supreme Court decision, *Sullivan v. Zebley* (1990). As a result of the Zebley decision, the *functional status* of children from low-income families, who had previously not been eligible for SSI because they were evaluated against stricter disability criteria than low income adults, was included in the disability assessment. Although the child's impairment must be comparable in severity to one that would prevent an adult from working, comparability under the new law was interpreted to mean that an impairment substantially reduces the child's ability to function independently and effectively in an age-appropriate manner (Perrin and Stein 1991). As a result of the outreach to potentially eligible children and their families mandated by OBRA89, the increased number of childhood impairment listings (from 4 to 11 general categories) and the rising rate of childhood poverty in the 1990s, there was a threefold increase in the number of children enrolled in SSI increased from 296,000 in 1989 to 893,000 children in 1994 (National Commission on Childhood Disability 1995). In 1989, approximately 51 percent of the children enrolled in SSI had physical impairments; by 1994, children with physical impairments composed approximately 39 percent of children enrolled, whereas children with mental impairments, including mental retardation, accounted for over 61 percent of enrollment.

In 1996, alarmed by the rapidly increasing SSI enrollment, Congress passed a new federal welfare law (PL 104-193), which dramatically redesigned the SSI program by cutting the cash assistance program for children with disabilities and restricting eligibility. This legislation established a more narrow definition of childhood disability based on more restrictive medical listings. In order to qualify for benefits, a child must have a "medically determinable physical or mental impairment which results in marked and severe functional limitations" of substantial duration. The Individualized Functional Assessment (IFA) was eliminated, and maladaptive behavior was deleted from the mental impairment listings.

EPIDEMIOLOGY OF SPECIAL HEALTH CARE NEEDS AMONG U.S. CHILDREN

Estimates of the number of children with special health care needs have been based on random samples of the population, medical records, demonstration projects, records of social and/or educational services, and reports of clinic enrollment. These disparate sources of data have led, not surprisingly, to widely varying estimates of the prevalence of chronic conditions among children. For example, a review of published studies showed estimates of the proportion of children with at least one chronic condition ranging from less than 5 percent to more than 30 percent (Newacheck and Taylor 1992).

National Health Interview Survey-Child Health Supplement

One of the most reputable sources of information about chronic health conditions among children is the Child Health Supplement of the National Health Interview Survey (NHIS-CHS 1988). The size of the population and the impact of chronic conditions have been estimated by analyzing data from household interviews with 17,110 respondents. The large sample size for this population-based survey lends credence to the supposition that conclusions drawn from these data will have substantial validity. Based on this survey, a study of the prevalence and impact of nine developmental disabilities concluded that 17 percent of children under 18 years of age had developmental disabilities (Boyle et al. 1994). Children with six conditions—cerebral palsy (prevalence = 0.2 percent), epilepsy or seizures (0.09 percent), blindness (0.08 percent), deafness or trouble hearing (0.18 percent), stammering or stuttering (0.13 percent), and other speech defects (0.17 percent)—considered to be developmental disabilities had substantially more doctor visits, hospital days, school-days lost, and repeated grades in school than children without these conditions.

Increasing the number of categories of chronic conditions examined to 19, Newacheck and Taylor (1992) estimated that 31 percent of children under 18 had one or more chronic conditions based on the NHIS-CHS. The authors suggest that even these estimates may understate the true size of the population with single and multiple conditions since the checklist did not include all childhood conditions, particularly those related to mental health. The most prevalent conditions included respiratory allergies (9.7 percent), asthma (4.2 percent), eczema and skin allergies (3.3 percent), frequent or severe headaches (2.5 percent), and speech defects (2.6 percent). Diabetes (0.1 percent), sickle cell disease (0.1 percent), and cerebral palsy (0.2 percent) were among the less prevalent conditions. The impact of chronic conditions varied. For example, 20 percent of the children with chronic illnesses were mildly affected, 9 percent of children experienced more than occasional bother or limitation of activity, but not both, and 2 percent were severely affected.

Chronic conditions do not impose the same burdens on the child and family. Some conditions may require frequent hospitalizations, or be disruptive for a family, whereas others may be managed more easily. The effect of different conditions on developmental progress would thus also be expected to vary. These considerations have stimulated efforts to classify children with chronic health conditions according to such variables as impact on the family, use of medical services, or the child's functional status. In other words, although they may suffer from distinct illnesses and disabilities, the daily experiences of children with special health care needs and their families may be very similar. For example, diabetes and sickle-cell anemia have very different etiologies and treatment protocols. But children affected by these conditions have in common school absences and the need for careful monitoring (Fowler et al. 1985). Conditions also have different ramifications depending on the age and stage of development of the child. Bronchopulmonary dysplasia usually requires fewer hospital visits as a child gets older, but the developmental delay associated with the condition may necessitate special education services when the child enters school (Farel et al. 1995). Federal laws, such as Title V, IDEA, and SSI, have also shifted the traditional orientation of identifying children with special needs from disease-specific listings to a focus on an individual child's needs for special services.

National Health Interview Survey on Disability

Recently Stein et al. (1993) developed a conceptual framework that cuts across diagnostic categories and provides a means for generating population-based estimates of the impact of chronic health conditions, including mental health, health, functional status, and family functioning, on children and their families. In lieu of specific diagnoses, the framework uses consequences of "chronic ongoing conditions" to identify children along such parameters as disability or functional limitation, dependency (e.g., medications, special diets, medical technology, assistive devices, personal assistance), and needs for services. Items based on this framework have been incorporated into the new National Health Interview Survey on Disability (NHIS-D 1994). The NHIS-D includes information for more than 60,000 children, enlarging substantially the 17,000 children surveyed in the NIHS-CHS supplement in 1988. Deliberately avoiding a unique definition of disability, the survey identifies children with disabilities or special needs through questions in the following areas: limitation of activity (from the NHIS core), impairments (for example, vision, hearing, mobility), activities of daily living (children > 5 years of age), a condition list, special health care needs, special education services, and early child development (Simpson, 1993). Preliminary analyses from this survey suggest that 16–18 percent of U.S. children under age 18 have chronic physical, developmental, behavioral, or emotional conditions that have some degree of functional impact or that require special services.

Projections of Incidence and Prevalence

The number of children with special health care needs is growing (Perrin et al. 1993). Increasing populations of children with special health care needs include those with HIV infection and children who are dependent upon advanced medical technology such as ventilators, gastrostomies, and tracheostomies (Palfrey et al. 1991). Improvements in the ability to diagnose some conditions (e.g., asthma, hearing impairments) and longer survival due to medical advances (e.g., cystic fibrosis) are credited in the increasing prevalence of certain diseases. Changes in prevalence rates for some chronic conditions and disabilities also speak to the success of programs with legislatively mandated outreach and child-find components.

The means for preventing some conditions are known. For example, the large percentage decline in spina bifida has been attributed to daily consumption of folic acid (Centers for Disease Control and Prevention 1992). Estimated to affect 1 in 1,000 births, fetal alcohol syndrome, which has been associated with mental retardation, birth defects, central nervous system impairment, and other cognitive and behavioral abnormalities, is preventable if alcohol is not consumed during pregnancy (Floyd et al. 1994). However, the means for primary prevention of most chronic conditions are unknown.

Racial and Socioeconomic Differences

Many of the same problems that undermine the ability to estimate the prevalence of chronic conditions among all children particularly hinder documentation of the prevalence of chronic health conditions among minority children. Health care practices and attitudes toward illness and disability vary among different cultures. However, the commitment to implementing culturally competent service systems requires understanding cultural variations in the use of health care and the impact and prevalence of chronic health and disabling conditions among minority populations. For example, Black and Hispanic parents are less likely than White parents to report that their children have developmental delays, learning disabilities, or emotional problems. Consequently, some disabilities, particularly learning disabilities, may not be accurately identified until a child reaches school age (Zill and Schoenborn 1990).

Using the 1988 NHIS-CHS, the prevalence of childhood chronic illness and the impact of chronic conditions on activity levels and utilization of health services were examined according to whether children were members of three different racial and ethnic groups: White non-Hispanic, Black non-Hispanic, or Hispanic (Newacheck et al. 1993). Families of White children were much more likely to report chronic conditions for their children than were families of Hispanic children or families of Black children. This difference was due in part to the likelihood that White families report and receive treatment for mild chronic conditions more frequently than do families of African American or Hispanic children. Children in White families were more likely to make use of ambulatory physician services than African American or Hispanic children, who were more likely to request care in hospital emergency rooms. Treatment of moderate and severe conditions was similar among groups.

Health insurance status varied among the three racial groups. Hispanic children with chronic illness were at greater risk for being uninsured than Black or White children, and less likely than Black children with chronic conditions to have health care services covered by Medicaid. Black and Hispanic children with chronic illnesses were far more likely to have their health care covered by Medicaid than White children with chronic illnesses (McManus and Newacheck 1993).

Children from minority populations and their families have traditionally been underserved because of poverty, ignorance of the health care system, and/or inability to communicate (Hutchins and Walch 1989). Minority children with chronic illnesses are at even greater risk for being underserved by the current health care delivery system (McManus and Newacheck 1993). Although ethnic minorities compose a growing proportion of the U.S. population, information about the prevalence and impact of chronic health conditions and disabilities among ethnic minority groups is limited (Patterson and Blum 1993). Recommendations for improving this situation include strengthening relationships between health care services and communities, using community outreach workers more systematically, and analyzing data from the NHIS-D which, with a sample of more than 60,000 children, will make it possible to improve understanding of African American, Asian, and Hispanic children with chronic conditions.

The burden of illness falls disproportionately on those who lack resources to marshal and pay for health care services (Egbuonu and Starfield 1982; Starfield 1982; Wise and Meyers 1988). Using national health examination and household interview data, a recent analysis of differences between poor and nonpoor children described the particular problems that arise from the intersection of poverty and chronic illness in children. An analysis of national survey data that collected health examination (National Health Examination Survey 1966–1970; National Health and Nutrition Examination Survey I 1971–1974; National Health and Nutrition Examination Survey II 1976–1980) and household interview data (NHIS Child Health Supplement, 1988) concluded that low-income children not only have a greater proportion of specific health problems such as higher levels of vision and hearing problems, oral health problems, non-acne skin lesions, and elevated blood lead levels than higher income children, but they are also affected more severely (Newacheck et al. 1994). Children from low-income families (<$10,000 annually) were more than twice as likely to be limited in school or play activities and six times more likely to be reported in only fair or poor health compared to children with chronic conditions from families with higher incomes of (>$35,000 annually) (Newacheck 1994).

SPECIFIC CONDITIONS AND CONCERNS

Abuse and Neglect among Children with Special Health Care Needs

Children with chronic conditions and disabilities are disproportionately maltreated compared to the general child population (Garbarino 1987; Crosse et al. 1994). A recent report of children for whom maltreatment was substantiated estimated the incidence to be 36 per 1,000 children with disabilities—a rate 1.7 times greater than that for the nondisabled childhood population (Crosse et al. 1994).

Retrospective studies have been unsuccessful in disentangling the extent to which maltreatment is a cause or a result of disability. In some instances, abuse and neglect may cause disabilities; in other situations, a chronic health condition may be a risk factor for maltreatment. Child Protective Service workers reported that a chronic condition precipitated maltreatment for 67 percent of maltreated children with serious emotional disturbance, 76 percent of those with a physical health problem, and 59 percent of those with hyperactivity (Crosse et al. 1994).

Identification of maltreatment among children with special needs is problematic for several reasons. For example, lower expectations of a child's developmental achievement and communication skills may prevent identification of maltreatment (Ammerman and Van Hasselt 1989). It is difficult to place children with special needs, particularly those with complex medical needs, in foster homes (Jaudes and Diamond 1985). Families with children with disabilities report social isolation (Embry 1980) and lack of access to appropriate community resources such as child care enjoyed by families of children who are not disabled (Crosse et al. 1994).

Prevention of Secondary Conditions

Chronic health conditions may generate secondary conditions that continue to reduce the child's health status. Arguing that disability is not solely a medical issue, the Institute of Medicine prepared an agenda for preventing primary chronic health conditions from contributing to further deterioration in health status, functional capacity, and quality of life, or in other words, becoming secondary conditions (Pope and Tarlov 1991). The strategies for reducing the incidence and severity of preventable secondary conditions include developing a national disability surveillance system, eliminating the barriers to access to care (including the standard of "medical necessity" applied by most insurance agencies), research that emphasizes longitudinal studies, and the education of health professionals. Although health promotion and disease prevention are national health priorities, only 3 percent of all health expenditures are directed to prevention (Thacker et al. 1994).

In 1988, the Centers for Disease Control and Prevention initiated a Disabilities Prevention program in the Center for Environmental Health and Injury Control to provide a national focus for the prevention of primary and secondary disabilities, to build capacity at the state and community levels to maintain programs to prevent disabilities, and to increase the knowledge base necessary for developing and evaluating effective preventive interventions (Houk and Thacker 1989). The mechanics of this program include grants to support the development of state-level disabilities prevention offices, and recent funding has emphasized prevention of secondary conditions.

Mental Health

Chronic illness affects the mental health of many children and their families (Drotar and Bush 1985; Silverman and Koretz 1989). Children with chronic health conditions have twice the risk for maladjustment as children without chronic conditions (Pless and Nolan 1991). In fact, medical advances have developed far faster than understanding of their emotional impact. While the association between chronic illness and poor mental health has been documented, identification of high-risk characteristics, evaluations of intervention strategies, and assessment of needs for mental health services has not advanced (Pless and Nolan 1991). In a study of children with diverse chronic conditions (cystic fibrosis, cerebral palsy, multiple handicap, and spina bifida), Breslau (1985) concluded that cerebral involvement (specifically, mental retardation) was a significant predictor of emotional problems. A study by Pless (1984) provided some evidence that children with sensory impairment are at increased risk for emotional problems. However, there is little evidence that specific health conditions are precursors to mental health problems. Examining adaptation to chronic illness or evidence of resiliency may be a more productive route to understanding adjustment to chronic illness than indicators of psychopathology (Rutter 1987). The specific influences of the health care, school, and community environments on the mental health and psychosocial adjustment of children with chronic health conditions and their families must be illuminated.

Adolescents with Special Needs

Over 85 percent of children with chronic conditions will survive into early adulthood; approximately 31.5 percent of adolescents in the United States have one or more chronic health conditions (Blum et al. 1993; Okinow 1994). Achievements in medical technology and public attitudes that have improved survival and community responsiveness to many children with chronic conditions have not been translated into comprehensive services for adolescents with special needs. Chronic health conditions or disabilities that continue through adolescence compound the complex adolescent tasks of achieving independence, developing strong peer relationships, and becoming oriented toward work and career interests.

The risks for poor outcomes are high among adolescents with special health care needs. Teenagers with special needs miss more school (Blum et al. 1993) and have a higher high school dropout rate (Okinow 1994). Fewer attend postsecondary education schools or programs than their healthy peers (Fairweather and Shaver 1991). In fact, adolescents with disabilities participate in postsecondary education at one-quarter the rate of their healthy peers. Adolescents with special needs also face adversity in the work force. They have more economic instability (Okinow, 1994), higher levels of unemployment (Wehman et al. 1988), and earn lower wages than their nondisabled peers. Youth with special needs also have more psychosocial problems and tend to be more socially isolated (Newacheck et al. 1991; Farrison and McQuiston 1989). Adolescents with chronic illnesses report greater body dissatisfaction and engage in more high-risk weight-loss practices than adolescents without chronic illnesses (Neumark-Sztainer et al. 1995). Utilization of health care services and financial barriers are also different for adolescents with special health care needs. They use more medical services and appear to lack primary care to a greater degree than younger children with special needs (Newacheck et al. 1991; Blum et al. 1993). One out of seven youths is uninsured (Newacheck 1989).

Although transition from childhood to adulthood is a process that occurs for all teenagers, comprehensive transition services that incorporate health, education, vocation, and social domains are critical for adolescents with special needs. A recent survey of public agencies regarding services for adolescents with special needs revealed that most programs focus on specialty services that are central to their particular mission and are relatively uninformed about the extent to which their services duplicate or address gaps in what is offered to this population. Across six public programs serving the adolescent population, 85 percent of the directors reported that the infant-toddler population receives the greatest programming emphasis. Only one-fifth of the agencies surveyed had conducted a needs assessment for youth with special needs (National Center for Youth with Disabilities 1993). Interagency planning to bridge the gap between services for children and services for adults is essential for delivering comprehensive services to adolescents and reaping the benefits of programs that were designed to improve the ability of youth with disabilities to lead productive, independent lives.

Home Care for Children Dependent on Technology

Medical technology is necessary to maintain health and improve life for many children. According to the Office of Technology Assessment (U.S. Congress 1987), children who are technology dependent need both a medical device "that compensates for the loss of normal use of a vital body function, and daily skilled nursing care to avert death or further disability" (p. 13). This population includes children who use ventilators, require prolonged intravenous administration of nutritional substances or drugs, use devices for respiratory or nutritional support such as tracheostomies or tube feedings, and children with prolonged dependence on other medical devices, such as apnea monitors or urinary catheters. Medical technology for this population is now more available, advanced, portable, and cost-contained (Adam 1989). The population of children who are dependent upon medical technology is expected to grow.

The benefits of home care include improvements in quality of life, health status, nutrition, growth, and psychosocial development (Fields et al. 1991). Decreased rehospitalization rates, length of hospitalizations, inappropriate use of the emergency room, increased use of primary care providers, and prevention of complications of the primary diagnosis are all associated with home care (Bock et al. 1983; Goldberg et al. 1984).

Despite ample documentation of the benefits of home care for a growing population, a number of issues require attention (Leonard et al. 1989). Although the improvements in anticipated lifespan and quality of life for children with chronic health conditions are due in large part to advances in medical care and technology, reliance on the highly specialized, fragmented service system that has evolved for children dependent on technology presents a serious barrier to comprehensive community-based services. The delicate balance between a family's available resources and the complex demands of the child's illness must be assessed accurately to implement effective discharge planning and follow-up services.

CURRENT AND EMERGING ISSUES

Civil Rights for Children with Special Health Care Needs

Several legislative initiatives address specifically the civil rights of individuals with disabilities and have implications for protecting the interests of children and young adults with special needs. Section 504 of the Rehabilitation Act of 1973

(PL 94-271) is neither an education law nor a federal grant program. Paralleling the language in the Civil Rights Act of 1964, Section 504 established rights and entitlements for persons with disabilities. For example, under this law, acts of discrimination and failure to provide an appropriate public education to eligible students are perceived as violations of basic civil rights and can be addressed through this legislation. Section 504 has the potential to cover a broader spectrum of students and scope of activities than IDEA. The definition of who qualifies as an "individual with a disability" is more inclusive than IDEA, and many children who are not considered eligible for special education or related services under IDEA are covered under Section 504. Students who fit the Section 504 definition are those with a disability (physical or mental) that substantially limits one or more major life activities. Students who "have a history of" or are "regarded as" having a disability are included. For example, students with attention deficit hyperactivity disorder (ADHD), or students with physical disabilities or sensory impairments who may only need accommodations for physical access or alternative methods of communication, qualify for services through Section 504 even if they do not meet the criteria specified under special education legislation.

In amendments to DD legislation in 1975, Congress established Protection and Advocacy systems in every state to pursue legal, administrative, and other appropriate remedies to protect the rights of persons with disabilities. Over the course of the implementation of special education legislation, some families have used state Protection and Advocacy programs to assist with developing an IEP for their children.

The *Americans with Disabilities Act of 1990* (ADA) was designed to protect people with mental or physical disabilities from discrimination based on disability. The ADA requires public accommodations, including child care centers, to make reasonable modifications in policies, practices, and procedures to accommodate individuals with special needs. Necessary changes for child care centers may include curriculum adaptations, removal of physical barriers, additional staff training, alteration of staffing patterns, and adaptive equipment.

Systems Development

Children with chronic conditions and their families need a range of services that is currently provided by an array of programs. Although separate but overlapping policy and legislative initiatives have identified populations in need of services and have authorized funding for infrastructure development at the community and state levels, gaps and duplications in services persist. Whereas Title V programs were initially the primary provider and coordinator of services for CSHCN, these programs are now one player, albeit one with a leadership mandate, among many programs, agencies, organizations, and professionals involved with these children and their families. Appreciation of the fact that children with chronic health or disabling conditions have needs beyond medical treatment stimulated program expansion in several sectors. Recognition that service delivery is more effective and efficient when directed toward the needs of children and their families rather than being based on condition lists has led to the identification of *systems development* as a long-term solution. The development of service delivery systems (Objective 17.20) is one of the Year 2000 Health Objectives (U.S. DHHS 1991) and the primary objective for children with special health care needs. Requirements for program accountability under OBRA89 all emphasize the development of responsive, community-based service systems. Before a comprehensive system of service delivery can be developed, the target population must be defined. Currently, there are 50 definitions of disability among 11 federal laws and programs addressing the needs of this population (Domzal 1995).

In response to the concern of state Title V programs that the concept of systems development has not been articulated consistently or specifically enough to provide direction, the Maternal and Child Health Bureau (MCHB) developed a definition of children with special health care needs. Definitions based solely on conditions or diagnostic lists were rejected as being too unwieldy. Definitions based on functional status alone were eliminated in that they would not include children whose disabilities have been alleviated by treatment or the continued use of special services. The following definition, drafted by the MCHB (U.S. DHHS 1995), is being discussed by state programs:

> Children with special health care needs are those who have or are at increased risk for chronic physical, developmental, behavioral, or emotional conditions and who also require health and related services of a type or amount beyond that required by children generally.

While very broad, a definition such as this is consonant with the population described in diverse federal laws and promises to provide useful guidance for strategic planning.

MCHB is also developing indicators to measure and collect information about systems development activity in the states. What the state is doing to develop systems at the state level and to support community-level systems development can be described in terms of types of collaborative activity among health, education, social service, other public agencies, and the private sector. Specific activities include formulating policies and priorities, managing and administering ongoing programs, developing standards for services, and determining if collaboration involves assessing needs and resources. Indicators to address integration across categorical service programs of primary, secondary, and tertiary care, and across all community service delivery programs, are also being developed. Community systems indicators address (1) early identification and referral systems; (2) primary and specialized health service networks; (3) family satisfaction and quality of care; (4) coordination of primary, specialized, and related services; and (5) family participation. Systems development indicators will make it possible for states and communities to document strengths in relationships among programs, target areas of particular concern, and develop outcome measures.

Family-Centered Care

Increasing attention to the needs, customs, and rights of families of children with chronic illnesses has shifted traditional intervention strategies and roles for families to a new philosophy of care. Once considered solely as recipients of services, parents are viewed as partners in a collaborative relationship with professionals. This approach affirms the central role of families for a child's care and enables families to serve as the primary decision makers for their children. Balancing professional perceptions with a family's sense of what is important for their child involves promoting and nurturing more collaborative roles among providers and parents (Shelton et al. 1987).

Operationalization of family-centered care has roots in parent-to-parent support and information groups at the local level and legislative and judicial processes at the state and national levels. The importance of common experience among parents of children with special needs has been described as the wellspring for the movement to improve the accessibility, accountability, and responsiveness of family-centered services (Pizzo 1983; Pizzo 1987).

Family-centered care figures prominently in early intervention legislation and recent amendments to Title V. In OBRA89, programs supported by Title V funds were required to provide and promote family-centered, community-based, coordinated care. Special education legislation, under IDEA, requires that each infant or toddler receive a multidisciplinary assessment and that services appropriate to meet the child's unique needs are documented in a written, individualized family service plan (IFSP), which includes parents in its development.

Through parents' organizations, litigation, and their own lobbying, families have become effective advocates for better services for their children. Parents of children with disabilities sued successfully for the same rights to public education as children without chronic conditions (Pennsylvania Association for Retarded Children v. Pennsylvania, 334 F. Supp. 1257 E. D. Pa. 1971). A class action brought by families whose children were being denied disability benefits changed substantially the way in which children's disabilities were assessed (Sullivan v. Zebley, 1990). One family's identification of obstacles to caring for a medically fragile child at home generated amendments to the Medicaid statute (Beckett 1989). Using the same skills and techniques that led to successful campaigns for education rights (e.g., IDEA) and civil rights (Americans with Disabilities Act,

1990), many families are involved in improving access to health services for their children. In 1993, representatives from Family Voices, a national grassroots organization started by families of children with special needs, participated in a White House briefing with senior health policy analysts to discuss the implications of health care reform.

Families have become an integral part of training programs for pediatric professionals (DiVenere 1993). Parents also serve as advisors for state Title V program development by reviewing policies and administrative practices that ultimately shape service delivery for children with special needs. A survey conducted in 1992 revealed that parents in 50 states were members of advisory committees or task forces, and families in 46 states were involved in their state's MCH Block Grant application process (Wells et al. 1993).

One of greatest challenges to implementing family-centered care is recognizing and responding to cultural diversity among families. There is considerable cultural variation in the conceptualization of chronic illness. As a result, the choice of services and the means for their implementation may vary with a family's cultural background (Carrese and Rhodes 1995; Gostin 1995; Groce and Zola 1993). The organization of service delivery systems must reflect sensitivity to cultural diversity in program planning, implementation, and monitoring (Groce 1990). For example, New Mexico, a state with a high proportion of Native American families, was unable to comply with the two-day federal requirement for referrals to early intervention programs for children whose assessment revealed the probability of a developmental delay. The state was threatened with a withdrawal of funding for its Part H Infant and Toddler program. The governor responded that the two-day limit was neither reasonable nor realistic for many Native American families who needed more time to discuss referrals with their extended tribal families before giving consent (Policy Clarification 1991).

Financing of Care

Health care expenditures for children with disabilities are three times higher than those for nondisabled children; 80 percent of this difference is attributed to greater use of hospital care, physician services, and prescribed medicines (Newacheck 1994). The number of children with disabilities requiring repeated hospitalization is relatively small, but, as a group, accounts for one-third of the days all children spend in hospitals, and their stays in the hospital are on average twice as long. Further, they visit physicians twice as often as children without disabilities and pay higher charges (Newacheck and McManus 1994). The cost for care is high and recurring.

In addition to specialized medical services, children with chronic disabilities and their families have continuing needs for medications, special education, and specialized appliances as well as for allied health services such as occupational therapy, physical therapy, and speech therapy. Many families experience severe financial stress trying to meet their children's needs because coverage from health insurance and Medicaid is insufficient.

Advances in understanding the appropriate composition of health care services for children with special health needs have generated new programs and sources of financing. Although access to services has increased substantially in the past decade, these gains may be jeopardized by current legislative initiatives to include this population in Medicaid managed care plans. While for many children, managed care means that they will be enrolled in plans that improve the quality and continuity of their health care, health care in organized delivery systems—particularly ones where providers are prepaid—may be inadequate for children with chronic health conditions and disabilities. Within a managed care setting, children with special needs may be undertreated because providers lack financial incentives to provide continuing treatment or referral to specialists and because families lack the resources to overcome administrative obstacles.

A recent report argued that the narrow subspecialist model for providing services to children with special health care needs should be expanded in order to ensure access to primary care services, developmentally appropriate assistive technology, and community-based family support programs. Several strategies for ensuring quality of care include enrolling children with special health care needs under an appropriate benefits package, standards of care that extend beyond the traditional medical model, and indicators for family-centered care. More research is needed to identify how managed care plans address financial risk, prevent morbidity, and enhance the quality of life (Harris-Wehling et al. 1995).

Managed care plans are a way for states to improve access to insurance for more low-income individuals while curtailing spending for health care. These rapidly occurring changes in the health care system have significant implications for maintaining the quality and comprehensiveness of care for children with special health care needs. The process of transition to a managed care environment for this population of children requires careful attention. Standards for care and access to pediatric specialty care providers, traditionally hallmarks of Title V programs, may be sacrificed to cost containment (Fox et al. 1993). Emphasis on cost containment may preclude referrals to ancillary and wrap-around services needed by this population. Title V programs for children with special health care needs have an important leadership role in monitoring the cost of participating in managed care plans for families of children with special health care needs. Fox et al. (1994) urge Title V CSHCN and Medicaid programs to collaborate in addressing issues related to enrollment of children with special needs and their families, provider networks, clarity of contracts with managed care plans to ensure commitments, definitions of medical necessity, adequacy of capitation rates, and costs to families.

Among primary concerns about the impact of managed care plans for children with special health care needs, the American Academy of Pediatrics' Committee on Child Health Financing (1995) noted the limited quality-of-care measures for children. Characteristics of managed care plans such as disruptions in provider-patient relationships, barriers to appropriate pediatric referrals, and delays in treatment authorization undermine current concepts of appropriate continuing care for this population. Other concerns consistently expressed include the extent to which managed care plans protect the central role of the family in planning and implementing services for their children. The expanding role of managed care plans as a financing mechanism for children with special health care needs requires diligent monitoring, the active involvement of families, and strong program leadership.

CONCLUSION

A growing number of children have special health care needs. Improved understanding of this diverse population of children and their families has generated clearer expectations about the characteristics of appropriate services and inspired commitments to the health and welfare of these children. Such expectations have reinforced the urgency of better linkages among health, mental health, education and social services, partnerships between the private and public sectors, and support for the development of community-based services. Affirmation of the importance of comprehensive and continuous care at each developmental stage in the life span requires that current deliberations and decisions about the financing of care for this population are monitored and that leadership roles at state and community levels are reinforced.

REFERENCES

Adam, H.M. 1989. Pediatric home care: An institutionally-based outreach program. In *Caring for children with chronic illness: Issues and strategies,* ed. R.E.K. Stein, 161–172. New York: Springer Publishing Company.

American Academy of Pediatrics, Committee on Child Health Financing. 1995. Guiding principles for managed care arrangements for the health care of infants, children, adolescents, and young adults. *Pediatrics* 95:613–615.

Americans with Disabilities Act, U.S. Code Vol. 104, sec. 12101 (1990).

Ammerman, R.T., and V.B. Van Hasselt. 1989. Abuse and neglect in psychiatrically hospitalized multihandicapped children. *Child Abuse and Neglect* 13:335–343.

Beckett, J.E. 1989. With a parent's eye. In *Caring for children with chronic illness: Issues and strategies*, ed. R.E.K. Stein, 110–119. New York: Springer Publishing Company.

Blum, R.W. et al. 1993. Transition from child-centered to adult health-care systems for adolescents with chronic conditions. *Journal of Adolescent Health*, 14:570–576.

Bock, R.H. et al. 1983. There's no place like home. *Children's Health Care* 12:93–96.

Boyle, C.A. et al. 1994. Prevalence and health impact of developmental disabilities in US children. *Pediatrics* 93:399–403.

Breslau, N. 1985. Psychiatric disorder in children with physical disabilities. *Journal of American Academy of Child Psychiatry* 24:87–94.

Carrese, J.A., and L.A. Rhodes. 1995. Western bioethics on the Navajo reservation: Benefit or harm? *Journal of the American Medical Association* 274:826–829.

Centers for Disease Control and Prevention. 1992. Recommendations for the use of folic acid to reduce the number of cases of spina bifida and other neural tube defects. *Morbidity and Mortality Weekly Report* 41:1–7.

Crosse, S.B. et al. 1994. *A report on the maltreatment of children with disabilities*. Washington, DC: National Center on Child Abuse and Neglect.

DiVenere, N.J. 1993. Parents as educators of medical students. In *Families, physicians and children with special health needs: Collaborative medical education models*, eds. R. Darling and M. Peter, 101–108. Westport, CT: Greenwood Publishing Company.

Domzal, C. 1995. *Federal statutory definitions of disability*. Falls Church, VA: Conwal Incorporated.

Drotar, D., and M. Bush. 1985. Mental health issues and services. In *Issues in the care of children with chronic illness, issues and strategies*, eds. N. Hobbs and J. Perrin, 514–550. San Francisco: Jossey-Bass.

Education for All Handicapped Children Act. Public Law 94-142 (1975).

Egbuonu, L., and B. Starfield. 1982. Child health and social status. *Pediatrics* 69:550–557.

Embry, L. 1980. Family support for handicapped preschool children at risk for abuse. In *New Directions for Exceptional Children*, Vol. 4, ed. J. Gallagher, 12. San Francisco: Jossey-Bass.

Fairweather, J.S., and D.M. Shaver. 1991. Making the transition to postsecondary education and training. *Exceptional Children* 3:264–269, December/January.

Farel, A.M. et al. 1995. Very-low birthweight infants at seven years: An assessment of the health and neurodevelopmental risk conveyed by chronic lung disease. *Journal of Learning Disabilities*, in press.

Farrison, W.T., and S. McQuiston. 1989. *Chronic illness during childhood and adolescence: Psychological aspects*. Newbury Park, CA: Sage Publications, Inc.

Fields, A.I. et al. 1991. Outcome of home-care for technology-dependent children: Success of an independent, community-based case management model. *Pediatric Pulmonology* 11:310–317.

Floyd, R.L. et al. 1994. Fetal alcohol syndrome. In *From data to action*, eds. J.S. Marks and L.S. Wilcox, 343–350. Atlanta, GA: Centers for Disease Control and Prevention.

Fowler, M.G. et al. 1985. School achievement and absence in children with chronic health conditions. *Journal of Pediatrics* 106:683–687.

Fox, H.B. et al. 1993. Health maintenance organizations and children with special health needs: A suitable match? *American Journal of Diseases of Children* 147:546–552.

Fox, H.B. et al. 1994. *A preliminary examination of state Medicaid waiver programs and children with special health care needs*. Washington, DC: Fox Health Policy Consultants.

Garbarino, J. 1987. The abuse and neglect of special children: An introduction to the issues. In *Special children—special risks: The maltreatment of children with disabilities*, eds. J. Garbarino et al., 3–14. New York: De Gruyter.

Goldberg, A.I. et al. 1984. Home care for life-supported persons: An approach to program development. *Journal of Pediatrics* 104:785–795.

Gostin, L.O. 1995. Informed consent, cultural sensitivity, and respect for persons. *Journal of the American Medical Association* 274:844–845.

Groce, N. 1990. Comparative and cross-cultural issues. *Disabilities Studies Quarterly* 10:1–39.

Groce, N.E., and I.K. Zola. 1993. Multiculturalism, chronic illness, and disability. *Pediatrics* 91: 1048–1055.

Harris-Wehling, J. et al. 1995. *Strategies for assuring the provision of quality services through managed care delivery systems to children with special health care needs: Workshop highlights.* Washington, DC: Board of Health Care Services, Institute of Medicine.

Houk, V.N., and S.B. Thacker. 1989. The Centers for Disease Control program to prevent primary and secondary disabilities in the United States. *Public Health Reports* 104:226–231.

Hutchins, V., and C. Walch. 1989. Meeting minority health needs through special MCH projects. *Public Health Reports* 104:621–626.

Ireys, H.T. 1980. *The Crippled Children's Service: A comparative analysis of four state programs.* Mental Health Policy Monograph Series No. 7. Nashville, TN: Vanderbilt Institute for Public Policy Studies, Vanderbilt University.

Jameson, E.J., and S.C. King. 1989. The failure of the federal government to care for disabled children: A critical analysis of the Supplemental Security Income Program. *Columbia Human Rights Law Review* 20:309–342.

Jaudes, P.K., and L.J. Diamond. 1985. The handicapped child and child abuse. *Child Abuse and Neglect* 9:341–347.

Leonard, B.J. et al. 1989. Providing access to home care for disabled children: Minnesota's Medicaid model waiver program. *Public Health Reports* 104:465–472.

Massie, R., and Massie, S. 1975. *Journey.* New York: Alfred A. Knopf.

McManus, M.A., and P. Newacheck. 1993. Health insurance differentials among minority children with chronic conditions and the role of federal agencies and private foundations in improving financial access. *Pediatrics* 91:1040–1047.

Mesibov, L. 1994. What's so special about special education? *School Law Bulletin,* Summer.

National Center for Youth with Disabilities. 1993. *Teenagers at risk. A national perspective of state-level services for adolescents with chronic illness or disability.* Minneapolis, MN.

National Commission on Childhood Disability. 1995. *Supplemental Security Income for Children with Disabilities Report to Congress.* Washington, DC: Government Printing Office, October.

National Health Examination Survey. 1966–1970. Rockville, MD: National Center for Health Statistics.

National Health and Nutrition Examination Survey I. 1971–1974. Rockville, MD: National Center for Health Statistics.

National Health and Nutrition Examination Survey II. 1976–1980. Rockville, MD: National Center for Health Statistics.

National Health Interview Survey-Child Health Supplement. 1988. Rockville, MD: National Center for Health Statistics.

National Health Interview Survey-Disability Supplement. 1994. Rockville, MD: National Center for Health Statistics.

Neumark-Sztainer D. et al. 1995. Body dissatisfaction and unhealthy weight-control practices among adolescents with and without chronic illness: A population-based study. *Archives of Pediatric and Adolescent Medicine* 149:1330–1335.

Newacheck, P.W. 1989. Adolescents with special health needs: Prevalence, severity, and access to health services. *Pediatrics* 84:872–881.

Newacheck, P.W. 1994. Unpublished analysis. Institute for Health Policy Studies, University of California, San Francisco, mimeo.

Newacheck, P.W. et al. 1991. Prevalence and impact of chronic illness among adolescents. *American Journal of Diseases of Children* 145:1367–1373.

Newacheck, P.W. et al. 1993. Ethnocultural variations in the prevalence and impact of childhood chronic conditions. *Pediatrics* 91:1031–1039.

Newacheck, P.W., et al. 1994. Health status and income: The impact of poverty on child health. *Journal of School Health* 64:229–233.

Newacheck, P.W., and M.A. McManus. 1994. *A current profile of children with disabilities*. San Francisco: Institute for Health Policy Studies, University of California.

Newacheck, P.W., and W.R. Taylor. 1992. Childhood chronic illness: Prevalence, severity, and impact. *American Journal of Public Health* 82:364–370.

Okinow, N. 1994. Transition of youth with special health care needs. In *Maternal and Child Health Practices*, 4th ed., eds. H.M. Wallace et al., 754–763. Oakland, CA: Third Party Publishing Company.

Omnibus Budget Reconciliation Act of 1989 (OBRA'89). United States Code 701, sec. 501.

Palfrey, J.S. et al. 1991. Technology's children: Report of a statewide census of children dependent on medical supports. *Pediatrics* 87:611–618.

Patterson, J.M., and R.W. Blum. 1993. A conference on culture and chronic illness in childhood: Conference summary. *Pediatrics* 91:1025–1030.

Pennsylvania Association for Retarded Children v. Pennsylvania (334 F. Supp. 1257 E. D. Pa., 1971).

Perrin, E.C. et al. 1993. Issues involved in the definition and classification of chronic health conditions. *Pediatrics* 91:787–793.

Perrin, J., and R.E.K. Stein. 1991. Reinterpreting disability: Changes in Supplemental Security Income for children. *Pediatrics* 87:1047–1051.

Pizzo, P. 1983. *Parent to parent: Working together for ourselves and our children*. Boston, MA: Beacon Press.

Pizzo, P. 1987. Parent to parent support groups: Advocates for social change. In *American Family Support Programs*, eds. L. Kagan et al., 228–245. New Haven, CT: Yale University Press.

Pless, I.B., 1984. Clinical assessment: Physical and psychological functioning. *Pediatric Clinics of North America* 31:33–45.

Pless, I.B., and T. Nolan. 1991. Revision, replication and neglect—research on maladjustment in chronic illness. *Journal of Child Psychology and Psychiatry* 32:347–365.

Policy Clarification (1991). *Early Childhood Report*, Vol. 2. Horsham, PA: LRP Publications, p. 11, August.

Pope, A.M., and A.R. Tarlov, eds., 1991. *Disability in America: Toward a national agenda for prevention*. Washington, DC: Institute of Medicine, Committee on a National Agenda for Prevention of Disabilities.

Rehabilitation Act of 1973. U.S. Code. Vol. 16, sec. 504.

Rutter, M. (1987). Psychosocial resilience and protective mechanisms. *Am Journal of Orthopsychiatry, 57,* 6–331.

Shelton,T.L. et al. 1987. *Family-centered care for children with special health care needs*. Washington, DC: Association for the Care of Children's Health.

Silverman, M.M., and D.S. Koretz. 1989. Preventing mental health problems. In *Caring for children with chronic illness: Issues and strategies,* ed. R.E.K. Stein, 213–229. New York: Springer Publishing Company.

Simpson, G. 1993. *Determining childhood disability and special needs children in the 1994–95 NHIS Survey on Disability.* Paper presented at the winter meeting of the American Statistical Association, Fort Lauderdale, FL, January.

Starfield, B. 1982. Family income, ill health, and medical care of US children. *Journal of Public Health Policy* 3:244–259.

Stein, R.E.K., et al. 1993. Framework for identifying children who have chronic conditions: The case for a new definition. *Journal of Pediatrics* 122:342–347.

Sullivan v. Zebley. 1990. 88 U.S. 1377 (1990).

Thacker, S.B. et al. 1994. Assessing prevention effectiveness using data to drive program decisions. *Public Health Reports* 109:187–194.

Trohanis, P.L. 1995. *Progress in providing services to young children with special needs and their families.* Chapel Hill, NC: National Early Childhood Technical Assistance System (NEC*TAS), University of North Carolina at Chapel Hill.

Walker, D.K., and F.H. Jacobs. 1984. Chronically ill children in school. *Peabody Journal of Education* 61:29–71.

Wehman, P. et al. 1988. *Transition from school to work. New challenges for youth with severe disabilities.* Baltimore: Paul H. Brookes Publishing Co.

Wells, N. et al. 1993. *Families in program and policy: Report of a 1992 survey of family participation in State Title V Programs for Children with Special Health Care Needs.* Boston, MA: National Parent Resource Center, Federation for Children with Special Needs.

U.S. Congress, Office of Technology Assessment. 1987. Technology-dependent children: Hospital v. home care—a technical memorandum. Washington, DC: Author.

U.S. Department of Health and Human Services. U.S. Public Health Service. 1987. *Surgeon General's Report: Children with special health care needs.* Rockville, MD.

U.S. Department of Health and Human Services. U.S. Public Health Service. 1991. *Healthy People 2000: National Health Promotion and Disease Prevention Objectives—Full Report, with Commentary.* Washington, DC: Government Printing Office.

U.S. Department of Health and Human Services, Maternal and Child Health Bureau. 1995. *Children with special health care needs draft definition.* Rockville, MD: Author, mimeo.

U.S. General Accounting Office. Comptroller General. 1981a. *Disparities still exist in who gets special education.* Washington, DC: Government Printing Office.

U.S. General Accounting Office. Comptroller General. 1981b. *Unanswered questions in educating handicapped children in local public schools.* Washington, DC: Government Printing Office.

Wise, P., and A. Meyers. 1988. Poverty and child health. *Pediatric Clinics of North America* 35: 1169–1186.

Zill, N., and C.A. Schoenborn. 1990. Developmental, learning, and emotional problems. *Health of our nation's children, US, 1988.* Advance data from vital and health statistics, No. 190. Hyattsville, MD: National Center for Health Statistics.

CHAPTER 12

Issues in Maternal and Child Nutrition

Barbara A. Laraia and Janice M. Dodds

INTRODUCTION

Nutrition is a critical component in any discussion of the health status of the maternal and child health (MCH) population. Physical growth is anticipated and desired in all subgroups of children and among pregnant women. Women who are between pregnancies or who do not become pregnant during their childbearing years focus on achieving or maintaining their optimal nutrition status. Good nutrition is biologically central to growth in that it provides the elements for building and repairing tissue and is required for the metabolic processes that mediate tissue development. If there is not adequate repair or growth, the body becomes dysfunctional. An inadequately nourished child becomes a sick child, one who listens poorly in school or is absent from school. Prolonged, inadequate nutrition during pregnancy and early childhood can affect the brain's development and functioning. In older children and adults, malnutrition can give rise to cardiovascular disease, and an excess of certain nutrients can accelerate the disease process in cancer-prone sites.

Underlying the following discussion, but beyond the scope of this textbook, is basic nutrition assessment methodology including dietary intake, growth status, and tissue levels of nutrients. Measures of dietary intake include three-day food records, food frequency, 24-hour recall, and dietary history techniques. Measures of growth, such as height and weight, can be combined into a body mass index (BMI) or compared to a growth chart. There are also tissue measures such as bioelectrical impedance to measure fat and muscle, bone densitometry, and biochemical measures of serum levels such as hemoglobin, hematocrit, cholesterol, triglycerides, vitamin A, protein, and glucose.

The knowledge base of nutrition is expanding at an accelerated rate with the application of technology to all phases of research into metabolism, food composition, dietary intake, and food behavior. Each of these areas is relevant to MCH issues.

The chapter begins with three salient MCH nutrition issues. Historically, getting enough calories in amount and type that support health has been a problem in the United States. One continues to see hunger among families with children confronting a variety of social and environmental problems including poverty, absent nutrition education, the disintegration of families and communities, and inadequate accessibility to service programs. An even greater problem in terms of frequency is childhood obesity. Although the federal government has established in *Healthy People 2000* (U.S. DHHS 1992) that the United States should decrease obesity among children and adults by the year 2000, at a midpoint evaluation, it continues to rise. The combination of factors that support this trend are discussed in this chapter, including sedentary lifestyles, widespread food availability, and a bewildering variety of food products. Lastly, this section closes with the issue of breastfeeding. The evidence of the positive impact of breastfeeding for any length of time continues to mount, yet the prevalence of breastfeeding in the United States is inadequate. The issue of breastfeeding provides an excellent example of the problems and potential of population-level strategies to support the individual nutrition decisions that families make. Without community support for breastfeeding, mothers and families would find it difficult to sustain.

Food and nutrition policies and programs are built from two dietary strategies, the Recommended Dietary Allowances (RDAs) and food guides. The RDAs provide the scientific foundation for all judgments about the adequacy of dietary intake. A food guide is the consumer information that advises people about their food selection over the course of a day. The Basic Four Food Groups prevailed for a number of years but were replaced in 1993 by the Food Pyramid. Government food and nutrition programs also articulate national policy. Three such programs, heavily used by women and children—the Special Supplemental Food Program for Women, Infants, and Children (WIC), School Meal Programs, and the Food Stamp Program—are described below.

Food and nutrition problems are often difficult to solve because of the number of factors that play a role in their etiology and maintenance. The Social Process Model described at the end of this chapter is an ecological model that, when applied to food and nutrition systems, can describe the diverse factors that may be thwarting or impeding solutions. The model describes three processes in sociological systems—the economic, the political, and the cultural. When the Social Process Model is used to describe the food and nutrition systems, the absence or overactivity of a process can illuminate the source of a problem.

THREE MCH NUTRITION ISSUES

Hunger in America

Hunger from the 1930s to 1960s

Hunger has existed throughout U.S. history. The nation has grappled with being hungry as the pioneers built this country, through war and famine, and as a result of poverty. It is in more recent history—1930s to present—that the country has struggled to make sense of why a nation with so much still cannot meet the needs of the least of its citizens.

It was during the Depression of the 1930s that federal domestic food assistance was first developed as a way to meet the needs of the unemployed and to answer the emotional outrage that the problem of hunger created. Communities battled the problem by starting soup kitchens, canneries, gleaning projects, and food baskets. Yet this was not enough. The agricultural sector had been concerned about large food surpluses throughout the 1920s. In the 1930s, food rotted while many Americans went hungry. The government tried to control the agricultural problem by price-depressing farm surpluses. Finally came the disposal of farm surpluses, backed by the Agriculture Department, to maintain the income of large-scale commercial farmers. The Agriculture Committees in Congress appropriated money, coined "farmers' money," to support this disposal. This became "the paradox of want amid plenty."

The first attempt at federal food assistance was through the Red Cross during the Hoover Administration (1929–1933). This measure was resisted by both Hoover and Congress until they were confronted by the cost of surplus storage, the waste caused by rodents, insects and decay, and the outrage of the American people. Finally, wheat from the Farm Board was distributed to the unemployed.

During the Roosevelt Administration (1933–1945), a continuous food assistance program was created. Congress had made many unsuccessful attempts at trying to deal with the problems of both hunger and surplus food. In the end, Roosevelt announced that the government would purchase a "wide variety" of surplus and have it distributed to the unemployed. The surplus commodity procurement and distribution project was formed and lasted for 30 years. Even today focusing on surplus crops and not on the nutritional needs of the citizenry is still a fundamental problem (Poppendieck 1992).

During the 1930s, 1940s, and 1950s, the government continued to address hunger and nutrition through the distribution of surplus agricultural commodities. (See Exhibit 12–1.) After World War II, the continued food shortage of the poor was not addressed until President Kennedy, in response to a campaign promise, outlined a program to expand food distribution by piloting the Food Stamp Program in eight counties. In 1964, under President Johnson, the Food Stamp

Exhibit 12–1 Selected Events in the History of Federal Policies To Address Hunger in the U.S.

1930	USDA and Federal Emergency Relief Administration distribute surplus agricultural commodities as food relief through Federal Surplus Relief Corporation.
1933	Congress creates the Agricultural Adjustment Administration to control farm prices and production and the Federal Surplus Relief Corporation to distribute surplus farm products to needy families.
1935–42	Congress provides for continued operation of Federal Surplus Commodities Corporation which, under USDA, purchases commodities for distribution to state welfare agencies.
1936–42	Amendments to *Agricultural Act* permit food donations to school lunches.
1939–43	Federal Surplus Commodities Corporation initiates experimental food stamp program.
1946	National School Lunch Program established.
1954	Special Milk Program established.
1955	USDA determines that average low-income family spends one-third of after-tax income on food.
1961	President Kennedy expands use of surplus food for needy people at home and abroad and announces eight pilot food stamp programs.
1964	Congress establishes the national Food Stamp Program. Social Security Administration establishes poverty line at three times the cost of USDA's lowest-cost Economy Food Plan. Since 1969, values have been adjusted according to the Consumer Price Index.
1966	*Child Nutrition Act* passes. President Johnson outlines Food for Freedom program.
1968–70	Ten-State and Preschool Nutrition Surveys and *Hunger, USA* report evidence of malnutrition among children in poverty.
1968–77	Senate establishes Select Committee on Nutrition and Human Needs to lead nation's anti-hunger efforts.
1969	President Nixon announces "war on hunger"; holds White House Conference on Food, Nutrition, and Health. USDA establishes Food and Nutrition Service to administer federal food assistance programs.
1971	Results of Ten-State Survey released to Congress indicate high risk of malnutrition among low-income groups.
1972	Congress authorizes Special Supplemental Food Program for Women, Infants, and Children (WIC).
1975	School Breakfast Program initiated, becomes permanent.
1977	*Food and Agricultural Act* and Child Nutrition and National School Lunch Amendments passed.

continues

Exhibit 12–1 continued

1981	USDA establishes a small demonstration project for commodity distribution, the Special Supplemental Dairy Distribution Program.
1981–82	Congress passed Omnibus Budget Reconciliation Acts, Omnibus Farm Bill, and *Tax Equity and Fiscal Responsibility Act* which eliminate, restrict, and reduce food and income benefits.
1983	The Special Supplemental Dairy Distribution Program becomes institutionalized as the Temporary Emergency Food Assistance Program (TEFAP).
1984	President's Task Force on Food Assistance finds little evidence of widespread or increasing undernutrition but concludes that hunger exists and is intolerable in the U.S.
1986	General Accounting Office finds that methodologic flaws discredit findings of the Physician Task Force on Hunger that hunger is prevalent in counties with low food stamp participation rates.
1988	DHHS publishes *Surgeon General's Report on Nutrition and Health*, which states that lack of access to an appropriate diet should not be a health problem for any American. Congress passes the *Hunger Prevention Act*, increasing eligibility and benefits for Food Stamps, Child Care, and TEFAP programs.
1989	House Select Committee on Hunger holds hearings on food security in the U.S.
1991	*Mickey Leland Childhood Hunger Relief Act* (HR-1202, S-757) introduced.

Source: Reprinted with permission from M. Nestle and S. Guttmacher, Hunger in the United States: Rationale, Methods, and Policy Implications of State Hunger Surveys, *Journal of Nutrition Education* 24(1), p. 185, © 1992, Society for Nutrition Education.

Program became permanent, and in 1966 the School Breakfast Program was established.

The 1960s brought about much change, but the single most powerful event that caused the public to refocus its concern over hunger was the release by the Field Foundation of *Hunger, USA* in 1968 (Citizens Board, 1968). This report, and its accompanying television documentary, showed widespread malnutrition and hunger in the rural South, and once again raised national recognition of hunger.

Hunger Held in Abeyance—1970s

The Select Committee on Nutrition and Human Needs, chaired by Senator George McGovern, was appointed by the Senate the same year that *Hunger, USA* was released. Its charter was to eliminate hunger. Food assistance for families, children, and the elderly was expanded. The WIC and congregate and home-delivered meal programs were initiated, and the school lunch program was expanded. In 1978 the Field Foundation sent its hunger investigation teams back to the same sites they had visited in 1968–1969. They found hunger had greatly diminished and nutrition programs were reaching the at-risk communities they had studied. As a result, hunger was considered to be virtually abolished in America during the 1970s (Brown and Allen 1988; Nestle and Guttmacher 1992).

Re-emergence of Hunger—1980s

During the early 1980s, there were many studies and reports documenting a resurgence of hunger in America, especially among families with children. Among the organizations reporting on hunger were the U.S. Conference of Mayors, the U.S. Department of Agriculture (USDA), the U.S. General Accounting Office (GAO), the United Church of Christ, the Salvation Army, the Working Group on Hunger and Poverty of the National Council of Churches, Bread for the World, the Citizens Commission on Hunger in New England, Save the Children Foundation, Second Harvest, the Food Research and Action Center (FRAC), and the Physicians' Task Force on Hunger in America. A faltering U.S. economy, accompanied by cuts in federal assistance programs, had increased the demand on emergency food during this time.

President Ronald Reagan appointed a Task Force on Food Assistance in 1983 as a result of the attention many of these studies and reports drew to this issue. The task force confirmed that serious hunger exists in America, but stated it could not determine to what extent (Brown and Allen 1988).

One of the largest obstacles in studying hunger was the lack of a clear definition and an acceptable measure of hunger. In 1984 the Connecticut Association for Human Services—with the help of a distinguished panel of child health and research experts—developed a scientifically valid design for a study of hunger among low-income families with children under age 12. A national replication of this study, known as the Community Child Hunger Identification Project or CCHIP, was initiated in 18 sites across the United States under the coordination of the FRAC (1991).

Present Happenings—the 1990s

The first CCHIP study was conducted from February 1989 to August 1990. It was unique in using a uniform definition of hunger and applying it to a nation-wide study. It saw "hunger" as "the mental and physical condition that comes from not eating enough food due to insufficient economic, family or community resources." The study used eight questions to establish whether the condition of hunger was present. A score of five or more positive responses shows that there is food shortage. Four or fewer responses show that the household is at risk for hunger. (See Exhibit 12–2.)

Exhibit 12–2 CCHIP Hunger Questions

1. Does your household ever run out of money to buy food to make a meal?

2. Do you or adult members of your household ever eat less than you feel you should because there is not enough money for food?

3. Do you or adult members of your household ever cut the size of meals or skip meals because there is not enough money for food?

4. Do your children ever eat less than you feel they should because there is not enough money for food?

5. Do you ever cut the size of your children's meals or do they ever skip meals because there is not enough money for food?

6. Do your children ever say they are hungry because there is not enough food in the house?

7. Do you ever rely on a limited number of foods to feed your children because you are running out of money to buy food for a meal?

8. Do any of your children ever go to bed hungry because there is not enough money to buy food?

Source: Data from Community Childhood Hunger Identification Project: A Survey of Childhood Hunger in the U.S., p. 104, Food Research and Action Center, 1991, Washington, D.C.

The key findings from the first CCHIP study, which concluded in 1991, were:

- Hunger prevalence rates, when applied to national population data, yield estimates of 5.5 million children younger than 12 years old who are hungry. In other words, one in eight children under 12 in the United States is probably hungry. Using the same rates, "in addition, approximately six million children under 12 are at risk of hunger because their families are experiencing food shortage problems" (FRAC 1991, p. 16). Therefore 11.5 million children under 12 are at risk; one in four is likely to experience one food shortage problem in the course of the year.
- Hungry children have more health problems than the nonhungry, and these affect school attendance. "When compared with children from nonhungry low-income families, children from hungry families were more likely to suffer from infection-based health problems and were two to three times more likely to show symptoms of low energy stores. Additionally, they are more than 3 times more likely to suffer unwanted weight loss, more than 4 times

as likely to suffer from fatigue, about 3 times as likely to suffer from irritability, more than 12 times as likely to report dizziness, more than 2 times as likely to have frequent headaches, about 2 times as likely to have ear infections, about 3 times as likely to suffer from concentration problems, and about 2 times as likely to have frequent colds. They miss 1.5 more days of school per year than nonhungry children" (FRAC 1991, p. 16).

- Twelve percent of all families with children younger than 12 years old in the United States experience hunger, with an additional 28 percent of families estimated to be at risk of hunger. Altogether, 40 percent of these families are hungry or at risk of experiencing hunger.

In addition to the ongoing CCHIP project there were three other events that took place in the 1990s. During 1990, Brown University held the World Hunger Conference. During the conference it was decided that the United States needed to come up with a "declaration" to eliminate hunger in the United States, just as the Bellagio Declaration attempts to halve world hunger by the year 2000. The "Medford Declaration to End Hunger in the U.S." was written at Tufts University as a result. The declaration proposes two steps: to use existing programs to ensure that food is available, and to increase the purchasing power of U.S. households. The Medford Declaration states that "we can begin with children . . . and we can virtually eliminate domestic hunger by 1995" (Medford Declaration 1992, p. 240).

In 1992 a food security indicator was developed to assess women and children who are food secure/insecure. In-depth interviews were conducted and qualitatively analyzed to create a conceptualization of two levels of food security—individual and household. From this conceptualization a survey tool was designed to measure household, women's, and children's food security. The definition of food security derived from this study was "the inability to acquire or consume an adequate quality or sufficient quantity of food in socially acceptable ways, or the uncertainty that one will be able to do so" (Radimer et al. 1992, p. 395). More work is needed to demonstrate the association between food insecurity and hunger (Campbell 1991).

Suggestions/Interventions

Hunger affects children physically, mentally, emotionally, and psychologically. If hunger persists, potential health care needs and the decrease in productivity that accompany prolonged hunger burden the economy. Combating hunger starts at the local level. People can do several things to help fight against hunger: find out where soup kitchens and Food Banks are located; investigate other food programs, such as gleaning projects and food rescue programs; most importantly, know that although people don't want to be poor and hungry, they often need professionals' support to break barriers. A qualitative study of hunger conducted in

North Carolina found that barriers to getting help and relieving hunger included pride, the stigma of poverty, transportation, staff attitudes at social services, and discrimination. During the focus groups that the North Carolina Hunger Project held, participants frequently cited their desire for all of the public assistance programs to be more supportive of men and women who are making an effort. They also stated that as soon as they "get ahead," their benefits are cut immediately, often leaving them further behind. (See Exhibit 12–3.)

The Other Extreme—Obesity in America

Introduction

Once a sign of wealth, obesity is a growing concern in most industrialized countries because it is a risk factor for many chronic diseases. Obesity is associated with coronary heart disease, hypertension, noninsulin dependent diabetes mellitus, certain cancers, and gallbladder disease. Obesity is also associated with psychosocial problems.

Prevalence and Incidence

Overweight is usually defined by a BMI of at least 27 to 30 kg/m². By this definition more than 25 percent of women and 31 percent of men over 18 years of age are considered overweight in the United States. Severe overweight is indicated by a BMI greater than 30 kg/m², which is present in 12 percent of the U.S. population (National Research Council 1989).

The prevalence of overweight in the U.S. adult population is alarming because of its impact on health, and it leads us to assess the risk of obesity among children. The prevalence of overweight among children 6 to 11 years old has increased by 54 percent between 1963 and 1980 (Gortmaker et al. 1987; Pipes 1989). It has risen by 39 percent in adolescents between 12 to 17 years old (Gortmaker et al. 1993; Pipes 1989). Currently, 27 percent of children and 21 percent of adolescents are obese. It is most likely that anywhere from 25 percent to 50 percent of obese children become obese adults, although this proportion has been reported as high as 74 percent. More striking, 70 percent of obese adolescents become obese adults. Conversely, 30 percent of adults who are obese were obese as children. The most important factor in determining a child's propensity for adult obesity is the age of onset and severity of obesity. The older the individual and the more severe the obesity at onset, the more difficult to reverse the outcome (Dietz 1987).

Since obesity has a potentially lasting effect from childhood, the difference between overweight and overfat is important for purposes of counseling and treatment (Dietz and Robinson 1993). *Overweight* is defined by a 20 percent increase in weight for height above ideal weight. However, weight for height does not

Exhibit 12–3 North Carolina Childhood Hunger Project Checklist

1. Implement a period of transition to independence and financial stability.
   * Decrease benefits incrementally as families' incomes increase.
   * Increase Aid to Families with Dependent Children benefits to the poverty level.
   * Increase food stamp benefit levels based on the U.S. Department of Agriculture Low Cost Food Plan (LCFP).
   * Increase federal and state funding for the Special Supplemental Food Program for Women, Infants and Children (WIC).
   * Promote breastfeeding as a means to reduce hunger in infants.

2. Expand the food buying power of low-income families to improve the nutrition of their children.
   * Increase the minimum wage to a level that allows a working family to meet its basic needs. The minimum wage should be linked to the Federal Poverty Guidelines.
   * Repeal the sales tax on food.
   * Establish funding for a supplemental nutrition assistance program that would enable food banks and pantries to purchase and distribute food orders that are more nutritionally complete.

3. Ensure that the social services available to families in need are user-friendly.
   * Activate the public relations campaign geared toward changing public perceptions of food stamp users so that current and potential recipients will receive benefits without embarrassment.
   * Encourage schools to be flexible in implementing the School Breakfast Program, particularly in regard to scheduling.
   * Develop a public relations campaign so that students can participate in school meal programs without embarrassment.
   * Establish customer service training for all workers and volunteers in food assistance programs.
   * Encourage local WIC agencies to offer extended hours for all services.

4. Institute education programs to assist parents and families in gaining the skills needed to better support and manage their households.
   * Implement nutrition education in school curricula.
   * Implement nutrition education programs for the clients of food assistance programs.

5. Publicize and support the programs and agencies available to help families in need.
   * Establish a Food and Nutrition Task Force in each county to identify the specific issues it faces and their solutions.
   * Aggressively increase the awareness of the Summer Food Program year round among potential sponsors and expand outreach to eligible individuals so that they may take advantage of the program.
   * Establish a Governor's Task Force on Hunger with the mission of stimulating responses to alleviate and prevent hunger and monitor the situation in the state.

Source: Reprinted with permission from Hidden Hunger: The Face of Hunger Among Families and Children in North Carolina, p. 70, Department of Nutrition, School of Public Health, University of North Carolina, © 1995, Janice Dodds.

directly measure body fat. Therefore, excess weight may be due to a large body frame and may not represent a long-term problem. Body fat is measured by triceps skinfold thickness; *obesity* is defined as a triceps skinfold measurement greater than the 85th percentile for age. A child who is overweight but has triceps skinfold thickness measurements within normal limits should be counseled differently than one who is overfat.

Epidemiologically, obesity occurs more in the northeastern part of the United States, followed by the Midwest, then the South, and finally the West. The environmental effects that are strongest are found within the family. Family patterns of inactivity, parental obesity, increased socioeconomic class, higher parental education, and smaller family size are all associated with childhood obesity. Sixty to 70 percent of obese adolescents have one or both parents who are obese. Furthermore, 40 percent of obese adolescents have obese siblings. Many people think that obese children may have "metabolic" or "glandular" disorders, but in reality less than 1 percent have these severe types of problems (Dietz and Robinson 1993).

Theories of Etiology

There is no clear understanding of why obesity occurs, and unfortunately there is no one successful treatment for obesity. There are many theories purporting to account for the increase in obesity in recent history, and most are sketchy at best. The majority of these cite both a genetic and an environmental component to obesity. One theory is that obesity has increased with an increase of available calories per capita while there has been a decrease in energy expenditure. Available calories increased from 3,100 calories per capita in 1950–1959 to 3,700 calories in 1990. During this time the percentage of calories available from fat remained consistently 40 to 43 percent of the diet. The per capita consumption of meats, fats, flour and cereal products, and caloric sweeteners have all increased between 1970 and 1992. Per capita egg consumption has decreased, while dairy products, aside from an increase in milk, have remained constant. In beverage consumption, the greatest increase has been in soft drinks, which increased from 24.3 gallons per capita in 1970 to 44.1 gallons in 1992. Fruits and vegetables all increased during this same time period (U.S. Bureau of the Census 1994). The increase in the amount of food available and the increase in the amount of food consumed has a direct impact on weight management in America.

Studies have shown diet to be directly linked to obesity, to chronic diseases such as cardiovascular disease (CVD), and to some cancers. While for most of its history the United States has been concerned that its citizens get enough food, the concern now focuses on "optimal" intake, which may be less food. Current dietary recommendations suggest no greater than 30 percent of calories in the diet be from fat. Moreover, studies show that a diet containing less than 20 percent of calories from fat can reverse disease processes. Needless to say, this greatly differs from the 40–43 percent fat diet Americans currently are eating. It has been suggested that a clear definition of "optimal" intake reflecting a lower percentage of dietary fat might help direct public policy in combating the ill effects of obesity and some chronic diseases (Wynder et al. 1992).

An example of how focusing on lower "optimal" intake could help modify policy can be found in the school lunch program. The fat content of school lunches exceeds current dietary recommendations of 30 percent or less total fat and 10 percent or less saturated fat. They contain an estimated 39 percent of energy from total fat and 21 percent of energy from saturated fat. A menu that often contains ground beef is a major contributor to the total fat. A study by Snyder et al. (1994) showed a reduction in total and saturated fat by cooking, draining, and rinsing the meat with water. Draining and washing allowed an additional 25 to 30 percent reduction in fat after cooking while maintaining nutritive values of iron and niacin in school lunch ground beef. Innovations such as these can contribute to the reduction of the fat content of school meal programs (Snyder et al. 1994).

The greatest environmental influences on children are their parents. In a study by Klesges et al. (1991), the impact of parental influences on food selection in young children was evaluated. A wide range of foods was offered to children for lunch independent of their mothers, then again with the understanding that their mothers would monitor their selection, and finally mothers were allowed to modify the choices of their children. This study showed that when children chose foods freely, their diets were less nutritious than when there was a threat of their mothers' watching or when their mothers modified the diet. Twenty-five percent of calories came from added sugar when children selected their own lunches. The meals were more nutritious when modified by the mothers. These were lower in total calories, lower in calories from saturated fats, and had lower sodium content. Yet even though these meals were lower in total calories and saturated fat, foods highest in nutrient content still were not selected. The overall results reveal first that children do not choose nutritious foods on their own, and second that mothers focus on lowering calories but not on increasing high nutrient dense foods (Klesges et al. 1991). Beyond food selection, parents influence children's eating behavior by verbal prompting at mealtime, adult eating behavior, and the use of food for rewards and punishments.

Inactivity and a sedentary lifestyle also contribute to obesity. Studies by Gortmaker et al. (1990), and by Kotz and Story (1994), show that increased television viewing increases the prevalence and severity of obesity. This may be explained by an increase in the number of inactive hours, as well as the effect on children of high-calorie food commercials. Viewing time has increased from 18 hours per week in 1968 to 25 hours per week in 1983. Viewing time may currently be as high as 40 hours per week, not including video movies, video games, or computer games (Gortmaker et al. 1990). A study by Kotz and Story (1994) reviewed a total of 997 commercials selling a product during 52.5 hours of Saturday morning children's television. Of the commercials, 56.6 percent were for food, 33 percent were for toys, and 10.2 percent were for other items. Of the food advertisements, 43.6 percent were for foods that contained fats and sweets; 35.7 percent were for breads, cereals, rice, and pasta. Of the latter group, 23 percent were for high-sugar cereals. Fast-food restaurants comprised 10.8 percent of the commercials, and milk, cheese, yogurt, meats, eggs, nuts, and frozen meals totaled less than 10 percent of all commercials. Needless to say, the overall picture of food commercials does not comply with the USDA Food Guide Pyramid's recommendations. Food commercials encourage consumption of the foods least necessary in one's diet, namely fats and sweets. Television viewing has been associated with not only an increased consumption of advertised foods, but an increase in children's requests for and parents' purchase of these foods.

Consequences

As mentioned, obesity is associated with coronary heart disease, hypertension, noninsulin dependent diabetes mellitus, certain cancers, and gallbladder disease. Both adults and children can experience hypercholesterolemia, hypertriglyceridemia, Blount disease and other bone diseases, and respiratory complications directly related to obesity. Obesity is also associated with psychosocial problems.

Problems with body image and discrimination have been well documented. A study conducted in 1967 by Stunkard and Burt showed that the development of a negative body image takes place most often during adolescence (Stunkard and Burt 1967). And while other studies have shown that overweight individuals have no greater psychological disturbances than do nonobese persons, all studies have shown evidence of strong prejudice against obese persons as young as six years old. Children have reported words such as "lazy," "dirty," "stupid," "ugly," and "lies" when describing silhouettes of obese children (Wadden and Stunkard 1985). Discrimination against the obese was revealed in a 1966 study by results that showed less obesity in colleges than in high schools even though obese and nonobese high school students showed no differences in academic criteria or application rates (Canning et al. 1966). Gortmaker et al. found social and economic consequences of obesity in adolescence. Obese women were less often married, had lower incomes, and a higher rate of poverty than nonobese women when controlling for socioeconomic status and aptitude (Gortmaker et al. 1993).

Interventions

Studies have shown that there is no easy treatment for obesity. One of the most effective approaches thus far is a family-based behavioral intervention that employs nutrition, exercise, and parent/child involvement (Epstein et al. 1990a; Epstein et al. 1990b). Another approach is the SHAPEDOWN program that incorporates cognitive, behavioral, and affective techniques to help make small modifications in the diet (Mellin et al. 1987).

The absence of a successful treatment for obesity makes preventive measures even more important. Reducing excessive caloric intake by reducing fat in school lunches, decreasing television viewing time, and implementing nutrition education for families are good beginnings. Furthermore, the amount of exercise must also increase. Physical education during primary and secondary school are very important. Decreasing the amount of television viewing time will aid in a decrease in sedentary activity and lower exposure to inappropriate food commercials. Interactive nutrition education during school can help reinforce and shape a child's eating habits. Having children involved in the solution is necessary in order to create the most effective change possible. Optimal diet and exercise are still the best preventive tools!

The Issue of Breastfeeding

Introduction

The issue of breastfeeding has become very complex in America's recent history. Although no longer an established practice in the United States, breastfeeding is widely agreed to be the best form of nourishment for a baby. Not only does breast milk have all the necessary nutrients in the correct proportion, it also has antibacterial factors and immunoglobulins to protect the infant. These biologically active constituents of breast milk are absent from formula. Since the advent of formula at the turn of the century, the use of breastfeeding has fluctuated greatly. The industrial revolution, urbanization, glass bottles, rubber nipples, pasteurization, and refrigeration are only some of the influences that have increased "artificial" feeding. Whereas 58 percent of American women were still breastfeeding in 1911, this figure had declined to only 38 percent by 1946, and was 52 percent in 1989 (Worthington-Roberts and Williams 1989). The focus of this section is to review the multiple barriers to successful breastfeeding that have prevented this country from reaching the national goal of 75 percent breastfeeding among new mothers, and to offer some suggestions for changing and combating these barriers. Contraindications to breastfeeding will also be reviewed.

Background

Despite all that is known about the benefits of breastfeeding, the practice has declined among women in the United States (Worthington-Roberts and Williams 1989). At one point there had been an increase in breastfeeding incidence, from the all-time low of 18 percent in 1966 to about 59 percent in 1984. In 1988 there were reported declines to 55 percent (Rassin et al. 1993; Worthington-Roberts and Williams 1989) and 52 percent in 1989 (Rassin et al. 1993). The Ross

Laboratories Mother Surveys in 1984 found that indicators for breastfeeding were race, maternal education, maternal age, and geographic region. Namely, college-educated and White women and those in western states breastfed more; Black women, those younger than age 20, and those with less education breastfed less often. Breastfeeding incidence is also declining among Hispanic women in spite of their strong cultural belief in this practice (Worthington-Roberts and Williams 1989; John and Martorell 1989). Rassin et al. (1993) found a decrease in breastfeeding among Hispanics with increased acculturation in the United States.

Currently, the American Academy of Pediatrics, the American Dietetic Association (ADA), and the Surgeon General all endorse breastfeeding as the optimal feeding method for healthy infants. *Healthy People 2000: National Health Promotion and Disease Prevention Objectives* (U.S. DHHS 1992) targets as a main objective "(to) increase to at least 75 percent the proportion of mothers who breastfeed their babies in the early postpartum period and to at least 50 percent the proportion who continue breastfeeding until their babies are 5 to 6 months old" (p. 379). Baseline was 54 percent at discharge from birth site and 21 percent at 5 to 6 months in 1988 for all discharges, Black and White. The baseline for Black mothers is 25 percent at discharge from birth site and 8 percent at 5 to 6 months old in 1988. For Hispanic mothers the baseline was 51 percent and 16 percent, respectively, and for American Indian/Alaska Native mothers it was 47 percent and 28 percent, respectively.

The American Academy of Pediatrics (AAP) supports exclusive breastfeeding for the first six months of life. The definition of exclusive breastfeeding is that no other form of milk or food be used for the first four months, and that breast milk be used until one year (or until the infant is weaned). In other words, no formula, cow's milk, or other milk substitute is recommended during the first year of life. Many studies have looked at breastfeeding using loosely constructed definitions; any breastfeeding, breast- and bottle-feeding, or breastfeeding for three to six months are all considered "breastfeeding." To see the effect of breastfeeding more clearly, however, many studies have used the more narrow definition of exclusive breastfeeding.

There are many reasons the AAP so strongly encourages exclusive breastfeeding. Among them are the aforementioned properties of breast milk that protect infants against disease in general and infectious disease in particular. The protective action of breast milk is well documented during the first year of life. The potential long-term protective effects are not known. One topic of current research is to investigate the relationship between breast- or bottle-feeding and childhood obesity. Work done by Prentice and others (1988) suggests that the British Department of Health and Social Services (DHSS) and the Food and Agriculture Organization/World Health Organization/United Nations University (FAO/WHO/UNU) both recommend dietary allowances for children that overestimate energy need. The DHSS and FAO/WHO/UNU used estimates based on modified Atwater factors derived from adult diets and by the assumption that breast milk was 20 percent more energy dense than currently is known to be the case. Then the FAO used a 5 percent inflation factor above these estimates. This led to an 8 percent to 17 percent increase in energy allowance, between one month and three years, compared to what Prentice et al. (1988) found by directly measuring energy expenditure through the use of doubly labeled water ($^2H_2{}^{18}O$).

A recent study conducted by DARLING (Davis Area Research on Lactation, Infant Nutrition, and Growth) investigates differences between exclusively breast-fed infants and bottle-fed infants. In it, Dewey et al. (1993) found that breastfed infants are significantly leaner than bottle-fed infants during the first year of life. The greatest difference was evident between 9 and 15 months of age. Infants were found to grow at about the same rate until four months old. At 12 months, however, 15 percent of the formula-fed infants had weight-for-length greater than the 90th percentile as opposed to 7 percent of the breastfed infants. This group of children will be followed until 3.5 years of age. The differences in body fatness will continue to be measured and will hopefully give insight into the difference between breast- and bottle-feeding with regard to childhood (and probably adult) obesity and health.

Barriers to Breastfeeding

Many of the initial barriers to breastfeeding operate before a woman becomes pregnant and while she is pregnant. Studies show that the sooner a woman makes a decision to breastfeed the more likely she is to breastfeed (Freed et al. 1992). Studies also show that this decision is oftentimes not encouraged or supported properly by the woman's health care provider and is influenced greatly by her "significant other." Many health care practitioners agree that "breast is best" but send a double message when they do not counsel on breastfeeding during prenatal visits.

Information is often given in the form of educational materials that may reinforce fears and frustrations associated with breastfeeding. These materials may use well-dressed, attractive models that in turn reinforce the idea that only confident, affluent women are successful at breastfeeding (Bryant et al. 1992). Often information regarding breastfeeding is not consistent. Advice may vary from "don't feed any supplement," to "top off each breastfeed with a bottle"; from "feed for 10 minutes on each breast" to "let the baby feed as long as he/she wants" (Ellis 1992a). A new mother can be left feeling confused when she receives varied information from several sources.

Furthermore, hospital policies can greatly deter any decision to breastfeed once the baby is born. The most negative policies are "separation of mothers and infants, regular feeding intervals, timed feeds, routine or sporadic supplementation with artificial feeds, exclusion of lay support people, and the provision of equivocal information, either oral or written, regarding infant feeding" (Ellis 1992b, p. 554). Policies such as giving a free formula gift at discharge are not consistent from one hospital to another. Snell et al. (1992) found a significant decline in breastfeeding among Hispanic women who were given a free formula sample. Additional studies have been cited that show a significant decrease in breastfeeding in the first month when formula samples were given, and significant declines in women who are from lower socioeconomic backgrounds, who are less educated, and who experience post-partum illness. However, at least three studies have shown no difference in breastfeeding between women who received a gift pack at hospital discharge and those who did not (Snell et al. 1992).

Other hospital policies, such as separating baby and mother after birth, lead to a more difficult time breastfeeding. The early introduction of bottles has been shown to interfere with the prolactin reflex and also to reduce the duration of breastfeeding. Prolactin is the hormone that stimulates the breast's milk-producing alveoli and is released in response to its stimulation. This "let-down" reflex may be interrupted because of interference with "proper" sucking. The sucking movement has been said to be different for a bottle and for a breast, leading to difficulty or "nipple confusion" for the baby. Poor suckling may also occur when a baby is more easily rewarded by the rapid emptying of a bottle (Newman 1990).

The WHO/UNICEF's (World Health Organization/United Nations International Children's Emergency Fund) "Ten Steps to Successful Breastfeeding" can be used by hospitals and birthing centers as a standard of practice for more successful breastfeeding outcomes. Based on these guidelines and other criteria (such as no free formula samples), a hospital can work toward a "Baby Friendly" UNICEF designation. First, a self-appraisal tool is used to establish how baby friendly an institution is to start. This assessment tool can then be used to work toward a more baby friendly state. Once the majority of the questions of the assessment tool are answered "yes," the institution can proceed with an external assessment conducted by a multiprofessional team with expertise in breastfeeding and lactation. After the team observes and questions the administrators, staff, and patients, the institution can be designated a "Baby Friendly" place by UNICEF. If the institution does not meet the baby friendly external assessment criteria, which are an 80 percent adherence to the UNICEF criteria (see Exhibit 12–4) and at least a 75 percent exclusive breastfeeding rate, the administrators can sign a certificate of commitment to put in place the necessary changes by a specified date (Jones and Green 1993).

In a meta-analysis by Pérez-Escamilla et al. (1994), hospital-based breastfeeding interventions, such as the ones that follow the WHO/UNICEF recommendations, are found to have a beneficial effect on lactation success. This was found strongly among first-time mothers. Their results showed that commercial dis-

Exhibit 12–4 Ten Steps to Successful Breastfeeding

1. Have a written breastfeeding policy that is routinely communicated to all health care staff.
2. Train all health care staff in skills necessary to implement this policy.
3. Inform all pregnant women about the benefits and management of breastfeeding.
4. Help mothers initiate breastfeeding within 30 minutes of birth.
5. Show mothers how to breastfeed and how to maintain lactation even if they should be separated from their infants.
6. Give newborn infants no food or drink other than breast milk, unless medically indicated.
7. Practice rooming-in, allowing mothers and infants to remain together, 24 hours a day.
8. Encourage breastfeeding on demand.
9. Give no artificial teats or pacifiers (also called dummies or soothers) to breast-feeding infants.
10. Foster the establishment of breastfeeding support groups and refer mothers to them on discharge from the hospital or clinic.

Source: WHO/UNICEF (1989). *Protecting, Promoting and Supporting Breastfeeding: The Special Role of Maternity Services.* Geneva: World Health Organization. Used with permission.

charge packs had a negative effect on successful breastfeeding. Rooming-in and breastfeeding support had a positive effect on breastfeeding among first-time mothers. Lastly, breastfeeding on demand had a positive effect on successful lactation (Pérez-Escamilla et al. 1994).

Apart from hospital policies and protocols, societal and political influences also have a bearing on breastfeeding success. The value placed on breastfeeding is reflected in workplace policies and state legislation. The presence of women in the work force has increased since the Industrial Revolution, and it continues to climb at a fast pace. In 1977, 32 percent of women with a child less than one year of age worked outside the home. In 1982, the percentage had increased to 43 percent and by 1989 the number rose to 52 percent. Employment of mothers of infants and young children could be detrimental to successful breastfeeding. However, there is a paucity of conclusive evidence to show that this is true. What has been shown is that some types of work interfere with breastfeeding more than others. A study by Kurinij and others (1989) of women from Washington, D.C., showed that both black and white women returning to a professional job had a longer duration of breastfeeding after leaving the hospital compared to women returning to sales or technical jobs. The author suggests that professional women have more control over their situation and can achieve a balance between the demands of the job and the demands of breastfeeding, whereas the women who hold clerical, sales, or technical positions have little control over their environment and have more difficulty acclimating to the demands of the job and of breastfeeding (Kurinij et al. 1989).

A study by Moore and Jansa (1987) surveyed 29 Fortune 500 companies and phone-interviewed 12 of the companies known to support breastfeeding to examine the types and prevalence of policies that help to support women who breastfeed. The study was small and not generalizable. It did, however, find that of the 25 who responded to the mailed surveys 48 percent had refrigeration, 14 percent allowed infants to breastfeed at work, 14 percent had health care professionals on site, and five percent had electric breast pumps. None had either day care or breaks for breastfeeding. Of the 12 companies interviewed by phone, 63 percent had refrigeration, 43 percent provided space to breastfeed, 75 percent had health care professionals, and 50 percent had electric pumps. Again, none had either day care or breaks for breastfeeding. The authors note that there is not generalized support for breastfeeding, nor is there a national parental leave policy for this purpose. Since the country is without a standard of procedure for maternity leave and breastfeeding practice, obtaining the goal of increasing breastfeeding incidence to 75 percent by the year 2000 will be very difficult. Additionally, there needs to be more research in this area, with the involvement of institutions, to measure effectiveness of breastfeeding programs (Moore and Jansa 1987).

Beyond the hospital and the workplace, social influences on breastfeeding can include use of the law. Currently four states protect the right of women to breastfeed in public: Florida, New York, North Carolina, and California. Until 1994, when Florida passed a law to enhance breastfeeding services in hospitals, encouraging "Baby Friendly" designations, and permitting breastfeeding in public, breastfeeding was officially viewed as indecent exposure by this state as it is in many others. New York, North Carolina, and California have followed Florida's example.

Within the Hispanic population there has been a marked decline in breastfeeding. The strongest association with this decline is with increased acculturation. The Mexican-American component of the Hispanic Health and Nutrition Examination Survey (HHANES-MA) was used to study the incidence and duration of breastfeeding. It was shown that English-speaking Hispanic households, which reflect a high degree of acculturation, had a lower rate of breastfeeding than did Spanish-speaking households. Furthermore, when the head of the household identified himself/herself as a Mexican-American, another indicator of acculturation, there was a negative association with breastfeeding compared to those designating themselves as Mexican, Hispanic, Chicano, Puerto Rican, Cuban, or of another country (John and Martorell 1989). A study by Rassin et al. (1993) also found that individuals with a lower level of acculturation—as measured by language, time in the United States, and association with other Hispanic people—breastfed more. Clearly, modern American society works in a myriad of ways to discourage breastfeeding, even among those culturally predisposed to breastfeed. Effecting change and promoting breastfeeding challenges the public health establishment and the nation.

Contraindications

Physiologically, almost all women can breastfeed. Ninety-nine percent of women who try breastfeeding are successful. There are very rare instances when a woman cannot breastfeed due to pathophysiological reasons. There are other reasons, however, that a woman may not be able to breastfeed or should be advised against breastfeeding. Four such contraindications are most notable. The first three are: when a mother is addicted to drugs, such as cocaine or phencyclidine (PCP); when a mother takes more than a minimal amount of alcohol; or when a mother is receiving certain therapeutic or diagnostic agents, such as radioactive elements and cancer chemotherapy.

In addition, women infected with human immunodeficiency virus (HIV) should not breastfeed to avoid transmission of HIV to a child who may not be infected (ADA 1993). Note, however, that this is not the case in situations where there is an otherwise high infant morbidity and mortality due to infectious diseases and malnutrition (ADA, 1993; Kennedy et al. 1990; U.S. DHHS 1992). A meta-analysis of four studies of women who seroconverted to HIV positivity postnatally, either through blood transfusion at birth or by heterosexual transfer, showed that the estimated risk of transmitting HIV through breast milk is 29 percent (95 percent CI 16–42 percent). This study also revealed that breastfeeding, when there was a positive HIV status prenatally, increased the risk of transmission in utero or during delivery by 14 percent (95 percent CI 7–22 percent) (Dunn et al. 1992). The exact mechanism of transmission is not known. It is believed that transmission may take place upon contact with the HIV before the mother makes antibodies, or when the mother is manifesting disease symptoms. In any case, where high infant death rates are attributable to infectious diseases, namely diarrhea, the mortality rate from bottle-feeding can be as high as 15/100,000, with a relative risk of 4, producing twice as many deaths (Kennedy et al. 1990). Therefore, the risk of not breastfeeding outweighs the risk of infection with HIV, and breastfeeding should be promoted, even where the HIV epidemic is severe (Dunn et al. 1992; Goldfarb 1993; Kennedy et al. 1990).

POLICIES AND PROGRAMS

Introduction

Nutrition policy and programs are greatly influenced by agriculture policy, food policy, and politics (Johnson 1994; Pinstrup-Andersen 1993). The issue of food access and availability has become emotionally, morally, and economically based. This section will review the history and application of two nutrition policies—the food guide pyramid and the RDAs. Furthermore, two examples of program delivery to achieve these policies will be illustrated in the context of MCH.

There are two primary nutrition program strategies in the United States: education or dietary guidance and the delivery of food, in bulk or prepared. Nutrition programs usually consider both. Generally, if food is delivered, it is not without dietary and nutrition information. In the recent past nutritionists emphasized nutrition in education strategies; however, there is a growing trend to emphasize making food nutritious, tasty, convenient, and easy to prepare. Such messages are more likely to be received with enthusiasm and to succeed in terms of participation and dietary change.

Dietary Guidance

Within the discipline of nutrition there are two central tools that are the basis of food and nutrition education—the food guide and the RDA. The food guide describes the type of food and amounts for daily consumption. Currently the Food Guide Pyramid (Figure 12–1), which divides food into five categories with a sixth being foods to avoid or eat in small amounts, is the basis of the U.S. government's nutrition education policy.

Food Guides

History and Purpose

Food guides were first developed in the United States in 1923 and consisted of five groups, later organized into seven. They were developed to help lay people ascertain whether they were eating enough of the right foods to prevent nutrition deficiencies. During the war years food was more scarce, and careful planning was necessary in order to maintain nutrition adequacy in the population. In fact, it was the discovery that more men than expected failed their physical examinations because of undernutrition that led, after the war, to the establishment of the national school lunch and milk programs to prevent this problem in the future.

In the 1950s, when the food guide grouping was reorganized and simplified from seven groups to four, it became known as the Basic Four and was central for nutrition education in schools. Nearly every adult was taught the Basic Four, and it was used by food companies in their advertising and packaging. It was not until the early 1970s that nutritionists recognized that excess food intake rather than deficiencies was the primary dietary problem in the United States. Since the Basic Four did not include fat or sugar, people assumed they could eat as much of these as they wanted. The shift to address excess dietary intake began with the publication of Dietary Goals by the Senate Select Committee on Hunger in 1977 (U.S. Senate Select Committee 1977). It was not until the 1980s, when the administrative arms of the government, USDA and the U.S. Department of Health and Human Services, officially released the Dietary Guidelines and established them as policy, that programs began to teach moderation energetically. However, the Dietary Guidelines are not helpful in planning a meal, a day's intake of food, or a weekly food list. For that reason USDA released the Food Pyramid in 1992, which provides dietary guidance to those who wish to eat for their own health and to assist others in doing so. (See Figure 12–1.)

Policy and the Pyramid

As mentioned earlier, nutrition policy is influenced by agriculture policy, food policy, and politics. The changes in the Food Guide Pyramid were scrutinized and debated at every turn. Agricultural interests had a substantial influence on the changes (Nestle 1993). Two commodity groups, dairy and meat, resisted the efforts to limit consumption of their foods even though scientific evidence showed a strong association between animal fat, notably saturated fat, and CVD. Initially dietary cholesterol alone was the focus for dietary change, and people were advised to eat no more than three or four eggs a week. As studies demonstrating the relationship between saturated fat and CVD proliferated, nutritionists began advising individuals to reduce cholesterol *and* saturated fat by selecting reduced fat milk, preferably skim milk, low fat yogurt, and limiting meat intake to two to three ounce portions a day—red meat only three times a week. By 1990 meat consumption was down from 158.7 pounds per capita in 1970 to 130.2 pounds per capita (Raper et al. 1992). Egg consumption has also decreased, from 39.2 pounds per capita in 1970 to 29.6 per capita in 1990. In the mid-1980s, meat consumption leveled off as a result of a high visibility media campaign but resumed its decline after 1985. The dairy industry now offers several reduced fat milks, from among which consumers should select products containing 1 percent milkfat or less. In 1970 whole milk consumption was 2181.2 pounds per capita. In 1990 it was 90.4. Low fat milk went from 50.8 pounds per capita to 131.6.

Implications for MCH

Nutrition has become one of four factors that consumers use in selecting food products, the others being taste, convenience, and price (Food Marketing Institute 1995). For this reason, after the release of the Pyramid, it quickly appeared on food packages. Consumer materials produced by the food industry and trade associations appeared even before USDA materials. The adoption of this new dietary guidance material was immediate and pervasive. The categories of the pyramid are based enough on visible characteristics that children can learn them as well as adults. It can be used both to categorize items in a snack or meal and as a basis for art activities and trips to stores, expanding children's familiarity with foods. The pyramid is the basis of team games in school and the content of games modeled after television quiz shows. The *Journal of Nutrition Education* publishes reports of these applications regularly, which can be accessed through the Educational Resource Information Center (ERIC).

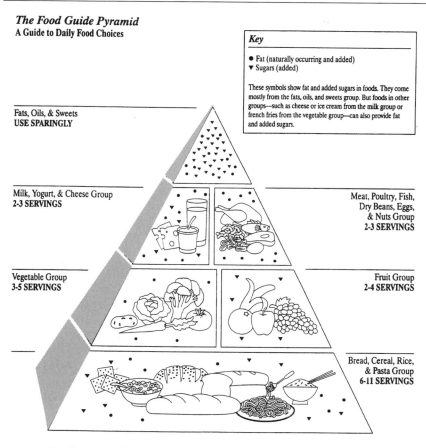

The Food Guide Pyramid
A Guide to Daily Food Choices

Key

● Fat (naturally occurring and added)
▼ Sugars (added)

These symbols show fat and added sugars in foods. They come mostly from the fats, oils, and sweets group. But foods in other groups—such as cheese or ice cream from the milk group or french fries from the vegetable group—can also provide fat and added sugars.

Fats, Oils, & Sweets
USE SPARINGLY

Milk, Yogurt, & Cheese Group
2-3 SERVINGS

Meat, Poultry, Fish,
Dry Beans, Eggs,
& Nuts Group
2-3 SERVINGS

Vegetable Group
3-5 SERVINGS

Fruit Group
2-4 SERVINGS

Bread, Cereal, Rice,
& Pasta Group
6-11 SERVINGS

Looking at the Pieces of the Pyramid

The Food Guide Pyramid emphasizes foods from the five major food groups shown in the three lower sections of the Pyramid. Each of these food groups provides some, but not all, of the nutrients you need. Foods in one group can't replace those in another. No one of these major food groups is more important than another—for good health, you need them all.

Figure 12-1 The USDA Food Guide Pyramid. *Source:* Reprinted from the USDA.

Recommended Dietary Allowances (RDAs)

History and Purpose

The second tool integral to food and nutrition education in the United States is the RDAs. The RDAs differ from the Food Guides by focusing on specific nutrient intakes instead of food portion sizes. Adopted in 1941 after the National Nutrition Conference RDAs were published by the Food and Nutrition Board of the National Academy of Sciences, they are reviewed every 10 years. As the standard against which dietary adequacy is measured, RDAs include the vitamins, minerals, and calories for which there are enough data to establish a recommended daily dietary intake for various age and gender groups. One or two nutrients are added with each revision as the scientific literature provides adequate evidence of the critical role of those nutrients and the amount the human body requires.

Characteristics

In the most recent publication of the RDAs there were 19 nutrients with recommended values. There were also seven nutrients with ranges that are likely to be important, but for which there is not enough evidence to establish recommended values.

Issues

While the field of nutrition describes the nutritional status of the population more precisely each year, the food supply is changing at a rapid pace. Computer technology is providing the system to distribute quickly new information about the nutrient content of foods. The *Food Labeling Act of 1992* mandated a rapid change in the nutrition information required on food labels. Food composition analysis technology and rapid information exchange made implementation possible within the proposed time frame of two years. With the advent of methods to substitute noncaloric sweeteners for sugar and to introduce fat substitutes with acceptable texture and flavor compounds, food product innovations multiplied in food markets.

Research studies have shown associations between dietary intake and certain disease conditions. Scientists often assume that the nutrient they know something about is the factor that is making the difference. However, this is not always the case. For example, studies show an inverse association between cruciferous vegetables and the development of cancer. Scientists assumed that beta-carotene, which was high in those vegetables, was the factor that made the difference. A clinical trial was mounted among a large population in New England where one group received a large dose of beta-carotene and another group did not. In preliminary results the experimental group did not do any better or worse than the control (Lappe 1982). Very likely there are other constituents in the vegetables and combinations of constituents that make the difference. Because of issues such as these, the best dietary recommendation to the public is to eat whole foods, close to where they were grown.

Implications for MCH

The RDAs are used as the criteria for nutrient adequacy in the meals served in the School Meals Program and for menu systems used in the Food Stamp Program. There are several caveats for the use of these standards. They are for healthy individuals, they are for groups of people, and they should be compared to dietary data that include several days of intake or a large sample. The Percent Daily Values that are computed from the RDAs are used as the standard. See Chapters 5 and 8 for nutrition problems among children and adolescents.

Three Food and Nutrition Programs
Special Supplemental Food Program for Women, Infants, and Children (WIC)

History

Assurance of food availability to low-income or disenfranchised populations is a growing concern in the United States. (See Hunger Section above.) Nutrition problems—either deficiencies or excesses—have been identified but are difficult to combat because of the many barriers to food access. There may not be enough money to purchase the food, or the population may live in a neighborhood where the food is not sold or is too high-priced. These factors are described in more detail above. At the 1969 White House Conference on Food, Nutrition, and Health, this problem was made very clear and led to the expansion of the Food Stamp Program and to the WIC, renamed in 1994 as the Supplemental Nutrition Program for Women, Infants, and Children. Studies have demonstrated the effect of inadequate nutrition during pregnancy on birth outcomes, including lower birth weight and prematurity. Inadequate nutritional intake by newborns and older infants also puts normal development at risk because of the rapid brain growth that occurs from birth until age two. Along with the possibility of nutritionally compromised brain growth, the most common nutrient deficiency of children below five years of age, iron deficiency, may further jeopardize cognitive development. Therefore, children below five years of age are included in the WIC population because of the potential harm that undernutrition has on growth and learning.

Characteristics

The WIC program was designed to give a woman and/or a child's caretaker a voucher or "check" with a list of approved foods and amounts to be purchased at participating food stores. A certain amount of food is approved for the certified person for six months, at which time she needs to return for recertification. For pregnant women and children, those foods are milk, eggs, cheese, cereal, and fruit juice. The food store has a list of brands that are acceptable for purchase. The determination is based on their concentration of the target nutrients—protein, iron, calcium, and vitamin C. Breastfeeding mothers may continue to get food supplements for up to six months postpartum. Infants may be given the infant formula that meets their needs, and foods are added progressively up to age one. Each participant or caretaker in the program must have two nutrition education program contacts every six months, when she must return to the agency for recertification. If the food supply is not limited among these participants, after six or 12 months on the program the nutritional risk is often rectified. However, if the participant leaves the program, she is likely to be back in several months because her low income puts her at nutritional risk again.

Eligibility for WIC is met in most states if the pregnant woman, infant, or child has an income below 185 percent of poverty and has a nutritional risk factor that includes specific medical conditions or an inadequate diet. In 1993 approximately 54 percent of eligible pregnant women were being served, 93 percent of eligible infants, and 49 percent of eligible children (FRAC 1993). The WIC program requires referral for medical services, so many programs are associated with primary health care for children and women.

Policy Implications/Evaluation

WIC was controversial from its inception (Brown et al. 1992). Although the purchase of foods included in the program supported domestic agriculture, critics of the program protested its "free lunch" appearance. In order to answer questions about the benefits of the WIC program, a large, national evaluation, funded by USDA, was designed and conducted by Dr. David Rush and the Research Triangle Institute. The study demonstrated that infants whose mothers were on the WIC program weighed an additional 28 grams at birth, a statistically significant difference. In addition, other studies showed that a one dollar investment in WIC was worth three dollars of Medicaid money saved in hospital costs that the lower weight infants would have incurred without WIC (Buescher et al. 1993).

Whether a food was included in the WIC program became big business because of the volume of food being purchased by program participants each month. Breakfast cereals were fortified with the nutrients to the level that made them eligible to be included on the WIC approved food lists. Iron was the most important nutrient. Infant formula vouchers were sought by mothers, and as infant formula steadily rose in price, the vouchers became very valuable. In addition, the WIC market share of infant formula was one-third of the total sales.

Infant formula rebates, which began in 1988, forced the formula companies to bid for a state's business for one to five years. With three, and later four, formula companies putting in competing bids, the WIC program in the state could save substantial funds that could then be used to add more clients to the program.

Implications for MCH

Participants in WIC like the program, so it becomes a good drawing card for the population that MCH programs want to serve. For this reason, immunization, injury prevention, and early intervention programs are pairing up with WIC to increase its health promotion potential. Sometimes abuse of the program or lack of participation by eligible people may come to the attention of an MCH staff person. Referral of eligible people and notification of possible abuses to the WIC staff can lead to important improvements in the program. If a health facility for children or pregnant women doesn't have a WIC program or doesn't know where to refer clients to to find one, advocacy by MCH personnel on behalf of the program is needed.

School Nutrition Programs

History

Congress established the National School Lunch Program (NSLP) in 1946, recognizing that a large proportion of children were not receiving an adequate lunch and possibly less than desirable breakfasts and dinners. It passed laws and allocated funds to establish a program to make low priced milk available in all schools and a hot lunch in as many schools as possible. This program has grown so that 25,073,570 children in public and private schools participate in the NSLP. School districts are subsidized for all lunches. Some children receive a free lunch and some a reduced price lunch based on ability to pay. Forty-four percent of the children pay the "full charge," but even those lunches are subsidized a small amount.

Characteristics

Until 1995 participating school districts planned menus that followed the USDA criteria, and they were evaluated for approval by the State Education Agency. The guidelines required that a menu consist of five items—a protein food, bread, vegetable or fruit, dessert, and milk. In the 1970s plate waste (food being thrown away) in the school meal program was reaching unacceptable levels. There were efforts to design menus that children liked; however, this did not totally rectify the problem. Now the school meal regulations allow children to select three of the five items on the menu rather than requiring them to take all five, knowing that they were going to throw away at least two. Since 1995 school meal managers have been able to plan their menus using the food groups or to meet a nutrient standard—e.g., one-third of the RDA for each required nutrient. This will require a nutrient calculation of each menu, which is now feasible with computerized nutrient analysis software. However, implementation of the nutrient method will require training of school food service managers, since a significant proportion of them across the country will be unfamiliar with computer technology.

The impetus for this change is again a problem of excess rather than deficiency. The fat, salt, and sugar content of school meals has grown to unacceptable levels. In an effort to serve food that children will eat, school food managers have found that this is most likely to be pizza, french fries, hamburgers, hot dogs, and a la carte items such as ice cream, cookies, and candy. However, these foods are all high in one or more of the items to avoid. Although this is a dilemma for the school meal program, the problem extends well beyond the schools. This means that there are a substantial number of young people now, and there will be more in the future, who have poor food habits. They will not try new foods, they have developed a one or two taste palate, and they have no idea how to start or where to go should they want to try new foods. Fat, salt, and sugar are problems because their high satiety value (feeling full) moves other nutrients out of the diet. Indeed, individuals with these food habits are deficient in vitamins and minerals that are critical for their health and the health of children they will raise. They are more susceptible to CVD and cancer at an early age. This is a problem that every MCH professional needs to deal with whether through parents, teachers, physicians, or the children themselves.

Even if the school meal program were one that nutritionists could endorse, one that offered foods that school children liked, those children who receive free or reduced price meals have to deal with the stigma attached to their participation by virtue of the payment arrangement. The only way to do away with the stigma is to give everyone a free meal, or have everyone pay the same low price by first getting the money into the hands of the poor children.

The Food Stamp Program

Purpose

The Food Stamp Program (FSP) is the primary government program designed to improve the nutrition of low-income individuals and families. In general, households with incomes below 135 percent of poverty are eligible for food stamps. The amount is revised each year after July when the annual poverty income guidelines are released by the Department of Labor. At the food stamp office, the household's net income is calculated and the program assumes that 30 percent of the income is spent on food. The difference between the amount of money available and the cost of the Thrifty Food Plan prepared by USDA is the value of the food stamps issued to the household (Cleveland and Kerr 1988). "Certification" of the household can be for 1 to 24 months. Prior to the expiration of the certification, the household is notified and a household member may make an appointment with the program to apply for recertification.

Characteristics

Food stamps can be used to purchase most foods at participating stores. They may not be used to purchase items such as diapers, cigarettes, household cleaning supplies, pet food, prepared foods, or alcoholic beverages. Participating stores are interviewed and monitored by the USDA. If a store is found to be violating the rules, it will be discontinued from the FSP. If the store also redeems WIC vouchers, the WIC program discontinues automatically.

Issues

There are two ongoing issues with the FSP. One is the stigma associated with using the coupons, and the second is fraud. The more common acts of fraud are selling food stamps for cash and use of food coupons for disallowed items. Theft is a personal hazard for recipients. Currently a number of states are using the results of pilot studies to implement a debit card issuance system. The debit card minimizes sale for cash and theft since an identification verification will be necessary for its use. A recipient will receive a debit card to use at the food store in place of food stamp coupons. This will also decrease stigma since debit cards are becoming available for use in food stores generally, and many stores are already using credit cards. The threat of being discontinued from the program is the incentive for food stores to not overcharge the FSP. Nutrition education with cost and health in mind is necessary for food stamp recipients so they will receive the largest nutritional benefit from the food purchased.

The amount of money issued to the recipient is also a problem. The program assumes that the difference between the Thrifty Food Plan amount and the food stamp value issued is spent on food. In fact, the money available in a household is frequently used for emergencies that arise such as transportation to employment or to a health appointment, school fees for trips or special services, and household bills such as telephone, heat, and or power. In addition, the Thrifty Food Plan requires economical food purchasing, planning, and time for preparation since many of the menus use recipes requiring preparation "from scratch." (The estimated per meal per person value is approximately 84 cents [Cleveland and Kerr 1988].) When middle or upper class individuals follow the menus and recipes prescribed for food stamp participants, their comments include that they are possible to do, but that the menus are boring, there is no allowance for eating out, every household member must carry lunch made at home, and that preparing the meals requires too much time.

Periodically it is recommended that the program be "cashed out," i.e., included in the welfare benefit a household receives. However, recipients, particularly mothers, insist that the program retain the food coupons or debit cards so the benefit must be spent on food; therefore, the recipient could not be forced to yield to pressures that it be spent on other expenses. As it is now, the value of the food stamp benefit issued is less than the cost of the Thrifty Food Plan, so it is not surprising that households, particularly those who are eating at emergency food locations, report that the food stamps don't last the month.

THE SOCIAL PROCESS MODEL: AN APPLICATION

Introduction

The ultimate objective of public health nutrition programs is to maintain and improve the nutritional well-being of the population. As a professional one often will focus on a subgroup of the population, such as pregnant women and infants, school children, or all of the people in a geographic area, whether a neighborhood or a state. Food, the basic component of nutrition, is consumed differently by different people for a number of reasons. As a professional whose purpose it is to see that every person knows what he/she should eat and how one can purchase or grow and/or prepare it, one will need to review a number of factors in the population in order to determine whether the population's nutritional well-being is adequate. Recently a model has been developed that addresses and organizes three factors, or "basic dynamics," of a society—the Social Process Model. (See Figure 12–2.)

The basic dynamics from which the Social Process Model is constructed include economic, political, and cultural processes. Each of the processes in turn includes three underlying activities: the economic process (resources, production, and distribution); the political (order, justice, and welfare); and the cultural process (wisdom, style, and symbols).

The Social Process Model is a basic organizational tool used to extend the description of a community from one dimension to a nine-dimensional design. It is brief enough to be remembered but inclusive enough to expand a discussion or plan to be multidimensional. It triggers the user to see the "big picture," to identify network possibilities, and to form well-rounded coalitions for stronger program impact. Thinking from a multidimensional context leads to more effectively integrated programs, and the synergy from this connected activity energizes participants and programs. Breadth is critical in nutrition planning as the reader will see below because, even when people know what they should eat, this knowledge alone cannot improve nutritional well-being (Foster 1992). Foods needed may not be available in the stores where people shop or sell for a price they can afford. People may not have money to buy the food or may not know how to prepare it. Perhaps their family is unfamiliar with the food and won't eat unknown foods.

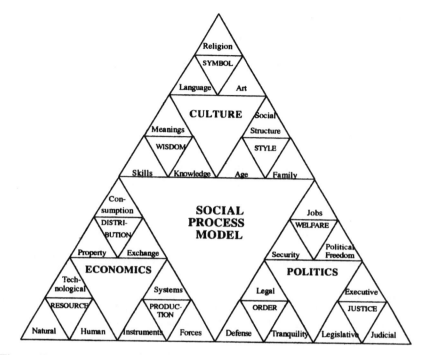

Figure 12–2 The Social Process Model.

Economic Process

A community's economic, political, and cultural processes are present in community systems. The *Economic Process* in a community is the system that delivers resources (material and human), by producing usable products, and distributing them throughout the community. One can use the process to describe the economic activity of the population or community that affects the food and nutrition systems. The questions that describe the process include

- What is the rate of employment?
- Where do residents work?
- What are the residents' occupations?
- What major businesses or employers are in the community?
- What is the number of employees at each?
- What are the transportation systems that the food producers, distributors, and consumers depend upon?

Political Process

The *Political Process* in the community is the system that maintains order and justice and responds to the community's concerns and needs, including systems that provide for the general welfare of the citizens (both resources and services), such as those that ensure the availability of health services and housing for the community. The elected representatives as well as government agencies are obligated to allocate public revenues in a way that meets the community's needs, and they are responsive to the will of the majority. The model describes a community's political process by supplying specific data to answer the following questions:

- Who are the elected representatives of the area?
- Who are the food, welfare, or health legislative aides?
- Which public agencies provide income maintenance services, and where are they located?
- What are the health facilities in the community—acute care, preventive care, extended care facilities?
- Are there public residential facilities—correctional, rehabilitation, psychiatric?
- What citizen committees are there advising local or state health services? Who are the people on the committees? Do they have a nutrition committee? Who are the staff people for these committees?
- What is the housing stock like in the area?
- Is there a local newspaper? What is its reach, number of subscribers? Is there a food and nutrition column?
- Which newspaper and which column is most popular in the community?

Cultural Process

The *Cultural Process* in the community, which affects nutrition, includes the educational systems for all ages; social groups, based on (but not limited by) ethnicity, age, occupation, and gender; and symbolic activities, which include art, language, and religious institutions. As with economic and political processes, data about the cultural process will answer the following questions:

- What are the agencies (with a contact person) that provide child day care both in homes and in centers?
- Who is on the community school board?
- Who is the superintendent, the school lunch supervisor, and the principal of the schools?
- What is the reading level of each grade? What is done, and when, with children who are not reading at grade level?
- How are children who don't speak English handled?

- Are there computers in the schools?
- How much television do children watch? Do they have homework?
- What recreation is there?
- What is the educational level of the adults in the community?
- How many children are in an average family? How many single parent families are there?
- Are there different neighborhoods that hold to ethnic traditions? What are they, where are they, and what are some of their centers of community activities?
- What happens to old people? What happens to teenagers? Are there gangs? Are children left unsupervised?
- What happens to the women? Do they work?
- What professional groups are there for people to be a part of? What voluntary/civic groups are there, and who can join?
- How many religious buildings are there? What faiths are represented and what are their numbers?
- Are there libraries? Art galleries? Are there murals in the community? What does the space look like—is it cluttered, lush, clean, or filthy; are there litter barrels or is there only litter; do the drains in the street work? Are there parks? What condition are they in? Who uses them?

Application of the Social Process Model to Food and Nutrition Systems

Within each of the economic, political, and cultural processes described above, there are food and nutrition systems. The food supply system of the community is part of the *Economic Process* and is described by answering these questions:

- Are there food-producing areas in the vicinity—farms, gardens?
- From how far away does the food come—from where and how much?
- Are there farmers' markets? Is the food warehoused and, if so, where and for how long?
- How does the food get into the area?
- Where are the major distribution points? Are they in the vicinity or outside the area?
- What is the profile of retail food stores, including specialty shops like bakeries, fruit and vegetable stores, meat shops? Are there thrift stores?
- Are there large national chain supermarkets? Are there local chain food markets? Are there small groceries?
- How do prices on several common food items, like milk, bread, dry cereal, apples, etc., compare? Are some small groceries more costly than others?
- What is the quality of the food?
- Describe the restaurants of the area, and categorize them as inexpensive, mid-range, or expensive in price.

- Do people outside of the area come to the area to eat?
- Are there diners, coffee shops, and low-cost ethnic restaurants?
- What restaurant chains are in the community?
- What are the prices of several common items such as hamburgers, milk, coke, fries, and salad?

Several of the food and nutrition programs whose data are collected in the *Political Process* have been discussed, specifically WIC and school nutrition programs. They are categorized as political because they are directly controlled by the electoral process, not the free enterprise system that controls the marketplace. However, since these programs provide a source of food, they are indirectly included in the food supply system. In the Political Process the focus is on the location and number of nutrition personnel. Beyond food and nutrition education programs requiring nutritionists, the primary location of nutritionists is in health care services and residential units. Nutritionists may be found in private nutrition practices, physician practices, ambulatory care facilities, health centers, health departments, health maintenance organizations, acute care hospitals, residential institutions such as correctional and child care, and special rehabilitative residences for alcohol abuse, psychiatric illness, and other chronic health problems. Additionally, nutritionists are employed by social service agencies and agencies for the elderly. The following questions can be asked:

- Do all stores take food stamps and WIC vouchers?
- Who are the nutritionists in the area? Where do they work?

Within the *Cultural Process* there are multiple mechanisms, organizations, and institutions whereby nutrition information can be delivered, including regular meetings or informal gatherings. The schools are a natural setting for disseminating information, both in classrooms and lunchrooms. The following questions are asked to assess where nutrition information is or can be disseminated.

- Is there a district curriculum coordinator of nutrition, science, or health who can facilitate the use of nutrition curriculum materials by teachers?
- Is there a nutrition committee that makes recommendations about lunch items? Is there a system designed to better meet the needs of students and teachers? Have the schools had some special food and nutrition events?
- Have the elderly meal programs, the day care programs for preschoolers, and after-school programs had nutrition education events?
- Is there a local dietetic association? Are there food and nutrition members of the local home economics association? Is there a Society for Nutrition Education affiliate or members? Do local food and nutrition councils serve as a source of nutrition information and resource people?
- Are there nutrition professional training programs, which would be a source of student trainees who could carry out programs in the community?

- What ethnic events occur in the community and what are the most popular foods served at them?
- Are there religious organizations and service organizations that offer free public gathering space in the community? Are they available for nutrition education events?
- Is there an artists' group that has shown an interest in food and food-related themes in its work or other activities?
- Is there dramatic activity where food might be a theme, or could food be related to the dramatic activities?

With this description of the community, a professional can develop a plan, set priorities, select areas of work, and recruit community members and leaders to develop interventions in some detail. The Social Process Model can assist in the analysis of a community as well as provide a framework for organizational purposes. From an analytical perspective one can review each of the processes in the community identifying overactive, missing, or adequate activities. For example, the *Economic Process* in nutrition includes agriculture and all of the issues around environmental tradeoffs to produce foodstuffs required by a population. In the 1960s there was a strong shift to vegetarian practices when consumers realized that it took 16 bushels of grain to produce one pound of meat (Lappe 1982). Food processing issues arise, including the energy used to process a food and ship it from parts quite distant to the consumption point. Finally, there are many issues surrounding the retailing of food: advertising, location of grocery stores, quality of product provided, point of purchase education, transportation, and storage.

Regarding nutrition, the *Political Process* centers on accessibility and availability of the food supply. Examples of inequity of access occur due to class, race or ethnicity, gender, and age. Rooted in the Political Process, food assistance programs also relate to the distribution of food (economic) and the knowledge and acceptability of the program (cultural). There are also issues of access to information, which appear in the numerous barriers confronted when accessing the welfare system (political). Computers and mail systems to provide information are integral to the proper operation of the political process.

The *Cultural Process* has historically been the primary focus of nutrition professionals. This includes nutrition education regarding knowledge and skills about nutrients and cooking. Where the food is eaten—home, school, or in restaurants—is critical for the design of interventions. The reasons why people eat and the meaning the food has for a person is critical. Food can be symbolic, representing something such as celebration, love, repentance, or guilt. To the extent that it does represent something cultural, food becomes a critical component in communication or art.

FUTURE ISSUES

The nutrition problems of women are often identified at the time of their pregnancies when they are likely to see a nutritionist or other health professional who screens and assesses their nutritional status. However, the recommended time to achieve long-term dietary change is during the interconceptional period and/or during family planning care rather than during pregnancy. Therefore, the nutrition programs in interconceptional care are the preferred locations for the implementation of dietary change strategies. These strategies include environmental changes as well as behavioral changes among women. For example, the importance of folic acid in the first two months of a pregnancy means that women need to be eating an adequate diet which, loosely defined for folic acid, means five servings of fruit and vegetables, including dark green vegetables and at least six servings of grain products a day. Because the diets of women in general are inadequate in folic acid, vitamin supplementation or folic acid fortification of a commonly eaten food product is a public health nutrition strategy being discussed at this time. If women were eating nutritionally adequate diets, these strategies would be unnecessary. Hence a primary prevention dietary strategy for the future is effective nutrition programs during interconceptional care.

Adequate growth among all of the MCH populations was discussed in this chapter, and it will continue to be an issue. As public health professionals we have not yet stopped the steady increase of obesity among women and children. The practices that produce this steady rise are linked to the availability of food in retail markets, the high-priced, effective food advertising campaigns, the high-stress lives that families lead, and the decreased physical activity of the nation. Although it is the individual who puts the food into his or her mouth, the forces listed above exert powerful influences on that action. The environmental strategies of public health nutrition are needed in order to create a climate that gives consumers a chance to make healthful choices. As discussed in this chapter, the reverse of obesity, excessive thinness, also persists in our society and requires environmental changes that promote diverse and realistic body images, particularly for young women. Basic to both of these situations is the need to promote healthful food choices at all points of purchase. The increasing popularity of eating outside of the home means that we need to pay attention to all prepared food outlets. This includes "take-out" food that may be eaten at home as well as restaurants and the food programs that have made significant contributions to the nutritious intake of women and children. The NSLP reaches 25 million children each day and needs to model health-promoting food choices. It has been reduced to paying its own way and has become dependent on the purchase of high fat, high sugar food items to balance the budget. A recent survey reported on National Public Radio of the U.S. population reports that 35 percent of the respondents eat pizza for breakfast.

This is one indication of the extent to which food choices are no longer traditional. Nontraditional food patterns can support health but programs of dietary change need to deal with the real dietary practices and forces that promote those practices. Consumers, including women and children, are increasingly forced into a daily food pattern that does not support their health.

Finally, public health professionals must be vigilant both about the nutritional quality of available food and the accessibility of nutritious food. There are issues regarding what is added to a food during its growth and manufacture, e.g., pesticides, and what is taken out in processing that may not yet have been identified as necessary for growth. Issues of equity in access in nutritious, affordable food in rural areas and low income urban centers continue to plague our efforts to support health through an adequate dietary intake. Nutrition science has made important contributions to the growth and development of the maternal and child population. The strategies to implement the science to date have primarily been through individual efforts by the practitioner and the patient. The future requires that we step back, design, and implement primary and secondary prevention strategies that will ensure healthful food choices for women and children in particular.

REFERENCES

Anonymous. 1993. Position of the American Dietetic Association: Promotion and support of breast-feeding. *Journal of American Dietary Association* 93:467–469.

Brown, J.L., and D. Allen. 1988. Hunger in America. *Annual Review of Public Health* 9:503–526.

Brown, J.L. et al. 1992. The politics of hunger: When science and ideology clash. *International Journal of Health Services*, 22:221–237.

Bryant, C.A. et al. 1992. A strategy for promoting breastfeeding among economically disadvantaged women and adolescents. *NAACOG's Clinical Issues* 3:723–730.

Buescher, P.A. et al. 1993. Prenatal WIC participants can reduce low birth weight and newborn medicine costs: A cost-benefits analysis of WIC participants in North Carolina. *Journal of American Dietary Association* 93:163–166.

Campbell, C.C. 1991. Food insecurity: A nutritional outcome or a predictor variable? *Journal of Nutrition* 121:408–415.

Canning, H. et al. 1966. Obesity—its possible effect on college acceptance. *New England Journal of Medicine* 275:1172–1174.

Citizens Board of Inquiry into Hunger and Malnutrition in the U.S. 1968. *Hunger, U.S.A.* Boston: Beacon Press.

Cleveland, L., and R.L. Kerr. 1988. Development and uses of the USDA food plans. *Journal of Nutrition Education* 20:232–238.

Dewey, K.G. et al. 1993. Breast-fed infants are leaner than formula-fed infants at 1 year of age: The DARLING study. *American Journal of Clinical Nutrition* 57:140–145.

Dietz, W.H. 1987. Childhood obesity. *Annual NY Academy of Science* 499:47–54.

Dunn, D.T. et al. 1992. Risk of human immunodeficiency virus type 1 transmission through breastfeeding. *Lancet* 340:585–588.

Ellis, D.J. 1992a. Supporting breastfeeding: How to implement agency change. *NAACOG's Clinical Issues* 3:560–564.

Ellis, D.J. 1992b. The impact of agency policies and protocols on breastfeeding. *NAACOG's Clinical Issues* 3:5552–5559.

Epstein, L.H. et al. 1990a. Five-year follow-up of family-based behavioral treatments for childhood obesity. *Journal of Clinical Psychology* 58:661–664.

Epstein, L.H. et al. 1990b. Ten-year follow-up of behavioral, family-based treatment for obese children. *Journal of American Medical Association* 264:2519–2523.

Food Marketing Institute. 1995. *Trends in the U.S.* Washington, DC: Research Division, The Institute.

Food Research and Action Center. 1991. *Community childhood hunger identification project: A survey of childhood hunger in the U.S.* Washington, DC: Author, March.

Food Research and Action Center. 1993. *WIC works, Let's make it work for everyone.* Washington, DC: Author.

Foster P. 1992. *The world food problem: Tackling the causes of undernutrition in the third world.* Boulder, CO: Lynne Rienner Publishers, Adamine Press.

Freed, G.L. et al. 1992. Prenatal determination of demographic and attitudinal factors regarding feeding practice in an indigent population. *American Journal of Perinatology* 9:420–429.

Goldfarb, J. 1993. Breastfeeding. AIDS and other infectious diseases. *Clinical Perinatology* 20:225–243.

Gortmaker, S.L. et al. 1987. Increasing pediatric obesity in the U.S. *American Journal of Diseases in Children* 141:535–540.

Gortmaker, S.L. et al. 1990. Inactivity, diet, and the fattening of America. *Journal of American Dietary Association* 90:1247–1252.

Gortmaker, S.L. et al. 1993. Social and economic consequences of overweight in adolescence and young adulthood. *New England Journal of Medicine* 329:1008–1012.

John, M., and R. Martorell. 1989. Incidence and duration of breast-feeding in Mexican-American infants, 1970–1982. *American Journal of Clinical Nutrition* 50:868–874.

Johnson, S.R. 1994. How nutrition policy affects food and agricultural policy. *Journal of Nutrition* 124 (Suppl 9):1871–1877.

Jones, F., and M. Green. 1993. Baby friendly care. *Canadian Nurse* 89:36–39.

Kennedy, K.I. et al. 1990. Do the benefits of breastfeeding outweigh the risk of postnatal transmission of HIV via breast milk? *Tropical Doctor* 20:25–29.

Klesges, R.C. et al. 1991. Parental influence on food selection in young children and its relationships to childhood obesity. *American Journal of Clinical Nutrition* 53:859–864.

Kotz, K., and M. Story. 1994. Food advertisements during children's Saturday morning television programming: Are they consistent with dietary recommendations? *Journal of American Dietary Association* 94:1296–1300.

Kurinij, N. et al. 1989. Does maternal employment affect breast-feeding? *American Journal of Public Health* 79:1247–1250.

Lappe, F.M. 1982. *Diet for a small planet.* New York: Ballentine Books.

Medford Declaration to end hunger in the U.S. 1992. *Nutrition Reviews* 50:240–242.

Mellin, L.M. et al. 1987. Adolescent obesity intervention: validation of the SHAPEDOWN program. *Journal of American Dietary Association* 87:333–338.

Moore, J.F., and N. Jansa. 1987. A survey of policies and practices in support of breastfeeding mothers in the workplace. *Birth* 14:191–195.

National Research Council, Committee on Diet and Health. 1989. Obesity and eating disorders. In *Diet and Health*. Washington, DC: National Academy Press.

Nestle, M. 1993. Food lobbies, the food pyramid, and U.S. nutrition policy. *International Journal of Health Services* 23:483–496.

Nestle, M., and S. Guttmacher. 1992. Hunger in the United States: Rationale, methods, and policy implications of state hunger surveys. *Journal of Nutrition Education* 24:185–225.

Newman, J. 1990. Breastfeeding problems associated with the early introduction of bottles and pacifiers. *Journal of Human Lactation* 6:59–63.

Pérez-Escamilla, R. et al. 1994. Infant feeding policies in maternity wards and their effect on breastfeeding success: An analytical overview. *American Journal of Public Health* 84:89–97.

Pinstrup-Andersen, P. 1993. *The political economy of food and nutrition policies.* Baltimore: The International Food Policy Research Institute.

Pipes, P.L. 1989. *Nutrition in infancy and childhood,* 4th ed. St. Louis, MO: Times Mirror/Mosby College Publishing.

Poppendieck, J.E. 1992. Hunger and public policy: Lessons from the great depression. *Journal of Nutrition Education* 24:6S–11S.

Prentice, A.M. et al. 1988. Are current dietary guidelines for young children a prescription for overfeeding? *Lancet* 2:1066–1068.

Radimer, K.L. et al. 1992. Understanding hunger and developing indicators to assess it in women and children. *Journal of Nutrition Education* 24:36S–44S.

Raper, N. et al. 1992. *Nutrient content of the U.S. food supply, 1909–1990.* Washington, DC: USDA, Home Economics Research Report No. 50.

Rassin, D.K. et al. 1993. Acculturation and breastfeeding on the United-States-Mexico border. *American Journal of Medical Science* 306:28–34.

Snell, B.J. et al. 1992. The association of formula samples given at hospital discharge with the early duration of breastfeeding. *Journal of Human Lactation* 8:67–72.

Snyder, M.P. et al. 1994. Reducing the fat content of ground beef in a school food service setting. *Journal of American Dietary Association* 94:1135–1139.

Stunkard, A., and V. Burt. 1967. Obesity and the body image: II. age at onset of disturbances in the body image. *American Journal of Psychiatry* 123:1443–1447.

U.S. Bureau of the Census. 1994. *Statistical abstract of the U.S. 1994.* The National Data Book, 114th ed. Washington, DC: Government Printing Office.

U.S. Department of Health and Human Services. Public Health Service. 1992. *Healthy People 2000: National health promotion and disease prevention objectives.* Boston: Jones and Bartlett, Publishers.

U.S. Senate Select Committee on Nutrition and Human Needs. 1977. *Dietary goals for the U.S.* Washington, DC: Government Printing Office.

Wadden, T.A., and A.J. Stunkard. 1985. Social and psychological consequences of obesity. *Annals of Internal Medicine* 103:1062–1067.

Worthington-Roberts, B., and S.R. Williams. 1989. *Nutrition in pregnancy and lactation,* 4th ed. St. Louis, MO: Times Mirror/Mosby College Publishing.

Wynder, E.L. et al. 1992. Nutrition: The need to define "optimal" intake as a basis for public policy decisions. *American Journal of Public Health* 82:346–350.

CHAPTER 13

International Maternal and Child Health

B. Cecilia Zapata and Charles J. M. Godue

INTRODUCTION

At the eve of the twenty-first century, an estimated 5.6 billion children, women, and men live on earth (UN, 1994). During the last three decades, the world has undergone far-reaching health and demographic changes. Although significant progress has been made in health-related fields including public health, medicine, and medical technologies and progress is evident at country as well as international levels, the benefits of these advances are not distributed globally. Worldwide, many countries face economic crises, but developing countries are experiencing particularly unfavorable economic conditions. Absolute poverty has increased in many countries. At the same time, the basic resources needed for the well-being of future generations are being depleted at an alarming rate. While everyone will be affected by the depletion of resources, women and children are most at risk due to their subordinate position in most societies. In an effort to assume social and political responsibility, the world community is beginning to appreciate the need for increasing international collaboration to address economic and social issues of sustainable environments including health, economic development, poverty, and equity. In the international arena, women, mothers, and children are greatly affected by worldwide political, social, and economic changes. Thus, maternal and child health (MCH) is directly linked to international health.

One cannot do justice to the complex field of international MCH in one chapter. Accordingly, this chapter will look at a historical perspective on international health and then highlight MCH issues and strategies. The chapter objectives are to view international MCH within a broader perspective and to search for similarities and differences that increase our capacity to resolve problems and address issues affecting these populations in the international MCH arena.

INTERNATIONAL HEALTH: IN SEARCH OF A NEW PARADIGM

The Evolution of International Health: A Brief Historical Overview

Recounting the history of international health represents a complex and somewhat arbitrary task because it relies on what we mean by international health and what we identify as international health activities. Definitions are closely related to the nature of the international system and of the relationships among countries. The modern *nation-state* (to be referred to as *country* or *nation*) formalized around three central features: a clearly defined territory; a population unified by shared symbols and history; and the existence of a legitimate authority for maintaining order within established boundaries. Different nations aimed at being independent and self-sufficient while simultaneously competing with each other for primacy and dominance. By the beginning of the twentieth century, there were only approximately 60 nation-states in the world, and almost one-third of the world's population lived under colonial rule. In the absence of an over-arching international authority, countries were virtually in a permanent state of war with their neighbors. Trade and war constituted the major modes of relations between the countries and the means to acquire wealth and expand territorially. However, periods of peace and relative tranquility allowed trade to flourish during the colonial era.

War and Trade

It should be no surprise then that international health activities from the seventh to the early twentieth centuries could hardly be divested from the interests of war and trade between nations. The development of international health during the colonial era was the result of ferocious competition among western countries. These rivalries fueled major scientific discoveries.

Western Europeans began to research tropical diseases and thus developed *tropical medicine* in order to protect their own people, including military attachés, living in the colonies. For example, in Africa, residential segregation was implemented to protect White colonists from vector-borne diseases like yellow fever (Patterson 1981). In addition, a number of schools of tropical medicine were built in this period. The focus of these schools was on the nature, origin, and transmission of diseases that were new and dangerous to Europeans and were therefore lumped together under the term "fevers." These schools were unconcerned with the introduction into the colonies of European diseases (measles, smallpox, and sexually transmitted diseases (STDs)) that had a devastating impact on local populations. Slowly tropical medicine and public health interventions extended to native populations.

The transmission of diseases from the colonies to the European nations was of greater concern, and the fears grew rapidly with the intensification of trade. As a protective measure, ships were quarantined. Sanitary authorities forced vessels to stay at sea until the crew was either cured or dead. The pressures placed on sanitary authorities by trading companies were considerable. Quarantines did not have a scientific base due to the lack of knowledge concerning disease transmission. At the time, keeping infected individuals isolated was the main mechanism to limit the spread of cholera and the plague. It was not until the First International Sanitary Conference convened in Paris in 1851 that western European nations felt it necessary to adopt and implement a common sanitary code to improve the salubrity of ports and establish fair and consistent measures of quarantine to protect their respective populations (Basch 1990; Howard 1975).

It is interesting to note that similar processes took place in the newly independent countries in the Americas. Brazil and Argentina adopted quarantine policies during the second half of the nineteenth century. An international conference was held in Santiago de Chile in 1887 to discuss measures aimed at controlling diseases while protecting trade among the countries of the southern hemisphere. Similar motives prompted the creation, in 1902, of the Pan American Sanitary Bureau, the oldest international health organization still in existence. A Pan American Sanitary Code was developed in large part to facilitate commerce among different countries within the Americas. Through this code, importance was given to the reporting of prevailing sanitary conditions in the ports and territories, the investigation of outbreaks of communicable diseases, and the promotion of sanitation of the ports. The United States, as a major power in the region, was the unequivocal leader in these endeavors. During the first 30 years of its existence, the director of the Pan American Sanitary Bureau was the surgeon general of the United States. From 1947 to 1959 this post was held by a career professional from the Rockefeller Foundation (Wegman 1977).

The Spanish-American War (1898) and the construction of the Panama Canal at the beginning of the century best illustrate the significance of international health activities for war and trade. The war, which pitted the United States against Spain, was a clear manifestation of the Monroe Doctrine that warned colonial powers not to interfere in the free western and southern hemispheres and protected huge U.S. sugar investments in Cuba. During this war, the United States lost 968 men in battle while 5,438 died from infectious disease. This fact made the United States realize its need to address sanitation and public health issues if venturing overseas (Fee 1987). The construction of the Panama Canal was costly. The company (Compagnie Universelle du Canal Interoceanique) responsible for constructing it declared bankruptcy in 1888, and almost 20,000 workers died from malaria and yellow fever. The vector of malaria and yellow fever was discovered by Carlos Finlay in Cuba and confirmed by Walter Reed in 1902. As a result, a number of ordinances were implemented to eliminate the vector and make the Panama Canal a reality.

The U.S. Presence

Tropical medicine never really got adopted in the Americas, probably because the United States considered it closely related to the colonial enterprises of European nations. The term *international health* first appeared and gradually gained ground following the establishment in 1913 of the International Health Commission (the Commission) of the recently created Rockefeller Foundation. This Commission was crucial in the eradication of hookworm disease. Its main purpose was to extend to other countries the acquired knowledge by the former Rockefeller Health Commission in the United States (Ettling 1981).

Armed with the fascinating and rapidly growing scientific discoveries regarding the transmission of infectious diseases and a genuine belief that progress would result from the development of science, the Commission strove to improve the health situation in Latin America and China. The Commission thought that diseases afflicting human populations were the main impediment to social and economic development. In Latin America, the explicit goal of the Commission was accompanied by other powerful interests, namely the progressive assertion of the American presence in the continent, the displacement of European influence (both cultural and scientific as well as economic), and the promotion and protection of American investments in the region (Solorzano 1992).

The diseases to be tackled by the Commission were selected with great care. In its effort to find the "magic bullet" to control or eliminate a disease, the Commission considered the scientific evidence pointing to an infectious agent and the availability of an intervention to limit its transmission. At the same time, it targeted health problems that had been the object of little attention by European schools. For example, yellow fever and bubonic plague, two deadly diseases, were given high priority because of their impact on trade through the paralysis of ports. Similarly, ankylostomiasis and malaria were of major concern because they affected the productivity of the work force by causing chronic anemia. The Commission achieved unparalleled influence in the region through its field interventions, the development of a network of schools of public health, and its close relationship with the Pan American Sanitary Bureau in the first half of the century.

European colonial powers were fundamentally concerned with preserving the health of colonial administrators and military personnel in Africa, the Middle East, and Asia. Simultaneously, American philanthropical foundations were reaching out to the populations in Latin America. Preoccupied with the implementation of technical solutions to complex health problems in order to allow social and economic development to take place, the foundations' officials interpreted their relative failures in dealing with these problems as a consequence of innumerable obstacles linked to so-called retarded societies in much need of modernization.

"Never Again"

Referring to the twentieth century, British Nobel Laureate William Golding said, "I can't help thinking that this has been the most violent century in human history." The world renowned French agronomist Rene Dumont described it as follows: "I see it only as a century of massacres and war" (Hobsbawm 1994, p. 1). In the aftermath of World War II, nations gathered and created the United Nations (UN)—a vehicle for peace and conflict resolution between nations and the protection of human rights. The political institutions of the UN dealt with security issues, while the specialized agencies attached to it fostered the cooperation necessary to face problems in the specialized areas. The World Health Organization (WHO) was thus founded in 1948 to promote and protect the health of all peoples. The United Nations International Children's Emergency Fund (UNICEF) was created the same year to provide some relief to the thousands of orphans and abandoned children as a result of the war in Europe.

The UN system was built on the premise that sovereign nation-states were the primary units of the international system and were represented by their political authorities, put in place with different degrees of legitimacy. Newly independent countries maintained arbitrary borders dictated by the former colonial powers. The challenge was (to employ an expression used years later during the Somalian civil war), *nation building*. It is important to understand that the WHO, as all specialized agencies of the UN system, was intended to function as an intergovernmental institution with a general assembly made up of the political representatives of each member state. The system operates as a forum for discussion and policy making by national health authorities, while the secretariat has the responsibility to implement the resolutions and deliver appropriate technical cooperation to the governments in order to achieve common goals. A good example of this is the 1978 Conference of Alma-Ata, Kazakhstan, which established the common goal of *Health for All 2000* and gave top priority to the strategy of primary health care (PHC). The assumption was quite linear in its logic—if top national health authorities of member countries agree on a common goal and a proper strategy and provide the required technical cooperation to implement them, focusing on countries in greater need and with less institutional capacity, then the goals will be achieved. In practice, the more vertical the programs and the more technical in nature, the more likely their specific objectives would be attained, even with minimal involvement and sometimes in spite of national health authorities. This logic raised key questions regarding the sustainability of the programs at the end of the 1980s.

The Third World and the Cold War

In addition to the creation of the UN after World War II, four changes in the international situation had major influences on international health activities.

First, the world had become qualitatively different in that it was no longer euro-centric; the relegation of West European nations to the rank of second-level pow-ers precipitated the end of the colonial system. Second, the United States and the Soviet Union emerged as the new major players on the world scene, resulting in a bipolar world system that led to the Cold War. Third, in between East and West emerged the developing countries, also known as the *Third World*, striving to find their place between the two superpowers in order to attract the means of economic and social development. These developing countries were quickly transformed into the operational theaters of the Cold War and used by the superpowers. Fourth, the world as a whole achieved unprecedented growth.

Within this complex web of relation, control, and influence, international health activities took place. By the 1950s the bilateral aid agencies in most west-ern industrialized nations, including the United States and Canada, were created. The foremost concerns in world politics were geopolitical in nature, more so in many cases than trade or economical interests. Depending on their role in the strategic confrontation between East and West, *Third World* countries were given or denied technical and financial assistance. Authoritarian and antipopular gov-ernments were actively supported, if not put in place, on the basis of their ideolo-gies. Substantial amounts of financial aid were channeled to such countries in the name of development but in reality to ensure their political stability and obedi-ence. This bogus situation made the work of the WHO quite difficult, in that it had to convince repressive regimes of the value of implementing health goals they had approved in the General Assembly.

Because of the availability of new funding for international health programs, a growing number of U.S. schools of public health got involved in overseas activi-ties and developed specialized postgraduate training in international health. For these schools, international health essentially meant public health for poor coun-tries (Godue 1992). The study of international health consisted of learning how to implement public health interventions to control infectious and other diseases in the context of innumerable economic, social, and cultural obstacles and resis-tances. By the same token, such training was judged adequate to deal with health problems of national minorities. The main assumption was that so-called back-ward Third-World economies could catch up with the proper transfer of knowl-edge and technology.

International Health in a Changing International Environment

The end of the Cold War has alternately generated or accelerated the pace of profound changes with potentially far-reaching consequences on international health activities and our understanding of international health. Of three changes, the first two, globalization and transnationalization, relate to major trends in the international environment, and the third, national security, to policy making.

Interdependence and Globalization

Interdependence is not a new phenomenon, but its intensification in recent years makes it a dominant characteristic of the world system in the post–Cold-War period. Interdependence means that each country renounces the aim of attaining self-sufficiency and a hegemonic position through the forceful appropriation of other countries' territory, population, or resources (Rosecrance 1986). In their search for security, countries shift their competition from war to trade, implying an acceptance of a differentiation of functions between the countries on a global scale, each one exploiting their competitive advantage in relation to the others in an open market. Interdependence should not be understood as a symmetrical power relationship between trading countries; conflict of interest is an omnipresent feature of the increasing mobility of peoples, goods, and services.

The peaceful resolution of conflicts requires a negotiated set of rules and norms agreed upon by participating countries and the eventual creation of international institutions for the surveillance and implementation of these rules. These agreements imply the delegation of some part of the sovereignty of a state to a supranational entity. In return, these agreements allow the opening of borders and economic integration. Intense economic competition and the development of transportation and communication technologies affect the circulation of ideas, peoples, capital, goods, and services on an unprecedented scale. Globalization refers to the fact that in recent years, the world has become more of a single operational unit (Hobsbawm 1994). There might not be a new world order, but there will be a more orderly world.

Globalization has major implications for people's health that can be regrouped as follows: increased mobility and velocity of transfer health risks between countries; increased exchanges of goods and services between countries in response to health problems; a changing role of national governments in the health sector; and a modified role for international organizations, multilateral in nature. The very relationship between health and development itself is changing as the health status of a country's population and the ability to limit the costs of health care are considered essential advantages in globalized competition. At the same time, societies seem to be more polarized between those who can and those who can not make it in such a competitive world, adding strength to the debate about equity in health.

Transnationalization

At the same time that interdependence and globalization call into question the very meaning and roles of the countries and international organizations, there is a burgeoning of horizontal relationships and linkages between individuals, institutions, and community organizations. This encompasses the so-called civil society on the one hand and private enterprises at the international level on the other. The term "post-international politics" has been coined to describe these changes. According to Rosenau (1990), "The very notion of 'international relations' seems obsolete in the face of an apparent trend in which more and more of the interactions that sustain world politics unfold without the direct involvement of Nations or States" (p. 480).

Parallel meetings of citizens and interest groups held during international summits and conferences are interesting manifestations of this phenomenon. The proliferation and growing strength of international nongovernmental organizations (NGOs) represent another example of transnationalization. One should, for example, consider their active and predominant role during the military intervention in Somalia. Furthermore, easy and inexpensive ways of communication between health workers from different countries through electronic networking challenge health information and reporting systems at the national level, as the recent outbreak of Ebola virus has shown in Zaire. It might be easier for a health worker in a Zairian village to communicate with an infectious disease expert in the United States than with his own national health authorities. One ought to therefore appreciate how much of a powerful advantage it is for a given country to have the ability for institutions and citizens to link effectively with field health workers of other countries and to make proper use of gathered information for the protection of its own population.

National Security

National security now includes public health, demographic, and environmental issues. The inclusion of threats to health in foreign policy considerations can be attributed in large part to the reduction of the international tensions that marked the end of the Cold War, which occupied the central and strategic components of policy making. Because of emerging health problems occurring on a world scale and the velocity of the potential transmission of disease between countries, it is imperative that the new health problems be given due attention in the framing of foreign policy because they cannot simply be met by the use of military force (Hamilton 1994). The altered agenda of national security to include public health issues signifies that public health policy need not be conceived strictly within national borders. Trends such as interdependence and transnationalization demand greater analysis of external and global threats to health and the articulation of a coherent response from the international community. In a sense, the borders become blurred, as does the distinction between the "We" and the "Others".

Analysis of the transactions that take place among countries and of the international community and its people's health will continue to challenge the traditional approaches to international health.

INTERNATIONAL ISSUES IN MCH

International health comparisons are difficult to perform due to differences in reporting systems and data collection, medical and health recordkeeping, limitations in research (methods, measurements, and definitions), and social and political constraints among others (Parkin et al. 1989). Despite these limitations, health comparisons have enabled the countries to become cognizant of the disparities, such as gender inequities and the availability of resources experienced by the haves and have-nots. International comparisons direct policy makers, international organizations, and individual countries to seek alternatives to common problems and to tailor health strategies to an individual country's needs.

Maternal Mortality and Morbidity

Maternal Mortality

Today's goal of obstetrical practice is to make every attempt to ensure that a woman is not impaired at the end of her pregnancy and delivery, and that she has a healthy, live infant. The management of pregnancy and labor becomes key in having these outcomes (Leigh 1986). Nonetheless, pregnancy and/or childbirth under some circumstances are the main cause of morbidity and mortality among 700 million women of reproductive age in the developing world (Williams et al. 1994).

Underreporting maternal deaths is a common occurrence in many countries, and the main reasons are: (1) incomplete investigation of death (autopsy and diagnosis) affecting the information entered in the death certificate, (2) inability or lack of knowledge about the pregnancy status, (3) the legal and economic constraints about reporting a death (limited number of days to report the death of a family member, paying a registration fee), and (4) distance and lack of transportation to appropriate registering office (Williams et al. 1994). The exact number of women who die of pregnancy-related causes is unknown. Worldwide, there are approximately 500,000 women dying unnecessarily each year from preventable causes associated with pregnancy and childbirth (Rosenfield 1989; Smyke 1993). Maternal mortality accounts for the first or second cause of death among women age 25 to 34 (Winikoff 1990). The African continent alone accounts for about 150,000 maternal deaths per year, and sub-Saharan Africa has the highest rates, 570 to 700 deaths per 100,000 live births (AbouZahr and Royston 1991). The discrepancy between developed and developing countries is approximately 10 times higher for maternal mortality than it is for infant mortality (Nowak 1995). The fact is that obstetric emergencies account for 75 percent of all maternal deaths. The main causes of maternal mortality in developing countries are hemorrhage, septic abortions, eclampsia, infection, and obstructed labor (Nowak 1995), while in developed countries they are hemorrhage and thromboembolic disease or amniotic fluid embolism (Sudström-Feigenberg 1988).

Nowak (p. 780) has addressed the impact that economic development has on maternal mortality. "One of the bonuses of living in a wealthy country is a relatively safe childbirth. For most women living in poor countries, however, being pregnant is all too often a life-threatening condition. Pregnancy is a risk factor for women's health, and unsafe abortion is one of the main contributors to women's morbidity/mortality." Countries such as Sweden and Brazil illustrate the role of unsafe abortion in women's lives. Sweden has had a decline in maternal mortality since the 1970s. The average maternal mortality in Sweden has been five a year. In 1974, the Swedish Parliament approved a new Abortion Act, making abortion no longer a crime but free on demand up to the eighteenth week of gestation. The Abortion Act was accompanied by another act on birth control, which made family planning information and services available and free of charge. The idea was that if abortion was free on demand, the society had an obligation to make contraception equally accessible. Family planning services were integrated with maternal health care all over the country (Sundström-Feigenberg 1988).

Abortion, illegal in Brazil, is the main cause of emergency visits by women of reproductive age. Analysis of hospital admissions (1980–1985) suggests 822 abortions for each 1,000 live births. Abortion has been labeled the "country's largest endemic" (Giffin 1994, p. 358). In contrast, abortion is legal in India, but approximately five to six million unsafe abortions are performed yearly. They contribute to about 15,000 to 20,000 abortion-related deaths per year (Karkal 1991).

Maternal mortality can be measured in three possible ways: life-time risk, maternal mortality ratio, and maternal mortality rate. The risk of dying from pregnancy-related causes is not equally distributed worldwide. The maternal mortality lifetime risk for an African woman is 1 in 21; an Asian woman has a 1 in 54 lifetime risk of dying, while a northern European woman has a one in 10,000 lifetime risk of dying due to pregnancy/childbirth (Nowak 1995). The maternal mortality ratio (maternal deaths in one year/100,000 live births) summarizes the hazards of pregnancy and also reflects obstetrical care. The maternal mortality rate (maternal deaths in one year/per 100,000 women age 15–44) reflects both the pregnancy hazards and the frequency of exposure to the risks of pregnancy. The maternal mortality ratio can be reduced by improving obstetric care for pregnant women, while the rate can be altered by improving obstetric care and by reducing the chances of getting pregnant (Fortney et al. 1988).

Ascertaining maternal mortality has been a difficult task. The traditional surveillance methods do not seem to yield the information needed to fully comprehend the magnitude of the problem in countries with insufficient surveillance and reporting mechanisms. Through the Safe Motherhood Initiative, an effort has been made to address maternal mortality including data collection and surveillance. The Safe Motherhood Initiative originated from the Safe Motherhood Conference held in Nairobi, February 10–13, 1987. The participants from 37 countries, the Director-General of WHO, the President of the World Bank, the Assistant Executive of United Nations Population Fund (UNFP), and the Administration of the UN Development Program passed the initiative. There are several methods to gather data on maternal mortality. The Sisterhood method and Maternal Mortality Audit are two of these to be used in areas without easy access to the information (Shahidullah 1995; Mari Bhat et al. 1995; Graham et al. 1989).

Maternal Morbidity

Apart from the known risks confronted by many women during pregnancy and childbirth, maternal morbidity can be classified in three areas: pregnancy and childbirth morbidity, infectious morbidity, and nutritional morbidity. This chapter will briefly discuss only pregnancy and childbirth morbidity, and infectious morbidity.

Pregnancy and childbirth morbidity. Given the lack of access to prenatal and intrapartum care for many women, the investment in costly technology, such as electronic fetal monitoring, is counterproductive until the majority of women have access to safe and appropriate care. Table 13–1 summarizes the health status of women and mothers in various regions of the world.

Pregnancy and prenatal care. There is evidence that prenatal care offers the best hope for the prevention of morbidity and mortality for women and infants. However, we are not as sure about what content, frequency, and approach of prenatal care has the best impact. We know that women who receive first trimester

Table 13–1 Health Status of Women in Various Regions

| Region | Life expectancy at birth (years) 1985–90[1] | Maternal mortality per 100,000 live births 1988[2] | Percent women age 15–49 with hemoglobin below normal[3] | | |
			Pregnant <11g/dl	Non-pregnant 12g/dl	All women
Asia	64	380	59	44	45
Africa	54	630	51	40	42
Latin America	70	200	41	30	34
Developed countries	77	26	17	12	12

Sources: 1. United Nations, Department of International Economic and Social Affairs (1991). *UN World Population Prospects 1990.* New York, NY: Author.

2. *Weekly Epidemiological Record* (1991). New estimates of maternal mortality, 66, 346.

3. World Health Organization (1992). *Prevalence of nutritional anaemia in women in the world.* Unpublished document, WHO/MCH/MSM/92.2.

prenatal care have better pregnancy outcomes than women who receive late or no prenatal care. Many women do not participate in prenatal care because for them pregnancy is a normal process that does not require the services of a medical provider. Other women are discouraged because of the time and effort involved in prenatal care. According to Kestler (1993), waiting time is one of the factors influencing women's decisions in seeking prenatal care. Low-risk pregnant women receiving prenatal care had to wait 71 to 190 minutes to be seen, and the average time in contact with clinical personnel was only 17 to 21 minutes. The waiting time for women labeled high-risk was 81 to 147 minutes, while the actual time spent with a health provider was 23 to 25 minutes. If seen by a physician, the woman only got care for an average of 11 to 15 minutes. The services and time expended with the health care provider have been identified by women as dehumanizing, fragmented, and provided in a routine manner regardless of the level of risk (Kestler 1993). In most countries, women's perceptions of prenatal care consistently differ between what care they get and what they expect.

Prenatal care differs among countries and within countries. For example, prenatal care in Latin America for the most part is "medical-curative-institutional" in its approach. The present prenatal care model is clinic- or hospital-based, has a physician as the provider, and is oriented solely to monitoring the well-being of the fetus (Langer et al. 1993). This type of care rarely takes into consideration the health and psychosocial needs of parents-to-be, or the health of the woman (Kestler 1993; Langer et al. 1993). In contrast, Sweden has a clear division of labor between the midwife and the physician in the provision of prenatal care. Midwives are responsible for the basic health supervision, and the physician cares mainly for high-risk pregnancies and acts as a consultant in the event of complications (Sundström-Feigenberg 1988).

Sweden's utilization of midwifery services is exemplary. The midwife takes ample time on the first prenatal visit to obtain a complete health and medical history. Laboratory tests are obtained to ascertain blood group, Rh-status, rubella immunity, and syphilis. Women at risk of human immunodeficiency virus/ acquired immune deficiency syndrome (HIV/AIDS) are checked for human T-cell Lymphotrophic Virus-3 (HTLV 3), and a lung X-ray is done for high-risk immigrants from countries where pulmonary tuberculosis is common. Follow-up visits include blood pressure, urine test, and uterine/fetal growth. In addition, the midwife talks to the parent(s)-to-be about adjustments to the pregnancy and preparation for delivery. The midwife assesses uterine growth by measuring the symphysis-fundus height and plotting it on the Gravidagram. This is an inexpensive, easy-to-use, and accurate way to detect accelerated or retarded fetal growth (Sundström-Feigenberg 1988). Midwives provide care addressing biological, psychological, social, and economic needs of parents-to-be, empowering parents throughout the reproductive process. During the pregnancy, the mother-to-be is assessed for various risk factors, and the midwife decides if the woman needs special care, consultation with a physician, a social worker or a psychologist, or hospitalization.

In addition to traditional known factors influencing the pregnancy, parents-to-be face an array of other factors such as social isolation, poverty, violence and abuse, alcohol and/or use of illicit drugs, smoking, environmental and occupational exposures, and immigration and migration. Recently, Zapata and colleagues identified sociopolitical violence as a risk factor for pregnancy complications. Sociopolitical violence was the main predictor of pregnancy complications among a healthy cohort of pregnant women (Zapata et al. 1992). The management of pregnancy needs to take on these risk factors to successfully accomplish its task (Sundström-Feigenberg, 1988).

Traditionally, hospital delivery assigns women the social role of being a patient, which means passivity, dependence, compliance, and trust (Midmer 1992). The hospital-based midwife is a bridge between the hospital environment and the parents-to-be's needs, expectations, and hopes.

Countries with excessive reproductive mortality, such as Brazil, have been pioneers in the development of the best mix of prenatal care, labor/delivery, and neonatal care technologies aimed at minimizing the number of deaths while, at the same time, being affordable in relation to resources available and appropriate in respect to the conditions and settings (Panerai et al. 1991).

Brazil has developed a basic package of technologies. It contains three interrelated phases: (1) prenatal care (health education in pregnancy, management of suspected premature labor, management of hypertension, prevention and treatment of infections of the gravida, and management of premature rupture of the membranes); (2) labor and delivery (support of inevitable home delivery, institutional vaginal delivery, local obstetric anesthesia and analgesia, enforcement of asepsis and antisepsis, Caesarean section delivery); and (3) neonatal care (support for newborn home care, initial care of the newborn, adequate feeding technique, prevention and treatment of neonatal infections) (Panerai et al. 1991). The basic package is the most effective intervention in areas with limited resources. In addition to the basic package, three other low-cost activities are proposed: referral system for pregnant women, treatment of respiratory conditions, and prevention of infections. The order of interventions is to start with the institutionalization of the basic package at the national level, and then to institutionalize the three other low-cost activities in the order above. Together, they will contribute to significant declines in mortality among mothers and infants.

Childbirth

Prenatal care is one part of the mother-to-be's and fetus' health equation, and childbirth is the other. The appropriate use of existing human resources is fundamental to prenatal and delivery care for women and their newborns. The midwife is a human resource used in the provision of prenatal care and delivery services in many developed and developing countries. There are two types of midwives, the empirical or traditional midwife and the midwife or nurse midwife (i.e., Sweden's midwife). A term widely used is *Traditional Birth Attendant* (TBA), and it encompasses traditional midwife, indigenous midwife, and empirical midwife. She is a wise woman of the community who is often sought by mothers-to-be for assistance throughout the pregnancy and delivery. TBAs all share a main skill, assisting women in childbirth. Most TBAs do not have formal schooling in the development of their skills; however, they are aware of their limitations and instinctively or from experience are able to identify potential risks and complications. Moreover, some countries have trained their TBAs to identify at early stages high-risk patients (Hyppolito 1992). In contrast, the midwife or nurse midwife is a woman who has medical training to provide women's health care, prenatal care, and delivery to low-risk women. Another important role of the TBA, midwife, or nurse midwife who attends a woman throughout labor is to provide her with physical and emotional support.

Cultures such as the Arabic culture have women who have knowledge and experience in assisting deliveries but are not TBAs. For example, in Yemen they are called *Jidda* (grandmother), and they see this role as one of the many duties women perform and not as a job. In fact they are not paid money or in-kind for their services. The Jidda's most important roles are to provide emotional support during labor and to cut the cord (Scheepers 1991). This woman may be the mother-in-law, the mother of the pregnant woman, or an older woman unrelated to the pregnant woman. These women are referred to as "they who cut the cord." In comparison to Sudan and Egypt, where women earn their living from assisting births, in Yemen they work for the promise of rewards given in the afterlife for a good deed done on earth (Scheepers 1991).

Although a large number of women have uncomplicated deliveries, some do experience complications. Obstructed labor is one of the most serious complications if available obstetrical services are not available. Women who have had prolonged or obstructed labor may have injuries that may not be life threatening but will have serious social consequences. The most common injury is vesico-vaginal fistula (VVF). It is an abnormal opening between the bladder and the vagina which results in urinary incontinence (Lawson 1989; Margolis and Mercer 1994). Factors associated with VVF are age (young), first pregnancy or subsequent pregnancy for a woman with the condition, prolonged labor, poverty, female circumcision, short stature, lack of education, lack of transportation, lack of appropriate health services, and women's low social status. Most women with VVF experience lifetime health problems and social isolation if the condition is not surgically treated. Sufficient evidence exists on the magnitude of maternal mortality and morbidity and on the knowledge and technology necessary to avoid senseless deaths, illness, and disability related to pregnancy and childbirth.

Infectious disease morbidity. Worldwide, STDs are the most commonly reported infectious diseases. In 1990, the annual total of STDs were trichomoniasis (120 million cases), genital chlamydia (50 million cases), genital pappillomavirus (30 million cases), gonorrhea (25 million cases), genital herpes (20 million cases), syphilis (3.5 million cases), chancroid (2 million cases), and HIV infection (1 million cases). It is believed that there is great underreporting of STDs due to gender biases in health and screening services (WHO 1992). For discussion of STDs, please refer to Chapter 10.

Child Health

What are the odds that an alive infant will survive to old age or even to the fifth birthday? The decline in infant and child mortality in developed countries has been to a great extent accomplished by the extensive use of the classic health technologies (such as clean water supply, environmental sanitation, personal hygienic practices, improved nutrition, education, and vaccination) in conjunction with improved standard of living and educational achievements (Ramalingaswami 1986). For the developing world to adequately address infant and child mortality, the implementation of traditional health technologies must be incorporated first; otherwise, the utilization of highly expensive modern technologies will prove to be counterproductive.

Newborns are at risk of respiratory distress syndrome. Assessment of fetal lung maturation is key to its prevention and appropriate treatment. It can be done through the determination of the association between a given lecithin/sphingomyelin ratio in the amniotic fluid and maturation of the fetal lung, or through the foam test. The foam test technique requires basic laboratory equipment, available at low cost, while the lecithin/sphingomyelin ratio requires advance laboratory technology. In developing countries where anywhere from 40 to 90 percent of women deliver at home or at maternity facilities with few resources and technology, the foam test can prevent infant morbidity (Faúndes et al. 1988).

Poverty and Education

Two powerful indicators of poverty are high infant mortality and high female illiteracy. Women are the poorest of the poor, and they work long hours, sacrificing their health and compromising their children's health. Recommended actions to address the feminization of poverty are: (1) readily available, accessible, and affordable preventive and curative services in areas of great need; (2) fair pay for women who do remunerative work; (3) provision of breastfeeding time and space in the working environment for nursing mothers; and (4) development of income-generating and literacy programs for women. The implementation of these recommendations is feasible, cost-efficient, and cost-effective. Kerala State, and Jamkhed, Maharashtra State, in India are two examples of how social action can affect the status of women and the health of the population (Arole and Arole 1994; Ramalingaswami 1986).

Poor women and children are the targets of illness and disease year round. The scarcity of drinking water during the dry season has been associated with diarrhea and Guinea worm, while malaria, onchocerciasis, and hookworm are known to be prevalent in the rainy season (Scheer and Ebrahim 1985). The accessibility to clean water, often taken for granted in industrialized nations, is one of the greatest contributors to child health. Worldwide, 1.2 billion people do not have access to clean water, and 1.9 billion have inadequate sanitation (Smyke 1993). The interaction between inadequate water supply and poor sanitation is worsened in urban areas by overcrowding and the precarious nature of most slum housing.

Worldwide it is the children under five and the poor who experience the greatest burden of illness and disease. Mortality of children under five accounts for 50 percent of all mortality in many areas. This creates a vicious circle of high fertility rates to compensate for high mortality rates. In our times, the surviving children are saved through the "magic bullets" of modern medicine without addressing the cycle of the *poverty syndrome*. Morbidity and mortality among infants, children, and mothers are to be "seen not in isolation but as part of the major problems of poverty" (Ramalingaswami, 1986, p. 1185). For health to be more than a goal, women, mothers, and children must be the central foci of the health system.

Most infant and child morbidity and mortality are preventable, yet the story is one of missed opportunities (Ramalingaswami 1986). For example, the use of oral rehydration (glucose-salt mixture) at the early stages of a diarrhea attack can lower the death rate associated with dehydration/diarrhea. Vaccines are the most universal cost-effective public health mechanism to combat illness, disability, and death. Complete and timely vaccination can break the damaging malnutrition and infection dyad (Fryer 1991). It is estimated that over 50 percent of child mortality and most growth retardation are caused by the synergistic effect between malnutrition and infections (Ramalingaswami 1986).

Infant mortality tends to be directly associated with high female literacy rates (Fryer 1991; Ramalingaswami 1986). Parental education as a pathway to influence mortality and fertility has been recognized for many decades. A quote from 1934 illustrates the relationship between women's education, fertility, and mortality.

> It would seem that when a community has gained the knowledge and acquired the habits necessary to reduce the death rate it will sooner or later gain the knowledge and acquire the habits necessary to reduce the birth rate. There may be time lag between the two processes, but both of them in a large share are the outcome of education (Cleland and Van Ginneken 1988, p. 1357).

Parental education as a child survival protective factor was identified recently. Traditionally, education was considered as a proxy indicator of socioeconomic status. Hence, the inverse relationship between education of parents and infant/child mortality was interpreted solely on economic terms. It was not until 1979 that Cadwell demonstrated that the mother's education was itself the most important predictor of child survival (Cleland and Van Ginneken 1988).

Cochrane et al. (1990), in a cross-country data analysis, have consistently found a linear relationship between maternal education and childhood mortality with an average 7–9 percent decline of infant/child mortality ratios with each one-year of attainment in mother's education. Although we do not know what specifically about maternal education works, findings show that women's education is strongly associated with declines in childhood mortality and less with infant mortality.

The universality of the relationship between women's education and child survival is less obvious when sex differentials in childhood mortality are taken into account. Studies conducted in the 1980s found that in some cultures the relative disadvantage of daughters may worsen among better educated or more wealthy families. Das Gupta (1987) found that educated mothers render their knowledge and skills selectively in favor of children of the preferred sex.

There are some extremely complex situations that have not been totally unraveled by research. For example, there is not a consensus in research findings about the effects of women's paid work on child survival or of employment status on fertility. Cross-cultural research addressing the universality of specific indicators is warranted, in order to shed light on international health policies and strategies.

Child Survival

Some common trends affecting infant and child mortality within the developing world are undernutrition, overcrowding, lack of a safe water supply, poor environmental sanitation, low levels of education (especially among women), lack of or incomplete vaccination among children, and synergism between malnutrition and illness (Fryer 1991). GOBI is a program advocated by UNICEF to address these and other threats to healthy child development in the developing world. GOBI has four components:

- Growth monitoring
- Oral rehydration
- Breastfeeding
- Immunization

This program fits beautifully within the PHC strategy. It is inexpensive and does not require alterations of the cultural fabric of most countries. As with PHC, this program requires middle-level health workers who serve as a bridge between communities and health institutions, and who can provide information and services to rural, peri-urban, and urban populations. GOBI is most effective when the health system has the following elements established: planning, management, and infrastructure. Most countries have integrated into their primary health care services the growth monitoring, oral rehydration, and immunization activities, while breastfeeding has been viewed as a selective activity. This section will consider breastfeeding issues, while aspects related to growth monitoring, oral rehydration, and immunization will be addressed throughout the chapter.

Breastfeeding

The promotion of breastfeeding in maternity wards has been endorsed by many governments, and by international organizations such as WHO, the World Bank, and UNICEF. In 1989, WHO and UNICEF issued "ten steps to successful breastfeeding," recommendations to be implemented in maternity wards (UNICEF, 1995). The main recommendations were training of health personnel on breastfeeding, early contact and initiation of breastfeeding, total rooming-in, on-demand breastfeeding, breastfeeding guidance by health personnel, and elimination of supplementary formula bottles during hospital stay and at hospital discharge (Perez-Escamilla et al. 1992). Hospitals that implemented the recommended steps in their maternity wards are labeled *baby-friendly* hospitals. Worldwide, 3,000 baby-friendly hospitals have been established (UNICEF 1995). Presently, 130 countries are participating. In the industrialized world, Sweden has taken the lead while the United States lags behind. The United States has not designated any hospital baby-friendly, has not established breastmilk substitute regulations, and has not provided minimum maternity benefits.

Long-term breastfeeding has been associated with primiparous, rooming-in women who have had breastfeeding guidance. However, multiparous women are not influenced as much by breastfeeding guidance. It may be that women with one or more children develop their infant feeding behaviors by their own previous experiences and time demands rather than by rooming-in and breastfeeding guidance.

The length of breastfeeding varies by geographic location. For example, the median duration of breastfeeding in urban areas was 6.5 months, 10 months in the slums (peri-urban), and in rural areas 14 months. Most children were bottle and breastfed even in rural areas (Bågenholm et al. 1987). Women who were working for pay and living in the slums reported having a conflict between their work and breastfeeding their infants/children (Bågenholm et al. 1987).

Culture and religion influence breastfeeding practice. For example, the Quaran recommends breastfeeding for two years, and cultural beliefs indicate that the breast milk of a woman who experiences fear, anger, or sickness is not suitable food for the infant/child (Bågenholm et al. 1987).

The 1985 report by UNICEF, "The State of the World's Children," stated, "A revolution in child survival is beginning to go around the world . . . (I)f its low cost techniques are to fulfill their potential to save millions of children's lives, then the focus of health care must be shifted from institution to family" (UNICEF 1985, p. 1). However, this "revolution" relies on women who historically have been the ones caring for the sick in their families and communities. Child survival proponents do not take into account that women from developing countries work longer hours than men in order to fulfill their domestic roles and participate in remunerated work (Adagala 1991; Babb 1987; Canadian Council 1991; Feijoo and Jelin 1987; Flores and Bonilla 1991; Khan et al. 1990; Raikes 1989; Ramalingaswami 1986; Vlassoff and Bonilla 1994). The burden of such revolution cannot be placed just on women. They have already contributed more than their share in the quest for child survival.

MCH Strategies

Primary Health Care

The thirtieth annual World Health Assembly (1977) unanimously declared as its decided goal "the attainment by all citizens of the world by the year 2000 of a level health that will permit them to lead a socially and economically productive life" (Basch 1990, p. 200). This was the birth of Health for All 2000 (HFA) and a programmatic target of the WHO. After several conferences (Brazzaville, Washington, Alexandria, Manila, New Delhi, New York, and Halifax), the one that crowned HFA was the International Conference on Primary Health Care held September 6–12, 1978, in Alma-Ata, Kazakhstan. This conference, cosponsored by WHO and UNICEF, had representation from 143 countries and 67 organizations. It was this conference that declared health to be a universal human right.

PHC is also known as community-based primary health care (CBPHC) or community health care program (CHCP). The PHC strategy rests on the utilization of middle-level personnel and low-cost, effective strategies to provide health coverage to the population. The use of middle-level health personnel has historically provided health care in rural areas without access to physicians and nurses. For example, the *feldsher* has provided middle-level health care for over a century in Russia and the former Soviet Union, as has the *barefoot doctor* in the People's Republic of China and traditional midwives throughout the world (Iyun 1989). Care delivered by community health workers (CHWs), also known as Health Promoters, has become increasingly trendy in the implementation of PHC.

The CHWs have different responsibilities, including the education of women in relation to the causation and prevention of common childhood and maternal diseases, child and maternal immunization, family planning and child spacing, nutrition, oral rehydration, prenatal care, and sanitation. The CHW in many countries is trained in the treatment of minor illnesses, prenatal care, low-risk deliveries, detection of risk and medical referral, and the cleaning and suturing of superficial wounds (Iyun 1989).

Another resource to be embraced by PHC is faith healers and/or traditional healers (Hyppolito 1992). Many cases of infant and children's respiratory infections and/or gastroenteritis leading to dehydration are first brought by the parents to these healers. Their training in simple prophylactic measures for treatment of dehydration and the recognition of cases needing medical assistance has proved to be equally beneficial for the healer, the child, and the health care system (Hyppolito 1992).

PHC can lower maternal morbidity and mortality through the use of middle-level health personnel and the use of appropriate techniques and hygiene (Leigh 1986). One of those techniques is the partogram, a graphic record of the progress of labor. The partogram uses the cervical dilation, the descent of the presenting part, and the frequency of uterine contractions to access the normal progress of labor and to recognize at early stages abnormal labor. This technique well used has had an impact on early referrals and unnecessary performance of Caesarean section (Leigh 1986).

Timely and adequate transportation of individuals needing medical care has direct implication for morbidity and mortality (Mir 1989). Pregnant women and infants are two at-risk groups. By the time the affected person arrives at the referral facility, the condition could have gotten worse. For example, hypothermia is the main cause of neonatal mortality among infants being transported (Mir 1989).

Cultural understanding and respect for traditional practices related to pregnancy and childbirth are key in training middle-level personnel, including CHWs and/or midwives and TBAs. Yemen serves as a good example. In this country, conflicts have arisen because *assistance* to women in labor is not viewed as the specialty of one or two women in a village but as an activity to be carried out by any woman who is not afraid to cut the cord. According to the cultural norms, attending a birth is a deed to be redeemed in the afterlife. Trained TBAs charge for their services, and consequently are rarely accepted by women who honor their traditional childbirth practices. Although TBAs may be the personnel preferred by PHC to attend deliveries, cultural practices and beliefs need to be taken into consideration when implementing PHC interventions and services to avoid placing CHWs and/or TBAs in tense relationships within their communities.

CHWs have many obstacles in performing their jobs. Among them are community expectations, self-medication by clients, lack of support from the ministries of health/surgeon general, lack of supervision, and lack of skills and means to fully address the needs of their communities. In many places CHWs have to compete with unscrupulous drug peddlers and with the availability of drugs without medical prescription. The lack of support from health officials compounded with unscrupulous business people contributes to the demoralization and attrition of CHWs.

Some Illustrations of PHC in Different Settings

PHC provides a unique entry point for avoiding missed opportunities by using low-cost technologies like oral rehydration for diarrhea, early diagnosis and treatment of common childhood illness and infections, well-child care for promoting growth and development, maternal and women's care, nutrition counseling, and reproductive health services. PHC can also contribute to the prevention of low birth weight by addressing the attitudes and perceptions of mothers and the traditions and cultural taboos regarding pregnancy, childbirth, and infant care (Ramalingaswami 1986).

The contrast between two states in India, Kerala and Uttar Pradesh, will help illustrate the influence of PHC and women's education on infant mortality. Both states are poor, but Kerala has high female literacy, and women there have access to well-developed PHC services. In Uttar Pradesh, women are illiterate and do not have access to health care facilities (Ramalingaswami 1986). In addition, the mean age of marriage for women in Kerala is higher than in any other place in India. The infant mortality rates in Kerala are 41 (rural) and 34 (urban), and the rates for Uttar Pradesh are 187 (rural) and 159 (urban).

Countries throughout the world have launched PHC as a vehicle to provide access to health care for their populations. Nigeria has embraced the PHC concept for both rural and urban areas as part of the package of "HFA" after the identification of serious health equity gaps. To improve child survival, Nigeria has opted for the control of communicable disease. The following findings in one of the country's regions were key in the development of PHC in Nigeria. Adekolu-J. (1989) found that out of 4,940 pregnancies, 412 ended in abortions. About 97 percent of births (4,508) were at home, assisted by traditional midwives. In addition to childbirth services, TBAs provide maternal and postnatal care to over 80 percent of women. Child spacing between one to three years was desired by 95 percent of the women. In fact, the women believed that a child would die if he or she were not two years old before the birth of the next baby. It is common knowledge that child survival decreases with subsequent pregnancies. In this region, child survival was less than 50 percent after the fifth pregnancy. Furthermore, 85 percent of deaths that occurred among children were caused by fevers, followed by gastrointestinal conditions and upper-respiratory infections. In addition, Adekolu-J. found that in this area female circumcision was almost 100 percent. TBAs are key in the performance of female circumcision. (For discussion of the implications of this cultural practice, please refer to Chapter 10.)

Zimbabwe is trying to change a legacy of abuse and neglect inherited from colonial times. Priorities for the country have been set and include primary education, improved water supply and distribution, free health care, adoption of the PHC strategy (including the expanded program on immunization), diarrheal disease control, nutrition, growth and development and child spacing, building rural health centers and hospitals, and human resources training, including village health workers (Sanders and Davis 1989). When compared with other developing countries, Zimbabwe presently has relatively low mortality, less infectious/communicable/environmental disease, and safer water supply and sanitation. However, the country has high levels of undernutrition, in spite of having a good food supply (Nkrumah and Nathhoo 1987).

Most examples of PHC are based on governments' implemented programs. The following illustrates a private effort to address the health of workers' families through PHC. A company in Peru spent $1.7 million in medical care and welfare services for its workers and families (Foreit et al. 1991). However, infant and child morbidity and mortality was still high. The factors contributing to high infant mortality (120/1,000) included lack of well-baby care, low vaccination coverage, high incidence of diarrhea and respiratory infections, overmedication, and use of inappropriate medicines. In addition only 5 percent of children (age one to four) were fully vaccinated. One quarter of those children got measles (Foreit et al. 1991). Physicians employed by the company to provide health services stated they did not have time for preventive care, and they believed that mothers would not use well-baby care. Children under five (17 percent of the population being served) accounted for 50 percent of all clinical visits (Foreit et al. 1991).

After the company established a PHC program, 75 percent vaccination coverage for children (age one to four) was achieved. Virtually all children under age one have been vaccinated on time. Children have been enrolled in the growth monitoring program, including 90 percent of children under age one and 35 percent of children age one to four. Children with third and second-degree malnutrition were enrolled in a nutritional rehabilitation program, and 2,258 cases of respiratory infections and 1,233 cases of diarrhea were treated during 1989. The mean number of antibiotics prescribed for respiratory infections and diarrhea declined from 1.5 to 0.5 (Foreit et al. 1991).

To have access to private health coverage does not guarantee adequate preventive health care services. Preventive health care using PHC can be provided at modest cost. Parents took advantage of the available well-baby services and had no complaints about the reduction of medications, including antibiotics.

Access to PHC services that include public health interventions has contributed to reducing nearly two-thirds of the risk of dying in the first year of life, worldwide vaccination coverage of approximately 80 per cent of children against childhood diseases, and lowering morbidity and mortality for children under five years of age. These impressive results are due to the use of oral rehydration therapy, growth and development programs, nutrition, and affordable health services.

Reproductive Health

During the past three decades, the international community has undergone incomparable demographic, technological, economic, political, and environmental change. Worldwide changes have created a milieu where attitudes regarding reproductive health have been challenged, resulting, "*inter-alia*, in the new comprehensive concept of reproductive health" (UN 1994, p. 3). The International Conference on Population and Development in Cairo was the pinnacle where reproductive health as a concept and as an ideology was discussed in an international forum. Hence, reproductive health has been defined as:

> a state of complete physical, mental and social well-being and not merely the absence of disease or infirmity, in all matters relating to the reproductive system and to its functions and processes. Reproductive health therefore implies that people are able to have a satisfying and safe sex life and that they have the capability to reproduce and the freedom to decide if, when and how often to do so. Implicit in this last condition are the rights of men and women to be informed and to have access to safe, effective, affordable and acceptable methods of family planning of their choice, as well as other methods of their choice for regulating fertility which are not against the law, and the right access to appropriate health-care services that will enable women to go safely through pregnancy and childbirth and provide couples with the best chance to have a healthy infant. In line with the above definition of reproductive health, reproductive health care is defined as the constellation of methods, techniques and services that contribute to reproductive health and well-being through preventing and solving reproductive health problems. It also includes sexual health, the purpose of which is the enhancement of life and personal relationships, and not merely counseling and care related to reproduction and sexually transmitted diseases (UN 1994, p. 38).

This conceptualization of reproductive health provides for a framework directly linking reproductive rights and freedom to women's status and empowerment thoughout the life cycle. The new redefinition of reproductive health has been the basis for a paradigm shift in which reproductive health includes antenatal care, family planning, sexual health, parenting education, Pap smears (women age 25–60 years), inclusion of psychosocial aspects of health, and services targeting youth, women, and men related to reproductive health (Sundström-Feigenberg 1988).

Tsui (1995) proposes the following framework to conceptualize and implement the different features of the new reproductive health paradigm (Figure 13–1). The main assumption of this framework is that sexual relations are to be free from unwanted/unplanned pregnancies and diseases/infections.

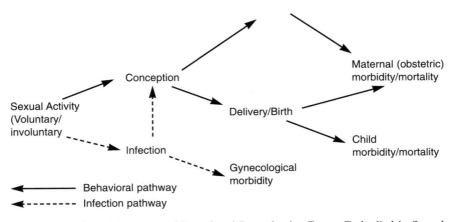

Figure 13–1 Causal Sequence of Sexual and Reproductive Events Embodied in Sexual and Reproductive Health Statutes. *Source:* A. Tsui, unpublished, 1995.

Tsui's eight dimensions framework includes the following main health activities or interventions.

1. Sexual activity is directly impacted by sex education services.
2. Conception is affected by family planning.
3. Infection is impacted by STD/HIV/AIDS screening and prevention programs.
4. Gynecological morbidity is indirectly affected by these screening and preventing programs.
5. Abortion is affected by its legal status and the services available to treat postabortion complications, which affect maternal morbidity and mortality.
6. Maternal morbidity and mortality are impacted by Safe Motherhood programs.
7. Delivery/birth is impacted by safe pregnancy interventions (e.g., attended deliveries).
8. Child morbidity and mortality are affected by child survival programs and interventions.

Today women's reproductive health is an important indicator of human rights (Center for Reproductive Law and Policy 1994). It is common to have a Women's Office at the Health Ministries in most Latin American countries. Furthermore, countries such as Brazil have a National Council of Women's Rights in the Justice Ministry and have established special women's police stations (Giffin 1994). In addition, countries such as Brazil, Colombia, Chile, and Venezuela have incorporated women's legal gains into their constitutions. Women are slowly gaining a new set of citizenship rights. In spite of these gains, women experience inequities that are deepened by the privatization of health care and increasing poverty (Giffin 1994).

One major consequence of privatization is that, for women, fertility control has been separated from routine health care. Poor and better-off women alike have been forced to meet their reproductive needs through private means. The women who can pay have access to fertility control, and if needed, to private abortion clinics. However, poor women without access to private family planning services, or the Caesarean and sterilization route, put their health and their lives at risk by depending on friends, neighbors, and drugstores/pharmacists for abortions. Brazil offers a good illustration of the impact of privatization on women's fertility control. In this country, the fertility rate dropped 75 percent between 1970 and 1990. This decline was accomplished through two main methods, the use of the pill and sterilization. In 1986, 66 percent of sterilizations were carried out in private institutions (43 percent of them free of charge), and 23 percent were performed in public or publicly supported units. In the northern states, approximately 76 percent of sterilizations were free of charge. São Paulo alone had a 93 percent increase between 1981–1989, and in the northeast an increase of 78 percent was observed during a six-year period. In addition, 75 percent of all sterilizations have been performed during childbirth, normally on women having Caesarean sections. One wonders if coercion has been part of the rise in sterilization (Giffin 1994). What remains clear is that insofar as medical services are less accessible, fertility control will continue to be a problem for women's reproductive health.

Globally, increasing numbers of women have entered the paid labor force in response to a decline in the purchasing power of family income. The fact that women are performing remunerated work and are having fewer children has not been sufficient for them to escape poverty (Giffin 1994). The increasing rates of child labor and abandonment point in the direction of the deteriorating situation faced by women and their families worldwide (Giffin 1994).

Internationally, the lack of information on causes and prevalence of reproductive health problems has been labeled *abysmal ignorance* and women's reproductive health itself a *silent emergency* (Giffin 1994). Given that suffering has been seen universally as inherent in women's reproductive lives and that women have been expected to be private on sexual matters, reproductive health has been shunted to the realm of informal cultural processes worldwide (Giffin 1994). As a result, formal women's health activities became an alternative perspective. A reproductive health paradigm has the potential to address inequities in health.

Women's participation in the paid labor force and the use of fertility control have not contributed to women's equality or liberation. On the contrary, these social practices represent a redistribution of gender roles, in which women have a double burden. Women lack power in sexual relationships and family decision making. A gender approach to health calls for empowerment of women by the inclusion of social gender roles at every stage of health and development programs.

INNOVATIVE TRENDS

Fascinating innovations and interventions are being implemented to address problems affecting the health of women, children, families, and communities through health, education, and development interventions and projects. Among those innovations are women and community empowerment projects, setting up local co-ops, and credit and income-generating projects. However, few projects are directed to teenagers and/or children. The following project is an example of the creative ways in which children can become a vehicle for health.

Children can be facilitators of healthy practices and multipliers of health knowledge. Interactive radio methodology has proven to be cost-effective for improving efficiency, accessibility, and quality of education in developing countries (Fryer 1991). In 1987, Bolivia became the first country in Latin America to use interactive radio to teach mathematics and geography at the primary school level. By 1989, Bolivia was the worldwide pioneer in applying interactive radio technology to primary school health education. Through the program, children became catalysts in the transmission of health-related practices and knowledge to family members. Approximately 10,000 fourth-grade and fifth-grade students in 250 schools have participated. Parents support the program. Children who have participated have influenced health practices, personal hygiene, and adequate treatment of diarrhea in their homes and communities.

SPECIAL POPULATIONS

Some groups are often overlooked, underserved, and without political clout. Among those are indigenous people, people with disabilities, street children, migrant populations, and refugees. Refugees are the population we will choose to illustrate some of the barriers faced by such neglected groups.

War, internal conflicts, natural disasters, and poverty have created groups of displaced people without a country or a home they can call their own. There are approximately 15 million refugees in the world, and 80 percent of them are women and children (Smyke 1993). Refugee women are often sexually abused and many times are expected to exchange sex for food or medicine (Williams et al. 1994). Despite the hardships and abuse, most refugee women possess great strengths, which have contributed to their abilities to survive their settlement ordeals and to help each other to build their lives and communities. Despite the will to survive, most refugees find it very difficult to reconcile their cultural conceptualization of health and healing with that of the host countries (Mahowald

1993). Common problems faced by refugees are depression, alienation, anxiety, abuse, fear, and overcrowding (Williams et al. 1994).

Information on and research about the effects of international migration on refugee children's health outcomes are very limited (Moss et al. 1992). Socioeconomic factors appear to be most important in explaining variation in weight-for-age, and a combination of approximate and socioeconomic variables was the most important predictor of diarrhea and respiratory illness. Migration itself appears to have very little explanatory power. In Belize, for example, health services are available to the whole population regardless of legal status, including refugee status. This may be different in other countries such as the United States, where undocumented persons are not always eligible for the health coverage offered by the government, having lost access to most publicly supported medical care (except emergency care) under welfare reform legislation in 1996.

High compliance with bacillus Calmette-Guérin, diphtheria, tetanus, pertussis, and polio vaccination suggests that immigrant mothers may be more efficient in obtaining preventive care or that health services may be providing sufficient outreach for infants. Low levels of measles immunization (age one) may indicate that as children grow, the utilization of preventive services decreases (Moss et al. 1992). Unmet needs are reflected in the frequent visits for primary health care (recorded in the health card) and the high frequency of diarrhea and respiratory infections. This study supports findings from other studies identifying the importance of parental education, income, and birth spacing in reducing infant and child morbidity and mortality.

NGOs and international human rights groups and organizations have been the main forces making these populations visible, bringing them into the international agenda, and denouncing abuses and violations inflicted upon them. Slowly, public health practitioners have become actively involved with indigenous people, people with disabilities, street children, migrant populations, and refugees in addressing those issues impacting on their health and well-being.

INTERNATIONAL HEALTH: IN NEED OF A NEW CONCEPTUAL FRAMEWORK

Prerequisites for a New Framework

Reflecting on international dynamics and circumstances, international health activities are getting more complex. Our vision of international health as a field of training and practice is equally challenged, and it requires a more coherent construct. In this dynamic political and social climate, it is not enough to think of international health as conventional technical assistance or cooperation in health that flows from the developed northern nations to the underdeveloped southern nations. Nor is it appropriate to limit international health to public health for the poor and the cultural "other," from an ethnocentric and a sociocentric perspective.

International health, as a field of study, contributes to our understanding of threats to health resulting from the new international framework enabling us to better appreciate its potential impact on health and disease. It assists us in identifying opportunities for action and in developing a coherent response to face these threats. In this context, we think of international health as a deliberate effort to improve people's health. Let's review some of the prerequisites and assumptions that are the building blocks for this conceptualization.

First, nations remain for the foreseeable future the basic units of the international system and the main actors in international relations (*The Economist* 1995). However, the roles of nations are undergoing profound transformations along two main lines: (1) sovereign states are delegating part of their traditional responsibilities and prerogatives to supranational entities in exchange for access to certain benefits, usually expanded market opportunities; and (2) new technologies have enabled civilian actors to relate internationally without government interference. Additionally, multinational corporations, some more powerful than some governments, are expanding and challenging policies. When it comes to the safety and welfare of their citizens, the nations still remain the dominant players. Nevertheless, international health needs to be conceptualized from the perspective of the country, both as the principal unit of analysis and the most relevant entity for policy making. That is to say, geographical borders still matter.

Second, enormous imbalance of power exists among nations. Weaker countries are more porous to external influences than the more powerful, and their capacity to articulate an appropriate response in the international community is equally limited. These uneven distributions of power not only manifest themselves in the bilateral relations between two countries, but also in the ability of the most powerful ones to direct the policies of multilateral organizations toward their own interests and vision. This can be done through budget reductions of the international organizations whose policy making reflects the principle of the equality of nations and a strengthening of those institutions where decisions are made on the basis of contribution in capital resources.

Third, centering on the interactions and transactions occurring between countries, the model of international health is collaborative and dynamic. Such an approach values the relationships of nations with each other and the world system as a whole rather than regarding internal processes within given countries as independent and self-contained phenomena. In order to explain the vulnerability of nations to external determinants and their abilities to give a proper response in the international community, we must understand the internal dynamics of countries. Historically, international health has been more interested in understanding the specificities of health problems within developing countries and proposed solutions and interventions directed at internal explanatory factors.

Fourth, there is a dual purpose to international health. As mentioned earlier, international health activities have been tied to war and trade. Such activities simultaneously sought a *health objective* and a *relation objective*. Then *health objectives* were primarily related to domestic protection and benefit of foreign populations while *relation objectives* varied from policies of confrontation, accommodation, or cooperation. The objectives were often interrelated according to the interests of the country and context. As we have previously seen, the first International Sanitary Conferences and Organizations were primarily concerned with the sanitation of ports as vehicles to facilitate trade between nations, although the health of sailors and other citizens likely benefited from these actions indirectly. Though no one doubted that other interests (both economic and political) were at stake, the stated objectives of the philanthropic institutions for their international health activities were the improvement of the health of populations through technical and financial assistance. Accordingly, international health activities, by their very nature, always carried with them a dual purpose. Lastly, moral or ethical components need to be an integral dimension of the framework, not only in terms of human rights but also of a nation's rights.

International Health and the National Interest

International health, from the perspective of national interest, should be looked at as the articulation of two functions, one *analytical* or *intelligence* and the other *operational* or *policy*. The intelligence function refers to the institutional capacity of the nation to gather relevant and critical information on external phenomena capable of impacting on the health of its population either directly or indirectly and to assess the magnitude of the risks involved. The policy function represents the institutional ability of a country to design and implement a proper and effective response to health threats and problems in the international community. Figure 13–2 illustrates these functions. The rectangle represents the country while the arrows are the international transactions.

Let's consider the intelligence function. The phenomena to be analyzed and monitored are of two general types, *intentional* and *nonintentional* (Panisset 1992). Intentional phenomena are those whose explicit objectives relate to the improvement of the health of the population. Broadly speaking, these phenomena correspond to technical and financial cooperation in health, be it from nongovernmental organizations, another country or group of countries, or from international institutions such as WHO and the World Bank. The intelligence function facilitates crucial understanding of the cooperation being offered, its appropriate-

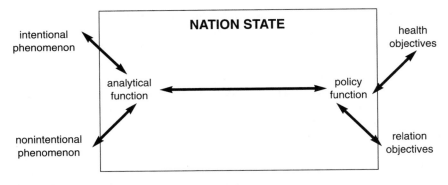

Figure 13–2 International Health and National Interest

---

ness, and programs under consideration for that country. At the same time, relation objectives of these organizations or countries have to be explored and clarified, along with their potential consequences for the national interest (Ratcliffe 1985). We must distinguish between assistance and cooperation. Cooperation connotes counterparts of a joint operation of a program, while assistance implies a rather passive role of the "recipient" country, which allows substitutive activities to take place within its territory or the transfer of models and technologies.

Nonintentional phenomena refer to external events whose explicit or primary objectives are other than health, but which potentially impact people's health. For the sake of clarity, we will modify *Rovere's Model*. This model refers to external determinants as the *international dimensions of health* and delineates four sets of potential impacts within a national entity (Rovere 1992). The first set potentially affects the health of the population (the internationalization of risks, be they biological, chemical, physical, or behavioral in nature). These risks might be limited in scope, like a toxic spill between two bordering countries. Risks may be regional such as the cholera epidemic in Central and South America, or they may be global such as the world epidemic of tobacco (Council 1990), the depletion of the ozone layer, or population growth (Wallack and Montgomery 1992). They include the movement of people (travel, tourism, migration, and refugees), and the movement of dangerous substances, industry, propaganda, and cultural penetration.

The second set relates to the organization and delivery of health care services—the Exporting Health Services Model (Rovere 1992). The medical-industrial complex plays a central part as international health insurance companies or hospital chains increase their share of foreign markets due to the privatization of the health sector currently taking place in many countries. Thirdly, the promotion and sale of medical knowledge, services and technologies, including drugs, has a major impact on the development of national health resources. Arguably, these phenomena could be considered "intentional" because they directly relate to health care. Nevertheless, we tend to view them as nonintentional because the primary purpose of the companies producing these goods or services is for profit rather than the health and well-being of the population.

Lastly, the development of social and economic policies within national boundaries is heavily influenced by external factors and, in turn, has serious consequences on the health, equity, and quality of the health care services provided. Governments are being pressured to privatize and decentralize. The structural adjustment programs promoted by the International Monetary Fund during the 1980s were partly aimed at achieving privatization and downsizing. Furthermore, a commercial or military embargo imposed on a country can have serious consequences not only on its accessibility to health devices and technologies, but also on its social and economic policies.

The policy function refers to the formulation of an international health policy which should be analyzed along two main axes. First of all, the raison d'être of these policies is the pursuit of health objectives. In turn, they might be concerned with the protection of that country's population or, alternately, with the improvement of the health status of another country. However, an international health policy can be examined for its relation objectives. An example of this is how international health activities support the foreign policy of a country by contributing to the development of political, diplomatic or commercial relationships.

From the standpoint of a donor nation, the analytical function can proceed in a proactive way by identifying external risks and their potential consequences for the country's health. It may work alternately in a reactive fashion by investigating the international dimensions of a specific health problem. The same attributes apply to policy making. The quality of the institutional articulation and networking of the intelligence and policy functions is crucial in protecting the country's population from external risks or in maximizing international opportunities to improve the welfare of its citizens. Both functions require knowledge pertaining to public health and international relations, and collaboration between experts in both fields. The efficiency of the country in that respect is also largely a tribute to its ability to mobilize and network NGOs and citizens around these functions.

The imbalance of power between countries expresses itself in its differential vulnerability to external determinants and the ability of one or several countries to convince other international actors to support their interests. External interests will influence and determine the welfare of the population of a weak country and the quality of its health services. As a result, its ability to articulate a coherent international health policy will be minimal. It is important to understand that a poor country is not the same as a weak country when dealing with public health and foreign policy issues. The strong sense of purpose and shared identity compensates for limited wealth. For example, Cuba is a poor country, but it is not a weak country when providing health care and implementing health policies for its people (Feinsilver 1993).

CONCLUSION

Today, international health is a worldwide reality due to the interconnecting factors shared by people and governments. Globalization has been a critical component changing traditional international health's scope (from the notion of dependence to that of interdependence) and its approach (from a view of homogeneity to diversity, and from assistance to cooperation). During the past 30 years, MCH has made significant gains; however, the health of women, mothers, and children lags behind in most countries. Issues of equity affect these groups in both industrialized as well as developing countries.

REFERENCES

AbouZahr, C., and E. Royston. 1991. *Maternal mortality: A global fact-book*. Geneva: World Health Organization.

Adagala, K. 1991. Households and historical changes in plantations in Kenya. In *Women, households and change,* eds. E. Massini and L. Stratigos, 158–179. Toyko: University of Tokyo and United Nations.

Adekolu-J., E.O. 1989. Maternal health care and outcomes of pregnancy in Kainji Lake area of Nigeria. *Public Health* 103:41–49.

Arole, M., and R. Arole. 1994. *Jamkhed: A comprehensive rural health project*. London: The Macmillan Press, Ltd.

Babb, F. 1987. *Between field and cooking pot: The economy market women in Peru*. Austin: University of Texas Press.

Bågenholm, G. et al. 1987. Child feeding habits in the People's Democratic Republic of Yemen. I. Breast and bottle feeding. *Journal of Tropical Pediatrics* 19:208–212.

Basch, P.F. 1990. *Textbook of international health*. New York: Oxford University Press.

Canadian Council for International Co-operation. 1991. *Two halves make whole: Balancing gender relations in development*. Ottawa: MATCH International and Association Québécoise des Organismes de Coopération Internationale.

Center for Reproductive Law and Policy, International Program. 1994. *The Cairo Conference, a programme of action for reproductive rights? Reproductive freedom at the UN*. New York: UN, October.

Cleland, J.G., and J.K. Van Ginneken. 1988. Maternal education and child survival in developing countries: The search for pathways of influence. *Social Science Medicine* 27:1357–1368.

Cochrane, S.H. et al. 1990. The effects of education on health. *World Bank Staff Working Paper No. 405*. Washington, DC: World Bank.

Council on Scientific Affairs. 1990. The worldwide smoking epidemic. *Journal of American Medical Association* 263:3312–3318.

Das Gupta, M. 1987. Selective discrimination against female children in rural Punjab, India. *Population Development Review* 13:77.

Economist, The. 1995. The nation-state is dead. Long live the nation-state. December 23–January 5, 15–18.

Ettling, J. 1981. *The germ of laziness.* Cambridge, MA: Harvard University Press.

Faúndes, A. et al. 1988. Maternity care in developing countries: Relevance of new technological advances. *International Journal of Gynecological Obstetrics* 26:349–354.

Fee, E. 1987. *Disease and discovery.* Baltimore and London: The Johns Hopkins University Press.

Feijoo, M., and E. Jelin. 1987. Women from low income sectors: Economic recession and democratization of politics in Argentina. *The invisible adjustment and the economic crisis.* Santiago, Chile: Alfabeta, 27–54.

Feinsilver, J.M. 1993. *Healing the masses: Cuban health politics at home and abroad.* Berkeley, CA: University of California Press.

Flores, C., and E. Bonilla. 1991. The impact of the demographic transition in the Colombian family. In *Women, households and change,* eds. E. Massini and L. Stratigos, 30–62. Tokyo: United Nations Press.

Foreit, K.G. et al. 1991. Cost and benefits of implementing child survival services at a private mining company in Peru. *American Journal of Public Health* 81:1055–1057.

Fortney, J.A. et al. 1988. Maternal mortality in Indonesia and Egypt. *International Journal of Gynecological Obstetrics* 26:21–32.

Fryer, M.L. 1991. Health education through interactive radio: A child-to-child project in Bolivia. *Health Education Quarterly* 18:65–77.

Giffin, K. 1994. Women's health and the privatization of fertility control in Brazil. *Social Science Medicine* 39:355–360.

Godue, C. 1992. International health and schools of public health in the United States. In *International health: A north south debate.* Human Resources Development Series, No. 95. Washington, DC: Pan American Health Organization, Regional Office of the World Health Organization, 113–26.

Graham, W. et al. 1989. Estimating maternal mortality: A sisterhood method. *Studies in Family Planning* 20:125–135.

Hamilton, L.H. 1994. A democratic look at foreign policy. *Foreign Affairs* 9:32–51.

Hobsbawm, E. 1994. *The age of the extremes. A history of the world, 1914–1991.* New York: Pantheon Books.

Howard, J.N. 1975. *The scientific background of the international sanitary conferences, 1851–1938.* Geneva: World Health Organization.

Hyppolito, S.B. 1992. Alternative model for low risk obstetric care in third world rural and peri-urban areas. *International Journal of Gynecological Obstetric* 38 (suppl):S63–S66.

Iyun, F. 1989. An assessment of a rural health program on child and maternal care: The Ogbomoso community health care program (CHCP), Oyo State, Nigeria. *Social Science Medicine* 29:933–938.

Karkal, M. 1991. Abortion laws and the abortion situation in India. *Issues in Reproductive and Genetic Engineering* 4:223–230.

Kestler, E. 1993. Wanted: Better care for pregnant women. *World Health Forum* 14:356–359.

Khan, M.E. et al. 1990. Work pattern of women and its impact on health and nutrition: Some observation from the urban poor. *Journal of Family Welfare* 36:3.

Langer, A. et al. 1993. The Latin American trial of psychosocial support during pregnancy: A social intervention evaluated through an experimental design. *Social Science Medicine* 36:495–507.

Lawson, J. 1989. Topical obstetrics and gynecology-3-vesico-vaginal fistula: A tropical disease. *Transactions of the Royal Society of Tropical Medical Hygiene* 83:454–456.

Leigh, B. 1986. The use of partograms by MCH aides. *Journal of Tropical Pediatrics* 32:107–110.

Mahowald, M.B. 1993. *Women and children in health care: An unequal majority.* New York: Oxford University Press, 242–54.

Margolis, T., and L.J. Mercer. 1994. Vesico-vaginal fistula. *Obstetrical Gynecology Survey* 49: 837–844.

Mari Bhat, P.N. et al. 1995. Maternal mortality in India: Estimates from a regression model. *Studies in Family Planning* 26:217–232.

Midmer, D.K. 1992. Does family-centered maternity care empower women? The development of women-centered childbirth model. *Family Medicine* 24:216–221.

Mir, N.A. 1989. Transport of sick neonates: Practical considerations. *Indian Pediatrics* 26:755–764.

Moss, N. et al. 1992. Child health outcomes among Central American refugees and immigrants in Belize. *Social Science Medicine* 34:161–167.

Nkrumah, F.K., and K.J. Nathhoo. 1987. Recent trends in child health and survival in Zimbabwe. *Journal of Tropical Pediatrics* 33:153–155.

Nowak, R. 1995. New push to reduce maternal mortality in poor countries. *Science* 269:780–782.

Panerai, R.B. et al. 1991. Estimating the effectiveness of perinatal care technologies by expert opinion. *International Journal of Technology Assessment in Health Care* 7:367–378.

Panisset, U.B. 1992. Reflections on health as an international issue. *International health: A north south debate.* Human Resources Development Series, No. 95. Washington DC: Pan American Health Organization, Regional Office of the World Health Organization, 165–191.

Parkin, D.W. et al. 1989. What do international comparison of health care expenditures really show? *Community Medicine* 11:116–123.

Patterson, K.D. 1981. *Health in colonial Ghana: Disease, medicine, and socio-economic change, 1900–1955.* Waltham, MA: Crossroads Press.

Perez-Escamilla, R. et al. 1992. Effect of the maternity ward system on the lactation success of low-income urban Mexican women. *Early Human Development* 31:25–40.

Raikes, A. 1989. Women's health in East Africa. *Social Science Medicine* 28:447.

Ramalingaswami, P. 1986. The child as a focus for health promotion in the developing world. *Social Science Medicine* 22:1181–1186.

Ratcliffe, J. 1985. The influence of funding agencies on international health policy, research and programs. *Mobius* 5:93–115.

Rosecrance, R.N. 1986. *The rise of the trading state.* New York: Basic Books.

Rosenau, J.N. 1990. *Turbulence in world politics: A theory of change and continuity.* Princeton, NJ: Princeton University Press.

Rosenfield, A. 1989. Maternal mortality in developing countries: An ongoing but neglected epidemic. *Journal of American Medical Association* 262:376–379.

Rovere, M. 1992. International dimensions of health. *International health: A north south debate.* Human Resources Development Series, No. 95. Washington, DC: Pan American Health Organization, Regional Office of the World Health Organization, 149–164.

Sanders, D., and R. Davis. 1989. The economy, the health sector and child health in Zimbabwe since independence. *Social Science Medicine* 27:723–731.

Scheepers, L.M. 1991. Jidda. The traditional midwife of Yemen? *Social Science Medicine* 33:959–962.

Scheer, P., and G.J. Ebrahim. 1985. Factors affecting child health in a traditional West African society. *Journal of Tropical Pediatrics* 31:77–82.

Shahidullah, M. 1995. The sisterhood method of estimating maternal mortality: The matlab. *Studies in family planning* 26:101–106.

Smyke, P. 1993. *Women and health.* Atlantic Highlands, New Jersey: Zed Books, Ltd.

Solorzano, A. 1992. Sowing the seeds of neo-imperialism: The Rockefeller Foundation's yellow fever campaign in Mexico. *International Journal of Health Services* 22:529–554.

Sundström-Feigenberg, K. 1988. Reproductive health and reproductive freedom: Maternal health care and family planning in the Swedish health system. *Women and Health* 13:35–55.

Tsui, A.O. 1995. *Causal sequence of sexual and reproductive events embodied in sexual and reproductive health status.* Paper presented at the Panel on Reproductive Health, Committee on Population, National Research Council, Washington, DC.

UNICEF. 1985. *The state of the world's children 1985—Part I.* Statement by James P. Grant, Executive Director. New York.

UNICEF. 1995. *The progress of nations: The nations of the world ranked according to their achievements in child health, nutrition, education, family planning, and progress for women.* New York.

United Nations. 1994. *Program of action of the United Nations International Conferences on Population and Development,* Unedited Version. New York: Author, September 30.

Vlassoff, C., and E. Bonilla. 1994. Gender-related differences in the impact of tropical disease on women: What do we know? *Journal of Biosocial Science* 26:37–53.

Wallack, L., and K. Montgomery. 1992. Advertising for all by the year 2000: Public health implications for less developed countries. *Journal of Public Health Policy* 13:204–223.

Wegman, M.E. 1977. A salute to the Pan American Health Organization. *PAHO Bulletin* XI:297–302.

Williams, C.D. et al. 1994. *Mother and child health: Delivering the services,* 3d ed. New York: Oxford University Press.

Winikoff, B. 1990. Women's health in the developing countries. In *Health care of women and children in developing countries,* eds. H.M. Wallace and K. Giri. Oakland, CA: Third Party Publishing Company.

World Health Organization. 1992. *Women's health: Across age and frontier.* Geneva: World Health Organization.

Zapata, B.C. et al. 1992. The influence of social and political violence on the risk of pregnancy complications. *American Journal of Public Health* 82:685–690.

PART IV

Maternal and
Child Health Skills

CHAPTER 14

Research and Evaluation in Maternal and Child Health

There is a general problem about who should be labeled a MCH research worker. My definition is anyone working on health issues involving mothers and children on a population basis, rather than as individuals or small groups.

Haggerty, 1981

INTRODUCTION

Maternal and child health (MCH) research is a collaborative process, like most good research today. In compiling this chapter I have relied upon many different MCH researchers to contribute a section based on the particular expertise of each. The contributors include faculty with backgrounds in medicine, social work, health services research, epidemiology and, of course, MCH. Each section's author or authors are identified at the beginning of that section—Ed.

THE RESEARCH QUESTION
Sandra L. Martin

In any research endeavor, the research question that is posed should guide all methodological activities undertaken in the research process (e.g., design of the study, data collection, data analysis, interpretation of study findings, etc.). Therefore, posing of the research question is one of the most important undertakings in any MCH research study, including the evaluation of MCH programs.

When posing a research question, it is helpful to keep in mind two characteristics of high-quality research questions, namely, the significance of the research question and the feasibility of addressing the research question. Each of these characteristics will be briefly discussed.

The Significance of the Research Question

The research question must be of great enough significance to the field of MCH to justify undertaking the research project. In other words, the question must be an important one, and finding the answer to the research question must somehow advance the field of MCH. This advancement of the field may take many different forms including, but not restricted to, the development or refinement of theories pertinent to MCH, estimating the extent of a health problem of unknown magnitude (including needs assessments and prevalence studies), identifying risk and/or protective factors associated with the health status of women and children, and evaluating the effectiveness of MCH programs and interventions.

Significant research questions also may be characterized as being somewhat unique in that they have never, or rarely, been posed or addressed before. Some research questions in MCH are truly unique in that no prior research has ever addressed the question. For example, recent investigations focusing on human immunodeficiency virus (HIV)-positive pregnant women posed novel research questions concerning the effectiveness of particular drugs in decreasing the extent of HIV transmission from the mother to the infant. It is more often the case that very important research questions addressed in MCH investigations have been examined in past studies; however, the later studies may incorporate methodological advances in the study design that justify re-examination of the issue. For example, several recent investigations have revisited the effectiveness of prenatal care visits in enhancing the health of pregnant women using new methodologies.

Another characteristic of significant research questions is that they are well-grounded in theory and/or that they are based on a well-formulated conceptual model (Earp and Ennett 1991). There is no one theoretical or conceptual perspective that underlies all of the possible areas of research within the broad field of MCH. Therefore, research within MCH draws upon theories and models that have been developed within a multitude of disciplines including epidemiology, health behavior, psychology, demography, biology, etc.

The Feasibility of Addressing the Research Question

The feasibility of adequately addressing the research question is of paramount importance in any type of research. Even the most interesting and significant questions are not worth pursuing if they cannot be reasonably addressed within the context of a research study. Several issues should be examined in assessing the feasibility of addressing the research question including, but not limited to, the five issues outlined here, namely, (1) whether the constructs implied by the research question can be operationalized, (2) whether data pertinent to the research question are accessible, (3) whether the research question is testable, (4) whether there are ethical issues inherent in addressing the research question, and (5) whether the significance of the research question justifies expenditure of the amount of resources necessary to address the question.

For a research question to be feasible, the researcher must be able to *operationalize* the constructs (or ideas or terms) contained within the research question (Wicker 1992). This means that the researcher must be able to develop a working definition for each of the terms contained within the research question. For example, if the following research question is posed, "What is the prevalence of homeless women within the United States?," the researcher must be able to clearly define what he/she means by the term *homeless women*. Several reasonable definitions for "homeless women" may be formulated, such as "all women living in homeless shelters on a particular date," "all women living on the street or in homeless shelters on a particular date," etc. Often, as in this case, there may be many reasonable ways to operationalize/define a particular construct/term, and different definitions will result in different answers to the research question.

In order for a research question to be feasible, the data (or information) needed to address the research question must be accessible to the researcher. This may be new information collected by the researcher in order to address the research question (e.g., the researcher may conduct his/her own survey, the researcher may observe the behavior of families during some task, etc.), or the researcher may review already existing information that has been collected by another person/agency for some other purpose (e.g., the researcher may review patients' hospital records to abstract pertinent information, the researcher may analyze research data that were originally collected to address some other research question, etc.).

Feasible research questions include those which can be "tested" in the context of a research study. Often, MCH research questions are framed in terms of testable hypotheses (or propositions) that may be refuted (or accepted) based on the study findings (Bauman 1980). For example, it would be possible to design a study to examine the following testable hypothesis: "Pregnant women who smoke cigarettes have babies of lower birth weight than do pregnant women who do not smoke cigarettes." In order to test this hypothesis, the researcher could compare the weights of infants of women who smoked during pregnancy with the weights of infants of women who did not smoke during pregnancy. In contrast, the following statement would not be classified as a testable hypothesis: "It should be illegal for women to smoke during pregnancy." Since this latter statement implies an attitude (or value judgment), it is not a testable hypothesis that could be refuted in the context of a research study.

While many of the research questions posed in the field of MCH take the form of hypotheses, which may be tested using research methods, other equally pertinent research questions may be posed as inquiries concerning estimation of the extent of a condition within a particular study population. Typically, these research questions focus on estimating the incidence or prevalence of a particular disease, disorder, or problem (Kleinbaum 1982). For example, a research question may ask, "What is the prevalence of domestic violence among married couples in the United States?" In this case, the research question is still "testable" in the sense that research methods may be used to estimate the extent of domestic violence within the population of interest.

Although all research questions should be significant, research questions vary in their degree of significance. In general, the degree of significance of the research question should be positively correlated with the amount of resources (e.g., time, money, personnel, etc.) expended to address the research question. In other words, it is feasible to allocate a small amount of resources to address a research question of moderate significance, while spending a greater amount of resources on addressing a research question of greater significance. For example, it may be of greater significance to the field of MCH to address research questions concerning the effectiveness of programs that are in place nationwide (e.g., programs such as the Supplemental Food Program for Women, Infants and Children [WIC]) than to address questions concerning the effectiveness of programs that serve a much smaller local community. Although research questions focused on the effectiveness of both of these programs may be viewed as significant, the relatively greater significance of learning about the effectiveness of a nationwide program compared to a local program would justify a greater research expenditure on the nationwide program.

Finally, most research conducted within the field of MCH relies upon information that will be, or has been, collected concerning people (e.g., surveys of the attitudes or behaviors of adults or children, review of the medical records of children or adults, etc.). It is important to examine whether ethical concerns will arise by addressing such research questions. As discussed in the next section, the researcher must ask whether addressing the study question will place any of the study participants at more than *minimal risk*. Federal regulations define the "minimal risk" of participating in a research study as being not greater than the probability and magnitude of the anticipated risks of harm "ordinarily encountered in daily life or during the performance of routine physical or psychological examinations or tests" (U.S. DHHS 1981, p. 8373). Therefore, the researcher must consider whether a research study may be designed so as to address the research question while minimizing the risk to the study participants.

RESEARCH ETHICS
Jonathan B. Kotch

Introduction

Researchers in MCH have special obligations to their subjects who, in many cases, are infants and children below the age of consent, or pregnant women, whose participation in research may have implications for the outcome of their pregnancies. Contemporary concerns regarding protecting the interests of children and other dependents who may be research subjects may be traced back to the Willowbrook experiments of the 1950s, when institutionalized, mentally retarded children were deliberately exposed to hepatitis virus for the purpose of observing the natural history of the disease in this special population (Beauchamp and Childress 1994). Sensitivity to protecting human research subjects from exploitation is now institutionalized in the requirement that research involving human subjects must be approved by institutional review boards (IRBs). This is in large part a consequence of the report of the National Commission for the Protection of Human Subjects of Biomedical and Behavioral Research, commonly known as the Belmont Report. That report proposed three principles for considering the ethics of a research proposal, namely, beneficence, autonomy, and justice (King and Churchill 1994; National Commission 1978). Intersecting these principles are the competing interests of society, the parent(s), the child, and the researcher. These interests will be discussed in the context of the three principles.

Principles of Biomedical Research

Beneficence

Beneficence of course is the principle that the research should benefit the actors involved, especially parent(s) and child(ren), but also society as a whole, at the same time as it adds to our scientific knowledge. In the ideal world it is the potential for the research to add to our scientific knowledge that motivates the researcher(s). Therefore, should the research be successful, the researcher(s) may be presumed to have benefited as well.

In the calculus of IRBs, it is not sufficient to demonstrate a benefit, but the benefit must outweigh the risk to the participants. Some authorities argue that any nontherapeutic research that does not benefit the child subjects themselves is unethical no matter what the benefits to society may be (Ramsey 1970). Others would admit the possibility that, if the risk to the child subjects were no more than minimal ("nearly that of the subject's ambiance . . . " [Englehardt, 1978, pp. 8–34]), a direct benefit is not required. In the case of therapeutic research, on the other hand, risk may be more than minimal provided that an intervention holds out the prospect of direct benefit. A distinction is drawn here between therapeutic and nontherapeutic research precisely because in much MCH research involving primary data collection by survey, there is no intervention, and consequently no direct benefit to subjects. To have to justify research that involves interviews, observation, or testing of children on the basis of a direct benefit would disqualify much of the work that MCH researchers do.

There are risks, of course, even in nontherapeutic research. These risks are primarily those of disclosure, i.e., breach of confidentiality. It is an absolute obligation of researchers to protect the confidentiality of subjects or to inform the subjects ahead of time as to what information might be at risk of disclosure. For example, child abuse researchers are more and more asking children directly about their experience of abuse (e.g., Finkelhor and Dzuiba-Leatherman 1995). All states in the United States have reporting laws that require that knowledge of abuse be reported to Child Protective Services. If the research is not protected by a Certificate of Confidentiality (Melton 1990) from the U.S. Public Health Service, the researcher(s) may be obligated to report child abuse discovered in the course of the child interview. In this case the researcher must specify this possibility in the informed consent instrument signed by the parent, and in the assent required of children over the age of seven.

Other potential risks include labeling, mental anguish, stigmatization, overtesting, and invasion of privacy. For example, either the parent or the child may experience mental anguish should the survey elicit painful memories. In this case, as in the case of labeling, stigmatization, overtesting, and invasion of privacy, researchers are expected to specify the risks in the informed consent and assent statements. Quantifying such risks is not an exact science, but two dimensions, the magnitude of the risk and the probability of an adverse outcome of the research, must both be considered, along with the risk of not doing the research. Should the risks be more than minimal, nontherapeutic research involving children would not be ethically justifiable.

Autonomy

The autonomy principle requires that researchers respect their subjects as persons. Persons, including children, must be treated as ends, not means. This principle is operationalized when subjects voluntarily give their informed consent to participate. This is not a trivial consideration in the case of children, who cannot themselves give informed consent. Parents are considered qualified to give "proxy consent" on behalf of their children for one of several reasons. First, the parents are presumed to be acting in the best interests of the child (National Commission 1978). Alternatively, the parent of a child older than an infant might believe that the child would give its informed consent if it could. A third possible justification is that the parent believes that the child would wish to do what he or she ought to do, and that participation in research in which the risk is not more than minimal is a manifestation of the obligation to share the common burden of medical progress that is for the benefit of all (McCormick 1974).

There is a problem, however, inherent in the nature of informed consent, if full disclosure of the purpose of the research would itself be an ethical harm to the subject. For example, what if full disclosure would itself be a painful reminder of undesirable parental characteristics, such as the fact that they abuse their children (Kinard 1985), or if full disclosure would subject participants to ridicule or stigma if the true nature of the study were known, e.g., a study about children with AIDS? When full disclosure is deemed risky for adult subjects, limited disclosure in the informed consent instrument may be justified, provided that subjects are debriefed at the end of the study. But is the same procedure valid in the case of research for which parents provide proxy consent for their children to participate? Partial disclosure limits the extent to which parents can stand up for the best interests of their children. Parents may need to be told more about the true nature of the study in question in order to exercise fully their roles as guardian when it comes to proxy consent.

Justice

The principle of justice requires that research subjects be treated fairly. In MCH and other human research, fair treatment begins with nondiscriminatory, nonarbitrary subject selection. That is, potential eligibles are selected for participation on the basis of objective criteria that are reasonably connected with the aims of the research, and eligibles have an equal chance of being recruited. The decision to use children as research subjects should itself be based upon specific criteria. Giertz (1983) articulates several preconditions for using children in nontherapeutic research, including that the research cannot be accomplished using adults, that there is no clinical or animal model, and that the benefits outweigh the risks. Dworkin (1978) adds that the research cannot be illegal.

There is the possibility that *not* conducting some forms of medical research, such as clinical trials on children, may itself be unjust. Such limits on the participation of children in medical research would lead to the growth of the "therapeutic orphan" problem. Certain therapies might never be available to children because the therapies could never be adequately tested on children to determine their safety and effectiveness. Similarly, innovative public health interventions including such services as home visiting or nutrition supplementation might never be proven effective were there no possibility for their scientific evaluation. Public health researchers therefore have an obligation to conduct research using child subjects in order to demonstrate the success, or futility, of a service that might benefit children as a whole, even though the participants may not themselves benefit.

The use of randomization as a fair mechanism for selection of subjects is itself controversial. In order to be ethical, random allocation of child subjects to a program or service that may prove to be beneficial is only justifiable when the potential benefits of the service or program are unproven, when the services would be unavailable to all in absence of the research, and when there is an equal chance of selection into the intervention group. Finally, at the end of the study (or before the end if the interim results show unequivocal success of the intervention), there must be an opportunity for controls to benefit.

Conflicts of Interest

The above principles may help in sorting out inevitable conflicts that arise in the course of MCH research. The first such potential conflict may arise between the interests of the parent and the child. An example is the case of knowledge of child maltreatment that may be the result of the data collection process. In this case the autonomy of the parent conflicts with beneficence toward the child. In order to protect the child from further abuse, the parent's confidentiality may have to be breached. However, it is not a simple decision. Reporting abuse may not in fact result in a benefit to the child (National Research Council 1993), whereas breach of confidentiality is a clear ethical harm. Furthermore, were the child the source of the information that led to the report, that child might be at risk of recrimination from the perpetrator(s) of the abuse.

Similarly, there may be a conflict between full disclosure of the aims of a research project and the interest of society (and the researcher) in completing the study. Again, child abuse research provides an example. To disclose to potential parent subjects that child abuse is the explicit focus of the research might lead to difficulty in recruitment, especially of those with a history of abusing children. Such a study might never be accomplished were full disclosure required. In this conflict between the autonomy of the subject parent (the right to full disclosure) and a benefit to society (increased knowledge about child abuse), if only minimal risk is anticipated and subjects are fully debriefed at the end of the research, the study might be pursued ethically. But what if the study were to lead to a child abuse report, which from the subject parent's point of view would be a harm? Such a subject would clearly not have volunteered to participate had he or she known the true nature of the research.

There may be a similar conflict between child autonomy and social benefit, as in the case of a parent whose consent is sought to use umbilical cord blood in a clinical experiment that might lead to saving the life of an anonymous third party. Does the parent have an obligation to volunteer a child for a research study "for the good of society," or would the parent be justified in refusing on behalf of the newborn whose own wishes on the subject would not possibly be known? Finally, there may be a conflict between a potential benefit to the child subject and society's interest in successfully completing a research project. The possibility that food supplementation may be withheld from poor children is one of the reasons why a nationwide, randomized study of the effect of WIC on children (as opposed to the effect of WIC on pregnant women and infants) has never been done. But at the same time there is very little scientific information on the impact of childhood WIC (U.S. Department of Agriculture 1992).

Research which is not ethical is not good research, no matter the results. MCH researchers in particular have an obligation to women and children to set a standard for the conduct of research that is both scientifically strong and ethically sound. Other fields that use women and children in their research can only benefit from this example.

PROJECT IMPLEMENTATION AND DATA MANAGEMENT FOR SURVEY RESEARCH
Jane Stein

Introduction

Much of what is taught and written about research is focused on the preliminary stages of question formulation and project and instrument design and on the penultimate data analysis stage. The actual carrying out of the project is perhaps too practical and pragmatic to receive much academic attention. However, those who learn to do research "on the job" and those who are forced to carry out a project without training quickly recognize the need for guidance and for guidelines.

Project implementation includes several phases: the set-up phase, where hiring, space allocation, and orientation to the project take place; the instrument pretest and redesign phase; the data collection phase; the data management phase; the data analysis phase; the interpretation, writing, and dissemination phases; and the shut-down phase. These are not necessarily consecutive and obviously overlap with some aspects of project design. The focus of this section is data management, a key and undervalued component of the implementation of a research or evaluation project. Critical elements of other phases will be addressed as well.

Project Administration

Research and evaluation projects vary enormously in how they are structured and in their size and complexity. Yet even small projects require a lot of nurturing. Research is generally a group process, and its success depends greatly on the principal investigator's (PI) skills and interests. Most PIs are juggling many activities. One key to a successful project is to hire a competent, experienced Project Manager who gives as much time to the project as the project can afford—at least 51 percent. This person should complement the PI—managing details and keeping on schedule if the PI is a visionary, or handling external relations and staff nurturing if the PI is detail- and number-oriented. The project staff should function as a team, meeting regularly (at least biweekly) and keeping one another informed about problems and successes. The budget, the project timeline, and the literature should be reviewed on a regular basis, with all staff members alerted to potential delays or financial difficulties. Monitoring, in the form of minutes, documented decisions, and completion dates, should be formalized and maintained. Above all, credit should be generously given for work well done, and each staff member's work should be valued and appreciated.

Data Collection

There are many possible pitfalls for projects that collect primary data, only some of which can be anticipated. One important preventive measure is to be sure that the proposed study population is in fact available and of the size expected. This is particularly crucial to patient or client studies where providers overestimate the numbers. Another controllable factor is the instrumentation—is it a reasonable length, is it well organized and worded, will it keep the interest of the study population? Less controllable but also vital in a site-based study are the relationships with the site staff. They must be convinced of the value of the project if they are to take on extra tasks or interact with research staff during the course of the day.

In a mailed survey, the principal issues concern a good cover letter that entices the subject to respond to the survey and procedures for logging in received forms and for following up with nonrespondents in order to achieve an acceptable response rate.

For either telephone or in-person interviews, the selection, training, and monitoring of interviewers must be well thought through, and staff turnover must be anticipated. Using videos for training, creating, and updating interviewer manuals will help (1) during the original training, which may take several sessions if not all interviewers can come at one time, (2) during regularly scheduled training updates, which can uncover misunderstandings and unexpected events, (3) and during the training of replacement interviewers. Interviewer procedures should be clear and systematically described. Particular attention should be paid to correct and consistent use of subject identifiers, procedures for minimizing and coding missing information, and the collection of information on nonrespondents. Above all, interviewers need a responsive and responsible supervisor, particularly if the interviews are being conducted in person and at some distance from the project headquarters.

Data collection instruments need almost as much tender, loving care as interviewers. Careful procedures should be established and followed with regard to their daily review by the interviewer, their transmission to the project headquarters, their second review and precoding (if necessary) by project staff, their transfer to data entry, and their storage for easy access during the data processing stage. If possible, some logging procedures should be implemented so that the location and status of any form could be determined at any time. On the other hand, those procedures should be minimally cumbersome to the staff. A team orientation will pay off at this stage, reducing the possibility that one group—interviewers or data processors or programmers—will be overly critical of or feel competitive with another group.

Data Management

Data management actually begins at the data collection stage with the forms management just described. It also encompasses data entry, data editing, and preliminary and final data analyses. The work may be done in phases by specialists or by one staff person. Two issues should be given priority: (1) the people doing this work should be experienced, or, if not, they should be very well supervised by someone who is, and (2) they should be treated as integral members of the research team. The more they understand and feel part of the project, the better and more efficient will be the handling of the data.

Accuracy is more important in data entry than is speed, but as the keyer can only key what is on the form, careful prior review is essential. Data entry software can greatly facilitate the data entry process and ensure more accurate data. Look for programs that incorporate data editing at data entry. This will enable checking for some common coding or keying errors such as out-of-range values, multiple responses to a question with mutually exclusive responses, or incorrectly administered skip patterns. However, the keyer must have been given procedures for dealing with such problems, such as flagging the problem and keying a missing value in the computer, or checking with the interviewer or supervisor before continuing. Whenever possible, each form should be keyed and verified—entered a second time, by a second person if possible. If this is not possible, all of the data should be hand-checked for accuracy.

If these procedures are followed, the data should be fairly clean by the time they arrive on the computer of the person who will edit them and run the preliminary analyses. However, this part of the process will still be time-consuming. Often as much as 70 or 80 percent of data processing time is spent cleaning, editing, and reducing data. As is true throughout a research project, good and current documentation is essential at this stage. This begins with well-documented programs and data files and with a log of data management activities.

The general process encompasses moving from data entry files, which contain all of the data from each questionnaire, to one or more analysis files which contain the data needed for analyses in a form that expedites those analyses. The data entry files are usually raw data, in text format. The first step is usually to convert these into a statistical file that is read and managed by a statistical program. During the course of this conversion, each variable will be given a name and a longer label for better identification, and each of the values of each noncontinuous variable will be labeled. The project will benefit if all those who will be involved in the analysis phase agree to the names and labels selected. It also encourages a sense of group ownership of data that will make the analysis steps less open to conflict. From the start, a log containing information about each computer job—the name of the job, the date run, the input file, the output file if applicable, the number of cases read in and written out, and the main tasks accomplished—should be maintained. This implies that each time data are manipulated, the work should be done by a program and not interactively. The programs themselves provide documentation about what has been done to the data. They should contain comments about the steps taken, clear titles, the name of the programmer, and the date run. Listings of the programs should be collected and kept in a binder. Never should a project trust a programmer's memory or allow for interactive modification of data.

The next step is to perform a fairly standard set of edits. The first is to check for the correct number of records in the file and the correct series of identifiers. Then each variable is checked to see that the values are "legal," that missing values have been correctly handled, and that the range of values for an unbounded variable such as age or income seems reasonable. Detected errors are corrected, based on decisions made or at least approved by the research staff. Pairs of related variables are then examined to check for consistent responses and proper skip patterns. These should be determined by the research staff based on their understanding of the relationships among the variables. After further corrections, the data are ready for preliminary evaluation. Is a variable potentially useful or does it have too many missing values or too little variation? Are its values distributed as expected? Dropping useless variables early on is highly recommended.

The next step includes variable transformation and reduction—recoding variables into categories, changing the direction of the values of a variable, and creating scales and composite variables. Again, this is an interactive process with input from the research staff. These new variables are edited just as were the original variables.

When this data cleaning process is complete, it is time to begin preliminary analyses. A well-organized project will have an analysis plan and will have assigned the variables to predefined analytic dimensions. Analyses should proceed dimension by dimension before looking across dimensions. Univariate descriptive analyses will be followed by bivariate analyses, and each dimension will be reviewed to decide which are the key variables for final analysis. If the population is stratified by one or more categorical variables, the data should also be examined in stratified analyses. Whenever possible and useful, graphics should be reviewed to help the research staff visualize the data. It is important that each member of the analysis group becomes familiar with the data at the variable level. If they are not, the interpretation of more complicated analyses is often faulty and full of conflict.

The next task is to create one or more analysis files that will be used for the final analyses. This may be done by a programmer or by qualified research staff. It is essential that these analyses be carefully documented as well, since these runs will provide information used in papers and reports and may be needed to provide backup justification and explanation for data tables and figures. Procedures should also be in place with regard to the storage of paper output so that it can be easily located and retrieved.

The final step in the data management process is to create a codebook that can be used by the staff for the analysis phase and by others in the future when the staff may have moved on to other jobs. This codebook should contain a list of all of the variables by name and label and the final file in which they are located. Each variable should be documented by its univariate statistics, and created or recoded variables should be accompanied by descriptions of how they were generated.

Projects do end but hardly ever die. Papers get written, reports and presentations are given, and other studies are designed based on the results of previous projects, often long after the project has closed down. The better the conduct and documentation of a project, the more likely it is to provide useful information and to have a lasting impact.

Conclusion

The steps described above are basic. If a project is longitudinal or multisite or includes a large number of instruments per subject or has multiple units of analysis, many other complications will arise. However, this is only meant to be a brief introduction to what is an important but neglected part of research. While the entire process of project implementation and data management is key to research and evaluation, it is not the part that tends to excite researchers, and it is certainly not what they were trained to do. However, it does take skill and thoughtfulness and some obsessiveness. All too many good research ideas have been buried by poorly managed projects and by bad data management. While funders and reviewers evaluate hypotheses, designs, and analysis plans, they rarely concern themselves with the day-to-day management of projects. Therefore, it is up to the PI and the project staff to properly value and carry out this part of the project.

THREATS TO ACCURATE INTERPRETATION OF SECONDARY DATA
Greg R. Alexander and Donna J. Petersen

A crucial step in the development of a research or evaluation design is the selection of a data source. Researchers must decide whether to collect their own data or to use an existing database. Good quality secondary databases, covering in detail a wide array of MCH populations and topics, increasingly are becoming available to researchers at a time when research funding for primary data collection is being constrained (Gable 1990). Researchers must choose not only between using primary and secondary data. They must also be prepared to justify their choices in terms of data acquisition costs, study duration costs, the quality, completeness and availability of needed data elements, and the potential validity and broad generalizability of results.

The use of secondary data for research is attractive for several reasons. The extended time required for the collection of primary data is saved, and the costs associated with data collection are accordingly diminished (Stewart 1984). To the extent that a secondary database can answer the same research question more quickly and at lower cost, the funder of the research receives better value for the research investment. Moreover, secondary databases can often provide extensive information on a large number of cases. Population-based secondary data, such as vital records, provide multiyear data on entire populations. Nationally representative surveys, e.g., the National Maternal and Infant Health Survey, offer extensive collections of variables (Sanderson et al. 1991). The results of studies using these databases have broad generalizability, compared to the more limited representativeness of studies using primary data collected from a single local population. Therefore, secondary data analysis may confer several advantages during times of fiscal constraints on research dollars. (A list of secondary databases and potential sources of secondary data is provided in Appendix 14–A.)

Notwithstanding these attributes, there are several problems associated with the use of secondary data. The analysis of secondary databases requires access to and mastery of the use of computer hardware and statistical analysis software. While mainframe computers are often required to analyze large secondary databases, this is rapidly changing with the development of more advanced personal computers and the availability of data sets on CD-ROM. These advancements have reduced the costs of secondary data analysis but have not lessened the level of statistical computing and research methods skills needed to manage, analyze, and interpret these data sets.

Being restricted to the variables contained on the data set is a basic limitation of secondary data. The primary collection of data affords researchers the opportunity to select their own variables of interest and decide how these variables will be collected and coded. This allows researchers to proceed from a theoretical or conceptual model to the determination of the operational definitions that will be employed to collect specific data elements or values from each individual case. In contrast, researchers using a secondary database must work with the data elements that are available. This presents a scientific and creative challenge.

In order to move beyond simply documenting and describing the contents of an existing database, researchers using secondary data must also start from a theoretical base with specific research hypotheses in mind. Being unable to specify the operational definitions of their research constructs, they must move backward from the available data elements to determine if the existing variables can be used, manipulated, or combined in such a manner as to provide conceptually valid indicators that will be useful for their own research purposes. This task involves both science and ingenuity. For example, the reported biological age initially collected on a database can be reformulated in a secondary analysis as a measure of legal status or age of majority. Income and occupation variables can be combined into a measure of status inconsistency. The art of secondary data analysis entails the creative reconceptualization and manipulation of existing variables into cogent new measures. When elegantly done, it would almost appear that the original data elements were collected for the specific purpose of the secondary analysis.

Of major concern in the use of secondary data is the difficulty inherent in using and interpreting data elements that have been collected, coded, and recoded by others. In order to appropriately analyze secondary data or to interpret the results of such analyses, a good working knowledge of the database is essential. This includes an understanding of variable definitions, the completeness and accuracy of reporting, and variable recoding strategies. As decisions about data measurement may produce unexpected biases, the credible use of secondary data for research and policy requires an in-depth assessment of the data, a careful and detailed documentation of the data coding procedures, and a cautious interpretation of the results.

Potential Threats to Accurate Data Interpretation

There are many potential threats to the accurate interpretation of secondary data. Whereas these threats are not different from those found in the interpretation of primary data, the finished appearance of a secondary database or analysis may make them less apparent. The remainder of this section will be devoted to identifying a number of the fundamental threats to the accurate interpretation of these data. These fundamental threats are listed in Exhibit 14–1. Several state vital record databases will be used to illustrate these threats. State vital record data, specifically Certificates of Live Birth and Infant Death, are probably the most commonly used data for MCH research, planning and evaluation, and needs assessment efforts, despite the many questions raised regarding their accuracy.

In drawing attention to inherent problems in vital record databases, one risks damping enthusiasm for their use. However, these data are extremely useful. Due to their coverage of entire populations over time and the increasing application of error checking programs by states, vital record data sets may offer benefits not available in hospital or medical record databases.

Exhibit 14–1 Potential Threats to Accurate Data Interpretation

Missing Data	Interpreting Large and Small Numbers
Out-of-Range Data	Concept Validity
Bivariate Inconsistency	Equating Risk with Cause

Missing Data

The first threat to accurate data interpretation involves the completeness of data reporting and the treatment of missing data. Missing or incomplete data can create major interpretation problems as it is uncertain if cases with missing data are similar to or markedly different from those with completely recorded information. Often at issue is whether it is appropriate to calculate rates and percentages from only those records or cases where data exist. There are good reasons to assume that cases with missing data are different from those with complete data. For example, several studies have noted that women whose birth certificates are missing gestational age data are more likely to have lower educational attainment and other lower indicators of socioeconomic status (Buekens et al. 1984; David 1980; Taffel et al. 1982; Wenner and Young 1974). As these women may have a higher risk of preterm delivery, we may suspect that cases with missing gestational age information may actually have a different gestational age distribution than those with this information reported.

Sometimes the issue of missing data is obscured by the way in which data are combined or presented. A notable example is the Institute of Medicine's (IOM) "Index of Adequacy of Prenatal Care" (Kessner et al. 1973). In this index, cases with missing prenatal care data were traditionally classified as receiving inadequate prenatal care, while cases with missing gestational age data were excluded from the index. Using Minnesota data from 1990–1991 (Table 14–1), we observe that, depending on the treatment of missing cases, the proportion of infants with mothers adequately utilizing prenatal care is either 62.9 or 74.5 percent. If the 15.7 percent with missing data have the same pattern of prenatal care utilization as those with completed data, then the 74.5 percent figure may be a good estimate of adequate prenatal care use. However, if cases with missing data are slightly less likely to adequately utilize prenatal care, then the 74.5 percent would be an overestimate.

Missing data on the date of last normal menses (DLNM), needed for the calculation of the gestational age interval, which in turn is used to compute adequacy of prenatal care indices, is a well-recognized problem. Nationwide, approximately 20 percent of birth certificates have missing or incomplete DLNM data

Table 14–1 Adequacy of Prenatal Care, 1990–1991 Minnesota Live Births

All Cases	*Only Complete Cases*
62.9% Adequate	74.5% Adequate
21.4% Less Than Adequate	25.5% Less Than Adequate
15.7% Missing	

(Taffel et al. 1982). A previous report on DHHS Region III states indicated variations in missing DLNM data ranging from approximately 5 to 30 percent (Alexander et al. 1990a). Reporting also varies by year. In South Carolina, the percent missing DLNM data was 31 percent in 1974 and less than 3 percent in 1990 (Alexander 1990b). As the percentage of missing adequacy of prenatal care data will exceed the percentage of missing gestational age data, an abrupt change in the proportion missing DLNM data, or major differences in the percent missing between population groups, can lead to the misinterpretation of prenatal care statistics (Alexander et al. 1991). In secondary analyses, careful attention must be given to the proportion missing and the treatment of cases with missing values in the computation of new variables, and indices should be clearly reported.

One accepted method for dealing with missing DLNM data is to impute a gestational age. There are two commonly used methods for this: the Day 15 method and the Preceding Case method (Alexander et al. 1990b). The choice of which, if any, imputation method to use is not without consequence. An investigation of 12-year trends in preterm delivery contrasted preterm percentages based on no imputation and by each of the above imputation schemes (Alexander et al. 1990b). Different trends emerged. The preterm percentages based on no imputation increased over the period. The Preceding Case method preterm percentages exhibited little if any change, while the Day 15 method preterm percentages decreased over time.

Out-of-Range Data

Out-of-range data present another fundamental problem for secondary data analysis. The proportion of out-of-range data is often not reported, as a convention for defining such data may not exist. Out-of-range data are those considered biologically implausible, or those outside the normally expected limits. This is mainly a problem with continuous variables. The problem with defining out-of-range data is determining the specific values that define the limits of the valid range. For example, while 10–50 years may seem like a reasonable range to use to define valid age of mother data, recent reports of live births to an 8-year-old and to surrogate grandmothers have increased the difficulty in selecting these cutpoints. As some health status measures are typically described in terms such as

"<2,500 grams" for low birth weight or "<37 weeks" for preterm delivery, improbable and clearly erroneous values may be inadvertently included in the calculation of these percentages unless precise limits are set that define the data values considered plausible. If cases with out-of-range values are included in the calculation of percentages and rates, e.g., preterm and very low birth weight, the resulting rates may be inflated.

Out-of-range data are a particular concern for investigations of cases at the extreme tails of distributions, e.g., very low birth weight, macrosomia, very preterm and postterm delivery, preteen pregnancy, and intrauterine growth. When secondary data are used for investigations of these topics, decisions made regarding the treatment of out-of-range data should be well-documented.

Bivariate Inconsistency

A data value may appear accurate until compared with another; then, it may become apparent that one is incorrect. This threat to accurate data interpretation is known as bivariate inconsistency. A fairly typical example of this is a case with a birth weight of 3,700 grams and a gestational age of 22 weeks. Such combinations are a little more than unusual. Tables have been developed to identify cases with implausible or inconsistent birth weight and gestational age values (Alexander et al. 1996). Other combinations of variables that can be checked for inconsistency include maternal age and parity and age and education. Checking for bivariate inconsistency is a good strategy when employing a secondary database and can reveal important information about the potential accuracy of the data that would not be evident from merely assessing the proportion missing or out-of-range.

Interpreting Large and Small Numbers

The next threat to accurate data interpretation involves large and small numbers. One attractive attribute of vital record databases is that they represent whole populations and, as such, contain a large number of cases from which to draw inferences. Nevertheless, in spite of the large numbers involved, many of the health status indicators monitored, e.g., infant deaths, are relatively rare events. Infant death rates, either based on a small number of births or a small number of deaths, are subject to considerable fluctuation. Highs and lows may not be reflective or typical of prevailing trends.

Large numbers are also a problem. Reliance on statistical tests can interfere with the appropriate interpretation of the data. It must be remembered that statistical testing is most useful for samples. For large populations, the majority of statistical comparisons will be significant based on large numbers alone. While so called significant, they may not signify a meaningful public health concern. For example, using data from Hawaii (Table 14–2), we note that the infant mortality rates vary significantly by military status among Whites, although the actual dif-

Table 14–2 Infant Mortality Rates by Military Status and Ethnicity, 1979–1989 Single Live Births to Adult, Married Hawaii Resident Women

	White	*Black*
Military	6.8	9.7
Nonmilitary	5.1	16.8
Significance	p>0.01	NS
N=	52,720	5,333

ference is relatively moderate. Among Blacks, the difference in infant mortality rates by military status is quite marked, but not significant. The differences in the number of live births among military-status and ethnic groups underlie the results of the significance tests.

Concept Validity

The selection of a health status indicator for research, evaluation or needs assessment involves a good conceptualization about what the indicator measures. At issue here is concept validity, and this can be a fundamental predicament in interpreting data. For example, gestational age refers to a unit of time between conception and birth, but this term is commonly used to refer to a host of other measures of fetal and newborn physical and neurological maturity that are highly correlated with but conceptually distinct from gestational age (Alexander and Allen 1996; Alexander et al. 1995). Furthermore, the use of neonatal-postneonatal time periods to differentiate endogenous-exogenous causes of death has been a hallmark in perinatal research but has recently been soundly criticized as no longer a conceptually valid approach (Kirby 1993).

Sometimes the stated title of the indicator may seem out of line with the strategy employed to measure it. The term "teen pregnancy" is a good example of a health status indicator without a well-established measurement convention. Thirteen to 19 years of age is technically the teenage years but less than 18, the age of minority, is often used in research. As seen in the Minnesota data presented in Table 14–3, the risk of low birth weight to the infant of a 19-year-old mother is quite distinct from that of a 13-year-old. The inclusion of 18- and 19-year-old mothers into the teenage group greatly inflates the numbers and percentages of teen mothers, while reducing the level of the associated risks observed to the group.

One focus of investigations into the impact of prenatal care utilization is a discussion of the conceptual premise for the various indices that are used to describe prenatal care use (Alexander and Kotelchuck, 1996). In Table 14–4, low and very low birth weight percentages are displayed by two different indices: (1) a modification of the original IOM index developed in the 1960s, and (2) an updated ver-

Table 14–3 Low Birth Weight by Age of Mother, 1990–1991, Single Live Births to Minnesota Residents

Age of Mother	Number	Percent LBW
12	4	25.0%
13	32	15.6%
14	146	8.2%
15	417	9.4%
16	1105	9.1%
17	1842	8.2%
18	2998	7.7%
19	4154	6.3%
<18	3546	8.7%
<20	10,698	7.5%

sion of this index using the latest standards for prenatal care visits recommended by the American College of Obstetricians and Gynecologists (ACOG). Note that the strength of the relationship between adequacy of prenatal care and birth weight is dependent on the index used. The ACOG index results in a lower proportion of cases in the adequate category, and the adequate category no longer has the lowest percentage of moderately low birth weight infants. There is little relationship to very low birth weight by either index.

Concept validity should not be confused with content validity. Some indices or measures do not provide a full coverage of the concept they measure. For example, prenatal care utilization indices only address the quantity of visits and do not consider the quality or content of care received. They may also exclude other forms of prenatal care.

Equating Risk with Cause

Another threat to data interpretation involves delineating between causal factors and risk factors. Rarely are we investigating *causal relationships*, e.g., a relationship where a variable is a direct biological cause. Most investigations focus on *risk factors*, e.g., factors that are associated with an increased chance of a poor outcome. While a characteristic may be a risk factor, not all individuals with that factor will experience negative outcomes.

In these data from Minnesota (Table 14–5), low birth weight percentages by age of mother and prenatal care utilization are examined. Teen mothers (<18 years of age) have a higher percentage of low birth weight (8.71 percent) than adult mothers (4.09 percent). Nevertheless, nearly 95 percent of total low birth weight births occur to adult mothers. If all teen pregnancies could have been eliminated,

Table 14–4 Very Low and Moderately Low Birth Weight Percentages by Two Measures of Adequacy of Prenatal Care Utilization, 1990–1991 Single Live Births to Minnesota Resident Mothers

	Modified IOM			ACOG		
	Percent	%<1,500	%1,500–2,499	Percent	%<1,500	%1,500–2,499
Adequate	62.93	0.47	2.49	41.52	0.70	3.33
Intermediate	17.25	0.68	4.34	38.66	0.31	2.42
Inadequate	3.75	0.40	5.69	3.75	0.40	5.69
No Care	0.49	8.39	13.04	0.49	8.39	13.04
Missing	15.58	1.76	5.45	15.58	1.76	5.45
	100.00			100.00		

Table 14–5 Low Birth Weight by Age of Mother and Prenatal Care, 1990–1991 Single Live Births to Minnesota Resident Mothers

Age of Mother	% Distribution	% LBW	% LBW Distribution
<18	2.69	8.71	5.61
18+	97.31	4.09	94.39
Prenatal Care			
Adequate	62.93	2.96	44.52
Intermediate	17.25	5.02	20.69
Inadequate	3.75	6.09	5.46
No Care	0.49	21.43	2.50
Missing	15.58	7.20	26.82

the number of total low birth weight infants during this period would have been reduced by only 5.6 percent.

Similarly, note the higher low birth weight percentages to mothers with no or inadequate prenatal care. Nearly two-thirds of the low-birthweight infants are to mothers with adequate or intermediate utilization of prenatal care. Certainly, young age of mother and no prenatal care utilization, as measured here, are associated with low birth weight. Still, it cannot be concluded that elimination of both of these risk factors will reduce even 10 percent of the low birth weight problem.

Conclusion

Secondary databases can be very important for research, planning, evaluation, and needs assessment in MCH. These databases can provide powerful evidence for new policy initiatives or justification for ongoing program activities. However, it should also be stressed that the use of these databases entails complex measurement issues. Knowledge of the database and the coding of the variables contained therein is essential to the prevention of simplistic and erroneous interpretations of the data.

EVALUATION RESEARCH
Joseph Telfair

Introduction

Much of what drives the field of MCH are concerns about the effective delivery and assessment of services (in the form of programs) for women, infants, children, adolescents, and families. Because of this service-based orientation, the process, utility, and implications of assessment become vital. Evaluation research, like other applied research, is primarily concerned with outcome data and the use of these data to influence program and policy development. Rossi and Freeman (1993) point out that "evaluation research is a robust area of activity devoted to collecting, analyzing, and interpreting information on the need for, implementation of, and effectiveness and efficiency of intervention efforts to better the lot of humankind by improving social conditions and community life" (p. 3). In the field of MCH, evaluation plays a key role in determining the validity and reliability of programs and services. This section will provide an overview of the practice and art of evaluation research* as applied to the field of MCH and will cover three main areas: (1) content focus, purpose, types, and procedures; (2) establishment of parameters; and (3) key problems and issues.

Content Focus, Purpose, Types, and Procedures

Content Focus

From the outset it is important to understand the fundamental difference between *evaluation* or *evaluation research* (both terms will be used) and *basic (social) research*. These differences are outlined in Table 14–6 developed by Miller (1991). Table 14–6 illustrates that basic research, often called *pure research*, is primarily concerned with seeking new knowledge and explanation of observed phenomena, whereas interventions to address a problem and focus on outcomes are not (necessarily) of interest (Babbie 1983; Miller 1991; Rossi and Freeman 1993). Evaluation, as a form of applied research, is concerned with providing information that is both useful and can be applied to social problems faced by and/or being addressed by MCH agencies and programs. It has as its primary interest the results of the rigorous and systematic assessment of an intervention's (activity of the program or agency) ability to produce change. As such, the focus of evaluation is the systematic use of social research methodologies "to judge and to improve the planning, monitoring, effectiveness, and efficacy of health, education, welfare, and other human service programs" (Rossi and Freeman 1985, p. 19; Miller 1991).

Purpose of Evaluation

One purpose of evaluation is answer some very basic, but often difficult, questions about the agency or program role in addressing a target problem and the potential for producing change. Some of the difficult questions that arise involve the kind of change desired, the means by which the change is to be brought about,

---

*The reader is referred to the references at the end of this chapter for excellent books covering the field of evaluation.

Table 14–6 Research Design Orientations

Defining Characteristic	Basic (pure)[a]	Applied (policy-action-useful)[b]	Evaluation (assessment-appraisal)[c]
Nature of the problem	Basic scientific investigation seeks new knowledge about social phenomena, hoping to establish general principles with which to explain them.	Applied scientific investigation seeks to understand a demanding social problem and to provide policy makers well-grounded guides to remedial action.	Evaluative research seeks to assess outcomes of the treatment applied to a social problem or the outcome of prevailing practices.
Goal of the research	To produce new knowledge including discovery of relationships and the capacity to predict outcomes under various conditions.	To secure the requisite knowledge that can be immediately useful to a policy maker who seeks to eliminate or alleviate a social problem.	To provide an accurate social accounting resulting from a treatment program applied to a social problem.
Guiding theory	Selection of theory to guide hypothesis testing and provide reinforcement for a theory under examination.	Selection of a theory, guidelines, or intuitive hunches to explore the dynamics of a social system.	Selection of a theory to fit the problem under assessment. Watch for ways to hook findings to a new theory or an established one.

continues

| Appropriate techniques | Theory formulation, hypothesis testing, sampling, data collection techniques (direct observation, interview, questionnaire, scale measurement), statistical treatment of data, validation or rejection of hypotheses. | Seek access to individual actions and inquire what actors are feeling and thinking at the time; elicit the attributions and evaluation made about self, other, or situational factors; regard crucial explanations as hypotheses to be tested. | Use all conventional techniques appropriate to the problem. |

[a] Kaplan, A. (1964). *The Conduct of Inquiry.* San Francisco, CA: Chandler; Dubin, R. (1969). *Theory Building.* New York: Free Press.
[b] Coleman, J.S. (1972). *Policy Research in the Social Sciences.* Morristown, NJ: General Learning Press; Argyris, C., Putnam, R. and Smith, D.M. (1985). *Action Science.* San Francisco, CA: Jossey-Bass; Lawler, E.E., III and Associates (1985). *Doing Research That Is Useful for Theory and Practice.* San Francisco, CA: Jossey-Bass; Freeman, H.E., Dynes, R.R., Rossi, P.H., and Whyte, W.F. (Eds.) (1983). *Applied Sociology: Roles and Activities of Sociologists in Diverse Settings.* San Francisco: Jossey-Bass.
[c] Lauffer, A. (1994). *Assessment Tools,* Vol. 30. Beverly Hills, CA: Sage; Luck, T.J. (1955). *Personnel Audit and Appraisal.* New York: McGraw-Hill; Juster, F.T. and Land, K.C. (Eds.) (1982). *Social Accounting Systems: Essays on the State of the Art.* New York: Academic Press.

and the signs by which such change is to be recognized. Several basic questions (Herman et al. 1987) to be addressed are:

1. Should the program be continued or discontinued?
2. What needs to done to improve the practices and procedures of a program, and how can it be done?
3. What specific programmatic strategies or techniques need to be added or dropped?
4. Can the program be replicated elsewhere?
5. Are program resources being allocated/used appropriately within program (are resources adequate)?
6. What is the nature and scope of the problem requiring action?
7. What program activities or interventions may be undertaken to improve the problem significantly?
8. What is the appropriate target population for the program or intervention?
9. Is the program or intervention being implemented in the ways envisioned?
10. Is the program or intervention effective?
11. How much does the program or intervention cost?
12. What are the program's or intervention's costs relative to its effectiveness and benefits?

A second purpose of evaluation is to address the social accountability issues inherent in applied work. Many programs are instituted with the hope that they will effectively ameliorate a specific problem (e.g., teenage pregnancy) or address a long-standing issue. Nonetheless, the basis for assessing the short- and long-term outcomes of these programs are not always clearly defined or agreed upon by those involved, the stakeholders. This dilemma requires that the evaluation endeavor be comprehensive and flexible enough to anticipate and address a number of key accountability issues that define MCH programs. These are:

1. to ensure that target programs achieve maximum effectiveness
2. to be accountable to funders
3. to influence policy makers
4. to enhance the standing of the target agency/program
5. to understand and appreciate the extent and effectiveness of the services provided to clients

Evaluation, as pointed out by Herman et al. (1987), is an endeavor that is partly social, partly political, and partly technical. As such, evaluation has a range of primary targets (stakeholders) that are invested in products of its endeavors. These primary targets and descriptions of each (Rossi and Freeman 1985; Suchman 1967) include:

1. *Policymakers and decision makers:* persons responsible for deciding whether a programs is to be instituted, continued, discontinued, expanded, or curtailed
2. *Program sponsors:* organizations that initiate and fund the program to be evaluated
3. *Evaluation sponsors:* organizations that initiate and fund the evaluation (Sometimes the evaluation sponsors and the program sponsors are identical.)
4. *Target participants:* persons, households, or other units who participate in the program or receive the intervention services under evaluation
5. *Program management:* group responsible for overseeing and coordinating the intervention program
6. *Program staff:* personnel responsible for actual delivery of the intervention (e.g., teachers)
7. *Evaluators:* groups or individuals responsible for the design and/or conduct of the evaluation
8. *Program competitors:* organizations or groups that compete for available resources
9. *Contextual stakeholders:* organizations, groups, individuals, and other units in the immediate environment of a program (e.g., local government officials or influentials situated on or near the program site)
10. *Evaluation community:* other evaluators, either organized or not, who read and evaluate evaluations for their technical quality.

This level of accountability often leads to a greater emphasis on the social and political elements of evaluation. However, technical rigor remains a crucial part of the work of evaluators, particularly in determining and implementing the type of evaluation approach most suitable for addressing key program problems and issues.

Types and Procedures of Evaluation

Often evaluation design utilizes a broad band of methodological procedures, most notably triangulation methodology (integration of quantitative and qualitative methods) as discussed by Miller (1991), Morse (1991), and Patton (1990). Determination of the type of evaluation approach to be utilized in the assessment of MCH agencies and programs must be based on a joint review and understanding of the goals and objectives of the program/agencies by the participants, staff, administrators, and the evaluator. Once this understanding is achieved, one or a combination of the following types of evaluation approaches can be used:

1. *Monitoring* does not necessarily involve a formalized evaluation schedule or set of procedures but allows for the assessment of whether or not an inter-

vention or program is operating in conformity to its design for reaching its specified target population.

2. *Needs assessment* involves the identification process of describing problems of a target population and the assessment of the importance and relevance of the problems and solutions of those needs. A needs assessment answers the question, "What do we need to do?"

3. *Process evaluation* refers to evaluation activities related to target identification and assessment of the appropriateness of services, programs, or interventions. Process evaluation answers the questions, "What services are actually being delivered and to whom?" and "Is the program happening?" and "Is there a program design and is it working as planned?"

4. *Formative evaluation* refers to evaluation activities related to the provision of information that allows program/intervention planners and implementers to make decisions regarding the improvement or refinement of a developing or ongoing program. This type of evaluation is ongoing and allows for the design and implementation of mechanisms to test for the maximum effectiveness of a program. A process evaluation answers the question, "Which works better?"

5. *Summative (or outcome) evaluation* refers to evaluation activities related to the provision of information that allows program/intervention planners and implementers to assess the overall quality and impact of a program for the purposes of accountability and policy. Summative evaluation answers the questions, "Did the program make a difference?" and "What immediate changes did clients make?"

6. *Impact evaluation* refers to evaluation activities related to the provision of information that allows program/intervention planners and implementers to assess the extent to which the program or intervention caused change in a desired direction in a target population. Impact evaluation also answers the question, "Did the program make a difference?" However, here the evaluator's interest is in the program's *ultimate* impact—what longer term changes occurred?

7. *Cost-effectiveness or cost benefit evaluation* compares program costs with expected benefits or compares the cost differences of alternative program or intervention strategies. Cost-effectiveness or cost benefit evaluation answers the question, "At what price does program or intervention success or failure occur?"

8. *Program implementation evaluation* examines the extent to which programs actually operate consistent with the objectives and procedures originally devised for them. Program implementation evaluation answers the question, "Is the program working as planned?"

Besides obtaining clarity on the types of evaluation needed to address MCH problems and issues, evaluators must have clarity in the basic terminology and definitions used in developing evaluation designs. Based on the program evaluation literature, the basic terminology, definitions, and examples of their applications to MCH issues are as follows:

1. *Intervention* is any planned effort designed to produce intended changes in a target population, e.g., a school-based pregnancy prevention program.
2. *Target populations* are the persons, households, organizations, communities, or other units at which programs or interventions are directed.
3. *Target problems* are conditions, deficiencies, or defects at which programs or interventions are directed, e.g., teen pregnancy or drug use.
4. *Goal* is a broad statement of a desired health or social status outcome. The statement does not necessarily need to be in measurable terms. For example, "to reduce the teen pregnancy rate among adolescents (14–17 years old) in the North Charleston School District #4 through school and community prevention efforts" is a goal.
5. *An Objective*:
    a. at the *program level* is a specific, measurable statement of desired change in knowledge, behavior, biomedical measures, or other intermediate characteristics that are expected to occur because of the intervention. For example, "the high school drop-out rate due to (teen) pregnancy in North Charleston School District #4 will decrease by 10 percent by June 30, 1997" is a program-level objective.
    b. at the *operational level* is a specific, measurable statement of activity (tasks) to be carried out by the program. For example, "280 female participants will be enrolled in the North Charleston School District #4 pregnancy prevention program" is an operational-level objective.
6. *Tasks or program elements* are identifiable and discrete intervention activities carried out by designated program personnel (or others) for the purpose of achieving the program objective(s). Tasks or program elements are what the program will do to achieve the objective(s). It is important to remember that each task must be linked to a specific objective.
7. *Indicator* is a measurable expected program outcome that corresponds to the cognitive, health, or social condition of the population targeted by the program for intervention. Indicators are what the evaluator is going to measure. For example, knowledge of HIV/acquired immune deficiency syndrome (AIDS), rates of violent behavior, rates unwanted/unintended pregnancies, etc., are indicators.
8. A *target* is a numerical value (quantity or amount [count]) that indicates the minimum desirable level of achievement for a particular activity (task) or indicator (outcome). As part of the operational-level objective, a target is usually linked with a date of anticipated achievement. For example, a 10

percent reduction in missed parenting group sessions by the sixth month of the program is a target.
9. A *program impact model* is the formal statement about the expected relationships between a program or intervention and its designated goals and objectives. It is the strategy that outlines and operationalizes the process of evaluating the link between goals and objectives set forth during the planning process and what is actually happening.

Once the participants, program staff, and evaluator have determined the type of evaluation to be used and have obtained a mutual understanding of the evaluation terminology and definitions, the last content and procedure issue to address is to decide what to actually measure and observe that will provide comprehensive data to catalogue the effectiveness of the program intervention. Herman et al. (1987) and Blalock (1990) have noted five components of a program that could be assessed to provide broad-based data for evaluation. These program components are as follows:

1. *Context characteristics* require attention to the setting or context (framework) within which a program must operate. They include the complex network of sociopolitical factors that influence almost all programs (e.g., power leadership, communications) as well as program-specific factors, such as class size, time frame within which the program must operate, budget, and specific incentives. It is especially important to get accurate information about aspects of the context that you suspect might affect how a program operates and its success.
2. *Participant characteristics* require attention to such things as age, sex, socioeconomic status, language dominance, ability, attendance record, attitudes, preconceptional health, and background/experience. It is sometimes important if a program shows different effects with different groups of clients.
3. *Characteristics of program implementation* require attention to the program's principal activities, services, processes, materials, staffing, and administrative arrangements. In summative evaluations, these will usually be the processes and characteristics that distinguish the program from other similar ones. In formative evaluations, these will usually be those aspects of the program that are most problematic.
4. *Program outcomes.* In most evaluations it is important to want to measure or observe the extent to which the program goals have been achieved. This requires that the evaluator must be alert to unanticipated outcomes (*positive and negative*) and consider both long- and short-range outcomes that focus the evaluation on agreed-upon goals and objectives.

5. *Program costs* address the question of what are the required resources and relative cost-effectiveness of competing alternatives. In considering program costs, Herman et al. (1987) state that it is important to gather situation-specific data about obvious costs (staff time, materials, equipment, facilities) and indirect, opportunity, and other hidden costs.

Establishing the Parameters of the Evaluation

Once the content focus, purpose, and types and procedures of an evaluation have been determined and agreed upon, establishing the parameters (context and "boundaries") (Herman et al. 1987; Rossi and Freeman 1993; Suchman 1967) of the evaluation presents the next challenge. Establishing parameters of the evaluation requires all involved in the evaluation process to outline the methodological elements of the evaluation process and allows for all involved to have an agreed-upon course of action that increases the probability of the success of the program/intervention and the usefulness of the outcome data. As such, the process of establishing the parameters includes establishing contextual and specification (guidelines) parameters, as well as selecting appropriate methods, design issues, and guidelines for data collecting and analysis.

Establishing the Contextual Parameters

Constituting parameters for the evaluation of MCH programs or interventions involves (1) determining the program goals and objectives; (2) carefully defining the target population; (3) defining the program-specific tasks, that is, the principal activities or services to be provided to meet the objectives and the expected progress based on the implementation of these activities or services; (4) determining the resources available—these include financial, personnel, agency, and other supports—as well as materials to use; (5) determining the frequency and duration of the intervention to be provided; (6) determining the person(s) responsible for implementation of the overall program and/or specific intervention; and (7) developing the evaluation plan.

Establishing Specifications

In addition to setting up the context of the evaluation process, certain specifications must be adhered to in establishing the "boundaries" (Herman et al. 1987) of the evaluation.

1. The evaluation should be tied to the overall goals of the program and specific interventions.
2. The evaluation should be broad-based and take into consideration the range of desired outcomes, be they short- or long-term.

3. Goal attainment at all levels should be documented through the measurement of specific program and operational level objectives.
4. The evaluation should examine the process by which outcomes are achieved (particularly in relation to the measurement of core [overall] indicators).
5. The data from the evaluation should be used in an ongoing fashion to improve programs. As with the contextual parameters, these specifications will increase the probability that the social and political components of the evaluation will be addressed.

Selecting the Appropriate Evaluation Methods

Once the context and boundaries of the evaluation have been secured, the evaluator must determine the appropriate methodological and design (logistical) considerations that will guide the evaluation process. The primary methodological considerations include the following:

1. Tasks should be fleshed out into a clearly specified, program-sensitive set of data collection procedures and, where relevant, measurement instruments.
2. Attention must be paid to the specific aspects of program context, processes, and outcomes on which the assessment will focus.
3. Attention must be paid to the best feasible methods to measure or otherwise observe those program tasks (i.e., specific measurement instruments you will purchase or develop and/or sources of information for other data collection methods).
4. Attention must be paid to the design and sampling plan for administering or enacting chosen assessment methods.
5. Attention must be paid to the logistical plan that will allow for the completion of evaluation tasks within a specified schedule.
6. Attention should be focused on collecting information of greatest interest and utility to primary users (targeted populations and stakeholders) about the most significant aspects of the program or intervention and its outcomes and that this is done in a way that ensures the quality, validity, and reliability of the information collected.

Determining Design Issues

Shortell and Richardson (1978) and Cook and Campbell (1979) advise that, independent of the research design chosen by the evaluator (experimental or quasi-experimental), the validity and reliability of the design must be of primary concern. Concerns with ensuring validity must address two questions:

1. To what extent are the program or intervention effects really due to the program or intervention rather than competing explanations? (in basic research, this is an issue of causality)
2. To what extent can results be generalized to other situations?

In addition, threats to the internal and external validity of the design must be addressed, particularly if a quasi-experimental design is chosen. Concerns with ensuring the reliability of the evaluation design must answer the question, To what extent has the assessment of the measure(s) being used, the target of the intervention, costs, logistics, time, and previous appraisals of reliability been made? Further discussion of design reliability issues can be found elsewhere in this chapter.

Data Collecting and Analysis Parameters

Lastly, given the applied nature of evaluation research and the emphasis on identifying and obtaining outcome data that are useful and relevant to stakeholders connected to the program, delineating data collection and analysis guidelines is crucial. The following guidelines are suggested.

1. Focus data collection where it is most likely to uncover program effects (if any occur). Ask, *"Which objectives are most likely to show change?"*
2. Try to collect a variety of information, particularly if multiple methods are being used to achieve a similar objective (e.g., *using both a group and one-to-one counseling to increase the self-esteem of female teenagers*).
3. Try to think of imaginative (and credible) ways to detect achievement of program objectives. Ask, *"What best illustrates the success of the innovative methods we have developed to achieve our objectives?"*
4. Collect information to show that the program at least has done no harm to the target population.
5. Measure or observe what is essential, as well as what is thought to be in the interest of the sponsor and other stakeholders.
6. Try to measure or observe things that will advance the development of target services or other outcomes linked to the target program(s).
7. Focus data collection where it is most likely to uncover program effects, if any occur.
8. Try to collect a variety of information (triangulation), i.e., *try to find useful qualitative (process) and quantitative (counts) information that is going to be collected anyhow. This provides the advantage of presenting a thorough look at the program or intervention.*

Involving the program staff in the process of implementing these guidelines will assist the evaluator in ensuring their successful completion.

Key Evaluation Problems and Issues

As has been discussed in this section, evaluation research takes place in a dynamic social and political environment. As such, there is a myriad of logistical problems and issues that must be recognized and addressed if the outcomes of the evaluation are to be useful, practical, and relevant. These problems and issues fall into two categories: (1) data- and measurement-specific, and (2) program- and stakeholder-specific problems and issues.

Data- and Measurement-Specific Problems and Issues

Because evaluation (as discussed in this section) often does not take place in a controlled environment, is very reliant on the participants and/or program staff for its implementation, and often utilizes more than one data collection method, ensuring scientific rigor becomes a real challenge. To ensure rigor, the evaluator must both anticipate and address (as part of the evaluation process) the following problems and issues: (1) establishing the parameters for a comparison group; (2) establishing a measurement design agreement between program staff and/or stakeholders and evaluator; (3) establishing parameters of adequacy of program or intervention effects; (4) establishing accountability roles and tasks of persons involved in the data collection process; and (5) identifying data collection issues and strategies such as (a) availability, use, and advantages/disadvantages of rec-ollected data (archival records, agency's administrative records, unobtrusive [qualitative] measures); (b) original (routine, ongoing) data collection; (c) use and advantages/disadvantages of interview questionnaires; (d) use and advantages/disadvantages of self-administered questionnaires; (e) use and advantages/disadvantages of telephone interviews; and (f) establishing the parameters for data analysis and use.

Program- and Stakeholder-Specific Problems and Issues

Because of the emphasis on social and political accountability that surrounds the information produced by the evaluation endeavor, there exist a number of logistical and reporting problems and issues that arise. As Rossi and Freeman (1993) point out, evaluators usually find themselves confronted with individuals, groups and/or agencies that have competing views on the use and appropriateness of the evaluation process and its results. In order to conduct their work with a reasonable degree of rigor and effectiveness, evaluators must understand their relationship with stakeholders *and programs*, as well as stakeholder *and program* relationships with one another (Rossi and Freeman 1993). The following are stakeholder- and program-specific problems and issues the evaluator must address at the outset or as a part of the evaluation process:

- agreeing to a set of indicators that allows for the separation of program generalities from those describing program performance or effect
- agreeing to a set of specific outcomes that, if achieved, will allow for agreement that programmatic objectives are being achieved
- agreeing to and delineating which important dimensions of program objectives need to be identified, including:

- specification of the nature or content of the objective (in what areas is the intervention intended to produce changes)
- ordering of objectives (at which level of specificity the objective is stated)
- agreeing to and outlining the number of objectives (most programs have more than a single objective)
- agreeing to and specifying the target group
- agreeing to and specifying the expected short-term versus long-term effect(s)
- agreeing to and specifying the expected magnitude of interventive effect(s) (how large an effect is expected?)
- agreeing to and specifying the stability of interventive effect (how long is/are the effect(s) intended to last?)
- establishing agreement as to the level of interrelatedness of objectives (the objectives may be highly related and similar to each other or unrelated and dissimilar)
- establishing agreement as to the hierarchy (importance) of each objective
- agreeing to and specifying the unexpected (unintended and unanticipated) consequences of the intervention

Conclusion

Use of evaluation information is dependent upon the social and political context in which the endeavor take place. As with all forms of applied research, evaluators must be vigilant in appraising the environment of those involved with the work (stakeholders). Further, use of evaluation results for decision making and program development must be of primary concern if changes in these programs are to reflect the needs of its participants and if the changes are to have the desired effect.

REFERENCES

Alexander, G.R., and M.C. Allen. 1996. Conceptualization, measurement and use of gestational age: I. clinical and public health practice. *Journal of Perinatology* 16:53–59.

Alexander, G.R., and M. Kotelchuck. 1996. A comparison of prenatal care indices: Classification of adequacy of prenatal care use. *Public Health Reports* 111(5):408–418.

Alexander, G.R. et al. 1990a. *The Region III Perinatal Data and Chart Book.* Special Report. Baltimore: Region III Perinatal Information Consortium.

Alexander, G.R. et al. 1990b. Gestational age reporting and preterm delivery. *Public Health Reports* 105:267–275.

Alexander, G.R. et al. 1991. Sources of bias in prenatal care utilization indices: Implications for evaluating the Medicaid expansion. *American Journal of Public Health* 81:1013–1016.

Alexander, G.R. et al. 1995. Discordance between LMP-based and clinically estimated gestational age: Implications for research, programs and policy. *Public Health Reports* 110:395–402.

Alexander, G.R. et al. 1996. A U.S. national reference for fetal growth. *Obstetrics and Gynecology* 87: 163–168.

Babbie, E. 1983. *The practice of social research.* 4th ed. Belmont, CA: Wadsworth Publishing Co.

Bauman, K.E. 1980. *Research methods for community health and welfare.* New York: Oxford University Press.

Beauchamp, T.L., and J.F. Childress, eds. 1994. *Principles of biomedical ethics.* 4th ed. NY: Oxford University Press.

Blalock, A.B. 1990. *Evaluating social programs at the state and local level.* Kalamazoo, MI: W.E. Upjohn Institute.

Buekens, P. et al. 1984. Epidemiology of pregnancies with unknown last menstrual period. *Journal of Epidemiology and Community Health* 38:79–80.

Cook, T.D., and D.T. Campbell. 1979. *Quasi-experimental design and analysis issues for field settings.* Skokie, IL: Rand McNally.

David, R.J. 1980. The quality and completeness of birthweight and gestational age data in computerized birth files. *American Journal of Public Health* 79:964–973.

Dworkin, G. 1978. Legality of consent to non-therapeutic medical research on infants and young children. *Archives of Disease of Childhood* 53:443–446.

Earp, J.A., and S.T. Ennett. 1991. Conceptual models for health education research and practice. *Health Education Research* 6:163–171.

Engelhardt, H.T. Jr. 1978. Basic ethical principles in the conduct of biomedical and behavioral research involving human subjects. In National Commission for the Protection of Human Subjects of Biomedical and Behavioral Research. *The Belmont report: Ethical principles and guidelines for the protection of human subjects of research,* Appendix Vol. I. DHEW Publ. No. (05) 77-0012. Washington, DC: Government Printing Office, pp. 8-1–8-45.

Finkelhor, D., and J. Dzuiba-Leatherman. 1995. Children as victims of violence. *Pediatrics* 94: 413–420.

Gable, C.A. 1990. Compendium of public health data sources. *American Journal of Epidemiology* 131:381–394.

Galai, G., and M. Yehiele. 1995. The role of public health schools in meeting the needs of rapidly developing communities. In *Race and ethnicity in America: Meeting the challenge in 21st century,* eds. G. Galai and M. Yehiele, Washington, DC: Taylor and Francis.

Giertz, G. 1983. Ethical aspects of paediatric research. *Acta Paediatrica (Oslo)* 72:641–650.

Haggerty, R.J. 1981. Challenges to maternal and child health research in the 1980s. In *Research priorities in maternal and child health. Report of a conference,* ed. L.V. Klerman, 245–251. Waltham, MA: Brandeis University and Office of Maternal and Child Health/HSA/PHS/USDHHS.

Herman, J.L. et al. 1987. *Evaluator's handbook.* Newbury Park, CA: Sage Publications.

Kessner, D.M. et al. 1973. Infant death: An analysis by maternal risk and health care. In *Contrasts in health status,* Vol I. Washington, DC: Institute of Medicine, National Academy of Sciences.

King, N.P., and L.R. Churchill. 1994. *Ethical principles guiding research on child and adolescent subjects.* Paper presented at "A Conference on Ethical, Legal, and Methodological Implications of Directly Asking Children about Histories of Maltreatment," Chapel Hill, NC, December 12.

Kinard, E.M. 1985. Ethical issues in research with abused children. *Child Abuse and Neglect* 9: 301–311.

Kirby, R.S. 1993. Neonatal and postneonatal mortality: Useful constructs or outdated concepts? *Journal of Perinatology* XIII:433–441.

Kleinbaum, D.G. et al. 1982a. Measures of disease frequency: Incidence. In *Epidemiologic research: Principles and quantitative methods.* New York: Lifetime Learning Publications, 96–116.

Kleinbaum, D.G. et al. 1982b. Other measures of disease frequency. In *Epidemiologic research: Principles and quantitative methods.* New York: Lifetime Learning Publications, 117–139.

McCormick, R. 1974. Proxy consent in the experimental situation. *Perspectives in Biology and Medicine* 18:2–20.

Melton, G.B. 1990. Certificates of confidentiality under the public health service act: Strong protection but not enough. *Violence and Victims* 5:67–71.

Miller, D.C. 1991. *Handbook of research design and social measurement,* 5th ed. Newbury Park, CA: Sage Publications.

Morse, J.M. 1991. Approaches to qualitative-quantitative methodological triangulation. *Nursing Research* 40:120–122.

National Commission for the Protection of Human Subjects of Biomedical and Behavioral Research. 1978. *Ethical principles and guidelines for the protection of human subjects of research.* DHEW Publication No. (OS) 77-0012. Washington, DC: Government Printing Office.

National Research Council. 1993. *Understanding child abuse and neglect.* Washington, DC: National Academy Press.

Patton, M.Q. 1990. *Qualitative evaluation and research methods,* 2nd ed. Newbury Park, CA: Sage Publications.

Ramsey, P. 1970. Consent as a canon of loyalty with special reference to children in medical investigation. In P. Ramsey, ed. *The patient as a person.* New Haven, CT: Yale University Press.

Rossi, P.H., and H.E. Freeman. 1985. *Evaluation: A systematic approach,* 3rd ed. Beverly Hills, CA: Sage Publications.

Rossi, P.H., and H.E. Freeman. 1993. *Evaluation: A systematic approach.* 5th ed. Newbury Park, CA: Sage Publications.

Sanderson. M. et al. 1991. The 1988 national maternal and infant health survey: Design, content and data availability. *Birth* 18:26–32.

Shortell, S.M., and W.C. Richardson. 1978. *Health program evaluation.* St. Louis, MO: C.V. Mosby.

Stewart, D.W. 1984. *Secondary research: Information sources and methods.* Applied Social Research Methods Series, Vol. 4. Beverly Hills: Sage Publications.

Suchman, D.A. 1967. *Evaluative research: Principles and practice in public service and social action programs.* New York: Russell Sage Foundation.

Taffel, S. et al. 1982. A method of imputing length of gestation on birth certificates. *Vital and Health Statistics.* Department of Health and Human Services, Data Evaluation and Methods Research Series 2, No. 93.

U.S. Department of Agriculture, Food and Nutrition Service. 1992. *WIC Child Impact Study.* RFP No. FNS 92–009CAW. Alexandria, VA: Author.

U.S. Department of Health and Human Services. 1981. Final Regulations amending basic HHS policy for the Protection of Human Research Subjects. *Federal Register* 46 (no. 16): 8366–8388.

Wenner, W.H., and E.B. Young. 1974. Nonspecific date of last menstrual period: An indication of poor reproductive outcome. *American Journal of Obstetrics and Gynecology* 120:1071–1079.

Wicker, A.W. 1992. Getting out of our conceptual ruts: Strategies for expanding conceptual frameworks. In *Methodological issues and strategies in clinical research,* ed. A.E. Kazdin, 41–61. Washington, DC: American Psychological Association.

MCH-Related Secondary Data Sources

A. National Vital Records (NCHS)

1. Live Births
2. Fetal Deaths
3. Induced Abortions
4. Infant Deaths
5. Marriages
6. Divorces
7. Linked Live Birth-Infant Deaths

B. National Health and Medical Records Surveys (NCHS)

1. Hospital Discharge Survey
2. Family Planning Reporting Survey

C. National Population-Based Surveys (NCHS)

1. National Health Interview Survey
2. National Health and Nutrition Examination Survey
3. Hispanic Health and Nutrition Examination Survey
4. National Survey of Family Growth
5. Ambulatory Medical Care Survey
6. Nursing Home Survey
7. Medical Care Utilization and Expenditure Survey
8. Survey of Personal Health Practices and Consequences
9. National Maternal and Infant Health Survey, 1988
10. Longitudinal Follow-Up to the National Maternal and Infant Health Survey

D. Other Sources of National Data Sources

1. Census Bureau

2. Centers for Disease Control and Prevention (CDC)
   a. Pregnancy Risk Assessment and Monitoring System
   b. Pregnancy and Infancy Nutrition Survey
   c. Behavior Risk Factor Surveys
   d. Developmental Disability Surveillance
   e. Teenage Pregnancy Surveillance
   f. Birth Defects Monitoring
3. Consumer Product Safety Commission
4. FBI: Uniform Crime Reports
5. National Institute of Occupational Safety and Health (NIOSH)
   a. Traumatic Occupational Fatality
   b. Fatal Accident Circumstances
6. U.S. Department of Agriculture: WIC
7. Indian Health Service

E. State and Local Data Sources

1. State and local health and social service programs
   a. Prenatal care programs
   b. WIC
   c. Immunization
   d. Child abuse reporting
   e. Foster care
   f. Juvenile corrections
   g. Social services
   h. Adoptions
   i. Child health
2. State Medical Societies
3. State Hospital Associations
4. School Systems
5. Community Health Centers
6. Poison Control Centers
7. State Registries: tumor, cancer, birth defects
8. State Medicaid
9. State Vital Records
10. Medical Registry Boards
11. Police and Fire Departments
12. Wildlife, Hunting and Boating Departments

F. Other Data Sources

1. Insurance Companies
2. Private medical records
3. Hospital and HMO medical records

CHAPTER 15

Planning and Monitoring Maternal and Child Health Programs

Mary D. Peoples-Sheps

INTRODUCTION

Program planning skills are essential to the practice of maternal and child health (MCH). Regardless of political climate, economic context, or cultural milieu, MCH professionals are called upon repeatedly to plan programs and to monitor progress toward achievement of program objectives. In the past few years, critical functions of the program planning process, assessment and assurance, have been reemphasized by the Institute of Medicine in its landmark report, *The Future of Public Health* (Committee 1988), and by the U.S. Public Health Service in its listing of 10 Essential Public Health Services (Essential Public Health Services Work Group 1994). At the time of this writing, an adaptation of the 10 essential services for MCH is under development (Tipton 1995). At least 6 of the 10 services involve program planning.

Program planning is pervasive because it serves as a bridge between and among theories, measurement sciences, substantive content, and actual practice of public health. In a sense, program planning offers an overarching framework within which many public health functions are carried out. The model of program planning most often recommended for public health is called *rational planning* (Backett et al. 1984; Blum 1983; Kettner et al. 1990; Williams et al. 1991). Simply stated, rational planning is a process for influencing certain outcomes, or ends, by instituting appropriate interventions, or means. It is rational in that the means and the ends correspond as well as current knowledge and circumstances allow.

The ideas expressed in this chapter were developed over a number of years in collaboration with many students and colleagues. To all of them I am grateful, but special thanks go to Mary Rogers, DrPH, Vangie Foshee, PhD, Eugenia Eng, DrPH, and Deborah Bender, PhD. Their unique skills and perspectives have enriched my understanding of rational program planning in countless ways.

Rational planning is carried out through a series of integrated steps described in this chapter. The logic of each step and its relationship to the other steps are explored, and some tools for conducting specific activities are presented. Most of the steps in the planning process, however, require additional knowledge and skill. Analytic expertise, including capabilities in epidemiology, biostatistics, decision analysis, evaluation research, and computer-based data management, are at one end of a continuum of useful skills (Gilbert and Specht 1977). At the other end is interactive expertise. Program planning must occur in a social and political context with extensive participation of individuals who have a stake in the problem to be addressed and in its solution. Mobilizing communities, forging partnerships, and working together effectively require specialized techniques in group process, community development, and leadership. The extent to which analytic techniques or interactive techniques are required in a given planning process depends upon many factors, such as the type of problem to be addressed, the data available, and political interest. The goal, of course, is to produce a program based on sound analysis and embraced by enough constituents to be implemented smoothly and carried out effectively. Some involvement of both analytic and interactive techniques at each step of the planning process is usually required to reach this goal.

Program planning is often conducted in two domains simultaneously. The first domain is one of action in which the analytic and interactive techniques required to accomplish each step in the process are applied. The other domain is communication. To obtain financial support and to meet reporting requirements, planning activities must be communicated well, either verbally or in written form. Communication of the important aspects of the planning process requires writing and presentation skills, which can be enhanced by tools that promote a systematic approach to the planning process. Samples of some tools are exhibited in this chapter. They serve as markers of progress and working summaries in the action domain and as vehicles for presenting complex information in the communication domain.

Figure 15–1 is a diagram of the critical steps in program planning. The steps in Figure 15–1 are presented in a circular format to show that the process is continuous; that is, the last step, evaluation, produces information required to inform the next round of problem assessment. The circular model is also intended to demonstrate that there are at least six points of entry to the planning process. The most appropriate place to start depends upon the stage of development of the program. For example, planning to address an emerging problem begins with assessment of the problem whereas planning in the context of well-understood problems and ongoing programs may begin with setting new objectives or adjusting the program to stay on track.

In addition to having multiple points of entry and continuity from one round to the next, the planning process is also iterative. That is, there is movement back and forth among the steps for the purpose of revision and refinement. Iteration is a necessary activity in program planning because new information that affects

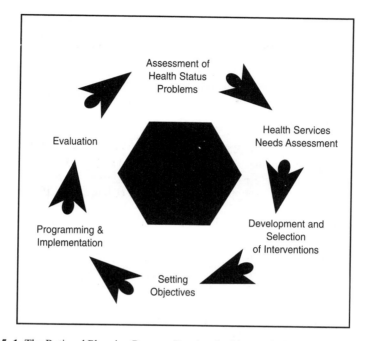

Figure 15–1 The Rational Planning Process. Reprinted with permission from M.D. Peoples-Sheps, A. Farel, C. Medins, and M.M. Rogers, *Assessment of Health Status Problems*, p. 4, © 1995, The University of North Carolina at Chapel Hill School of Public Health.

earlier steps continues to emerge throughout the process. Iteration ensures that each step uniquely influences and is influenced by the steps that both precede and follow it. The greater the amount of iteration in the planning process, the closer the plan comes to being truly rational.

The planning model shown in Figure 15–1 encourages development of creative and comprehensive programs to prevent health problems of mothers and children. It is useful for addressing health status problems that range from the very simple to the most complex. The framework is also flexible enough to be used at local, state, and federal jurisdictional levels. These characteristics are demonstrated in the following sections.

ASSESSMENT OF HEALTH STATUS PROBLEMS

Assessment of health status problems is the foundation step for the entire planning process. This step involves identification and, if necessary, ranking of MCH problems and an examination of the causes and risk factors for each of the problems that are considered high priority. Through this process, the precursors of the problem and their relationships to each other and to the problem are identified or updated (Backett et al. 1984; Blum 1974). Assessment of health status problems has four dimensions: perception, verification, prioritization, and analysis.

Problem Perception

To perceive that a problem exists, it must be recognized. A problem may be defined as an unacceptable gap between the real (what is) and the ideal (what should be). In the field of MCH, a health problem is identified when the actual level of health status of a population of mothers or children is different from the ideal level.

Perception of a health status problem generally occurs in one of the following ways:

- An individual or a community develops an impression that there is too much of an adverse health condition. The actual level of the condition is compared with the standards of the perceiver and an unacceptable gap between the real and the ideal is identified.
- A statewide or community assessment illuminates a problem. This process is conducted by health departments, community agencies, or advocacy groups, sometimes because of a required assessment, such as the one for the MCH Block Grant application. A variety of health problems, risk factors, and services are examined for the purpose of identifying MCH problems. Methods range from routine surveillance of health indicators to focus groups and key informant interviews.

While some latitude in labeling health problems is wise and practical, it is important not to define a health service deficiency (e.g., lack of services for . . .) as a health status problem. When a health service deficiency is identified as a problem, the only possible response is to provide the missing services, which may not be the most effective or appropriate way to improve health status. By focusing on health status as the problem, opportunities to intervene in many ways will be illuminated. These intervention opportunities may include, but will not be limited to, predetermined ideas about which services should be implemented.

Problem Verification

Verification of health status problems occurs concurrently with problem perception. Several objective aspects of the problem are examined for the purpose of determining whether or not observed levels really constitute a problem. Aspects that must be examined are extent, variation across population groups and geographic areas, duration, and expected future course. Questions that should be answered in order to verify that a problem exists are:

- *Extent.* What is the incidence or prevalence of the problem? How many people are affected?
- *Variation.* How does the extent of the problem vary across population groups (e.g., specific racial or age groups) and geographic areas? Does the problem affect some people and not others?
- *Duration.* How long has the problem been at the observed level? In what ways have levels changed over time?
- *Expected future course.* What is likely to happen to the problem if no intervention takes place? How will sociodemographic changes in the community influence the problem over the next 5 years? 10 years?

The existence of a health status problem is verified if the incidence or prevalence of the condition is worse in the population of concern than it is in the general population or in another group serving as a standard for comparison. The assessment of variation in extent may reveal that the population most affected by the health condition is an identifiable subgroup of the entire population. The problem is verified further if the assessment suggests that it has worsened or has been at the same unacceptable level for some time, and/or if it is likely to worsen in the future.

Setting Priorities among MCH Problems

Every local community, each state, and the nation usually have more MCH problems than they have human, financial, and other resources to address them. This necessitates ranking of the problems in order to decide how to allocate resources. Setting priorities can occur at several stages of the planning process and, indeed, the priorities may even be set by an outside body (e.g., funding agency, legislature, state health agency, managed care organization). If an agency is setting its own priorities, it is most efficient for the process to occur before too much investment is made in further analysis of the problems and needs.

Numerous criteria and the perspectives of many individuals should be considered when health problems are being prioritized. Some criteria may appear initially to be noncontroversial. For example, problems that have serious consequences are often considered more important than those with less serious consequences, and problems that have been increasing in magnitude may be assigned a higher priority than those that are decreasing. Each of these criteria, however, may have controversial aspects. In the first case, the most serious problems may affect only a small proportion of the population. In the second situation, the rate of increase or decrease may modify conclusions about the trends.

It is important to include as many of the people who have an investment in the problem/issue as possible in the process of setting priorities among health problems. Representatives of state and local agencies, other public and private organizations, members of the MCH community, and private citizens should be involved. But when such groups convene, discussions and decisions may be dominated by individuals with especially persuasive and/or persistent verbal skills. In such a milieu, important aspects of the problem may never emerge. To allow a variety of perspectives and criteria to be fully represented, a framework that encourages expression and consideration of all of them in a balanced, rational way is essential.

The development of a simple matrix can meet this need (Spiegel and Hyman 1978; World Health Organization 1984). Table 15–1 shows a matrix with several of the problems of contemporary concern to MCH programs in the left-most column. Heading the other columns are criteria that might be used to prioritize the problems. There is no ready-made set of criteria that will apply in all situations, and criteria will differ from place to place and over time, depending on the important issues of the day. Two potentially useful criteria were mentioned above: the seriousness of the consequences of the problem and the direction of trends (improving or worsening). Another important one is the extent of the problem (the proportion of people affected and/or at risk). Other criteria may be found in written and unwritten policies. For example, problems that have been identified in *Healthy People 2000* (U.S. Department of Health and Human Services 1991) are priorities for all federal agencies. Within state and local areas, similar sets of objectives or special reports may focus on certain problems, and these should be taken into account. The acceptability of addressing a problem may also be an appropriate criterion. For example, such controversial problems as smoking and adolescent sexual behavior should be considered in light of the ability of the jurisdiction to accept any attention or interventions directed to them.

Discussion of criteria to guide the ranking of problems places the decisions to be made within a broad framework that discourages a focus on irrelevant aspects of individual problems. A lively debate here may lead to new insights and much more informed decisions about which health problems to address. The matrix in Table 15–1 facilitates the discussion by providing for assignment of a yes/no or high/low score in each cell. The problems with the highest total scores are accorded highest priority according to the chosen criteria.

Problem Analysis

Once the highest priority problems have been identified, each problem must be analyzed to understand its precursors and consequences and the direction and strength of the relationships among them. This aspect of health status problem assessment is crucial for linking health status problems to appropriate interven-

Table 15–1 Matrix of MCH Problems by Prioritizing Criteria Using 0 = No (Low) and 1 = Yes (High) Scores

	Criteria						
Health Problem	Severe Consequences	Trends Increasing	Extent (High Incidence/ Prevalence)	In HP 2000	In State Priorities	Acceptability to Citizens	Total
Low birth weight	1	1	1	1	1	1	6
Infant mortality	1	0	1	1	1	1	5
Vision impairments	0	0	0	0	0	1	1
Hearing impairments	0	0	1	1	0	1	3
HIV	1	1	0	1	0	0	3
Childhood communicable diseases	1	1	0	1	1	1	5
Adolescent pregnancy	1	1	0	1	1	1	5
Adolescent smoking	1	1	1	1	0	0	4
Injuries							
Intentional	1	1	1	1	1	1	6
Unintentional	1	1	1	1	1	1	6

Source: Reprinted from M.D. Peoples-Sheps, A. Farel, and I. Ahluwalia, *Needs Assessment: Resource Handbook,* p. 24, 1994. Maternal and Child Health Bureau, Health Resources and Services Administration, Public Health Service, U.S. Department of Health and Human Services.

tions. If a problem is not well defined, it is not likely to be solved. Unfortunately, this step is often omitted in busy health agencies.

There are many ways to analyze health problems. The approach recommended here forces consideration of a broad range of precursors and consequences that represent all relevant domains (e.g., physical, behavioral, psychological, social, environmental). The central feature of the approach is a diagram that helps to conceptualize the dimensions of the problem and that can be used as a reference throughout the planning process.

A problem diagram has four components: the problem, precursors, consequences, and linkages (Blum 1974). There is no intrinsically correct or incorrect way to develop one of these diagrams. The goal is to find the most revealing way to show how the precursors and consequences relate to each other. In the diagram, the problem itself is generally identified in the middle, preceded by the precursors and followed by consequences. Arrows indicate linkages among these factors, some of which are well accepted, while others may be hypothesized. A sample problem diagram, for low birth weight (LBW), is illustrated by Figure 15–2.

Precursors

The precursors of the problem are factors that have been associated with the problem. Some of them are directly related to the pathological processes that lead to the problem. Others are not as directly linked; instead, they influence the precursors that have a more direct effect. Still others, like race and marital status, may be associated with the problem statistically, but they are considered markers for other unknown or unmeasured phenomena.

At the direct level, the factors describe individuals and may be biological, medical, or behavioral. While there may be two or more levels of these factors, they have the most influence on the problem. In Figure 15–2, maternal/fetal health status represents biologically occurring events, such as third trimester bleeding, that contribute directly to LBW. Other direct precursors include such behavioral risks as smoking, alcohol and drug use, and poor nutritional habits. These behaviors influence LBW through physiological processes.

Socioeconomic, psychological, and familial factors are usually at the next (secondary) level. Preventive health services that are known to be associated with the problem also may be secondary precursors. These secondary factors are often, although not always, precursors to the direct factors. For LBW, psychological stress, lack of social support, and lack of prenatal care are a few of the secondary precursors that exert their influences through the direct precursors. For example, lack of early, continuous, and comprehensive prenatal care can affect behavioral risks; a woman in need of a drug abuse treatment program may not get referred for treatment to modify her behavior if she is not seen in prenatal care. Tertiary factors tend to be more of a societal, policy, and environmental nature. As shown in Figure 15–2, racism and discrimination, poverty, and political climate are ter-

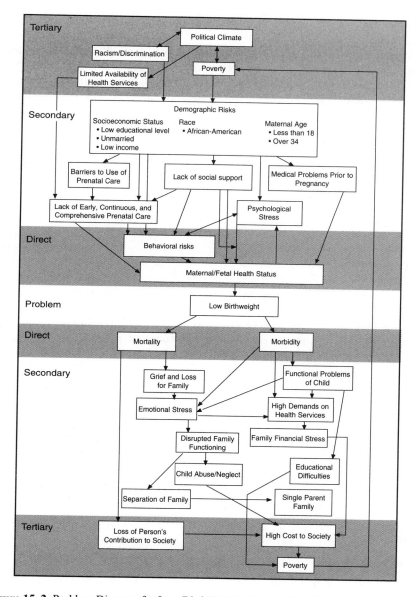

Figure 15–2 Problem Diagram for Low Birth Weight. *Source:* Reprinted from *Assessment of Health Status Problems* by M.D. Peoples-Sheps, A. Farel, and M.M. Rogers (1996). Rockville, MD: Maternal and Child Health Bureau, Health Resources and Services Administration, Public Health Service, U.S. Department of Health and Human Services, p. 15.

tiary factors. Like direct factors, both the secondary and tertiary categories often have multiple levels.

Identifying the linkages among the precursors and the problem requires familiarity with the epidemiology literature and an understanding of the concept of *relative risk*. Relative risk, which is measured by an odds ratio, is an indicator of the strength of association between a risk factor and a health problem. It is the ratio of the incidence of the problem in the population of people with the risk factor to the incidence in the population without the risk factor (Backett et al. 1984). Literature that reports results of studies of risk factors for a health problem can be used to identify risk factors for the problem diagram. Relative risk indicators can also help in determining the potential impact of intervening at a specific precursor. For example, if maternal smoking has a higher relative risk for LBW than maternal alcohol consumption, an intervention directed toward smoking cessation for pregnant women would potentially have more of an impact on LBW than an intervention focused on reducing alcohol consumption.

To link factors to each other, additional research may be necessary. If the problem has a behavioral component (and most do), there are theories of human behavior, many of which have been tested empirically, that specify what factors contribute to certain behaviors and how these factors relate to each other (Dignan and Carr 1992; Glanz et al. 1990). For example, current theories of social support and stress guided the development of the LBW diagram in Figure 15–2. Social support is viewed as having a direct effect on maternal/fetal health status, a buffering effect on the impact of stress, and an indirect effect on maternal/fetal health status through behaviors such as utilization of prenatal care and behavioral risks.

Consequences

Consequences are the effects of the problem on individuals, families, and society. They provide significance to the problem as shown in Figure 15–2, where the impact of having a LBW infant is evident in emotional and financial stress and, possibly, disruption of the family unit. Like precursors, consequences can be categorized according to direct, secondary, and tertiary levels, each representing one or more domains that are increasingly removed from the problem. Note that the consequences of one cycle of the problem may become precursors of the next as indicated by the arrow connecting poverty in the consequences to the same factor in the precursors.

Reality Checking

The diagram prepared so far may be derived from published literature. It is a solid beginning but not a finished product. A complete problem analysis is refined by discussions with people involved with the problem, by examination of extent, duration, and likely future course of the precursors and consequences, and through statistical analysis of the precursors in that population. This refinement stage will allow identification of precursors and consequences that are especially prevalent in the population of concern as well as those that do not apply. For example, smoking is a well-accepted precursor of LBW. But if few people in the population under study smoke, this precursor is not likely to have a significant effect on the incidence of LBW in that population.

Importance of Understanding Precursors and Consequences

Both precursors and consequences play critical roles in the rational planning process. Precursors:

- constitute a framework for identifying alternative interventions that either modify the risk factors or compensate for those that cannot be modified
- identify the hypothetical relationships from which the program hypothesis is developed
- link the assessment phases of planning to program design and implementation

Moreover, by analyzing a broad range of precursors from different domains, interventions with multiple components can be devised. These often attack several precursors with greater probability of success than single component interventions.

While precursors are in many ways the base from which program planning unfolds, consequences serve a very different, but equally important, function. They encourage recognition of the problem and, if they are significant and/or extensive, they may form the rationale that convinces policy makers and funding agencies that the problem must be addressed.

Finding the Data

Often the data required for assessment of health status problems are available from federal sources, such as those described in *Principles and Practice of Public Health Surveillance* (Teutsch and Churchill 1994); *From Data to Action: CDC's Public Health Surveillance for Women, Infants and Children* (Wilcox and Marks 1995); and *Needs Assessment: Resource Handbook* (Peoples-Sheps et al. 1994). Data sources that are specific to states and local areas may be identified by state centers for health statistics. If data of acceptable quality are not available, collection of primary data should be considered. This is a decision that should be made carefully and in consultation with experts in qualitative and quantitative data collection, since collecting data is expensive, and producing data of high quality depends upon well-conceived and executed methods.

HEALTH SERVICES NEEDS ASSESSMENT

Health Services Needs Assessment is the second step in the planning process (Figure 15–1). This step involves identification and assessment of the services that can address precursors of the health problem and, through them, reduce the incidence of the problem itself. The assessment of needs for health services is generally approached from four perspectives: normative, expressed, relative, and perceived (Bradshaw 1972).

Normative Needs

Normative needs for services are assessed by comparing services that address precursors of the problem and are actually available to the population of concern with standards indicating what services should be available. To do this, of course, standards must be found or developed. Standards may be established by custom, authority, or general consensus (Kettner et al. 1990). For many MCH problems, formal standards for service delivery have been developed. These standards for services are often promulgated by professional organizations and public health groups to foster adequacy and quality of care. Good examples of standards are in *Healthy Communities 2000: Model Standards* (American Public Health Association 1991), which was developed to complement *Healthy People 2000* (U.S. Department of Health and Human Services 1991). For new and emerging problems, formal service standards may not yet be established, but it may be possible to draw from standards for services to address a similar problem. For example, violence between dating couples is an emerging problem for which there are as yet no standards for services. However, other forms of physical abuse have been recognized for a long time; thus, standards for interventions to prevent family violence may be adapted for dating violence until more specific standards are developed.

Another source of standards for services is consensus. This means that there is general agreement about what kinds of services or interventions should be available to address a particular problem. Development of consensus on standards for services is a process that begins with a review of the problem, especially the precursors that are prevalent in the geographic area or population group in which the problem exists. Every precursor is, potentially, a factor that can be altered by an intervention and, therefore, a starting point for identifying interventions.

Identifying potential interventions is one of the most creative parts of the planning process. It challenges the planner not only to think about what has been done in the past to alleviate the problem, but also to create interventions that have not yet been tried but could, conceivably, address precursors of the problem. This is an especially productive process when people with different perspectives are involved. Potential interventions should be identified systematically to minimize the possibility of overlooking a particularly effective option. A systematic approach involves three activities.

1. List points of intervention. With some obvious exceptions (e.g., race, ethnicity), the precursors of the problem are factors that can be altered by inter-

ventions, although some of the precursors may have such low prevalence that they should not be considered seriously. After these are removed from consideration, the remaining precursors should be organized in a format that will encourage recording of a broad spectrum of intervention possibilities. One approach is to develop a continuum of precursors that more or less follows the order of the precursors in the problem diagram (e.g., tertiary, secondary, direct precursors). Table 15–2 shows this approach using a subset of the precursors from Figure 15–2.

2. List potential interventions next to each precursor. The interventions should be specific to each precursor rather than interventions that will affect it through others. For example, in Table 15–2, interventions to improve knowledge and understanding of the importance of prenatal care correspond specifically to one barrier to use of prenatal care. An improvement in knowledge and understanding should have an indirect effect on use of prenatal care, whereas the interventions that correspond to the lack of prenatal care precursor should have direct effects on that precursor. When appropriate, interventions should include a substantive type (e.g., educate) and a mode (e.g., via mass media) of intervention.

3. Review the potential interventions for feasibility. Once the list of interventions is complete, they can be grouped by substantive type (e.g., social support) and mode (e.g., through home visits). It may also be appropriate to delete some potential interventions at this point because they are completely unacceptable: illegal, politically insensitive, or outrageously expensive. It is important to make these decisions with care. Sometimes an intervention that appears inappropriate at first will appear more feasible after further consideration.

When these activities are undertaken by a group of planners, the resulting list of interventions can be used as a supplement to professional standards for services in the assessment of normative needs.

Acquiring and developing the standards for services is the first part of assessing normative needs. The second part involves comparison of the services that are actually available with those recommended in the standards. Thus, an assessment of normative needs results in a statement about whether or not the interventions available to the population of concern are consistent with the recommendations of professional organizations and with the ideal interventions that the planning group has developed by consensus. The interventions that are not available, or are available only in part, represent unmet needs from a normative perspective.

Assessment of normative needs generates useful information, but it also harbors an important limitation. The normative standards that are based on professional judgment may reflect the biases of the individuals who developed them by

Table 15–2 Relationship of Potential Interventions to Selected Precursors

Precursor	Potential Intervention
Barriers to use of prenatal care	
Limited understanding of the importance of prenatal care	Education through mass media, in schools, and clinics Role modeling in schools, clinics Individual counseling when pregnancy test is positive
Lack of transportation	Van service from health center Vouchers for public transportation Individual counseling re: transportation to prenatal care Services provided in neighborhoods, worksites, homes
Inability to pay	Counseling and assistance to: • obtain financial assistance • budget more effectively
Lack of social support	Patients with commonalities (e.g., adolescents, primiparas) grouped in same clinic sessions Regular visiting in home by nurses or trained lay people Big Sisters linkage (for adolescents) Significant family and friends involved in care Individual counseling and assistance to remain in school
Lack of early, continuous, and comprehensive prenatal care	Waiting time for a first prenatal care appointment decreased by adding clinic sessions Linkage and referral patterns across services (medical, social, nutritional, behavioral) established or reinforced Neighborhood outreach to identify early pregnancies and follow up missed appointments Financial or gift incentives for keeping prenatal appointments Mail or telephone follow-up of missed appointments

continues

Table 15–2 continued

Precursor	Potential Intervention
Behavioral risks	
Smoking	Literature about smoking in pregnancy
	Education in schools, clinics, mass media
	Individual advice/counseling from prenatal providers
	Group behavior modification
	Combination of individual counseling, group support, and mail and telephone reminders
Drug use	Education in schools, clinics, mass media
	Drug treatment program for pregnant women
Inadequate nutrition	Nutrition counseling (individual, group)
	Assistance to obtain food stamps
	WIC enrollment

overemphasizing some criteria at the expense of others. For example, the standards developed by professional groups may overemphasize the interventions that their profession has to offer, such as more medical interventions and fewer social services recommended in standards created by medical professional organizations. This bias in published standards can be offset by the standards developed by consensus in a planning group representing diverse perspectives.

Expressed Need

Expressed need is sometimes referred to as demand. It represents the services people actively seek. Expressed need is usually measured by use of services (e.g., the number of people who access a service). Those who receive the service are counted in utilization rates. The assumption underlying this perspective is that receipt of services is synonymous with needs being met. Those who do not receive the service presumably continue to have unmet needs. Some obvious limitations of the expressed need perspective are: (1) demand often expands to meet supply, (2) needs are not necessarily met even when services are rendered, and (3) those who do not seek services are not represented in this estimate, and they may have very different needs than those who do seek services. An assessment of expressed need usually involves an analysis of the use of available services (identified in the assessment of normative needs) by relevant characteristics of the population (e.g., number of children 0–3 years receiving specified services).

Relative Need

Relative or comparative need is the need identified when services available to one population are compared with those available to another group, such as the population of a similar jurisdiction. In general, the lesser served are considered to have unmet needs. The information resulting from an assessment of relative need has limitations because the services that establish the standard (i.e., the services in the comparison area) may not be the most appropriate ones. For example, preventing severe asthma attacks that require hospitalization may be aggressively addressed in one population by early identification and treatment of attacks. Primary care services to provide these interventions may be widely available, while primary prevention, such as education and assistance in reducing exposure to irritants, may be relatively unavailable. An assessment of relative need using the services available to this population as standards would be biased in favor of primary care interventions.

Perceived Need

Perceived or felt need is what people say they need. Information about perceived need can be gathered through a variety of means, many of them qualitative, from people at risk, from people with the problem, and/or from service providers. Perceived needs are limited by the expectations of the individuals from whom perceptions are solicited. They may be underestimated (1) if subjects are unaware of options available to them, (2) if they choose not to admit that they are in need, or (3) if they really do not know they are in need. The needs may be overestimated if the perceptions are based on unreasonable norms or expectations.

Summary of Unmet Needs

Each of the four categories of needs has limitations, and no lone perspective can independently identify all service needs that are not met by existing interventions in a community. But, with information from each category, a list with the following unmet needs can be developed:

- interventions that are viable, but do not exist in the community at all
- interventions that exist in the community but need to be modified to meet normative standards completely
- interventions for people who are turned away from existing services
- interventions that raise the level of services in the community to the level in a comparison community
- interventions that address perceived needs for services

It is not unusual for the list to include contradictory information. For example, the assessment of normative needs may show that smoking cessation programs are available for pregnant women in the community, but the perceived needs assessment may indicate that most pregnant women think there is a need for smoking cessation interventions that is not being met. Contradictions like this provide an opportunity to explore the needs for service in greater depth. In this case, the true shortcoming may be in terms of knowledge about available programs, referrals to them, and/or financial coverage of those services.

With the discrepancies in the list resolved and redundancies across categories removed, a final list of unmet needs for services is easily developed. This is the list that serves as the starting point for the next step in the planning process.

The two "assessment" steps—of health status and of health services—are sometimes grouped together under the rubric "needs assessment." A distinction between these two elements is made here because the two concepts and their corresponding assessment methods differ considerably. Regardless of terminology, both of these steps are essential components of the assessment required to understand the nature of the problem and to determine the extent to which existing services are addressing the problem. Where existing services fall short, unmet needs become apparent, and interventions can then be developed to meet these unmet needs.

While many individuals are involved in the earliest stages of problem identification, they usually do not have a mandate to develop a plan to address the problems they identify. The planning team with this charge should be formed when the existence of a problem and the need to develop a plan to address it are clear. The team should consist of knowledgeable individuals, each with an essential point of view and/or analytic or interactive skill. The team should be balanced so that all skills can be put to use, but none will dominate. In addition to individuals with specific planning and content expertise, the team should include professionals from agencies that may be called upon to contribute to the solution to the problem, as well as people with a personal knowledge of the problem.

DEVELOPMENT AND SELECTION OF INTERVENTIONS

The third step in the planning process is the development and selection of interventions. At this stage, the planners have a good understanding of unmet needs for services to address the health problem. Services that do not exist at all have been identified as well as others that are in the community but are not functioning well, or are functioning well but covering only a portion of the people in need. As the process unfolds, most planners have a preference for the type of intervention they would like to implement. This is expected since members of the planning group are often chosen because they represent different constituencies, each of which sees the problem and its solution differently. Rather than jumping into the fray with a favorite argument, however, it is prudent to proceed within a framework that allows all relevant objective information and points of view to be taken into account. A framework for this step in the planning process involves three activities: development of interventions, selection of criteria for decision making, and assessment of the interventions according to the criteria. The final step is completed when an intervention is selected.

Development of Interventions

Development of interventions involves sorting the list of unmet needs according to relevant categories. Categories that are frequently used include substantive type of intervention (e.g., education, legal services, psychosocial support, training of providers, changing laws), delivery mode (e.g., individual encounter, mass media, lobbying), administrative responsibility (e.g., schools, health departments, social services, churches), and target population (e.g., adolescents, professionals, community, legislators). Within one category, each intervention can then be linked to characteristics from other categories so that combinations that may logically form coordinated programs are grouped together. Table 15–3 shows how the same interventions can be linked in three different ways: by type of intervention, administrative responsibility, and mode of delivery. Once the interventions are linked in ways that might logically form programs, they can be reviewed for overall feasibility. For example, an educational program that involves three modes of delivery (the first program organized by type in Table 15–3) may require administrative support from several agencies. If multiagency involvement is not a possibility, then this program should not be considered further, although its component interventions may be considered within other programs such as the health center and high school programs in the second column in Table 15–3.

This process of grouping interventions into categories, linking characteristics across categories to form programs, and screening to eliminate impossible options serves to reduce the number of alternatives from which one will be selected. This is an important step because making a selection from fewer options is more manageable than selecting from many. The process usually engenders a great deal of discussion that allows misunderstandings to surface while specifying the operational characteristics of alternatives, so each is clearly differentiated from the others. This feature also aids decision making. At this point, each program should be operationalized enough to characterize it according to the criteria to be used to select one program for implementation.

Criteria for Selection

Criteria that are frequently used to guide selection of programs are effectiveness, cost, feasibility (administrative, political, technical), acceptability, and other

Table 15–3 Three Alternatives for Linking the Same Interventions to Form Programs

By Type of Intervention	By Administrative Responsibility	By Mode of Delivery
Education regarding importance of prenatal care and behavioral risks via mass media, formal programs in schools, and home visiting	Neighborhood health center: prenatal care in local storefronts, home visiting to high-risk prenatal patients and prenatal education	Mass media: education regarding importance of prenatal care and behavioral risks Classroom: education regarding importance of prenatal care and behavioral risks
Social support by home visitors	High school: prenatal care and education	Home visiting: education, social support, prenatal care
Prenatal care in homes, worksites, neighborhood storefronts, and schools	Family services agency and the local university: prenatal care in worksites supplemented by home visiting by lay visitors	Clinics in worksites, neighborhood storefronts, and schools: prenatal care

criteria of key funding sources, the community, the state, and other relevant groups. Effectiveness refers to the extent to which the program is likely to be successful in improving the health status problem to which it is addressed. In addition to the actual efficacy of the intervention, this criterion must account for expected penetration of the target population, the time that might elapse before any effects are seen, and side effects. Ideally, effectiveness is estimated from evaluation studies of the effectiveness of this or a similar program on a similar population. Unfortunately, this type of information is rarely available, and the planner must estimate from much less reliable sources.

The criterion of cost is more easily measured than effectiveness, but some thought should be given to what costs are under consideration. Often in program planning, costs to the agency or organization (e.g., salaries, benefits, equipment, supplies, transportation, communication) are the main considerations. However, there are many instances (e.g., neonatal intensive care services supported by public funds) in which costs to the client, family, or society are equally important. The degree to which costs are detailed at this point depends on the needs of the decision makers. Sometimes, a ballpark figure that allows gross discrimination among alternative programs will suffice. Other times a detailed budget may be necessary to facilitate the decision.

Cost and effectiveness are necessary but usually not sufficient to make a decision among alternative interventions. A low-cost, highly effective service is of no value if it cannot be implemented. Feasibility is critical. There are three feasibility criteria that are frequently used: administrative, political, and technical. Administrative feasibility refers to the extent to which there is a structure in place to carry out such essential administrative tasks as organizing, monitoring, billing, personnel management, planning, and day-to-day oversight. If a structure is in place, can it absorb a new program? If there is no structure, is it feasible to develop one? Political feasibility, or the extent of support or opposition each program will encounter from various interest groups, authorities, and community members, is a critical factor for many MCH programs. Interventions that address adolescent sexual behavior, some family planning options, and ethical issues related to neonatal care and genetics are examples that require careful consideration of political feasibility. Technical feasibility measures the availability of the human and technical resources required to carry out the program. Technical feasibility is often of major consequence in rural areas where resources are not plentiful and, as in some developing countries, they cannot be obtained easily.

The five criteria described above are basic to most decisions. Others, such as accessibility of services and involvement of various individuals, organizations, or groups, are often used as well. A criterion of emerging importance is the extent to which a program fosters organizational collaboration or partnerships. Depending on the priorities of the organization, these relationships may be among public agencies or between public and private organizations. Another criterion of importance to MCH agencies and programs is the ability of the intervention to encourage development of systems of care, especially for children with special health care needs.

Assessment of Program Alternatives According to the Criteria

Applying the criteria to program alternatives in order to select one for implementation is the third activity in this step of the planning process. There are many ways to do this, ranging from highly interactive discussions through highly analytic quantitative procedures that require computer software. The most important ingredients for a sound decision are a systematic process and participation from many stakeholders. The criteria-weighting method (Spiegel and Hyman 1978), described in part for prioritizing health problems, can be adapted for selecting interventions as well. This method promotes systematic consideration of each criterion, weighted according to its relative importance. And the process can be structured so that it encourages participation but allows verbal dominance to be controlled.

Table 15–4 is an example of criteria weighting. The criteria discussed above are listed in the left column of the matrix. Each criterion has been assigned a set of scores ranging from 1 (least consistent with the criterion) to 4 (most consistent). The next column indicates the weight assigned to each criterion. Weights are used when one or more criteria are considered more important than the others. In this case, the weights range from 1 (important) to 3 (most important). Technical feasibility is weighted 1 while both effectiveness and cost have been assigned weights of 3.

The next section of the matrix identifies three programs under consideration. Each program has two columns. The first includes a raw score on each criterion. A definition for each score is given at the bottom of the table. For example, the "1" in the effectiveness/education program cell should be interpreted thus: "The education program has a 50 percent chance of improving the problem." The second column under each program consists of weighted scores, that is, the product of the weight of each criterion and the corresponding raw score. The results of this analysis demonstrate the role that weights can play in the process. Note that the total raw scores for both education and prenatal care programs are identical. The weighted scores, however, give the prenatal care program the edge because it scored high on effectiveness, which also had a heavier weight.

Making a decision about which program to implement is one of the most important aspects of the planning process, on a par with defining the problem correctly in the first place. Regardless of the analytic methods used to facilitate decision making, a great deal of discussion among representatives of all groups with a stake in the decision is imperative. The criteria weighting method pro-

Table 15–4 Criteria Weighting Method for Selecting a Program for Implementation

| | | Programs[3] | | | | | |
| | | Education | | Social Support | | Local Delivery of Prenatal Care | |
Criteria[1]	Weight[2]	Raw Score	Wtd. Score	Raw Score	Wtd. Score	Raw Score	Wtd. Score
Effectiveness	3	1	3	3	9	4	12
Cost	3	3	9	4	12	2	6
Administrative feasibility	2	2	4	3	6	2	4
Political feasibility	2	2	4	4	8	1	2
Technical feasibility	1	4	4	4	4	3	3
Total		12	24	18	39	12	27

[1]Criteria:

Effectiveness:
4 = Highly effective, long-lasting
3 = Effective, duration of effects uncertain
2 = Good chance of improving the problem
1 = 50 percent chance of improving the problem

Political feasibility:
4 = Acceptable to all constituents
3 = Acceptable to most constituents; little active opposition
2 = Acceptable to some constituents; little active opposition
1 = Unacceptable to most constituents

Cost:
4 = Very inexpensive
3 = Affordable
2 = Expensive
1 = Very expensive

Administrative feasibility:
4 = Fits easily in existing administrative unit
3 = Minor modifications in administrative unit required
2 = Difficult to administer
1 = Impossible to administer

Technical feasibility:
4 = Technology and human resources readily available
3 = Technology available; human resources not available
2 = Technology not available; human resources available
1 = Technology and human resources not available

[2]Weights:
3 = Most important
2 = Very important
1 = Important

[3]Program characteristics are summarized in Table 15–3 under "Type of Intervention."

vides an ideal framework for organizing such discussions (World Health Organization 1984).

SETTING OBJECTIVES

When the health problem was first identified, it was possible to develop an objective with an appropriate health status indicator and target. Often, however, this step is implicit because no other objectives can be developed until a program is selected for implementation.

Objectives are statements of purpose. What is to be accomplished? How is it to be done? By what date? To what extent? Objectives that are clearly and logically constructed are a blueprint for the program. In addition, objectives can be used by administrators for decision making and resource allocation. If something about the program does not align with the objectives, then either the activities or the targets need to be changed. Thus, objectives are a framework around which the program is constructed and amended. Objectives also can be used as standards for comparison to assess the program's progress. There are two critical aspects to setting objectives: constructing a program hypothesis and developing the components of objectives.

Program Hypothesis

The program hypothesis is the conceptual framework that links the program's activities to improvements in the health status problem. The hypothesis is made up of a set of objectives that have hierarchical relationships to each other and reflect the relationships of the precursors of the problem. That is, an intervention is expected to modify the precursor to which it is addressed, which in turn will start a chain reaction of modifications among the precursors that link it to the health status problem. Therefore, each of the intervening precursors could be reflected in an objective.

A framework for understanding the concepts behind a program hypothesis is illustrated by Figure 15–3. A program provides one or more activities or services, which are expected to produce outcomes in the form of changes in some characteristics of those who receive the services. Characteristics targeted for change by health programs might include knowledge, behavior, and biochemical levels in the body. By altering these characteristics in some manner, it is expected that specific aspects of the health status of recipients will improve, ultimately improving the general health status of the community. The specific population represented at each level may vary but the principle that achievement of one level constitutes the means for achieving the next higher level is the core of a sound program hypothesis.

To promote clarity, labels have been given to the objectives. The labels used here are intended to reflect the purpose of each level. Operational objectives refer

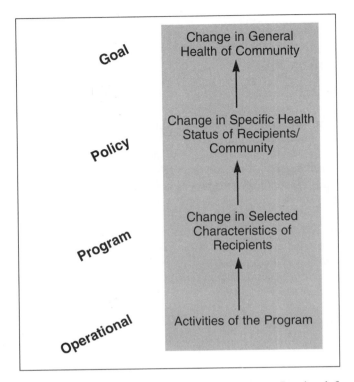

Figure 15–3 Components of a Program Hypothesis. *Source:* Reprinted from *Setting Objectives* by M.D. Peoples-Sheps, E. Byars, M.M. Rogers, E.J. Finerty, A. Farel, p. 7, with permission of the University of North Carolina at Chapel Hill School of Public Health © 1995.

to the actual operations, or activities, of the program. Program objectives represent the effects of receiving the activities or services of the program. These correspond to the changes in specific characteristics of recipients, such as knowledge, behavior, or biochemical measures that are expected to occur because of the specific program. Policy objectives are at the next higher level. These are the objectives that correspond most closely to the health problem itself. The term *policy* is used here because these objectives reflect what needs to be accomplished but not how the accomplishments will be realized. The "how-to's" are reflected in operational and program level objectives. In this labeling scheme, the goal is expected to be achieved through accomplishment of the policy objectives. It is a broad statement of desired health status, as distinguished from another broad domain, such as economic growth or improved social welfare. A program hypothesis that corresponds to the problem in Figure 15–2 is shown in Figure 15–4.

Components of Objectives

Each objective is composed of one subject and one or more targets. Subjects can be indicators or activities. For policy and program objectives, the subject is

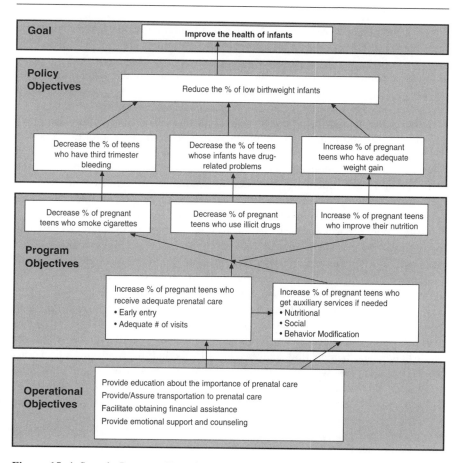

Figure 15–4 Sample Program Hypotheses. *Source:* Adapted from *Setting Objectives* by M.D. Peoples-Sheps, E. Byars, M.M. Rogers, E.J. Finerty, A. Farel, p. 9, with permission of the University of North Carolina at Chapel Hill School of Public Health © 1995.

an indicator of a specific health or health-related condition. The subjects of operational objectives are activities that will be done as a part of the program. Indicators and activities must be measurable, with acceptable and unacceptable levels of achievement. This is an obvious statement but one that too often goes unheeded. The major difficulty is that some concepts, like stress for example, can be measured in a number of ways, each of which may have different standards for acceptable and unacceptable levels. Selection of an appropriate measure requires consideration of the cost and feasibility of required data collection methods as well as the reliability and validity of the measure itself.

The way in which an indicator will be measured must be specified before the target of the objective can be set. A target is a numerical value that indicates the minimum desirable level of achievement for a particular activity or indicator. A target may have two parts: a quantity or amount (e.g., 20 percent) and a date of anticipated achievement (e.g., by the end of month 3). Usually program and policy objectives are written for the life of the program, whereas the operational objectives may have shorter, often one year, time frames. This is because program activities may change from year to year by design or because of developments encountered as the program is implemented. For example, a program may be designed so that recruitment of clients is a major activity in year 1, to be replaced in year 2 with service delivery activities. Alternatively, it may be found that by the end of year 1 recruitment has not been as productive as expected, so different recruitment activities are added to the operational objectives. In both cases, the operational objectives would change from year 1 to year 2.

Targets play a particularly important role in the type of evaluation known as monitoring. The most difficult aspect of setting targets is deciding what is a desirable level of achievement. Help in this task can be found through a variety of sources. When targets are absolute numbers of program activities, such as the number of encounters with clients, individuals with experience delivering similar programs can provide useful insights. These sources may also be helpful when estimating the percentage of change for indicators of program and policy objectives. Relevant literature in the field, such as evaluations of similar programs, time studies, and patient flow analyses can also be helpful when these decisions are to be made. Two widely available public health references should always be consulted when setting objectives. The targets in *Healthy People 2000* (U.S. Department of Health and Human Services 1991) correspond to program and policy objectives for many MCH programs, and those in *Healthy Communities 2000: Model Standards* (American Public Health Association 1991) correspond to operational objectives.

The targets proposed in these references are not universally transportable, but they provide benchmarks from which appropriate targets for a given program can be derived. Other factors to consider when setting targets include the speed with which the program will become fully operational, whether some negative effects are expected before seeing positive ones (e.g., often programs that rely on reporting of cases see an increase in cases reported because the intervention is now available before they see a decrease due to the intervention itself), and if there is a reason to set targets particularly high or low. In the end, the levels selected for targets are usually derived from a synthesis of the data and guidance available at the time. In the next round of planning, experience with the new program will inform these decisions.

PROGRAMMING AND IMPLEMENTATION

The objectives form a blueprint for the program, which must be elaborated in detail so that it can be implemented. This fifth step of the planning process, programming and implementation, has three distinct parts: program design, implementation planning, and budgeting.

Program Design

Many factors must be taken into account when designing a program. Typically, they fall into four categories: activities, clients, organization, and personnel. The key activities of the program are specified in the operational objectives. Elaboration of each of them is required at this point. This task should be undertaken by individuals with the knowledge and skills to design the intervention according to relevant theories and practice standards. Often these individuals are members of the profession that will deliver the intervention. For example, health educators may be best qualified to design behavior modification interventions because they are trained in this area, while public health nurses are in a similar position with regard to home visiting interventions. Regardless of professional identification, the appropriate experts to design the intervention should be brought into the team at this stage if they are not already members.

Complementary components of the program also require designing and description. If a core intervention involves modification of smoking behavior, meetings at clients' homes may be required which, in turn, implies that such other components as communication (to schedule appointments) and transportation need attention. Alternatively, if the intervention is to be offered in an agency setting, space and scheduling may be critical considerations.

Two tools that are helpful at this stage are written procedures and flow charts (Spiegel and Hyman 1978). Written procedures are clear and concise statements about activities to be done, including exactly what tasks are involved, the sequence they should follow, and who is responsible for them. Flow charts offer another way of accomplishing the same result. These charts show the sequence of activities in diagrammatic form. They are especially useful when depicting several parallel sets of activities.

A particularly important aspect of program design is coordination of the program's activities. For a program to function smoothly, components must work together (e.g., the personnel department and the service delivery unit or various service units, each providing a different type of service) and must have specific mechanisms for ensuring unimpeded interactions. These mechanisms should be detailed as procedures for routine coordination, like referral procedures from one clinic to another. In addition, there should be a procedure for handling the atypical problems that will arise.

The program must fit with the characteristics of the clients in order for it to function well. If the first language of the target group is not English, then bilingual providers, or at least interpreters, should be hired. If the intervention is targeted to mothers of young children, provisions for child care should be taken into account. Many of these characteristics were identified when the health problem was analyzed, but identification of others may require interviews or focus group discussions with members of the target population.

In the selection of interventions, consideration was given to both administrative and technical feasibility. The issue at that stage was the extent to which administrative structure and technical capability existed or could be developed. Now, these capabilities must be operationalized. The planners need to consider whether the new initiative should be integrated into an existing organizational unit, adding to or drawing from available human resources. There is often some economic advantage to this approach, but there is also a risk that the program will become indistinguishable from the other programs in the unit. An alternative is to structure the program as a demonstration project by setting it up as an organizationally distinct, short-term initiative. One reason to take a demonstration project approach is to retain the totality of the intervention so that it can be rigorously evaluated. From an administrative perspective, demonstration projects often have high visibility, are not tied to the peculiarities of an ongoing bureaucracy, and are allowed considerable organizational autonomy. All of these characteristics tend to encourage creativity within the project. On the other hand, there are disadvantages of demonstration projects. Since they may require the same types of staff as ongoing units, duplicating functions may be wasteful and inefficient. High visibility may bring negative attention. Also, demonstration projects sometimes become elitist and entrenched in their own institutional culture, thus losing the creativity and flexibility for which they are best known.

Traditionally, MCH programs have been offered in either the public or the private sector. As new types of health care organizations dominate the field and as public-private partnerships are encouraged from many sides, new challenges for organizational structure are emerging. Planners of MCH programs must give particular attention to clarifying the advantages and disadvantages of placing programs in emerging organizations, perhaps with little knowledge of, or experience with, MCH interventions. In situations where staff members are shared by partnering organizations, chains of authority and responsibility as well the percent effort to be devoted to the program must be explicit.

With the program's activities and organizational structure specified, the types and numbers of personnel can be determined. Alternative types of providers should be discussed by the planning team so that the final selection represents the best fit of provider training and experience with the job to be done. The number of personnel required should be estimated by determining how much of the service each staff member can provide vis-à-vis the total amount that needs to be done. Supervisory responsibilities and time commitments are taken into account when estimating expected productivity of staff members. These estimates should be calculated as carefully as possible since underestimates could cause serious delays in achievement of operational objectives that will then have adverse effects on program and policy objectives.

The universal tool for linking staff members to program activities and to organizational structure is the position description. Most organizations and agencies have standard formats for position descriptions, which include job title, minimum and desired qualifications, chain of command, and job functions and responsibilities. Because position descriptions reflect many decisions made in the process of program design, they are critical links in the planning process. They can also serve an important role for the individuals who fill the positions in that they link those individuals to the program's specific operational objectives and through them to the overall program hypothesis.

Thoughtful attention to the program's activities, the target population, the organizational structure, and program personnel will lead to a thorough explication of the program. Such extensive immersion in the complexities of the program often fosters emergence of new objectives, another manifestation of the iterative nature of the rational planning process.

Implementation Planning

Activities, clients, organizational placement, and personnel are requirements of the ongoing program. They are distinct from the resources and another set of activities necessary to implement the program. Resources are the equipment, personnel, arrangements, and other items required to begin program operations. Implementation activities are the tasks that must be done in order to have the resources available to start the program. Having designed and described the program (above), this is the logical next step. The distinction between ongoing program activities and resources/implementation activities is illustrated below.

Assume that an operational objective for a program involves providing transportation to a clinical service. In designing the program, decisions regarding when to offer transportation and the number of people who would have to be transported when the program is operating were made. This is the information needed to determine the resources to launch the program. Resources in this case include vehicles, insurance, drivers, and schedules for the service. Implementation activities are the tasks required to have these resources when they are needed. Vehicles will have to be purchased or leased, or perhaps a contract with a transportation service could be arranged. Drivers must be hired and insurance obtained. A schedule must be developed. Accomplishment of each of these tasks will require other tasks, all of which must be specified with due consideration to organizational norms and constraints. If, for example, the organization will not allow the purchase of vehicles, this must be taken into account.

Obviously, the resources required for implementation must be available when the program is to start. Scheduling implementation activities to meet program start dates can be challenging. For each activity, the length of time required to accomplish it and its sequence relative to the other activities must be determined. In addition, responsibilities for each activity should be assigned. If many people are working on implementation, several chains of activities can be carried out concurrently.

If the number of implementation activities is relatively small (about 20–40), they can be easily organized in a diagram that shows at a glance when each should start and be completed. Ordering the activities may be considerably more difficult when there are a great number, especially if many of them should be undertaken concurrently. In this case, a project management tool will facilitate the task. These tools are widely available in computer software (Rasmus 1988) They are based on the Program Evaluation Review Technique (PERT) (Schaefer 1987), which can also be accomplished by manual calculations. Whichever approach is used, the end result is a schedule that shows what needs to be done, when to start and stop, and who is responsible.

Budgeting

Most organizations and funding sources have required formats for budgets. In general, the budget has two parts, personnel and nonpersonnel. The personnel section has entries for each type of personnel (by name if known), the number of each type, percent time devoted to the program, salary, and benefits. Nonpersonnel items include equipment, supplies, travel, communication, contractual arrangements, and other items specific to the program. A budget using these categories is called a line item budget. It may be developed for the entire program or for each of the operational objectives. When developed for each operational objective, it is possible to see how much each program component will cost. This approach makes it easier to make decisions about where to trim costs if it becomes necessary to do so.

Estimating the cost of each item is fairly straightforward. The key is to obtain costs from the correct source; for example, the personnel department of the organization is usually the best source for salaries and benefits, while distributors are more reliable sources for nonpersonnel items. Cost estimates for each item are then multiplied by the quantity required of that item. Changes in costs over the budget period, such as salary raises and airfare increases, must be built into the estimates. Some costs that may not be immediately obvious are (1) items that will be needed later in the budget period for phased-in services, (2) costs of evaluation, and (3) implementation expenses. All of these should be included in the budget.

In addition to cost estimates, it is sometimes necessary to distinguish between requested funds and donated funds. This distinction is used when a proposal for the program is being submitted to an outside funding source for consideration. Funding sources are often interested in the extent to which the applicant organization will support the program. *Donated* refers to the applicant's contributions. *Requested* funds are those the applicant is requesting from the funding source.

The costs identified above are direct, that is, the costs expected to be incurred while implementing and conducting the program. But the direct costs of a specific program or project may not represent all of its costs. For example, housing, utilities, and equipment are often used by several programs and may not be included in the direct costs of any of them. Some funding agencies will pay a percentage of direct costs to compensate for the indirect costs incurred by the new program. Specifications for calculating indirect costs vary across agencies and should be obtained from them directly when needed (Kiritz 1979).

The budget is one of the most essential components of the planning process. If the budget is omitted or poorly executed, all of the preceding work amounts to no more than wishful thinking. Like the objectives and program hypothesis, the budget provides a blueprint of the plan. It can help to clarify roles and responsibilities as proportions of effort are estimated. It can also contribute to cost awareness among the participants in the process. Working through budget details may produce some fresh ideas or new perspectives on other parts of the plan, thus offering another opportunity for iteration.

EVALUATION

The evaluation plan, which is the last step in the program planning process, is too often omitted due to lack of time or lack of appreciation for its importance. Yet program evaluations make significant contributions to many segments of MCH activities. For example, evaluation results inform the next round of planning, identify if the program is going awry so it can be corrected, and produce information used for decision making by managers, policy makers, funding agencies, and the public. The evaluation plan should be an integral part of the program plan. If the planning process is conducted as described in this chapter, completing an evaluation plan is straightforward because two of the key prerequisites for evaluation, a logical program hypothesis and measurable objectives, are already developed.

There are two major strategies for program evaluation: evaluation research and monitoring (DeFriese and Beery 1983). Evaluation research involves the application of social science research methods to determine whether a program causes observed effects. Planning for evaluation research involves development of (1) a research design, (2) a recruitment plan, (3) a data collection plan, and (4) an analysis plan. These steps are described in detail in books on evaluation research (Fink 1993; Patton 1990; Rossi and Freeman 1993). Evaluation research is the strategy to use when the effectiveness of a new program (e.g., a demonstration project) must be determined. For many programs, however, the evaluation question is not whether the program caused the effects, but whether the program (which is already known to have the capacity to be effective) was conducted as planned. Answering this question does not require the sophisticated methods, expertise, time, and financial resources required for evaluation research. Rather, monitoring is the evaluation strategy for the job.

Monitoring involves assessment of progress toward achievement of the objectives of a program. Monitoring tries to ensure that the objectives are met. By monitoring the extent to which targets are achieved, MCH staff can determine whether the program has fallen short on some objectives. If it has, this information should trigger an in-depth search for the reasons the expected targets were not achieved. This search, in turn, is part of the health problem and service assessments in the next round of planning.

A formal process for monitoring is a useful adjunct to the concept itself. This begins with the objectives of the program and involves developing formulas to measure progress, assigning weights, and developing data collection plans. These are illustrated in Table 15–5.

Developing Formulas To Measure Progress

There are three types of formulas, each based on the principle that a score of 1.00 is complete accomplishment (Guild and Gillings 1983). A score of 0.99 or lower signifies that the activity or indicator fell short of the target; a score that exceeds 1.00 indicates greater than expected achievement. The simplest type of formula is to score 1.00 if the target is reached and 0.00 if it is not reached. This formula can be used with any type of target, but it does not allow for an indication of partial progress toward achievement of the objective.

A second type of formula can be used when the target is a date. A score of 1.00 is given if the activity is completed at the projected time, and 1.00± the propor-

Table 15-5 Monitoring Plan for Selected Objectives of Social Support Program To Reduce Low Birth Weight

Activity/Indicator	Target	Formula To Measure Progress	Weight	Data Source/Data Collection Plan
Operational Objectives:				
Provide education about the importance of prenatal care	100% of pregnant teenagers will receive one educational session on the importance of prenatal care	% who receive one educational session/100	1	Maternity Information System
Provide/ensure transportation to prenatal care if needed	95% of visits when transportation is needed will have transportation provided or ensured	% who have transportation provided or ensured/95	2	Maternity Information System
Provide basic emotional support and counseling through in-person encounters with Resource Mothers	90% of pregnant teenagers will have one encounter per week	% who have one encounter per week 90	2	Maternity Information System
Program Objective:				
Percent of pregnant teenagers who smoke cigarettes	40% of pregnant teenagers who smoke will reduce the number of cigarettes smoked per day	% who reduce the number of cigarettes smoked per day/40	3	Maternity Information System
	10% of pregnant teenagers who smoke will quit smoking	% who quit smoking/10	3	Maternity Information System
Policy Objective:				
% of low birth weight infants	15% reduction	% reduction/15	NA	Birth Record Files

Source: Peoples-Sheps, M.D., Rogers, M.M., and Finerty, E.J. (1990). *Monitoring Progress Toward Achievement of Objectives.* © The University of North Carolina at Chapel Hill, School of Public Health, pp. 6, 8, 10, with permission.

tional equivalent of the number of months or weeks early or late is given for over- or underachievement. For example, if the target is one year from now, a reasonable formula for accomplishment would be 1.00 ± 0.08 because 0.08 is the decimal equivalent of 1/12 or 1 of 12 months.

A third type of measure can be used when the target is a percent, proportion, or number. A score is calculated by dividing the level of actual achievement by the level of anticipated achievement.

Assigning Weights

Weights are used to show that accomplishment of some objectives is relatively more important than accomplishment of others. For example, some objectives may represent precursors that have stronger relationships to the problem than others. Accomplishing these objectives may be critical to improving the problem or accomplishing policy objectives. Therefore, these critical objectives should have greater weight when assessing overall program accomplishments than others. Weights are assigned on a scale agreed upon a priori by the planning group.

Developing a Data Collection Plan

Identifying the data source and, if no source exists currently, the data collection plan during the planning process helps to ensure that data will be available for monitoring. It is not uncommon for programs to have elaborate objectives but no plans for collecting or accessing the data necessary to monitor achievement of the objectives. It may be discovered at a much later date that the required data are not available.

If primary data collection is planned, the data collection tool should be identified and plans for administering it should be thought out. Often, specific items on the tool will correspond to specific objectives. These relationships should be acknowledged explicitly in a table or narrative description so that anyone charged with carrying out the monitoring phase of the program has a well developed set of guidelines to follow.

Achievement Scores

Table 15–5 shows all the components discussed above for monitoring a set of objectives. This type of table would be developed for each set of objectives (i.e., operational, program, policy) as the program is planned. The formulas are then used to evaluate progress toward achievement of the objectives at specified points in time. To appreciate the importance of the resulting information, it is helpful to see the type of information that can be derived. Table 15–6 is a sample table that

Table 15–6 Summary of Progress Toward Achievement of Selected Objectives at the End of Year 1

Activity/Indicator	Target	Formula To Measure Progress	Weight	Results	Achievement Score
Operational Objectives:					
Provide education about the importance of prenatal care	100% of pregnant teenagers will receive one educational session on the importance of prenatal care	% who receive one educational session/100	1	95%	0.95
Provide/ensure transportation to prenatal care if needed	95% of visits when transportation is needed will have transportation provided or ensured	% who have transportation provided or ensured/95	2	75%	0.79
Provide basic emotional support and counseling through in-person encounters with Resource Mothers	90% of pregnant teenagers will have one encounter per week	% who have one encounter per week/90	2	70%	0.78
Program Objective:					
Percent of pregnant teenagers who smoke cigarettes	40% of pregnant teenagers who smoke will reduce the number of cigarettes smoked per day	% who reduce the number of cigarettes smoked per/day/40	3	25%	0.63
	10% of pregnant teenagers who smoke will quit smoking	% who quit smoking/10	3	8%	0.80
Policy Objective:					
% of low birth weight infants	15% reduction	% reduction/15	NA	12%	0.80

Source: Peoples-Sheps, M.D., Rogers, M.M., and Finerty, E.J. (1990). *Monitoring Progress Toward Achievement of Objectives.* ©The University of North Carolina at Chapel Hill, School of Public Health, pp. 6, 8, 10, with permission.

might be developed to summarize accomplishments at the end of one year. The first four columns are identical to those in Table 15–5. The fifth column shows the actual value (result) attained for each target in year 1 of the program. The sixth column, labeled Achievement Score, shows the score produced when the formula for the measure is applied. For example, for the third objective, the target was 90 percent but only 70 percent was accomplished. Achievement was 70/90 or 0.78. This value is less than 1.00, thus indicating that the program fell short of its target, although progress was made. In addition to calculating an achievement score for each objective, overall achievement scores can be calculated by summing the scores for each objective and dividing by the number of objectives to obtain an average. The weights can be applied by multiplying the score for each objective by the weight before summing. To obtain a weighted average, the sum of all weighted scores is divided by the sum of the weights.

Interpretation

The information derived from monitoring shows which objectives need more attention in subsequent years and whether any of them require less intensive work. Adjustments in resource allocations can be based upon the strengths and weaknesses of the program in meeting its objectives, but careful assessment of the reasons for shortfalls on objectives should be conducted before any decisions are made. There are many reasons why a program may not reach its targets. Inadequate funding—a primary reason—may take the form of insufficient resources across the board or misallocation of funds across objectives. It may be possible to detect misallocation if some targets are overachieved while others fall short. Other commonly cited reasons why programs may fall short in achieving objectives include: (1) lack of adequate knowledge about feasible target levels, (2) external factors that make it difficult or impossible to reach the target (e.g., inability to find the required type of personnel), (3) inaccurate measurement of the objective, and (4) a conceptual error in the program hypothesis.

Advantages and Disadvantages of Monitoring

As an evaluation strategy, monitoring has three important shortcomings: (1) it does not produce evidence of cause-effect relationships, (2) its results cannot be extrapolated from one program to another, and (3) there are no firm guidelines for interpretation of the scores. Interpretation must be done within the context of the specific program being evaluated. Even with these limitations, however, monitoring is a valuable tool for planning and management decisions. It produces information that can trigger adjustments in program operations. The same information can inform the assessment steps of the next planning cycle. Monitoring methods are flexible; they can be applied in whole or in part to meet the needs of each specific program. The process is inexpensive and can be used readily by anyone with entry-level training or experience. Finally and importantly, the monitoring process described above meets the requirements of most government and private foundation funding agencies.

CONCLUSION

For MCH professionals, the systematic steps of the rational planning process sometimes seem to get lost amidst the continuous demands of legislative mandates and administrative red tape. In the face of these realities of everyday life in busy agencies, however, mothers and children are encountering complex and multifaceted health problems. The challenge to MCH professionals is to develop, implement, and monitor programs to prevent those problems. Rational program planning provides a problem-solving analytic framework for meeting this challenge. It promotes deliberate decision making and development of creative and responsive programs of interventions, while operating comfortably in a social and political context. It uses many of the analytic and interactive techniques available to the field of public health, thus serving as a bridge between research and practice. Program planning methods can be used at any jurisdictional level (e.g., local, state, federal) and for any system of care (e.g., managed care organizations, traditional public health systems). The process is a dynamic one, involving both continuity and iteration, as well as the development of program plans that are intended to be changed. Over many years, MCH professionals have found that program planning skills are indispensable tools in their efforts to improve the health of mothers and children.

REFERENCES

American Public Health Association. 1991. *Healthy communities 2000: Model standards*, 3rd ed. Washington, DC: Author.

Backett, E.M. et al. 1984. *The risk approach in health care, with special reference to maternal and child health, Including family planning*. Public Health Paper 76. Geneva, Switzerland: World Health Organization.

Blum, H.L. 1974. *Planning for health: Development and application of social change theory*. New York: Human Sciences Press.

Blum, H.L. 1983. *Expanding health care horizons*, 2d ed. Oakland, CA: Third Party Publishing Company.

Bradshaw, J. 1972. The concept of social need. *New Society* 30:640–643.

Committee for the Study of the Future of Public Health. 1988. *The future of public health*. Washington: National Academy Press.

DeFriese, G.H., and W.L. Beery. 1983. Choosing an evaluation strategy. *Baseline* 1:1–6.

Dignan, M.B., and P.A. Carr. 1992. *Program planning for health education and health promotion*, 2d ed. Philadelphia: Lea and Febiger.

Essential Public Health Services Work Group. 1994. *Essential Public Health Services*. Paper prepared by the U.S. Public Health Service, August.

Fink, A. 1993. *Evaluation fundamentals: Guiding health programs, research, and policy*. Newbury Park, CA: Sage Publications.

Gilbert, N., and H. Specht. 1977. *Planning for social welfare*. Englewood Cliffs, NJ: Prentice-Hall, Inc.

Glanz, K. et al., eds. 1990. *Health behavior and health education: Theory, research and practice*. San Francisco: Jossey-Bass Publishers.

Guild, P.A., and D.B. Gillings. 1983. Goal-oriented evaluation as a program management tool. *Baseline* 1:1–6.

Kettner, P.M. et al. 1990. *Designing and managing programs: An effectiveness-based approach*. Newbury Park, CA: Sage Publications.

Kiritz, N.J. 1979. Program planning and proposal writing. *The Grantsmanship Center NEWS*, 71–79.

Patton, M.Q. 1990. *Qualitative evaluation and research methods*. Newbury Park, CA: Sage Publications.

Peoples-Sheps, M.D. et al. 1994. *Needs assessment: Resource handbook*. Rockville, MD: Maternal and Child Health Bureau, USDHHS.

Rasmus, D.W. 1988. Making it happen. *MACazine*, 21–24.

Rossi, P.H., and H.E. Freeman. 1993. *Evaluation: A systematic approach*. 5th ed. Newbury Park, CA: Sage Publications.

Schaefer, M. 1987. *Implementing change in service programs: Project planning and management*. Newbury Park, CA: Sage Publications.

Spiegel, A.D., and H.H. Hyman. 1978. *Basic health planning methods*, Germantown, MD: Aspen Publishers.

Teutsch, S.M., and R.E. Churchill, eds. 1994. *Principles and practice of public health surveillance*. New York: Oxford University Press.

Tipton, M. 1995. Growth from the maelstrom: Revisiting public MCH program functions, *CityLights* 4:2.

U.S. Department of Health and Human Services. 1991. *Healthy people 2000: National health promotion and disease prevention objectives*. DHHS Publication No. (PHS) 91-50212. Washington, DC: Government Printing Office.

Wilcox, L.S., and J.S. Marks. 1995. *From data to action: CDC's Public Health Surveillance for Women, Infants and Children*. Atlanta, GA: Centers for Disease Control and Prevention, USDHHS.

Williams, H.S. et al. 1991. *Outcome funding: A new approach to targeted grantmaking*. Rensselaerville, NY: The Rensselaerville Institute.

World Health Organization, Division of Family Health. 1984. *A workbook on how to plan and carry out research on the risk approach in maternal and child health including family planning*. Geneva, Switzerland: Author.

Glossary of
MCH Acronyms
and Abbreviations

AAP	American Academy of Pediatrics
ACOG	American College of Obstetricians and Gynecologists
ADA	American Dietetic Association
ADA	Americans with Disabilities Act
ADC	Aid to Dependent Children
ADHD	Attention Deficit Hyperactivity Disorder
AFDC	Aid for Families with Dependent Children
AFP	Alpha-Feto-Protein
AHTP	Adolescent Health Training Program
AIDS	Acquired Immune Deficiency Syndrome
AMA	American Medical Association
AMCHP	Association of Maternal and Child Programs
ATMCH	Association of Teachers of Maternal and Child Health
ATSDR	Agency for Toxic Substances and Disease Registry
AZT	Azydothymidine
BDMP	Birth Defects Monitoring Program
BMI	Body Mass Index
BWSM	Birth Weight Specific Mortality
C & Y	Children and Youth
CAPTA	Child Abuse Prevention and Treatment Act
CBPHC	Community-Based Primary Health Care
CCHIP	Community Child Hunger Identification Project
CCS	Crippled Children's Services
CDF	Children's Defense Fund
CDC	Centers for Disease Control and Prevention
CHCP	Community Health Care Program
CHW	Community Health Worker

CPS	Child Protective Services
CSHCN	Children with Special Health Care Needs
CVD	Cardiovascular Disease
DARLING	Davis Area Research on Lactation, Infant Nutrition, and Growth
DCP	Disabled Children's Program
DD	Developmental Disabilities
DES	Diethylstilbestrol
DHHS	Department of Health and Human Services (U.S.)
DHSS	Department of Health and Social Services (UK)
DLNM	Date of Last Normal Menses
DPT	Diphtheria/Pertussis/Tetanus
EEPCD	Early Education Program for Children with Disabilities
EHA	Education of the Handicapped Act
ELBW	Extra Low Birth Weight
EMIC	Emergency Maternity and Infant
EMS	Emergency Medical Services
EPSDT	Early and Periodic Screening, Diagnosis, and Treatment
ERIC	Educational Resource Information Center
FAO/WHO/UNU	Food and Agriculture Organization/World Health Organization/United Nations University
FAPE	Free, Appropriate Public Education
FDA	Food and Drug Administration
FNS	Food and Nutrition Service
FPL	Federal Poverty Line
FRAC	Food Research and Action Center
FRC	Family Resource Center
FSP	Food Stamp Program
GAO	General Accounting Office
GAPS	Guidelines for Adolescent Preventive Services
GOBI	Growth Monitoring, Oral Rehydration, Breastfeeding, Immunization
HCFA	Health Care Financing Administration
HFA	Health for All (by the year 2000)
HHANES	Hispanic Health and Nutrition Examination Survey
HHANES-MA	Hispanic Health and Nutrition Examination Survey-Mexican American
HHS	Health and Human Services
Hib	Haemophilis influenza type b
HIV	Human Immunodeficiency Virus
HDL	High Density Lipoprotein

HMO	Health Maintenance Organization
HRSA	Health Resources and Services Administration
HRT	Hormone Replacement Therapy
HTLV 3	Human T-cell Lymphotrophic Virus-3
IAC	Inter-African Committee (on traditional practices affecting the health of women and children)
ICD	International Classification of Diseases
ICD-CM	International Classification of Diseases-Clinical Modification
IDEA	Individuals with Disabilities Education Act
IEP	Individualized Education Plan
IFA	Individualized Functional Assessment
IFSP	Individualized Family Service Plan
IHS	Indian Health Service
IOM	Institute of Medicine
IRB	Institutional Review Board
ISP	Individual Service Plan
IUD	Intrauterine Device
IUGR	Intrauterine Growth Retardation
IV	Intravenous
LBW	Low Birth Weight
LCFP	Low Cost Food Plan
LDL	Low Density Lipoprotein
LEAP	Leadership Education for Adolescent Programs
LMP	Last Menstrual Period
M & I	Maternal and Infant
MACDP	Metropolitan Atlanta Congenital Defects Program
MADDSP	Metropolitan Atlanta Developmental Disabilities Surveillance Program
MCH	Maternal and Child Health
MCHB	Maternal and Child Health Bureau
MLBW	Moderately Low Birth Weight
MMR	Measles/Mumps/Rubella
MMWR	*Morbidity and Mortality Weekly Report*
NASHS	National Adolescent School Health Survey
NBW	Normal Birth Weight
NCCAN	National Center on Child Abuse and Neglect
NCHS	National Center for Health Statistics
NGO	Nongovernmental Organization
NHANES	National Health and Nutrition Examination Survey
NHI	National Health Insurance

NHIS	National Health Interview Survey
NHIS-CHS	National Health Interview Survey-Child Health Supplement
NHIS-D	National Health Interview Survey-Disability
NHS	National Health Service
NICHD	National Institute of Child Health and Human Development
NICU	Neonatal Intensive Care Unit
NIH	National Institutes of Health
NIMH	National Institute of Mental Health
NIOSH	National Institute of Occupational Safety and Health
NMCUES	National Medical Care Utilization and Expenditure Survey
NMIHS	National Maternal and Infant Health Survey
NRC	National Research Council
NSLP	National School Lunch Program
OBRA	Omnibus Budget Reconciliation Act
OEO	Office of Economic Opportunity
OMH	Office of Minority Health
OTA	Office of Technology Assessment
PCP	Phencyclidine
PEPI	Postmenopausal Estrogen-Progestin Intervention
PERT	Program Evaluation Review Technique
PHC	Primary Health Care
PHS	Public Health Service
PI	Principal Investigator
PL	Public Law
POPRAS	Problem-Oriented Prenatal Risk Assessment System
RDA	Recommended Dietary Allowance
RDS	Respiratory Distress Syndrome
REACH	Resources for Enhancement of Adolescent Community Health
RTI	Reproductive Tract Infection
SAM	Society for Adolescent Medicine
SBHC	School-Based Health Center
SES	Socioeconomic Status
SGA	Small for Gestational Age
SIDS	Sudden Infant Death Syndrome
SIPP	Survey of Income and Program Participation
SMR	Severe Mental Retardation
SPCC	Society for the Prevention of Cruelty to Children

SPRANS	Special Projects of Regional and National Significance
SSA	Social Security Act
SSI	Supplemental Security Income
SSI/DCP	Supplemental Security Income/Disabled Children's Program
STD	Sexually Transmitted Disease
STI	Sexually Transmitted Infection
TBA	Traditional Birth Attendant
TEFAP	Temporary Emergency Food Assistance Program
UAF	University-Affiliated Facility
UN	United Nations
UNFPA	United Nations Population Fund
UNICEF	United Nations International Children's Emergency Fund
USC	United States Code
USDA	United States Department of Agriculture
VBACS	Vaginal Birth after Cesarian Section
VLBW	Very Low Birth Weight
VVF	Vesico-Vaginal Fistula
WIC	Special Supplemental Food Program for Women, Infants, and Children
YRBSS	Youth Risk Behavior Surveillance System

INDEX